This volume covers the background to the Victorio Campaign of 1879-1881. In the early 1870s, a mixture of diplomacy and successful military campaigning by General George Crook led to the formation of several reservations for various Apache groups such as the Mescalero, Chiricahua and Western Apaches. Almost before the ink was dry on these treaties, an effort was made to rationalise this arrangement by placing the Apaches upon one reservation (the concentration policy). The first reservation to close was the Fort Bowie reservation, which belonged to the Chokonen (Central Chiricahua) Apaches. Some chose to resist, and this resistance – combined with the continued drive for concentration – brought about the closure of the Chihenne (Eastern Chiricahua) Apache reservation at Ojo Caliente, New Mexico, in 1877 and their removal to the San Carlos reservation in Arizona. The Chihennes were led by Victorio, Nana and Loco at this time, and they chose to accept the move, even though this was to the territory of the Western Apaches (with whom they often had a mutually hostile relationship). The land they were allocated was not healthy and a deadly feud between the Chihennes and the San Carlos Apaches quickly flared up; in September 1877, Victorio led a large portion of his people off San Carlos and tried to return to Ojo Caliente. Between 1877 and 1879, Victorio and his followers resisted their removal back to San Carlos – periodically fleeing and raiding mainly in Mexico to survive; they minimised hostile activity in the USA in order to keep alive their hopes of a return to Ojo Caliente. By August 1879, Victorio gave up hope that a return to Ojo Caliente was possible and declared war on the USA, as well as continuing their conflict with the Mexicans. Between September and December 1879, Victorio and his warriors – no more than 150 strong (and often as little as 50) – inflicted a number of defeats upon the Ninth Cavalry, US citizen volunteers and Mexican State troops. By the end of this volume, they had taken refuge – undefeated – in Northern Mexico and were poised to return to continue their battle with the USA for the return of their reservation. This research will outline the previously unreconstructed and sophisticated strategies and tactics utilised by Victorio, Nana and their followers to defeat every opponent sent against them.

Dr Robert N. Watt is a lecturer in the Department of Political Science and International Studies (POLSIS) at the University of Birmingham, UK. His main area of research is into the Apache Wars of 1860-1886, with particular reference to the Victorio Campaign of 1879-1881. He has made numerous archive and field trips to the USA and has visited most of the areas where the Victorio Campaign took place – including Tres Castillos in Northern Mexico, where Victorio was killed in October 1880. He has published articles on Victorio, the Apaches and the US Army in *Small Wars & Insurgencies*, *The New Mexico Historical Review*, *War in History*, *Southwestern Historical Quarterly* and *The Journal of Military History*. He has also published two books with Osprey on the *Apache Warrior* and *Apache Tactics* and taught a module on American Indian Wars for the History Department, the University of Birmingham. He has also published an article on the Red Army in the Second World War and has lectured on Soviet Deep Battle/Operations for a module in the same department.

‘I WILL NOT SURRENDER THE HAIR OF A HORSE’S TAIL’

The Victorio Campaign 1879

Robert N. Watt

Helion & Company Limited

Helion & Company Limited
Unit 8 Amherst Business Centre
Budbrooke Road
Warwick
CV34 5WE
England
Tel. 01926 499 619
Email: info@helion.co.uk
Website: www.helion.co.uk
Twitter: @helionbooks
Visit our blog http://blog.helion.co.uk/

Published by Helion & Company 2017. Reprinted in paperback 2019
Designed and typeset by Mach 3 Solutions Ltd (www.mach3solutions.co.uk)
Cover designed by Paul Hewitt, Battlefield Design (www.battlefield-design.co.uk)

ISBN 978-1-913118-28-0

British Library Cataloguing-in-Publication Data.
A catalogue record for this book is available from the British Library.

Contents

List of Plates

'These monochrome photos were originally in colour. If you wish to have colour copies of these photos email me at r.n.watt@bham.ac.uk. Please note that any further use of these photos is strictly forbidden unless given the express permission of the author.

List of Contemporary Photographs

List of Maps

In colour section

Key to Maps

Map 2.1 Horseshoe Canyon

A Horseshoe Canyon Spring.
B Dry Arroyo.
C Boulders on the right and higher ridge occupied by the Apache warriors overlooking the spring.
D Boulders on the left and much lower ridge also occupied by the Apaches.
E Modern dirt road running up the canyon.
F Trail left by the Apaches going to the spring.
G Trail left by the Apaches leaving the spring. It parallels the inward trail (F) for some distance before veering off to the right and proceeding into the mountains.
H Once out of sight of the inward trail the Apaches circle round to positions C and D and conceal themselves.
I Russell's detachment following the inward trail (F) and spotting the outward trail (G) and they decide it is safe to water their horses and are ambushed at the spring.

1 This map covers the majority of the geographic area encompassing the events outlined in this trilogy. It is intended to provide the reader an overview or master map for the Victorio Campaign.

I have made strenuous efforts to pinpoint the broad locations of places mentioned in this narrative. However, some places, particularly small ranches mentioned in US army scouting reports, were often only temporarily occupied before the occupants moved on 'to a better place'. I even came across a reference to a 'Watt's Ranch'. While I was able to narrow the location to somewhere between the southern reaches of the Black Range and Cooke's Range, I was unable to pinpoint it and therefore it is not included on the map. Therefore, some of the more obscure locations mentioned in this trilogy are not entered on this map simply because I've been unable to pinpoint an approximate location.

Map 7.1 McEvers' Ranch

The Hillsboro posse was probably ambushed only a few hundred yards from McEvers' Ranche where the road curves round between a cienega and some low but steep hills and ridges approximately fifty feet in height. Around Point A the posse was probably ambushed by Apache warriors stationed at Points B, C and D. There are many natural firing positions at all these points and their victims would have found themselves under fire from three directions from above and at close range. Any survivors could have taken cover in the cienega. Today there is a lot of cover in this marshy area. If Victorio had stationed a couple of warriors at Point E any survivors could have been effectively pinned down in this area. Point F is slightly higher but set back from the site but would have provided an excellent vantage point from which Victorio or whoever directed this ambush could signal instructions to his warriors

Map 4.1 Victorio Campaign

Place	Grid
Alamillo	B9
Alamosa & Alamocita	F37
Aleman Well	J42
Alma	E15
Annaya Spring	F31
Apache Spring	N85
Ascension	M93
Belen	B6
Brockman's Mill	J55
Cañada Alamosa	F34
Carizalillo Spring	M79
Carrizo Spring	F26
Casas Grandes	Q95
Chamberino	J71
Chase's Ranch	F19
Chihuahua City	U105
Chivatito (Chivalo?)	Q121
Chloride & Winston	F20
Cienega Apache	F23
Clifton	E14
Cow Springs	H77
Coyame	T122
Cuchillo	F36
Cuidad Guerrero	U104
Deming	J78
Dona Ana	J66
Eagle Springs	R90
El Carmen	S99
El Carrizal	Q107
El Colorado	J62
El Lucero	Q110
El Paso	M81
El Paso Del Norte	M82
El Rito	B4
Fort Bayard	H52
Fort Bliss	M80
Fort Bowie	H75
Fort Craig	F29
Fort Cummings	J125
Fort Selden	J65
Fort Stanton	G47
Fort Sumner	C13
Fresno Springs	N87
Galeana	Q97
Garcia	B3
Georgetown	H53
Gold Dust	J39
Guadalupe	M113
Hacienda Corralitos	Q94
Hermosa	F18
Hillsboro	J40
Hudson's Hot Springs	J56
Hueco Tanks	M83
Janos	P92
Jaralosa	J59
Juan Mata Ortiz	P96
Kingston	J41
Knight's Ranch	H126
La Joya	B8
La Luz	F45
La Mesilla	J68
Laguna Colorada	R117
Laguna De Patos	Q109
Laguna de Guzman	M128
Laguna de Santa Maria	M130
Laguna el Cuervo I	R134
Laguna el Cuervo II	T132
Laguna el Uno	T133
Laguna la Vieja	Q131
Laguna las Flores	Q111
Laguna Palomas	M127
Laguna Salada	R118
Laguna Spring	J74
Lake Valley	J57
Las Cruces	J67
Las Lunas	B5
Las Palomas	F38
Lincoln	G48
Lloyd's Ranche	J63
Lower & Upper Plaza	E16
Magdalena	B10
Malpais Spring	F43
Mason's/Slocum's Ranche	J64
McEvers' Ranche	J58
Mescalero Agency	G46
Monica Spring	F25
Mule Springs	J124
Namiquipa	S103
Nutt Station	J135
Ojinaga	T123
Ojo Caliente N.M.	F24
Ojo Calientes TX/Mex	R116
Ojo Caliente Mex	Q106
Ojo del Carrizo	T120
Old Fort Quitman	N89
Old Fort Tularosa*	E17
Ortega	S101
Paraje	F30
Picacho	J70
Pinos Altos	H50
Placitas	F35
Polvadera	B11
Quemado	A1
Rattlesnake Springs	N86
Roswell	G49
Rincon	J61
Sabinal	B7
Samalayuca	M115
San Antonio	F27
San Buenaventura	S98
San Ignacio	M114
San Jose NM	F33
San Jose Mex	Q108
San Lorenzo	S100
San Marical	F28
Santa Barbera/Barbara	J60
Santa Clara	S102
Santo Tomas	J69
Seboyeta	B2
Shaw's Ranch	F21
Shedd's Ranch	J72
Sherman's Cienega	E22
Silver City	H51
Slocum's/Mason's Ranche	J64
Socorro	B12
Soldiers Farewell	H76
Sulphur Spring	N84
St Nicholas Spring	J73
Thompson's Ranch	J54
Tinajas De Cantarrecio	M112
Tinaja De Las Palmas	N88
Toussaint's Ranch	F32
Tres Castillos	T119
Tulerosa	F44
Upper & Lower Plaza	E16
Vado De Santa Maria	Q129
Van Horn Wells	R91
Winston & Chloride	F20
Ysleta	M136

Note:

* To minimise confusion between Tularosa, site of the Chihenne Reservation Agency in the early 1870s and Tularosa the site of a Mexican village adjacent to the Mescalero Apache reservation, I have decided to refer to the former as Tularosa and the latter as Tulerosa. No doubt this will cause some annoyance to New Mexican readers but it should minimise confusion for a more general readership.

Rivers

1 Rio Bravo/Rio Grande
2 Rio Salado
3 Gila River
4 Rio Tularosa
5 San Francisco River
6 Rio Penasco
7 Seven Rivers
8 Black River
9 Rio Corralitos
10 Rio Santa Maria
11 Rio Concho
12 Pecos River

Mountain Ranges

A1 Gallo Mts
A2 Escondido Mtn
A3 Mangas Mts
B1 Cebollita Mesa
B2 Sierra Lucero
B3 Datil Mts
B4 Gallinas Mts
B5 Bear Mts
B6 Sierra Ladrones
B7 Polvadera Mtn
B8 Socorro Peak
B9 Los Pinos Mts
B10 Manzano Mts
B11 Plains of San Agustin
E1 San Francisco Mts
E2 Tularosa Mts
E3 Mogollon Mts
E4 Kelly Mts
E5 Saliz Mts
E6 Brushy Mts
E7 Mogollon Rim
E8 Nantanes Mts
E9 Gila Mts
E10 Elk Mts
E11 Pelona Mtn
E12 Horse Mtn
F1 Luera Mts
F2 Black Range (North)
F3 San Mateo Mts
F4 Cuchillo Negro Mts
F5 Fra Cristobal Mts
F6 Magdalena Mts
F7 San Andres Mts (North)
F8 Oscura Mts
F9 Lava Flow
F10 The Jornada Del Muerto
F11 Lava Bed
G1 Lone Mtn
G2 Patos Mtn
G3 Carrizo Mtn
G4 Vera Cruz Mts
G5 Capitan Mts
G6 Sierra Blanca
G7 Sacramento Mts (North)
H1 Pinaleno Mts
H2 Cabezas Mts
H3 Peloncillo Mts (North)
H4 Whitlock Mts
H5 Pyramid Mts
H6 Big Burro Mts
H7 Little Burro Mts
H8 Cow Springs Mtn
H9 Victorio Mts
H10 Pinos Altos Mts
H11 Stein's Peak
H12 San Simon Valley
J1 Black Range (South)
J2 Cooke's Range
J3 Caballo Mts
J4 Berenda Mtn
J5 Sibley Mtn
J6 Nutt Mtn
J7 Goodsight Mts
J8 Little Florida Mts
J9 Florida Mts
J10 Sierra De La Uvas
J11 Rough & Ready Hills
J12 Sleeping Lady Hills
J13 West Potrillo Mts
J14 Picacho Mtn
J15 San Diego (Round) Mtn
J16 Point of Rocks
J17 Dona Ana Mts
J18 San Andres Mts (South)
J19 Organ Mts
J20 The White Sands
J21 Robledo Mtn
J22 Cooke's Peak
J23 San Augustin Pass
K1 Sacramento Mts (South)
K2 Guadalupe Mts (North)
K3 Brokeoff Mts
L1 Dragoon Mts
L2 Mule Mts
L3 Swisshelm Mts
L4 Perilla Mts
L5 Chiricahua Mts
L6 Peloncillo Mts (South)
L7 Animas Mts
L8 San Luis Mts
L9 Little Hatchet Mts
L10 Big Hatchet Mts
L11 Alamo Hueco Mts
L12 Cedar Mts
L13 Sulphur Springs Valley
L14 San Bernardino Valley
L15 Animas Valley
L16 Playas Valley
L17 Hachita Valley
M1 Sierra La Rancheria
M2 Sierra El Presidio
M3 Sierra Juarez
M4 Sierra Las Conchas
M5 Sierra Los Muertos
M6 Sierra Guadalupe
M7 Cerro La Rosina
M8 Sierra Boca Grande
M9 Sierra Las Lilas
M10 Sierra El Cartucho
M11 Sierra San Blas
M12 Sierra La Nariz
M13 Cerros Prietos & Sierra El Malpais
M14 Sierra Los Borregos
M15 Cerros El Venado
M16 Sierra Alta
M17 Sierra Samalayuca
M18 Carrizallio Hills
M19 Tres Hermanas Mts
M20 East Potrillo Mts
M21 Franklin Mts
M22 Sierra el Fresno
M23 Hueco Mts
M24 Sandhills
N1 Cornudas Mts
N2 Guadalupe Mts (South)
N3 Delaware Mts
N4 Sierra Prieta
N5 Sierra Diablo
N6 Baylor Mts
N7 Apache Mts
N8 Beach Mts

N9 Sierra Blanca
N10 Finlay Mts
N11 Malone Mts
N12 Quitman Mts
N13Sierra San Ignacio
N14 Sierra La Amargosa
N15 Devil's Ridge
Q1 Sierra La Candelaria
Q2 Sierra La Alcaparra
Q3 Sierra San Ignacio
Q4 Sierra San Rafael
Q5 Sierra Vado
Q6 Sierra Los Arados
Q7 Sierra El Chivo
Q8 Sierra Santa Lucia
Q9 Sierra Rancheria
Q10 Cerro El Chile
Q11 Sierra San Miguel
Q12 Sierra El Chilicote
Q13 Sierra China
Q14 Sierra Santo Domingo
Q15 Sierra El Capulin
Q16 Sierra La Escondida
Q17 Cerros El Gregorio
Q18 Sierra America
Q19 Cerros Los Caballos
Q20 El Barreal
R1 Sierras San Jose Del Prisco & Las Vacas
R2 Sierras Carrazalillo &El Pino
R3 Sierra El Hueso
R4 Sierra La Lagrima
R5 Sierra La Pelea
R6 Sierra La Chocolata
R7 Sierra El Fierro
R8 Sierra El Hacha
R9 Sierra Los Lamentos
R10 Sierra El Perdido
R11 Sierra El Alambre
R12 Chispa Mt
R13 Eagle Mountains
R14 Carrizo Mts
R15 Wylie Mts
R16 Davis Mts
R17 Van Horn Mts
R18 Sierra Vieja
R19 Cuesta Del Burro
S1 Sierras San Joaquin & El Cristo
T1 Sierra Tosesihua
T2 Sierra El Jabali
T3 Sierras El Rayo, La Vibora & Las Escaramuzas
T4 Sierra La Aguja
T5 Sierra Los Clanes
T6 Chinati Mountains

Map 9.1 Morrow's Campaign – September–October 1879 Campaign

1.	23-24 Sept.	Morrow marches his battalion from Fort Bayard to McEvers' Ranche. They are joined by some civilian volunteers from Georgetown.
2.	24 Sept.	Enroute to McEvers' Ranche, at Thompson's Ranche on the Mimbres River, Morrow sends Lts Blocksom & Gatewood with their Apache scout companies over the Black Range. They will arrive at the headwaters of the Las Animas River from the west.
3.	25-26 Sept.	Morrow leaves McEvers' Ranche and moves his battalion up to Las Animas Canyon from the east in the hope of trapping Victorio between his battalion and the Apache scouts.
4.	26 Sept.	Morrow receives news of the discovery of a large trail left by the hostile Apaches in the Seco Creek from Lt. Blocksom's Apache scouts.
5.	28 Sept.	Morrow catches up with his Apache scouts 12 miles north of Seco Creek probably in the vicinity of the Palomas River. The scouts had discovered Victorio's camp but fail to surround it during the night of the 28–29 of Sept.
6.	29-30 Sept.	Morrow's battalion engages Victorio's Apaches approximately 8 miles north of the camp on the Palomas River. This probably places it somewhere along the South Fork of the Rio Cuchillo Negro.
	1-2 Oct.	Morrow's forces again attempt to surround Victorio's camp located less than four miles from the camp assaulted on 29 October. Unfortunately, no direction is given so the camp could be either north or west of this location. The Apache scouts capture a Warm Springs Apaches woman and child who state that Victorio is intending to move west into the Mogollon Mts.
	3 Oct.	Morrow's Apache scouts scout the area and confirm that Victorio appears to be making west towards the Mogollon Mts.
7.	4 Oct.	Morrow's troops arrive at Ojo Caliente.
8.	5 Oct.	Morrow arrives at Shaw's Ranch on the North Star Road.
9.	6 Oct.	Morrow's force reaches Sherman's Cienega and is joined by reinforcements from Fort Bayard led by Capt. Purington. Neither force had seen any sign of hostile Apaches and Apache scouts are sent back into the Black Range. The scouts eventually discover that Victorio had moved into the San Mateo Mts.

9.	10 Oct.	Lt. Gatewood's scouts discover Victorio's trail as it leaves the San Mateo Mts.
10.	11 Oct.	Morrow returns to Ojo Caliente and spends the next day replenishing his supplies.
11.	12 Oct.	Morrow reaches Chases' Ranch on the Cuchillo Negro River.
12.	15 Oct.	Morrow's forces arrive at the recently burned McEvers' Ranche.
13.	16-18 Oct.	Apache scouts, sent out from McEvers' Ranche arrive at Lloyd's Ranche discover the trail of the Apaches going into the Goodsight Mts. They leave the trail and make for Fort Cummings for supplies where they are joined by the rest of Morrow's Battalion who marched directly from McEvers' Ranche.
14.	19-20 Oct.	Gatewood's Apache scouts are sent south to the Florida Mts and spend the following day searching this range.
15.	21 Oct.	Gatewood moves on to the Tres Hermanas Mts. where he is joined by the rest of Morrow's battalion
16.	22 Oct.	The command moves to a camp next to the Laguna Palomas. Gatewood's scouts are sent to scout along the Rio Corralitos.
17.	23 Oct.	During Gatewoods' absence Morrow, from his camp at Laguna Palomas, spots smoke in the Potrillo Mts.
	24 Oct.	Gatewood is sent to scout the Potrillo Mts but returns to report no sign of the Apaches.
	25 Oct.	Morrow returns to the Potrillo Mts. with his command and discovers a four-day old camp.
	26 Oct.	Further scouting in the Potrillo Mts. reveals a second abandoned campsite.
18.	27 Oct.	Victorio's Trail is pursued south through the Sand Hills in Northern Chihuahua.
19.	27-28 Oct.	Morrow engages Victorio and Juh's warriors probably in the hills in front of the Sierra San Blas.
20.	28 Oct.	Morrow breaks off and makes for the Rio Corralitos for water.
21.	30 Oct.	Morrow arrives back at the Laguna Palomas.
22.	2-3 Nov.	Morrow's battalion returns to Fort Bayard.

Map 9.2 Cuchillo Negro

Top: Blocksom & Gatewood's Apache scouts fan out in search of Victorio's Chihenne Apaches. Lt's Blocksom & Gatewood's Sixth Cavalry Detachment & Morrow's Ninth Cavalry command settle down for breakfast. Victorio's warriors having waited until the Apache scouts have long gone, infiltrate down the sides of the canyon.

Middle: The hidden Apaches pick off a single Ninth Cavalryman left on guard above Morrow's camp and at the same time open fire upon both encampments. Both camps and the ground in between are caught in a heavy crossfire and pinned down for almost an hour. The Chihenne Apaches occupy particularly strong positions on Hills One & Two.

Bottom: Blocksom's & Gatewood's Sixth Cavalry detachment storms Hill One and opens fire upon the hostile Apaches on Hill Two. Some of Morrow's Ninth Cavalrymen are able to launch a counterattack up the canyon side onto Hill Two just as the Apache scouts return. In the face of this counterattack, Victorio's warriors pull back and disappear back up into the mountains.

Map 12.1 Candelaria Mountains

Once the men from Carrizal were firmly inside the segment of the canyon chosen for the ambush, Apache warriors stationed at the top and bottom of the trap, (Green Dots) and the Apache sharpshooters (Blue Dots) opened fire to prevent the Mexicans from fleeing along the canyon in either direction. In this opening fusillade the horses were the primary targets. Seeing an apparently obvious source of cover, the Mexicans took cover (Green Arrows) in the rocks to their left. At that point the majority of the Apaches (Red Dots) opened fire from above and behind them. With little or no cover from the Apache rifles, the first party from Carrizal was ultimately wiped out.

There was a slight variation in the destruction of the second party. The Apaches remained hidden until these men had gathered up the bodies and were in the process of burying their comrades. Being aware of the traditions of their enemies the Apaches had probably waited until they were presented with a compact group of men clustered around the grave site before they opened fire. Some of the survivors managed to break out of the trap only to be run down and killed. There is some dispute within the sources as to whether the second group was wiped out. At least thirty Mexican Irregulars were killed in this double ambush.

List of Figures

List of Tables

Preface & Acknowledgements

My interest in the Apache Wars was triggered as a child by a TV series called 'The High Chaparral'. My mother, Heather Neill Watt, now a retired history teacher, encouraged my passion for history at an early age. When she saw a film or television programme spark any interest in me, a non-fiction book, or more, would appear within days. She taught me that the historical facts were as interesting, if not more so, than the fiction. She also taught me to never rely upon one source and to read as much as one could on whatever topic had grabbed my attention.

My interest in Victorio was sparked when my late father, John (Ian) Rankin Watt, let me stay up to watch a film called 'Hondo' which was very rarely shown on UK television in the early 1970s. He thought it was a great John Wayne movie, yet for me it was Michael Pate's portrayal of Victorio, as a tough but fundamentally honourable man, that made a lasting impression. Only days later a book on the Apache Wars mysteriously appeared. After reading the book (long since lost) it was clear to me that there was little information about Victorio and I wanted to know more about him. This mystery was somewhat solved almost twenty years later by my discovery, in 1991, of Stout's 'Apache Lightning' which led me on to Dan L. Thrapp's work 'Victorio and the Mimbres Apaches'.

Therefore, I will start by acknowledging the influence of two individuals whom I never had the pleasure of meeting: Dan L. Thrapp and Eve Ball. Dan Thrapp pioneered the study of the Apache Wars and it was his books which finally confirmed my interest in this fascinating period of history. Eve Ball managed to preserve invaluable Apache testimony before it was lost and has made an incalculable contribution to our knowledge of the Apache point of view.

Many people have helped me on my way over the years through either the sustained encouragement of close friends or sage advice from colleagues at various conferences or gatherings over the years. I am bound to have forgotten people so apologise in advance for any omissions. As such, I would like to thank the following persons: Julian Greaves, Guy Wishart, Mike Snape, Armin Grünbacher, Victoria Henshaw, Steven Campbell, Fiona and Meirion Jeffreys, Kira Watt, Sam Watt, Kim Watt, Maureen Waugh, Mike Nellis, Cornelia Navari, Nigel Dorrington, Professor Jim Storr, Professor Hew Strachan, Robert M. Utley, Frank Brito, Deni Seymour, Eleanor King, Allan Radbourne, J.R. Absher, Jim Bowman, Jim Winder, Lance Robert Blyth, Layton Hooper, Edward Hull, Roy Marcot, Harley Shaw, Alun Evans, George Hackler, Ron Burkett, Rod Millar, Joe Arcure, Alan Ferg, Anthony Romero, Frank Parrish, Paul Magid, James Kornberg, Craig McEwan, Mike Fitzgerald, Ces Moore, David Glantz, Stuart Britton, Scott Forsythe, Jonathan Boff, Dan Whittingham, Steve Dobrott, Tai Kreidler, Brecken Uhl, Dr Samuel Watson, Andrew Taylor, Thomas T. Smith, Richard Johnson, Anastasia Nesvetailova, Anthony Hopkins, Luis Perez, Louis Kraft, Greg Michno, John Monnett, Richard Denning, Patrick Campbell, Ian Hall, Ray Boyles, Richard North, Paul B. Rich, Will Sulkin, Martin Windrow, Marcus Cowper, Bruce Vandervort, Paul Andrew Hutton, Peter MacDonald, Chuck Rankin.

I should also mention several groups of people who have also encouraged my research. The Western Writers of America, the Hillsboro Historical Society, the Order of the Indian Wars, University of Birmingham's War Studies Seminar attendees, the Military History Society of the West Midlands Police and the October Club. The Red Lion, Vicarage Road, Kings Heath,

Birmingham UK also deserves an honourable mention as a great place to unwind and relax of a Friday evening.

Special thanks must go to Duncan Rogers at Helion for taking on this large project. Helen Hancock did an outstanding job copy-editing this manuscript. Thanks to Kim McSweeney for her impressive efficiency and speed in completing the final version of this book. Ana Clamont drew up some wonderful maps for my journal article on Grierson Versus Victorio based on my hand-drawn maps. George Anderson also did an outstanding job in converting my hand-drawn maps/diagrams into the versions you see in this volume.

Singular mention must also go to Professors Paul Jackson, David Marsh and Stuart Croft. In 2000, I wrote a draft essay on 'Why the Victorio Campaign was important'. All three separately read and commented upon this article and actively encouraged me to pursue this research. This work would probably not have been pursued without their encouragement at this nascent stage.

Paul Jackson and Dr John Bourne also conspired to keep me in academia by pointing me in the right direction for getting my first article on the Apaches published in 2002.

Professors David Marsh, Colin Hay and David Dunn supported my research at key points in its development and this is thoroughly appreciated.

Particular mention also has to be made of the sustained encouragement, support and criticism from William A. Dobak and Katharine Franklin. Ed Sweeney has been an outstanding friend, supporter and critic. Professors Robert Wooster and Jerry Thompson have also been particularly strong supporters of my research. Stephen H. Lekson has given me great encouragement and also lent me an unpublished article which significantly changed how I viewed the history of the Chihenne Apache. Craig Springer has sent me a number of snippets of information that filled in several specific gaps in my knowledge of the Victorio Campaign. Both Professor Durwood Ball and Sherry Robinson have the quiet ability to see through to, and advise on, the key arguments and interpretations of my research.

I would also like to thank Jim McKechnie and Hazel Knox, whose module on Developmental Psychology I took as an undergraduate at the University of Paisley in 1990-91. They showed me that different cultures have different ways of thinking and that differences do not necessarily denote superiority. They planted the seed that made the investigation and interpretation of Chiricahua Apache strategies and tactics, from their point of view, a key element of this research.

A very special mention must go to Dan Aranda, Emilio Tapia, Eric and Kathy Fuller, Bill and Jill Cavaliere, Karl Laumbach, Lynda A. Sánchez, Juan Rojelio, Mary Williams, Kevin Bowler, Berndt Kuhn, Bernd Brand, Bob Roland, Spike Flanders, James Irby and Diana Hadley. I have made eight field trips to New Mexico and Arizona since 2005 and they could not have made me feel more welcome. More importantly, by getting me into 'the field' to visit the locations where events occurred, they have fundamentally influenced my understanding and interpretation of the Victorio War. There is far more to the study of history than dusty archives and every historic location visited has provided valuable additional insight into those events.

Nevertheless dusty archives are enormous fun and a number of people have made my life in the archives a most rewarding (and easier) experience. Richard Wakefield, Jay Van Orden, Katherine Reeve, Laraine Daly Jones, Laura Hoff and Bruce Dinges at the Arizona Historical Society. Laurence S. Creider at the University Library, New Mexico State University, Las Cruces. Michael Musick, Jill Andrea and Deanne Blanton at the National Archives, Washington DC, Daisy Njoku at the Smithsonian, Ann Wellborn and LaRena Miller at the Geronimo Springs Museum, Truth or Consequences, New Mexico and Tomas Jaehn at the Fray Angélico Chávez History Library, Santa Fé, New Mexico.

I've already mentioned Dan Aranda of Las Cruces NM but he deserves singular attention. Dan is the most important influence on my research. He is a gold mine of information about New Mexico's frontier history. When Ed Sweeney put me in touch with Dan around 2002, I suspect that neither of them realised that this was to be the tipping point which changed what was an intriguing project into sustained academic archive and field research. Without Dan's insight, advice and encouragement, I would not have finished this work. He also does a very good impression of a rattlesnake so be warned.

Lastly, I could not have completed this research without the support and encouragement of my wife, Catherine Edwards. She's kept me going when I'm at my lowest ebb. She also has the greatest store of involuntary knowledge about the Chihenne Apaches, the Ninth Cavalry etc. I cannot understand how that could have happened.

A final comment on my interest in Victorio also underlines the reason for writing this book. Whilst Thrapp answered many of my questions several remained unanswered. Having completed my current research some of these mysteries have still not been solved and I hope some questions will remain for future research whether undertaken by myself or others. There is no substitute for digging through the voluminous primary sources and walking the ground where events occurred; I found that they invariably challenged most of the secondary sources. Nor should the reader assume that this work is the definitive work on this conflict. I have very occasionally been confronted by outraged individuals who challenge my interpretations on the basis of 'that is not what Thrapp says in his book'. I suspect that the latter would not claim to be the last word on the topic, nor do I claim such omniscience. If, on reading this work, you see any anomaly or contradiction, do not be afraid to do your own research and challenge my interpretations. I may have uncovered new material and developed new or different interpretations of events from those previously published. Yet I strongly believe that history should not be presented as complete when published and neither should you make that assumption.

The main reason for writing a trilogy on the Chihenne Apache resistance from 1877 to 1881 is quite simple. Since starting this research virtually everybody I have met has heard of Geronimo but few were aware of Victorio. This was a war in which the Apaches gained a military draw with the USA and Mexico. Yet in some ways they won quite an important political victory of sorts in forcing an end to the policy of concentrating the Apaches on one reservation in Arizona, or worse. The US army singularly failed to defeat the Chihenne Apaches and their allies from 1879-1881. Therefore, it is clear if one has heard of Geronimo one really ought to know Victorio. In writing a history of the Victorio Campaign, I hope to not only change that perception but show why we should be aware of Victorio's importance as a Chihenne Apache leader. In doing so, I hope that other names such as Nana, Van Patten, Hatch, Morrow, Terrazas, Denny, Kaytennae, Samaniego, Parker, Cooney, Grierson, to name but a very few, become more than small footnotes in the history of the struggle for Apacheria.

Author's Notes

The hostilities known as the 'Victorio war' or 'Victorio campaign' are usually accepted as having occurred between 4 September 1879, when Victorio raided Ojo Caliente, and 15 October 1880, when he was killed at Tres Castillos, Chihuahua Mexico. However, the campaign will be better understood if we include the period leading up to Victorio's breakout from San Carlos in September 1877, and that of the attacks by Nana (Victorio's successor), which lasted until August 1881. Certainly, the 'accepted' period does highlight the most sustained period of warfare between the Ninth Cavalry and those Apaches led by Victorio; and if we adhere strictly to the period of Victorio's involvement in this campaign, our interest should end with his death in October 1880. However, Victorio's second in command, Nana (sometimes spelled Nané or Nani), a very old and experienced warrior, re-grouped at least some of the Warm Springs Apaches and launched a spectacular long-range raid into New Mexico in 1881. The political goal of the return of their Ojo Caliente reservation had not changed with the death of Victorio. This counterattack, launched after the major setback of Victorio's death, should be included in any study of the Victorio Campaign. Moreover, due to the manner of Victorio's ultimate defeat, the US authorities were still unsure as to whether Victorio had indeed been killed at the point when Nana launched his raid.[1] In fact, at least one officer described his own participation in the 'Victoria' campaign as lasting from 3 October 1879 to 1 October 1881.[2]

There can also be potential confusion relating to place names. There are three 'Ojo Caliente's' in this trilogy. Luckily they are situated in New Mexico, Chihuahua and Texas and can be easily delineated. However, Tularosa/Tulerosa can refer to two locations within New Mexico. I've seen both sites spelled with this variation. One refers to the location of the Chihenne reservation in 1872-74 near modern-day Aragon NM. The other refers to a village adjacent to the Mescalero Reservation. While there are the two variations in spelling both are more commonly referred to as 'Tularosa'. However, in an effort to avoid confusion among readers outside New Mexico, I have chosen to refer to the Chihenne Reservation as 'Tularosa' and the village near the Mescalero Reservation as 'Tulerosa'. I apologise in advance for any annoyance caused.

Finally, the majority of the primary sources surveyed were hand-written and very occasionally I simply could not decipher the handwriting. Where this is the case, whether quoting them in the text, footnotes or in the appendices/original documents, I have denoted this by using groups of four or more question marks (????).

1 See Thrapp, 1974, p.310.
2 Personal File Louis H. Rucker, NARA Wash. D.C., RG94 Entry 297 Box 180.

1

The Role of Politics and History: Has the Victorio Campaign Been Neglected?

There is a long history of hostility between the American Indians known as Apaches and their Spanish (later Mexican) neighbours, with Spanish records listing encounters with consistently hostile warriors from the time of the first settlement of what is now the southern United States of America.[1] However, it was when the Apaches encountered the Anglo-Americans, in the late nineteenth century, that they were finally forced to surrender their way of life. This book will examine the experience of the people who can broadly be termed the Warm Springs or Chihenne Apaches, under the leadership of Victorio and Nana, and their allies among the Chiricahua and Mescalero Apaches, in their warfare with the Anglo-Americans and Mexicans, from 1879 to 1881. The conflict between the Apaches and the Anglo-Americans is generally agreed to have been ignited by with the Bascom Affair of 1861,[2] in which Lieutenant George N. Bascom, a US army officer, accused Cochise, chief of the Chiricahua Apaches, of raiding and kidnapping. An attempt by Bascom to seize the Apache leader failed, following which both sides executed hostages and unleashed over a decade of sustained guerrilla warfare which affected large tracts of south eastern Arizona and south western New Mexico. The conflict radiated out through other Apache groups related to Cochise's Chiricahuas, including the Warm Springs Apaches, led at that time by the redoubtable Mangas Coloradas. During the 1860s, while hardly acting in concert, the Apaches in general refused to bow to federal United States authority.

Three reasonably simultaneous factors broke this deadlock. With the ending of the Civil War, in 1865, the United States was able to devote more military resources to the Southwest.[3] By the 1870s, the effects of a campaign of attrition were beginning to tell, and the Apaches were more receptive to peace overtures. Second, the USA initiated a peace process in the early 1870s, and many Apaches, including Cochise, accepted reservations scattered across the area that had come to be designated Apacheria. Finally, others refused to accept these reservations and, between 1872 and 1874, General George Crook led a sustained attack on those holding out. Significantly, Crook realised that the best strategy to combat Apache guerrillas was to use Apache scouts to spearhead campaigns by US soldiers. He kept his scouts and troops in the field throughout the year, and succeeded in convincing the Apaches that they could not keep to their old way of life. By 1874, the Apache Wars seemed to be over.[4]

---

1 See Worcester, 1941; pp.1-14; Johnson, p.148; Woodward, p.3.

2 Hostilities between the Apaches and the USA did not flare up overnight, and there had been hostile encounters before 1860. Yet I think it is safe to say that the point of no return was crossed with this encounter. See Sweeney, 1991, p.119 & 1998, pp.399-400.

3 This is, of course, in relative terms. Between 1865 and the Victorio Campaign, the US army and others would argue that the US government did not direct sufficient military resources to Apacheria. For example, see comments in Thrapp's *Conquest of Apacheria* on the incident in which Apaches led by Juh ambushed and killed Lt Cushing in 1871.

4 See Ogle, 1970, pp.114-117 for a summary of these operations.

However, a decision to generally concentrate the Apaches on just one reservation thwarted this potentially peaceful solution. A combination of forcing together Apache tribal groups who considered each other to be enemies and failure by the federal authorities to deliver promised resources resulted in disaster. Disillusioned, the Apaches left the reservation in increasing numbers, and a series of breakouts culminated in the Victorio Campaign of 1879-81.[5]

The Victorio Campaign should be regarded as a key episode in the history of the Apache Wars, and as the beginning of the failure of the US federal authority's 1870s concentration policy.[6] Nevertheless, the campaign itself has largely been forgotten, certainly when compared with the later Geronimo campaigns. To view this omission in terms of comparative analysis of individual Apache leaders, however, is too narrow an approach.[7] The reasons for this collective amnesia are complex; but politics is the common denominator. While this volume is a history of the Victorio Campaign, other disciplines, including developmental psychology and sociology, will be drawn on where relevant. For example, the ideas of sociologists Emile Durkheim and Max Weber are very useful in considering the interplay between the Apache and the US army notions of warfare, and how these views affected the two sides' ability to confront one another. However, it is the field of 'politics' that will best enhance our understanding of the history of the campaign. Therefore, some effort should be expended in attempting to define 'politics'.

The first point to be made is that the only certainty about attempts to define politics is that debate and disagreement will ensue. The study of 'politics', 'political science' or 'government' is a constantly evolving discipline, with a number of ideas competing to explain what politics is in theory and how it works in practice. The diversity of the conceptions of politics available, certainly from a 'western' perspective, can be demonstrated by a brief comparison of the views of Bernard Crick and Carl von Clausewitz.

Crick argues that politics is an activity which involves the conciliation of differing interests within a given community.[8] He rejects the notion that politics involves a 'struggle for power'.[9] At the other end of the spectrum, Clausewitz argues that war is an integral element of politics:

> War can never be separated from political intercourse, and if, in the consideration of the matter, this is done in any way, all the threads of the different relations are, to a certain extent, broken, and we have before us a senseless thing without an object.[10]

---

5 This is a somewhat potted account of the Apache Wars up to 1879. Those interested in more detailed accounts of this period should consult the following: Thrapp's *Conquest of Apacheria*', *Victorio and the Mimbres Apaches* (chapters I-XVII), and *Al Sieber*, Lockwood's *The Apache Indians*, Bourke's *On the Border with Crook* and Worcester's *The Apaches: Eagles of the Southwest* etc. See bibliography.

6 More details of the concentration policy will be given in chapter 5. Suffice to say that this policy attempted to place the various Western and Chiricahua Apache bands on one reservation at San Carlos. This concentration of diverse Apache bands was a recipe for hostilities. However, there were other factors. The San Carlos site was hardly the best real estate in Arizona. And attempts to turn the Apaches into peaceful farmers were not only hampered by this factor but by a failure of the US federal government to provide sufficient resources, as promised under the treaty. Pusillanimous and short-sighted attempts to force Victorio's people to move to San Carlos turned out to be the final straw and heralded a further 10 years (1876-83 and 1885-6) of sustained guerrilla warfare between the US and Mexican military and the Chiricahua Apaches.

7 For example, Claridge argues that Victorio has been neglected by history in comparison with Geronimo. (Claridge webpage; See also Royal City News webpage; Thrapp cited by Herb Whitney The Arizona Republic 31 Aug., 1986)

8 Crick, 2005 p.7.

9 Crick, 2005 p.5.

10 Clausewitz, 1968, p.402.

This brief comparison of the ideas of Crick and Clausewitz illustrates the difficulty for those who attempt an exact definition of politics, for there is none that is universally accepted. Some of the best examples of this aspect of the study of politics are contained in two collections of essays edited by Adrian Leftwich, both entitled 'What is Politics?'[11] These essays outline clearly their authors' conceptions of how 'the political' should be defined. The key point that emerges is that each person's definition will be governed by their beliefs as to how their world is, or, more accurately, should be, organised. These definitions can be seen in the various authors' conceptions of how local or national government should work, and in their discussions of rival abstract, moral generalisations concerning issues such as 'freedom', 'liberty', and 'equality'.

In invoking this debate, I offer my own definition of politics, and give a brief overview as to how this may help develop a more robust historical interpretation of the Victorio Campaign. This approach may appear subjective, or unscientific; but in developing it I draw on both Crick and Stewart Russell. Crick argues that to allow natural-science-style theorising or party dogma to determine what is the legitimate study of politics 'becomes discredited if the authority of the teacher or the curiosity of the students is tied tightly to a particular cause or orthodoxy.'[12] Russell argues that it is down to the individual researcher to 'reconstruct and argue a process,'[13] although whilst Russell is concerned with the study of the impact of new technology on society, my focus is on the application of politics to the history of the Victorio Campaign.

To help outline this point of view, I shall return to Leftwich, who, in his own writing, argues that 'politics' can be found everywhere; it is a process which involves the interaction of different interests. And, unlike Crick, Leftwich includes conflict within this view of politics, arguing that:

> the way people use and distribute resources – their politics – also helps to explain the problems which occur within or between societies, institutions or groups, whether it be unemployment, war, famine disease, overcrowding or various forms of conflict.
>
> The central point to emphasize at this stage is that the *politics* of societies – *not* their government, but it includes that – is at every level and in every sphere inextricably involved with how resources are used, produced, organized, distributed and redistributed, and by whom and with what consequences.[14]

If we accept Leftwich's argument that all human society is inherently political through its control over, use of, and distribution of, resources[15] then this can be applied to the two main opponents in the Victorio Campaign. The tight-knit groups of Apache guerrillas, and their social support networks, tried to marshal their resources against the various organs of the US government: the US army; and the Departments of State and the Interior. This description helps us see that a military history of any war or campaign becomes, to paraphrase Clausewitz, a 'thing without sense' if we fail to take account of the political factors influencing the course of events. Moreover, the politics of this conflict do not just result from the interplay of different political cultures: Apache, Mexican and Anglo-American. There are, as we shall see, political conflicts within each culture concerning the use and distribution of resources. For example, where the USA is concerned, this

11 See, Leftwich, A. (Editor), 1984, *What is Politics? The Activity and its Study* (Blackwell: Oxford) & 2004, *What is Politics? The Activity and its Study* (Polity: Cambridge).

12 Crick, 2005, p.vii.

13 Russell, 1986, p.342.

14 Leftwich, 1983, p.12.

15 Leftwich, 1983, makes a very convincing case for the role of politics in such diverse societies as the !Kung-San of the Kalahari (1983, chapter 2, pp.28-42), the Aztecs of Central America (chapter 3, pp.44-63), the Maasai (chapter 4, pp.64-77) and *The Politics of European Expansion, Conquest and Control*' (chapter 7, pp.117-156).

brings into stark relief another political debate: that between the elements that have become known as 'structure' and 'agency.'[16] Very briefly, this refers to the issue of how far human agents can exercise autonomy while attempting to follow the rules of the structures within which they work. In this example, how far did laws laid down by Congress, government department policy, or orders from higher up the chain of command affect the relative autonomy of individual actors in the US army?. The relative autonomy of certain US army actors in pursuing Apaches across the international border between Mexico and the United States is a very good example of the dynamic interplay of agents and the structures they inhabit.

Politics impacts on the Victorio Campaign in two broad ways. First, politics clearly has an effect on the origins, progression and outcome of the campaign itself. We shall examine these factors in greater depth, as and when they arise, in the main body of this history of the Victorio Campaign. However, politics also influences how this campaign is remembered today. Political factors are key to understanding why this campaign has been relegated to a relatively obscure position in the history of the Apache Wars of 1860-1886. History itself has become a 'collection of resources', the importance of which interested parties can emphasise or, as in the case of the Victorio Campaign, deny. The relative obscurity of this campaign is probably the result of the US army's role in evaluating its success, or lack of it, in the aftermath of the campaign.

In the years preceding the Victorio Campaign, the US army was the subject of political controversy concerning its military efficiency. The Sioux and Nez Perce Campaigns of 1876-7 and 1877 respectively had resulted in several clear defeats by well-armed and motivated warriors defending their families, land and freedom. The image of a 'modern' army failing to quell 'ignorant savages' was hardly one the US army wished to cultivate. Rather, the aim was to present to the world a modern, professional army that could compare itself favourably with its European equivalents. In the Victorio Campaign, while the setbacks it suffered were hardly as spectacular as those of the two earlier campaigns, the US army did suffer several humiliating defeats at the hands of Victorio's warriors. For almost a year, the army was unable to inflict more than minimal casualties on the Apaches. Yet, in the military history of the Old West, the Victorio Campaign is eclipsed by the preceding Sioux and Nez Perce campaigns, and by the following Geronimo Campaign. Why? Thomas Cruse, a veteran of later Apache Wars including the Victorio Campaign, makes an interesting comment concerning the Victorio Campaign:

> When we were making up the list of Indian campaigns for the Pension Office in 1895, much to our amazement we discovered that our campaign against Victorio was not listed as an "Indian Campaign!" Why one never knew. The Bannock Campaign, the Ute Campaign, and several others not nearly so disastrous or far-reaching were so listed.[17]

Historians William A. Dobak and Thomas D. Phillips also note that the lack of official recognition for an Apache campaign between 1876 and 1881 meant that no soldiers involved, bar one company of the African American Ninth Cavalry Regiment that had served in the Ute Crisis of 1879, could claim to be Indian War veterans.[18]

To find an answer to the question that baffled Cruse, we should turn to the realm of politics, and the fact that the US army's activities failed to enable the federal government to provide a clear-cut

16 See for example Hay, 1995, pp.189-206 & McAnulla, 2002, pp.271-291.

17 Cruse, 1987, p.86 & p.176. On the US Army Center of Military History's webpage, there is an interesting collection of histories of US army units. Appendix 4 to this collection of documents lists 77 'Dates of Important Campaigns'. The Apache Wars have one entry dated 1861-90. Yet an expedition lasting less than one month in September 1875 'against Indians in eastern Nevada' is also listed.

18 Dobak & Phillips, 2001, pp.272-273.

Plate 1.1 The Black Range Mountains between West Diamond Creek and the headwaters of the Cuchillo Negro River. The Black Range and San Mateo mountains formed the northern refuge of the Chihenne Apaches in the 1860s and 70s. The stereotypical image of the Chiricahua and Western Apaches is of a hardy desert people. The reality is that they lived in these mountains but knew how to survive in the surrounding arid desert country. (Photo: author)

Plate 1.2 This photo, taken in the same area, shows the difficult nature of the terrain through which the US army had to pursue Apaches. It also shows the type of ridge tops that the troops could find held against them. (Photo: author)

political settlement to the Victorio Campaign of 1879-81. In the earlier operations against the Sioux and their allies, and against the Nez Perce, the US army had eventually delivered military, and thus political, victories. The operations against the Apaches that followed the Victorio Campaign resulted in negotiated surrenders the last of which, in 1886, was casually reneged upon by the US government. In other words, politically, they managed to 'deliver the goods' to the US federal government. This tended to negate the impact of any operational failures that occurred along the way. However, the fact that Victorio met his ultimate defeat at the hands of Mexican state militia indicates that the US army had failed to bring their campaign to a satisfactory political conclusion with either a military victory or a negotiated return to the reservation.

This political failure offers a very clear reason for the relative obscurity of the campaign. It was hardly in the interests of the US army to draw attention to its failures. Indeed, there were even blatant attempts to obscure these failures, the most obvious being the 'creative' accounts of certain 'sweeping victories' that were accompanied by inflated numerical estimates of Apache warriors present – and killed. There is also a suspicion that the US army was occasionally careless in terms of reporting its own casualty figures. The reason for the relative obscurity of the Victorio Campaign may thus partially lie in a reluctance on the part of the army to highlight its inability to bring the exploits of Victorio, whom many considered an 'ignorant savage', to an end. Another political point we shall examine is that it may have been expeditious for officers within these regiments to play down their setbacks in order to avoid supplying ammunition to those opposed to the use of African Americans as front-line troops.

There were also numerous political obstacles that faced the US army during the time they were prosecuting the war against the Apaches. These included internal factors, such as fragmented command structures, inefficient logistics and poor communications, and external factors related to these, such as the role of Congress and its funding of the army. Other external constraints included relations between the Department of the Interior, the Department of State, and the Department of War. The Republic of Mexico, at both federal and state levels, represented another set of actors whose willingness to facilitate or hinder efforts to defeat the Apaches proved to be subject to their own political dynamic. And, finally, the US army had to contend with obstacles presented by its own citizens based in the Territories of New Mexico and Arizona, from the ambitions of governors and the comments of regional newspapers to the actions of individual citizens. These constraints will be discussed in chapter 3.

Another reason for the lack of attention paid to the Victorio Campaign is, surprisingly, the central role played in it by African American and Mexican actors. The African American role in the Victorio Campaign comes principally through their membership of the Ninth and Tenth Cavalry Regiments. A number of issues concerning this will be covered in chapter 3, where we shall consider more general factors relating to the US army's attempts to combat Apache guerrillas. However, it should be noted here that, paradoxically, reasons for the relative obscurity of the Victorio Campaign lie in the increasing popular awareness of the African American role in the American Indian wars in the aftermath of the American Civil War. This awareness carries with it both a benefit and a cost.

That the African American role in frontier history has finally been recognised as a key addition to our general knowledge of this period. The Victorio war was the only campaign against American Indians between 1865 and 1891 where African American troops spearheaded the US army's efforts. For this reason, the involvement of the Ninth Cavalry as individual officers and men in the Apache War of 1877-81 has been well documented – although the regiment's performance *as a whole* during this campaign has been less studied. However, whilst the participation of the 'Buffalo Soldiers' has drawn particular attention to the Apache Wars of the 1870s and 1880s, this attention has been used mainly as a means by which to emphasise the achievements of the men of the Ninth and Tenth Cavalry. Whilst it is true that the Apache War of 1879-81 provides a fertile source of examples of the bravery, resourcefulness and other admirable qualities of these troops, in reality the Buffalo Soldiers were often, though not always, outfought by Victorio, his guerrillas and their allies. Thus the focus on one neglected ethnic group's role in frontier history has, at best, meant that insufficient attention has been paid to the determined resistance of another ethnic group in defence of their way of life. At worst, some of the focus on the Buffalo Soldiers has been used as a springboard for a modern political agenda which, in lauding the qualities of one ethnic group, has scant regard for how its portrayal of historic events may undermine their current efforts to cultivate political allies amongst Native Americans.

Where Mexican and Mexican American involvement in the campaign is concerned, these participants may be the victims of a combination of their own success and Anglo-American perceptions of their culture. There is a tendency for Mexican involvement in the Apache Wars to be viewed with little interest, with disdain, or even with utter contempt. General William Sherman is said to have recommended a second war with Mexico to force the latter to take back New Mexico.[19] However, this supposed attitude has to be balanced with one indicated in the following communication, in which an application by Lieutenant W.W. Tyler, Ninth Cavalry, for sick leave then retirement on grounds of ill-health is rejected on behalf of Sherman by the Adjutant General of the Army:

> [This application] has been disapproved by the General of the Army, who directs me to say that, in his opinion, there is no healthier country on earth than New Mexico; that Lieut. Tyler can not be retired at this time and should render the best service he possibly can in return for his pay.[20]

This reaction to apparent malingering on the part of one of his junior officers suggests that contrary opinions voiced by Sherman on the Territory of New Mexico were probably mediated by a concern with politics in Washington DC.

Nevertheless, negative attitudes tended to prevail. George Hand, a Union soldier serving in Arizona and New Mexico in 1862-4, epitomized this attitude:

> All the sentinels were Mexicans and very poor soldiers. It requires a man to make a soldier and if we were to depend on such specimens for our liberties, we would certainly want for them.[21]

Corporal E.A. Bode, in 1880, reported that 'their only good habit was the cleanliness of their clothing.'[22] Meyer recorded that there were two stereotypes: polar opposites generated by a distant legacy of the wars of religion between 'Protestant England and Catholic Spain.'[23] Thus, Mexican Americans were seen as:

> Untrustworthy, villainous, ruthless, tequila-drinking philandering *machos*, or as courteous, devout, and fatalistic peasants who are to be treated more as pets then people.[24]

Of course, both stereotypes justified the need for Anglo-Americans to dominate political processes in the areas they inhabited. White makes the point that racial stereotypes, as applied to both

19 See Outside View of New Mexico/General Sherman's Opinion webpages.

20 Townsend to Comdg General, Department of the Missouri (Hereafter referred to as 'DoM'), 25 October 1879 in *Letters Received, Dept. of Missouri 1868-98*, RG 393, Entry A1-1 2601, Box 85.

21 Carmony, p.166.

22 Smith, 1994, p.141.

23 Meyer, p.75.

24 Meyer, p.76.

Plate 1.3 Remains of a house belonging to Roque Ramos, an ex-Chihenne Apache captive. While this structure dates from after the Victorio War, it gives a good idea of the appearance of the isolated Mexican ranches in the USA which carried on illicit trade with the Apaches until 1881. (Photo: author)

Plate 1.4 Torreon, Lincoln, New Mexico. This was originally built as a refuge for the local population from the Apaches. (Photo: author)

American Indians and Mexican-Americans, reveal a hierarchy of their perceived utility according to Anglo-American economic values.[25] Myers argues that the change in power relations after the Mexican-American War of 1846-1848 was a 'change from the easygoing Mexican way to the avaricious, restless, dog-eat-dog Yankee mode.'[26] While acknowledging that the Anglo-American way had its negative aspect, this statement maintains the old stereotype of Mexican American attitudes. This characterisation fails to recognise the political and economic disadvantages that the Mexican federal and state authorities faced in comparison with the United States. When the Mexican federal or state authorities did manage to put troops into the field, some of these units were very effective indeed.[27] Yet even these efforts were often dismissed as ineffectual by Anglo-American commentators whose own troops' military efforts were hardly more successful.[28] Indeed, the fact that Victorio was finally killed by Chihuahua state troops must have been something of a 'final straw' for the US army, underlining its supreme embarrassment over its own failure to catch this wily guerrilla leader.

There was a much deeper political element to the role of the Republic of Mexico during the Victorio Campaign, and this concerned on-going diplomatic relations between Mexico and the United States. These were often tense, a direct consequence of the Mexican-American War of 1846-48, in which the United States had taken control of almost a third of Mexico's territory. The Chiricahua Apaches' home ranges straddled this new international border, and they were quick to recognise and exploit this fact. If either country maintained strict border controls and forbade its neighbour's forces to pursue the Apaches into its own territory, this gave the Apaches a huge advantage, allowing them to shake off pursuit by crossing an artificially created political boundary line.[29]

The challenge presented to the United States and Mexico was how willing each would be to allow the other's forces to cross the international line in 'hot pursuit' of Apaches. This issue dominated both nations' efforts to subdue the Apaches. The fact that they eventually managed to reach a formal agreement allowing US troops to pursue Apaches deep into Mexico must rank alongside the deployment of Apache scouts as one of the decisive factors that allowed the USA to prevail over the Chiricahua Apaches. During the Victorio campaign, these negotiations were still on-going and revolved around the issue of national sovereignty.

The Chiricahua and Chihenne Apaches also had a fundamentally complex relationship with the Mexican settlements, ranchers and traders who lived in and around their home ranges. The two groups were equally willing to engage in trade or to slaughter each other indiscriminately, often 'at the drop of a hat', in what could be termed a 'trade/hate'[30] relationship. The Victorio Campaign was no exception. Victorio, while raiding other Mexican communities on both sides of the border, maintained cordial trading relations with specific New Mexican and Old Mexican settlements.[31]

25 White, 1986, pp.399-401.
26 Myers, 1968, p.5.
27 See comments by Cocker, pp.201-202.
28 See Finerty, p.252; Bourke, 2001ii, p.352 & p.362.
29 See comment by Schwatka, 1887, p.42.
30 See Sweeney, 1991, chapters 3-6 & 1998 especially pp.110-113 chapters 3-6 & 8-9 particularly pp.187-188. His two books illustrate this paradoxical relationship between the Chiricahua Apaches and the Mexican settlements in Sonora and Chihuahua in the 1840s and 1850s. This situation was also known to the US army in the 1860s. For example, it was reported that the Apaches were currently at peace with the town of Janos and thus had a ready market for goods stolen in the USA. (Capt. Moore, Thirty-eighth Infantry, CO Ft Cummings to Lt E. Hunter, Acting Assistant Adjutant General (AAAG), District of New Mexico (hereafter referred to as DoNM), 27 November 1868 in Letters sent Vol. 3 June 24 1867–Jan 20 1869, in HQ Records of Fort Cummings, New Mexico, 1863-1873 & 1880-4, National Archives, Washington D.C. (Hereafter referred to as NA), RG393, M1081, Roll 1; pp.141-145)
31 This was a common tactic during the 1870s; Hughes notes that the Nedni Apaches maintained the same relationships with the town of Janos in Chihuahua (2001, p.133).

He maintained good relations with the nearest Mexican community, at Cañada Alamosa,[32] and also traded with some Mexican settlements along the Rio Grande valley in return for providing them with 'protection'.[33] In addition, the Apaches maintained friendly relations with selected Mexican shepherds who roamed over their home territory.[34] From all these sources, the Apaches could gain food, guns and ammunition. One Maximiano 'Max' Madrid recalled that Victorio had advised his trading partners to wear a 'white handkerchief' on their hats, so that his warriors would know them to be friends.[35] However, there was obviously a calculated risk to this relationship. Below the Mexican border, Victorio maintained the same type of relations with some Mexican communities as he did with the above mentioned communities north of the border. Here, however, Victorio banned his warriors from consuming alcohol to prevent treachery, as there seems to have been a constant risk that the Mexicans would turn on the Apaches while they were under the influence, in order to collect the scalp bounties periodically offered by the state governments of Chihuahua and Sonora.[36]

Finally, one observer, Lieutenant Charles Gatewood, who commanded a company of Apache scouts during part of the Victorio campaign, argued that the Apache Wars seemed to have provided both Anglo-Americans and Mexicans with cover to carry out inter- and intra-ethnic feuding and blame any associated killings on the Apaches.[37] He also noted that some ranchers, without specifying Mexican or Anglo-American, may have profited from selling guns and ammunition to the Apaches, while others attempted to profit from the presence of the US army. For example, they were not above spreading exaggerated, or even completely false, rumours about Apache raids in order to charge exorbitant prices for supplying fodder to US army detachments subsequently stationed on their ranches. If the US army ignored some of these claims, they were excoriated for failing to protect defenceless citizens and their ranches.[38]

The above political factors lead directly into the second reason for the Victorio campaign's relative obscurity: the somewhat distorted overall historical analysis of the Apache Wars. This interpretation of the Apache Wars focuses on the immediate, rather than the cumulative, reasons for the collapse of the peace forged with the Apache tribes in the mid-1870s. The flashpoint is assumed to be an Apache scout mutiny at Cibecue, and the almost simultaneous flight of many Chiricahuas from San Carlos in August and September, 1881. While this was the breaking point in relations between the Apaches and the Anglo-Americans in general, it was no sudden explosion. The seeds of the conflict were sown in 1876, when many Chiricahua Apaches refused to accept removal from their previously designated reservation to the San Carlos Reservation. It was further attempts to concentrate the Warm Springs Apaches in 1877 that culminated in Victorio's war of 1879-1880, and this period saw hostilities reach a peak reminiscent of the early 1860s, when Cochise and Mangas Coloradas declared war on the Anglo-Americans.[39]

32 Kaywaykla, 1963, p.67; Ball, 1970, p.57; Worcester, p.216; According to a 'Ghost-Town' website entry, Cañada Alamosa was founded in 1856, being renamed Monticello in 1881. It should be noted that such relations were not always so cordial. Wilson reports that between 1860 and 1867 a combination of severe flooding which destroyed their crops and Apache raiding caused its temporary abandonment in 1867 (pp.336-337).

33 Ball, 1970, p.18.

34 Sonnichsen, p.190; Wellman, 1957, p.149; Longstreet, pp.90-91.

35 Cited in Bryan, 1998, p.125.

36 Ball, 1970, p.74.

37 Gatewood, p.103.

38 Gatewood, p.103.

39 Hunter makes the point that the two most important periods of warfare between the Anglo-Americans and the Apaches were those with Cochise and Victorio. It is also worth noting that Hunter defines both Cochise and Victorio as Chiricahua Apaches (1944, p.299).

Indeed, this campaign is a much-neglected aspect of the Apache Wars, eclipsed by the events starting on 31 August 1881, when the army intervened against a religious leader on the San Carlos reservation. In the ensuing fracas at Cibecue Creek, Apache scouts mutinied, killing seven US cavalrymen and one officer. In return, the army shot dead the leader of the religious movement and several other Apaches.[40] This resulted in a year-long conflict between the Western Apaches and the US army, culminating in the Battle of Big Dry Wash in 1882.[41] Increased US army activity in response to the crisis then precipitated the flight of Juh, Geronimo and many Chiricahuas from San Carlos into Mexico on 30 September and 1 October 1881.[42] Having fled from San Carlos, the two leaders, allied with Nana's remaining Warm Springs Apaches, returned to San Carlos in 1882 and forcibly removed many of the Chiricahuas, including those Warm Springs Apaches under the leadership of Loco who still remained on the reservation. These events are all cited as reasons for the return of General George Crook to New Mexico and Arizona. In the early 1870s, Crook had proved spectacularly successful in combating these supreme guerrilla warriors.[43] There were two reasons for this: Crook often relied on Apache scouts from rival sub-groupings to combat whichever group he was pursuing; and he kept his word concerning the treatment he promised both his Apache allies and his enemies. Having been so successful in the past, Crook was an obvious choice to take command of this situation. His campaigns against these last Apache holdouts in 1883 and 1885-6 are well known, and it is not the purpose of this book to question the reasons for his return. As C.M. Robinson III rightly argues, the events at Cibecue were a 'defining moment' in relations between the Apaches and the United States.[44]

However, the reasons for Crook's return given by most historians tend to focus on immediate events (Cibecue, and the flight of the Chiricahuas) rather than cumulative ones.[45] The Cibecue incident was a flashpoint caused by the routine breaking of promises made to the Apaches by the US authorities between 1871 and 1876 in exchange for the former's agreement to accept concentration on the San Carlos Reservation. Yet if we examine the subsequent 1877-81 period in more detail, we can see that the attempt to place the Apaches on a single reservation had failed long before the Cibecue mutiny. Conflict between 1876 and 1881 was anything but sporadic, and was provoked almost wholly by the political drive to 'concentrate' the Apaches. In fact, the Victorio campaign saw warfare between the Chiricahua Apaches and the Anglo-Americans return to levels of intensity not seen since the early 1860s.

---

40 See Thrapp, 1972, chapter 2; Thrapp, 1967, chapter XVII; Cruse, 1987, chapters IX-XIV; Thomas Cruse was a 2nd lieutenant in the Sixth Cavalry who, as we shall see, saw service in the Victorio Campaign, and he provides an eyewitness account of the later events at Cibecue (sometimes spelled Cibicu). His memoir *Apache Days and After* is essential reading for any student of this period. While he is sometimes vague and sometimes in error as to the chronology of events in general, his account of this particular event is clear. The Officer in charge, E.A. Carr, was court martialled as a result and Cruse, being a prime witness, would surely have had access to these documents when recounting his version of the Cibecue fight.

41 See Thrapp, Al Sieber, chapter XV; Thrapp, 1967, chapter XIX.

42 Thrapp, 1972, p.49; see also the detailed account of this flight by Collins in his book *The Great Escape.*

43 See Thrapp; 1964, and 1967.

44 C.M. Robinson III, p.253.

45 Clendenen and Wormser are good examples of this tendency to analyse the immediate. The former concentrates most of his analysis of the Apache Wars from Cibecue to Geronimo's final surrender. (Clendenen, pp.96-112) The Victorio Campaign merits half a page, and the man himself is wrongly identified as a Mescalero Apache. (Clendenen, p.95) Yet his book focuses upon the relationship between the US army and Mexican irregulars. As we shall see, the Victorio Campaign itself forms an important chapter in the history of such relations. Wormser, mentions Victorio by name only once, in reference to a particular skirmish in May 1880. (Wormser, p.431) And he devotes only a single sentence to the Victorio Campaign. (Wormser, p.386) Yet his analysis of the Apache Wars is determined by the participation in them of General Crook (Wormser, pp.333-346 & pp.366-383).

Plate 1.5 Stein's Peak on the Butterfield Trail. The ruins in the foreground belong to the stage station. The establishment of travel routes into and beyond Apacheria was one of the first indications that US 'manifest destiny' had arrived to confront both Mexican and Apache. (Photo: author)

Plate 1.6 Ruins of the original Fort Bowie from circa 1862; another sign of American intentions to take control of Apache territory. (Photo: author)

Between September 1879 and 1881, Victorio and his successors waged a virtually incessant guerrilla war, causing economic chaos and many fatalities in southern New Mexico, south eastern Arizona, western Texas, and the State of Chihuahua in Mexico. The US army, while making sterling efforts to combat Victorio's warriors, proved unable to defeat them decisively, losing several (by Apache Wars standards) pitched battles. The survivors of Victorio's resistance did not surrender until 1883, when General Crook confronted them in their Sierra Madre strongholds and his troops finally gave the government a political victory. Had General Crook not acted so decisively to end the Chiricahua threat in 1883, the preceding Victorio Campaign offers a clear indication of what might have occurred.

The Victorio campaign had a major, cumulative effect on the direction of hostilities between the Apaches and the US federal government from 1882 onwards. However, historical accounts of the Apache Wars generally fail to recognize this.

There is another consistent oddity about accounts of the Victorio campaign given in sources covering 1876-81. There are two problems with this literature. The first concerns the tendency of some historians to acknowledge the Victorio Campaign, but to deplore this conflict as a tragedy. This allows them to give a minimal summary of the campaign before moving on to more 'interesting' events. In other words, whether consciously or not, a 'let us move on to examine the campaigns the US army ultimately won' approach to the history of the Apache Wars has been adopted. Lockwood, one of the first to attempt a history of the Apaches in the 1930s, is a prime example of a historian wishing to draw a veil over the events of 1879-81:

> The career of this supremely daring and capable Apache chief [Victorio] was nearing its end. Such strategy and endurance, such command over a handful of desperate warriors, such defiance of interminable mountains and arid desert, and such victory over superior numbers of white foes armed and equipped with the best that a civilised nation could provide or invent has rarely been equalled in the records of savage warfare – perhaps never surpassed. To follow the fights and the retreats, the ambushes and the flights, the pillage, the wounds, the torture, and the slaughter through which this flaming savage rode as on a red whirlwind would require a volume. Already both writer and reader are weary of the frightful details of the insane and savage warfare so long waged between the white man and the Apache.[46]

This summary raises several issues. Victorio's skills are acknowledged but not elucidated, and he is dismissed as a savage. There is no mention of the fact that the majority of the front-line US troops in this campaign were African Americans. Nor is there any reference to the Mexican involvement. The discourse creates an exaggerated impression of a dichotomy between 'civilisation' and 'savages', as opposed to offering a considered and dispassionate analysis.[47] While there do appear to have been instances of torture, the narrative's picture of a general descent into an orgy of violence is unsustainable.

A crucial point may be drawn from Lockwood's last sentence. The historian and his readers are weary of the horror and the madness of the conflict. However, this may be an indication of the influence of an 'official' US or Anglo-American political perspective on the Victorio campaign. Where the United States is concerned, its long history of warfare with the American Indians is punctuated by acts of often ferocious brutality and treachery. However, in most of these conflicts, ultimately, there is a result in favour of the United States. The darker aspects of this warfare may thus often be obscured by a discourse of gallant US soldiers and citizens ultimately bringing 'civilisation' to the

46 Lockwood, pp.229-230.

47 We shall examine and challenge the popular image of Victorio as a 'savage' who routinely tortured his captives in the following chapter.

ignorant savage. In the Victorio Campaign, neither the US army nor any US citizen paramilitary organisation inflicted a crushing defeat – or even surrender – on the Apaches. In effect, from an Anglo-American point of view, there is no glory to be gained from anything that occurred before or during this campaign. The US authorities created the conflict by breaking promises made to the Apaches. In the campaign itself, the US army proved unable either to defeat the guerrilla tactics of the Apaches, or to force them to surrender through a strategy of attrition. It is not possible, therefore, to point to a final triumph in the campaign of 1879-81. On these grounds alone it is not surprising that this campaign has been eclipsed by other – more 'successful' – campaigns.

There is another, more important, aspect to Lockwood's approach to the Victorio Campaign, – that it has encouraged other writers – possibly unconsciously – to ignore it. For example, E.E. Dale, in his *The Indians of the Southwest*, ignores Victorio and sums up the campaign, inaccurately, in three lines.[48] However, Lockwood's approach, and the possible historical bias behind it, are not the only influences at play here. Another possible factor is a conflict between the Department of the Interior and the War Department that was described in a later historical account written by a former Indian agent, John P. Clum.

It should be noted that Clum, while Apache agent at San Carlos in 1874-7,[49] was a very effective reservation agent. However, during those years he engaged in a vigorous feud with the US army and the War Department concerning the army's authority to intervene in matters on an Apache reservation, which was the responsibility of the Department of the Interior. The memory of this feud, together with his unwavering promotion of the Apache concentration policy, continued to affect Clum's writings as a historian in the 1920s and 30s, with the result that these offer a very distorted account of Apache-US relations between 1876 and 1881.

Clum portrays the US army as inherently anti-Apache, and makes a very clear, and often convincing, case for considering the treatment meted out to the Apaches to be unjust, and the result of having two separate government departments operating on the reservation – a charge that was, incidentally, repeated by General Crook in 1882.[50] Indeed, Clum may have had some grounds for his argument that Cibecue and the flight of the Chiricahuas resulted from a blunder on the part of the US army. Yet, he fails to make any effort to determine why the US army acted as it did.[51] He also portrays the years 1874-81 as a time of peace which was suddenly shattered by the US army's stupidity.[52] He singles out Geronimo as the prime mover of events post-1881, and argues that, after the Apache leader was captured at Ojo Caliente in 1877, he should have been dealt with appropriately, that is, handed over to the civilian authorities at Tucson where he would undoubtedly have been executed. In effect, Clum implies that if this had been done, the Apache Wars of 1881-6 would not have occurred.[53] This argument is simply not sustainable. The years 1874-81 were not years of peace, as his description of the events of 1876 and 1877 attests. Many Chiricahua Apaches did not accept the efforts to concentrate them in one location, and chose to resist.[54] General Crook later noted that many of the Chiricahuas had, by 1883, been at war with the United States for

---

48 Dale, Chapter VII 'The Army and the Apache, 1869-86', p.107.

49 Clum, 1928, p.7.

50 See in particular Clum, 1929ii, p.231; Crook to Acting Adjutant General (AAG), HQ Division of the Pacific, (hereafter referred to as 'MDoP'), Presidio of San Francisco, Cal. 9 September 1885, Manuscript Reports, Department of Arizona (hereafter referred to as 'DoAz') 1880-1885, NA, RG393, Part 1 Entry 187, pp.5-21.

51 Clum, 1929ii, p.153, p.222 & p.223.

52 Clum, 1929ii, p.219.

53 Clum, 1929ii, p.218.

54 See Opler, 1938, p.361.

approximately 15 years.[55] The Chihenne (also known as the Warm Springs or Eastern Chiricahua) Apaches did not universally accept their removal, and many of them, led first by Victorio and then by Nana, resisted efforts to remove them to the San Carlos Reservation, waging a guerrilla war that was particularly intense and destructive in the years 1879-81. It is this supposed 'peaceful' situation, which influenced the US army's alleged over-reaction at Cibecue in 1881.[56] Are we to believe that the sustained guerrilla warfare of the Victorio campaign of 1879-81 had no influence on their actions? Clum may be correct in stating that those Apaches who had accepted settlement at San Carlos had seen seven years of peace. In February 1880, the editor of the *Grant County Herald* argued that, while he endorsed the pursuit of Apaches onto their reservations, San Carlos should not be invaded, as there had been no trouble there for five years, due to the reservation's Indian police. If the US army were to move onto San Carlos, this situation could be destroyed.[57] However, this misses the point that many of these peaceful Apaches were settled on land they themselves had previously occupied. Moreover, their warriors, if they felt the need to wage war, could find more than enough warlike employment as police or scouts within and beyond San Carlos, dealing with those Apaches who were resisting the efforts of the Department of the Interior to close their reservations. His argument that peace reigned presents a rather distorted picture of events.

Similarly open to question are Clum's claims that if the arrest of Geronimo had been properly handled at the time, it could have prevented the Apache Wars of 1881-6. By the time Clum published his recollections, in the late 1920s, Geronimo had become a symbol of Apache resistance through the notoriety he gained among Anglo-Americans for being popularly perceived as the last to surrender.[58] However, killing Geronimo in 1877 would not have prevented the conflicts with Apaches that occurred between 1881-4 and 1885-6. The Apache Wars of 1876-86 were not a reflection of US army incompetence or brutality; nor did they reflect the malign influence of a single Apache 'Napoleon of Crime': Geronimo. There is also some question as to whether Geronimo was a key leader in the period 1881-3. There were other Apaches who had equal, if not greater, status than he , such as Juh, Nana, Kaytennae, Chihuahua, Josanie, and the somewhat controversial Chato. In the final breakout, in 1885-6, it was Chihuahua and Josanie who wreaked major havoc in their attacks, not Geronimo.[59] With or without Geronimo, a large section of Warm Springs Apaches and other Chiricahuas would not have accepted removal to San Carlos in 1876 or 1877, and would have supported any leaders who resisted.

Convinced by his considerable success on the San Carlos reservation, Clum refused to countenance the fact that the wider policy of concentration was a war-provoking blunder on the part the Department of the Interior. As an employee of that Department, Clum wholeheartedly embraced the concentration policy; yet San Carlos was not the home of the Chiricahuas, and the resistance of Victorio and other leaders was a reflection of the failure of this policy. For those Apaches who accepted life on the reservation, their subsequent experience was of corruption among the agents who succeeded Clum and of failure by these people to support the peace forged in the mid-1870s. In the case of the Cibecue incident, discontent centred on the long-term failure of the Department of the Interior to fulfil its treaty obligations to the Western Apaches. The incident was not provoked by the US army or the Department of War. When Clum was in charge, he was honest and fair

55 Crook to AAG, HQ MDoP, Presidio of San Francisco, Cal., 9 Sept., 1885, Manuscript Reports, DoAz, 1880-1885, NARA, Wash, D.C., RG393, Part 1 Entry 187, p.15.

56 Opler and Opler p.29; see also Reeve, p.309.

57 'Fighting Indians on Reservations', *Grant County Herald*, 7 Feb., 1880.

58 See Cocker, p.191: See also Claridge webpage.

59 Crook, in September 1885, did not view Geronimo's breakout as having any of the significance of earlier conflicts. (Crook to AAG, HQ MDoP, Presidio of San Francisco, Cal., 9 Sept., 1885, Manuscript Reports, DoAz, 1880-1885, NA, RG393, Part 1 Entry 187, p.39) See Thrapp, 1988, p.549.

Plate 1.7 Tenth Cavalry enlisted men's quarters, Fort Davis, Texas. (Photo: author)

Plate 1.8 Monument to Corporal Clinton Greaves who won the Medal of Honor when attacked by a superior force of Chiricahua Apaches whilst on patrol in the Florida Mountains, 26 June 1877. (Photo: author)

in his dealings with the Apaches. General Crook, on investigating the causes of the hostilities of 1881, found that even those Apaches who had not gone to war with the United States after Cibecue were very discontented with the failure of the Office of Indian Affairs (OIA) to meet its treaty obligations.[60] This was not down to the army, but was a result of, to use Clum's own phrase, 'misrule', by corrupt Indian agents and their superiors. The one period after Clum's departure when the reservation was run with honesty was after one agent and his associates had been dismissed and the US army provided an officer to run the reservation until the corrupt officials could be replaced.[61]

In other words, the OIA's stubborn determination to concentrate the Apaches was central to the Apache conflicts of 1876-86;[62] and the OIA's failure to adequately supervise and control its employees' activities was another major factor in the outbreak of warfare. This does not exonerate the US army from blame for its specific actions in moving onto the reservation and precipitating hostilities. Ogle points out that individual officers, both in reaction to the presence of the Apache shaman at Cibecue and in the immediate aftermath of the battle, seemed more concerned with achieving a military solution, and thus inflamed the situation.[63] However, the army was by no means responsible for the conditions which had provoked the Apaches in the first place.

Clum must be given great credit for what he did as agent at San Carlos. However, his analysis of the reasons for the hostilities of 1881, and beyond, does not stand up to scrutiny; and as a primary source of material on the Apache wars, he may bear a great deal of responsibility for the distorted historiography which condemns the Victorio campaign to relative obscurity. He failed to see that significant numbers of Chiricahua Apaches never had anything like the enthusiasm he himself had for his erstwhile employer's policy of concentration. He dismisses Victorio as a 'desperate renegade',[64] although he had earlier described him as 'the recognized chief of the Warm Springs Indians.'[65] His use of the term 'renegade' suggests a man leading a small band of outlaws who had been rejected by their own people, rather than one with a following the size of that attracted by Victorio. Thus, if uncritically reviewed, the work of Clum the historian presents a significantly distorted picture of events in which the participation of Clum the Indian agent deserves a lot of credit.

These problems with an historical analysis of the period 1876-81 leave a vast gap in the narrative. Historians Anne F. Hyde and William Deverell argue that the significance of 'The West' in American History contributes to discussion of a diverse range of contemporary issues, such as gender, ethnicity, class, and political grouping.[66] One of the factors linking 'The West' to these issues is the exercise of 'state power'[67] and its interaction with each topic.

If we adopt an idea of the significance of western frontier history which includes all of its participants, bounded by an overall 'power-relations' narrative, a different story may emerge. Nobody has tried to synthesise the perspectives of the various cultures involved in a military history of this campaign.[68] The literature tends to focus on specific aspects, rather than producing a campaign overview. For example, *The Buffalo Soldiers* by Leckie focuses on the involvement of the Ninth and Tenth Cavalry Regiments' involvement in the Victorio Campaign. However, in dealing with the campaign

60 See Bourke, 1980, pp.435-437; Lockwood, pp.257-259; Thrapp, 1967 pp.258-259; Ogle; 1940, pp.216-217; Worcester, 1979, pp.259-261; Cruse, 1987, p.181; (For a review of a range of illegal practices, see Ogle, 1958, pp.86-90, 91-93 & 99-100.

61 Ogle, 1958, pp.90-91.

62 Thrapp, 1967, pp.165-166; Worcester, 1975, pp.34-35; Hatfield, p.55.

63 Ogle, 1958, pp.96-97.

64 Clum, 1928, p.35.

65 Clum, 1928, p.35.

66 Hyde & Deverell, p.305.

67 Deverell, p.39.

68 See comments at end of this chapter.

itself, Leckie provides an uncritical and sometimes inaccurate narrative.[69] General overviews of the Apache wars[70] or the US army between 1865 and 1890[71] also tend to provide a descriptive analysis. Such criticism can even be levelled at historians Dan L.Thrapp and Joseph A. Stout, whose work does focus on the Victorio Campaign in some detail.[72] This lack of interest in detail can also lead to gaps or inaccuracies in the narrative, and result in somewhat distorted and/or descriptive accounts of events. If we are aware of the Apache principles of war, it is possible to advance interpretations of their actions in particular instances. In researching the Victorio Campaign, it is all too common to find historians making the same mistakes as the US army in failing to understand the Apaches by failing to apply general knowledge of Apache stratagems to specific incidents.

The failures of historians as outlined above have led to a frustrating consistency in the literature, which generally acknowledges Victorio as a supreme guerrilla strategist and tactician,[73] yet offers minimal explanation of his specific actions in the light of such talent. Why was Victorio such a successful guerrilla? No matter what the focus of a particular work, the casual acceptance of Victorio's skills as given betrays a tendency to describe rather than interpret events. Sources which focus on the Apaches as a whole tend to highlight their expertise in guerrilla warfare. Yet where Victorio is the focus of attention, this knowledge is rarely explicitly applied. Armed with such knowledge, the researcher can go beyond describing events, and can offer an active interpretation of these, and of how they combined to form what we now know as the Victorio campaign. In telling a detailed story of the campaign as a whole, we can reconstruct a number of strategies and tactics deployed by Victorio which reveal him to be more than deserving of the very high respect he is accorded.

To return to the point made by Deverell, from an Anglo-American point of view, and certainly from a power-relations point of view, the Victorio Campaign has become significant for all the wrong reasons. It reflects a failure to exercise state power successfully. Yet for African American, Apache and Mexican participants, and more importantly for the descendants of these, their ancestor's involvement in this campaign is surely of significance. Some Anglo-Americans, now as then, may wish to forget this campaign. Other social groups, however, may want to be reminded of their roles in this episode of American history. This is not to say that the existing literature is poor. Many contributions have a wide framework for their analysis and, as such, they usually offer valuable background source material. However, in referring to the Victorio campaign itself, these books, read in conjunction with each other and with primary sources, reveal different accounts of the unfolding of events, different cultural perspectives, and most importantly, portray inaccurate versions of events. The question arises of why the secondary sources are so problematic. The suspicion is that this is because the original secondary historic record of this period portrays the Victorio campaign as not particularly important, and that this perspective has not been seriously challenged. For this reason, I have tried to reconstruct a history of the campaign based upon primary sources, in order to avoid the distractions of the secondary resources.

With this approach, there is an issue of the type primary source material to use, and the US military archives have revealed a rich fund of information relating to the Victorio campaign. There is a concern amongst historians that to utilise these sources is to take a very biased approach – one described as 'boots & saddles' – to the study of the American Indian wars. There is obviously

69 See Leckie, 1967 & 2003 Chapters VIII & IX; The same can be argued in reference to Billington's work on the Buffalo Soldiers.
70 For example, see Thrapp, 1967, and Worcester, 1979.
71 Utley, 1973.
72 Thrapp, 1974 & Stout 1974.
73 Strategy refers to manoeuvres implemented out of sight of the enemy; tactics refer to manoeuvres carried out in sight of the enemy.

some cause for anxiety here, but only up to a point. Two counter arguments spring to mind. First, this study stems from the author's interest in military history, and in the clash between two very different military cultures. The US military records for this period are voluminous, and they cannot be ignored. Moreover, they were not produced from one source; nor do all the records originate with the US army. Second, the debate should focus not upon *whether* military archives have been used, but on *how* these sources have been used. The role of politics again comes to the fore, and researchers know that many written records are almost certainly biased and were written with an eye to history. To minimise the impact of such bias, researchers are advised to check a variety of different archive sources; and to interview, if it is feasible, as many as possible of those who participated in the events being researched. We are also encouraged to study 'policy intent' statements and documents, and to contrast these with statements and documents dealing with the outcome of the policy in question.

These methods, with the obvious exception of interviewing participants, have been applied in the use of military records of the Victorio Campaign. Documents which were written in advance of projected military operations, and letters and telegrams sent and received during those operations, were looked at in the context of how events were subsequently reported. This process revealed that the planning and implementation of military operations against the Apaches during this period were not nearly as straightforward as the US army would have us believe. This result is perhaps not surprising in itself; but, so far, little effort has been made to delve into this military archive material. The material also shows that the US army was very good at passing on information from non-military sources, such as local US citizens and organs of state such as the Departments of State and the Interior. To suppose that, by using the military sources the researcher is only accessing the US army's perspective on the Victorio Campaign, is an assumption that must be challenged.

For all the reasons outlined above, a fresh military history of the Victorio campaign is long overdue. The campaign has not been forgotten; but it does not occupy as prominent a place as it deserves in the history of the American Indian wars.

2

The Warm Springs and Chiricahua Apache Guerrillas

> When you see Apache "sign", be keerful; 'n' when you don' see nary sign be more keerful.
>
> (Joe Felmer, US army officer and scout)[1]

Apache Principles of War

Apache methods of waging war were a crucial factor in the lack of attention given to the Victorio campaign. There are three key issues to be discussed here: first, the nature of Apache warfare; second, the use of Apache scouts; and third, the role of torture, and atrocity in general.

Apache War and Society

J M White makes the point that North American Indian warriors all had a broadly similar approach to warfare – one governed by their own social context, and which was completely alien to European principles of war.[2] Common to most American Indian warfare was the principle of maximum damage inflicted for minimal loss sustained.[3]

Despite this common legacy, Apache warfare developed a form that was radically different from, for instance, the brashness of Plains Indian warfare, or the chivalry of the Nez Perce Indians. If the Apache principles of warfare had to be summed up in a sentence, they would be expressed as: 'Kill as many of your enemies as you can, but don't be such a fool as to get killed yourself.'[4] War as experienced by both the Apaches and their enemies did not lend itself to displays of 19th century romanticism. The Apaches were never numerous enough to indulge in show-off tactics or chivalry. Nor did they ever have the numbers, the military cohesion, or the inclination, to inflict a defeat as severe as that meted out to Custer's troops. In effect, the never numerous Apache warriors waged a form of total warfare where all members of their perceived enemy were potential targets.[5] RK Evans describes them as fighting 'under the black flag.'[6] This had two important effects: Apache warfare tended to impact more heavily on the economic activity of their opponents, in comparison to that of other hostile American Indians; and they were not as vulnerable to US army 'total war' countermeasures as other groups.[7]

---

1 Dan L. Thrapp, 1967, p.66.
2 White, 1979, pp.114-139.
3 White, 1979, p.115.
4 Watson, 2001, p.646.
5 See Opler, 1996, p.335 & p.343.
6 Evans, 2001, p.608.
7 See Crook, 2001iii, p.603.

The caption to this photograph reads: "Chape an Apache Indian. A reward was offered for his father's scalp so he killed his father and brought his head in so he could get the reward." (The National Archives)

Raiding and warfare were so central to the life of a Chiricahua Apache warrior that the anthropologist M. E. Opler covers this aspect of Apache life under 'Maintenance of the Household.'[8] Moreover, both Opler and G.Goodwin (author of '*Western Apache Raiding and Warfare*') state that 'raiding' and 'warfare' constituted two different acts for the Apaches. The former meant taking property from an enemy; the latter consisted of deliberately seeking out an enemy and killing him.[9] This does not mean that enemies were not killed during a raid; and war was often launched as a result of deaths sustained during raiding expeditions.[10] However, what we must note is that raiding and warfare were very calculated acts on the part of the Apache. Their aim was to enable the Apache warrior to provide for his dependants and live to continue such provision.

Training

From a fairly young age, Apache boys were trained in the skills required to become a warrior.[11] When a young Apache was considered ready for action, he would volunteer to accompany established warriors on four raids. If he successfully completed this apprenticeship, he would be consid-

8 Opler, 1996, pp.323-354; see also Spicer, p.243; Alonso, p.26; Cocker, p.213; Loring, 2001, p.185.

9 Opler, 1996, pp.334-335; Goodwin, p.16.

10 Goodwin, pp.17-18; Opler, 1996, p.335.

11 See Opler & Hoijer, pp.618-619; Shipp, 2001, p.519; Ball, 1970, p.29 & p.159; Opler & Hoijer, p.619; Opler, 1996, pp.67-68; Thrapp, 1974, p.10; Sweeney, 1991, p.13; Sweeney, 1998, pp.23-25; Cocker, p.195; Robinson, p.5; Loring, 2001, p.185.

ered a warrior in his own right.[12] Once a raiding party had agreed to accept the boy, his family would outline his duties to him – duties as an assistant to the warriors, but not a direct participant in the raid. They would also indicate the risks of such a venture.[13] Finally, a local shaman would advise him of his spiritual duties and how to use certain equipment unique to the novice warrior.[14] This instruction was reinforced by warnings of the dire consequences of being found wanting during these four expeditions. Failure would mark the individual for life, in the eyes of the tribe, as unreliable and untrustworthy.[15] In fact, throughout his childhood the young Apache was surrounded by rituals and folktales which emphasised his future role as an adult Apache.[16] Needless to say, such ceremonies and legends underlined the virtues of discipline, obedience, forbearance and respect.[17]

Use of the Environment

The Apaches knew the flora and fauna of their environment with an intimacy that enabled them to survive in their often inhospitable land.[18] An Apache eyewitness of the Victorio campaign, James Kaywaykla, noted that Anglo-Americans often failed to detect the presence of sub-surface water. 'Many perished, when by digging two or three feet they could have obtained water.'[19] This superior knowledge also allowed the Apaches to pollute obvious water sources if closely pursued by their enemies.[20]

The Apaches were able to use the stars for guidance,[21] though it should be noted that they were reluctant to engage in night fighting. Kaywaykla stated that this was because they were wary of rattlesnakes, which they believed to be more active at night.[22] And Opler recounts a tale of the folk character 'Coyote', who accidentally released 'darkness' upon the world. 'This [darkness] is acceptable only to the night prowlers and fierce animals; the birds and the small harmless creatures desire daylight.'[23] This reluctance to fight at night was also well known in the folklore of the American West. Kansas firearms manufacturer Roy E. Weatherby, interviewed about his experiences on the western frontier, recalled in 1938 that during the Apache Wars the stage lines often ran at night in an effort to avoid attack;[24] and the historian Charles Collins also mentions the reluctance of Apaches to move, let alone fight, in darkness due to a fear of 'ghosts'.[25] However, there may also have been another very practical reason for avoiding night fighting: the warriors did not want to

12 Opler & Hoijer, p.620.
13 Opler & Hoijer, p.620.
14 Opler & Hoijer, p.620.
15 Opler & Hoijer, p.621.
16 Sweeney, 1991, pp.10-12; Sweeney, 1998, pp.19-20.
17 Sweeney, 1991, p.12; Sweeney, 1998, pp.19-20.
18 See Bourke, 1980, p.36; Cremony, pp.296-297; Opler, 1996, p.185 & p.348; Worcester, 1975, p.26; Sweeney, 1998, pp.21-22.
19 Ball, 1970, p.74; Bourke, 1980, pp.36-37; Opler, 1996, p.348.
20 Laumbach, p.100.
21 Opler, 1996, p.348.
22 Ball, 1970, p.16; see also Ball, 1980, p.23 & p.93; Haley, 1981, p.279. Rattlesnakes were not the only dangerous fauna at large; there were venomous (though not necessarily fatal) spiders, scorpions and centipedes. For example 'Jose Valdez, of Santa Fé, was bitten by a spider no larger than a fly last week and died in an hour and a half' (*Thirty Four*, 30 July 1879).
23 Opler, 1996, pp.196-197.
24 American Life Histories: Manuscripts from the Federal Writers' Project, 1936 to 194 webpage – Incidents of the Early '80s webpage; see also American Life Histories webpage – The Alma/Alms Massacre; and Abran Miller's testimony; Bourke, 2001i, p.141; Finerty, 2001, p.249.
25 Collins, 1994, p.86; See also Thrapp, 1973, p.15 & p.24; Thrapp, 1972, p.55: Loring, 2001, p.187; Rice, 2001, p.504.

Plate 2.1 The western end of Cooke's Canyon, where the Apaches' use of landmarks to move through their territory can be clearly demonstrated. The shadowy ridge on the horizon, seen through the notch in the ridge on the southern side of the canyon, is the Florida Mountains, approximately 25 km distant. To their right, the three peaks of the Tres Hermanas Mountains, approximately 50 km away, can just be distinguished. (Photo: author)

Plate 2.2 This photo, taken from almost the same position previous one, illustrates the different weather conditions that can be encountered in the Southwest. The previous photo was taken on 20 September 2005. This photo was taken on 4 October 2015. (Photo: author)

waste precious ammunition without clear targets.[26] Exceptional leaders could sometimes persuade their warriors to fight at night; but fear of being unable to detect potentially dangerous fauna, the need to save ammunition, and fear of the 'spirits' of the dark, tended to preclude night fighting. However, if the Apaches felt threatened, they would readily move to a safer location during the hours of darkness.

Apache skills in concealment are legendary, even in locations where the observer would judge cover to be non-existent:

> they are the most dangerous antagonists in the world, so far as ambush is concerned. You may ride right through their country and never see head nor hand, so perfectly do they conceal themselves, and you can ride right into an ambush when you least expect. The first indication you are likely to have is the ping of a rifle bullet.[27]

Apache warriors habitually improved the defences of their positions by constructing small rock emplacements.[28] US army captain and diarist John Gregory Bourke recorded at least one incident, in 1883, in which Mexican troops were deceived by emplacements covered in vegetation. When Sonoran state troops who were pursuing the Apaches got to within point blank range, the concealed warriors rose up and delivered a deadly volley which killed four men and severely wounded two more. The emplacements had been sited to catch the Mexicans from the front and both flanks. By the time the survivors and some reinforcements had reorganized their pursuit, the Apaches had made their escape.[29] General Crook also mentioned Apache warriors ambushing a wagon train on a flat plain by throwing dust over themselves and tying tufts of grass to their heads.[30] US volunteer officer John C. Cremony described the use of a system of smoke signals, and of stones and branches laid out so as to convey messages to their accomplices without betraying their presence to their enemies.[31] Mirrors were also used to coordinate ambushes.[32] The US army learned to start patrols during the hours of darkness to avoid being spotted by Apaches.[33] Apache camps were sited in easily defended positions, often improved by defensive stone emplacements of the type described above. Sentries were usually posted on high ground close to the camp to give the group warning of imminent danger. Sites were also selected for concealment purposes. Thus, while campsites were easily defended, they would be difficult to spot in the first place. Another ploy was for family groups to camp far enough apart to prevent the whole camp being taken in a surprise attack; but these individual emplacements were also intended to be close enough to render

26 Robinson, p.192.

27 Howard cited in Cozzens, 2001, p.390; See also Eaton, 2001, p.181; Finerty, 2001, p.258; Bourke, 1980, p.37; Opler, 1996, p.185: Nickerson, 2001, p.107. It is also worth noting Cremony's description of a demonstration given to him by Quick Killer, a Mescalero Apache, of the latter's ability to conceal himself (Cremony, pp.290-291).

28 Thrapp, 1974, pp.264-265, Collins 1994, pp.77-78, 84 & 86; Gillett, 1976 p.187; Laumbach, p. 53 & p.100; Finerty, 2001, p.259; Barnes, 2001i, p.275; Bourke, 2001ii, p.369; Ludwig, 1993, Figures 9, 16 & 17.

29 Bourke, 2001ii, p.354.

30 Crook, 2001i, p.402.

31 Cremony, pp.179-80 & p.233; see also Ball, 1970, p.6; Opler, 1996, pp.346-347; Worcester, 1975, p.26; McKenna, p.57.

32 Ball, 1970, p.6; Ball, 1980, p.66; Opler, 1996, pp.347-348; In a Survival Documentary on BBC2, 21 December 1999, it was stated that mirror signals can be observed up to 80 miles away from their source by aircraft. William Neifert, a US army Signals Corpsman manning a heliograph station, recorded that he could see at least 50 miles and more from his station (2001, p.559).

33 Carr, 2001, p.32.

each other support during an attack.[34] Victorio had a reputation for building small emplacements to improve the defensive properties of a campsite as one of his first priorities, no matter how temporary the site.[35] Crook also noted that raiding parties would often travel at night, but at daybreak they would seek high ground, concealing themselves during the day but alert for any activity by enemies in their neighbourhood.[36] Apache warriors also placed great store on the possession of a good pair of field glasses[37] or a telescope.[38]

Women and Warfare

An understanding of Apache women's role in maintaining their family and the group's warriors is also central to understanding the effectiveness of the Apaches' guerrilla tactics. Apache women were responsible for gathering, preparing and storing food stocks,[39] for childcare, for preparing hides, and for making clothes and footwear.[40] D.C. Cole argues that the warriors were less likely to survive on their own over long periods, as it was their womenfolk who had an intimate knowledge of food gathering, preparation and preservation, particularly where the local flora was concerned.[41] As with adolescent boys, girls were given vigorous physical training[42] and were also taught how to use weapons.[43] They also had to be capable of moving over the same rough terrain as the warriors to avoid their enemies.[44] In general women were considered subordinate to men, though they were sometimes permitted to contribute to councils held by the warriors.[45] Apache women could be beaten for disobeying their spouse, and if they committed adultery they might end up having their noses cut off.[46] It is also clear, however, that if faced with such treatment, woman did not have to meekly accept it.[47] Finally, Kimberley M. Buchanan effectively sums up the role of Apache women as being fully integrated with that of the men. 'Hunting, raiding and warring were the three central features of Apache life. In order for a band to survive, both males and females participated in these activities.'[48]

Apache men and women sometimes operated in two separate groupings, and as we shall see, this was a strategy adopted by Victorio several times during his campaign. While the women and children, usually accompanied by a small number of older warriors, took care of the gathering and preparation of food and clothing, the rest of the warriors hunted and raided. The US army scout Al Sieber noted that younger Apache warriors, being without dependents, could not always be relied upon to defend family groups, whereas older warriors would defend their own families.[49] Sieber also reckoned that Apache warriors tended to operate in groups that were fairly closely related to each

34 Bourke, 2001ii, p.361, p.362 & 364; See also Elliott, 2001, p.433; Davis, 2001, p.493; Crook, 2001ii, p.579; Daly, 2001, p.466.
35 Thrapp pp.264-265 Gillett, 1976 p.187 references Laumbach, p.53 & p.100.
36 Crook, 2001iii, p.599.
37 Davis, 2001, p.493; Ball, 1970, p.13.
38 'A Talk with Na-na'. Lt Buck, 13th Infantry, Socorro, NM, 14 August 1881 in The *Army & Navy Journal*, Vol.19, 10 September 1881, p.125.
39 Opler, pp.354-372; Stockel, 1991, p.10 & 14; Sweeney, 1998, pp.21-22.
40 Stockel, 1991, p.18.
41 Cole cited in Stockel, 1991, p.15.
42 Opler, p.416.
43 Robinson, p.5.
44 Stockel, 1991, p.31; Buchanan, p.19 & p.20.
45 Ball, 1970, p.21 & p.128; see also Opler, p.142; Stockel, 1991, p.17.
46 Stockel, 1991, p.18: Opler, p.410.
47 Opler, p.401, p.410 & 411; Stockel, 1991, p.23.
48 Buchanan, p.18.
49 Sieber, 2001, p.293.

Plate 2.3 The vast distance that can be seen looking east from the heights of the southern Black Range or Mimbres Mountains. The Caballo Mountains can be seen in the middle horizon and are approximately 50 km away (as the crow flies). The San Andres Mountains marching along the far right and left horizon are at least 100 km distant. (Photo: author)

Plate 2.4 The view from the southern end of the Potrillo Mountains across the desert westwards towards the Florida Mountains. The latter are just visible rising above the haze on the horizon. The Apaches could traverse this arid terrain with ease, but it posed a formidable obstacle to many of their enemies. (Photo: author)

other.[50] When moving their families from one location to another, they would focus their attacks away from the intended travel route. This had the additional benefit of focusing their enemies' efforts on warriors unencumbered by dependants. These warriors would keep tantalisingly ahead of their pursuers, occasionally engaging in low-risk rearguard actions. Their opponents often assumed that such delaying actions were intended to give the families time to escape, and this encouraged them to continue their pursuit till exhausted. In effect, the warriors adopted a simple decoy tactic designed to protect their own logistic resources while wreaking havoc on those of their enemies.

Leadership

While the hereditary passing of positions of power from father to son was by no means unknown, leaders were usually elected by the warriors.[51] Successful candidates would have built up a reputation for success in war and wise counsel. However, the sons of established leaders obviously benefitted from being trained by individuals who could pass on their own successful experience.[52] An Apache war leader whose warriors suffered what were perceived to be unnecessary fatalities would soon lose his position of respect. Opler makes it quite clear that a leader's powers were not absolute, and were the result of 'a process in which birth and wealth have their place, but in which ability and personal magnetism are always the leavening factor.'[53] The Apache leader was the product of a long training programme and sustained reputation among his following based on his perceived success.[54] Successful war leaders often directed operations well into their 60s and 70s. This success was measured against the basic maxim of Apache warfare: inflict maximum damage while sustaining minimal loss. While European-led troops may have accepted the loss of casualties in combat, Apaches viewed fatalities as something to be avoided at all costs. The economic impact on the rest of his family of the loss of a warrior was of paramount importance to the Apaches, where it was of little concern to 'professional' European military units. This concern about casualties led to an extremely careful approach to raiding and warfare.

Tactics

Tactics can be divided into three categories: evasion, ambush and attack.

Evasion

When pursued or surprised by their enemies, the Apaches would scatter and reform at pre-arranged rendezvous points. It was standard practice to agree a rendezvous point in advance of any move, or as they settled down to camp.[55] Whether moving as a family unit or as a war party, they would have scouts posted in advance, flank guards and a rear guard (see Figure 2.1).[56] Not only would this system provide early warning of an attack, it could also allow some of the warriors time to find positions from which to fight a delaying action (see Figure 2.2) To be able to successfully evade

50 Bourke, 2001ii, p.371; See also Debo, 1976, p.265.
51 Ball, 1980, pp.43-45; Opler, 1996, pp.462-471.
52 Sweeney, 1991, pp.12-13; Sweeney, 1998, pp.23-24.
53 Opler, 1996, p.470; See also comments by Laumbach pp.101-103.
54 Sweeney, 1991, p.xiv.
55 Opler, 1996, p.346; Ball, 1970, p.4; Sonnichsen, p.134; Bourke, 2001ii, p.350; Adam, 2001, p.420; Daly, 2001, p.453; Davis, 2001, p.491, p.492 & p.493; Shipp, 2001, p.518; Pettit, 2001, p.533; Crook, 2001ii, pp.578-579; Crook, 2001iii, p.597 & p.599; Crook to AAG, HQMDoP, Presidio of San Francisco, Cal. 9 Sept., 1885, NA, RG393, Part 1 Entry 187, Manuscript Reports, DoAz, 1880-1885, p.4.
56 See Davis, 2001, p.493.

their enemies required an intimate knowledge of the landscape.[57] Small pouches holding food were carried by Apache children in case their group had to scatter quickly.[58] Caches of food, cloth, utensils, weapons and ammunition would be secreted throughout their home ranges.[59]

The Apaches also had a very different attitude towards horses from that of the Plains Indians. In warfare, the horse was more of a means to an end than a source of currency or status. Apaches would often outdistance their pursuers through riding their horses into the ground and stealing more if required.[60] Horses also provided a ready source of food.[61] Their attitude towards horses also placed Apache warriors at an advantage over their US cavalry opponents. The latter could not, in pursuit of the Apaches, routinely run their horses into the ground. The artist Frederic Remington noted an attitude among the US cavalry that '[n]o pains are spared to prolong the usefulness of an Army Horse.'[62] When pursuing Apaches, the US cavalryman usually had a single mount and his officers would often be faced with a choice between preserving horses, and thus losing contact with the enemy, or having to explain equine casualties to the Quartermaster General.

Ambush

The practices described above combined to produce in the Apache warrior a truly deadly adversary. His ambush tactics epitomised his people's principles of war. A lightning strike delivered before his opponents had detected his presence was the classic Apache tactic. Therefore, most attacks and ambushes were initiated by warriors fighting on foot. While not unknown, fighting from horseback was the exception rather than the rule. Ambushes were usually intended to cripple their enemies' ability to give pursuit. This often involved the Apaches targeting the enemy's horses in the opening seconds of an ambush, a tactic that further underlines differences between the Apaches and the Plains Indians of the same period. There were probably a number of people who survived to old age because Apache warriors had aimed at their horses. There is some dispute as to the accuracy of Apache warriors when using firearms. Some commentators have argued that they were very poor shots.[63] On the other hand, General Crook states that Apache warriors were 'good marksmen.'[64] It may well be that many of their victims did not realise the significance of having their horse shot out from under them during an Apache ambush.

The author visited a number of the ambush sites selected by Victorio and Nana, and one of the things that immediately struck him was that, *at first glance*, these locations did not look particularly dangerous. When examined more closely, however, it was obvious that the highly innocuous appearance of the terrain must have been one of the reasons for its selection in the first place. The deepest canyon, or the high mountain stronghold, was not necessarily the most dangerous terrain in Apacheria.

If a first strike routed or paralysed their foes, Apache warriors were quite willing to follow up their success and inflict further damage, provided there was minimal loss on their own side. If this involved several hours' careful preparation before they closed in and finished off the survivors of the

---

57 Keith H. Basso demonstrates just how intimate with the land the Apaches are, even today, in a fascinating project in which the Apache geography of the Cibecue region was reconstructed.

58 Robinson, p.7.

59 Ball, 1970, p.3 & pp.19-20; See Opler, 1996, p.371 for a detailed description of the methods the Apaches used to cache supplies. Robinson details the discovery and contents of a cache discovered in the Goodsight Mountains in 1915 (pp.31-32).

60 Crook, 2001iii, p.599; Evans, 2001, p.605.

61 Evans, 2001, p.606.

62 Remington, 1888-9, p.899.

63 See for example Finerty, 2001, pp.258-259; Pettit, 2001, p.535.

64 Crook, 2001i, p.404.

first attack, then they were willing to spend this time. Equally, if an ambush failed, it had usually been mounted in such a way as to allow the Apaches to fade back into difficult terrain before an effective counter attack could be organised, again minimising their own casualties.

The Apaches also used decoys to lure their opponents into an ambush. However, such moves on their part were more subtle than similar tactics deployed by the Plains Indians against the US army. Apache decoys would show themselves, but pretend that they were not aware of the presence of their enemies. The intention was to lull their foes into a false sense of security and coax them

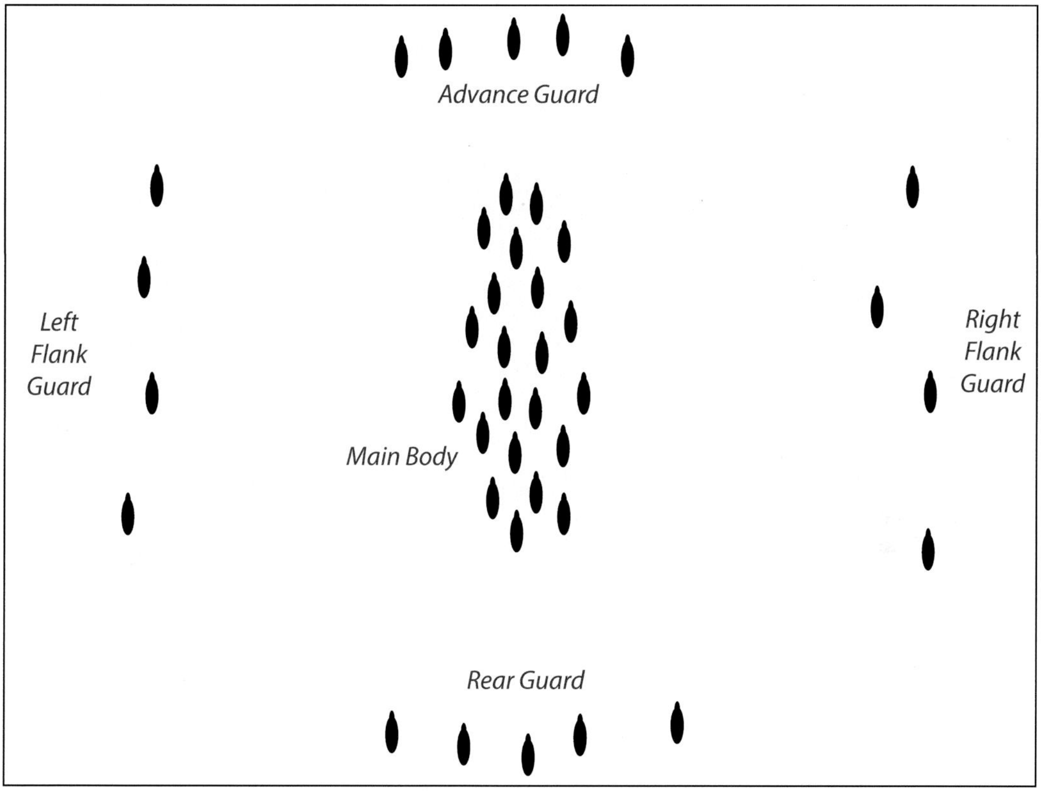

Figure 2.1 Apache Order of March.

Notes:
Direction of March: It should be noted that should a threat be detected then the advance, rear and flank guards can change roles depending upon the new direction chosen to avoid this threat. For example if the route of march is suddenly changed to move to the right; the right flank guards become the advance guards, the rear guard becomes the right flank guard and so on. Any changes to the numbers in each changed grouping can be filtered through as the Apaches continue in their new line of march.

Main Body: This could be made up of either:

1. a small group of warriors escorting a large group of women and children;
2. a small group of warriors driving stolen stock; or
3. a larger group of warriors either setting out on, or returning from, a raid.

Depending upon terrain and circumstance, the gaps between the main body and its advance, flank and rear guards could be measured in yards or miles. There is also an implicit use of the four sacred directions for protection in such a formation.

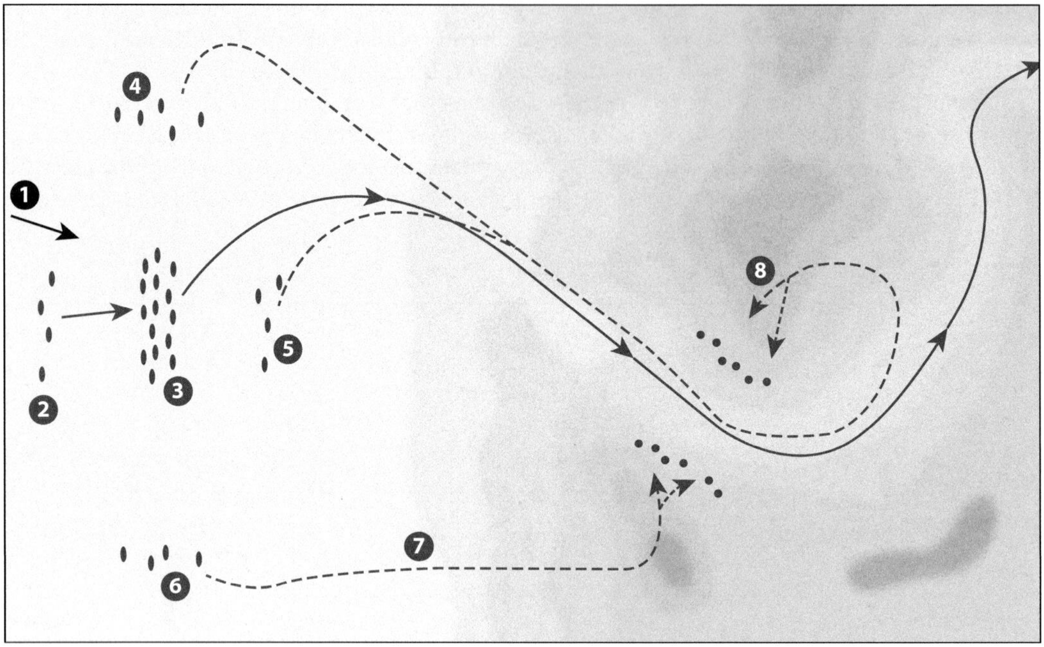

Figure 2.2 Apache Evasion and Ambush Tactics.

Notes:

Enemy forces (1) are detected by the left flank guard (2) who raise the alarm. The Apaches can choose to scatter and rendezvous at a pre-arranged location.

However, if the terrain suits, the Apaches can attempt to pull their pursuers into an ambush as follows. At the first alarm, the left flank guard joins the main body (3) and helps screen its retreat towards a pass in the mountains. The advance guard (4), the right flank guard (5), and the rear guard (6) race ahead to a suitable spot and set up an ambush for their pursuers without leaving their quarry any indication of their impending ambush, by using a different route (7) and/or doubling back (8) to reach their positions.

onto terrain they might otherwise have avoided.[65] At least one example – that of the ambush and killing of Lieutenant Howard B. Cushing by Juh, in 1871 – involved the use of women as 'innocent' decoys.[66] A further example of the Apaches' decoy skills can be seen in a particularly cunning ambush that was perpetrated on a pursuing US cavalry detachment on 21 October 1871. (See Figure 2.3) The Apache war party left a trail leading straight into a box canyon which contained a waterhole in its depths. The 21-man US cavalry detachment arrived at the mouth of the canyon to find a trail leading away from, as well as entering, the canyon. Assuming that the Apaches had left, and requiring water themselves, they entered the canyon. No sooner had they started watering their horses than they were ambushed by the Apaches, who had indeed left the canyon, but had travelled only a short distance, turning up into the mountains and returning to occupy the heights surrounding the waterhole. In the event, while the Apaches caught their pursuers completely off-guard, they inflicted few casualties, though the skirmish lasted for four hours and the troops fired approximately 2,000 rounds of ammunition. Nevertheless, the US army detachment's Anglo-

65 Opler, 1996, pp.345-346.

66 Thrapp and Barney outline the classic example of an attempt to trap the small US detachment commanded by Lt Cushing in 1871. While the trap was detected, Cushing was killed leading his detachment to safety (Thrapp, 1967, pp.72-77; Barney, pp.25-27).

American scout was killed and a soldier badly wounded. Despite claims to the contrary, the Apaches probably escaped with few, if any, injuries.[67] Even when US cavalry detachments tried to prevent such ambushes, the intimate knowledge of the terrain possessed by the Apaches could often foil any countermeasures. On 14 May 1885, a detachment of the Fourth Cavalry attacked and scattered a group of Chiricahuas in a dawn attack. Later that day, the same detachment was ambushed as they watered their horses in a canyon. This was despite the detachment commander taking the precaution of putting out an advance guard and flankers. The Apaches managed to use the rough terrain to slip behind the advance guard and between the flank guards. In a lightning strike, they shot dead two soldiers and wounded three more during what was described as 'a stiff fight.'[68] There was no mention of any equine casualties, but one can be fairly certain that these were a high-priority target. The key result from the Apaches' point of view was the abandonment of the pursuit by the cavalry detachment.

The patience involved in pursuing the principle of maximum-damage-minimal-loss ethos can be illustrated by an ambush sprung by Chihuahua and his warriors on a supply train guarded by eight soldiers from the Fourth Cavalry on 8 June 1885. The Apaches reached a point above the camp undetected. They waited until the troopers took a meal break, and despite the presence of a sentry, they managed to crawl to within a few feet of the soldiers. Their opening volley killed four or five men and routed the others, following which they ransacked the wagons, then burned them.[69] The loot included the troopers' personal arms, and they may have managed to gain some ammunition supplies, though one of the survivors stated that that some of the ammunition stored in a wagon had exploded as he was making his escape.[70]

Attack

If Apache warriors launched an attack, this was designed to panic and rout their enemies without placing the attackers in a position where they could sustain heavy casualties if their opponents stood their ground. This was a particularly effective tactic with the advent of reliable, breech-loading weapons which could be reloaded on the run. Using difficult terrain, the Apaches could launch a sustained infiltration attack that would give the impression of a far greater number than were actually present.[71] There are several accounts left by both settlers and soldiers who were convinced they were being attacked by large numbers of Apache warriors when this does not appear to have been the case. This may reflect a tendency to enhance the heroic status of the participants; but it may also indicate the successful use of tactics to convey the impression of far greater numbers of warriors than were actually present.

These tactics also demonstrate that psychological warfare was a key element in the Apaches' maximum-damage-minimal-loss principle. If their enemies' resolve could be broken at long range, the Apaches were less likely to sustain casualties in gaining a victory. Equally, if their opponents were not 'psyched out', the attack could be aborted before there were any casualties.

Nature or Nurture: Comprehending the Apache Guerrilla

Yet anthropologist Greville Goodwin argued that the Apache guerrilla is often presented as an enigma in historical accounts of the Apache Wars:

67 Barney, 1996, pp.22-24; Sweeney, pp.326-327.
68 Benson, 2001, pp.553-554.
69 Elliott, 2001, pp.431-433.
70 Jett, 2001, p.496.
71 Robinson, p.39.

> All too often, "the Apache" has been portrayed as a figure barren of ideology, devoid of values, and somehow – miraculously – exempt from the inevitable constraints imposed by membership in a society. He is a man without culture and therefore he is an impossible man.[72]

Thus, whilst the Apaches are acknowledged to have been expert guerrillas, they are often portrayed as super-human, in an effort to explain why small groups could thwart Anglo-American attempts to subdue them. Yet this representation also diminishes the Apaches' skills, implying they were the result of inherent traits.[73] So, on the one hand their expertise has been acknowledged, whilst at the same time their skills have been presented as inherited or innate rather than developed and learned. This misses the key fact that Apache expertise was adaptable to changing events. Guerrilla warfare, as practised by the Apaches, was a calculated act governed by years of careful training which was flexible enough to allow individuals to adapt and easily disseminate relevant information in the light of new experiences. The expertise required to survive in the Apaches' environment was beyond mere inherited ability; it was the product of clear thinking by intelligent and adaptive human beings.

Developmental psychologist Jean Piaget's concept of a 'formal operational stage' in human development may help us to understand the Apaches' success. During this stage, the child/adolescent begins to develop abstract reasoning.[74] One controversy concerns whether all human beings attain this highest level of reasoning. There are several facets to this debate, in which it is argued that many members of US society and other cultures, particularly non-literate cultures, fail to reason at this level.[75] Piaget posits that one reason for this apparent failure is that many people use this level of reasoning only selectively, at times when they are confronted by matters which deeply interest them or are critical to their continued survival.[76] A study by psychologists Tulkin and Konner from 1973 found that Bushmen demonstrated this tendency, using abstract thinking when tracking prey, a skill crucial to their survival.[77] Examples of operational reasoning by Apaches can be seen in the warriors' rapid adoption of breech-loading weaponry, and in the way they adapted their tactics to this technology. Historian Frank R. Safford notes that, as early as 1872, the Chiricahua Apaches were well-equipped with 'improved breech-loading guns.'[78] Even more impressive was their swift recognition of the telegraph as a source of danger. The initial response was to destroy the wires and poles. However, once they realised the speed with which these lines could be repaired, they would still cut the lines, but would then splice the cut wire with rawhide. Their enemies would be aware that the lines had been cut; but locating the site of the break would be very time-consuming.[79] Despite these examples of operational reasoning, there was a popular conception at the time that 'the Indian requires about the same treatment as a child.'[80]

As the above-mentioned examples show, the Apache warrior focused his formal operational thinking on the pursuit of guerrilla warfare, and his Anglo-American, African American and Mexican opponents often found themselves at a disadvantage through this behaviour, and through their own unfamiliarity with the principles of Apache warfare. Where these opponents failed to prevail, this may be put down to their dismissal of the Apaches as less developed human beings, and/or unwillingness or inability to adapt their own principles of war in the face of Apache

72 Goodwin, 1998, p.11.
73 see for example, Loring, 2001, p.195; Shipp, 2001, p.519.
74 Shaffer, 1999, pp.251-255.
75 Shaffer, 1999, p.255.
76 Shaffer, 1999, p.255.
77 Shaffer, 1999, p.255.
78 Safford, 2001, p.129; See also comment by Crook, 2001ii, pp.571-572; Crook, 2001iii, p.596 & p.603.
79 Ball, 1970, p.177; Barnes, 2001ii, p.620; Faulk, 1969, p.47.
80 Elliott, 1948, p.101.

guerrilla tactics. The Apaches' most dangerous opponents were those who recognised what they were up against, and themselves drew on operational reasoning. It is only when we acknowledge the centrality of raiding and warfare to the Apaches' culture that we can recognise the source of their expertise in guerrilla warfare. Apache guerrillas were the products of formal operational thinking and a culture of leadership that operated largely on merit. Thus, their thinking was often more flexible than that which governed their opponents' military operations. The Apaches fought specifically to their own strengths, waging guerrilla warfare on their own terms and not allowing their opponents to set the agenda. The clearest indication of this is the US army having to resort to Apache scouts to combat Apache opponents. The US failure to achieve a victory in the face of the guerrilla warfare tactics used by Victorio and Nana is central to the relative obscurity of the two leaders' campaigns. If the US army could not achieve a victory over the Apaches, there were no 'stirring' stories to be told to the taxpayers.

Therefore, in order to survive, the never numerous Apache warriors waged a flexible form of total warfare, which was constantly evolving in the light of experience.[81] More importantly, all members of all Apache groups owed their survival to hunting, gathering, raiding and trade. Throughout the Apache Wars, small groups of intelligent, well-armed and motivated Apache guerrillas would paralyse economic activity in large tracts of present-day Arizona, Chihuahua, New Mexico and Sonora.[82] This did not endear them to a culture whose strongest objective was the economic development of virgin territory. As late as the 1930s, veteran pioneer J.F. Henderson declared that: 'An Indian is the biggest coward in the world unless he has all the advantage or can do his dirt in a sneaky ways.'[83] However, it would be a blind observer who did not notice that, under the pretext of 'civilising the savage', US and Mexican citizens were more than willing to employ the same techniques of total war.[84]

Equally, the reader should not be deceived by biased sources as to the courage of individual Apache warriors. To the Apaches, courage was a means to an end rather than an end in itself. Opler notes that there was nothing more dangerous than a wounded Apache trying to give his companions a chance to escape by delaying the enemy.[85] This was a point appreciated by a few of their more perceptive opponents. Bourke[86] argued that:

> The Apache was in no sense a coward. He knew his business, and played his cards to suit himself. He never lost a shot, and never lost a warrior in a fight where a brisk run across the nearest ridge would save his life and exhaust the heavily clad soldier who endeavoured to catch him. Apaches in groups of two and three, and even individual Apaches, were wont to steal in close to the military posts and ranchos, and hide behind some sheltering rock, or upon the summit of some conveniently situated hill, and there remain for days, scanning the movements of the Americans below, and waiting for a chance to stampede a herd, or kill a herder or two, or "jump" a wagon train.[87]

81 See Opler, 1996, p.335 & p.343.

82 See in particular comments by Evans, 2001, p.607; See also Elliott, 1948, p.93; Crook, 2001i, p.403; 2001ii, p.585; Clarke, 2001, pp.630-631.

83 American Life Histories webpage; see also The Alma/Alms Massacre Testimony.

84 See Cocker, 1999, p.214.

85 Opler, 1996, p.349; See also Cremony, p.227-228.

86 Bourke was an officer who served under Crook in both his 1870s and 1880s operations against the Apaches. He was Crook's ADC for 15 years and left several detailed accounts of Apache customs and operations mounted against Apaches by the US army.

87 Bourke, 1980, p.37 See also Gen. Raguero cited in Cozzens, p.387; Merritt, 2001, p.156; Cremony, p.180; George A. Forsyth, most famous for his leading role in the Beecher's Island Fight against Cheyennes and Lakotas in September 1868, commanded the Fourth Cavalry stationed in Apache

However, not all their opponents appreciated the skill and planning driving the Apaches' style of warfare. Cavalry officer Charles P. Elliott[88] stated that:

> The Apache Indian is as perfect a savage as this country has ever produced, and it is impossible to conceive of greater cruelty and less natural affection in any creature that walks on two legs. The fiendish cruelties committed by them when on the warpath give one a creepy feeling while among them, and when a son brings in his father's head on which a reward had been placed, not because he had trouble with him, but because he happened to know where he was in hiding and wanted the reward, it makes one doubt whether they are human.[89]

John F. Finerty, an experienced war correspondent for the *Chicago Times*, described the Apaches in similar terms to Elliott.[90] He dismissed their failure to mount an assault on Fort Apache, in the aftermath of the scout mutiny at Cibecue Creek, as the result of not having 'the requisite amount of "sand" for such an operation.'[91] Another soldier, Corporal Clarence Chrisman, interpreted the Apache maximum-damage-minimal-loss principle as displaying reluctance to attack US troops.[92] This misinterpretation is echoed in comments made about Victorio in the *Weekly New Mexican*:

> [H]e [Victorio] has been extremely suspicious of White men, and for years after coming on the reservation at Canada would never show himself in town when Americans were present. This extreme caution was so often exercised that he acquired the reputation of being an arrant coward, a reputation which he rather encouraged and gloried in – Mesilla News.[93]

The misinterpretation of the Apaches' 'bravery' was only one facet of a wider misunderstanding of the rules governing their warfare. Thrapp gives two examples of the US army's tendency to misconstrue their skirmishes with Apaches:

> The word 'routed' was the customary euphemism meaning the soldiers had lost contact.[94]
>
> The Indians 'carried off their dead and wounded', which as most Army men know was a euphemism for; 'We don't know whether we hit any of them, but at least we hold the field.'[95]

In reporting on a clash between Juh's Chiricahua Apaches and two detachments of the Sixth Cavalry at K-H Butte on 2 October 1881, Finerty acknowledged the prodigious but ineffective fire of both sides, with the cavalrymen expending over 4,000 rounds of ammunition 'without discernible effect.'[96] He excused the troopers as having being faced with targets hardly visible in their cover. However, he did acknowledge the Apaches' skills in guerrilla warfare, and expressed his

country in the 1880s. (Dixon, pp.147-148) See Dixon 1994 for full biography. See also succinct comment by Ayers, p.263; Worcester, 1975, p.26.

88 Elliott was an officer in the Fourth Cavalry from 1883 till his retirement in 1898. He was detached from the Fourth Cavalry soon after his arrival at Fort Lowell in 1883 to serve as a provost officer on the San Carlos Reservation. As such he would have had very close contact with Apache warriors during the last phase of the Apache Wars. However, he does not seem to have felt the need to familiarise himself with Apache culture (See Elliott, 1948, pp. 94-95).

89 Elliott, 1948, p.101.

90 Finerty, 2001, p.242; See also comments by Lloyd, 2001, p.326.

91 Finerty, 2001, p.243.

92 Chrisman, 2001, p.542.

93 'Victoria the Indian Chief *Weekly New Mexican* 18 October 1879 in The Walter Lowry Finley Collection.

94 Thrapp, 1974, p.263.

95 Thrapp, 1967, p.206.

96 Finerty, 2001, p.258.

Plate 2.5 Rattlesnakes are one of the reasons why Apaches were very reluctant to fight at night. Rattlesnakes are predators that are most active at night, and when neither human nor snake sees the other, and direct contact is unintentionally made, the snake will usually strike. This is a Western Diamondback photographed in Cooke's Canyon. (Photo: author)

Plate 2.6 Pronghorn antelope photographed in Nogal Canyon, the San Mateo Mountains, New Mexico. The Southwest USA and Northern Mexico support a wide range of flora and fauna. This allowed the Apaches to support themselves quite easily in what, at first glance, seems very inhospitable country. (Photo: author)

relief that they had only killed one sergeant and wounded four troopers. Finerty noted two other points: the fact that the Apache warriors were fighting a rearguard action to cover the escape of their families; and the large number of cavalry mounts killed in the action.[97] However, he failed to spot the significance of the latter point. The Apaches were directing their fire at the horses in what turned out to be a successful attempt to cripple any subsequent pursuit.

In another instance where those people who made an effort to engage with an alien culture developed a better understanding of the Apaches, William D. Fuller[98] also noted examples of poor marksmanship by the Apaches, but added that they were 'more certain shots, since they will not fire until almost upon the object.'[99] Fuller reported that, in hunting also, the Apaches would attempt to creep into close range before firing. This was in spite of the fact that the rifles being used were effective over a much greater range than that favoured by the Apaches. For their first shot, the Apaches preferred to, if possible, rest their weapon on a rock or a cut branch to steady their aim.[100] The above observation that the Apaches preferred to utilise their firearms at close range finds a possible echo in a report in the *Army and Navy Journal*, where it was noted in an account of shooting by Plains Indians that the subjects appeared to have removed the sights from their rifles, giving rise to the statement that 'evidently the Indians did not desire to waste their ammunition (which they probably obtained with more or less difficulty) at long ranges.'[101]

Perhaps the most interesting description of the Apaches comes in a statement alleged to have been made by General Crook in 1872:

> The Apache is as much worse than the Sioux as the hyena is worse than the tiger. Bloodthirsty, cruel, cowardly, treacherous, implacable, incapable of gratitude or any other generous emotion, he has all the ferocity of the most savage wild beast, intensified by the worst human passions and rendered more formidable by human cunning. The outrages perpetuated by Apaches upon the bodies of their living and dead victims would be utterly incredible if they were not strictly authenticated. Their insensibility to kindness, and their total lack of gratitude is only paralleled among meaner brutes.[102]

The political context of this statement should be carefully considered. If Crook made or authorised this statement, it does not reflect his later evaluations of Apache guerrillas. However, at the time he made it, Crook was strongly opposing a peace mission, headed by General Oliver Otis Howard, which threatened to disrupt his intended operations against the Apaches. If he did genuinely think the Apaches were such paragons of bestiality, he soon changed his mind, ultimately reversing his original description to describe them as tigers rather than hyenas.[103]

97 Finerty, 2001, pp.257-259.

98 Fuller recorded his observations from a hunting trip with Apaches and this was first published in 1872. Cozzens also notes that 'Internal evidence suggests Fuller to be the author of this article' (See Cozzens, 2005, p.524).

99 Fuller, 2005, p.467.

100 Fuller, 2005, p.466 & 467.

101 'Arms used by Indians' *Army and Navy Journal,* Vol.17, 25 Oct., 1879, p.225.

102 Crook, or Bourke attributed in Cozzens, 2001, p.113.

103 See original comment by Crook, 2001iii, p.602 see also 2001ii p.571 & p.576. For a comprehensive description of the challenges of Apache warfare see Crook, 2001iii, pp.597-598; see also comments Crook, 2001iii, pp.602-603.

The Role of Apache Scouts

One of the decisive tactics employed by the Anglo-Americans in the Apache wars was the use of Apache warriors not only to locate Apaches but also to actively fight them.[104] As noted earlier, General Crook's exploitation of hostilities within and between various Apache bands had proved spectacularly successful in the early 1870s. By 1886, Crook had concluded that, for the Americans to operate successfully against Apaches, some degree of tribal disintegration must take place, with a tribe, or section of a tribe, being pitted against one or more other tribes or sections.[105] The Americans' use of Apaches in the Victorio campaign was to be equally critical. A company of sixty-five Apache scouts inflicted what was probably Victorio's heaviest defeat on US territory *without* the presence of regular US troops, a fact which the US army was somewhat reluctant to acknowledge at the time. Lieutenant Thomas Cruse, who saw service in the Victorio Campaign, argued that Apache scouts attached to US army troops and mule trains were crucial factors in wearing down the Apaches.[106] These detachments of Apache scouts, US cavalry and mule packers avoided the use of cumbersome wagons and carried only the bare essentials (food and blankets) when in the field.[107] James Kaywaykla noted the particular hatred independent Apaches reserved for Apache scouts.[108] Nana is reported to have referred to Apache scouts as 'bloodhounds.'[109] As members of the same culture, these scouts knew how to survive, track and fight Apaches far more effectively than did US troops. In operational terms, Apache scouts were the most effective weapon in the US army's arsenal, often foiling ambushes which the army would not have detected. The Apaches also found it far more difficult to break contact with US army units accompanied by these scouts. They tended to avoid engaging such units unless they were forced to do so, or were absolutely sure of their chances of victory. However, as the Victorio Campaign would demonstrate, not all US army commanders accepted General Crook's views concerning the key role of Apache scouts. Colonel Eugene A. Carr, commander of the Sixth Cavalry stationed in Arizona Territory during the campaign, was firmly of the opinion that Apache scouts should only be used to locate Apache warriors: it was the job of the accompanying troops to fight these belligerents.

However, the Victorio Campaign reveals a complex situation with regard to American use of Apaches, and the reader should not be deceived by terms such as 'quisling' or 'turncoat' when applied by later commentators to these Apache scouts. As noted above, it was General Crook's opinion that, in many cases, enthusiastic service by Apache scouts merely reflected long standing inter- and intra-tribal conflicts. There were a number of occasions during the 1879-81 period when Apache scouts acted in their own interests, and did not serve their employers as well as might have been expected. On one occasion, a scout company was suspected of having led a detachment of Ninth Cavalry in New Mexico Territory back along a false trail towards the scouts' own reservation in Arizona Territory to coincide with their discharge date.[110] On another occasion, it appeared that a scout detachment had opened fire prematurely in order to warn independent Apaches of their presence, thus allowing the latter to escape.[111] Some scout detachments were also accused of giving

104 See Crook, 2001ii, p.586 & p.587; Crook, 2001iii, p.598.

105 Crook, 2001iii, pp.597-598; see also comments Crook, 2001iii, pp.602-603.

106 Cruse, 1987, pp.54-55.

107 Letter 5 January 1879 in MacPherson Letters 1 January 1879 to 3 September 1880, University of Virginia at Charlottesville.

108 Ball, 1970, p.33.

109 'A Talk with Na-na'. Lt Buck, 13th Infantry, Socorro, NM, 14 August 1881 in The *Army and Navy Journal*, Vol.19, 10 September 1881, p.125.

110 Thrapp, 1974, p.245.

111 Captain Henry Carroll's report letters and telegrams sent by the battalion on the Southern Pacific Railroad at Separ NM September–November 1881, in NA, RG391, Entry 921, pp.11-12; See also Daly,

false reports,[112] trading ammunition with independent Apaches,[113] or even serving on both sides at different stages of the Apache Wars.[114] Indeed, it was later suggested, during 1881, that some Chiricahua Apaches had enlisted as scouts simply to get a better picture of how their opponents operated and what their weaknesses were, so that this knowledge could be exploited at some future point. As we shall see, one of the key stumbling blocks to a peaceful resolution to the Victorio Campaign was the US authorities' unwitting, or even blind insistence, that Victorio settle on the San Carlos reservation. What the authorities did not know was that during his first forced transfer to San Carlos, in 1877, a lethal feud between his following and some of the Western Apaches already settled on the reservation had blown up, which meant that by 1879-80 Victorio knew that if he accepted settlement on the reservation, his days would be numbered.

Finally, the readiness with which some Apache scouts were willing to serve the Anglo-Americans was not always indicative of overall loyalty to the US army. In some instances, a lack of enthusiasm on the part of the scouts could probably be attributed to an increasing dissatisfaction with the treatment they received on their reservations. It could also be credited to a lack of faith in the US army's perceived ability to defeat Victorio in the field. Whether being led by an Apache or an Anglo-American, and notwithstanding any particular feud some of the scouts may have had with Victorio, if Apache warriors felt that they were being badly led, their enthusiasm for the campaign would have quickly faded.

Torture Atrocities

There is a myth that, during his last campaign against the Mexicans and Americans, Victorio turned into an embittered monster who routinely tortured captives. The Apaches had always had a reputation for cruelty, and it was not surprising that they retaliated harshly against the Spaniards, the Mexicans and finally the Anglo-Americans. Indeed, a belief that this was the way the Apaches behaved was ingrained in the minds of those recalling their experiences in the Old West in the 1930s.[115]

Allegations that Victorio routinely inflicted the cruellest tortures upon his opponents are found in several sources.[116] Wright, a scout employed by the US army in 1885-6, recounted the story of a Fourth cavalryman tormented to death at the hands of Victorio;[117] but the account is hearsay, in that Wright was not its original source. It also comes across as an exaggerated tale designed to scare green recruits for the amusement of 'old hands'. Those recounting such stories could expect them

---

2001, p.487.

112 See Letters and Telegrams sent by the Battalion on the Southern Pacific Railroad at Separ NM September–November 1881, NA, RG391, Entry 921 p.15; See also comments by Shipp 2001, p.524 &525 Pettit, 2001, p.535 See also Benson, 2001, p.553; Maus, 2001, pp.248-249.

113 Daly, 2001, pp.465-466.

114 On 7 October, 1881, Jack (Long?), the First Sergeant of Lt Bailey's scout company reported to Major Biddle that one Chiricahua and eight Warm Springs 'called Chiricahuas' deserted this afternoon. (Col MacKenzie citing Major Biddle's Report, 7 October 1881, NA, RG393, Part 1, Entry 181, p.186) 'The scouts claimed to have killed one; certainly they had the discharge paper of one of Lieut. Guilfoyle's scouts.' (Captain Carroll's Report in Letters and Telegrams sent by the Battalion on the Southern Pacific Railroad at Separ NM September–November 1881, NA, RG391, Entry 921 p.13)

115 See American Life Histories webpage: Old Timers Dictionary, Early Days Around Silver City, Early Days in Silver City and Grant Co.; J.C. Brock, Louie Taren, Mrs OS Warren, Jose Apodaca entries; Evans, 2001, p.608.

116 Brown, 1970, pp.399-400; see also Gibson, p.77; Wellman, 1957, pp.164-165; Balmer, p.7.

117 Wright, 2001, p.498.

to be widely believed.[118] Later historians such as Paul Wellman, spoke of Victorio as 'an implacable enemy and his cruelty was notorious.'[119] J.H. Byler, interviewed in the 1930s, remembered someone known as 'old Victor…an old Apache with the wildest instincts.'[120] Colonel Benjamin Grierson, commander of the Tenth Cavalry, normally sympathetic towards his American Indian opponents, is reported to have considered Victorio to be 'brutal and degenerate.'[121] This evaluation of Victorio seems to have been taken from a comment by historian Frank M. Temple and not directly attributed to Grierson.[122] However, it is clear that captives taken by Apaches *were* sometimes brutally tortured.[123] On his first long patrol in February 1880, Lieutenant Cruse reported that the graves of men described as 'tied to cactus and roasted to death' and 'staked out on an ant heap and left' during the Apache warfare of the 1860s could still be seen in the cemetery at Fort Bowie.[124]

So, although many stories were exaggerated by their enemies, it has to be acknowledged that some Apache warriors did use torture as a means of intimidating their enemies. Writing in the second half of the 20th century, historians, Thomas E. Mails and David Roberts make this point very clear.[125] However, both authors indicate that these acts have to be carefully considered as part of a range of guerrilla tactics deployed by the Apaches and were not indicative of an innate predisposition to savagery. Daklugie, son of Juh,[126] does not deny torture but makes the point that it was not as widespread as some would have us believe, and that such acts were often acts of revenge for equally appalling acts perpetrated on the Apaches.[127] He also stated that the Chiricahua and related bands were particularly warlike and fought against the Anglo-Americans for as long as they could. In doing so he stated that: 'We had the Sioux beat [for cruelty], especially the Nednhi and Chiricahua. The Warm Springs too. They were brave warriors and real fighting men.'[128] This statement does suggest that such cruelty was an acceptable, even if not an obligatory, option for the Apaches. However, it must be remembered that cruelty was not an inherent trait: many Apache warriors did not indulge in this practice, and they were not censured by their peers for their forbearance.[129] Some Chiricahua Apaches may have viewed such acts as a perfectly legitimate terror tactic to deter invaders. Their reputation for this behaviour was even acknowledged by other Apaches. John Rope, a Western Apache scout with General Crook in 1883, made the following comment: 'I had never fought the Chiricahua and did not know how mean they were, so I was always in the front.'[130]

However, documents of the time make it crystal clear that the Apaches did not possess a monopoly on deliberate cruelty. For example, Roberts recounts the killing of two Apache infants

118 Neifert records the 'ribbing' of new recruits on arrival in Apacheria by both veterans and civilians usually involving lurid tales of Apache atrocities (2001, p.558).

119 Wellman, 1957, p.176. This narrative has also been repeated in the recent *Idiot's Guide to the Old West.* (p.345) The Electric Scotland.Com website dateline for October 1880 states that: 'Victorio Apache chief/murderer, killed by Mexican army.'

120 See American Life Histories webpage.

121 Fort Davis Museum webpage.

122 Temple, 1959, p.111.

123 Sweeney, 1991, p.172 & p.295; Sweeney, 1998, p.409.

124 Cruse, 1987, p.60; See also commentary by Niefert, 2001, p.558 & Wright, 2001, p.498.

125 Thomas E. Mails, pp.310-311 & Roberts, Chapter 3.

126 Juh was a very active war leader from at least the 1860s through to his death from natural causes in 1883. He was widely respected as an able strategist. His son Daklugie proved to be a valuable source in the early 1950s for Eve Ball's book, *Indeh*, published in 1980. He died in 1955. See Thrapp's work on Juh included in the bibliography.

127 Ball, 1980, p.83.

128 Ball, 1980, p.78.

129 Thrapp, 1974, p.12.

130 Goodwin, p.156.

in 1864 by someone he calls 'Sugarfoot Jack'.[131] This was clearly someone belonging to the Anglo-American culture that would have presented itself as above such acts at the time. However, to project today's morality back through time fails to recognise that many of the people engaged in this conflict thought scruples about 'humane behaviour' had no relevance in dealing with those they perceived as 'savages'.[132] It is also worth noting that, while the Apaches rarely scalped their enemies, this did not deter Anglo-Americans or Mexicans from scalping dead Apaches,[133] often in response to scalp bounties offered at various times by the Chihuahua and Sonora state governments. Due to their beliefs about contact with the dead[134] the Apaches were very reluctant to scalp a fallen enemy. Experienced frontier dwellers were aware of this reluctance, but were equally aware that the Apaches were capable of inflicting far worse on live captives.[135] Thrapp makes a useful distinction between the warfare of the 1860s and early 1870s, which was intended to drive the Apaches onto reservations, and the wars arising from breakouts from various reservations in the later 1870s and 1880s.[136] It may have been that torture was more likely to be used by the Apaches in the earlier phase of warfare, when it would have been designed to discourage intruders from invading their sovereign territory. Such practices may have had less utility in the latter phase of the Apache wars, unless the Apaches felt secure in a position. Where speed and secrecy were often essential, the use of torture as a tactic was likely to be less useful. Indeed, at least one source claims that torture had no place among some Apache tribes.[137]

In respect of the Victorio Campaign, a detailed examination of the available information gives no evidence of Victorio's alleged descent into an orgy of cruelty. However, it does show that Victorio and his followers were capable of inflicting high casualties on their enemies, and it is accounts of such punishment which probably gave rise to the story that Victorio was particularly cruel. Have we forgotten Victorio and his warriors because they were erroneously thought of as unbearably cruel? It is probably more accurate to suggest that Victorio has been overlooked because he was too successful. A contemporary newspaper article argued that:

> Victorio pursued a Fabian[138] policy. He kills people, loses few men himself, is fierce in battle, cautious in retreat, wears his opponents out, keeps them chasing through the mountains on fruitless errands until their horses become useless, and out generals their generals.[139]

It is also a measure of the success of Apache society in general that, in order to defeat its members, the US army had to become Apaches. They recruited large numbers of Apache scouts to spearhead their efforts against independent Apaches. These units were led by US army officers and civilian scouts who had made the effort to engage with a culture very alien to their own. In the face of the strategy and tactics employed by the Warm Springs and Chiricahua Apaches, this engagement, and the adaptations it led to were essential to their success in finally defeating the guerrillas.

131 Thrapp, 1967, p.32; Roberts, 1998, p.47; Cocker, pp.187-188.
132 See comment by Richard Hofstader in Deverell, p.35.
133 Barnes, 2001i, p.278.
134 See for example Stockel, 2004, p.64.
135 Barnes, 1982, p.81.
136 Thrapp, 1964, p.214.
137 See Loring, 2001, p.187.
138 'Employing a cautiously persistent and dilatory [delaying] strategy to wear out an enemy' (Concise Oxford Dictionary, 8th Edition, 1991, Edited by R.E. Allen, (BCA: London)).
139 Las Vegas Gazette cited in 'By Telegraph' *Grant County Herald,* 15 May 1880; Pope's Annual Report Year ending 22 September 1880, NA, RG393, Part 1, Entry 2546, p.613; Report of General John Pope, 22 September 1880, in Annual Reports of the War Department (AR-WD), 1880, NA, M997, Roll 35, 1880 Vol. I, pp.88-89.

Plate 2.7 Sotol Plant photographed in Magdalena Gap, New Mexico. Lance shafts would be made from the stalk. Lances were generally used on foot and wielded two-handed. The Hollywood image of the Apache warrior fighting from horseback, while not completely false, was not the norm for the Apaches, who preferred to fight on foot. (Photo: author)

The terms 'strategy' and 'tactics' are sometimes thrown about with little attempt to differentiate between the two. If one defines strategy as 'manoeuvring out of sight of the enemy' and tactics as 'manoeuvring within sight of the enemy', we can say that they had a clear notion of both concepts. For example, this can be illustrated by the way the Apaches would strategically and tactically target their opponents' horses. A frequent strategy employed by Victorio was to lead his opponents for long distances over difficult terrain, so as [indirectly] to exhaust, if not kill, their horses. The deliberate shooting of horses in the opening moments of an ambush was a direct tactic. Thus, with regard to horses, the Apaches employed both strategies and tactics geared to undermining their opponents' ability to operate against them. Part of their success was often the result of an unwillingness on the part of their opponents to make a concerted effort to understand Apache principles of war. This is not a criticism that could be levelled at the Apaches, as their adoption of breech-loading technology and understanding of the implications of the telegraph illustrate.

Given that, in our first chapter, much was made of the importance of political concepts for an understanding of the Victorio campaign, our discussion of the Apaches will not be complete until an effort has been made to understand them from a political point of view. It is, however, the ideas of one of the founding fathers of sociology, Emile Durkheim, that perhaps give us the best insight into the political organisation of Apache society. Durkheim argues that there are two types of social solidarity: mechanical and organic.[140] The Apaches represent a mechanical society – that is, one where there is little diversity in roles (most men being hunters and/or guerrillas), and where the society is small enough for most members to know each other personally. With the Apaches, it was the focus on raiding and warfare as a key element of their mechanical solidarity which produced such fearsome guerrillas. The expression of their social solidarity took the form of personal loyalty to known leaders and an accepted set of cultural norms concerning training, perceived success and promotion based on merit.

Pitted against the Apaches, the US army represented another form of social solidarity. The army was one of many organs making up the US state, and thus represented an element of what is known as organic solidarity. A society that has organic solidarity has, through developments in technology and an increasing diversity in the range of occupation open to individuals, grown out of a mechanical expression of solidarity to an 'organic articulation of free individuals pursuing different functions but united by their complementary roles.'[141] Therefore, a member of the US army might have expressed a broad loyalty to the United States in the same manner as a merchant, a lawyer, or a labourer in that society might have done. However, the scale of this society meant that each individual was more likely to express a meaningful personal solidarity with the particular organ of society to which she or he belonged than to the state in general. Thus a member of the US army fighting the Apaches might have had a conception of solidarity with the United States, but might also have held members of the Department of the Interior in contempt for their perceived misguided policy towards American Indians – an attitude that might have been reciprocated by members of that Department. The United States of America, vast in comparison to anything experienced by the Apaches, developed a broad conception of the role of its armed forces, which was open to interpretation by different organs of the US state. This raised a number of political challenges for the US army over and above the one posed by the Apaches, and will be the subject of the next chapter.

140 See Nisbet, 1966, pp.84-85; Morrison, 2006, pp.160-168; Callinicos, 1999, pp.127-128 for an overview of the concept of mechanical and organic solidarity.

141 Nisbet, 1966, p.84.

3

Political Constraints on the US Army

When the US army encountered the Apaches in the Southwest, many of their problems stemmed from the attitude they adopted to people whom many of them regarded as 'primitive savages'. The post-Civil War US army's abiding concern was with its professional standing as compared with that of European regular armies. This did not prepare it for conflict with the Apaches or other American Indians. For example, if we use the term 'principles of war' or 'principles of warfare' in relation to the US army and its Apache opponents, we refer to the education received by each side to prepare it for the successful waging of warfare. Historian Robert M. Utley argues that the US army was preparing for future, conventional warfare while ignoring the 'unconventional wars of the present;'[1] and Jerome Greene points out that 'treatises dealing with the formal methodology of Indian warfare were virtually non-existent.'[2]

In the years following the American Civil War, military research geared towards the development of a modern professional army was actively encouraged by General Sherman, and included the sending of officers to observe foreign regular forces at work.[3] These efforts to develop principles of war were made in the context of a fighting force that, as Utley and other authors argue, had adopted the 'total war' techniques developed by General Sherman during the latter part of the Civil War. 'Total war' techniques aimed at the use of overwhelming force in the destruction of the enemy's economic as well as military resources. While the post-Civil War army was cut back drastically by Congress, elements of this strategy can still be seen at work in winter campaigns against the Plains Indians, despite the severe cuts in the resources available to the US army.[4] It was these techniques that were adopted by a US army that had only limited resources at its disposal when campaigning against American Indians.

This is not to say that no research on frontier campaigning was published at the time; but these publications were generally seen as an interesting diversion rather than serious military science. Utley pinpoints the efforts of a few individual officers, such as de Trobriand and General Crook, to develop specific Indian fighting techniques.[5] Reedstrom examines the development of US cavalry tactical manuals from 1779 onwards and notes the inclusion of frontier service sections in these manuals from the 1860s on.[6] However, it should be noted that these sections formed only a small element in much wider ranging conventional cavalry tactical manuals. *A Handbook for Officers and*

1 Utley, 1973, p.44.
2 J.A. Greene's Foreword to E.S. Farrow, *Mountain Scouting: A Handbook for Officers and Soldiers on the Frontiers* (Norman The University of Oklahoma Press 2000) First published in 1881 p.3 see also pp.7-8.
3 See R.E. Reedstrom, Chapter 14 pp.147-153.
4 See also Janda, Lance. "Shutting the Gates of Mercy: The American Origins of Total War, 1860-1880" *The Journal of Military History*, Vol. 59, Issue 1 (Jan 1995), p.7-26 for further details.
5 Utley, 1973, pp.52-53.
6 Reedstrom, 1990, Chapter 14 pp.147-153.

Soldiers on the Frontier was published in 1881[7] by E.S. Farrow. In general terms, this is a fascinating survival guide for the frontier. However, it has two serious flaws. First, it reads as an attempt to interpret unconventional warfare in conventional terms. Second, in attempting to generalise about American Indian tactics and strategy, it fails to prepare officers and soldiers for campaigns against specific American Indian tribes. Farrow's manual holds little information which would have helped US soldiers fight the Apaches and, in any case, appeared too late to be of any use for troops fighting Victorio and Nana between 1877 and 1881.

The preceding chapter suggested that it was Apache guerrilla warfare techniques which caused so many problems for the US army. While a number of US army officers did understand the formidable challenges presented by such warfare, many more did not, preferring to assume that the Apaches were inferior, primitive, savage or, at best, unsophisticated. This charge of misunderstanding the Apaches can also be laid against some historians. For example, Driver argues that, in comparison with the Plains and Eastern Woodland Indians, the Apache and Navajo had weaker notions of warfare.[8] Turney-High uses Jicarilla Apache folklore to generalize about the Apaches, and argues that they had virtually no notion of planning, or of the value of their own lives.[9] If nothing else, the previous chapter gives details of the level of planning prevalent, at least amongst the Western and Chiricahua Apaches, and indicates that the preservation of Apache lives was one of the basic principles behind this planning.

In addition to revealing a widespread contemporary ignorance of the sophisticated guerrilla war culture of the Chiricahua Apaches, a study of the Victorio Campaign highlights a number of other challenges presented to field officers that were parallel to, but no less serious than, those posed by their Apache opponents. At first glance, there would seem to be a diverse range of challenges confronting the military. A common denominator, however, is their political nature, although they can be divided into internal and external factors (see Figure 3.1).

Problems that can be categorised as internal were caused by the manner in which the US army was organized. Those units (primarily the Ninth Cavalry) sent to face the Apaches had to contend with a higher command that was concerned with the creation of a 'European' army, a fragmented command structure, and limited resources. Limited resources were a central problem during the Victorio Campaign in that Apache tactics caused the Ninth cavalry heavy horse and pack mule casualties, thus stretching supplies of these animals beyond breaking point. This was a situation which was exacerbated, rather than created, by Apache guerrilla tactics.

The problem of limited resources indicates the first of a number of external factors: that of congressional and constitutional budgetary and numerical constraints on the army. A further related factor was the involvement of two other US government agencies: the Department of the Interior and the State Department. The Department of the Interior, through the Office of Indian Affairs, was responsible for Indian Policy in the United States. The involvement of the State Department highlights a further diplomatic constraint on the ability of the US army successfully to prosecute the war against Victorio and Nana: the involvement of the Republic of Mexico, which was caused by the fact that the Apaches claimed territory in both republics. To complicate matters further, the Mexican involvement brought in agencies and actors at both the federal and state levels in both countries. For various reasons, the issue of the 'hot pursuit' of Apaches across the international border proved to be a major obstacle for the US army during the Victorio Campaign.

---

7 Farrow, E.S. (2000), *Mountain Scouting: A handbook for Officers and Soldiers on the Frontiers: Foreword by Jerome A. Greene* (University of Oklahoma Press: Norman) First published New York 1881.

8 H.E. Driver, *Indians of North America* (The University of Chicago Press: London) pp.353-379.

9 H.H. Turney-High, 1991, *Primitive War: Its Practice and Concepts* (The University of South Carolina Press: Columbia)p.124 & pp.210-211.

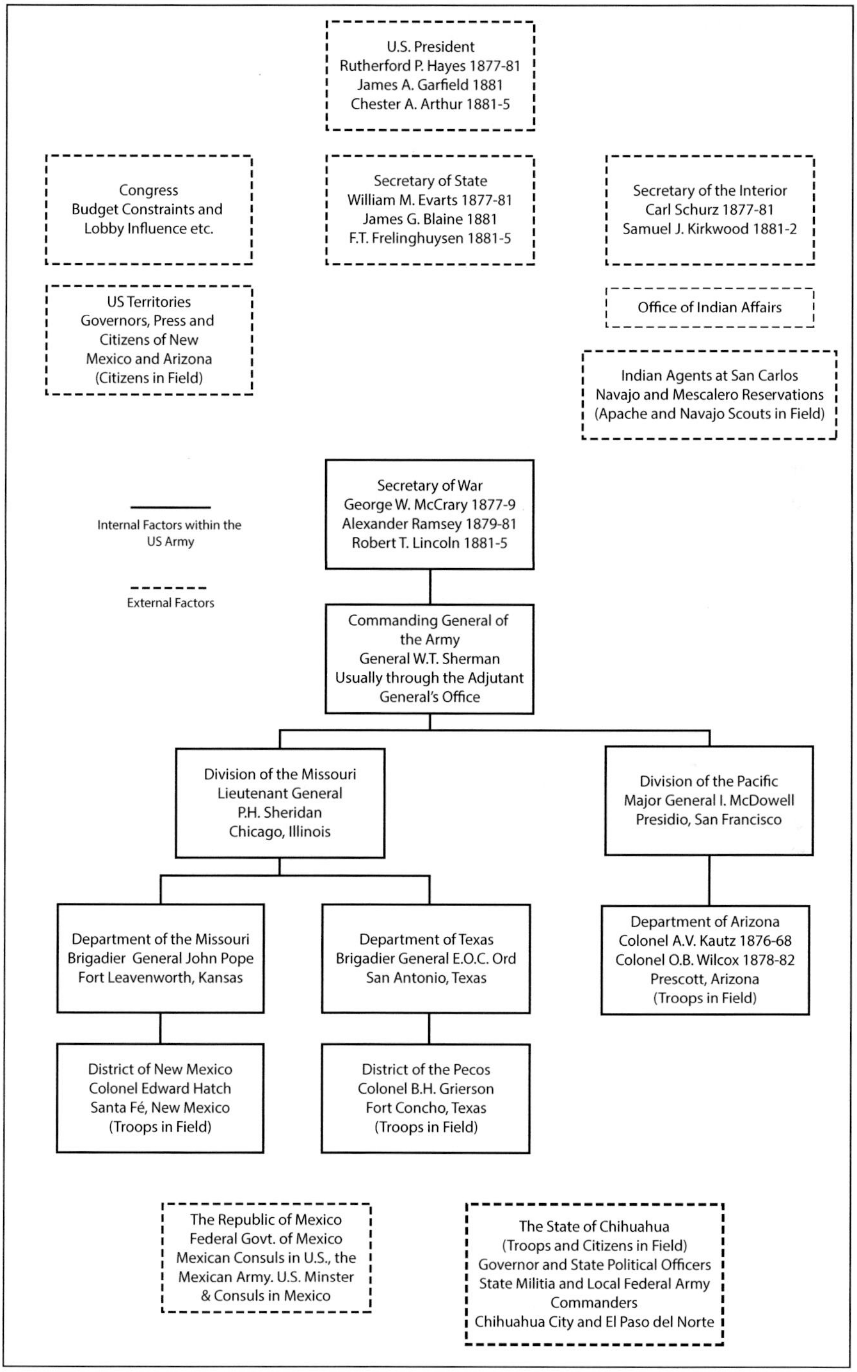

Figure 3.1 External and Internal Factors Influencing the US Army during the Victorio Campaign.*

* AR-WD 1876-1881, Bowles, N. (1998), *Government and Politics of the United States 2nd Edition* (MacMillan Press: Basingstoke) pp.22-23; Grant, A. (1994), *The American Political Process 5th Edition* (Dartmouth: Aldershot) pp.326-327; Chun, C.K.S. (2004), *U.S. Army in the Plains Indian Wars 1865-91 (Battle Orders Number 5)* (Osprey Publishing: Oxford) p.12, p.& p.26; Cabinet Members under Hayes/Garfield/Arthur www.infoplease .com

Finally, there was the involvement of US territorial (New Mexico and Arizona) and state (Texas) actors and agencies, namely governors and other political representatives, the press, state and volunteer troops, and citizens in general. Where the Ninth Cavalry was concerned, support from this quarter was at best rather lukewarm and at worst extremely hostile. The New Mexican press was particularly opposed to the Ninth Cavalry, and although it reserved most of its vitriol for its commanding officer, the ethnic origin of its rank and file was also utilised in newspaper vilification of army efforts to combat the Apaches.

However, as a final point, it should be noted that there were means by which the US army could, and during the Victorio Campaign sometimes did, circumvent such constraints.

Internal Political Constraints

In Pursuit of a 'European' US Army

The desire to create a US army which could hold its own against that of any of the European powers was one of Sherman's clearest post-Civil War goals. This desire probably dated back to the War of Independence, but had been reinforced by the political statement of the 1823 Monroe Doctrine[10] and its popular 1840s expression in the concept of 'manifest destiny'.[11] The potential threat posed by a European army had recently been reinforced by the French intervention in Mexico between 1862 and 1866. Indeed, in the immediate aftermath of the Civil War, the US army had demonstrated in strength along the Rio Grande frontier, and large amounts of US army surplus equipment 'mysteriously' ended up in the hands of the Mexican Republican army.[12] The Third Empire took the hint, and rapidly withdrew from Mexico,[13] though the rise of the Prussian state and its implications for the French may have had more influence in this decision.[14] This desire for an army which would be capable of defending the interests of the United States from European powers had to be balanced with the demands facing the US army when dealing with American Indians. In 1878, George W. McCrary, Secretary of War, announced that the War Department's – and hence the US army's – policy towards the American Indians comprised two elements: that there should be 'fair and just treatment of the Indians'; but that there should be 'prompt and effectual punishment of all acts of war on their part.'[15]

Where General Sherman's goals affected the US army units based in New Mexico Territory – the Ninth Cavalry, and the Fifteenth Infantry – was that the methods they adopted to combat Apache guerrillas undermined both regiments' military efficiency. In other words, the combat experience gained fighting Apaches did not prepare them to face a European opponent. This lack of a certain kind of proficiency was, on several occasions, criticised by General John Pope as leading to a lack of skill in manoeuvring as a regiment. General Pope usually[16] appreciated that

10 See Foster, 1900, pp.438-478; Fish, 1923, pp.203-219, 324-335 & 384-395; Latane & Wainhouse, 1940, pp.pp.169-196; Van Alstyne, 1978, pp.584-596; Rostow E.V., 1993, pp.144-149.

11 See Pletcher, 1978, pp. 526-534; Jones, M.A., 1983, p.177.

12 See Clendenen, C.C. (1969), *Blood on the Border: The United States Army and the Mexican Irregulars* (Collier-Macmillan: London) pp.57-58; Foster, 1900, pp.402-403.

13 See Foster, 1900, pp.402-403; Jones, 1983, p.394 (Note 3); Morison *et al*, 1977, *A Concise History of the American Republic* (Oxford University Press: New York) p.345; Rostow, 1993, pp.171-172 (Note 2).

14 Latane & Wainhouse, 1940, pp.415-416.

15 Report of Geo. W. McCrary, Secretary of War, in AR-WD 1878: NA, M997, Roll 30, 1878 Vol. I-II, p.iv.

16 General Pope did not quite appreciate some of the basic principles of Apache strategy and tactics and thus, in at least two instances, pointed out to Colonel Hatch that if there were only about 50 Apache warriors, and Hatch had at least 10 times this number, he did not see what the problem was and why

his troops usually had to operate in scattered detachments to stand any chance of catching their Apache opponents, or at least of limiting the latter's freedom of action. However, he clearly thought that the long-term effects of the implementation of such tactics would have a very detrimental effect upon the ability of the Ninth Cavalry to engage a 'modern' opponent. He argued that both the Ninth Cavalry and the Fifteenth Infantry should be transferred away from Apacheria in order to 're-establish discipline and tactical knowledge, which have been considerably impaired by the service they have had to perform for a number of years past.'[17] So not only was the Ninth Cavalry put under external pressure for not finishing off 'a handful of Apaches', but it also came under attack from within the army for not maintaining a peak of basic 'European' military efficiency. However, such efficiency could only be achieved by abandoning any pretence of defending the citizens of New Mexico from Apache guerrillas. This is not a point being made in hindsight: it is quite clear that personnel within the US army were aware that fulfilling specific frontier requirements meant that frontier regiments' experience would not match Sherman's long term goals.[18]

General John Pope. Commander of the Military Department of the Missouri. Pope partially understood the challenges of campaigning against Apache guerrillas. However, his failure to fully appreciate these problems sometimes led to his making unrealistic demands upon his subordinates, particularly Hatch, in New Mexico. (The National Archives)

Fragmented Command Structures

Command and communication structures were key elements of the Victorio Campaign. The US army's command structures were divided between the District of New Mexico, the Department of Arizona and the District of the Pecos. (See Figure 3.2.) The 1877-81 campaign against the Apaches involved three 'field' headquarters: two serving the Districts of New Mexico and the Pecos; and

more troops were required. (Pope to Hatch 7 August 1881, NA, RG393, Part 3, Entry 439, pp.137-138; See also later comments in Pope to R.C. Drum, Adjutant General (AG), Washington DC 21 August 1881, Letters Rec'd by the Office of the Adjutant General (AGO), 1881-1889. M689. Roll 44, Correspondence and reports mainly concerning efforts to capture Apache Indians who were terrorising the border region of the District of New Mexico, July-Dec. 1881). He also criticised Hatch for spreading his detachments too widely, leaving them unable to counter the Apaches, not appreciating that the Apaches would make every effort to avoid larger concentrations of troops (See Pope to Sheridan 1 July 1880, NA, RG393, Part 1, Entry 2546, pp.521-527).

17 General Pope, Headquarters (HQ), DoM Annual Report for Year ending 22 September 1881, NA, RG393, Part 1, Entry 2546, p.850; See also Pope to Sheridan 1 July 1880, NA, RG393, Part 1, Entry 2546, pp.521-527; Pope's Annual Report Year ending 22 September 1880, NA, RG393, Part 1, Entry 2546, p.613.

18 See, for example 'The Arizona Outbreak' in the *Army and Navy Journal*, 10 September 1881, p.120.

the third serving the Department of Arizona. Both the District of New Mexico and the District of the Pecos reported to the Division of the Missouri, via the Department of the Missouri and the Department of Texas respectively. The Department of Arizona reported to the Military Division of the Pacific. As the Victorio War developed, all three field headquarters found themselves having to combine their forces in an effort to combat the Apaches, though such coordination did not always run smoothly. Each headquarters made sterling efforts to communicate with the others, as well as up their own chains of command; but such efforts could be painfully slow once detachments in the field moved away from telegraph lines. Once detachments of troops were committed to field service, a great deal of luck governed the contacts between, for example, detachments of Arizona troops sent to intercept Apaches currently being pursued by troops from New Mexico.

As well as affecting contact between troops, this division of field headquarters also allowed individual commanders to play political games. When troops from the Department of Texas were earmarked for temporary service in the District of New Mexico, their commander, General E.O.C Ord, tried to argue that these troops should still be considered as under his direct orders. When this failed, Ord lobbied for a re-drawing of the boundary between the Districts of New Mexico and the Pecos, and had to be sharply reminded by General Sheridan that his job was to facilitate the pursuit of Apaches rather than to engage in personal empire building.[19]

Inefficient Logistics and Communications

Logistics were a key element for both sides in the Victorio Campaign; but the Apaches and the US army faced different logistical constraints. The former's Achilles heel was the maintenance of a secure and regular supply of ammunition for their breech-loading rifles. The latter was faced by the budgetary constraints laid down by Congress for the army each year. The continuous fielding of cavalry units and Indian scouts in pursuit of Apache guerrillas proved to be beyond the US army's capabilities several times during the campaign. Nor was this a new situation for the US army in Apacheria. In the fall of 1868, a scout from Fort Cummings noted that the men were suffering from lack of footwear, the stock at Fort Cummings having been already used up before the detachment set forth, and that this situation could not be alleviated by visiting either of two other posts (Goodwin and Bowie).[20]

For the maintenance of their horses and mules, the Ninth Cavalry depended on forage provided by a system of local suppliers.[21] Local citizens, not US army personnel, were appointed to act as contractors to supply this forage – an arrangement that was not the most efficient one for keeping

19 Whipple to Ord, Press Copies of Letters and Endorsements Sent, Military Division of the Missouri, (Hereafter referred to as MDoM), NA, RG393, Part 1, Entry 2539, Vol. 13, p.339; Whipple to Ord, 11 June 1880, 'Victorio Campaign, February 1879-November 1880' in "Special Files" Created by the MDoM, Records of US Army Continental Commands, 1821-1920, (Hereafter referred to as the 'Victorio Files') NA, RG393, M1495, Roll 14.

20 Capt. Moore, 38th Infantry, CO Ft. Cummings to Lt E. Hunter, AAA General, DoNM, 27 Nov., 1868 in Letters sent Vol. 3 June 24 1867-January 20 1869, in HQ Records of Fort Cummings, New Mexico, 1863-1873 & 1880-1884 NA, RG393, M1081, Roll 1, pp.141-145.

21 See the following for notice of appointment of local citizens as forage agents: Special Order 12, par 4, Feb. 11, 1879 NA, RG393, Part 3 Entry 450: see also Special Order 29, par 1, Apr. 2, 1879; Special Order 28, par 5 & 6, Apr. 18, 1879; Special Order 48, par 3, May 17, 1879; Special Order 67 par 3, July 21, 1879; Special Order 104, par 2, Oct. 20, 1879; Special Order 17, par 2, Feb. 5, 1880; Special Order 66, par 2, June 11, 1880; Special Order 114, par. 11, Sept. 23, 1880; Special Order 19, par's 3&4, Feb. 16, 1881; Special Order 80, par. 4, June 29, 1881; Special Order 101, par.4, Aug. 25, 1881; Such appointments could also be revoked: See Special Order 96, par 1, Sept. 30, 1879; Special order 71, par 8, June 28, 1880.

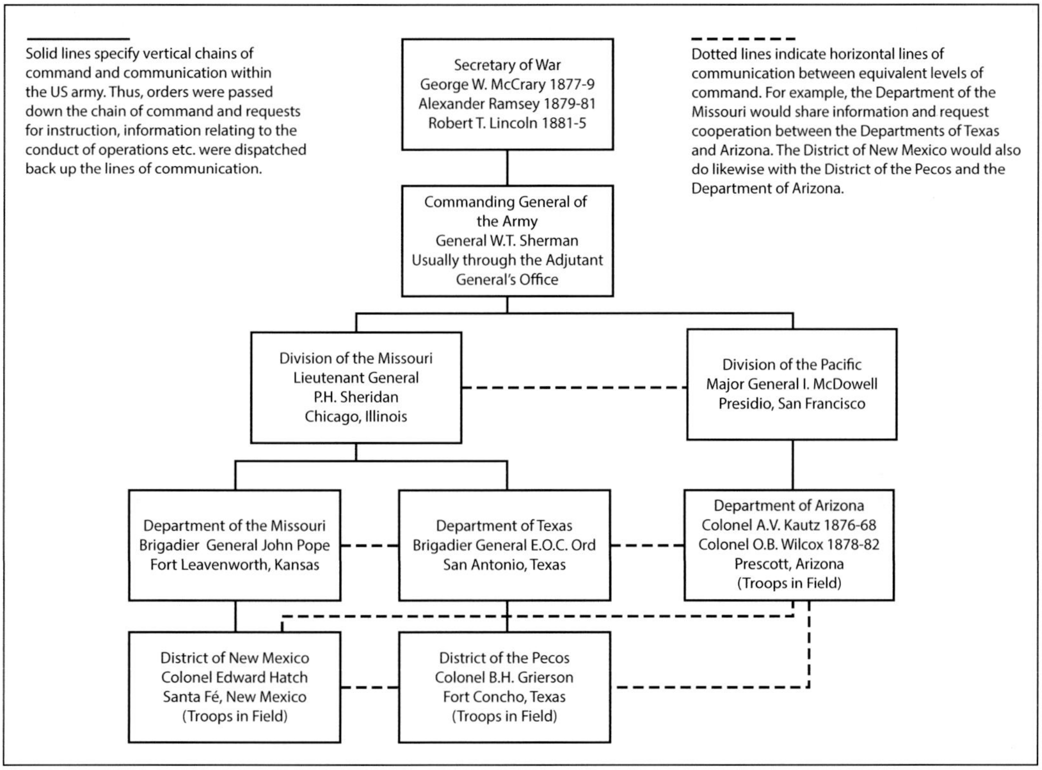

Figure 3.2 Vertical Chain of Command and Communication and Horizontal Lines of Communication within the US Army during the Victorio Campaign.*

* AR-WD 1876-1881, Bowles, 1998, pp.22-23; Grant, 1994, pp.326-327; Chun, 2004, p.12, p.& p.26; Cabinet Members under Hayes/Garfield/Arthur www.infoplease .com

cavalry in the field. Throughout the Victorio Campaign one can find orders both appointing[22] and revoking[23] forage contracts between New Mexican citizens and the US army. As we shall see, this system played a significant role in the failure of the plan to corner Victorio during April 1880.

When the regimental monthly and bi-monthly returns for the Ninth Cavalry are examined in detail, it becomes clear that the regiment was chronically short of horses. Between January 1879 and December 1881, it was only on rare occasions that the number of available men in each company was matched by the number of serviceable horses. This is an important issue that will be commented on at intervals as our examination of the campaign progresses, and will be considered in the final chapter of this volume. Colonel Edward Hatch also noted the poor quality of the

22 Special Order 12, par 4, Feb. 11, 1879 NA, RG393, Part 3 Entry 450: see also Special Order 29, par 1, Apr. 2, 1879; Special Order 28, par 5 & 6, Apr. 18, 1879; Special Order 48, par 3, May 17, 1879; Special Order 67 par 3, July 21, 1879; Special Order 104, par 2, Oct. 20, 1879; Special Order 17, par 2 Feb. 5, 1880; Special Order 66, par 2, June 11, 1880; Special Order 114, par. 11 Sept., 23, 1880; Special Order 19, par's 3&4, Feb. 16, 1881; Special Order 80, par. 4, June 29, 1881; Special Order 101, par.4, Aug. 25, 1881.

23 Special Order 96, par 1, Sept. 30, 1879, NA, RG393, Part.3, Entry 450; Special order 71, par 8, June 28, 1880, NA, RG393, Part.3, Entry 450.

majority of horses sent to the regiment, with most being either too small[24] or not used to the climate and rough terrain of the Southwest, so that often less than a full year passed before they became unfit for field service.[25] It should be noted that this situation predates the flare-up of hostilities between Victorio and the Ninth Cavalry in September 1879, and it was not a situation created by the Apaches but rather one born of poor logistical support. It showed that an already inefficient system of remounts was stretched beyond breaking point by the Apaches.

Target practice was not a routine exercise in the US army, and this was a result of the unrealistic allowances for ammunition set by Congress. In 1877, the Chief of Ordnance reported that the allowance of ten rounds per man per month for target practice was 'entirely inadequate', and the 'constant applications from the troops and from commanding generals for a larger supply clearly indicate its absolute necessity.'[26] It was noted that the ten rounds per man per month allowance used up three million cartridges per annum, and that the reserve stock of .45 calibre bullets was nine million.[27] The Chief of Ordnance recommended that Congress be made fully aware of this situation and asked to double the allowance for target practice, and, by implication, the reserve stock, in future congressional appropriations of money for the army.[28]

Logistical inefficiency was not the only problem facing the US army in the Southwest. As noted earlier, once US army detachments moved away from the telegraph lines, the speed of communication between these detachments slowed down considerably, undermining their ability to coordinate their efforts with maximum speed. The key role of Acting Assistant Adjutant General (AAAGs) and Acting Adjutant General (AAGs) in facilitating the coordination of US forces should not be underestimated. The practical function of AAAGs and AAGs was to coordinate the flow of information and orders up and down the chain of command, usually in letter or telegraph format. Thus, if we refer to Figure 3.2, and consider it alongside Table 3.1 below, we see that each district (New Mexico and the Pecos), department (Missouri, Arizona and Texas) and military division (Missouri and the Pacific) would have either an AAAG at district level or an AAG at department or division level. If the CO of the district, department, or division was in the field coordinating operations, he sometimes appointed a temporary 'AAAG in the field'. If the commander was absent for activities other than field operations, the AAAG or AAG would coordinate communication between the absent commander and both his superiors and subordinates. Thus, while the officer in charge of the district, department or division could leave his headquarters, the AAAG or AAG had to remain on site. The role carried a great deal of responsibility for the successful direction of field operations, the transmission of requests for additional logistical support and the circulation of reports from the individual detachment commanders.

Appreciating the role of the various adjutant general positions is important for historians of the Apache Wars. The difficulty facing the US army when trying to combat Apache guerrilla warfare cannot be grasped merely by examining the reports written after these operations were completed. The historian patient enough to sift through the correspondence (letters and telegrams) sent through the offices of the various assistant adjutant generals during the campaign sees clearly the difficulty of trying to coordinate different detachments in the field as fresh, and often unreliable, information

24 Hatch to AAG, DoM, Fort Leavenworth 3 Sept., 1879 in Letters Sent by the 9th Military Department, the Department of New Mexico, and the District of New Mexico 1849-1890, (Hereafter referred to as '9MD/DNM/DoNM'), NA, RG393,M1072, Roll 6, Jan-Oct 1879, Letter No.438, p.312.

25 Report of Maj. James Biddle 10 Sept., 1880, in AR-WD 1880, NA, M997, Roll 35, 1880 Vol. I, p.214.

26 Report of the Chief of Ordnance in Annual Reports of the War Department, NA, M997, Roll 29, 1877 Vol. III-IV, p.vi.

27 Report of the Chief of Ordnance in Annual Reports of the War Department, NA, M997, Roll 29, 1877 Vol. III-IV, p.vii.

28 Report of the Chief of Ordnance in Annual Reports of the War Department, NA, M997, Roll 29, 1877 Vol. III-IV, pp.vii-vii.

arrived. Moreover, from the historian's point of view, officers, and even non-commissioned officers, in the field who are addressing communications to their superiors are short of time, and are not necessarily writing with history in mind: they are simply giving the courier or wire operator as much information for the relevant headquarters as can be conveyed in the time available. Thus, it is essential that the historian knows the name and/or location of each AAAG or AAG. For example, 'Captain Loud, AAAG, Santa Fé' is often addressed by name only. He was also addressed as 'AG Santa Fé', 'AAG Santa Fé' or 'AAG SF'. It is only the knowledge that Santa Fé is the headquarters of the District of New Mexico that allows us to identify the messages that make up the flow of communications from various detachments through this headquarters.

Table 3.1 Summary of AAG/AAAG Personnel and Station 1879-81[29]

	AAG	AAAG	Station
Divn. of the Missouri	Colonel W.D. Whipple	–	Chicago, Illinois
Dept. of the Missouri	Major E.R. Platt	–	Fort Leavenworth, Kansas
Dept. of Texas	Major T. M. Vincent	–	San Antonio, Texas
Dist. of New Mexico	–	Lieutenant/Captain John S. Loud[1]	Santa Fé, New Mexico
	–	Lieutenant M.W. Day[2] Lieutenant Davis[3]	In the Field
Dist. of the Pecos	–	Lieutenant R.G. Smither	Fort Concho, Texas
	–	Lieutenant W.H. Beck[4]	In the Field
Divn. of the Pacific	Major J.M. Norvell	–	Presidio, San Francisco
Dept. of Arizona	Major J.P. Martin[5]	–	Whipple Barracks, Arizona
	–	Lieutenant John B.Kerr	Fort Lowell, Arizona
	–	Lieutenant John B.Kerr[6]	In the Field

Notes

1 1st Lt. John S. Loud was promoted to Captain on 1 Mar., 1880 (Army & Navy Journal, Vol.17, 13 March 1880, p.642).

2 2nd Lt. M.W. Day was Major Morrow's AAAG in the Field January/February 1880.

3 Davis was Col. Buell's AAAG in the Field during the expedition into Mexico. See Buell to AAG DoM, 20 Nov., 1880, Letters Received by HQ DoNM, September 1865-August 1890 NA, RG393, M1088, Roll 42, File 658-1658, January-April 1881.

4 Beck accompanied Col. Grierson during his field operations against Victorio in July/August 1880. See Grierson's Report of the Campaign in Western Texas, July –August 1880, submitted 22 Sept., 1880; NA, RG393, Part 1, Entry 2546, pp.639-644.

5 Cannot identify this officer with confidence from Heitman (Note 44). See entry for James Porter Martin in Altshuler, 1991, p.221 (Note 44).

6 Lt. Kerr accompanied Col. Carr into the field during the Buell expedition into Mexico. See Carr to AG Dept. Arizona, 19 September 1880, Troops in Southeastern Arizona, DoAz. of Arizona, NA, RG393, Part 1, Entry 232, Vol.8, September 6 1880 – December 12 1880, Letter No.569, pp.19-20.

Another facet of this approach is that the researcher begins to develop an understanding of US army operations against the Apaches *as they unfold*. The key documents are telegrams and letters

29 Derived from Altshuler, C.W. (1991), Cavalry Yellow & Infantry Blue: Army Officers in Arizona between 1851 and 1886 (Arizona Historical Society: Tucson); Heitman, F.B. (1903), Historical Register and Dictionary of the United States Army 1789-1903 (Government Printing Office: Washington D.C.)

generated before an operation and those sent as the operation progresses, and these documents can give a very different account from documents produced after the event.

There was also a political element to the job of AAAG or AAG. On at least one occasion, Captain John S. Loud, AAAG, District of New Mexico, exercised his discretion as to *when* to pass information up the chain of command to those in charge of the Department of the Missouri. During August 1881, he contacted his commander, Colonel Hatch who was absent coordinating the pursuit of Nana and his raiders, to inform him of an inconclusive skirmish with the same Apaches at Monica Springs.[30] Loud offered to delay the transmission of information up the chain of command, and stated, 'do you [Hatch] wish me to repeat to department headquarters and Genl Pope at Ft Garland will not do so until I hear from you.'[31]

Despite its apparent failure to tackle the fragmented command structure in Apacheria, the US army did at least attempt to institute as efficient a system of command, logistics and communication as such a structure would allow. However, it should be remembered that this less than ideal situation was created by the way in which Congress oversaw the US army's personnel and budget.

External Political Constraints

Congressional Constraints

The reason for the constraints placed on the army's budget and personnel by the US Congress lies in the origins of the American Republic. The members of Congress feared the threat that a standing army could pose to the Republic either on its own initiative or as a tool of others.[32] Therefore, they kept a close eye on the numbers employed in the army, and maintained a tight rein on its annual allocation of money, an attitude often described as 'niggardly'[33] in army circles. These constraints impacted very clearly on the army's ability to pursue the Apaches in New Mexico in two key areas.

First, strict adherence to a limit of 24,000 men in the army made it very difficult for *additional* Apache scouts to be recruited. While there was some dispute between field commanders as to the role played by Apache scouts when confronting Apaches, most officers serving in the campaign did not dispute the necessity for Apache scouts. However, the cap imposed by Congress on numbers serving in the army made it very difficult to authorise *additional* Apache scouts during a major campaign against Apaches. Thus, when experienced field commanders such as Colonel Hatch and Major Albert P. Morrow were pleading[34] with their superiors for more Apache scouts, it was this congressional limit that was responsible for the obstacles they encountered. They were informed by their superiors, from military department headquarters up through to the commanding general and on to the Secretary of War that such recruitment would take the army over the 24,000 men

30 This skirmish occurred on 3 August 1881. See Guilfoyle to AAAG Santa Fé, 6 Aug., 1881, NA, RG393, Part 3, Entry 439, pp.165-166; Loud to CO Fort Wingate, 10 Aug., 1881, Telegrams Sent DoNM, Vol.5, February-December 1881, NA, RG393, Part 3, Entry 431, p.318; Loud to Hatch, 10 August 1881, NA, RG393, Part 3, Entry 439, pp.734-735; See also Whipple to Sheridan (citing a report from Lt. Guilfoyle posted on 6 August from Ojo Setiemera?), 16 August 1881, NA, RG393, Part 1, Entry 2539, Press Copies of Letters and Endorsements Sent, MDoM, Vol. 14, p.584.

31 Loud to Hatch, 10 August 1881, NA, RG393, Part 3, Entry 439, p.735; See also Loud to Hatch, 12 August 1881, NA, RG393, Part 3, Entry 439, p.746.

32 Martin, J.K. & Lender, M.E. (1982), *A Respectable Army: The Military Origins of the Republic, 1763-1789* (Harlan Davidson: Wheeling Illinois) pp.8-9.

33 'The Arizona Outbreak' in the *Army and Navy Journal*, Vol.19, 10 September 1881, p.120.

34 As early as 15 June 1879, Morrow contacted the AAAG, DoNM, to ask for more Apache scouts. Letters Received by HQ DoNM, September 1865-August 1890, NA, RG393, M1088, Roll 37, File 658-1658, April-June 1879.

authorised by Congress, and it was thereby prohibited.[35] The only 'official' solution offered was to reduce the numbers of scouts employed in other military departments.

Second, the budget constraints imposed upon the army directly affected the Ninth Cavalry's ability to confront the Apaches. The Ninth Cavalry operated under a system whereby if a man could be mounted, only one horse was provided for him. The budget assigned to the army did not provide for a type of campaigning which required either the stabling of a large number of remounts at various posts in the war zone or each cavalryman being accompanied by several remounts while in the field. The existing system did not usually break down when the army faced Plains Indians; but it could not bear the additional strain imposed by the Apache approach to warfare, which identified cavalry mounts as their warriors' primary targets.

United States Government Departmental Politics

Three federal government departments were involved in the Victorio Campaign: the Department of the Interior, the Department of War, and the Department of State. The Department of War and the Department of the Interior, the latter through the Office for Indian Affairs (OIA), were both engaged in the debate concerning the settlement of the Warm Springs Apaches, and, generally, the Department of War favoured the establishment of a reservation for Victorio at Ojo Caliente in New Mexico, while the OIA continued to support a policy of concentrating Apaches on one reservation at San Carlos in Arizona.

The Department of State also became involved in the Victorio Campaign as a result of the direct involvement of the Republic of Mexico. The Warm Springs Apaches and the associated[36] Mescalero Apaches claimed territory on both sides of the international border. At first glance, it made sense for both republics to allow their troops to cross the border in pursuit of Apaches and to cooperate with each other in the face of a common enemy. However, elements within the Mexican political system were deeply suspicious of the United States' intentions concerning the integrity of Mexican territory. In this they had grounds for concern, since Mexico had lost approximately one third of its territory to the United States after 1848. More recently, the United States had flexed its muscles when, through the 'Ord Order', it had declared its right to engage in 'hot pursuit' of brigands and hostile Indians across the border. This was in response to Mexico's apparent failure to prevent such miscreants either from raiding across the border from Mexico into the United States or from seeking refuge from the US army below the border.

The Victorio Campaign focused attention on the issue of cross border cooperation between the United States and Mexico, and pursuing negotiations with the Republic of Mexico was part of the remit of the Department of State. For its part, the United States offered to recognise the recently constituted regime of Porfirio Diaz if the latter allowed the US army to cross the border to deal with Victorio and other Apaches, should the need arise. However, the Diaz government, which was deeply conscious of the need to preserve the integrity of the Mexican republic and their own internal political position, held out for reciprocal permission to cross the border.[37] Until such time as this stand-off could be resolved, the US army did not have the Mexican government's permission to pursue Victorio's warriors across the border. However, both the Mexican and United States

35 Sherman to Sheridan, 31 May 1880, NA, RG393, Part 1, Entry 2546, p.479 & p.480.

36 Some Mescalero Apaches allied with Victorio's Warm Springs Apaches against both the USA and Mexico. Other Mescalero Apaches elected to fight independently.

37 See Ruelas to Morgan, 23 July 1880, Morgan to Ruelas, 24 July 1880, 'Victorio Files' NA, RG393, M1495, Roll 14; See also Dinges, Bruce J. "The Victorio Campaign of 1880: Cooperation and Conflict on the United States-Mexico Border," *New Mexico Historical Review*, Vol. 62 No. 1, (January 1987), 81-94.

authorities recognised the Apaches as enemies. So, while denying US troops official permission to cross the border, the Mexican authorities were more than happy for their own troops to cooperate with them in pursuit of their mutual enemy, provided both forces remained within their own territory. Local contacts with the US army by both Mexican state and Mexican federal troops were encouraged to facilitate such cooperation.

The Republic of Mexico: Federal Government vs. State Warlord

There was another dimension to the tension between the United States and Mexico concerning the pursuit of independent Apaches across the international line. At that time, the federal government of Mexico had, at best, a loose hold over its border territories. In the State of Chihuahua, the governor was, in effect, an independent warlord running his own private feudal state. There was a widespread belief that certain towns near the US border had an unofficial but lucrative understanding with the Apaches, independent of their governor, that the Apaches could trade their plunder, with no questions asked, in return for buying guns, ammunition and alcohol.[38]

The federal Mexican government perceived that it was in its interests to maintain friendly relations with the United States and to encourage US investment in Mexico, particularly in railroad construction. The development of a rail network within Mexico would make it easier for the central Mexican authorities to curb the power of the state governors. Despite the advantages to be gained from such a relationship, the Mexican government had to steer careful course between encouraging US economic investment and provoking the nationalist element within the Mexican legislature.

Hostility and Prejudice: The Territorial Press and Citizens in New Mexico

To varying degrees, the press and citizens of the Territory of New Mexico presented some difficult obstacles that the US army had to overcome in its campaign against Victorio and his successors. The most serious challenge came from local citizens, usually with the active support of the territorial press. This challenge had three faces: criticism, misinformation, and illegal activity. The territorial press was highly critical of the conduct of the campaign by the US military. And both individual citizens and the press had a tendency to transmit what turned out to be either exaggerated or utterly false reports of Apache raids. Most seriously, there were a number of US citizens, both Anglo-Americans and Mexicans, who were willing to put guns and ammunition into the hands of Apaches.

The criticisms aimed at the US army during the Victorio Campaign fell into three broad categories: personal attacks upon Colonel Hatch; general condemnation of the US army's behaviour; and denigration of the Ninth Cavalry as an effective fighting force. Hatch was accused of misrepresenting the state of affairs in New Mexico to his superiors, and condemnation of him sometimes developed into a wider critique of the US army. A common criticism was that General Pope and the federal government in faraway Washington DC were indifferent to the plight of citizens in New Mexico Territory.[39] The Ninth Cavalry themselves came under some degree of attack, but not anything like the degree directed at their commander. The term 'Buffalo Soldier' was used rarely, and usually only as a term of quiet contempt within the local press. There was little positive contemporary usage of this term.[40] Most criticism levelled at the Ninth Cavalry labelled them as ineffective

---

38 Report of General Pope in AR-WD, NA, M997, Roll 30 1878 Vol. I-II, p.81.

39 See for instance Ashenfelter, Editor, *Grant County Herald*, 27 March 1880; *Thirty Four*, 12 May 1880.

40 See 'From Georgetown' *Grant County Herald*, 8 May 1880; Occasional, 10 June 1880, Georgetown N.M. 'How to Fight Apaches' Letter in the in the *Grant County Herald*, 12 June 1880.

in comparison to white troops.[41] Early in the campaign, although the press was inclined to dismiss the Ninth Cavalry,[42] at least one newspaper argued that the regiment should be given the chance to prove itself.[43] However, as the campaign progressed, positive feeling towards these troops largely disappeared. One article took comfort in the fact that at least the failure to defeat the Apaches had shown the use of 'the African' as a soldier to have been unsuccessful.[44] The Ninth Cavalry were even accused of throwing away cartridges and being chronically insubordinate.[45] At one point, one George Parker, a tracker, was described in the *Grant County Herald* as a 'full blooded negro' and one of the 'bravest of the brave', but he was presented as an exception to the rule.[46] Not only did hostile citizens publish various resolutions in the local press trumpeting their dissatisfaction, they even addressed at least one such communication to the President of the United States.[47]

Colonel Edward Hatch. Commander of both the Ninth Cavalry Regiment and the Military District of New Mexico. Hatch was an officer who understood the nature of Apache warfare but never had the resources to combat them effectively. Nevertheless he was politically inept in dealing with the local press and citizens in southern New Mexico which would increasingly hamper his efforts to combat the Apaches between 1879-1881. (The National Archives)

There were, however, some positive comments made concerning the Ninth Cavalry. One account argued that a white regiment would have been hard pushed to maintain its morale and willingness to fight at the level maintained by the Ninth Cavalry during the campaign.[48] Indeed, in November 1880, there even appears to have been an attempt by an Anglo-American to join the Ninth Cavalry as a recruit at Fort Cummings, prompting the commanding officer to contact the adjutant general in Washington to verify whether this was possible.[49]

41 See *Thirty Four*, 11 February 1880 and 24 March 1880; 'Mystery and History' *Grant County Herald*, 10 April 1880; 'Victory?' *Grant County Herald*, 17 April 1880; 'Town & County' *Grant County Herald*, 24 April 1880; *Thirty Four*, 5 May and 12 May 1880; *Grant County Herald*, 19 June 1880; 'Town & County', *Grant County Herald*, 31 July 1880; 'Town & County' The *New Southwest & Grant County Herald*, 16 July 1881.
42 See for instance *Thirty Four*, 12 November and 19 November 1879.
43 *Thirty Four*, 19 November 1879.
44 "In the Name of the Prophet! Figs!!" *Grant County Herald*, 27 March 1880. See also 'Not Prejudice', Ashenfelter, Editor, *Grant County Herald*, 27 March 1880 & Ashenfelter, Editor, *Grant County Herald*, 3 April 1880.
45 *Thirty Four*, 9 June 1880.
46 'Town & County', *Grant County Herald*, 15 May 1880.
47 Citizens Bailey etc. to President R.B. Hayes, Washington D.C., 10 May 1880, 'Victorio Files', NA, RG393, M1495, Roll 14; See also Silver City 7 June 1880 Resolution in the *Grant County Herald*, 12 June 1880; *Thirty-Four*, 16 June 1880; Hart, 1997, p.48.
48 See *Thirty Four*, 2 June 1880.
49 Dudley to AG Washington DC, 13 November 1880, Letter No. 148 Letters sent Vol. 7 October 25 1880–June 24 1881 in HQ Records of Fort Cummings, New Mexico, 1863-1873 & 1880-1884 NA,

Plate 3.1 Some of the ruins of Fort Cummings, an important army base in the 1860s, and temporarily re-activated in the war against Victorio in 1879-80 and the continued operations against Nana in 1881. Cooke's Peak is visible in the background. (Photo: author)

Plate 3.2 The US army often established temporary posts. These are the remains of one such post on the Alamocito River, to the northwest of Ojo Caliente, near the Datil Mountains. These temporary posts were often existing small civilian ranches or settlements used as staging posts by the army. This station was mentioned as being used in 1879 by troops searching for Victorio, and it was used again as a temporary base by soldiers campaigning against Nana in 1881. (Photo: author)

During the Victorio Campaign, the forms of misinformation circulated by citizens and press fell into two categories: those resulting from panic; and those resulting from a desire to make mischief. The more common of the two categories covered activities that could be ascribed to panic. The nature of Apache warfare was such that, while the actual damage inflicted was relatively limited, the psychological threat posed by these expert guerrillas could, and often did, paralyse economic activity in an area. The psychological stress experienced resulted in the production of scare stories which exaggerated the impact of an attack in reported casualties and number of Apaches involved. Other reports were based on completely erroneous sightings, where parties of mounted miners, traders or even US cavalry patrols were mistaken for Apache warriors.[50] Another relatively common trigger for a false alarm was citizens involved in hunting or target practice being mistaken for an attack.[51] There was even an instance where a small patrol of Tenth Cavalry and a group of three prospectors mistook each other for Apaches and headed to the nearest US army post to raise the alarm.[52] The end result of these false alarms was frantic messages sent by courier and/or telegraph demanding US army protection.

Officers from the Ninth Cavalry raised complaints about the level of false reporting of Apache threats throughout the campaign.[53] As we have seen, the Ninth Cavalry was already constrained by an inadequate logistics system. To see already limited resources being wasted in pursuit of non-existent Apache raiders was extremely frustrating. Such false reporting seriously hampered the Ninth Cavalry's ability to focus their forces on areas where Apache warriors were actually operating.

A much more insidious form of misinformation was the deliberate false reporting of Apaches. This was usually accompanied by vociferous demands that US troops be stationed in the locality. The motive was sometimes down to genuine panic; but often the aim was to exploit any detachments brought in by charging them exorbitant prices for food, which was often of poor quality, for fodder and for other supplies.[54] Misinformation, whether panic driven or deliberate, provided an additional and major obstacle to the effective prosecution of a campaign against the Apaches.

RG393, M1081, Roll 1.

50 See for instance Morrow to Loud AAAG, NA, RG393, Part 3, Entry 439, p.9 see also comment Hatch to Loud AAAG, NA, RG393, Part 3, Entry 439, p.129; Lt Emmett to Post Adjutant, Ft Bayard, 30 November 1879 in Letters Received, DoNM, September 1865-August 1890, NA, RG393, NA, RG393, M1088, Roll 39, October-December 1879; Ord to the AG, MDoM, 30 March 1880, NA, RG393, Part 1, Entry 2546, p.365; Loud to CO Fort Bayard, 6 May 1880, Telegrams Sent DoNM, Vol.3,Jnuary-November 1880 NA, RG393, Part 3, Entry 431, p.387; Taylor to AAAG, Troops in the Field, Fort Cummings, 16 November 1880, Humphrey to Dudley, 24 November 1880, both in Reports of Scouts 2 November 1880–1 August 1882, HQ Records Fort Cummings, NA, RG393, M1081 Roll 8 pp.2-3 & p.5.

51 See for example Gardner to The Adjutant, Battalion Ninth Cavalry, Separ S.P.R.R., N.M. 31 October 1881, DoM, Letters Received, 7320 DoM, 1881.

52 Capt. Carpenter, 10th Cavalry, Hot Springs Texas to AAAG, District of the Pecos (Hereafter referred to as 'DoP'), 22 Sept., 1880 in Register of Telegrams Rec'd 11 October 1879-8 October 1880, HQ DoP 1878-1881, NA, RG393, M1381, Roll 2, p.226, Letter No.398.

53 See for instance, Loud to CO Fort Wingate, 18 August 1881, Telegrams Sent DoNM, Vol.5, February-December 1881, NA, RG393, Part 3, Entry 431, p.340; Bradley to AAAG DoNM, 19 Aug., 1881 NA, RG393, Part 3, Entry 439, p.148; Bradley to AAAG DoNM, 19 August 1881 NA, RG393, Part 3, Entry 439, p.149; Smith? to Loud AAAG Santa Fé 17 August 1881, NA, RG393, Part 3, Entry 439, p.152; Loud to AAG, Fort Leavenworth 18 Aug., 1881, NA, RG393, Part 1, Entry 2546, p.900.

54 See Dudley to Chief Quartermaster DoNM, January 1881, where he registered a protest at a claim of $1568 submitted by one J.A. Miller for hay supplied to Fort Cummings. Dudley described the fodder as of 'very inferior quality.' Letters sent, Vol. 7 October 25 1880–June 24 1881, HQ Records, Fort Cummings, NA, RG393, M1081, Roll One.

Moreover, there was the existence of illicit trade networks which enabled the Apaches to trade their plunder for, amongst other goods, guns and ammunition.[55] If necessary, individuals involved in this trade were willing to take steps to protect their interests, and a small number of United States troops were killed or wounded at the hands of such people. Samuel Brown of F Company, Ninth Cavalry, was murdered by unknown persons in Tulerosa on 13 or 18 April 1880 near to the Mescalero reservation.[56] The assailants were suspected of being Mexican-American citizens. Corporal Samuel Myers was killed on 21 October 1880 while investigating the illegal sale of US government property at Upper Plaza in the San Francisco Valley. He was believed to have been killed by Mexican-American citizens.[57] A third Ninth cavalryman, Charles Cunningham, was badly wounded, on or around 1 January 1880, by a 'Mexican assassin.'[58]

The Apache guerrillas had two 'Achilles heels': the willingness of other Apache warriors to serve in the US army; and the lack of a regular supply of rifles and ammunition. Some of the citizens of the Territory of New Mexico were more than willing to alleviate any Apache shortage of modern munitions in return for personal gain. Almost certainly, some of the fatalities sustained by the Ninth Cavalry came from weapons placed in the hands of Apache warriors by illegal traders. Many of these traders would have been citizens the regiment was supposed to be protecting from these same Apaches. It is only fair to mention that other citizens in the territory did take steps to, at the very least, intimidate citizens suspected of trading with the Apaches.[59] US army post commanders were also warned to be very careful about to whom they sold obsolete arms.[60]

It is also worth mentioning the occasionally very unhelpful attitude of some citizens when requested to assist the Ninth Cavalry. Lieutenant Mathias W. Day reported that the 'colored' population of Las Vegas NM actively aided and abetted Ninth cavalry deserters, helping them to avoid falling into his hands.[61]

There were also instances where individual telegraph operators were reluctant to give military telegrams priority.[62] Captain Loud, AAAG for the District of New Mexico, contacted the

55 See US Attorney General for Territory of New Mexico to Hatch, 11 July 1879 in Letters Received DoNM, September 1865-August 1890, NA, RG393, M1088, Roll 38, July–Sept. 1879.

56 Record of Events April 1880 in Returns From Regular Army Cavalry Regiments 1833-1916, 9th Cavalry 1873-1880, NA, M744, Roll 88.

57 Humphreys to AAAG Santa Fé 1 November 1880, NA, RG393, Part 3, Entry 439, pp.650-652; Bi-Monthly Company Muster Rolls for Company M, 9th Cavalry, September-October 1880, NA, RG94; Record of Events Oct., 1880 in Returns From Regular Army Cavalry Regiments 1833-1916, 9th Cavalry 1873-1880, NA, M744, Roll 88.

It was decided to send a Ninth cavalry company out to Parson Williams Ranche from Fort Cummings and to pull out all Ninth cavalry detachments stationed along the San Francisco River. The officer in charge of the company was charged with investigating the death of Corporal Myers and submitting a report to District Headquarters. Once the investigation was completed the company was to return to Fort Cummings. (Loud to CO Fort Cummings, 10 November, 1880 in Letters Rec'd 1880-1881, HQ Records of Fort Cummings, New Mexico, 1863-1873 & 1880-1884 NA, RG393, M1081, Roll 5)

58 Bi-Monthly Company Muster Rolls for Company K, 9th Cavalry, May-June, NA, RG94.

59 Report from Andrew Kelley concerning illegal trade with Apaches at Cañada Alamosa as reported in *Thirty-Four*, 5 May 1880.

60 Field Order No. 10, HQ, DoAz in the Field, Camp Thomas, 15 September 1881, Special Orders 1879-1881, Dept. of Arizona, NA, RG393, Part 1, Entry 184.

61 Day to AAAG, DoNM, 19 October 1880 in Letters Received by HQ DoNM, September-August 1890, NA, RG393, M1088, Roll 41, July-December 1880.

62 Capt. Carroll, Ft Craig to AG DoNM, Santa Fé 12 October 1879 in Letters Received, DoNM, September 1865-August 1890, NA, RG393, M1088, Roll 39, October-December 1879; Loud to Robinson, ATSF RR, 19 August 1881, Telegrams Sent DoNM, Vol.5, February-December 1881, NA, RG393, Part 3, Entry 431, p.345; See also Loud to Hatch, Nutt Station, 19 August 1881, Telegrams Sent DoNM, Vol.5, February-December 1881, NA, RG393, Part 3, Entry 431, p.345.

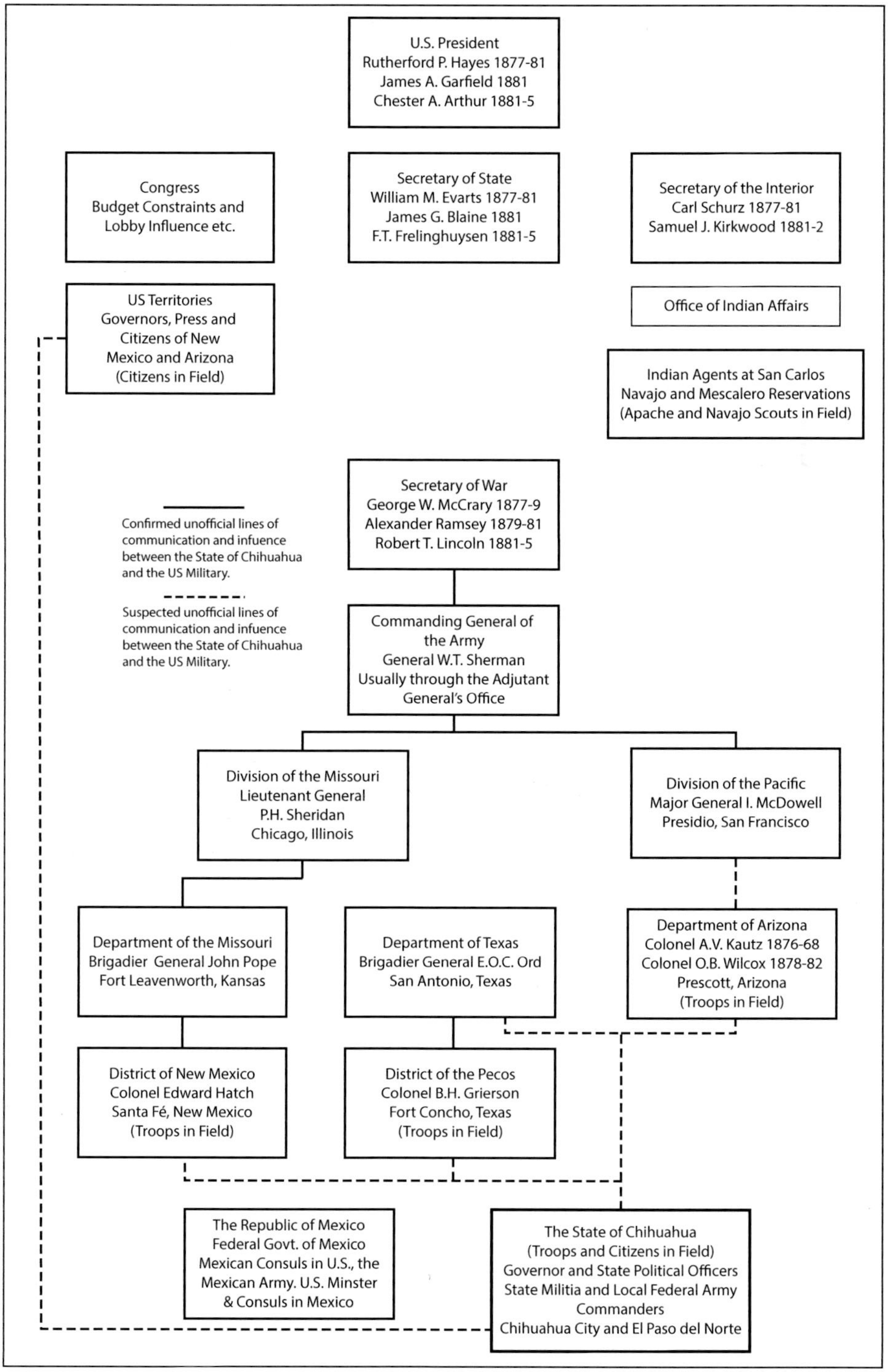

Figure 3.3 Unofficial US Political and Military Chains of Command, Communication and Influence during the Victorio Campaign 1877-81.*

* AR-WD 1876-1881, Bowles, 1998, pp.22-23; Grant, 1994, pp.326-327; Chun, 2004, p.12, p.& p.26; Cabinet Members under Hayes/Garfield/Arthur www.infoplease .com

Postmaster at Santa Fé to complain about a failure to deliver letters to recipients, pointing out that this caused 'embarrassment and inconvenience to the service' and that it 'was not the first instance of the kind.'[63] On one occasion, Colonel Hatch had to contact the general manager of the Atchison, Topeka and Santa Fé Railroad concerning an obvious unwillingness to cooperate on the part of their agent at San Marical concerning the transport of Ninth cavalrymen being sent to respond to Nana's raid in August 1881.[64] Equally, it has to be noted that other telegraph operators did their utmost to keep the line open for military traffic. Will C. Barnes remembered a number of occasions where he stayed long hours at his post waiting for the emergency call '39-39-39' and ready to transmit these messages as quickly as possible.[65]

Solutions

Some of the responses to constraints imposed by the various external factors on the US army's ability to prosecute a successful campaign against the Apaches highlight the *informal* or *unofficial* links between various actors. (See Figure 3.3.) US army detachments in 'hot pursuit' of Apaches often had no qualms about crossing the border during the Victorio Campaign. As we shall see, the army was also prepared to send private citizens as scouts across the international line, without necessarily notifying the Mexican authorities, in an effort to keep track of the movements of Apaches.[66]

A far more interesting informal development concerned the growth of 'unofficial' cooperation between local actors on both sides of the border. This was designed to circumvent the deadlock at federal level over the granting of official reciprocal rights for each country's forces to cross the border in pursuit of Apaches. This 'cooperation' culminated in the organising of a joint effort to trap Victorio by United States forces and Chihuahuan state troops. The expedition was organised through informal contacts maintained between certain actors and institutions on both sides of the border. It was driven by the conviction of local actors that they were faced by an urgent problem that they could not wait for the two federal governments to solve. This led to an acceptance that the constraints facing the US army should be tempered by an awareness that a political obstacle, whether it be a law or an institution, created by one group of actors could be challenged by other groups of actors. This appreciation of the role of power politics is central to an understanding of how, despite the presence of both internal and external obstacles, the US army was able to function more effectively than could have been predicted.

The remaining part of this book will concern itself with the background to, and history of, the Victorio Campaign. This chapter has not chosen to cover such detail as garrison life, health, and training in the US army; nor has it chosen to focus on the experience of the Buffalo Soldiers. First, there is a wealth of detail already written on these topics;[67] and second, a discussion of the political

63 Loud to Postmaster, Santa Fé, 15 June 1880 in Letters Sent by the '9MD/DNM/DoNM', NA, RG393, M1072, Roll 6, January 1880-August 1881, Letter No.290, p.187.

64 Hatch to General Manager, A.T.& S.F. Railroad, 13 August 1881, Miscellaneous Records 1868-1889, NA, RG393, Part 3, Entry 453.

65 Barnes, 1982, pp.37-38.

66 See for example Pope to Sheridan 1 July, 1880, NA, RG393, Part 1, Entry 2546, pp.521-527; See also Pope's Annual Report Year ending 22 September 1880, NA, RG393, Part 1, Entry 2546, p.613; Brinkerhoff to AAAG, Santa Fé (SF), 11 September 1880, NA, RG393, Part 3, Entry 439, pp.405-408; Bradley to Van C. Smith, 13 October 1881, Letters Received 1880-1, HQ Records Fort Cummings, NA, RG393, M1081, Roll 5; Van C. Smith to MacKenzie, 19 Nov., 1881, Letters Sent Vol. 8, 26 June 1881-2 April 1882, HQ Records, Ft Cummings, NA, RG393, M1081, Roll 1.

67 See for example Coffman, E.M., 1986, *The Old Army: A Portrait of the American Army in Peacetime 1784–1898*; Cozzens, P., 2005, *Eyewitnesses to the Indian Wars 1865-1890 Volume V: The Army and the Indian*; Knight, O., 1978, *Life and Manners in the Frontier Army*; Leckie, S.A., 1989, *The Colonel's Lady on the Western Frontier: The correspondence of Alice Kirk Grierson*; Rickey, D., 1963, *Forty Miles a Day on Beans*

constraints facing the US army gives us a far more robust insight into the latter's actions during the Victorio Campaign. Issues such as training, garrison life, Buffalo Soldiers and so on will be discussed where and when they become relevant, as the history of the Victorio Campaign unfolds.

---

and Hay; Smith, S.L., 1990, *The View from Officer's Row: Army Perceptions of Western Indians*: Tate, M.L., 1999, *The Frontier Army in the Settlement of the West*; Utley, R.M., 1967, *Frontiersmen in Blue*; Utley, R.M., 1973, *Frontier Regulars*; Wormser, R. 1966, *The Yellowlegs.*

For Buffalo Soldier literature see for example Billington, M.L., 1991, *New Mexico's Buffalo Soldiers 1866-1900*; Carroll, J.M.,1971, *The Black Military Experience in the American West*; Dobak, W.A. & Phillips, T.D., 2001, *The Black Regulars 1866-1898*; Fowler, A., 1996, *The Black Infantry in the West 1869-1891*; Kenner, C.L., 1999, *Buffalo Soldiers and Officers of the Ninth Cavalry 1867-1898*; Leckie, W.H. & Leckie, S.A., 2003, *The Buffalo Soldiers: A Narrative of the Black Cavalry in the West – Revised Edition*; Schubert, F.N., 1995, *On the Trail of the Buffalo Soldier: Biographies of African Americans in the U.S. Army 1866-1917*; Schubert, F.N., 1997, *Black Valor: Buffalo Soldiers and the Medal of Honor, 1870-1898*; Schubert, F.N., 2003, *Voices of the Buffalo Soldier: Records, Reports, and Recollections of Military Life and Service in the West.*

4

Origins of the Victorio Campaign: 1870 to 1877

> Envy, hatred malice, covetousness. Revenge, and falsehood, are very lively, but they cannot overturn one grand fact, Viz: that the wildest Apaches may be met and conquered, without arms, by God's Help.
>
> (General Oliver Otis Howard, 23 September 1873)[1]

The Ojo Caliente (Warm Springs or Mimbres) Apaches made up the easternmost segment of the Chiricahua Apaches, whose home range spread across the mountains of south-west New Mexico (including the San Mateos, the Black Range, and the Mogollon Mountains), centring on the hot springs at Ojo Caliente, and running south into Northern Mexico. Smith states that, in the 1830s, they tended to make raids into Mexico by congregating in and around the lakes (lagunas) of Northern Chihuahua – the i.e. Lagunas[2] de Guzman, Santa Maria and Patos. Using this area as their base, they would launch their raids deep into the south of Chihuahua.[3]

The Warm Springs Apaches' own name for themselves was the Chihenne,[4] and there are various versions of this spelling, e.g. Tcihene. Whatever the spelling, the meaning approximates to 'red paint people.'[5] The Warm Springs Apaches were also referred to as the 'Mimbres' and 'Ojo Caliente' Apaches by the Anglo-Americans. The Warm Springs Apaches often allied themselves with other Chiricahua bands and with wider groups of Apaches, particularly the Mescalero Apaches. However, we should be wary of how we understand the term 'allied'. In the Victorio Campaign, the southern Chiricahuas under Juh may have allied themselves with Victorio in October-November 1879, but they served as scouts against him later in the campaign. It is clear that the US army of the time regarded the Warm Springs Apaches as part of the Chiricahua Apaches, describing them as the 'Warm Springs Chiriguas,'[6] Other Apaches appeared to accept this definition, with, for example, the Apache first sergeant of an Apache scout company reporting, on 7 October 1881, that one Chiricahua and eight Warm Springs 'called Chiricahuas' had deserted from his company.[7]

However, at this point, we need to agree on terminology. There seem to have been four broad tribal groupings (Chokonen, Bedonkohe, Chihenne and Nedni's) that came under the umbrella

1 Howard to Commissioner of Indian Affairs (CoIA), 23 September 1873 (See Crook to AG Washington D.C., 8 December 1873 for a robust rejection of Howard's sentiment) both in Correspondence relating to the agreement with Cochise, Chief of the Chiricahua Apache, negotiated by Gen. Oliver O. Howard (hereafter referred to as 'Cochise-Howard Agreement', Letters Rec'd by the AGO, 1871-80, NARA, Wash. D.C., M666, Roll 123.

2 Laguna translates as 'lake'.

3 Smith, 1962, p.25; See also Laumbach, pp.105-106.

4 Ball, 1970, p.xiv; 1980, p.11.

5 Lekson, p.1.

6 Hatch to AAG, DoM, Fort Leavenworth, 14 August 1879 in Letters Sent by the '9MD/DNM/DoNM', NA, RG393, M1072, Roll 6, Jan-Oct 1879, Letter No.394, pp.280-282.

7 Col. MacKenzie citing Major Biddle's Report, 7 October 1881, NA, RG393, Part 1, Entry 181, p.186.

title of 'Chiricahua.'[8] It is sometimes argued that the Chokonen were the true Chiricahuas, but 'Chiricahua' is also used as a blanket term for all four groups.[9] It should be noted that each tribal grouping was further subdivided into what Edwin R. Sweeney terms 'sub-groups.'[10] Sweeney states that each local grouping was made up of 'between ten and thirty extended families.'[11] Exceptional leaders, such as Cochise, Mangas Coloradas and Victorio, could sometimes move beyond the leadership of a local group to gaining the allegiance of several such groups. There were close ties between these groups; and although this did not preclude hostile encounters between and within them, members of one of these bands who encountered warriors from one of the other three would be *more likely* to form an alliance with them, or remain neutral, than would be the case if they encountered warriors from wider Apache tribal groups.

By the beginning of the 1860s, Anglo-Americans (mostly miners, and some ranchers) were pushing into territory claimed by the Warm Springs Apaches in south-western New Mexico. Even earlier, from the late 1850s, Mexican-American farming communities pushed southwards along the Rio Grande into territory previously denied to them by Apache and Navajo raiders.[12] J.P. Wilson argues that this settlement was to some extent driven by the prospect of lucrative trade with local army posts and/or the Warm Springs Apache agency at Cañada Alamosa.[13] According to R. White, in the 25 years following the independence of Mexico from Spain, in 1821, land grants in the area that now forms New Mexico and Colorado generally moved north and east from Santa Fé. Yet there were also some grants made to the south, along the Rio Grande valley, as far as the current international border.[14] Both developments led to increased contact between the Warm Springs Apaches and Mexican/Anglo-Americans. As noted in chapter 1, the Apaches had a long running 'trade-hate' relationship with the Mexicans. By 1861, the Chiricahua Apaches were at war with the Anglo-Americans. While there had been skirmishes in the preceding decade, this general warfare was triggered by an attack by Anglo-American miners on an Apache camp on 4 December 1860 and by the Bascom Affair and its impact on Mangas Coloradas' closest ally, Cochise.[15] These incidents had unleashed the full fury of the Warm Springs Apaches against Anglo-American citizens for the first time.[16] Mangas Coloradas was taken under a truce flag in early 1863 by a US army detachment and was summarily executed that night on the orders of General Joseph West.[17]

By 1860, Victorio had already risen to a position of leadership amongst the Warm Springs Apaches. He was certainly a local group leader by the early 1850s, when he is noted as being approached to sign an 1853 treaty between the Apaches and the United States.[18] He was also present, in alliance with Mangas Coloradas and Cochise, on a series of raids which struck both Chihuahua

8 Ball, 1970, p.xiv; Buchanan, p.4.

9 See Hunter, 1944, p.299.

10 Sweeney, 1991, *Cochise: Chiricahua Apache Chief* (University of Oklahoma Press: Norman) p.5; 1998, *Mangas Coloradas: Chief of the Chiricahua Apaches* (University of Oklahoma Press: Norman) pp.5-9.

11 Sweeney, 1998, p.8.

12 Wilson, "How the Settlers Farmed: Hispanic Villages and Irrigation Systems in Early Sierra County, 1850-1900" *New Mexico Historical Review* Vol. 63, No. 4, (Oct 1988), pp.334-335.

13 Wilson, 1988, p.353.

14 White, R., 1991, *"It's Your Misfortune and None of My Own": A New History of the American West* (University of Oklahoma Press: London) p.51.

15 Sweeney, 1998, pp.395-396 & p.406.

16 Thrapp, 1974, p.73: Thrapp, 1967, pp.21-23; Utley, 1984i, p.66: Debo, p.61; Roberts, p37; Flanagan, p.341; Dunn p.326.

17 Clum, 1928, p.3; Thrapp, 1967, pp. 21-23; Thrapp, 1974, p.82-83; Sweeney, 1998, pp.455-460; Utley, 1967, pp.251-252; Utley, 1984i, p.67; Stout, pp. 29-30; Debo, pp. 69-71; Roberts, pp. 41-42 Flanagan, p.341; Dunn, p.333; Ball, 1980, pp.19-20; Myers, 1966ii, pp.299-300.

18 Sweeney, 1998, pp.272-273.

and Sonora in 1856.[19] Again in alliance with Mangas Coloradas and Cochise, Victorio, Nana and Juh are said to have led their own personal followings in an attack on Carleton's California Column at Apache Pass in July 1862.[20] By 1863, Victorio had risen to such a position of respect among the Chihenne Apaches that both he and Nana could attempt to persuade Mangas Coloradas against making the attempt to parley that led to his execution.[21] A camp, believed to be Victorio's, was attacked by Union cavalry in January 1863 and the latter claimed to have killed nine Apaches and wounded several more. However, the detachment's commander was sufficiently impressed to note its location on 'the most rugged, high and difficult mountains to ascend and pass I ever saw.'[22] One of Victorio's tactics commented on by his US army and Texas Ranger opponents almost two decades later was his careful siting of camps in easily defended terrain.[23] Later in 1863, Victorio and other leaders, including Cochise, struck back and raided southern New Mexico, and in one attack in July managed to kill Union Army Lieutenant L.A. Bargie.[24] In the aftermath of Mangas Coloradas' death, Victorio avoided peaceful contact with the Anglo-Americans until April 1865.[25] Victorio and other Warm Springs Apaches met with N.H. Davis, the Assistant Inspector General, at Fort Cummings,[26] to consider a move onto the Bosque Redondo reservation. Victorio indicated that the Warm Springs Apaches were willing to move on condition that they would be allowed to inspect the reservation.[27] However, the Apaches did not rendezvous with Davis for an inspection tour as promised.[28] In the light of the US army's treatment of Mangas Coloradas, their apparent compliance with Davis' request may have been a ploy to give the Warm Springs Apaches time and scope to evade the US troops at Fort Cummings. Later that year, Victorio made a second attempt to negotiate a peace with the Anglo-Americans at Pinos Altos. Here at least three Chihenne Apaches were killed and Victorio himself was wounded. This convinced Victorio that the Anglo-Americans did not want peace with the Chihenne Apaches, and in retaliation four soldiers were ambushed and killed and another wounded near Fort Cummings some weeks after this Anglo-American treachery.[29] The role Victorio played through the 1850s and 60s points to a steady rise in his influence among the Chihenne Apaches during this period. By 1870, Victorio was seen as the key leader among the Warm Springs Apaches.[30]

Towards the end of the decade, relations between the United States and the Warm Springs Apaches had improved sufficiently for the latter to accept a US Agent based at Ojo Caliente in 1869-70.[31] Assistant Inspector General Davis warned that such progress was driven by a desire for a temporary respite before the renewal of hostilities. He specifically maintained that, during 1870, Cochise had been able to send some of his dependents to the Cañada Alamosa reservation in New Mexico, leaving him free to pursue his war in Arizona. Davis also noted that Cochise

19 Sweeney, 1998, p.328.
20 Sweeney, 1998, p.430.
21 Sweeney, 1998, pp.446-447 & p.448.
22 Sweeney, 1998, p.460.
23 Thrapp, 1974, pp.312-313.
24 Sweeney, 1991, p.213; 1998, p.463.
25 Sweeney, 1991, pp.223-225; Miller, 1984, p.149; Haley, 1981, p.249.
26 This post was activated in 1863, abandoned ten years later in 1873. It was reactivated in response to Victorio's War in 1880. Unlike most army posts it was surrounded by a wall. It was built at the southern opening of Cook's Canyon, and overlooked a spring, on the Butterfield Trail and a popular ambush location once relations with the Apaches broke down in the early 1860s (See Boucher, *Real West* Apr., 1970).
27 Miller, 1984, p.149.
28 Miller, 1984, p.149.
29 Sweeney, 1991, p.240.
30 Ball, 1962, p.22 & 1970, p.48.
31 Ball, 1962, p.22; Haley, 1981, p.251.

Plate 4.1 Memorial erected to the four men killed by Chihenne Apaches in 1866. The inscription reads: 'SACRED TO THE MEMORY OF THOS RONAN AGED 45 LS HUNTER AGED 33 CHAS DEVLIN AGED 28 THOS DALY AGED 28 LATE PRIVATES OF CO G 1ST VETERAN INFANTRY CAL. VOLS. KILLED BY APACHES AT OAK GROVE NM JAN 17 1866.' (Photo: author)

Plate 4.2 The township of Cañada Alamosa. The Chihennes' first reservation was centred on this settlement. The town's inhabitants quickly gained a reputation for not asking too many questions concerning trade with the Apaches. A number of Mexican and early Anglo-American settlers were implicated in supporting a vibrant illicit trading relationship with the Warm Springs Apaches. (Photo: author)

and a number of his men apparently used the New Mexico reservation to rest and recuperate.[32] There is also evidence that at least some of the Warm Springs Apaches were content to accept a reservation in the United States while continuing to raid in Mexico. On 4 March 1871, eight US citizens were killed and their train ransacked by Apaches in the Galeana district of Chihuahua.[33] While these raiders were probably other Chiricahua Apaches, it was known that Victorio and other Warm Springs Apaches sometimes traded their plunder in the town of Galeana. The US Consul in Chihuahua City noted that the decline in the mining and stock-raising industries in Chihuahua State could be attributed to 'the want of a suitable market, and Indian depredations.'[34] This situation, he argued, could be reversed by opening up Chihuahua to the North American market by the construction of a railroad to the US border, and perhaps beyond.[35] Davis' warning was prompted by a new peace initiative launched in 1871. During August and September of 1871, Vincent Colyer, Secretary of the Board of Indian Commissioners, was instructed to tour Apacheria and establish a sufficient number of reservations for the Apaches. He recommended that at least four reservations be created, including one for the Warm Springs Apaches in New Mexico.[36] His mission was based on the principles laid down by the US federal government two years earlier:

> That they (the Indians) should be secured in their legal rights; located when practicable on reservations; assisted in agricultural pursuits and the arts of civilized life; and the Indians who should fail or refuse to come in and locate in permanent abodes provided for them would be subject wholly to the control and supervision of military authorities, to be treated as friendly and hostile as circumstances might justify.[37]

From 1870, the Cañada Alamosa Reservation contained approximately 1,200 Warm Springs Apaches, led by 'Victoria, Loco and Nanné, who nominally are at peace, though guilty of having committed several murders and many thieving depredations.'[38] Colyer also found 2-300 Mexican

32 Special Report of N.H. Davis, Inspector General in relation to Apache Indians in New Mexico, 25 October 1871, in Correspondence relating to the selection by Vincent Colyer of the Board of Indian Commissioners of sites for Apache Indian reservations at Tularosa Valley, and White Mountain, New Mexico Territory, and at Camp Grant and Camp Verde, Arizona Territory, 1871-72 (Hereafter referred to as 'Colyer Correspondence 1871-72', Letters Rec'd by the AGO. 1871-80, NA, M666, Roll 24.

33 Moye to the Second Assistant Secretary of State, 23 March 1871 in Consular Despatches Chihuahua Mexico 1830-1906, NA, M289, Roll 1.

34 Brown to Second Assistant Secretary of State, Washington D.C., 1 October 1871 in Consular Despatches Chihuahua Mexico 1830-1906, NA, M289, Roll 1.

35 Brown to Second Assistant Secretary of State, Washington D.C., 1 October 1871 in Consular Despatches Chihuahua Mexico 1830-1906, NA, M289, Roll 1.

36 See Delano to General Howard, 4 March 1872 in 'Colyer Correspondence 1871-72', Letters Rec'd by the AGO, 1871-80, NA, M666, Roll 24.

Colyer's original intention appears to have been to set up two reservations; one based around Camp Grant in Western Apacheria and another at its eastern extremity in New Mexico. (Colyer to Delano, Sec. of the Interior, 31 July 1871 in 'Colyer Correspondence 1871-72', Letters Rec'd by the AGO, 1871-80, NA, M666, Roll 24.) Having visited the area he recommended five reservations for Arizona (Colyer to Gen. Schofield, HQ MDoP, 19 October 1871 & Delano to the President of the U.S.A., 7 November 1871 in 'Colyer Correspondence 1871-72', Letters Rec'd by the AGO, 1871-80, NA, M666, Roll 24; See also Clum, 1928, p.3; Reeve, p.296; Thrapp, 1967, p.103; 1974, pp.138-139); Hurst provides a very useful summary of the build up to the Victorio Campaign in a 3 page web article (See Hurst (2) webpage).

37 Reeve, p.296; See also Delano to the President of the U.S.A., 7 November 1871 & G. Crook, Lt. Col. 23rd Infantry; General Orders No. 35, HQ DoAz, 27 December 1871 in 'Colyer Correspondence 1871-72', Letters Rec'd by the AGO, 1871-80, NA, M666, Roll 24. see also comments by Stockel, 1991, p.43.

38 Special Report of N.H. Davis, Inspector General in relation to Apache Indians in New Mexico, 25 October 1871, in 'Colyer Correspondence 1871-72', Letters Rec'd by the AGO, 1871-80, NA, M666, Roll 24.

farmers and traders settled in or around the village of Cañada Alamosa. He inspected the hot springs at Ojo Caliente 'which the Indians considered the heart of their traditional country.'[39] While Colyer found this projected site for a reservation to be far enough from Mexican settlers to avoid potential clashes, there was not enough land to support the occupants by farming.[40] Colyer travelled further north and west to the Tularosa valley, which was described as being 'remote from white settlements, surrounded by mountains not easily crossed' and as having 'sufficient arable land, good water, and plenty of wood and game.'[41] The Tularosa Reservation was designated on 29 August 1871 as the new reservation for the Warm Springs Apaches.[42] Any other independent Apaches still roaming in New Mexico were 'commanded' to report to this location. As long as they remained at peace, the resident Apaches were guaranteed protection by the US federal government. It was also stated that leaving dependents on the reservation while the warriors carried out raids would not be tolerated.[43] Governor William Anderson Pile of New Mexico Territory endorsed this agreement, arguing that every effort should be made to get those Apaches led by Cochise to settle there, as Cochise was 'the ablest and most desperate among the wild tribes of the west and has been thoroughly embittered against the whites by treacherous treatment at the time his brother-in law (Mangas Coloradas) was killed.'[44] Assistant Inspector General Davis was unimpressed with the choice, noting that the Tularosa reservation location was not likely to prove suitable for military operations, while presenting the Apaches with no obstacle to continuing their raids.[45] The numerous affidavits and letters submitted by US citizens suggest that Cañada Alamosa provided a base for significant raiding activity, which their agent, Orlando Piper, was unwilling or unable to confront.[46]

The Apaches themselves did not want to go, and military compulsion was advocated should they refuse to move. Concern was also expressed that the Tularosa area was both fertile and rich in minerals, and would soon attract ranchers and prospectors, which would eventually lead to strife. It was recommended by the army that the Cañada Alamosa reservation be fixed on for both economic and military considerations, because keeping the Apaches there would make it easier to contain any raiding activity.[47] Colyer himself thought that General Crook's recruitment of Apache scouts had become known to the independent Apaches, thus making their cooperation harder to secure as they

39 Thrapp, 1974, p.139; Haley, 1981, p.319.

40 Colyer to Delano, 26 August 1871 & Colyer to Schofield, 20 October 1871 in 'Colyer Correspondence 1871-72', Letters Rec'd by the AGO, 1871-80, NA, M666, Roll 24; Thrapp, 1974, p.139.

41 Colyer to Nathaniel Pope, Superintendent of Indian Affairs, New Mexico, 29 August 1871 in 'Colyer Correspondence 1871-72', Letters Rec'd by the AGO, 1871-80, NA, M666, Roll 24; See also Ogle, 1970, p.90; Reeve, pp.296-297; Thrapp, 1974, p.139; Ball, 1962, p.22; Kayser, 1973i, p.16.

42 Colyer to Nathaniel Pope, Superintendent of Indian Affairs, New Mexico, 29 August 1871 & Nathaniel Pope, Superintendent of Indian Affairs New Mexico to CO DoNM, 6 September 1871 in 'Colyer Correspondence 1871-72', Letters Rec'd by the AGO, 1871-80, NA, M666, Roll 24.

43 Delano to the President of the U.S.A., 7 November 1871 & General Orders No. 8, HQ, MDoM, 20 November 1871 in 'Colyer Correspondence 1871-72', Letters Rec'd by the AGO, 1871-80, NA, M666, Roll 24.

44 Pile to Fish, U.S. Secretary of State, 19 June 1871 in 'Colyer Correspondence 1871-72', Letters Rec'd by the AGO, 1871-80, NA, M666, Roll 24.

45 Special Report of N.H. Davis, Inspector General in relation to Apache Indians in New Mexico, 25 October 1871, in 'Colyer Correspondence 1871-72', Letters Rec'd by the AGO, 1871-80, NA, M666, Roll 24.

46 See numerous affidavits, letters and resolutions 'Colyer Correspondence 1871-72', Letters Rec'd by the AGO, 1871-80, NA, M666, Roll 24.

47 Special Report of N.H. Davis, Inspector General in relation to Apache Indians in New Mexico, 25 October 1871, in 'Colyer Correspondence 1871-72', Letters Rec'd by the AGO, 1871-80, NA, M666, Roll 24.

feared treachery.[48] The Camp Grant Massacre of April 1871 must also have been fresh in the minds of the Apaches. However, Agent Piper thought that part of this opposition could be the result of the Warm Springs Apaches' loss of the trading relations they had developed with the Mexican settlers and traders in Cañada Alamosa.[49] There appears to be a good deal of truth in this allegation. In April 1876, E.C. Kemble, an inspector for the Bureau of Indian Affairs, arrived at the Ojo Caliente agency to investigate widespread fraud.[50] Kemble described Cañada Alamosa as a haven for Mexicans trading alcohol and other unspecified goods for all manner of government property (openly displayed) which had originally been issued to the Apaches at Ojo Caliente.[51]

Despite their misgivings, the Apaches were persuaded to move to Tularosa and the removal was carried out in the spring of 1872.[52] Lieutenant Colonel Thomas Devin of the Eighth Cavalry was charged with completing the move, and he reported that Victorio, Loco and Gordo had eventually agreed to go, realising that they had no other option other than war. They agreed to the sending of the old and sick by road, in the charge of the army, but most of the Apaches made their own way to the new reservation, arriving there on 24 May.[53] The move was carried out without any problems arising;[54] but it soon became clear that the Apaches were very unhappy with the Tularosa site.[55] In 1872, General Howard had a long conference with Victorio, whom he viewed as very much in favour of peace – being principally concerned for the preservation of his tribe – and as exerting a restraining influence on his warriors.[56] This conference took place on 12 September 1872. General Howard interviewed Victorio, Loco, Nana, Gordo, Chevo and Lopez. The transcript of this meeting makes it quite clear that the Apaches did not want to remain at Fort Tularosa, citing the ill-health of their children, high mortality rates, impure water, adverse weather effects on their crops and lack of natural food sources. They clearly stated their desire to return to the Cañada Alamosa region.[57] In summing up the reasons for the Apache discontent, the conference reported that '[t]he people are all discontented, are leaving and Victorio cannot keep them together.'[58] General Howard promised that he would submit this request to the President for his approval.[59] In doing, so he may have unwittingly caused a political problem concerning the maintenance of the Tularosa reservation. He subsequently met an Apache leader called Sancho, as part of his peace commission in 1872, in the vicinity of the Cuchillo Negro area. General Howard gave Sancho permission to reside in the Cañada Alamosa area during this conference. This, as representatives from the Department of the Interior and the US army pointed out, undermined the whole rationale

48 Colyer to Delano 26 August 1871 in 'Colyer Correspondence 1871-72', Letters Rec'd by the AGO, 1871-80, NA, M666, Roll 24.

49 Thrapp, 1974, p.141; see also Ball, 1970, p.49; Reeve, p.293 & p.298.

50 See Kemble, 2001, pp.203-210.

51 Kemble, 2001, pp.204-205.

52 See Special Orders No.55, HQ DoNM, 9 Apr., 1872 & T.C. Devin Lt.Col. Eighth Cavalry to AAAG, DoNM, 27 May 1872 in 'Colyer Correspondence 1871-72', Letters Rec'd by the AGO, 1871-80, NA, M666, Roll 24.

53 T.C. Devin Lt.Col., Eighth Cavalry to AAAG, DoNM, 27 May 1872 in 'Colyer Correspondence 1871-72', Letters Rec'd by the AGO, 1871-80, NA, M666, Roll 24.

54 T.C. Devin Lt.Col. Eighth Cavalry to AAAG, DoNM, 27 May 1872 & Granger, Col. Comdg. DoNM to AAG, Ft. Leavenworth 21 June 1872 in 'Colyer Correspondence 1871-72', Letters Rec'd by the AGO, 1871-80, NA, M666, Roll 24.

55 Kayser, 1973i, p.19.

56 Thrapp, 1974, p.150; see also Ogle p.107; Reeve, p.300.

57 Howard to F.A. Walker, ColA, 7 November 1872 in 'Colyer Correspondence 1871-72', Letters Rec'd by the AGO, 1871-80, NA, M666, Roll 24; See also Misc. 2 Document.

58 See Misc. 2 Document – "Appendix A: Council of Mimbres Apaches held at Fort Tularosa September 11 [12] 1872" NA, RG 75 also in Arizona Historical Society Microfilm MC 4.

59 Howard to F.A. Walker, ColA, 7 November 1872 in 'Colyer Correspondence 1871-72', Letters Rec'd by the AGO, 1871-80, NA, M666, Roll 24.

for creating the reservation in the Tularosa Valley.[60] Nevertheless, the outcome of this conference was that if Cochise's Chiricahua Apaches could be persuaded to join Victorio's people, General Howard favoured the re-establishment of the reservation in the Ojo Caliente area.[61]

The conference between General Howard and the Apache leaders at the Tularosa reservation also indicates that at this point the US army thought that Victorio was the leading man amongst the Warm Springs Apaches. By this time, the war between the Chiricahua Apaches and the Anglo-Americans had taken its toll in over 10 years of conflict. Victorio, Cochise and other Apache leaders were actively considering a peaceful accommodation with the Americans. Victorio, in removing to Tularosa, was acting in good faith in trying to reach just such an accommodation. He could see a wider picture, with several possible choices, and chose to attempt a peaceful solution before he resorted to war.

Equally, it should be noted that Victorio was quite capable of taking advantage of the political divisions amongst his opponents. On 15 July 1871, Julian Chavez lost three oxen from his ranch on the Mimbres River and in company with Abeline Mejia and Luciano Montoya he pursued the raiders onto the Cañada Alamosa reservation. They arrived simultaneously with the raiders and successfully demanded the return of the oxen.[62] Then Chavez spotted an Apache riding a stolen horse belonging to him:

> on his complaint to the Agent, the latter ordered Alcalde Trujillo to have it returned, but he could not secure it from the Indians: Trujillo saw the Indian Chiefs Loco & Victoria, who told him that they could not secure the horse from the Indians as they showed fight to them, but if they could be furnished with twenty (20) soldiers to assist them they could get all the stock stolen from Citizens of Grant Co. and Agent Piper replied that he could not do so, for then all the Indians would leave the Reservation.[63]

As subsequent events would showed, the very idea that the combined forces of Victorio and Loco required outside help to enforce their will upon the Warm Springs Apache reservation beggared belief. Victorio had probably worked out that the Indian agent (an employee of the Department of the Interior through the Office of Indian Affairs) was very reluctant to call upon the services of the US army (employees of the Department of War). By proposing the intervention of US troops, Victorio and Loco were illustrating the weakness of their agent to their own followers. The Apaches did not like Piper,[64] probably because, in their eyes, he did not stand up to them. The agent seems to have been thoroughly intimidated by his charges.[65] This episode also reveals that, even when at

60 See for example Piper to N. Pope, Sup. Of Indian Affairs, New Mexico, 17 October 1872, Gen. Pope to Sheridan, 28 October 1872 & Gen. Pope to Sheridan, 11 December 1872 in 'Colyer Correspondence 1871-72', Letters Rec'd by the AGO, 1871-80, NA, M666, Roll 24.

Nathanial Pope did point out in response to these protests that General Howard was currently relying upon members of Sancho's band in his effort to contact Cochise and was effectively at their mercy. N. Pope strongly advised patience until Howard completed his mission (Pope, Sup. Of Indian Affairs, New Mexico to Col. Granger, CO DoNM, 24 October 1872 in 'Colyer Correspondence 1871-72', Letters Rec'd by the AGO, 1871-80, NA, M666, Roll 24).

61 Thrapp, 1974, p.151; Worcester, p.209.

62 Affidavit of Julian Chavez submitted 4 October 1871 in 'Colyer Correspondence 1871-72', Letters Rec'd by the AGO, 1871-80, NA, M666, Roll 24.

63 Affidavit of Julian Chavez submitted 4 October 1871 'Colyer Correspondence 1871-72', Letters Rec'd by the AGO, 1871-80, NA, M666, Roll 24.

64 Thrapp, 1974, pp.148-149.

65 See for example Affidavits of M. Cronin submitted 11 September 1871 & Julian Chavez submitted 4 October 1871 in 'Colyer Correspondence 1871-72', in Letters Rec'd by the AGO, 1871-80, NA, M666, Roll 24.

peace, the Apaches were ever vigilant for any sign of weakness which could be exploited to thwart attempts to control them. It is a measure of his political skill that it took until 1877 for Victorio to be provoked back into open warfare with the Anglo-Americans. However, we must acknowledge that it would be inaccurate to suggest that all was peace and quiet on the Cañada Alamosa and Tularosa reservations. In 1873 there were several instances of aggressive behaviour and continued raiding by Victorio's warriors.[66]

Benjamin Thomas left a detailed and often vivid account of his service as Indian agent at the Tularosa reservation during the period 1873-4. He probably gives the best account we have of somebody who had regular contact with Victorio before the latter commenced his final resistance to the United States. Yet as we shall see, Thomas did not really gain an understanding of his charges during his tenure in office. In January 1873, he reported that the Apaches were clearly unhappy with their reservation and requested that a quick decision be made as to whether they could return to Cañada Alamosa.[67] However, even the ever-vigilant Apaches could miscalculate the odds and rely too heavily on the political rivalries of their enemies. A couple of weeks later, Thomas requested two companies of troops to be stationed at the reservation as the Apaches were utterly contemptuous of his authority, refused to adapt to American ways, and when drunk on tiswin, 'almost enforce their claim to the control of the agency.'[68] Thomas observed that approximately one Apache a month was being killed during tiswin drinking sessions.[69] He proposed that the beef and flour ration be increased and the corn ration be reduced as the latter was being used to brew tiswin.[70] Thomas also antagonized the Apaches when he started to issue beef rations to individuals rather than turning the cattle loose to be shot down. Thomas countered that if he had used this method to supply the Apaches with beef, the leading warriors would have taken a disproportionate amount of meat. He also reported that many Apaches were using the reservation as a safe haven for their families while they went out on raids.[71] These charges were supported by his observations and various instances when troops and citizens followed the raiders to the edge of the reservation. In November 1872, Sergeant J.B. Cooney with 10 enlisted men of A Company, Eighth Cavalry, and a Mexican scout, followed the trail of a band of Apaches who had killed two men four miles from Fort Bayard. The trail was followed onto the Tularosa reservation.[72] On 19 March, three citizens from the settlement of Tulerosa near Fort Stanton, with an escort of five troops, traced four stolen horses to the reservation. Thomas met with Victorio and demanded their return. All four horses were returned within the week. Thomas also noted that increased cavalry patrols were having some effect when a party led by Ponco, which was heading out of the reservation to raid in Chihuahua, was fired on by troops in the vicinity of Cañada Alamosa and returned to the reservation.[73] In retaliation for Agent Thomas's exerting his authority and increasing US army activity around the reservation, the Apaches turned their attention to him. Thus, while Thomas could report that, as far as he was

66 See for instance Reeve, p.301; Thrapp, 1974, p.160.

67 Thomas (U.S. Indian Agent, Southern Apache Indian Agency) to Dudley (Superintendent of Indian Affairs), 13 January 1873 in Benjamin Thomas Papers AC221, Box 1 Folders 3 & 7 (Hereafter referred to as 'Thomas Papers'), Fray Anjelico Chavez History Library, Museum of New Mexico, Palace of the Governors, Santa Fé (Hereafter referred to as 'FAC-HL/MoNM/PoG/SF').

68 Thomas to Dudley, 22 & 31 January 1873 in 'Thomas Papers', FAC-HL/MoNM/PoG/SF.

69 Thomas to Dudley, 22, 31 January & 23 June 1873 in 'Thomas Papers', FAC-HL/MoNM/PoG/SF.

70 Thomas to Dudley, 8 March 1873 in 'Thomas Papers', FAC-HL/MoNM/PoG/SF.

71 Thomas to Dudley, 8 March 1873 in 'Thomas Papers', FAC-HL/MoNM/PoG/SF.

72 Return for November 1872 in Returns From U.S. Military Posts 1800-1916 Fort Bayard, New Mexico 1866-Dec. 1879, NA, RG393, M617, Roll 87.

73 Thomas to Dudley, 1 Apr., 1873 in 'Thomas Papers', FAC-HL/MoNM/PoG/SF.

Plates 4.3 and 4.4 Two shots of the interior of the northern Black Range near the ghost town of Hermosa in the heart of the territory claimed by the Chihenne Apaches. From the outside, these mountains look as if they are a long spine of rolling peaks, when in fact there are a lot of flat open areas in the interior of these mountains with good water sources and hunting. It should come as no surprise that the Warm Springs Apaches put up a spirited political and military resistance to removal from this area. (Both photos: author)

aware, the Apaches were not raiding outside of the reservation during the month of May 1873, he also had to put a guard on the reservation's store room to prevent an increase in theft.[74]

A new challenge for Agent Thomas arose in the form of a feud within the Warm Springs Apaches, and this focused on the activities of four brothers of whom the leader, Pajarito, was the son-in-law of Victorio. This individual had already killed a woman, and a man named 'Snaggle-Tooth Ponce'. On or around 23 June, Pajarito and his three brothers openly challenged the rest of the Apaches and fired several shots, which Thomas thought mortally wounded another Apache. Thomas refused to bring in the army to help deal with Pajarito and his brothers when asked to do so by Victorio and other leading men. Thomas argued that the Warm Springs Apaches were well enough armed to deal with these men.[75] This was a mistake. Thomas was perfectly correct in believing that the Apaches could take care of dissident members of their own tribe; but the Pajarito brothers were being used by the leading men of the Warm Springs Apaches to test the authority of the agent. The Apaches would not necessarily have appreciated the exact political issues between representatives of the War Department and the Department of the Interior, though as noted earlier, they were aware that there was a conflict between the agent and the army. The agent's refusal to call up what the Apaches would have regarded as his 'enforcers' was probably interpreted as a clear sign of weakness. Indeed, within two weeks, Thomas was asking for army protection as the Apaches were 'insolent and threatening' and claiming that 'arms are openly displayed to enforce their demands.'[76] The situation seemed to calm down after 'Colonel'[77] William Redwood Price, with one company of cavalry, passed through the reservation on his way to Fort Wingate. What the Apaches did not know was that the same officer was due to return in mid-July with three companies of cavalry, in order to demonstrate to the Apaches that it was not in their interests to raid off the reservation or threaten reservation employees.[78] In the meantime the Pajarito brothers returned to the reservation and seemed to have settled their differences with the rest of the Warm Springs Apaches. Trouble flared up again after a laundress was harassed by three inebriated Apaches. They had then threatened the corporal of the guard, who had attempted to intervene, at gunpoint. A subsequent attempt to arrest the culprits by the small army detachment stationed nearby failed, and during it an Apache woman was shot dead. Thomas finally managed to calm the situation down, but not before a number of threats were made against him by the Apaches.[79]

Thomas was not the only employee threatened by the Apaches:

> Several days ago one of the Indians fired an arrow at Dr Duane when he was entering their camp in answer to their call for professional service. About the same time an Indian fired an arrow at my interpreter and tried to fire one at the Beef Contractor's herder. The last Indian who leveled arms at me was killed by Capt. Chilson's party. When they have fired at any of the employees it has been without provocation and simply for their own amusement.[80]

It was a skirmish with Captain George W. Chilson of the Eighth Cavalry which brought matters on the reservation to a crisis. In July 1873, Captain Chilson responded to a stock raid on Shedd's Ranch led by a Warm Springs Apache called Sancho. The captain led a small detachment of 15

74 Thomas to Dudley, 5 & 31 May 1873 in 'Thomas Papers', FAC-HL/MoNM/PoG/SF.
75 Thomas to Dudley, 14 June 1873 in 'Thomas Papers', FAC-HL/MoNM/PoG/SF.
76 Thomas to Dudley, 26 June 1873 in 'Thomas Papers', FAC-HL/MoNM/PoG/SF.
77 Price, according to Heitman was, in fact a Major in the Eighth Cavalry but the Colonel probably refers to the highest rank he gained during the Civil War.
78 Thomas to Dudley, 28 June 1873 in 'Thomas Papers', FAC-HL/MoNM/PoG/SF.
79 Thomas to Dudley, 11 July, 1873 in 'Thomas Papers', FAC-HL/MoNM/PoG/SF.
80 Thomas to Dudley, 25 July, 1873 & Thomas' Monthly Report for July 1873 submitted 7 August 1873 in 'Thomas Papers', FAC-HL/MoNM/PoG/SF.

men, including three civilian volunteers, who caught up with the raiders 'somewhere near the Luera Mountains, west of the Cañada Alamosa' and killed three Apaches in the process of recovering the stolen livestock. Corporal Frank Brauting was also killed in the skirmish; but the most significant event was the wounding of an Apache who was Victorio's nephew.[81] The first Agent Thomas knew of the affair was the sounds of lamentation coming from one of the Warm Springs' camps. On investigation, he found Sancho with a wounded Apache recounting his skirmish with Chilson. Sancho had earlier left the reservation with five or six men and had returned with three, one of whom was wounded.[82] Two of Sancho's party were thought to have been killed.[83] On 23 July, Thomas interviewed Victorio and Loco in his office and 'told them' that he wanted to arrest Sancho and 'what I wanted them to do.'[84] Thomas knew that the head men of the Apaches had previously expressed a wish that 'bad Indians' be punished. He also recalled an earlier episode under Agent Piper where Victorio had offered to accompany troops to Sancho's camp and kill Sancho for stealing cattle. He assumed that the same feeling prevailed. To his surprise Victorio and Loco refused to arrest Sancho, arguing that they should be protected at the agency and that they would not allow Sancho to be arrested. When Thomas persisted in his attempts to have Sancho detained, Victorio and Loco left the building and, at their signal, the women and children departed, while the warriors armed themselves and mounted their horses. Thomas then reported that Victorio had confronted him to inform him that 'if I [Thomas] wanted to fight he was ready, or if the soldiers wanted to come here and fight, he was ready.'[85]

Loco, Chihenne Apache leader. History has been somewhat dismissive of Loco as a leader because of his efforts to negotiate peacefully with the US Government. This is a complete misreading of a very brave man who, in conjunction with Victorio and Nana, provided very effective leadership of the Chihenne Apaches in the 1870s. Remember this is the man who with Nana engaged the Pajarito brothers at close range to end the latter's leadership challenge. (The National Archives)

Thomas had miscalculated on two counts. First, he had failed to realise that he had already lost the respect of the Apache leadership. He was not in a position to issue demands to Victorio and Loco. Second, he may not have realised that the wounded Apache was the nephew of Victorio.[86]

81 Thrapp, 1974, p.160; 1988, p.263; Anon. 2 Document; See also comments by Price to AAAG, DoNM, 1 August 1873 in 'Cochise-Howard Agreement', Letters Rec'd by the AGO, 1871-80. M666. Roll 123.

82 Thomas' Monthly Report for July, 7 August 1873 in 'Thomas Papers', FAC-HL/MoNM/PoG/SF.

83 Price to AAAG, DoNM, 25 July, 1873 in Letters Received, DoNM, NA, RG393.

84 Thomas to Dudley, 25 July, 1873 in 'Thomas Papers', FAC-HL/MoNM/PoG/SF.

85 Thomas to Price 24 July, 1873 & Thomas to Dudley 25 July, 1873 & Thomas' Monthly Report for July, 1873 submitted 7 August 1873 in 'Thomas Papers', FAC-HL/MoNM/PoG/SF; Price to AAAG, DoNM, 25 July, 1873 in Letters Received, DoNM, NA, RG393.

86 It was almost a week later that Thomas transmitted this information to Col. Price. (Thomas to Price, 30 July, 1873 & Thomas' Monthly Report for July 1873 submitted 7 August 1873 in 'Thomas Papers', FAC-HL/MoNM/PoG/SF; See comments by Thrapp, 1974, p.160.

Uncles and nephews seem to have had a close relationship in Apache society,[87] and the wounding of his nephew may have hit Victorio hard. Where the Apaches had miscalculated was in their ignorance of the planned return of Colonel Price and 100 Eighth cavalrymen and 25 Navajo scouts, who suddenly descended on the agency. Price confronted Victorio and Loco, who refused to enter the agency buildings, no doubt fearing arrest, and a tense council was held outside. Between 30 and 40 armed Apaches attended this conference, with additional sentries stationed on the nearby hillsides to give early warning of any potentially hostile move on the part of Price's detachment. Victorio and Loco were described by Price as 'insolent', but he also got the impression that they were much surprised and alarmed by the sudden appearance of such a large body of troops within an hour of their defying the agent and challenging him or the army to a fight.[88] The Apaches refused to talk further until they had drunk some tiswin, and they agreed to return to the conference the following day.[89] This was a ruse to allow them to pull back into the hills. The next morning, Victorio sent word that he would talk in a canyon two miles from the agency. When Thomas, Price and 18 soldiers arrived, there were no Apaches to be found.[90] Prior to the attempt to meet with Victorio, it was Thomas's interpreter,[91] Robert H. Stapleton[92] who, that morning, had gone to meet Victorio, and who had brought back word that the latter was willing to meet with Price and five other men.[93] Seeing a larger number of men coming to the meeting, Victorio had probably suspected treachery and fled. On their return, Price's party managed to get between a small camp of Apaches and the surrounding hills and, at Thomas' request, arrested three men, though a further two escaped. Price, not being inclined to initiate hostilities, declined to open fire on these fugitives. Two youths and 30 women and children were also taken into custody. One of the men arrested was the person who, as noted earlier, had shot an arrow at interpreter Stapleton. This man turned out to be one of Pajarito's brothers.[94]

Price then ordered 60 men from two of his companies and 20 Navajo scouts to pursue the fleeing Apaches, and though they were led through the most difficult terrain, this detachment was able to catch up with and persuade small groups of Warm Springs Apaches, including Victorio, to agree that they would return to the agency.[95] Price recorded that, after his interview with Victorio, he was 'so frightened that he does not know what course to take.'[96] Again, this agreement appeared to be a ruse on Victorio's part to gain further time to re-group after this unexpected setback.

On his return to Tularosa, Price found Loco, with a few men and approximately 70 women and children, bivouacked near the agency buildings. Victorio and most of the warriors were reported to

87 See Opler, 1996, pp.55-58.
88 Price to AAAG, DoNM, 25 July, 1873 in Letters Received, DoNM, NA, RG393.
89 Thomas to Dudley, 25 July, 1873 & Thomas' Monthly Report for July 1873 submitted 7 August 1873 in 'Thomas Papers', FAC-HL/MoNM/PoG/SF; Price to AAAG, DoNM, 25 July, 1873 in Letters Received, DoNM, NA, RG393.
90 Thomas to Dudley, 25 July, 1873 & Thomas' Monthly Report for July 1873 submitted 7 August 1873 in 'Thomas Papers', FAC-HL/MoNM/PoG/SF.
91 Thomas to Price, 30 July, 1873 & Thomas' Monthly Report for July 1873 submitted 7 August 1873 in 'Thomas Papers', FAC-HL/MoNM/PoG/SF.
92 Thrapp, 1974, p.149.
93 Price to AAAG, DoNM, 25 July, 1873 in Letters Received, DoNM, NA, RG393.
94 Price to AAAG, DoNM, 25 July, 1873 in Letters Received, DoNM, NA, RG393; Price to CO Fort Bowie, 25 July, 1873 in 'Cochise-Howard Agreement', Letters Rec'd by the AGO, 1871-80, NA, M666, Roll 123; Kayser, 1973i, p.20; See also Anon. 2 Document.
95 Price to Thomas, 30 July, 1873 & Thomas' Monthly Report for July 1873 submitted 7 August 1873 in 'Thomas Papers', FAC-HL/MoNM/PoG/SF.
96 Price to Thomas, 30 July, 1873 in 'Thomas Papers', FAC-HL/MoNM/PoG/SF.

be camped 50 miles away on the San Francisco River.[97] The colonel decided that his arrival on the reservation had dealt with the crisis, and he departed, leaving one of his three cavalry companies to act under the orders of the agent, just in case hostilities flared up once more. Price thought that with his departure the disaffected Warm Springs Apaches would quietly drift back to the reservation.[98] Thomas was not so sure, and when Victorio did arrive back at the reservation, the agent got the distinct impression that he was not going to back down. Loco also stated that, as Agent Piper had previously deposed him as principal chief, he could not speak for Victorio's intentions.[99] On 5 August, Nana, Raffaelle and 20 other Apaches returned from a visit to the Chiricahua reservation. Nana, on hearing of recent events, promised Thomas that he would sort everything out, and the following day Victorio came in and had a conference with the agent. Two days later, Pajarito and a 'number of other young men' returned to the reservation. Thomas informed Victorio that he was no longer the head chief and had been replaced by Loco. Thomas also demanded the surrender of Sancho but was forced to conclude that Sancho had already made his escape.[100]

On 24 August, the Warm Springs Apaches finally dealt with the Pajarito brothers. An incident arose when the brothers announced their intention of going on a raid, and this was opposed by Loco. Pajarito's brother, Turevia, in a fit of anger, shot and wounded a woman; Pajarito then shot her dead. Both Loco and Nana immediately opened fire, and a general close-range battle erupted. Thomas reported that Pajarito, his brother Pajarito Chiquito, and a woman were killed in a fight in Victorio's camp. Turevia was severely wounded 'shot through the body', and the fourth brother was slightly wounded in the arm. Victorio was shot in the face with an arrow, Raffaelle had his leg broken by a bullet, a man named Jaralches was slightly wounded in the chest by an arrow, and an unnamed young warrior was badly shot through the elbow.[101] Thomas concluded that, since the Pajarito brothers had been the instigators of most of the trouble on the reservation in 1873, Loco and Nana had decided to 'rid the tribe of these four pests.'[102] He added that Loco was a distinct improvement on Victorio, as the former commanded more respect than the latter. He also noted that, although the tribe was split, with Victorio's faction licking their wounds after their defeat at the hands of Loco and Nana, they appeared to be settling their differences amicably.[103]

This narrative does not ring true on several counts. Had the break between Victorio and Loco and Nana been genuine, then Victorio would have been their prime target in the fight and would have been killed. The later close relationship between the three leaders suggests that this fight was a sham presented for Thomas's benefit. That is not to say that the fight itself was a pantomime, not least for the Pajarito brothers: the deception comes in how it was presented to Thomas *post-bellum*. There were a number of factors at play that stimulated the actions of Victorio, Nana and Loco during this period. Particularly important was the fact that Pajarito was beginning to gather together his own following, and throughout 1873 was making it clear that he was a potential challenge to the existing Warm Springs Apache leadership. The fact that Pajarito was Victorio's son-in-law may have meant that it would have been difficult for the latter, for personal reasons, to initiate action against him without support from other group leaders within the Warm Springs

97 Price to AAAG, DoNM, 1 August 1873 in 'Cochise-Howard Agreement', Letters Rec'd by the AGO, 1871-80, NA, M666, Roll 123.

98 Price to AAAG DoNM, 1 August 1873 in Letters Rec'd by the AGO, 1871-80, NA, M666, Roll 123.

99 Thomas to Dudley, 30 July, 1873 & Thomas' Monthly Report for July 1873 submitted 7 August 1873 in 'Thomas Papers', FAC-HL/MoNM/PoG/SF.

100 Thomas' Monthly Report for July 1873 submitted 7 August 1873 in 'Thomas Papers', FAC-HL/MoNM/PoG/SF See also Price to AAAG, DoNM, 1 August 1873 in 'Cochise-Howard Agreement', Letters Rec'd by the AGO, 1871-80, NA, M666, Roll 123.

101 Thomas to Dudley, 30 August 1873 in 'Thomas Papers', FAC-HL/MoNM/PoG/SF.

102 Thomas to Dudley, 3 September 1873 in 'Thomas Papers', FAC-HL/MoNM/PoG/SF.

103 Thomas to Dudley, 3 September 1873 in 'Thomas Papers', FAC-HL/MoNM/PoG/SF.

Plates 4.5 and 4.6. Two photos taken from the approximate location of Old Fort Tularosa where Victorio and Loco confronted Agent Thomas, only to be taken by surprise by Colonel Price and his troops. These photos give a good idea of the terrain into which the Chihennes fled after the unexpected arrival of so many US cavalrymen. (Both photos: author)

Apaches. This situation was also a good opportunity for the Warm Springs Apaches to test the role of Thomas as the head man with whom they must deal. The agent singularly failed the test when he refused to deal with the Pajarito brothers, and he thus lost the Apaches' respect; but at the same time he gave them the green light to deal with Pajarito themselves. In the meantime, the Sancho affair erupted and in this Victorio and Loco faced down Thomas, only to be taken by surprise by Colonel Price's fortuitous and somewhat coincidental arrival. It became clear to the Warm Springs Apaches that Victorio was being blamed by Thomas for this incident, and they went through the motions of accepting their leader's demotion in order to draw Thomas's attention away from him. However, the problem of the Pajarito brothers remained to be solved, and what better way would there be than to 'present' the brothers' killing as the rest of the Warm Springs Apaches putting the 'erring' Victorio in his place. Yet Victorio soon regained his standing with the agent. By April 1874, Thomas was again consulting Victorio over decisions affecting the whole of the Warm Springs Apaches.[104] Thomas had previously noted, in January 1874, that Victorio and 10 others had left the reservation to raid in Mexico for horses.[105] If Victorio's capital within the Warm Springs Apaches had sunk as low as Thomas thought it had, it would have taken more than one successful horse raid into Chihuahua to restore his prestige. Indeed, many years later, Joseph H. Ware, a soldier serving at Fort Tularosa during this period, strongly implied that while Loco was recognized as the official chief of the Warm Springs Apaches, he was not the man to whom most of the Apaches gave their allegiance, though he does not identify the man of whom he was speaking.[106]

As a postscript to this affair, Sancho, who had fled the reservation the previous summer, turned up on the reservation during June 1874 and offered the hand of peace to Thomas, which was accepted, although Thomas informed Sancho that he frankly doubted the latter's sincerity and that 'if he ever left the reservation without my pass I would do all I could to have him shot.'[107]

Things seemed to settle down on the reservation; but Thomas found that this apparent tranquillity did not usually work in his favour. He reported only limited success in encouraging the raising of crops, and recommended that the Apaches would profit from the raising of stock.[108] He failed to prevent the illegal selling of whiskey to the Apaches by Mexicans from the Rio Grande valley.[109] And his attempt to set up a school on the reservation also failed, due to the strong influence of the older leaders.[110] The root cause of these specific failures was that the Warm Springs Apaches continued to be opposed to the location of their reservation.[111] Thomas must have transmitted this discontent and its consequences back to his superiors, and a proposal for a move back to Ojo Caliente was favourably received by the Warm Springs Apaches in April 1874.[112] However, Thomas reported that their leader stated, 'Yes, but give us some place and let us remain there.'[113] Unfortunately, the agreement to abandon Tularosa for Ojo Caliente in 1874 was a purely economic decision, the Tularosa reservation's isolation being a drain upon federal resources.[114] Ogle also suggests that the proposed move back to Ojo Caliente represented an (unsuccessful) effort to break the 'illegal' trade in stolen property between Tularosa and the Chiricahua reservation in

104 Thomas to Dudley 18 Apr., 1874 in 'Thomas Papers', FAC-HL/MoNM/PoG/SF.
105 Thomas to Dudley, 31 January 1874 in 'Thomas Papers', FAC-HL/MoNM/PoG/SF.
106 Joseph H. Ware vs. the U.S. & Apache Indians, Depredation Claim No. 4584, 16E3/3/6/5 Box 375.
107 Thomas to Dudley, 12 June 1874 in 'Thomas Papers', FAC-HL/MoNM/PoG/SF.
108 Kayser, 1973i, p.21.
109 Thomas to Dudley, 31 March 1874 in 'Thomas Papers', FAC-HL/MoNM/PoG/SF.
110 Thomas to Dudley, 28 February & 31 March 1874 in 'Thomas Papers', FAC-HL/MoNM/PoG/SF.
111 See Thomas to Dudley, 28 February in 'Thomas Papers', FAC-HL/MoNM/PoG/SF.
112 Thomas to Dudley, 18 Apr., 1874 in 'Thomas Papers', FAC-HL/MoNM/PoG/SF.
113 Kayser, 1973i, p.22.
114 Reeve, p.303; Thrapp, 1974, pp.164-165; Ogle 1970, p.164.

southeastern Arizona.[115] Two months later, Thomas was informed that he should prepare to return the Warm Springs Apaches to Ojo Caliente.[116] This transfer was completed in the first half of September, and the first issue of rations at Ojo Caliente was made on 10 September 1874. Thomas was able to report that the Warm Springs Apaches were very happy.[117] They were so happy that by 19 September, Thomas had recovered 14 horses and mules stolen by Apaches and requested that the commanding officer at Fort McRae take custody of the beasts until the civil authorities could take charge of them.[118]

Dr James M. Laing, the doctor serving the Warm Springs Apaches in 1874, painted an interesting picture of his companions. On the positive side, he noted that, for the most part, they were very healthy and very moral, though he also noted the practice of cutting off the ears and noses of women caught in adultery and reported three cases of gonorrhoea[119] during this period. He also noted the Apaches' love of gambling, pitching flat rocks like quoits, and playing a hoop and stick game. In a report of how he had treated Victorio's son for a cut on the leg, he implied that Victorio was the leading man on the reservation. He also described the Warm Springs Apaches as filthy, and having seen them checking each other for parasites in ration queues, he described this activity as being 'after the fashion of monkeys, another argument in favour of Darwin's theory, though they have been sufficiently civilized not to eat these parasites as their prototypes do.'[120]

Unfortunately, the relatively idyllic life now enjoyed by the Chihenne Apaches had about two years to run before it was destroyed by the concentration policy promoted by the Department of the Interior. While this policy proved to be a key element in Victorio's decision to openly oppose the Anglo-Americans, the period from 1860 to 1876 had already taught him and his followers to be very wary when interacting with representatives of the United States. They had seen the fate of Mangas Coloradas; and Victorio had had a narrow escape from a parley in 1865. Once the Warm Springs Apaches had agreed to settle on a reservation, they were allocated land which did not suit them; and they were given leaders (agents) for whom they had little, if any, respect. Yet Victorio also learned that he had to be very careful in challenging an agent's authority. There was also the issue of corrupt reservation officials. Agent Piper had been 'retired' by November 1872. A temporary agent was briefly employed, and it was this agent who was replaced by Agent Thomas at the end of 1872.[121] On 15 November 1874, Thomas was moved on to become agent for the Pueblo Indians.[122] He was succeeded by John M. Shaw, who reported a huge rise in population at Ojo Caliente. Before he left, Thomas had reported his charges as numbering 400, of whom 175 were warriors. This had risen to 1,317 by the end of 1875.[123] Thrapp diplomatically hints at corruption – the claiming of supplies far in excess of the needs of the reservation's population and their subsequent sale for profit.[124] The Warm Springs Apaches were key players in what could be termed the 'black economy' in the surrounding territory, and would have been aware of this trade by the agent and his accomplices. This cannot have improved the standing of such actors in the eyes of the Apaches. From their point of view, such people were supposed to provide leadership; and one of the

115 Ogle, 1970, pp.137-138.
116 Dudley to Thomas, 20 June 1874 in 'Thomas Papers', FAC-HL/MoNM/PoG/SF.
117 Thomas to CoIA, 7 October & 2 November 1874 in 'Thomas Papers', FAC-HL/MoNM/PoG/SF.
118 Thomas to CO Fort McRae, 19 September 1874 in 'Thomas Papers', FAC-HL/MoNM/PoG/SF.
119 The previous year, the then medical officer on the reservation, Dr Duane, had noted their virtuous nature and a complete lack of syphilis amongst the Warm Springs Apaches (Duane to Thomas, September 1873 in 'Thomas Papers', FAC-HL/MoNM/PoG/SF).
120 Annual Report of Dr. James M. Laing, 31 August 1874 in 'Thomas Papers', FAC-HL/MoNM/PoG/SF.
121 Thrapp, 1974, pp.150-151 & p.157; Kayser, 1973i, p.20.
122 Thrapp, 1974, p.170.
123 Thrapp, 1974, p.170.
124 Thrapp, 170; see also Ogle, 1970, p.171; Worcester, p.198; Cocker, pp.218-220; Dale, pp.106-107.

components of such leadership was generosity concerning surplus resources. To use excess supplies for the enrichment of the agent and his accomplices was the antithesis of good leadership.

So far, relations with the United States were hardly smooth; but they had not led to open warfare. What the Apaches could not know about were the political negotiations which had commenced with Colyer's return to the capital. As his recommendations were being ratified in Washington in late 1871, changes to Colyer's plans were already being mooted. When General Howard was sent on his peace commission to Apacheria in 1872, the Secretary of the Interior asked him to consider:

> the propriety of inducing the nomadic tribes of Arizona to unite and accept a reservation further east, in the territory of New Mexico, where they may be more readily reached by the efforts of the Government and of philanthropic citizens, in the work of providing for their physical wants, and with a view to promoting their civilization.[125]

Failure, at the federal level of government, to appreciate that many Apaches would oppose their concentration triggered increasing levels resistance among the Warm Springs and other Chiricahua Apaches, and would culminate in the Victorio Campaign of 1879-1881.

125 Delano to Howard, 4 March 1871 in 'Colyer Correspondence 1871-72', Letters Rec'd by the AGO, 1871-80, NA, M666, Roll 24.

5

Concentration Policy: 1876-1877

Aside from the chronic issue of where to locate the Chihenne Apache reservation from 1872 onwards a more serious problem was the gathering momentum of the policy to concentrate the location of the Apaches.[1] In other words, a comprehensive solution to the location of all the Western and Chiricahua Apaches reservations was being considered by the Department of the Interior. While the concentration of the Chiricahua Apaches onto the San Carlos or Ojo Caliente reservations had been reflected upon for some time, the final decision appears to have been, once again, economic.[2] However, there were other factors other than economics at play in this situation. The Chiricahua reservation was too close to the Mexican border and did not have sufficient agricultural land.[3] Removal to another reservation might reduce cross-border raiding and encourage the adoption of a pastoral existence.[4] General Howard, in reaching his peace treaty with Cochise, had noted that approximately 50 Apache warriors had refused to accept this treaty and had departed for Sonora.[5] It could be argued that General Howard's peace mission had merely allowed Cochise to retire gracefully, while allowing other Chiricahuas the freedom to raid in Sonora. The booty taken in Mexico could be sold in New Mexico, allowing Cochise to deny responsibility for such activity on the part of Chiricahuas and other Apaches over whom he had little actual control. General Crook was openly contemptuous of this treaty, arguing that a lasting peace could only be brought through respect for the US army gained by military conquest.[6] Thus, for once, the Office of Indian Affairs' drive to concentrate the Apaches did somewhat dovetail with the ideas of the local US commanders, who saw both the Chiricahua and the Warm Spring Apache reservations as foci for continued resistance, undermining the military successes gained against other Apache tribes.[7]

However, the situation was affected by a far deeper, historical, attitude ingrained in many US citizens, who held that the 'New World' was 'there for the taking' from the 'savages'. Concentration was merely one link in a long historical chain of events designed to remove American Indians from possession of the land.[8] One only needs to recall the 'Monroe Doctrine' of 1823[9] and its logical

1 See Spicer, pp.251-252.
2 Ogle, 1970, p.164.
3 See Jeffords to Smith, CoIA, 30 November 1873 in 'Cochise-Howard Agreement', Letters Rec'd by the AGO, 1871-80, NA, M666, Roll 123.
4 Reeve, p.304.
5 Howard to CoIA, 23 September 1873 in 'Cochise-Howard Agreement', Letters Rec'd by the AGO, 1871-80, NA, M666, Roll 123.
6 See Crook to AAG, MDoP, 7 July 1873 & Crook to AG Washington D.C., 8 December 1873 in 'Cochise-Howard Agreement', Letters Rec'd by the AGO, 1871-80, NA, M666, Roll 123.
7 See Price to Commanding General, DoAz, quoted in Vandever, U.S. Indian Inspector to CoIA, 23 January1874 in 'Cochise-Howard Agreement', Letters Rec'd by the AGO, 1871-80, NA, M666, Roll 123.
8 Cocker, 1999, p.222.
9 See Van Alstyne, 1978, pp. 584-596.

progression in the term 'manifest destiny'[10] to remind oneself of the momentous forces of change confronting the Apaches.

The Closure of the Chiricahua Reservation

The dissolution of the Chiricahua reservation came about as a result of the killing of two men called Rogers and Spence on the reservation on or around 7 or 8 April 1876.[11] The men ran a stage station in the Dragoon Mountains, but were also suspected of supplying illicit whiskey[12] to the Apaches and of asking no questions as to the origins of the goods the latter offered in exchange. The two men were killed when they refused to sell more whiskey to a Chiricahua raiding party led by one Pionsenay.[13] A third man, Lewis, was also killed by the Chiricahuas 60 miles to the west of Fort Bowie.[14] The killers of Rogers and Spence were pursued by a detachment from Fort Bowie which caught up with the culprits but found them too numerous and too well-fortified in difficult terrain to be tackled.[15] John P. Clum,[16] the agent at the San Carlos reservation, wrote to the Commissioner of Indian Affairs asking for whatever support could be rendered in either soldiers or arms, or both, to arrest the culprits, who were believed to be drawing rations at the Chiricahua agency.[17] This attack was the moment for which both the army and the Office of Indian Affairs had been waiting. Orders were issued to remove the Chiricahuas to the San Carlos reservation. These orders instructed that the San Carlos Indian Police, commanded by Clum, should be issued with arms and ammunition to effect the closure of the reservation.[18] It had been assumed that Clum could implement this policy on his own, but in view of the fact that the Chiricahuas had not been subdued by the US army, it was decided that direct support from the Department of Arizona should be solicited.[19] The request for a loan of arms to the San Carlos Police was quickly authorized by the Secretary of War.[20]

---

10 See Pletcher, 1978, pp.526-534.

11 Kautz to AAG, MDoP, 23 October 1876 in 'Cochise-Howard Agreement', Letters Rec'd by the AGO, 1871-80, NA, M666, Roll 123.

12 Kautz to AAG, MDoP, 23 October 1876 in 'Cochise-Howard Agreement', Letters Rec'd by the AGO, 1871-80, NA, M666, Roll 123.

13 Report of Col. August V. Kautz, 15 September 1876 in AR-WD, NA, M997, Roll 26, 1876 Vol. I-II, p.98; Thrapp, 1974, pp.173-174.

14 Kautz to AAG MDoP, 30 June 1876 and Kautz to AAG, MDoP, 23 October 1876 in Correspondence relating to the removal of the Chiricahua Apache Indians to the San Carlos Indian Agency, Arizona Territory, 1876-77 (Hereafter referred to as 'Correspondence relating to Chiricahua Removal 1876-77'), Letters Rec'd by the AGO, 1871-80, NA, M666, Roll 265; Report of Col August V. Kautz, 15 September 1876 in AR-WD, NA, M997, Roll 26, 1876 Vol. I-II, p.98.

15 Kautz to AAG, MDoP, 23 October 1876 in 'Cochise-Howard Agreement', Letters Rec'd by the AGO, 1871-80, NA, M666, Roll 123.

16 Clum is a pivotal character in that he both participated in and subsequently wrote many articles concerning the Apache reservation system and wars of the 1870s and 1880s. As such, he deserves a huge amount of credit for his efforts to make the concentration policy work for the benefit of the Apaches. Unfortunately, his personal ambition combined with the collapse of the concentration policy has coloured his recollection of events.

17 Clum to CoIA, 13 May 1876 in 'Correspondence relating to Chiricahua Removal 1876-77', Letters Rec'd by the AGO, 1871-80, NA, M666, Roll 265.

18 Acting Secretary of the Interior to the Secretary of War, 9 May 1876 in 'Correspondence relating to Chiricahua Removal 1876-77', Letters Rec'd by the AGO, 1871-80, NA, M666, Roll 265.

19 Acting Commissioner Galpin to The Secretary of the Interior, 8 May 1876 and Governor Safford to CoIA, 6 May 1876 in 'Correspondence relating to Chiricahua Removal 1876-77', Letters Rec'd by the AGO, 1871-80, NA, M666, Roll 265.

20 Secretary of War to the Secretary of the Interior, 16 May 1876 in 'Correspondence relating to Chiricahua Removal 1876-77', Letters Rec'd by the AGO, 1871-80, NA, M666, Roll 265.

John Philip Clum was a very effective agent running the San Carlos reservation in Arizona. However, his enthusiasm for the concentration policy and his willingness to act independently to implement this policy was a major contributing factor in sparking the Victorio Campaign. (The National Archives)

In truth, the decision to abolish the reservation had already been made and all that was required was the justification supplied by Pionsenay and his men. The decision had been considered by the Office of Indian Affairs for some time, and the reservation's existence had been generally opposed by the army, despite its creation by General Howard. The origins of the closure probably dated back to 1873, when the Office of Indian Affairs had warned the then agent, Tom Jeffords that if Cochise could not stop the use of his reservation as a staging post for Apache raiders operating in both Sonora and New Mexico, they would consider acquiescing to General Crook's request to take the reservation under direct military control.[21] Jeffords claimed he had made efforts to stop such traffic, and that those responsible for such activity were from 'northern reservations.' Despite his advice to them to return to their reservation, Jeffords suspected that most of the raiding was being done by these Apaches who, passing through the Chiricahua reservation, were wittingly or unwittingly diverting the blame for their activities onto Cochise.[22] William Vandever, US Indian Inspector, visited Cochise in the company of Jeffords and found that there was no check upon the numbers of Apaches on the Chiricahua reservation, and little inclination on the part of Cochise or Jeffords to intervene in illicit raiding and trading. Vandever's immediate solution was to instruct Jeffords to withhold rations from those Apaches who had been assigned to the Tularosa reservation.

21 Edward Smith, Commissioner to Jeffords, 29 December 1873 in 'Cochise-Howard Agreement', Letters Rec'd by the AGO, 1871-80, NA, M666, Roll 123.

22 See Jeffords to Smith, CoIA, 30 November 1873 in 'Cochise-Howard Agreement', Letters Rec'd by the AGO, 1871-80, NA, M666, Roll 123.

His overall solution was to recommend that the Chiricahua reservation be moved away from the Mexican border, though, having subsequently visited the Tularosa reservation, he was inclined to blame Major Price's intervention for causing the problem in the first place.[23] It is only fair to note that Agent Thomas had contacted Price to say that the latter's appearance on the reservation had helped him remain in control of the Apaches at Tularosa. Thomas claimed that had Price elected to remain on the reservation for a couple of months, the process of reforming the Apaches would have been completed.[24] Price was inclined to blame 'interested parties surrounding the Reservations' for the false accounts passed to Vandever.[25] Thus despite the fact that the aims of both the Department of War and the Department of the Interior with reference to the future of certain Apache reservations appear to have coincided, this did not reflect a thawing of political relations between these two departments. Vandever was of the opinion that only peaceful means would prevail against the independent Apaches: 'The Apaches like all wild Indians are averse to work and inclined to war and pillage; feeding them tames their nature, but fighting them only stimulates their savage instincts.'[26] In contrast, General Crook was quick to point out that the success stories on some of the Apache reservations were only achieved after these Apaches had been soundly defeated.[27]

However, despite these polarised opinions on policy, the dissolution of the Chiricahua reservation suited both camps, and Clum was ordered to proceed with the closure.[28] Clum was supported[29] by a large military operation to blockade the reservation commanded by Colonel August V. Kautz, commander of the Department of Arizona.[30] This blockade was not consistently maintained: for example, Kautz strongly criticised Major Charles E. Compton, Sixth Cavalry, for failing to obey his instructions and allowing a large party of Apaches to leave the reservation.[31] At least one detachment had more success: on 9 June, Apache scouts led by Captain George Brayton intercepted a four-man raiding party returning from Sonora. Two of the Apaches fled towards the Chiricahua agency and were not pursued. Two attempted to flee away from the reservation and in 'quite a little skirmish' Brayton's Apache scouts killed them.[32]

Doubtless many senior officers in the army saw this operation as an essential component of their operations against the Chiricahuas.[33] Yet there was some disapproval of the concentration of the Apaches. Several months after the event, Colonel Kautz stated that:

---

23 Vandever, US Indian Inspector to CoIA, 23 January 1874 in 'Cochise-Howard Agreement', Letters Rec'd by the AGO, 1871-80, NA, M666, Roll 123.

24 Thomas to Price, 29 May 1874 in 'Cochise-Howard Agreement', Letters Rec'd by the AGO, 1871-80, NA, M666, Roll 123.

25 Price to Lt Mahnken, AAAG DoNM, 13 June 1874 in 'Cochise-Howard Agreement', Letters Rec'd by the AGO, 1871-80, NA, M666, Roll 123.

26 Vandever, US Indian Inspector to CoIA, 23 January 1874 in 'Cochise-Howard Agreement', Letters Rec'd by the AGO, 1871-80, NA, M666, Roll 123.

27 Crook to AG Washington D.C., 8 December 1873 in 'Cochise-Howard Agreement', Letters Rec'd by the AGO, 1871-80, NA, M666, Roll 123.

28 Clum, 1928, p.9.

29 Schofield to AG USA., 18 May 1876 and Kautz to AAG MDoP, 30 June 1876 in 'Correspondence relating to Chiricahua Removal 1876-77', Letters Rec'd by the AGO, 1871-80, NA, M666, Roll 265; Clum, 1928, p.9; Worcester, 1975, p.36; Haley, 1981, p.311.

30 Kautz to AAG MDoP, 30 June 1876 in 'Correspondence relating to Chiricahua Removal 1876-77', Letters Rec'd by the AGO, 1871-80, NA, M666, Roll 265.

31 Kautz to AAG MDoP, 30 June 1876 in 'Correspondence relating to Chiricahua Removal 1876-77', Letters Rec'd by the AGO, 1871-80, NA, M666, Roll 265.

32 Brayton, Captain 8th Infantry to AAG, DoAz, 30 June 1876 in 'Correspondence relating to Chiricahua Removal 1876-77', Letters Rec'd by the AGO, 1871-80, NA, M666, Roll 265.

33 One has to be somewhat wary of Clum's accounting of events. He rarely misses a chance to attack the higher echelons of the US army. Even when helping him, he often ascribes ulterior motives behind such gestures. I will also address this point in the conclusion of this work.

> I have not approved the concentration of large bodies of Indians of different tribes on one reservation, and would have advised against the removal of the Chiricahuas had I been consulted.[34]

One suspects that Kautz did, in fact, approve of the dissolution of the Chiricahua reservation, but had assumed that the Chiricahuas would be removed to Ojo Caliente, as had earlier been the intention of General Howard. It is also clear that the dangers of the policy of concentration were clear to some of the field commanders well in advance of the removal of the Warm Springs Apaches from Ojo Caliente to San Carlos in 1877.

In the meantime, the commander at Fort Bowie warned that if every available soldier was not deployed, any attempt to remove the Chiricahuas would unleash a full-scale war.[35] While this prediction can be argued to have been correct in the long term, the immediate effect of the proposed removal was to spark off a leadership battle. Those Chiricahuas who were inclined towards continued warfare were led by Eskinya and Pionsenay, and those in favour of peace and a removal to another reservation supported Cochise's son, Taza. On the evening of 4 June, the 'peace' faction prevailed by shooting dead several of the 'war' faction, including Eskinya, and wounding several more, including Pionsenay. The peace faction lost two men killed and several wounded.[36] The Chiricahua reservation was officially closed on 6 June 1876[37] and this was to have direct consequences for the Warm Springs Apaches on their reservation at Ojo Caliente. Some of the Chiricahuas from the war faction fled into Mexico;[38] others went to join their relations at Ojo Caliente. General John Schofield stated that there were 300 Apaches at Fort Bowie ready to move to San Carlos. He also estimated that 60 Apaches had fled either to Mexico or Ojo Caliente, and that the numbers of Chiricahuas on the reservation had been exaggerated.[39] It was reported by one G. King that at least 100 well-equipped Apache warriors had not surrendered and were threatening the countryside, and that those Chiricahuas who had been removed were mainly old men, women and children.[40] During the operation to remove the Chiricahuas, Major Compton and Captain Brayton had attempted to estimate the numbers of Chiricahuas, and could not account for more than 400 individuals. They openly doubted Jeffords' estimate that over 200 southern Chiricahuas had left for Sonora and that a Warm Springs leader with between 30 and 60 persons

---

34 Kautz to AAG, MDoP, 23 October 1876 in 'Cochise-Howard Agreement', Letters Rec'd by the AGO, 1871-80, NA, M666, Roll 123.

35 Schofield to AG U.S.A., 18 May 1876 in 'Correspondence relating to Chiricahua Removal 1876-77', Letters Rec'd by the AGO, 1871-80, NA, M666, Roll 265.

36 Kautz to AAG MDoP, 30 June 1876; See also Schofield to Adjt. US army Washington D.C., 7 June 1876 in 'Correspondence relating to Chiricahua Removal 1876-77', Letters Rec'd by the AGO, 1871-80, NA, M666, Roll 265; See also Report of Col. August V. Kautz, 15 September 1876 in AR-WD, NA, M997, Roll 26, 1876 Vol. I-II, p.98; Willcox to Fremont, Governor of Arizona Territory, 3 April 1880, NA, RG393, Part 1, Entry 169, Vol. 10, pp.137-140; See also Report of General O.B. Willcox, 11 September 1880, in AR-WD 1880, NA, M997, Roll 35, 1880 Vol. I, p.207.

37 Kautz to AAG MDoP, 30 June 1876 in 'Correspondence relating to Chiricahua Removal 1876-77', Letters Rec'd by the AGO, 1871-80, NA, M666, Roll 265; See also Clum, 1928, pp.15-16; Thrapp, 1974, pp.173-174; Ogle, 1958, p.83; 1970, pp.165-166; Wellman, 1957, p.145, Tate, 1977, p.108; Hughes, 2001, pp.136-137. Haley, 1981, p.311 claims that the reservation closed on the 4 of June but this was the date of the gunfight between the two factions. According to Kautz's report Clum had a conference with the Apaches on the 6 of June where they agreed to the move to San Carlos.

38 Schofield to Adjt. US army Washington D.C., 7 June 1876 in 'Correspondence relating to Chiricahua Removal 1876-77', Letters Rec'd by the AGO, 1871-80, NA, M666, Roll 265.

39 Schofield to AG Washington, 11 June 1876 in 'Correspondence relating to Chiricahua Removal 1876-77', Letters Rec'd by the AGO, 1871-80, NA, M666, Roll 265.

40 G. King, Hot Springs, Tres Alamos, Pima Co., Arizona to the Secretary of War, Washington D.C., 24 August 1876 in 'Correspondence relating to Chiricahua Removal 1876-77', Letters Rec'd by the AGO, 1871-80, NA, M666, Roll 265.

had been living on the Chiricahua reservation for three years but had fled when trouble flared up. Compton and Brayton concluded that only a small number of Chiricahuas under Juh, Geronimo and Ca-ca-ri-za[41] had gone to Sonora. Having contacted Clum and Colonel Kautz, and promised to bring in their people, they had quietly slipped away, having killed their dogs and abandoned their camp possessions. A trail of approximately 40 ponies was discovered making for Mexico, but the troops were two days behind and there was such a general lack of water in the area that they did not pursue the fugitives very far.[42] Kautz openly doubted Jeffords' estimate that over half the Chiricahuas had fled rather than remove to San Carlos and, in effect, suspected Jeffords of inflating the number to hide the fact that he had ordered more supplies than necessary while in charge of the Chiricahua reservation.[43] Kautz believed that some Apaches had fled under Juh, Geronimo and Nolgee to Sonora; but he also believed that some had made their way to the Warm Springs Apache reservation in New Mexico.[44] Troops in New Mexico were alerted, and A and C Companies, Ninth Cavalry, from Fort Bayard, and B Company, Ninth Cavalry, from Fort McRae, were sent out to scout for any Chiricahuas who might have strayed into southern New Mexico.[45]

The debate over the number of Apaches who had refused to go to San Carlos can be attributed to Jeffords not keeping an accurate account of the numbers of Apaches on the Chiricahua reservation. The dispute over the numbers of Chiricahuas who did and did not accept the move to San Carlos reinforces the impression that few, if any, people in the US government could accurately estimate the number of independent 'Chiricahua' warriors that were at large between 1876 and 1881.

By 1876, affairs on the Warm Springs Apache reservation at Ojo Caliente were also giving cause for concern for Colonel Hatch, in his position as commander of the District of New Mexico. The familial and trading links between the Chiricahua and Warm Springs Apache reservations had already led to some disturbances and fights among the resident Warm Springs Apaches. Prior to the closing of the Chiricahua reservation, Colonel Hatch visited Ojo Caliente, in an attempt to both assess and calm the situation.[46] He conferred with Victorio at Ojo Caliente, and found that the Apaches were in a belligerent mood, claiming that the government had reneged on its promises to feed them. The leading men of the Warn Springs Apaches openly declared that this situation had encouraged their warriors to renew raiding in order to survive. They also declared that those who remained were faced with starvation or taking charge of their own affairs.[47] Hatch noted that the Apaches still on the reservation were very well supplied with modern rifles (Sharps, Winchester and Springfield) and revolvers (Colt and Smith & Wesson),[48] and were thus in a position to return to their old way of life should they so wish.

---

41 Later identified as Nolgee by Kautz in communication sent to AAG, MDoP, 23 October 1876 in 'Cochise-Howard Agreement', Letters Rec'd by the AGO, 1871-80, NA, M666, Roll 123.

42 Compton to AAG, DoAz, 18 June 1876, Kautz to AAG MDoP, 30 June 1876 & Kautz to AAG, MDoP, 23 October 1876 in 'Correspondence relating to Chiricahua Removal 1876-77', Letters Rec'd by the AGO, 1871-80, NA, M666, Roll 265.

43 Report of Col. August V. Kautz, 15 September 1876 in AR-WD, NA, M997, Roll 26, 1876 Vol. I-II, pp.98-99.

44 Report of Col. August V. Kautz, 15 September 1876 in AR-WD, NA, M997, Roll 26, 1876 Vol. I-II, pp.98-99.

45 Record of Events, April 1876, Returns From Regular Army Cavalry Regiments 1833-1916, 9th Cavalry Regimental Returns 1873-1880, NA, M744, Roll 88.

46 Hatch to AAG, DoM, 20 May, 1876 in Letters Received, DoM 1868-98, RG 393, Entry A1-1 2601, Box 87: See also Reeve, p.305; Thrapp, 1974, p.175.

47 Hatch to AAG, DoM, 20 May, 1876 in Letters Received, DoM 1868-98, RG 393, Entry A1-1 2601, Box 87.

48 Hatch to AAG, DoM, 20 May, 1876 in Letters Received, DoM 1868-98, RG 393, Entry A1-1 2601, Box 87; See also Bourke's description of the heavily armed Apaches encountered in the Sierra Madre expedition of 1883, 2001ii, p.p.376, p.377 & p.379. It should be noted that in 1868 it was reported

Plate 5.1 and Plate 5.2 Two shots of the Chiricahua mountains in Cave Creek canyon. As with the Chihennes and their attachment to the Black Range, it should come as no surprise that some Chokonens were willing to resist removal from these mountains. (First photo: author; second photo: Catherine Edwards)

The premise behind the removal of these nomadic raiders from hindering the expansion of the United States was that, in return for the Apaches staying within the confines of their reservations, the federal government would undertake, in the short-term, to feed and clothe them. In the long-term, the government would provide the means through which the Apaches could be transformed into assimilated, self-sufficient farmers and ranchers. In theory, this policy seemed perfectly sound; but in practice it did not work, as too many Indian agents saw their postings as an opportunity for self-enrichment. They did not see the implications of their actions in cheating the Apaches for the long-term assimilation of the latter. Indeed, one suspects that they did not see the Apaches as candidates for integration, and made little effort to implement these long-term policy goals. They failed to realise that their charges were not 'ignorant savages' but a society with a highly developed culture whose members would quickly grasp the realities of their situation and act accordingly.

Yet Colonel Hatch reported that Victorio was still willing to try to maintain peace with the United States if he was treated as promised. Hatch even reported that Victorio and Nana killed four of their men and some of their followers who opposed Victorio's efforts to avoid war.[49]

In the aftermath of the closure of the Chiricahua reservation, there were a number of clashes between these independent Chiricahuas and the US army. Governor A.P.K. Safford of Arizona Territory complained that the operation to remove the Chiricahuas to San Carlos had been botched, and that by August 1876 several 'prospectors and travellers' had been picked off by renegade Chiricahuas.[50] Two miners named Todenworth and Keho were killed approximately 25 miles to the south of Fort Bowie, and a third man, Burrows, escaped to raise the alarm. A detachment of 20 Sixth cavalrymen buried the bodies and pursued the trail of an estimated five Apaches to the Sonoran line.[51] Colonel Kautz maintained that this was the only authenticated attack by Chiricahua Apaches since their removal.[52] However, there was evidence of raiding, and the trail of this activity appeared to lead back towards the Warm Springs Apache reservation at Ojo Caliente. Kautz reported that there was a raid in September 1876 in which a number of horses were driven off in the direction of New Mexico.[53] In New Mexico, Lieutenant H.H. Wright,

that "a number" of Spencer and Sharps cartridges had been found in an abandoned camp on the San Carlos River. (Capt. Moore, 38th Infantry, CO Ft. Cummings to Lt E. Hunter, AAA General, DoNM, 27 November 1868 in HQ Records of Fort Cummings, New Mexico, 1863-1873 & 1880-1884, NA, RG393, M1081, Roll 1.)

49 'Indian Warfare – Gen. Hatch's Opinion.' in the *Army & Navy Journal*, Vol.19, 7 January 1882, p.496; Hatch to AAG, DoM, Fort Leavenworth, 14 February 1880 in Letters Sent by the '9MD/DNM/DoNM', NA, RG393 M1072, Roll 6, Jan 1880-August 1881, Letter No.82, pp58-65; Hatch cited in Laumbach, pp.108-109 & p.123.

Hatch implied that he participated in this 1876 skirmish in the *Army and Navy Journal* article but makes no mention of his involvement in his 14 February, 1880 summary of relations with the Warm Springs Apaches from 1876 to February 1880 but this source is six years after the event and by this point Hatch, in the aftermath of his roasting at the hands of the territorial press during the Victorio Campaign, had a vested interest in portraying himself as martially as possible.

50 Safford to Kautz, 21 August 1876 in 'Correspondence relating to Chiricahua Removal 1876-77', Letters Rec'd by the AGO, 1871-80. NA, M666, Roll 265.

51 One Sgt. M. Robbins led ten men of Co. H & 10 men of Co. L, Sixth Cavalry, in pursuit of Apaches who had killed two men on 15 July. The detachment trailed the raiders to Sonora but failed to catch their quarry. They did find and destroy a cache of flour and mescal. (Record of Events July 1876, Returns From Regular Army Cavalry Regiments 1833-1916, 6th Cavalry Regimental Returns 1875 to 1880, NA, M744, Roll 63.)

52 Kautz to AAG, MDoP, 23 October 1876 in 'Cochise-Howard Agreement', Letters Rec'd by the AGO, 1871-80, NA, M666, Roll 123; See also Report of Col. August V. Kautz, 15 September 1876 in AR-WD, NA, M997, Roll 26, 1876 Vol. I-II, p.98.

53 Kautz to AAG, MDoP, 23 October 1876 in 'Cochise-Howard Agreement', Letters Rec'd by the AGO, NA, M666, Roll 123.

with A and C Companies, Ninth Cavalry, and Indian scouts, attacked an Apache camp on the Cuchillo Negro River on or around 25 September 1876. After the attack, 21 wickiups – Apache huts – were destroyed. District Headquarters approved Lieutenant Wright's actions, assuming that these had been the same Apaches reported to have been raiding the settlements on the Mimbres River.[54] Captain Henry Carroll with F Company, Ninth Cavalry, on a scouting trip into the Florida Mountains from Fort Selden, surprised four Apaches on 15 September, killing one and capturing their horses.[55] The acting Indian agent at San Carlos, one M.A. Sweeny, also claimed that most of the Chiricahuas who had not accepted the move to San Carlos were to be found at the Warm Springs Apache agency in New Mexico.[56] As 1876 drew to a close, General Pope was convinced that the Chiricahua Apaches in New Mexico and Arizona would continue to resist as long as they were allowed to retain their arms. He argued that the Apaches from Cañada Alamosa and Fort Stanton reservations did not need their firearms as there was insufficient wildlife to satisfy their food requirements, and all they used them for was to prey on those citizens living in the vicinity. His solution was to disarm them and concentrate them on the Fort Stanton reservation or elsewhere.[57]

The conflict with dissident Chiricahuas continued into January 1877. Lieutenant Wright had a sharp encounter when a group of Apaches led by Juh surrounded his detachment of six Ninth cavalrymen (C Company) and three Navajo scouts in the Florida Mountains on 24 January 1877. Wright reported that they shot their way out of the encounter, killing five Apaches and wounded several others. The detachment also captured 11 'animals', including six horses. The remaining Apaches pulled back to higher ground, opened fire and forced Lieutenant Wright to retreat from his already exposed position.[58] Reading between the lines, Wright's detachment probably caught the Apaches off guard but swiftly became the hunted and were lucky to get away with no casualties.

Earlier, on 9 January, Second Lieutenant J. Rucker, Sixth Cavalry, with 40 Apache scouts, nine enlisted men and three citizens, inflicted a sharp defeat upon a band of Chiricahuas, killing 10 and capturing their camp intact. Rucker's detachment had been following raiders who had stolen 21 horses from Samuel Hughes' ranch on 17 December.[59] Rucker's scouts tracked the Apaches to a camp which Rucker estimated was approximately 40 miles south of Ralston. Leaving their mounts under guard about six miles from the camp, the troops closed in during the night, on foot. The plan was for the scouts to occupy a hill 150 yards to the west of the camp, while Rucker and his troops occupied a hill 300 yards to the north of the camp. The scouts, under the command of a guide named Dunn, had orders to open fire on the camp at dawn, but launched their attack before Rucker had reached his position. A two-hour skirmish ensued as the Apaches took cover in the rocks and fought back. Dunn and his scouts made a number of probing attacks, but were driven back, with one scout corporal badly wounded. The deadlock was broken when Dunn and Rucker's men combined in a charge and scattered the Apaches. Rucker captured an Apache boy about

54 Personal File Henry H. Wright Box 334, NA, RG94 Entry 297.

55 Record of Events September 1876, Returns From Regular Army Cavalry Regiments 1833-1916, 9th Cavalry Regimental Returns 1873-1880, NA, M744, Roll 88.

56 Willcox to Fremont, Governor of Arizona Territory, 3 April 1880, NA, RG393, Part 1, Entry 169, Vol. 10, pp.137-140; See also Report of General O.B. Willcox, 11 September 1880, in AR-WD 1880, NA, M997, Roll 35, 1880 Vol. I, p.207.

57 Report of Gen. Pope, 26 September 1876 in AR-WD, NA, M997, Roll 26, 1876 Vol. I-II, p.449.

58 See various entries cited in Personal File Henry H. Wright Box 334, NA, RG94, Entry 297; The Ninth Cavalry Regimental Return for January 1877 notes a skirmish where Capt Beyer led an attack upon and Apache Camp in what looks to be the Boca Grande Mountains on January 28, 1877. Capt. Beyer was in the same company as Wright and the latter's skirmish is not mentioned so until further evidence to the contrary surfaces it will be assumed that this is a slightly garbled version of Wright's skirmish.

59 Report of Col. Kautz, 15 August 1877 in AR-WD, NA, M997, Roll 28, 1877 Vol. I-II, pp.135-136.

five-years old, subsequently identified as a nephew of 'Ger-on-i-mo.'[60] Forty-six horses and mules, a large amount of food and clothing, plus one Springfield rifle, a Sharps carbine, two Winchesters, and two revolvers were also captured.[61]

Reports from Mexico suggested that the Chiricahua and Warm Springs Apaches were also raiding there. One Moses Kelley sent word to Lieutenant John Bullis at Fort Clark in Texas that 300 'Gila' Apaches had raided the El Valle [Valley] de San Buenaventura and Galliana [Galeana?]. The Apache raiders were said to have been confronted by 100 Mexicans, whom they defeated in the ensuing fight, inflicting 18 fatalities. Kelley stated that the Governor of Chihuahua had sent a force of regular cavalry to support the 'ranchmen' but no further reports were received.[62]

The Warm Springs Apaches Are Removed to San Carlos

By early 1877 further reports filtered in that the Ojo Caliente reservation was harbouring known Chiricahua raiders.[63] In early February 1877, Apaches raided the San Pedro, Sonoita and Santa Cruz Valleys, killing seven and wounding four Mexicans, and stealing or killing 85 horses, mules and cattle. On 8 February, Lieutenant Rucker set out in pursuit of an estimated 15 to 35 Apaches. He followed their trail until it split, one party going south into Sonora while the other made for the Warm Springs Apache reservation. Rucker lost the latter trail approximately a day's march from Ojo Caliente. Three weeks later a patrol discovered a trail leading up from Sonora and making its way towards Ojo Caliente, but also failed to catch this party.[64]

Colonel Kautz sent Lieutenant Austin Henely, Sixth Cavalry, to investigate, and the lieutenant confirmed that Chiricahua raiders, including Geronimo, were using Ojo Caliente as a rendezvous point.[65] Of equal concern was the information that some of Victorio's warriors were allying themselves with the Chiricahuas in their depredations.[66] This information was passed from the War Department to the Secretary of the Interior, who informed the Commissioner for Indian Affairs. The latter contacted Agent Clum at the San Carlos reservation.[67] Clum was ordered to move to Ojo Caliente to arrest the Chiricahuas and remove them to San Carlos, to be held on suspicion of murder and thievery. Clum was also instructed to ask for military aid if required. Clum duly notified

60 As spelled in Rucker's original report. What is interesting is Rucker's attempt to present Geronimo as an Apache name not realising that 'Geronimo' was of Spanish origin.

61 Rucker to Post Adjutant, Camp Bowie, 14 January 1877 in 'Correspondence relating to Chiricahua Removal 1876-77', Letters Rec'd by the AGO, 1871-80, NA, M666, Roll 265; Reports & Tabular Statements of Scouting Expeditions 1867-91, Statement of 'L' Company, 6th Cavalry, Quarter ending March 31, 1877, NA, RG391 Entry 841; Record of Events January 1877, Returns From Regular Army Cavalry Regiments 1833-1916, 6th Cavalry Regimental Returns 1875 to 1880, NA, M744, Roll 63; Tate, 1977, p.110; Report of Lt. E.D. Thomas, 5th Cav., Act. Engineer Officer, 30 June 1877 in AR-WD, NA, M997, Roll 28, 1877 Vol. I-II, p.1450; Willcox to Fremont, Governor of Arizona Territory, 3 April 1880, NA, RG393, Part 1, Entry 169, Vol. 10, pp.137-140; See also Report of General O.B. Willcox, 11 September 1880, in AR-WD 1880, NA, M997, Roll 35, 1880 Vol. I, p.207.

62 Kelley to Lt Bullis Fort Clark TX, 16 September 1877, 'Disturbances at El Paso TX', 'Victorio Files', NA, RG393 M1495, Roll 14.

63 Report of Col. Kautz, 15 August 1877 in AR-WD, NA, M997, Roll 28, 1877 Vol. I-II, pp.135-136; Ogle, 1970, p.169; Worcester, 1975, p.36.

64 Report of Col. Kautz, 15 August 1877 in AR-WD, NA, M997, Roll 28, 1877 Vol. I-II, pp.136-137.

65 Report of Col. Kautz, 15 August 1877 in AR-WD, NA, M997, Roll 28, 1877 Vol. I-II, p.136; Willcox to Fremont, Governor of Arizona Territory, 3 April 1880, NA, RG393, Part 1, Entry 169, Vol. 10, pp.137-140; See also Report of General O.B. Willcox, 11 September 1880, in AR-WD 1880, NA, M997, Roll 35, 1880 Vol. I, p.207.

66 See Report of Col. Kautz, 15 August 1877 in AR-WD, NA, M997, Roll 28, 1877 Vol. I-II, pp.135-136; Clum, 1929i, pp.112-113; Ogle, 1970, p.169 & p.172; Thrapp, 1974, p.186; Worcester, p.199.

67 Clum, 1928, p.27; Ogle, 1970, p.172; Worcester, p.200.

both Colonel Kautz and Colonel Hatch of his request for cooperation in this matter.[68] On 3 April 1877, General Pope instructed Colonel Hatch to cooperate as fully as he could in the arrest of the renegades at Ojo Caliente and to take the opportunity to warn the Warm Springs Apaches that they should not allow such renegades to use their reservation as a refuge.[69] In a dramatic confrontation, Clum successfully arrested several Chiricahua leaders, including Geronimo. It was what happened in the aftermath of Clum's capture of the Chiricahua renegades that was to have a profound effect on Victorio's future relations with the United States. Clum made his arrests on 21 April 1877,[70] in accordance with his instructions from the Office of Indian Affairs. However, by 28 April 1877, Clum reported that, with the exception of some 'seventeen refractory members' whom he had arrested, the 434 Apaches at Ojo Caliente had 'consented' to a move to San Carlos.[71] In effect, the Warm Springs Apache reservation had been closed down.[72] This was not the expressed intention behind Clum's expedition to return the Chiricahua 'renegades' to San Carlos. Therefore, the decision to move Victorio's people and close Ojo Caliente seems to have been reached after Clum had arrived at Ojo Caliente.

Geronimo. A very controversial and divisive figure in the history of the Apache Wars. His continued resistance to the US and use of the Chihenne reservation at Ojo Caliente provided the justification that the US authorities needed to close this reservation in 1877. His actions certainly contributed significantly to the outbreak of the Victorio Campaign. (The National Archives)

It would appear that Clum, with perfectly good intentions, saw an opportunity to bring another band of wayward Apaches under his benevolent administration. Following this line of thought, he explained the removal as being down to his offering a 'common-sense' explanation of his reservation system to the Warm Springs

68 See CoIA to Clum, 20 March 1877, Clum to CoIA, 31 March 1877, CoIA to Secretary of the Interior, 2 April 1877, Clum to Hatch, 2 April 1877, Secretary of the Interior to Secretary of War, 3 April 1877 & Secretary of the Interior to the Secretary of War, 8 April 1877 in Correspondence relating to the arrest and removal of Geronimo's band of renegade Chiricahua Apache Indians from Ojo Caliente, New Mexico Territory, to the San Carlos Indian Agency, Arizona Territory, 1877 (Hereafter referred to as 'Geronimo File 1877'), Letters Rec'd by the AGO, 1871-80, NA, M666, Roll 326; Clum, 1928, p.27.

69 Pope to C.O. DoNM, 3 April 1877 in 'Geronimo File 1877', Letters Rec'd by the AGO, 1871-80, NA, M666, Roll 326.

70 Clum, 1929, pp.110-111.

71 CoIA to The Secretary of the Interior, 28 April 1877 & Secretary of the Interior to the Secretary of War, 28 April 1877 in 'Geronimo File 1877', Letters Rec'd by the AGO, 1871-80, NA, M666, Roll 326.

72 CoIA to The Secretary of the Interior, 28 April 1877 & Secretary of the Interior to the Secretary of War, 28 April 1877 in 'Geronimo File 1877', Letters Rec'd by the AGO, 1871-80, NA, M666, Roll 326.

Apaches, with particular reference to the 'head-count' to avoid false accusations of raiding.[73] That this action was independent can be deduced from the earlier communication from General Pope instructing Colonel Hatch to use the arrest of the Chiricahuas to remind the Warm Springs Apaches that raiding from their reservation would not be tolerated. There is no mention of the closure of the reservation. Moreover, Colonel Kautz, in relation to an accusation from Clum that no military assistance for the removal of the Warm Springs Apaches had been received from the Department of Arizona, stated that:

> As Agent Clum's dispatch of the 31st of March to me did not foreshadow the removal of all of the Indians from the Warm Springs Reservation to the San Carlos, I saw no occasion to march troops into the Department of Missouri where there were troops close at hand.[74]

The accompanying telegram from Clum to Kautz indeed makes no mention of the removal of the Warm Springs Apaches, only referring to the arrest of renegade Chiricahuas and related matters. Kautz reported to his superiors that he felt that Clum, in making such accusations, was trying to score another point in his feud with the Department of Arizona.[75] Kautz concluded that Clum was generally 'discourteous and offensive,' and stated that his apparent success on the reservation was down to 'several men of great personal influence among the Indians, who have had far more to do with their control than the agent.'[76] Kautz's evaluation of Clum is obviously clouded by his relations with the agent and is rather unfair, though we should remember that at least some of the Chiricahuas remember naming Clum the 'turkey gobbler'. Thrapp perhaps best sums up John Clum as:

> brash impudent, contentious, and nearly impossible to get on with, and he hated, or at least despised, the army. But he also was brave, intelligent, reliable in action, probably honest, and in sum, a fine agent.[77]

It is also clear that the Commissioner of Indian Affairs, while approving Clum's actions and subsequent recommendations, had been caught off guard by the latter's exercise in 'free enterprise'.[78] The commissioner acknowledged that Clum was 'acting under orders from this office,'[79] yet it was clear that Clum's superiors were as surprised at the closure of Ojo Caliente as the army. On 28 April, the Commissioner of Indian Affairs contacted the Secretary of the Interior to report that:

> I should be glad also if the Military would arrange for the custody of the Indians now reported by Agent Clum as prisoners, provided he so desires. The obscurity of his dispatch leaves me somewhat in doubt as to the exact nature of his plans and wishes or this request would be more specific.[80]

73 Clum, 1928, p.34; 1929i, pp.116-117; 1930ii, pp.80-82.
74 Kautz to AAG, MDoP, 11 May 1877 in 'Geronimo File 1877', Letters Rec'd by the AGO, 1871-80, NA, M666, Roll 326.
75 Kautz to AAG, MDoP, 11 May 1877 in 'Geronimo File 1877', Letters Rec'd by the AGO, 1871-80, NA, M666, Roll 326.
76 Report of Col. Kautz, 15 August 1877 in AR-WD, NA, M997, Roll 28, 1877 Vol. I-II, pp.140-141.
77 Thrapp, 1974, p.355, Note 33.
78 Smith, Commissioner, to Clum, Southern Apache Agency, April 17, 1877 via Fort Craig, Records of the New Mexico Superintendency of Indian Affairs, 1846-80, Microfilm Reel 24, Newberry Library, Chicago.
79 Secretary of the Interior to the Secretary of War, 28 April 1877 & CoIA to The Secretary of the Interior, 28 April 1877 in 'Geronimo File 1877', Letters Rec'd by the AGO, 1871-80, NA, M666, Roll 326.
80 CoIA to The Secretary of the Interior, 28 April 1877 in 'Geronimo File 1877', Letters Rec'd by the AGO, 1871-80, NA, M666, Roll 326.

Plate 5.3 The 'Hot Springs' at Ojo Caliente. When visited in 2005, the temperature was decidedly at the cold end of the water temperature spectrum. (Photo: author)

Plate 5.4 The remains of the buildings at Ojo Caliente, with the opening into the Cañada Alamosa Canyon just visible in the upper left of the photo. It was around these buildings that John Clum had his showdown with Geronimo and his followers. However, the more important event was Clum's 'persuasion' of the Chihennes to accept removal to the San Carlos Reservation. The presence of armed San Carlos Apache police was probably the real reason the persuasion was successful; but, it may never have occurred to Clum that he was intimidating the Warm Springs Apaches into leaving their land. (Photo: author)

Thus it was not until 1 May 1877 that General Sherman telegraphed General Philip Sheridan with instructions that Hatch should 'assist Agent Clum in his efforts to remove the Indians at the southern agency for the Apaches to the reservation at San Carlos."[81] Colonel Hatch pre-empted these instructions and was able to report, on 27 April 1877, that Major James Wade, in charge of the troops sent to Ojo Caliente, had disarmed and dismounted all Apaches found on the reservation and handed them over to Clum. Cavalry had been provided to accompany the Warm Springs Apaches and wagons had also been provided for those Apaches who had been arrested and were now in irons. Those cavalrymen not assigned to escort duty were then in pursuit of 'raiding parties.'[82]

Victorio and other leading Warm Springs Apaches might have advanced a very different interpretation of this episode. Despite the increasing involvement of Warm Springs Apache warriors in raiding, Victorio might have still been trying to reach a peaceful accommodation with the Anglo-Americans and thus have been willing to test Clum's arguments.[83] Yet, along with Geronimo and the other independent Chiricahuas, Victorio had been caught off guard by the sudden appearance of 100 well-armed San Carlos Apache policemen backed by the Ninth Cavalry. This show of force backed the Chihenne Apaches into a corner. From their point of view, Clum's 'persuasion' was backed by forces they could not oppose without sustaining unacceptable casualties. This was not Clum's intention, but this show of force was the critical factor which 'persuaded' the Warm Springs Apaches to relinquish Ojo Caliente and move to San Carlos. Victorio himself certainly viewed the removal as a temporary one, for he and his warriors cached their best arms in the environs of Ojo Caliente.[84] This lends further weight to the argument that their removal to San Carlos had more to do with being temporarily out-manoeuvred than with Clum's power of persuasion.

The capture of a number of noted Chiricahuas at Ojo Caliente and the removal of the Warm Springs Apaches to San Carlos did not mean that all of the Apaches had been rounded up. A detachment of Ninth Cavalry and Indian scouts skirmished with a group of Apaches on 5 May 1877, near Ojo Caliente, capturing two Indians and 'six animals.'[85] On 29 May 1877, two mail carriers were killed by Apaches within five miles of Fort Bowie. Soldiers from Fort Bowie followed these Apaches to the Animas Mountains before they scattered.[86] Just prior to Victorio's breakout from San Carlos in September 1877, a 21-man patrol from the Sixth Cavalry, in pursuit of Apaches, cornered Nol-gee, on 29 August, at Black Rock, Arizona Territory, forcing his surrender along with that of two warriors. Another 10 warriors surrendered the following day.[87]

81 Sherman to Sheridan, 1 May 1877 & Secretary of War to the Secretary of the Interior, 4 May 1877 in 'Geronimo File 1877', Letters Rec'd by the AGO, 1871-80, NA, M666, Roll 326.

82 Hatch to AAG, DoM, 27 April 1877 & Secretary of War to Secretary for the Interior, 12 May 1877 in 'Geronimo File 1877', Letters Rec'd by the AGO, 1871-80, NA, M666, Roll 326; See also Record of Events May 1877, Returns From Regular Army Cavalry Regiments 1833-1916, 9th Cavalry Regimental Returns 1873-1880, NA, M744, Roll 88.

83 See Victorio quoted by Clum, 1929i, p.116 & 1930ii, pp.80-82.

84 Abbott to AAG DoAz, 22 September 1877 in Correspondence relating to military operations against the Warm Springs Indians who fled from the San Carlos Indian Agency, Arizona Territory, 1877-79, (Hereafter referred to as 'Operations re Warm Springs Apaches 1877-79'), Letters Rec'd by the AGO, 1871-80, NA, M666, Roll 366; Thrapp, 1974, p.193; Roberts, p.173; Worcester, 1975, p.37.

85 Personal File Henry H. Wright Box 334, NA, RG94, Entry 297.

86 Report of Col. Kautz, 15 August 1877 in AR-WD, NA, M997, Roll 28, 1877 Vol. I-II, p.137.

87 Reports & Tabular Statements of Scouting Expeditions 1867-91, Statement of 'F' Company, 6th Cavalry, 3rd Quarter ending Sept. 30, 1877, NA, RG391, Entry 841.

Victorio Breaks Out of San Carlos

Approximately 250 Warm Springs Apaches burst out of San Carlos on 2 September 1877.[88] Some Chiricahua Apaches led by Pionsenay also left the reservation. The recently captured Nol-gee also fled when he discovered that Agent Vandever wanted to hold his band as hostage until the rest of the renegades returned.[89]

Victorio's stated desire was that he and his people should return and live in their old haunts, peacefully. There had also been at least two fatalities resulting from a feud between the Warm Springs Apaches and the White Mountain Apaches during Victorio's stay at San Carlos.[90] Clum speculated that the persistence of smallpox, first detected as he moved them to San Carlos, might also have encouraged the Chihenne Apaches to view the reservation as inherently unhealthy.[91] James Kaywaykla reported that Victorio, Nana and Loco had agreed to the breakout as a response to the lack of food supplies and the increasing incidence of malaria among their people.[92] Victorio, Nana and Loco were later interviewed at Fort Wingate, on 24 October 1877, and all three reiterated that they wanted a reservation at Ojo Caliente, though neither Victorio's nor Nana's statement gave any specific reason for leaving San Carlos. Only Loco hinted that there was some trouble with the Coyotero Apaches, and he did not want the portion of his family still at San Carlos to remain among the latter.[93]

The US army concluded that the breakout was inevitable, and could be attributed to a combination of the effects of forcing mutually hostile Apache bands into close proximity and corruption among reservation agency staff.[94] As far as Colonel Kautz was concerned, the concentration of the Apaches was partially motivated by territorial politicians who represented those citizens who would profit from the increased unrest such a process would cause.[95] Some blame was also apportioned to Pionsenay, who had returned to recruit more followers at San Carlos after successfully raiding in Mexico.[96] The final element was the resignation of Agent Clum, on 1 July 1877.[97] Clum was a victim of his own success with the Apaches. His constant feuding with the US army was increasingly accompanied by conflict with his own employers in the Office of Indian Affairs (OIA). This disagreement seems to have been provoked by the lobby power of local businessmen, who had become alarmed at the prospect of losing lucrative army contracts as the Apache threat diminished through Clum's administration. Clum resigned when it became

88 Tupper to Post Adjutant, Camp Grant, 18 September 1877, Hart, San Carlos Indian Agent to CoIA, 18 September 1877 & Hatch to AAG, DoM, 22 September 1877 in 'Operations re Warm Springs Apaches 1877-79', Letters Rec'd by the AGO, 1871-80, NA, M666, Roll 366.

89 McDowell, Major General to AG, Washington D.C. 11 September 1877 in 'Operations re Warm Springs Apaches 1877-79', Letters Rec'd by the AGO, 1871-80, NA, M666, Roll 366.

90 Kautz to AG DoP, 5 October 1877 & Name obscured by official Stamp to CO Fort Wingate 8 October 1877 in 'Operations re Warm Springs Apaches 1877-79', Letters Rec'd by the AGO, 1871-80, NA, M666, Roll 366; Thrapp, 1974, pp.193-194 & p.198; Goodwin, p.116; Reeve, p.308: Dunlay, p.169; Laumbach, p.159.

91 Clum, 1930i, pp.139-140.

92 Kaywaykla, 1962, p.23.

93 Statement of Apache Indian Chiefs, Fort Wingate, 24 October 1877 in Letters Received, DoNM 1877 (copy of document in supplied by Dan D. Aranda, Las Cruces, New Mexico).

94 Kautz to AAG, MDoP, 28 September 1877 Kautz to AG, DoP, 5 October 1877 in 'Operations re Warm Springs Apaches 1877-79', Letters Rec'd by the AGO, 1871-80, NA, M666, Roll 366; See also Report of Col. Kautz, 15 August 1877 in AR-WD, NA, M997, Roll 28, 1877 Vol. I-II, pp.140-141.

95 Report of Col. Kautz, 15 August 1877 in AR-WD, NA, M997, Roll 28, 1877 Vol. I-II, p.138.

96 McDowell, Major General to AG, Washington D.C. 11 September 1877 in 'Operations re Warm Springs Apaches 1877-79', Letters Rec'd by the AGO, 1871-80, NA, M666, Roll 366.

97 Haley, 1981, p.316; Tate, 1977, p.113.

clear that the OIA was no longer willing to support him.[98] His resignation removed a major obstacle for other OIA employees to feather their own nests at the expense of the Apaches. The month prior to Victorio's breakout, Lieutenant Lemuel Abbott, Sixth Cavalry, 'reported to the Assistant Adjutant General, Department of Arizona that Vandever, the Indian inspector at San Carlos, was negligent and that fraud, theft and robbery were rampant.'[99] Abbott clearly thought that Vandever, whether due to negligence or direct participation in these practices is not clear, was in large part responsible for the flight of Victorio's people, because he had failed to supply them with enough food.[100]

Victorio's flight was aided by the theft of horses from the White Mountain Apaches. The latter pursued the Warm Springs Apaches, bringing them to bay at Ash Creek on 3 September.[101] In the ensuing battle, the Warm Springs Apaches managed to hold off their pursuers until the latter ran out of ammunition. The White Mountain Apaches withdrew, having captured 30 women and children, 28 horses, and all the Chihenne Apaches' camp provisions.[102] Captain T.C. Tupper, with a detachment of Sixth Cavalry and Apache scouts, picked up the trail of the fleeing Apaches. Tupper reported that the trail could only be followed during the day. He also noted that a large number of Apaches had rendezvoused at the headwaters of the Rio Bonito, and from that place a clear trail of many people was followed for 30 miles, till it scattered as it reached Eagle Creek. Large signal fires were spotted to the south, on high peaks in the direction of Clifton, on the evening of 4 September. For the next 50 miles, no more than three animals could be discerned in any one of the many trails. By 7 September, the trails had merged once again, after leading Tupper's command over the roughest of terrain. On the following day, the trail divided into two, one going south, the other proceeding to the north east. Tupper divided his Apache scouts to pursue both trails.

Later that same day, the Apache scouts following the southern trail, who were commanded by Lieutenant Rucker, engaged in a five-hour running fight with a party of approximately 50 Apaches in the vicinity of the San Francisco River. The Apaches immediately scattered, but lost seven captured and, Tupper was fairly certain, five killed. The captives reported that some Apaches, led by Pionsenay, were travelling south, making for Mexico (these were presumably the ones attacked by Lieutenant Rucker), while the rest were trying to reach their old reservation in New Mexico. Pionsenay and his party may have been luckier than they imagined, as some of the Springfield Rifles supplied to the Apache scouts proved less than reliable, with a number failing to eject spent cartridges.[103] Tupper also discovered that the escape had been carefully planned in order to avoid raising the suspicions of the reservation authorities. The prisoners revealed that, for about 10 days prior to the breakout, small parties of Chiricahua and Warm Springs Apaches who intended to

98 Haley, 1981, p.316.

99 See detailed and damning report submitted by Lt. Abbott to the AAG DoAz on the 21 August 1877 concerning the lamentable state of affairs presided over by Vandever at San Carlos in 'Operations re Warm Springs Apaches 1877-79', Letters Rec'd by the AGO, 1871-80, NA, M666, Roll 366; Kautz to AAG, MDoP, 28 September 1877 in 'Operations re Warm Springs Apaches 1877-79', Letters Rec'd by the AGO, 1871-80, NA, M666, Roll 366; Hatfield, pp.34-35.

100 Abbott to AAG DoAz, 22 September 1877 in 'Operations re Warm Springs Apaches 1877-79', Letters Rec'd by the AGO, 1871-80, NA, M666, Roll 366.

101 Tupper to Post Adjutant, Camp Grant, 18 September 1877 in 'Operations re Warm Springs Apaches 1877-79', Letters Rec'd by the AGO, 1871-80, NA, M666, Roll 366.

102 Hart, San Carlos Indian Agent to CoIA, 18 September 1877 in 'Operations re Warm Springs Apaches 1877-79', Letters Rec'd by the AGO, 1871-80, NA, M666, Roll 366.

103 Tupper to Post Adjutant, Camp Grant, 18 September 1877 (including Lt Hanna's attached report) & Lt Hanna to Post Adjutant, Camp Huachuca, 28 September 1877 in 'Operations re Warm Springs Apaches 1877-79', Letters Rec'd by the AGO, 1871-80, NA, M666, Roll 366.

leave San Carlos had slipped away to quietly congregate at the headwaters of the Rio Bonito.[104] Having lost contact with the Apaches on the southern trail, Tupper and his scouts returned to follow up those Apache scouts sent after Victorio.

On 10 September 1877, Victorio was again cornered at the foot of the Mogollon Mountains,[105] this time by the San Carlos Apache Police, supported by those Apache scouts sent to follow the trail moving to the north east by Tupper. This time, Victorio lost one warrior and 11 women and children killed. Thirteen women and children, and six horses, were captured and returned to San Carlos.[106] Agent H.L. Hart, Clum's replacement, complained that the Apache scouts and the Sixth cavalrymen had not arrived in time to support the 23 men of the San Carlos Police, and this was the reason for their failure to capture the entire band.[107] The US army countered that the delay caused by the alarm being raised by 'runners' from the reservation had meant that too much time had elapsed for an effective pursuit to be mounted.[108] Captives taken in this skirmish informed Tupper that the Chihenne Apaches intended to reform in the mountains to the east of the San Francisco River. The day after the fight, Tupper scouted the area but found no signs of any rendezvous. Finding his scouts exhausted, he terminated his pursuit and returned to Arizona, though he noted that troops from Fort Bayard had picked up the trail a couple of days earlier and were in pursuit.[109] It was later estimated that of the 310 Warm Springs Apaches who had fled the reservation, 255 had managed to escape.[110]

Once again, Victorio had managed to break contact and disappear. To replace their lost horses, his warriors raided several ranches along the Arizona-New Mexico line, taking over 100 horses and killing at least 12 men.[111] As he entered New Mexico, Victorio found six companies of the Ninth Cavalry scouting for signs of the Warm Springs Apaches.[112] One detachment, under Lieutenant Wright, scouted between the Burro and Pyramid Mountains but found no sign of Apaches. Lieutenant W.H. Hugo, Ninth Cavalry, and a party of 'citizens' followed a trail, probably belonging to the Apaches led by Pionsenay, beyond Janos in Mexico, forcing the Apaches to

104 Tupper to Post Adjutant, Camp Grant, 18 September 1877 in 'Operations re Warm Springs Apaches 1877-79', Letters Rec'd by the AGO, 1871-80, NA, M666, Roll 366.

105 Captain Moore noted that the Mogollon Mountains were seventy miles long and thirty miles wide. (Capt. Moore, 38th Infantry, CO Ft. Cummings to Lt E. Hunter, AAA General, DoNM, 27 November 1868 in Letters sent Vol. 3, June 24 1867–Jan 20 1869, HQ Records of Fort Cummings, New Mexico, 1863-1873 & 1880-1884, NA, RG393, M1081, Roll 1, pp.141-145.)

106 Hart, San Carlos Indian Agent to CoIA, 18 September 1877 in 'Operations re Warm Springs Apaches 1877-79', Letters Rec'd by the AGO, 1871-80, NA, M666, Roll 366.

107 Hart, San Carlos Indian Agent to CoIA, 18 September 1877 in 'Operations re Warm Springs Apaches 1877-79', Letters Rec'd by the AGO, 1871-80, NA, M666, Roll 366.

108 Kautz to AAG, DoP, 4 October 1877 in 'Operations re Warm Springs Apaches 1877-79', Letters Rec'd by the AGO, 1871-80, NA, M666, Roll 366.

109 Tupper to Post Adjutant, Camp Grant, 18 September 1877 in 'Operations re Warm Springs Apaches 1877-79', Letters Rec'd by the AGO, 1871-80, NA, M666, Roll 366.

110 Hart, Indian Agent, San Carlos to Lt, Abbott, CO, Camp Thomas, 24 November 1878 in 'Operations re Warm Springs Apaches 1877-79', Letters Rec'd by the AGO, 1871-80, NA, M666, Roll 366.

111 Hart, San Carlos Indian Agent to CoIA, 18 September 1877 in 'Operations re Warm Springs Apaches 1877-79', Letters Rec'd by the AGO, 1871-80, NA, M666, Roll 366; Hatch to AAG, DoM, 22 September 1877 in 'Operations re Warm Springs Apaches 1877-79', Letters Rec'd by the AGO, 1871-80, NA, M666, Roll 366; Haley, 1981, p.319; Report of General Sheridan, 25 October 1877 in AR-WD, NA, M997, Roll 28, 1877 Vol. I-II, p.57.

112 Sheridan to Townsend AG, Washington DC, 18 September 1877, Sheridan to Townsend, 30 September 1877 & Platt AAG Ft Leavenworth Kansas to AAG, HQ MDoM, 6 September (should be October) 1877 in 'Operations re Warm Springs Apaches 1877-79', Letters Rec'd by the AGO, 1871-80, NA, M666, Roll 366; Record of Events October 1877, Returns From Regular Army Cavalry Regiments 1833-1916, 9th Cavalry Regimental Returns 1873-1880, NA, M744, Roll 88.

Plates 5.5 and 5.6 Two photos, one showing the Gila Wilderness (5.6), the other the Mogollon Mountains (5.5). It was into this terrain that the Chihennes retreated after their breakout from San Carlos and were so closely pursued by Apache police and the Sixth Cavalry that many chose to turn north and surrender temporarily at Fort Wingate. (Photos: author)

slaughter their extra horses.[113] Lieutenant Wright moved his detachment of Ninth cavalrymen and Navajo scouts north towards Fort Wingate, and on 9 October his men clashed with some Apaches near the Luera Mountains, north west of Ojo Caliente, killing two Apaches and capturing three horses.[114]

By the beginning of October 1877, approximately 150 Warm Springs Apaches, including Victorio, had surrendered at Fort Wingate.[115] By 11 October, that number had risen to 190 Apaches, with an additional 56 Apaches in negotiation for their surrender.[116] By the end of October, 46 of those Apaches had surrendered, bringing the total number of Warm Springs Apaches in custody to 233.[117] When Lieutenant M.B. Hughes, Ninth Cavalry, reported on the dismounting and disarming of the Warm Springs Apaches, on 10 November 1877, he reported the recovery of 36 horses, three mules and two burros[118] most of which were sent to Fort Craig, although six horses and one mule were given to the leading men of the Warm Springs Apache, namely Loco, Victorio, Nana, Esquine, Mangas and Thomaso. Lieutenant Hughes also recorded that six lances, eight bows, six muzzle-loading muskets, one Springfield rifle and one Sharps carbine, one 'Horse-pistol', one Colt and two Remington revolvers were handed over by the Apaches.[119] This paucity of arms strongly suggests that the Apaches had cached most of their arms either before surrendering at Fort Wingate, or even prior to their transfer to San Carlos.

Colonel Hatch issued instructions that the Apaches at Fort Wingate were to be treated as prisoners of war and supplied with food. They were also, on no account, to be allowed to 'affiliate' with the Navajo. General Pope informed his superiors that the Warm Springs Apaches 'have an invincible objection to returning to San Carlos Agency' and recommended that they, for the moment, be returned to Ojo Caliente,[120] though he had earlier stated that 'they cannot be trusted in any way, and if they are to be kept quiet, they ought to be stripped of weapons & ponies and kept substantially as prisoners.'[121] Colonel Hatch also suggested that if the Warm Springs Apaches were to be returned to Ojo Caliente, they should be encouraged to plant crops,[122] no doubt to facilitate their integration into American society. Colonel Hatch argued that the return of the Apaches to Ojo Caliente would encourage other small parties still hiding out in the mountains, or having reached the Mescalero reservation, to join their compatriots. It would also allow the US army in New Mexico and Arizona to focus their efforts on rooting out the remaining Chiricahua renegades who were based in Mexico, using the cross-border pursuit rules currently being followed by the troops

113 Wade, CO Ft. Bayard to AAAG Santa Fé, 22 September 1877 in 'Operations re Warm Springs Apaches 1877-79', Letters Rec'd by the AGO, 1871-80, NA, M666, Roll 366.
114 Personal Files: Henry H. Wright, Box 334, NA, RG94, Entry 297.
115 See Vandever, to CoIA, 29 September 1877 & Acting CoIA to the Secretary of the Interior, 1 October 1877, in 'Operations re Warm Springs Apaches 1877-79', Letters Rec'd by the AGO, 1871-80, NA, M666, Roll 366; Clum, 1930i, p.138; Thrapp, 1974, pp.201-202; 1967, pp.177-178; Ogle, 1958, pp.84-85; 1970, p.183; Billington, 1991, pp.53-54; Goodwin, p.308, note 39; Carter, USACMH, webpage; Moore, p.176.
116 Pope to AAG, MDoM, 18 October 1877 in 'Operations re Warm Springs Apaches 1877-79', Letters Rec'd by the AGO, 1871-80, NA, M666, Roll 366.
117 Sheridan to Townsend, Washington DC, 30 October 1877 in 'Operations re Warm Springs Apaches 1877-79', Letters Rec'd by the AGO, 1871-80, NA, M666, Roll 366.
118 Donkeys.
119 Lt. M.B. Hughes to CO Ojo Caliente, 10 November 1877 from documents sent to the author by Dan D. Aranda, Las Cruces N.M.
120 Pope to AAG MDoM, 18 October 1877 & Pope to AAG, MDoM, 5 November 1877 in 'Operations re Warm Springs Apaches 1877-79', Letters Rec'd by the AGO, 1871-80, NA, M666, Roll 366.
121 Report of General Pope 15 September 1877 in AR-WD, NA, M997, Roll 28, 1877 Vol. I-II, pp.135-136.
122 Loud to AAG, DoM, Fort Leavenworth, 30 January 1878 in Letters Sent by the '9MD/DNM/DoNM', NA, RG393, M1072, Roll 6, Letter No.6.

based in Texas.[123] Additional troops were sent to Fort Wingate to provide two companies to escort the Apaches back to Ojo Caliente.[124] Captain Hooker, Ninth Cavalry, was placed in command of the soldiers at Ojo Caliente and was charged with searching the Mimbres Mountains for any Apaches who had escaped in the pursuit from San Carlos. He was also to protect the local settlements from these Apaches. Hooker was instructed to feed those Apaches who had surrendered at Fort Wingate once they were delivered to Ojo Caliente.[125] Once operations were over, a seven-man detail from the Fifteenth Infantry was to be stationed at Ojo Caliente. Two Navajo scouts and two mule packers were also assigned to this post.[126]

The operations undertaken by the Ninth Cavalry to intercept the Apaches fleeing from San Carlos convinced Colonel Hatch that his cavalrymen should be supported by pack mules. Mules were not able to travel fast when hitched to a travois, or to carry enough when harnessed to a cart. The key to using them was in the proper packing of individual animals, to ensure that they went for as long as possible without breaking down.[127] This idea was not new. In 1868, when scouting the Mogollon and Florida Mountains, one Captain Alexander Moore of the Thirty-eighth Infantry had strongly urged that a corps of experienced Mexican packers and 'a sufficient number of extra mules should accompany the scouting party to alternate the packs. Scarcity of food in the country renders it most difficult to preserve the lives of animals.'[128]

By June 1878, there were reported to be 267 Warm Springs Apaches – 64 men, 106 women and 97 children – held at Ojo Caliente.[129] An additional 143 Warm Springs Apaches – 22 men, 63 women and 58 children – still resided at San Carlos.[130] This indicates a *known* population of 86 men, 169 women and 155 children. When compared with the 434 Warm Springs Apaches originally sent to San Carlos in 1877, this suggests an approximate population of around 400 in 1878. It also suggests a figure of about 60 adult males sufficiently active and inclined to fight. What is not known is the number of Warm Springs Apaches who evaded the original move to San Carlos in the first place. During the fighting between Victorio and the United States in 1879-1880, Apache recollections and contemporary sightings imply the presence of between 75 and 90 Warm Springs Apache warriors. This higher number could be a combination of warriors who never moved to San Carlos and some of the adolescent boys achieving warrior status between 1878 and 1879. It also indicates that throughout this period Victorio's resistance was supported by most Chihenne Apache warriors.

---

123 Hatch to AAG, DoM, 11 October 1877 in 'Operations re Warm Springs Apaches 1877-79', Letters Rec'd by the AGO, 1871-80, NA, M666, Roll 366.

124 Sheridan to Townsend, 13 October 1877 in 'Operations re Warm Springs Apaches 1877-79', Letters Rec'd by the AGO, 1871-80, NA, M666, Roll 366; Hatch, Ojo Caliente to CO Fort Wingate, 30 September 1877, Press Copies of Letters and Telegrams Sent by Commander Hatch in the Field 1877 Ojo Caliente, NA, RG393, Part 3, Entry 474, pp.1-2; Record of Events October & November 1877, Returns From Regular Army Cavalry Regiments 1833-1916, 9th Cavalry Regimental Returns 1873-1880, NA, M744, Roll 88.

125 Hatch, HQ in the field, Ojo Caliente to Hooker, 3 October 1877, Press Copies of Letters and Telegrams Sent by Commander Hatch in the Field 1877 Ojo Caliente, NA, RG393, Part 3, Entry 474, p.10

126 Date of Order not clear, Press Copies of Letters and Telegrams Sent by Commander Hatch in the Field 1877 Ojo Caliente, NA, RG393, Part 3, Entry 474, pp.1-2.

127 Hatch to Asst Quartermaster General, US army 31 January 1878 in Letters Sent by the '9MD/DNM/DoNM', NA, RG393, M1072, Roll 6, Letter No.36.

128 Capt. Moore, 38th Infantry, CO Ft. Cummings to Lt E. Hunter, AAA General, DoNM, 27 November 1868 in Letters sent Vol. 3 June 24 1867–Jan 20 1869, HQ Records of Fort Cummings, New Mexico, 1863-1873 & 1880-1884, NA, RG393, M1081, Roll 1, pp.141-145.

129 Name undecipherable, 1st Lt, 15th Infantry to Post Adjutant, 7 June 1878 in 'Operations re Warm Springs Apaches 1877-79', Letters Rec'd by the AGO, 1871-80, NA, M666, Roll 366.

130 Thomas Keam, Supt. of Apaches to Capt. A.E. Hooker, 21 January 1878 in 'Operations re Warm Springs Apaches 1877-79', Letters Rec'd by the AGO, 1871-80, NA, M666, Roll 366.

6

Phoney War, 1877–9

> The policy adopted by our Government in conducting Indian affairs has always seemed to us, criminal and absurd. The root of the evil, in our opinion, lies in the fact that we have acknowledged them as independent nations, and have made treaties with them as such. It would be just as sensible to treat with a band of horse thieves or brigands, who might be preying upon our citizens – or with communists who throng our elites, and only bide their time to destroy the property of others.
>
> (S.M. Ashenfelter, editor, *Grant County Herald*, Saturday 27 September 1879)

> The government promised those Indians that their reservation should be at Hot Springs N.M. The government built an Agency at a cost of from thirty (30,000) to forty (40,000) thousand dollars and directly broke faith with these Indians and ordered them to the San Carlos reservation. Nearly all of them told me that they had to die but once; that they would all die before they would live on the San Carlos reservation.[1]
>
> (John Ayer, former agent of the Warm Springs Apaches, reporting a conversation with some of these Apaches at Casas Grandes, Chihuhua in July 1879)

> I trust and believe that this will be the end of the trouble with these Indians.'[2]
>
> (S.A. Russell, Mescalero reservation agent, 30 June 1879)

While most of the Warm Springs Apaches had surrendered at Fort Wingate, skirmishes continued between Chiricahua renegades and the Sixth Cavalry. On 28 November 1877, a detachment of men from C, G and H Companies, Sixth Cavalry, and C Company, Indian Scouts from Fort Bowie, pursued some Apaches into Mexico. There, two skirmishes with Chiricahua Apaches took place, on 13 and 18 December. The first was only brief, with just one Chiricahua Apache killed. The second occurred at St Louis Pass, in Mexico, and here the detachment claimed 15 or 16 Apaches killed and one captured. A total of 60 horses and mules were also captured, and the Apaches' camp was destroyed.[3]

In fact, 1877 and the years immediately following were punctuated by low-level conflict between the US army and Apaches. This not only involved the Warm Springs Apaches of New Mexico but also radiated out to the west and east of their territory. As we have already seen, there was

1 Ayer to Col Hatch, 26 October 1879 in Letters Received by Headquarters District of New Mexico September 1865-August 1890, NA, RG393, M1088, Roll 39, October-December 1879.

2 Russell to Hatch, 30 June 1879 in Letters Received, DoM 1868-98, RG 393, Entry A1-1 2601, Box 87.

3 Record of Events December 1877 in Returns From Regular Army Cavalry Regiments 1833-1916, 6th Cavalry Regimental Returns 1875 to 1880, NA, M744, Roll 63; Reports & Tabular Statements of Scouting Expeditions 1867-91, Statement of Lt Rucker, 6th Cavalry, Quarter ending 31 December 1877, NA, RG391 Entry 841.

additional conflict with independent Chiricahuas in Arizona. To the east of the Rio Grande, the Mescalero Apaches were also active, raiding to the south and east into Texas and Mexico from their reservation situated to the south and west of Fort Stanton, New Mexico. In June 1877, a detachment of troops from Fort Davis, Texas, pursued some Apaches into the Guadalupe Mountains and recovered 12 stolen horses and mules.[4] Later in November, C Company, Tenth Cavalry, pursued a group of Mescalero Apaches into Mexico and fought an apparently bloodless skirmish with them on 29 November.[5]

This widespread Apache activity prompted General Edward O.C. Ord to initiate a thorough survey of the region.[6] This duty fell to Colonel Benjamin H. Grierson, as commander of both the District of the Pecos and the Tenth Cavalry. When time allowed, Colonel Grierson undertook some of this survey work himself;[7] otherwise it was devolved to his subordinates in the Tenth Cavalry.[8] The Tenth Cavalry's monthly return for 1878 shows that the regiment was regularly in the field 'in pursuit of hostiles.'[9] These expeditions were over and above the extensive scouting of the area by detachments of the Tenth Cavalry regiment. For example, when Lieutenant John Bigelow returned from a pursuit of Apache raiders in April 1878, he reported that he had discovered a spring while on the trail. Orders were passed to Lieutenant Mason Maxon to pinpoint the location of this spring, as it was thought that Bigelow might have stumbled across an established Mescalero raiding route.[10]

Throughout May and June 1878, detachments from several companies were sent out to scout the trans-Pecos region.[11] By August 1878, Colonel Grierson was able to notify his superiors of a comprehensive plan to use Tenth Cavalry detachments to map western Texas and deploy infantry detachments to picket known water sources in order to frustrate the easy passage of Apache raiders. In the first instance, he intended to keep six companies of cavalry with infantry detachments in the field until December 1878.[12] Grierson also employed a mixture of Anglo-American and Pueblo scouts to facilitate this activity.[13] However, such work did not always progress smoothly, with

4 Record of Events June 1877 in Returns From Regular Army Cavalry Regiments 1833-1916, 10th Cavalry Regimental Returns 1873-80, NA, M744, Roll 96.

5 Record of Events November 1877 in Returns From Regular Army Cavalry Regiments 1833-1916, 10th Cavalry Regimental Returns 1873 to 1880, NA, M744, Roll 96.

6 Vincent to CO, DoP, 30 April 1878 in Register of Telegrams Rec'd 23 January 1878-4 February 1881, HQ DoP 1878-1881, NA, M1381, Roll 2, p.19, Letter No. 40 ; Vincent, AAG, Department of Texas (Hereafter referred to as 'DoTx'), to CO, DoP, 11 March 1879 in Letters Rec'd File 19 March 1878-14 February 1881, HQ DoP 1878-1881, NA, M1381, Roll 2; McChristian, 1982, p.49; Temple, 1962, pp.86-7.

7 Capt. Thomas Lebo to Post Adjutant, Fort Davis, Texas, 16 February 1879, NA, RG393, Part 1, Entry 2546, pp.68-104.

8 Smither to Maxon, 9 May 1878, Letter No.6, and Smither to Norvell, 12 May 1878, Letter No. 7 in Letters Sent 31 January-15 September 1879, HQ DoP 1878-1881 NA, M1381 Roll 1.

9 Record of Events January-September 1878 in Returns From Regular Army Cavalry Regiments 1833-1916, 10th Cavalry Regimental Returns 1873-80, NA, M744, Roll 96.

10 Smither to Maxon, 19 May 1878, Letter No.8 in Letters Sent 31 January-15 September 1879, HQ DoP 1878-1881 NA, M1381 Roll 1.

11 See Smither to Maxon, 25 May 1878, Letter No. 10; Smither to Norvell, 26 May 1878, Letter No.15; Smither to McMartin via CO Fort Stockton, 26 May 1878 Letter No. 16; Smither to Norvell, 30 May 1878, Letter No.24 and Smither to Carpenter, 4 June 1878 Letter No.26 in Letters Sent 31 January 1878-15 September 1879, HQ DoP 1878-1881 NA, M1381 Roll 1.

12 Col Grierson to AAG, DoTx, 2 August 1878, Letter No.40 in Letters Sent 31 January 1878-15 September 1879, HQ DoP 1878-1881 NA, M1381 Roll 1.

13 Grierson to AAG, DoTx, 15 September 1878, Letter No.51 in Letters Sent 31 January 1878-15 September 1879, HQ DoP 1878-1881 NA, M1381 Roll 1.

Gabriel Monroe, S.E. Stilwell and John Briggs were stationed at Forts Concho, Stockton and Davis at $60 per month. Grierson also employed two Pueblo scouts called Bernado and Simon (Olguin?) whom he noted could only be recruited if they could scout together. They were paid $30 per month.

Captain Charles D. Viele of the Tenth Cavalry noting that his guide, Bernardo Leguin, was almost blind, and spoke and understood only a limited amount of English.[14]

Bad luck also played its part. On 17 November 1878, a patrol from Eagle Springs led by Captain Viele took up the trail of 40-50 animals in the Eagle Mountains. The trail was pursued north until 21 November, by which time the horses were exhausted. Viele's detachment had come close to catching up with the raiders, making camp within a mile of them in the early hours of the morning of 20 November; but the Apaches detected his arrival and decamped immediately. It was several hours before Captain Viele discovered the remains of their campsite.[15] Nevertheless, by the close of 1878, Colonel Grierson was able to report that 52 scouting expeditions, covering a combined distance of 24,469 miles, had been completed[16] (see also document file no. 1). Grierson clearly thought his efforts had been effective, and he informed his superiors of his intention to continue his active scouting and picketing strategy in the spring of 1879.[17]

The US army was not alone in its pursuit of Apache raiders. Between July and September 1878, Lieutenant John Tays, with three men of C Company, Frontier Battalion, Texas Rangers, from El Paso, twice failed to intercept raiders before they reached the Fort Stanton reservation.[18] During August, Lieutenant Tays lost one ranger in a gun battle with Mescalero raiders. The slain man's weapons and horse were taken, and the horse was later reported as having been seen at the Mescalero reservation.[19] The District of New Mexico was also concerned about the activities of the Mescalero Apaches. At least three parties of Mescalero raiders were followed onto their reservation between April and September 1878.

By June 1878, Colonel Hatch had established that there were no more than 50 independent Indians who had never registered at the agency living in the southern reaches of the Sacramento Mountains. He ordered Lieutenant Wright, with a detachment of Navajo scouts, to report to Fort Stanton and join a detachment of 50 men of the Ninth Cavalry. They were to sweep the area and compel these Indians to settle on the reservation.[20] In early August, F and H Companies, Ninth Cavalry, under Captain Henry Carroll, accompanied by Wright with his Navajo scouts, clashed with Mescalero Apaches in Dog Canyon, capturing 22 horses and mules and killing three Mescalero warriors, but losing Corporal Thomas Dale in the fray.[21]

See also AAG, DoTx, 8 August 1878 in Register of Letters Rec'd 23 March 1878-30 January 1881, HQ DoP 1878-1881, NA, M1381, Roll 2, p.6, Letter No.23; Vincent, AAG, DoTx to CO, DoP, 8 August 1880 in Letters Rec'd File 19 March 1878-14 February 1881, HQ DoP 1878-1881, NA, M1381, Roll 2.

14 Capt. Viele to AAAG, DoP, Fort Concho, Texas, January 1879, NA, RG393, Part 1, Entry 2546, pp.25-40.

15 Viele to AAAG, DoP, Fort Concho, Texas, 24 January 1879, NA, RG393, Part 1, Entry 2546, pp.25-40.

16 Grierson to AAG, DoTx, 28 December 1878, Letter No.70 and Smither – Tabular Statement of Expeditions, Scouts etc 1878, 28 December 1878 in Letters 31-January 1878-15 September 1879, HQ DoP 1878-1881 NA, M1381 Roll 1.

17 Grierson to AAG, DoTx, 6 March 1879, Letter No.6 in Letters Sent 31-January 1878-15 September 1879, HQ DoP 1878-1881 NA, M1381 Roll 1.

18 Gen. Ord to Maj. J.M. Vincent, Adjutant General's Office, State of Texas, 20 December 1878, NA, RG393, Part 1, Entry 2546, pp.9-11 and 14-15.

19 French to AAG, DoP in Register of Telegrams Rec'd 23 January 1878-4 February 1881, HQ DoP 1878-1881, NA, M1381, Roll 2, pp.65-66, Letter No.152; Ord to Maj. J.M. Vincent, Adjutant General's Office, State of Texas, 20 December 1878, NA, RG393, Part 1, Entry 2546, pp.12-13.

20 Capt. Loud to CO Fort Stanton, 13 June 1878 in Letters Sent by the '9MD/DNM/DoNM', NA, RG393, M1072, Roll 6, Letter No.280, pp.198-200.

21 Return for August 1878 in Returns From US Military Posts 1800-1916 Fort Stanton, New Mexico, January 1878-December 1887, NA, M617, Roll 1218: Record of Events August 1878 in Returns From Regular Army Cavalry Regiments 1833-1916, 9th Cavalry Regimental Returns 1873-80, NA, M744, Roll 88.

Where Victorio is concerned, he does not appear to have engaged in hostilities after his return to Ojo Caliente after surrendering at Fort Wingate. In the spring of 1878, Colonel Hatch was appealing for clothing to be provided for the women and children, who had survived the winter 'with old canvas;' and he also instructed the commander of Fort Craig to provide the Warm Springs Apaches with supplies that would enable them to begin to raise crops.[22] However, this 'tranquillity' was not to last. By July 1878 it was decided to move the Warm Springs Apaches back to San Carlos.[23]

This was not before much procrastination in Washington DC over what should be done with the Apaches at Ojo Caliente. It was mooted, at one point, that the Warm Springs Apaches be removed to Fort Sill in the Indian Territory.[24] Victorio and his people's continued problems were the result of individuals in Washington DC losing sight of policy concerning the Apaches in the wider 'ether' of policy making in general. The truth was that, at the federal level of government, the Warm Springs Apaches were a minor issue concerning the Departments of War and the Interior. Eventually, General Sheridan threatened to withdraw the US troops currently supervising the Apaches, whether or not the Indian Bureau sent personnel to take charge at Ojo Caliente.[25]

Sheridan's unsubtle effort to solve the problem backfired when his superior, the Secretary of War, George McCrary, recommended that the Warm Springs Apaches be 'turned loose with their own tribe, as I suppose they are no worse than the remainder of the tribe.'[26] As the rest of the Warm Springs and Chiricahua Apaches were then based at San Carlos, the Commissioner of Indian Affairs, E.A. Hayt, with the approval of the Secretary of the Interior, Carl Schurz, recommended that the Warm Springs Apaches be sent back to San Carlos.[27] Had the Secretary of War been more attuned to General Sherman's advice, and had that advice been more effectively transmitted in the first place, it seems unlikely that McCrary would have recommended this deportation. The return of the Warm Springs Apaches to San Carlos had been vigorously opposed by the commanders of the Departments of Arizona and the Missouri, through their respective divisional commanders, and the General of the Army.

The Secretary of the Interior's opposition to Ojo Caliente was based on a calculation of economic cost (the price of beef) which completely failed to account for the economic chaos which could, and

Hatch also mentions that Capt. Carroll had come up against a party of Apaches in the Guadalupe Mountains on 31 July 1878 killing 'some' Apaches and recovering one hundred animals, though this could be a garbled account of the skirmish in Dog Canyon. (Hatch to AAG, DoM, Fort Leavenworth, 1 October 1878 in Letters Sent by the '9MD/DNM/DoNM', NA, RG393, M1072, Roll 6, Letter No.437 pp.303-304; Hatch to AAG, DoM, 28 May 1879 in Letters Sent by the '9MD/DNM/DoNM', NA, RG393, M1072, Roll 6, January-October 1879, Letter No.257, pp.187-190.)

22 Hatch to AAG, DoM, Fort Leavenworth, 30 March 1878 in Letters Sent by the '9MD/DNM/DoNM', NA, RG393, M1072, Roll 6, Letter No.151.

23 Secretary of the Interior to Secretary of War, 18 July 1878 in 'Operations re Warm Springs Apaches 1877-79', Letters Rec'd by the AGO, 1871-80, NA, M666, Roll 366; See Gen. Pope, cited in Clum, 1930i, p.139; Moore, p.177; Haley, 1981, p.319.

24 See Secretary of the Interior to Secretary of War, 5 February 1878 where a great deal of discussion of the advantages and disadvantages of sending the Warm Springs Apaches to Indian Territory took place between November 1877 and March 1878 in 'Operations re Warm Springs Apaches 1877-79', Letters Rec'd by the AGO, 1871-80, NA, M666, Roll 366.

25 7th Endorsement of 24 June 1878 by Gen. Sheridan cited in Chief Clerk for the Secretary of War to the Secretary of the Interior, 8 July 1878 in 'Operations re Warm Springs Apaches 1877-79', Letters Rec'd by the AGO, 1871-80, NA, M666, Roll 366; Reeve, p.308.

26 McCrary to the Secretary of the Interior, 6 August 1878 in 'Operations re Warm Springs Apaches 1877-79', Letters Rec'd by the AGO, 1871-80 NA, M666, Roll 366.

27 CoIA to Secretary of the Interior, 14 August 1878 and Secretary of the Interior to Secretary of War 16 August 1878 in 'Operations re Warm Springs Apaches 1877-79', Letters Rec'd by the AGO, 1871-80, NA, M666, Roll 366.

did, result from concentrating the Apaches in general on a single reservation.[28] This was despite a report from Ojo Caliente clearly stating that great progress towards the 'civilising' and self-sufficiency of the Warm Springs Apaches at Ojo Caliente had been achieved after their return from Fort Wingate. Reports from the military also reiterated the Warm Springs Apaches' strong desire to stay at Ojo Caliente.[29]

The removal from Ojo Caliente was ordered in September 1878,[30] and was attempted in mid-October. Captain F.T. Bennett, I Company, Ninth Cavalry, was charged with escorting the Apaches to San Carlos, and was assisted by 20 Navajo scouts under Lieutenant Wright. This detachment of Navajo scouts was already at Ojo Caliente when Bennett's company arrived on 10 October. Colonel Hatch, in ordering Bennett to carry out the removal, did not anticipate trouble, as these Apaches had, in his opinion, been 'thoroughly disciplined' and had many women and children with them. Hatch thought that the younger men would be easily deterred from flight by the threat presented by the Navajo scout detachment.[31] General Pope agreed, noting that the Warm Springs Apaches were about to be returned to San Carlos and, while there had been some of the usual minor problems with these Apaches, there had been no 'serious outbreak,' and he did not foresee any further trouble.[32] Hatch also recommended selling Ojo Caliente as a stock ranch, stating that the five buildings built by the Department of the Interior were in good condition and that the army had added stables and corrals. He also added that this plot of land controlled the water supply for 15 miles around.[33]

Despite attempting to maintain complete secrecy,[34] Bennett found that the Warm Springs Apaches had been warned of his troops' arrival 10 days previously. He found the Chihennes utterly opposed to a return to San Carlos, which Bennett mistakenly informed them was their home. As Victorio and another leading man named Thomas [Tomas?] or Toggi were absent on a pass to Fort Wingate, the rest refused to make any decision until they returned and Bennett agreed to this delay. Two days later, Victorio and Thomas returned, and the same refusal was made, to which Bennett could only respond that this removal had already been discussed at the highest level, and that they had no option but to go to San Carlos. A couple of days later, Victorio promised Bennett that while against the move, he would not oppose the return to San Carlos, and that by the close of that day, 14 October, he would gather his people at the agency. Bennett, though somewhat suspicious, was lulled into a false sense of security by the finality of his orders and the reports he had received that the Warm Springs Apaches had been thoroughly cowed by the reverses they had suffered when they had broken out of San Carlos in September 1877.

---

28 ColA to the Secretary of the Interior, 23 July 1878 in 'Operations re Warm Springs Apaches 1877-79', Letters Rec'd by the AGO, 1871-80, NA, M666, Roll 366.

29 Letter from Capt. Charles Steelhammer, CO Ojo Caliente to Capt. Loud AAAG DoNM, 7 August 1878 in 'Operations re Warm Springs Apaches 1877-79', Letters Rec'd by the AGO, 1871-80, NA, M666, Roll 366; see also Loud to AAG DoM, Fort Leavenworth, 16 August 1878 in Letters Sent by the '9MD/DNM/DoNM', NA, RG393, M1072, Roll 6, Letter No.365, pp258-259.

30 See orders 18 September 1878 detailing 'I' Company, 9th Cavalry, as escorts for the Warm Springs Apaches being sent to San Carlos in 'Operations re Warm Springs Apaches 1877-79', Letters Rec'd by the AGO, 1871-80, NA, M666, Roll 366.

31 Loud to Bennett, 2 October 1878 in Letters Sent by the '9MD/DNM/DoNM', NA, RG393, M1072, Roll 6, Letter No.442 pp.307-308.

32 Report of Gen. Pope in AR-WD, NA, M997, Roll 30, 1878 Vol. I-II, p.39.

33 Hatch to W.M. Leeds, Acting Commissioner, Department of the Interior, 30 October 1878 in Letters Sent by the '9MD/DNM/DoNM', NA, RG393, M1072, Roll 6, Letter No.477 pp.333-334.

34 'The District Commander directs that the matter relative to removal of the Warm Spring Indians therein contained, will not be allowed to transpire and that you will take due precautions to prevent the information reaching the Indians in question before the Escort is on the ground to take charge of them.' (Loud to Lt Cornish 15th Inf, Ojo Caliente, 1 October 1878 in Letters Sent by the '9MD/DNM/DoNM', NA, RG393, M1072, Roll 6, Letter No.438 p.305.)

At 3 p.m. that afternoon, however, one of the Navajo scouts reached Bennett and reported that Thomas and two or three men had left Ojo Caliente. Bennett issued orders to Lieutenant Wright to take 10 of his Navajo scouts and six Ninth cavalrymen and to pursue them. Bennett also placed Loco and one Kiralchiddy, the latter also a leading warrior, under close guard. These events were seen by a Mescalero woman who had approached the captain to request that she return to the Fort Stanton reservation rather than be sent to San Carlos. The woman grabbed a horse and fled to the Warm Springs Apaches, loudly proclaiming their imminent deaths at the hands of the army. This caused a stampede, and by the time Bennett had restored order, he found that over 80 Apaches had fled. He placed the remaining 186 under guard. Lieutenant Wright had already managed to round up one woman and three children in the immediate aftermath of the stampede, but apart from a fleeting glimpse of an Apache warrior, no other trace could be found of those who had fled.

Bennett sent out two small detachments of Navajo scouts and Ninth cavalrymen commanded by Lieutenant Charles Merritt and Lieutenant Wright, but little or no sign of the Apaches was discovered.[35] Having reported his failure to catch the 80 who had fled, Bennett was instructed to take the remaining 186 Apaches to San Carlos.[36] It was thought that Victorio, with the 80 fugitives, had fled towards Fort Wingate, and that post was alerted and ordered to apprehend them should that be the case.[37] The fugitives consisted of three 'chiefs', 40 men and 40 women and children. The Apaches remaining at Ojo Caliente were so adamant that they did not want to go to San Carlos that it was decided they would have to be placed under armed guard for the duration of the trip.[38]

In the meantime, Victorio sent one of his men, Sanchez, into Ojo Caliente with word that he would return but needed two days to gather his people. In response, Bennett delayed his departure; but when Sanchez and his family managed to elude the guard on the night of 23 October, Bennett concluded that the whole story was a feint to allow Sanchez to recover his family and allow Victorio and the rest of the fugitives more time to make their escape. Two days later, Bennett finally set forth for San Carlos with his remaining prisoners. On the night of 28 October, some of the escaped Apaches made contact with Bennett's prisoners by shouting to them from the darkness, though Bennett's guard prevented any escape. Over the next two days, three warriors turned themselves in and were placed under arrest.[39] Twenty men, 77 women and 75 children[40] arrived back at San Carlos on 24 November.[41] If we include the three men who surrendered, Bennett should have arrived with 189 Apaches; but he handed over 172. This suggests some loss through death by

35 Bennett's detailed report to AAAG DoNM, 4 December 1878 in 'Operations re Warm Springs Apaches 1877-79', Letters Rec'd by the AGO, 1871-80, NA, M666, Roll 366; Thrapp, 1974, p.210.

Moore recounts a slightly different version of events in which Victorio, when informed of the deportation order, adamantly refused to go and fled into the mountains with approximately 80 Warm Springs Apaches. Seventeen more disappeared later, leaving 169 to be transported to San Carlos. (Moore, p.206; see also Haley, 1981, p.320) Laumbach states that about 250 Warm Springs Apache were at Ojo Caliente and that Victorio and over 80 Apaches including 50 warriors fled. This left 172 Apaches led by Loco with 20 warriors to make the trek back to San Carlos (Laumbach, p.128).

36 Gen. Pope to AAG, MDoM, 20 October 1878 in 'Operations re Warm Springs Apaches 1877-79', Letters Rec'd by the AGO, 1871-80, NA, M666, Roll 366.

37 Loud to CO Fort Wingate, 20 October 1878 in Letters Sent by the '9MD/DNM/DoNM', NA, RG393, M1072, Roll 6, Letter No.462 p.320.

38 Loud to AAG MDoM, 19 October 1878 in 'Operations re Warm Springs Apaches 1877-79', Letters Rec'd by the AGO, 1871-80, NA, M666, Roll 366.

39 Bennett's report to AAAG DoNM, 4 December 1878 in 'Operations re Warm Springs Apaches 1877-79', Letters Rec'd by the AGO, 1871-80, NA, M666, Roll 366.

40 Bennett's report to AAAG DoNM, 4 December 1878 and Hart, Indian Agent, San Carlos to Lt. Abbott, CO Camp Thomas, 26 November 1878 in 'Operations re Warm Springs Apaches 1877-79', Letters Rec'd by the AGO, 1871-80, NA, M666, Roll 366.

41 MacDowell to Sherman, 25 November 1878 in 'Operations re Warm Springs Apaches 1877-79', Letters Rec'd by the AGO, 1871-80, NA, M666, Roll 366.

natural causes on the march, but most of this discrepancy can probably be put down to further escapes made during the march to San Carlos.

The forced removal to San Carlos precipitated another series of raids by the fugitive Apaches. Colonel Hatch noted on 4 December 1878 that the Apaches, though raiding, had apparently not killed anybody.[42] Nevertheless, another report noted that during November and December 1878, Apaches raiders were active around Fort Bayard and were believed to be responsible for the death of several citizens. This report also noted that the Florida Mountains were a rendezvous point for these Apaches, and suggested it was inadvisable for small parties to journey near or through these mountains.[43] Surgeon MacPherson also reported that, sometime in December, a wagon train had been attacked at Ash Springs in the Stein's Peak Range, with several persons killed.[44] In the first half of January, near Fort Cummings, two men, Dave Sullens and 'Charlie', were reported killed by Apaches.[45]

Frank Clifford, whose memories were recorded circa 1940, recalled his experience of chasing Apache raiders who had stolen horses from around Hillsboro. One has to be wary of the effects of the passage of time on memory: Clifford refers to 'old Geronimo' as the leader of the Apaches during this time, when in fact he was referring to Victorio; he does not refer to specific years during his account of the conflict with the Apaches; and his memory of the time of year is also somewhat vague, with him ascribing some events to the spring when they occurred during the autumn. Therefore, it is difficult to pinpoint the exact timing of Clifford's experiences beyond sometime between mid-1878 and mid-1879. However, the one specific name he recalls in his brief account of the Victorio conflict is corroborated by US Army records (see next chapter). And his recollection of specific incidences is vivid but not prone to exaggeration. Clifford, a somewhat mysterious character who went through life under a number of aliases, was then living at Hillsboro and trying his luck with gold mining. His first encounter with the Chihennes occurred approximately two miles outside of Hillsboro, where he engaged in casual conversation with a Mexican:

> who had a sway-backed mare grazing in a little *vega* (meadow) nearby. Suddenly the Mexican gave a little "yip" and I whirled round and saw an Indian come running up to the mare. He put his hands on her flanks, sprang upon her, and went on, all in one movement, or so it seemed. That was the slickest getaway on a horse I ever saw.[46]

About 50 citizens gathered in Hillsboro and set out in pursuit of the Apaches, who had stolen a number of horses from the immediate area. Setting off in the mid-afternoon, they caught up with the raiders by the end of the day:

> when we sighted them and opened fire upon them at once. They immediately scattered and melted away into the under-brush and rock, a few of them driving on ahead the herd of stolen horses they had gathered. We could not follow the horse herd without exposing ourselves to be ambushed by the Indians, so we had to scatter them first.

---

42 Hatch to CO Company I, 9th Cavalry, Fort Wingate, 4 December 1878 in Letters Sent by the '9MD/DNM/DoNM', NA, RG393, M1072, Roll 6, Letter No.535 p.372; Thrapp, 1974, p.210; Reeve, p.308; Ogle, 1970, p.193; Worcester, p.217; Billington, 1991, p.54.

43 Report of Lt. Rogers Birnie Jr. Ordnance Corps, submitted 15 March 1879 in AR-WD, NA, M997, Roll 33, 1879, Vol. I-II, p.2223.

44 Letter 16 January 1879 in MacPherson Letters 1 January 1879 to 3 September 1880, University of Virginia at Charlottesville.

45 *Thirty Four*, 15 January 1879.

46 F. Clifford and F. Nolan (Ed.) , *Deep Trails in the Old West: A Frontier Memory*, (University of Oklahoma Press: Norman) p.48.

Plates 6.1 and 6.2 During 1877-1879, Victorio sought to minimise direct conflict with troops and settlers in the USA; but he did occasionally raid in northern Mexico. While several Mexican towns carried on a brisk trade with the Apaches, both sides were capable of turning on each other with little or no warning. This Church at Janos would have been used for the community's worship, but also as a place of refuge. Note the heavy doors, and most windows being placed high off the ground. (Photos: author)

> I don't know whether we killed any or not. I do know that one Indian was hit as he ran dodging up the mountain from cover to cover. It was a long shot, but we had one old buffalo hunter in the crowd who had his "Betsy" along with him. Those old buffalo guns were fine for long-range shooting. His first shot raised the dust ahead of the Indian. His second raised a puff of dust behind the red man. Then the old fellow chuckled, and said "I'll get him next time, boys. Got the range now!" Sure enough, the Indian dropped at his third shot, but was picked up and carried off by other Indians, so we didn't know if he was killed or not.[47]

The posse returned to Hillsboro when night fell, but eight men, including Clifford, resolved to return to the pursuit the following day. Tracking the Apaches into the Black Range, they followed their quarry several days before stopping at Fort Bayard to beg supplies from the army. The post commander, probably Major Morrow, 'laughed and told us we were wasting our time.' He informed them that the Apaches had traversed the area earlier, and that as they spoke the raiders would already be in Mexico. The men returned to Hillsboro empty-handed.[48]

Lieutenant Merritt, with I Company, Ninth Cavalry, and supported by Lieutenant Wright's detachment of Navajo scouts, was dispatched from Fort Wingate to Ojo Caliente on 4 December 1878 with orders to deal with these raiders, believed to be a combination of Warm Springs Apaches and Chiricahua renegades who had originally fled to Mexico in 1876.[49] Merritt subsequently reported that Nana had set up a base on the Mescalero reservation and commenced raiding along the Rio Grande.[50] Victorio was believed to have moved further south to raid in the state of Chihuahua. Merritt's source was a citizen called Green, who lost 15 horses but had enough support and courage to pursue the raiders to Nana's camp and recover the horses. Green, who did not see Victorio during the recovery of his stock,[51] may have belonged to a posse from Palomas who are on record as having followed 'Nani' and 'Tomasito' to the Mescalero agency in December 1878 to recover stolen stock.[52]

Green's intelligence concerning Victorio appears to have been reliable; and by January 1879, Apache raiders were active in the part of Chihuahua frequented by Chihenne Apaches. Governor Angel Trias of the State of Chihuahua reported several attacks by Apaches during January 1879 (see document file No. 2). On 2 January, near Temochic, a mule train belonging to Vacente Antillon was attacked, with two men killed, a further three reported missing, and the mules driven off. The Mexican town of Carrizal was attacked on 13 January, and 25 head of stock driven off. Nine of the animals had been individually tethered to the house doors of their owners. This prompted one Estaban Martinez of Carrizal to petition the State of Chihuahua for arms, as the lack thereof in Carrizal meant that the residents could not defend themselves, let alone retaliate against such raids. Six persons were reported killed and a further six missing in the Sierra Fierro (Iron Mountains),

47 Clifford, F. & Nolan, F. (editor) 2011, *Deep Trails in the Old West: A Frontier Memory* (University of Oklahoma Press: Norman) p.48.

48 Clifford, F. & Nolan, F. (editor) 2011, *Deep Trails in the Old West: A Frontier Memory* (University of Oklahoma Press: Norman) pp.48-49.

49 Hatch to CO Company I, 9th Cavalry, Fort Wingate, 4 December 1878 in Letters Sent by the '9MD/DNM/DoNM', NA, RG393, M1072, Roll 6, Letter No.535 p.372.

50 Lt. Merritt to AAAG, DoNM, 20 February 1879 in 'Operations re Warm Springs Apaches 1877-79', Letters Rec'd by the AGO, 1871-80, NA, M666, Roll 366.

51 Merritt, Ojo Caliente to AAAG DoNM, 20 February 1879 in 'Operations re Warm Springs Apaches 1877-79', Letters Rec'd by the AGO, 1871-80, NA, M666, Roll 366 and 'Victorio Files', NA, RG393, M1495, Roll 14; See also Thrapp, 1974, pp.212-214.

So far, there appears to be no record of whether Green recovered his stock through peaceful or violent means.

52 *Thirty Four*, 25 December 1878.

though the date of the attack is unclear. A small skirmish took place between two Apaches at Cantareccio on 18 January, with the Apaches escaping with two horses belonging to Roman Aranda; but the defenders prevented them from running off a further two horses. On or before 22 January, Miguel Otero's ranch was attacked with several herders killed and all his cattle run off. These attacks prompted appeals for arms and ammunition to be supplied to the people to enable them to defend themselves. One correspondent noted that 15 Remington rifles, assigned by the State of Chihuahua to their canton, had still not been delivered. It was proposed that, if state law allowed, a further 25 Remington rifles be bought by public subscription for the canton. It was even suggested that the Apaches be pursued into the United States, if this could be achieved without the creation of an international incident. The superiority of the arms carried by the Apaches was also noted, and the United States was widely blamed both for arming and for failing to control the Apaches.[53] Lieutenant Hugo was also reported to have found the remains of an unidentified man 'five miles east of the Corralitos River,' shot in the shoulder and thigh and believed to have been carrying a carbine when killed.[54] What Lieutenant Hugo was doing in Mexico was not explained. As we shall see, most of the identifiable locations noted above were certainly within the range frequented by Victorio and his warriors, though one or two of the raids could have been perpetrated by Mescalero Apaches. As a result of these communications, the Office of the Secretary of War and Marine of the Federal Government of Mexico 'recommended'[55] that the State of Chihuahua be provided with the arms requested for their civil defence forces.[56]

In November 1878, Nana ostensibly surrendered at the Mescalero reservation. This reservation, centred on the agency at South Fork, straddled the Sacramento Mountains to the east of the Warm Springs Apaches' home range. The arrival of Nana's band at the Mescalero reservation caused some friction between the War Department and the Office of Indian Affairs, until the former decided to let them remain where they were for the moment.[57]

Victorio reappeared with 22 warriors at Ojo Caliente on 7 February 1879, having finally returned from Mexico. The Apache leader had clearly made earlier contact with Lieutenant Merritt, as the latter had contacted District Headquarters, on 25 January, seeking instructions as to what to do with 25 Apaches who wished to surrender. He was instructed to treat these men as prisoners of war.[58] The Apaches rode to within hailing distance of the post at dusk and asked for a 'talk'. Merritt and the rest of the surprised garrison went on alert. Merritt and interpreter Andrew Kelley then walked out to meet Victorio and agreed to meet for a parley the following day.[59] Victorio

53 Original Reports numbered 1-7 forwarded by Angel Trias (7 February 1879) to Mr Ruelas, Minister for Foreign Affairs, Mexico, who submitted them (13 March 1879) to John W. Foster, Minister of the United States to Mexico, who in turn passed them on (15 March 1879) to William M. Evarts, US Secretary of State who finally passed them on to George W. McCrary, Secretary of War on 7 April 1879, NA, RG393, Part 1, Entry 2546, pp.119-149.

54 *Thirty Four*, 8 January 1879.

55 Garcia to Governor of Chihuahua, 6 March 1879, NA, RG393, Part 1, Entry 2546, p.143 & 144.

56 Original Reports numbered 1-7 forwarded by Angel Trias (7 February 1879) to Mr Ruelas, Minister for Foreign Affairs, Mexico, who submitted them (13 March 1879) to John W. Foster, Minister of the United States to Mexico, who in turn passed them on (15 March 1879) to William M. Evarts, US Secretary of State who finally passed them on to George W. McCrary, Secretary of War on 7 April 1879, NA, RG393, Part 1, Entry 2546, pp.119-149.

57 Townsend, AG to Lt Gen. P.H. Sheridan, 7 December 1878, NA, RG393, Part 1, Entry 2546, p.1.

58 Loud to Merritt, 31 January 1879 in Letters Sent by the '9MD/DNM/DoNM', NA, RG393, M1072, Roll 6, January-October 1879, Letter No.25 pp.19-20.

59 Merritt, Ojo Caliente to AAAG DoNM, 20 February 1879, 'Victorio Files', NA, RG393, M1495, Roll 14 7 and in 'Operations re Warm Springs Apaches 1877-79', Letters Rec'd by the AGO, 1871-80, NA, M666, Roll 366; see also Hatch to Pope, Pope to Townsend, 13 February 1879, NA, RG393, Part 1, Entry 2538, pp.26-27; see also Pope to AAG Chicago, 13 February 1879, 'Victorio Files', NA, RG393,

only agreed to stay at Ojo Caliente after Merritt and Kelley walked unarmed and unescorted up 'the highest mountain to the right' above Ojo Caliente to negotiate with the Apaches.[60] It was the accoutrements of this band of warriors that finally convinced Merritt that they had been in Mexico[61] (see document file no. 3). In July 1879, correspondence between the US Consul in Chihuahua and the State Department in Washington DC made general mention of two major raids into Chihuahua. It also made specific reference to an incident in which 20 Mexican citizens were killed by Apaches at Temosachic, sometime in the previous year.[62] Temosachic was certainly within the area of Chihuahua where Chihenne Apaches were known to both trade and raid, and thus Victorio may have been responsible for this attack while in Mexico.

It was probably during this interview with Merritt and Kelley that Victorio and his followers made it clear that 'they prefer death to being sent to San Carlos.'[63] Ever cautious, Victorio had left most of his current following and horses some miles off while he negotiated with Lieutenant Merritt. He immediately asked that he be allowed to contact Nana's following and ask them to join him at Ojo Caliente. This Merritt agreed to, with the clear understanding that, in the meantime, Victorio would not engage in any hostile actions. In fact, the sudden appearance of Victorio's party had placed the lieutenant in an awkward position. He was in possession of clear instructions to encourage the Apaches to cease raiding, and he was convinced that Victorio's expedition to Mexico had been to garner mounts and ammunition for a renewed round of fighting. It was also clear to him that Victorio was too wily to be arrested on the spot and taken into custody. So, Lieutenant Merritt felt that he had to negotiate a deal 'on the spot' or risk provoking a renewed round of raiding.[64] Hatch was not impressed with Merritt's decision not only to allow Victorio to surrender but also to allow the Apache leader to send runners to the Mescalero reservation to summon Nana and his followers to Ojo Caliente.[65] Hatch thought that Merritt had overstepped the mark by approving such a move without seeking higher approval. Nevertheless, he felt able to support the

M1495, Roll 14; Pope to Townsend, 18 February 1879 in 'Operations re Warm Springs Apaches 1877-79', Letters Rec'd by the AGO, 1871-80, NA, M666, Roll 366; Thrapp, 1974, pp.212-214; see also Thrapp, 1988, p.764 and p.976; Ball, 1962, p.23; Billington, 1991, p.87; Worcester, p.217; Record of Engagements, p.84; Record of Engagements with Hostile Indians within the Military Division of the Missouri from 1868 to 1882. Compiled from Official Records. HQ– Military Division of the Missouri, Chicago Illinois, 1 August 1882. (Hereafter referred to as the 'Record of Engagements').

60 Merritt, Ojo Caliente to AAAG DoNM, 20 February 1879, 'Victorio Files', NA, RG393, M1495, Roll 14.

61 Merritt, Ojo Caliente to AAAG DoNM, 20 February 1879, 'Victorio Files', NA, RG393, M1495, Roll 14; See also Hatch to Pope, Pope to Townsend, 13 February 1879, NA, RG393, Part 1, Entry 2538, pp.26-27; See also Pope to AAG Chicago, 13 February 1879, 'Victorio, NA, RG393, M1495, Roll 14; Thrapp, 1974, pp.212-214; see also Thrapp, 1988, p.764 and p.976; Ball, 1962, p.23; Billington, 1991, p.87; Worcester, p.217; Record of Engagements, p.84; Record of Engagements.

62 Scott (US Consul in Chihuahua City) to Hunter (Asst. Secretary of State) 20 July 1879 in Letters Received, DoM 1868-98, RG 393, Entry A1-1 2601, Box 83.

63 Pope to Townsend, 13 February 1879, NA, RG393, Part 1, Entry 2538, pp.26-27; See also Hatch to AAG DoM, 26 February 1879, 'Victorio Files', NA, RG393, M1495, Roll 14; Pope to AAG Chicago 13 February 1879 'Victorio Files', NA, RG393, M1495, Roll 14; Hatch to AAG Fort Leavenworth, 12 February 1879, Telegrams Sent DoNM, Vol.2, January-December 1879, NA, RG393, Part 3, Entry 431, p.31.

64 Merritt, Ojo Caliente to AAAG DoNM, 20 February 1879 'Victorio Files', NA, RG393, M1495, Roll 14.

65 Merritt's fifteen day safe conduct to two Apaches to visit Fort Stanton and return to Ojo Caliente with all the Warm Springs Apaches currently there to Ojo Caliente dated 27 January 1879 and Loud to Merritt, 18 February, 1879 in 'Operations re Warm Springs Apaches 1877-79', Letters Rec'd by the AGO, 1871-80, NA, M666, Roll 366; Loud to Merritt, 18 February 1879, 'Victorio Files', NA, RG393, M1495, Roll 14; Hatch to Lt Merritt, Telegrams Sent DoNM, Vol.2, January-December 1879, NA, RG393, Part 3, Entry 431, p.39.

Plate 6.3 The opening into the Cañada Alamosa Canyon as seen from the garrison at Ojo Caliente. Andrew Kelley and Lieutenant Merritt ascended the peak to the right to negotiate with Victorio on 8 February 1879. (Photo: author)

Plate 6.4 Anyone pursuing Apaches into the Black Range, as the small posse including Frank Clifford did in pursuit of their stolen horses, found this to be difficult terrain. There is excellent cover in the form of both thick vegetation and innumerable rocky outcrops, making pursuit a very dangerous undertaking. (Photo: author)

settling of the Warm Springs Apaches back on their old reservation and ordered supplies to be sent there for their sustenance. Hatch also added that if Victorio's people were to be transferred back to San Carlos, a company of Apache scouts from that reservation should be sent to help enforce their removal.[66]

> There is no question of these Indians resisting to the death in being moved there. If the order is to be carried out, we may as well accept the fact that many of these Indians must be killed; they have undoubtedly cached their arms and ammunition or left them concealed with two or three Indians. I believe it is preferable to have them as closely under guard as possible by the troops, until it is decided what is to be done with them.[67]

It was Victorio's unequivocal statement concerning his desire to remain at Ojo Caliente that probably prompted General Pope to immediately ask of his superiors, 'What disposition shall be made of these Indians?'[68] Early the following month, Pope endorsed Hatch's views concerning the establishment of a reservation at Ojo Caliente.[69] However, in April 1879, the Commissioner of Indian Affairs directed that all Warm Springs Apaches held by the US army be sent to the Mescalero reservation.[70] This *volte face* appears to have come from the realisation that the fundamental problem was the decision to send the Warm Springs Apaches to San Carlos. The Secretary of the Interior credited the advice given by Hatch and Pope in making this decision,[71] though Hatch only appears to have considered the implications of this policy change after the decision was made.[72] It was probably advice received from the Commissioner of Indian Affairs which influenced this decision. Not only did the Commissioner acknowledge that the Warm Springs Apaches were opposed to a move back to San Carlos; he also noted that they appeared to assimilate well with the Mescalero Apaches.[73] In doing so he dismissed Mescalero Agent Russell's concerns that the Warm Springs Apaches would exacerbate an already unstable situation if they were to settle on

66 Hatch to AAG DoM, 26 February 1879, 'Victorio Files', NA, RG393, M1495, Roll 14; Hatch to Lt DeLany, 15th Infantry, Fort Craig, 10 February 1879, Telegrams Sent DoNM, Vol.2, January-December 1879, NA, RG393, Part 3, Entry 431, p.30.

67 Hatch to AAG, DoM, 26 February 1879, 'Victorio, NA, RG393, M1495, Roll 14.

68 Pope to AAG, Chicago 13 February 1879, 'Victorio Files', NA, RG393, M1495, Roll 14.

69 Pope to AG of the Army via HQ MDoM, 7 March 1879; DoM, 26 February 1879, 'Victorio Files', NA, RG393, M1495, Roll 14.

70 Hoyt, Commissioner to Secretary of the Interior, 11 April 1879 'Victorio Files', NA, RG393, M1495, Roll 14.

71 Secretary of the Interior to Secretary of War, 20 May 1879 in 'Operations re Warm Springs Apaches 1877-79', Letters Rec'd by the AGO, 1871-80, NA, M666, Roll 366; see also Department of the Interior to Secretary of War, 20 May 1879 in Letters Received by HQ DoNM, September-August 1890, NA, RG393, M1088, Roll 37 April-June 1879.

72 Hatch to AAG Fort Leavenworth, 14 April 1879, Telegrams Sent DoNM, Vol.2, January-December 1879, NA, RG393, Part 3, Entry 431, pp.95-96; Pope to AAG MDoM, 15 April 1879 in 'Operations re Warm Springs Apaches 1877-79', Letters Rec'd by the AGO, 1871-80, NA, M666, Roll 366; Platt, AA General to AAG HQ MDoM, Chicago, 15 April 1879, 'Victorio Files', NA, RG393, M1495, Roll 14; See also Thrapp, 1974, p.215.

73 CoIA to the Secretary of the Interior 11 April 1879 in 'Operations re Warm Springs Apaches 1877-79', Letters Rec'd by the AGO, 1871-80, NA, M666, Roll 366; Platt, AA General to AAG HQ MDoM, Chicago, 15 April 1879, 'Victorio Files', NA, RG393, M1495, Roll 14; See also Loud to Hatch, 30 March 1879, Telegrams Sent DoNM, Vol.2, January-December 1879, NA, RG393, Part 3, Entry 431, p.84; Department of the Interior to Secretary of War, 7 March 1879 in Letters Received by HQ DoNM September-August 1890, NA, RG393, M1088, Roll 37 April-June 1879; Thrapp, 1974, p.215; Worcester, p.217; Record of Engagements, p.84.

his reservation. Russell also argued that while at Ojo Caliente the Warm Springs Apaches had behaved impeccably.[74]

Thus, while the Office of Indian Affairs and the Department of the Interior appeared to gain a firmer grip on reality, they still failed to appreciate the implications of closing the Ojo Caliente reservation, even when prompted in that direction by their own employees. The policy towards the Warm Springs Apaches was still driven by a desire to reduce costs. It had at last been tempered with the realisation that San Carlos was not an option; but the basic impetus for concentration remained.

However, the delays which accompanied this policy-making caused Victorio to become increasingly concerned about the US army's intentions towards him. On 23 March, he delivered an ultimatum stating that he would not come in to Ojo Caliente unless Hatch had a personal council with him, and this caused some consternation at District Headquarters.[75] Hatch had instructed Merritt to hold Victorio and his followers as prisoners of war, and had assumed that Merritt was actually holding them at Ojo Caliente.[76] In fact, Victorio and Merritt had entered into a 'gentleman's agreement' that the former would camp on his former reservation until the reservation issue was resolved. Unfortunately for Merritt, he had failed to inform District Headquarters of this arrangement. Victorio would never have agreed to be confined at the military post at Ojo Caliente, and it should be remembered that he had left enough warriors in the hills to see what reception he got when he approached Merritt in the first place. Having now realised their misinterpretation of Merritt's original communication, it was decided at District Headquarters that the garrison at Ojo Caliente should be reinforced by 50 men under either Major Morrow or Captain Charles Beyer, and Lieutenant Robert Emmet with 10 Navajo scouts.[77]

Such troop movements could not be hidden from the Apaches. Victorio, having seen what could happen to Apache leaders who fell completely into the power of the US army, was ever wary of the possibility of being imprisoned and even assassinated. Thus, on 15 April 1879, when the news that he was to be sent to the Mescalero reservation was received, he may have already become suspicious of the US army. He declared to Lieutenant Merritt that he would die before he complied with such an order. He and his adherents then fled into the San Mateo Mountains.[78]

A different story of the events surrounding the flight of the Warm Springs Apaches emerged after the event, with Lieutenant Merritt accused of being too drunk to perform his duties. Colonel Hatch instructed Captain Ambrose E. Hooker to verify an unofficial report concerning Lieutenant Merritt's conduct, according to which,[79] when Victorio refused to move to the Mescalero reser-

74 CoIA to Russell, US Indian Agent 16 April 1879 'Operations re Warm Springs Apaches 1877-79', Letters Rec'd by the AGO, 1871-80, NA, M666, Roll 366; see also E.A. Hoyt, Commissioner to Agent Russell, 16 April 1879 in Letters Received by HQ DoNM, September-August 1890, NA, RG393, M1088, Roll 37 April-June 1879.

75 Loud to Hatch, Fort Bayard, 26 March 1879, Telegrams Sent DoNM, Vol.2, January-December 1879, NA, RG393, Part 3, Entry 431, p.75.

76 See Telegrams Sent DoNM, Vol.2, January-December 1879, NA, RG393, Part 3, Entry 431, p.78.

77 Hatch to Morrow, Fort Bayard, 1 April 1879 in Letters Sent by the '9MD/DNM/DoNM', NA, RG393, M1072, Roll 6, January-October 1879, Letter No.191 p.139; See also Hatch to Beyer, 1 April 1879, Telegrams Sent DoNM, Vol.2, January-December 1879, NA, RG393, Part 3, Entry 431, p.101; Hatch to Lt Clark, 15th Infantry, Ft Craig, 24 April 1879, Telegrams Sent DoNM, Vol.2, January-December 1879, NA, RG393, Part 3, Entry 431, p.112.

78 Hatch to AAG Fort Leavenworth, 18 April 1879, Telegrams Sent DoNM, Vol.2,January-December 1879, NA, RG393, Part 3, Entry 431, p.102; Platt to AAG HQ MDoM, 18 April 1879, 'Victorio Files', NA, RG393, M1495, Roll 14 and 'Operations re Warm Springs Apaches 1877-79', Letters Rec'd by the AGO, 1871-80, NA, M666, Roll 366.

79 Hatch to Captain Hooker, Fort Union, 19 April 1879 in Letters Sent by the '9MD/DNM/DoNM', NA, RG393, M1072, Roll 6, January-October 1879, Letter No.165 p.117.

vation, Merritt, too drunk to take charge himself, left the rest of his company to surround the Apaches and detain them while he retired to his quarters indisposed.[80] The Apaches were not caught napping, and both sides opened fire. Three US army mounts were shot before the Apaches escaped. Merritt compounded this error by failing to organise a pursuit for a further 24 hours.[81]

The story of this episode offers a complete contrast to Merritt's cool and courageous dealings with Victorio in February, and may lend some weight to the allegations that the lieutenant was inebriated at the time. It may be no coincidence that Merritt also reported the loss of 'the corral,' to fire, on 15 April 1879, an incident in which a significant amount of forage was destroyed. The forage was of such an amount that District Headquarters sent a sternly worded message, reminding Lieutenant Merritt that forage was supplied when required by post commanders and that, therefore, the forage lost in the fire was not government property.[82] The fact that the fire and Victorio's escape took place on the same day, combined with the unofficial report that Merritt had been drunk on duty, cannot have made a favourable impression on headquarters. Papers relative to Merritt's 'misdemeanours while on duty at Ojo Caliente' were forwarded to Department Headquarters with a recommendation that he be tried at Santa Fé 'for the best interests of the service.'[83]

Hatch later reported that more information relative to this officer's conduct had come to light,[84] and commented that Merritt had handled the whole affair 'badly,'[85] and had been 'brought to trial and dismissed the service.'[86] In fact, Merritt had been charged with three specific instances of being drunk while in charge at Ojo Caliente. He was also charged, under the heading of misconduct, with two instances of 'failure to personally direct certain operations of the troops against hostile Indians.'[87] He was found guilty on all charges except for one of the charges of misconduct during operations against the Apaches, and was dismissed from the service.[88] Merritt committed suicide in Santa Fé on 12 December 1879.[89]

Captain Hooker, with E Company, Ninth Cavalry, was dispatched from Fort Union to take vigorous action against the Warm Springs Apaches. Hooker was ordered to try persuasion, and

---

80 Charge II, 2nd Specification, General Court Martial Orders No.59, 8 November 1879, HQ of the Army, AGO, Washington DC.

81 Charge II, 2nd Specification, General Court Martial Orders No.59, 8 November 1879, HQ of the Army, AGO, Washington D.C.; see also Hatch to Merritt 22 April 1879 Letters sent M1072 and 'Charges and Specifications against Lt Charles Merritt' 2 August 1879, Letters Received M1088; Record of Events Company I, Ninth Cavalry, March 1879, Returns From Regular Army Cavalry Regiments 1833-1916, 9th Cavalry Regimental Returns 1873-1880, NA, M744, Roll 88.

This loss was said to have occurred in March instead of April 1879. This could be to the result of a clerical error on the part of whoever compiled the monthly Regimental Return but it is slightly strange. The Court Martial Record also clearly states that this skirmish occurred on, or around, 8 March 1879. Yet it is clear from other documents that this skirmish was reacted to by District Headquarters on or around 18 April 1879.

82 Loud to Merritt, 22 April 1879 in Letters Sent by the '9MD/DNM/DoNM', NA, RG393, M1072, Roll 6, January-October 1879, Letter No.172, pp124-125.

83 Hatch to AAG, DoM, Fort Leavenworth, 1 July 1879 in Letters Sent by the '9MD/DNM/DoNM', NA, RG393, M1072, Roll 6, January-October 1879, Letter No.322, p.229.

84 Hatch to AAG, DoM, Fort Leavenworth, 1 July 1879 in Letters Sent by the '9MD/DNM/DoNM', NA, RG393, M1072, Roll 6, January-October 1879, Letter No.322, p.229.

85 Hatch to AAG, DoM, Fort Leavenworth, 14 February 1880 in Letters Sent by the '9MD/DNM/DoNM', NA, RG393, M1072, Roll 6, Jan 1880-August 1881, Letter No.82, pp58-65.

86 Hatch to Major J.J. Coppinger 10th Infantry, Acting Assistant Inspector General, DoM, 26 June 1880 in Letters Sent by the '9MD/DNM/DoNM', NA, RG393, M1072, Roll 6, Jan 1880-August 1881, Letter No.309, pp.199-201.

87 *Army & Navy Journal*, Vol.17, 29 November 1879, p.320.

88 Ibid.

89 *Army & Navy Journal*, Vol.17, 20 December 1879, p.380.

then force, to compel Victorio to seek terms. The fugitive leader and his men were then to be handed over to the Indian agent at the Mescalero reservation.[90] An Apache scout company from Arizona under Lieutenant Gatewood, Sixth Cavalry, was sent to reinforce the troops already at Ojo Caliente and was ordered to join the pursuit of the fugitive Apaches before they initiated any hostilities.[91] Gatewood's company[92] departed for Ojo Caliente on 23 April, and arrived on 2 May 1879.[93] Some concern was raised that some of the Apaches with Victorio at the time he fled were Warm Springs Apaches who had earlier been returned to the San Carlos reservation.[94] However, the San Carlos agent confirmed that all the Chihenne Apaches who had arrived in November 1878 were present at the reservation.[95] It was therefore concluded that if there were any Chiricahuas with Victorio, they were probably ones who had fled San Carlos some time before and were up from Mexico.[96]

Meanwhile, Victorio and other groups of disaffected Apaches continued their depredations, with various US army units in 'hot' pursuit.[97] In response to the news that 20 Warm Springs Apaches were said to have been raiding around Bacon Springs, Merritt, at this point still in command at Ojo Caliente, was instructed to put the Apache scouts into the field and spare no effort to recapture

---

90 Loud to Hooker, 19 April 1879 in Letters Sent by the '9MD/DNM/DoNM', NA, RG393, M1072, Roll 6, Jan-Oct 1879, Letter No. 166, pp.118-120.

91 Hatch to CO, Fort Union, 18 April 1879, Telegrams Sent DoNM, Vol.2, Jan.–Dec. 1879, NA, RG393, Part 3, Entry 431, p.104; Hatch to Major Compton, Fort Apache, 22 April 1879, Telegrams Sent DoNM, Vol.2, Jan.–Dec. 1879, NA, RG393, Part 3, Entry 431, p.108; Compton to Hatch, 22 April 1879, Field Records – Troops in Southeastern Arizona, DoAz, NA, RG393, Part 1, Entry 232, Vol.2, Sept 1 1878-27 May, 1879, Letter No. 132; Hatch to AAG Fort Leavenworth, 23 April 1879, Telegrams Sent DoNM, Vol.2, Jan.–Dec. 1879, NA, RG393, Part 3, Entry 431, pp. 109-112; Fort Wingate Jan–June 1879, Returns from U.S. Military Posts 1800-1916; NA, M617, Roll 1449; Special Order 28, April 18 1879, Paragraphs 2, 3, 4 & 7, NA, RG393, Part 3, Entry 450,) See also Hatch and Platt to AAG, HQ. MDoM, 18 April 1879 and 23 April 1879, and Whipple, AAG MDoM to AG of the Army, 24 April 1879, 'Victorio Files', NA, RG393, M1495, Roll 14; Hatch to AAG Fort Leavenworth, 18 April 1879, Telegrams Sent DoNM, Vol.2, Jan.–Dec. 1879, NA, RG393, Part 3, Entry 431, p.102; Hatch to CO Fort Wingate, 28 April 1879 in Letters Sent by the '9MD/DNM/DoNM', NA, RG393, M1072, Roll 6, Jan-Oct 1879, Letter No.200 pp145-146.

92 On 1 January 1879, Surgeon MacPherson detailed Gatewood's company as consisting of twenty-five Apache scouts, thirty-five Sixth Cavalrymen, six packers and a guide plus MacPherson himself as the only available doctor and Lt. Cruse as QM in the field. (Letter January 1, 1879 in MacPherson Letters 1 Jan 1879 to 3 September 1880, University of Virginia at Charlottesville) He later noted that the company was accompanied by thirty mules. (Letter 16 January 1879 in MacPherson Letters 1 Jan 1879 to 3 September 1880, University of Virginia at Charlottesville.) It should be noted that Cruse's own memoir state that he was ordered to Arizona on 30 September, 1879. (Cruse, 1987, p.21) See also comments made in the caption for the Photo on p.215 this volume

93 Compton to Hatch, 23 April 1879, Field Records – Troops in Southeastern Arizona, DoAz, NA, RG393, Part 1, Entry 232, Vol.2, Sept 1 1878-27 May, 1879, Letter No. 138; Compton, Field Records – Troops in Southeastern Arizona, DoAz, NA, RG393, Part 1, Entry 232, Vol.3, 27 May, 1879-3 July, 1879, Letter No. 175, pp.3-4.

94 Compton to Hart Indian Agent, San Carlos, 22 April 1879, Field Records – Troops in Southeastern Arizona, DoAz, NA, RG393, Part 1, Entry 232, Vol.2, Sept 1 1878-27 May, 1879, Letter No. 134.

95 Compton to Hatch, 24 April 1879, Field Records – Troops in Southeastern Arizona, DoAz, NA, RG393, Part 1, Entry 232, Vol.2, Sept 1 1878-27 May, 1879, Letter No. 141.

96 Compton to CO Fort Bowie 25 April 1879, Field Records – Troops in Southeastern Arizona, DoAz, NA, RG393, Part 1, Entry 232, Vol.2, Sept 1 1878-27 May, 1879, Letter No. 143 See also same entry Letter No.'s 133 & 134.

97 Compton to Major McLellan, CO Fort Bowie, & Lt. Blocksom, CO Company 'C', Indian Scouts, 25 April 1879, Field Records – Troops in Southeastern Arizona, DoAz, NA, RG393, Part 1, Entry 232, Vol.2, Sept 1 1878-27 May, 1879, Letter No.'s 143 & 144; See also Thrapp, 1974, p.216, 1967, p.181; Billington, 1991, pp.87-89; Worcester, p218.

them.[98] This time he was, if successful, to confine them as prisoners of war.[99] However, as was all too common during the Apache Wars, a number of detachments fanned out across south-western New Mexico and south-eastern Arizona and endured the heat and terrain but failed to find any trace of their opponents. Another report had it that 20 Apaches were raiding 20 miles to the east of Fort Wingate, at Crane's Ranch.[100] However, it was discovered that the depredations reported near Bacon Springs and at Crane's Ranch were fictitious – something that happened with annoying frequency during the Victorio Campaign.[101] Such rumours were, and would be, a major strain on the US army's efforts to combat Apache guerrillas.

In western Texas, as promised, Colonel Grierson renewed his policy of surveying and picketing the Pecos region, and by the end of March 1879 at least six detachments were in the field.[102] He also passed on the first detailed map of the area to the Department of Texas, and asked that a copy be furnished to all posts in the District of the Pecos.[103] News was also received that a proposed new fort, to be based on the eastern slopes of the Guadalupe Mountains, had received the support of General Ord.[104] Nevertheless, small parties of Mescalero Apache raiders continued raiding, one party being pursued on to the reservation by Lieutenant Bullis, who reached the agency on 7 March 1879.[105] Captain Viele, Tenth Cavalry, surprised two Mescaleros camped at Flat Rock, 'a day's march from the Guadalupe Mountains' on 13 April. The two men escaped, but their possessions and animals, two horses and two mules, were captured by the detachment.[106] Raiders stole 12 horses from Fort Davis on 5 May, and were pursued for 81 miles to the south-east before the Tenth Cavalry detachment had to pull up because their horses could go no further. The pursuers did force their quarry to abandon six of the stolen horses, but the raiders scattered into difficult terrain near Pena Blanco and were presumed to have escaped into Mexico.[107]

By mid-summer 1879, events in Mexico had also changed the pattern of raiding in western Texas. In December 1878, one Colonel Ortiz, commanding Mexican forces 'at Del Norte' clashed with Mescalero Apaches in Mexico, killing six and capturing 'eighty-six Indians, large and small...

---

98 Hatch to Merritt, Ojo Caliente, 27 April 1879, Telegrams Sent DoNM, Vol.2, Jan.–Dec. 1879, NA, RG393, Part 3, Entry 431, p.114.

99 Hatch to Merritt, Ojo Caliente, 30 April 1879, Telegrams Sent DoNM, Vol.2, Jan.–Dec. 1879, NA, RG393, Part 3, Entry 431, p.117.

100 CO Fort Wingate to AAAG, DoNM, 21 April 1879 in Letters Received by HQ DoNM, September-August 1890, NA, RG393, M1088, Roll 37 April-June 1879.

101 Hatch to Merritt, 3 May 1879, Telegrams Sent DoNM, Vol.2, Jan.–Dec. 1879, NA, RG393, Part 3, Entry 431, p.121; Lt Mitchell, 15th Inf. to Post Adjutant, Fort Wingate, 23 April 1879 in Letters Received by HQ DoNM, September-August 1890, NA, RG393, M1088, Roll 37 April-June 1879.

102 See Orders sent in Letters 11-13, 27 March & Letters 14-16, 28 March 1879 in Letters Sent Jan. 31 1878–Sept 15 1879, HQ DoP 1878-1881 NA, M1381 Roll 1.

103 Grierson to AAG, DoTx, 31 March 1879, Letter No. 25 in Letters Sent Jan. 31 1878–Sept 15 1879, HQ DoP 1878-1881 NA, M1381 Roll 1.

104 Smither to CO Company C, Tenth Cavalry, 28 March 1879, Letter No. 16 in Letters Sent Jan. 31 1878–Sept 15 1879, HQ DoP 1878-1881 NA, M1381 Roll 1.

105 Ord to AG, MDoM, 18 March 1879, NA, RG393, Part 1, Entry 2546, pp.105-107.

106 Carpenter to AAG, DoP, 20 April 1879 in Telegrams Sent 29 January 1878-April 21 1879, HQ DoP 1878-1881 NA, M1381 Roll 1, Telegram No. 63, p.184; Carpenter to AG, DoP, 20 April 1879 in Telegrams Rec'd , Jan. 23-July 31, 1878 & Oct. 1, 1878–May 17, 1880, HQ DoP 1878-1881, NA, M1381, Roll 3; Ord to AAG, DoTx, 21 April 1879, NA, RG393, Part 1, Entry 2546, pp.117-118; Tabular Statement of Expeditions and Scouts against Indians, &c., made in the Department of Texas, During the Year ending 30 September, 1880 (Hereafter referred to as 'Tabular Statement of Scouts, DoTx, 1880'), NA, RG393, Part 1, Entry 2546, pp.626-627.

107 Carpenter, Fort Davis to AAG, San Antonio, Texas, 10 May 1880in Telegrams Sent April 24, 1879-June 22, 1880, HQ DoP 1878-1881 NA, M1381 Roll 1, pp.14-15; Carpenter to AAAG, DoP, 10 May 1879 in Telegrams Rec'd , Jan. 23-July 31, 1878 & Oct. 1, 1878–May 17, 1880, HQ DoP 1878-1881, NA, M1381, Roll 3; Ord to AG, MDoM, 12 May 1879, NA, RG393, Part 1, Entry 2546, pp.150-151.

and that very few escaped.'[108] Another small band of cattle thieves were intercepted by a detachment of Mexican troops under the command of General Gerónimo Trevino and driven across the border.[109] A few Lipan Apaches also seem to have been operating in the area at the time, and in early March 1879 raided several ranches on the Mexican side of the border, prompting the local political officer to alert the US army. A small detachment was sent to oversee the relevant border crossings.[110] The Mexican response to the Mescalero and Lipan Apaches operating from their territory seems to have been enough to drive these Apaches north over the border, though, for the moment, it did not stop their raiding. In pursuing these raiders during the month of June, they achieved what the Tenth Cavalry reported to be a marked change in the chosen flight patterns of their quarry. Denied their markets in Mexico, they started to move their plunder north into New Mexico, finding a ready market in and around the Mescalero reservation.[111]

Even during Victorio's all too brief stay at Ojo Caliente in 1879, the border between Arizona and New Mexico was scouted by detachments from the Sixth Cavalry, who covered much ground but failed to contact any independent Apaches.[112] For example, C Company, under Captain Daniel Madden, made a round trip of approximately 279 miles from Camp Bowie to Knight's Ranch.[113] They then scouted the Gila between Knight's Ranch and Solliman's Store, and returned to Camp Bowie via Camp Grant and Point of Mountains.[114] Madden reported that 'during all these movements, no signs of Indians were discovered.'[115] A detachment of G Company set out from Camp Grant on 19 February, returning on 5 March 1879.[116] Following in Captain Madden's footsteps, Captain C.B. McLellan, with L Company, Sixth Cavalry, scouted southwards from Camp Bowie to the Burro Mountains between 17 and 31 March 1879.[117] Both detachments encountered a small picket consisting of Sergeant David Badie and five enlisted men of the Ninth Cavalry.[118] McLellan's detachment also encountered a party of Fifteenth Infantrymen from Fort Bliss

108 Mason, A.A.G. to AG, MDoM, Chicago, 30 December 1878, NA, RG393, Part 1, Entry 2546, p.16; See R.E. Moffitt to Lt. John L. Bullis, Fort Clark, Texas, 19 January 1879, NA, RG393, Part 1, Entry 2546, pp.20-24 for more details.

109 W.M. Evarts to George W. McCrary, Secretary of War, 19 December 1878, NA, RG393, Part 1, Entry 2546, pp.17-19.

110 E.O.C. Ord to AG, MDoM, 8 March 1879, NA, RG393, Part 1, Entry 2546, pp.62-64.

111 See correspondence concerning the pursuit of Apache raiders in June 1879, NA, RG393, Part 1, Entry 2546, pp.152-156; in particular see Ord to AG, MDoM, 18 June 1879, NA, RG393, Part 1, Entry 2546, pp.155-156.

112 See Compton to AAG, DoAz, 7 February 1879, Field Records – Troops in Southeastern Arizona, DoAz, NA, RG393, Part 1, Entry 232, Vol.2, Sept 1 1878-27 May, 1879, Letter No.46.

113 Knight's Ranche is noted as being north of Soldiers Farewell and Cow Springs. (Hatch to AAG, DoM, Fort Leavenworth, 21 September, 1880 in Letters Sent by the '9MD/DNM/DoNM', NA, RG393, M1072, Roll 6, Jan 1880-August 1881, Letter No.503, p.325.)

114 Compton to CO Company of Cavalry at Fort Bowie, 29 January 1879, Field Records – Troops in Southeastern Arizona, DoAz, NA, RG393, Part 1, Entry 232, Vol.2, Sept 1 1878-27 May, 1879, Letter No.41; Capt Madden to Maj. Compton CO Camp Apache, 14 February 1879, NA, RG393, Part 1, Entry 240 – This report includes a drawn map of this scout; Record of Events January 1879 in Returns From Regular Army Cavalry Regiments 1833-1916, 6th Cavalry Regimental Returns 1875 to 1880, NA, M744, Roll 63.

115 Capt Madden to Maj. Compton CO Camp Apache, 14 February 1879, NA, RG393, Part 1, Entry 240.

116 Lt ??Cheever?? to CO Camp Apache, 7 March 1879, NA, RG393, Part 1, Entry 240.

117 Record of Events March 1879, Returns From Regular Army Cavalry Regiments 1833-1916, 6th Cavalry Regimental Returns 1875 to 1880, NA, M744, Roll 63.

118 See Bi-Monthly Company Muster Rolls for Company B, 9th Cavalry, Jan/Feb 1879 in NA, RG94; Record of Events January to April 1879 in Returns From Regular Army Cavalry Regiments 1833-1916, 9th Cavalry Regimental Returns 1873-1880, NA, M744, Roll 88.

Plate 6.5 This is a different photo of the ruins at Ojo Caliente to contrast with that shown in chapter 4. This gives a better idea of the flat terrain surrounding the immediate area of the post where the bungled attempt to arrest Victorio and his followers was attempted in April 1879. (Photo: author)

Plate 6.6 Like most forts of the western frontier, Fort Davis was not surrounded by the 'traditional' wooden palisade, as most American Indians would not risk the losses which would be sustained in an attack. However, lack of a palisade made forts potentially vulnerable to stealthy groups of raiders seeking to steal munitions and/or stock. (Photo: author)

repairing the telegraph line near the Burro Mountains.[119] Between January and April 1879, B, C and G Companies, Ninth Cavalry, were to be found on regular scouting expeditions in southwestern New Mexico between the Arizona border and the Florida Mountains.[120] None of these US army detachments found any sign of Apaches.

In early May, prior to the arrival of Hooker's detachment, Lieutenant Merritt reported that Victorio and 40 warriors with Mescalero and San Carlos allies had gathered in the San Mateo Mountains to waylay a supply convoy travelling between Fort Craig and Ojo Caliente. However, as the convoy was accompanied by a strong escort detachment, the Apaches had aborted their intended ambuscade.[121] The Apaches did pick off one Lewis Wellington, who was riding on courier duty between Fort Craig and Ojo Caliente on or around 28 or 29 April 1879, and they stole his horse. Wellington was then the farrier to Emmet's Navajo scout detachment, but whether he was a civilian volunteer, a Ninth cavalryman or a Fifteenth infantryman is unclear.[122] The Apaches also picked off some civilians in the area, with Surgeon MacPherson reporting that the Apaches had killed four men before managing to evade Lieutenant Gatewood's scouts.[123] Interpreter Kelley also stated that a man named Duncan had been slain less than two miles from Ojo Caliente on 1 May 1879.[124] Later in May, one man was reported killed in the vicinity of Hillsboro. The Longfellow Mines were also reported to have been raided.[125]

Lieutenant Gatewood reported that at least 150 Warm Springs and Mescalero Apaches were based in the San Mateo Mountains. They were heavily armed and apparently eager for a fight with the Ojo Caliente garrison. As the latter consisted of approximately 50 men, including Navajo and Apache scouts, they had no intention of taking up the gauntlet until reinforced.[126] This information[127] prompted Hatch to order a detachment of troops from Fort Bayard to scout up the North Star Road towards Ojo Caliente. This was led by Lieutenant Hugo, who led his detachment as far as Camp Sherman via Georgetown, Willow Springs, Diamond Creek, Camp Vincent, and Shaw's Ranch, and returned, on 24 May, to report an abundance of pony tracks but no contact with Apaches.[128] Another detachment was sent to Old Fort Cummings.[129] This detachment,

119 Capt. McLellan to CO Camp Apache, 3 April 1879, NA, RG393, Part 1, Entry 240; Lt ??Cheever?? to CO Camp Apache, 7 March 1879, NA, RG393, Part 1, Entry 240; See also Compton to CO Company of Cavalry at Fort Bowie, 29 January 1879, Field Records – Troops in Southeastern Arizona, DoAz, NA, RG393, Part 1, Entry 232, Vol.2, Sept 1 1878-27 May, 1879, Letter No.41.

120 Record of Events January to April 1879 in Returns From Regular Army Cavalry Regiments 1833-1916, 9th Cavalry Regimental Returns 1873-1880, NA, M744, Roll 88.

121 Merritt to AAAG Santa Fé, 12 & 30 May 1879 in NA, RG393, Part 3, Entry 439, pp.183-185 & pp.202-203.

122 Return for May 1879 in Returns from U.S. Military Posts 1800-1916 Ojo Caliente, New Mexico, May 1879-Mar. 1882, NA, M617, Roll 877; *Thirty Four*, 7 May 1879; Report from Andrew Kelley concerning illegal trade with Apaches at Cañada Alamosa as reported in *Thirty-Four*, 5 May 1880. See also The Chronological List, p.42.

123 Letter 22 May 1879 in MacPherson Letters 1 Jan 1879 to 3 September 1880, University of Virginia at Charlottesville.

124 Report from Andrew Kelley concerning illegal trade with Apaches at Cañada Alamosa as reported in *Thirty-Four*, 5 May 1880.

125 *Thirty Four*, 26 November 1879.

126 Compton to AAG DoAz, 15 May 1879, Field Records – Troops in Southeastern Arizona, DoAz, NA, RG393, Part 1, Entry 232, Vol.2, Sept 1 1878-27 May, 1879, Letter No. 148.

127 Plus the probably erroneous news that there were Apaches at large in the Organ Mountains *Thirty Four*, 14 May 1879.

128 Hugo to Post Adjutant, 9 June 1879 in Letters Received by HQ DoNM, September-August 1890, NA, RG393, M1088, Roll 37, April-June 1879.

129 Loud to CO Fort Bayard, 5 May 1879, Telegrams Sent DoNM, Vol.2, Jan.–Dec. 1879, NA, RG393, Part 3, Entry 431, p.123; Compton to AAG DoAz, 15 May 1879, Field Records – Troops in Southeastern

commanded by Lieutenant Wright, arrived at old Fort Cummings on 7 May 1879. Up to 23 May, when the detachment returned to Fort Bayard, daily patrols were sent into Cooke's Canyon to the west and the Goodsight Mountains[130] to the east. Two scouting parties also penetrated Cooke's Range and the Florida Mountains. They found no sign of Apaches.[131] A third detachment left Fort Bliss to occupy the staging post of Martin's Wells (Aleman) and scout towards Fort McRae and Round Mountain.[132] Hooker was ordered to speed up his advance from Fort Union.[133] Merritt was instructed to locate and observe the independent Apaches, using the Apache scouts from Arizona, and to strike them hard once the additional troops had arrived.[134] On his arrival, Hooker ordered Merritt with all his mounted and dismounted men to thoroughly scout the San Mateo Mountains and the surrounding water sources 'with a view to the discovery and extermination of hostile Indians.'[135] In fact, Merritt's men had already discovered an eight-day-old trail which led towards the Mogollon Mountains.[136] Lieutenants Gatewood and Emmet, with their Apache and Navajo scout detachments and a squad of 15 men from Ojo Caliente, were sent in pursuit of Victorio on 10 May. Lieutenant Merritt guessed that this westwards movement was an attempt to remove those Warm Springs Apaches still residing on the San Carlos reservation.[137]

For some unknown reason, Hatch assumed that Victorio had turned to the south and was making for Mexico.[138] Hatch therefore concluded that Victorio had joined other 'renegade' Mexican Apaches, estimating the total number of independent Apache warriors at 100. He predicted that these Apaches would make small raids across the border, which would cause 'considerable annoyance to the settlements.' Such annoyance was offset by the fact that these Apaches were, in Hatch's opinion, encumbered by women and children, thus making it more difficult for them to elude pursuing troops, whose presence might even persuade the Apaches to surrender.[139] Hatch had also visited the apparently peaceful Warm Springs Apaches led by Nana and Tomas, who were currently settled on the Mescalero reservation. He had asked Tomas and five other Apaches to make contact with Victorio with a view to bringing about a peaceful end to the current hostilities.[140]

Arizona, DoAz, NA, RG393, Part 1, Entry 232, Vol.2, Sept 1 1878-27 May, 1879, Letter No. 148; Beyer to Wright, Special Orders No.44, 6 May 1879 in Letters Received by HQ_DoNM, September-August 1890, NA, RG393, M1088, Roll 37, April-June 1879.

130 These mountains are variously referred to as the 'Goodsight', 'Goodsite' or 'Good Sight' Mountains.

131 Wright to Post Adjutant, Fort Bayard, 23 May 1879 in Letters Received by HQ_DoNM, September-August 1890, NA, RG393, M1088, Roll 37, April-June 1879.

132 Loud to CO Fort Bliss, 6 May 1879, Telegrams Sent DoNM, Vol.2, Jan.–Dec. 1879, NA, RG393, Part 3, Entry 431, p.125.

133 Loud to Hooker, Los Lunas, 5 May 1879, Telegrams Sent DoNM, Vol.2, Jan.–Dec. 1879, NA, RG393, Part 3, Entry 431, p.124.

134 Loud to Merritt, Ojo Caliente, 5 May 1879, Telegrams Sent DoNM, Vol.2, Jan.–Dec. 1879, NA, RG393, Part 3, Entry 431, pp.123-124.

135 Order No.2, 20 May 1879, HQ, Troops in the Field, Ojo Caliente N.M., Special Orders Rec'd from Sub Commands, NA, RG393, Part 3, Entry 453.

136 Hatch to CO Camp Apache, 15 May 1879, Telegrams Sent DoNM, Vol.2, Jan.–Dec. 1879, NA, RG393, Part 3, Entry 431, p.131.

137 Merritt to AAAG Santa Fé 12 & 30 May 1879 in NA, RG393, Part 3, Entry 439, pp.183-185 & pp.202-203; Compton, Field Records – Troops in Southeastern Arizona, DoAz, NA, RG393, Part 1, Entry 232, Vol.3, 27 May, 1879-3 July, 1879, Letter No. 175, pp.3-4; Return for May 1879 in Returns From U.S. Military Posts 1800-1916 Ojo Caliente, New Mexico, May 1879-Mar. 1882, NA, M617, Roll 877.

138 Hatch to AAG, DoM, 26 May 1879, 'Victorio Files', NA, RG393, M1495, Roll 14.

139 Hatch to AAG DoM, 26 May 1879, 'Victorio Files', NA, RG393, M1495, Roll 14.

140 Hatch to AAG DoM, 26 May 1879, 'Victorio Files', NA, RG393, M1495, Roll 14 & 'Operations re Warm Springs Apaches 1877-79', Letters Rec'd by the AGO, 1871-80, NA, M666, Roll 366; Hatch to AAG, DoM, Fort Leavenworth, 26 May 1879 in Letters Sent by the '9MD/DNM/DoNM', NA, RG393, M1072, Roll 6, Jan-Oct 1879, Letter No.251, pp.181-182.

Lieutenant Gatewood followed Victorio, or at least some of his warriors, from Ojo Caliente to the vicinity of San Carlos [141] via Clifton, Arizona, before his men and animals succumbed to exhaustion and had to break off the pursuit.[142] In fact, the Longfellow Mine, noted above as having been raided, was about five miles from Clifton, Arizona, and was attacked on 15 May 1879 by the Chihennes being pursued by Gatewood.[143] The Warm Springs Apaches killed four herders and stole eight horses and 12 mules, though initially they were reported to have taken 80 animals.[144] The Apaches had led their pursuers over some of the roughest terrain in that part of the country, abandoning worn out horses when fresh horses could be stolen.[145] This expedition showed just how far these Apache raiders could travel in a short space of time, and is an early illustration of one of the most effective Apache tactics utilised repeatedly during the Victorio War Campaign.

From the Clifton area, the Apaches made towards the San Carlos reservation.[146] Thirty Warm Springs Apache warriors apparently managed to take two women and some children and to steal some horses and mules from the San Carlos reservation.[147] This was later denied by the Indian agent at San Carlos and General O.B. Willcox, but Major Compton was convinced that two women and two children had left the reservation and were now with Victorio.[148]

The US troops in Arizona were not slow in reacting. Lieutenant A. P. Blocksom's Indian scouts set out from Fort Bowie; and Lieutenant Howard, with D Company, Indian Scouts, was also tracking the Apaches, backed up by Captain W.L. Foulk. Meanwhile, A Company, Sixth Cavalry, from Fort Grant, under Captain Campbell, was ordered to make for Ash Spring in an effort to intercept Victorio. Captain Adam Kramer, with E Company, Sixth Cavalry, had left Fort Apache

141 Compton to Lt Blocksom & AAG DoAz, 15 May 1879, Field Records – Troops in Southeastern Arizona, DoAz, NA, RG393, Part 1, Entry 232, Vol.2, Sept 1 1878-27 May, 1879, Letter No. 152 & 153; Compton to Hatch NA, RG393, Part 3, Entry 439, p.196; Hatch to Wilcox, 21 May 1879, Telegrams Sent DoNM, Vol.2, Jan.–Dec. 1879, NA, RG393, Part 3, Entry 431, pp.141-142.

142 Letter 25 May 1879 in MacPherson Letters 1 Jan 1879 to 3 September 1880, University of Virginia at Charlottesville.

143 Email from Bernd Kuhn, 22 May 2012 who notes that the attack was perpetrated by Chihenne Apaches.

144 Compton to Lt Howard, CO Company 'D', Indian Scouts, 17 May 1879, Field Records – Troops in Southeastern Arizona, DoAz, NA, RG393, Part 1, Entry 232, Vol.2, Sept 1 1878-27 May, 1879, Letter No. 156 see also letter No. 158; Compton to CO Fort Grant, 17 May 1879, Field Records – Troops in Southeastern Arizona, DoAz, NA, RG393, Part 1, Entry 232, Vol.2, Sept 1 1878-27 May, 1879, Letter No. 155.; Compton, Field Records – Troops in Southeastern Arizona, DoAz, NA, RG393, Part 1, Entry 232, Vol.3, 27 May, 1879-3 July, 1879, Letter No. 175, pp.3-4; Willcox to Hatch, NA, RG393, Part 3, Entry 439, p.191 & Compton to Hatch, NA, RG393, Part 3, Entry 439, p.196; See also Letter 25 May 1879 where MacPherson mentions Victorio and his men killing four men near the Clifton Copper Mines in MacPherson Letters 1 Jan 1879 to 3 September 1880, University of Virginia at Charlottesville.

145 Compton, Field Records – Troops in Southeastern Arizona, DoAz, NA, RG393, Part 1, Entry 232, Vol.3, 27 May, 1879-3 July, 1879, Letter No. 175, pp.3-4.

146 Compton, Field Records – Troops in Southeastern Arizona, DoAz, NA, RG393, Part 1, Entry 232, Vol.3, 27 May, 1879-3 July, 1879, Letter No. 175, pp.3-4.

147 Willcox to AG, Presidio, San Francisco, 28 May 1879, NA, RG393, Part 1, Entry 169, Vol. 9, p.161; See also Willcox to Gen. Comd. DoNM, 19 May 1879, NA, RG393, Part 1. Entry 169, Vol. 9, p.171; See also comment by Hatch in Hatch to AAG DoM, 26 May 1879, 'Victorio Files', NA, RG393, M1495, Roll 14; McDowell to AG of the Army, 29 May 1879 in 'Operations re Warm Springs Apaches 1877-79', Letters Rec'd by the AGO, 1871-80, NA, M666, Roll 366; Hatch to AAG, DoM, Fort Leavenworth, 26 May 1879 in Letters Sent by the '9MD/DNM/DoNM', NA, RG393, M1072, Roll 6, Jan-Oct 1879, Letter No.251, pp.181-182.

148 Compton, Field Records – Troops in Southeastern Arizona, DoAz, NA, RG393, Part 1, Entry 232, Vol.3, 27 May, 1879-3 July, 1879, Letter No. 175, pp.3-4; Report of Gen. Willcox in AR-WD, NA, M997, Roll 33, 1879, Vol. I-II, p.164; See also Letter 25 May 1879 in MacPherson Letters 1 Jan 1879 to 3 September 1880, University of Virginia at Charlottesville.

and was scouting southwards towards the supposed location of the Apaches. A third Sixth Cavalry detachment, commanded by Captain Tupper, was made available for field service if required.[149]

Lieutenant Howard's detachment had picked up the trail of 17 Warm Springs Apaches, including two women, on the San Carlos reservation. The trail progressed east from the foot of Rocky Canyon. Howard also sent in word that Victorio was on the reservation and orders were issued to Captains Foulk and Tupper to intercept him.[150] The tracks of approximately 18 Apaches were discovered six miles east of Fort Grant, coming eastwards from Ash Creek, by Jones, a local prospector, and Jones followed this trail until it turned into the Gila Mountains. Two more Sixth Cavalry companies, one from Fort Grant (F Company) the other from Fort Apache (D Company) were mobilised to pursue this trail.[151] The latter company was ordered to pick up the trail at the mouth of Rocky Canyon and to follow it down Ash Creek Valley.[152] The trail was followed to water tanks[153] on the north side of the Gila Mountains, at which point the Apaches scattered.[154] Altogether, in May 1879, four companies, and in June 1879, six companies of the Sixth Cavalry were active scouting for Apaches along the Arizona-New Mexico line.[155]

Despite their failure to find any Apaches, this vigorous response from the troops in Arizona (in spite of a shortage of pack-mules to support the above scouting detachments) encouraged the Apaches to turn eastwards.[156] Lieutenant Blocksom's Apache scout detachment was given the specific credit for forcing this retreat.[157] As the Apaches were now moving back towards New

149 Compton to Willcox, 20 May 1879, Field Records – Troops in Southeastern Arizona, DoAz, NA, RG393, Part 1, Entry 232, Vol.2, Sept 1 1878-27 May, 1879, Letter No. 161; Compton to CO Fort Grant, 17 May 1879, Field Records – Troops in Southeastern Arizona, DoAz, NA, RG393, Part 1, Entry 232, Vol.2, Sept 1 1878-27 May, 1879, Letter No. 155; Willcox to General Comd. DoNM, 19 May 1879, NA, RG393, Part 1, Entry 169, Vol. 9, p.171; Compton to Lt Howard, CO Company 'D', Indian Scouts, 17 May 1879, Field Records – Troops in Southeastern Arizona, DoAz, NA, RG393, Part 1, Entry 232, Vol.2, Sept 1 1878-27 May, 1879, Letter No. 156; Compton, Field Records – Troops in Southeastern Arizona, DoAz, NA, RG393, Part 1, Entry 232, Vol.3, 27 May, 1879-3 July, 1879, Letter No. 175, pp.3-4; Willcox to Hatch, NA, RG393, Part 3, Entry 439, p.191 & Compton to Hatch, NA, RG393, Part 3, Entry 439, p.192.

150 Compton to CO Fort Thomas, 21 May 1879, Field Records – Troops in Southeastern Arizona, DoAz, NA, RG393, Part 1, Entry 232, Vol.2, Sept 1 1878-27 May, 1879, Letter No. 162; Compton, Field Records – Troops in Southeastern Arizona, DoAz, NA, RG393, Part 1, Entry 232, Vol.3, 27 May, 1879-3 July, 1879, Letter No. 175, pp.3-4; See also Letter 25 May 1879 in MacPherson Letters 1 Jan 1879 to 3 September 1880, University of Virginia at Charlottesville.

151 Compton to CO Fort Grant, 27 May 1879, Troops in Southeastern Arizona, DoAz, NA, RG393, Part 1, Entry 232, Vol.3, 27 May, 1879-3 July, 1879, Letter No.173; Compton, Field Records – Troops in Southeastern Arizona, DoAz, NA, RG393, Part 1, Entry 232, Vol.3, 27 May, 1879-3 July, 1879, Letter No. 175, pp.3-4; Compton to CO Fort Bowie, 29 May 1879, Troops in Southeastern Arizona, DoAz, NA, RG393, Part 1, Entry 232, Vol.3, 27 May, 1879-3 July, 1879, Letter No.176, p.4.

152 Compton to CO Fort Thomas, 27 May 1879, Troops in Southeastern Arizona, DoAz, NA, RG393, Part 1, Entry 232, Vol.3, 27 May, 1879-3 July, 1879, Letter No.174.

153 'Tanks' usually refer to natural pools of water caught in depressions or holes in rocks.

154 Compton to Lt. Howard CO Company 'D', Indian Scouts, 30 May 1879, Troops in Southeastern Arizona, DoAz, NA, RG393, Part 1, Entry 232, Vol.3, 27 May, 1879-3 July, 1879, Letter No.181, pp.7-8.

155 See Record of Events May & June 1879 in Returns From Regular Army Cavalry Regiments 1833-1916, 6th Cavalry Regimental Returns 1875 to 1880, NA, M744, Roll 63.

156 Compton, Field Records – Troops in Southeastern Arizona, DoAz, NA, RG393, Part 1, Entry 232, Vol.3, 27 May, 1879-3 July, 1879, Letter No. 175, pp.3-4.

157 Willcox to AG, Presidio, San Francisco, 28 May 1879, NA, RG393, Part 1, Entry 169, Vol. 9, p.161; See also Willcox to Gen. Comd. DoNM, 19 May 1879, NA, RG393, Part 1. Entry 169, Vol. 9, p.171; See also comment by Hatch in Hatch to AAG DoM, 26 May 1879, 'Victorio Files', NA, RG393, M1495, Roll 14; McDowell to AG of the Army, 29 May 1879 in 'Operations re Warm Springs Apaches 1877-79', Letters Rec'd by the AGO, 1871-80, NA, M666, Roll 366.

Mexico, General Willcox told Hatch that he would cooperate with the New Mexico troops.[158] On 30 May 1879, he telegraphed Hatch to argue that:

> there can be no peace until Warm Springs Indians whose families are at San Carlos are either killed, captured or induced to come in. To this end as soon as the present movement is over efforts should be made in concert with Hatch Comd Dist NM to ascertain the place where these Indians are supposed to be bound and a concerted movement will be made against them as soon as our men and animals are rested.[159]

Colonel Orlando Bolivar Willcox commanded the Military Department of Arizona from 1878-1882. During 1879-1881, troops from his Department were regularly called upon to support the troops in New Mexico. (The National Archives)

Bearing this instruction in mind, Compton was instructed to coordinate his efforts with Colonel Hatch to take joint action against the Warm Springs Apaches.[160]

Victorio's return towards his Black Range strongholds via the Mogollon Mountains was also reported to Major Morrow at Fort Bayard. Morrow had received news that American citizens had shot and killed four Apaches and sustained two wounded in a recent skirmish in the San Francisco Valley, after a ranch had been ransacked and the owners had been wounded but able to make their escape[161] (see document file no. 4). The major thought that he could head the Apaches off at Diamond Creek between the Mogollons and the Black Range Mountains. He ordered Lieutenant Patrick Cusack to ride to Fort Cummings from Fort Bliss with A Company, Ninth Cavalry, and Lieutenant Emmet to maintain his pursuit, while he sent C Company, Ninth Cavalry, under Captain Charles Beyer, to march to Diamond Creek to intercept the Apaches.[162]

---

158 Willcox to AG, Presidio, San Francisco, 28 May 1879, NA, RG393, Part 1, Entry 169, Vol. 9, p.161; See also Willcox to Gen. Comd. DoNM, 19 May 1879, NA, RG393, Part 1. Entry 169, Vol. 9, p.171.

159 ? to Compton, Fort Apache, 30 May 1879, NA, RG393, Part 1, Entry 169, Vol. 9, p.168; Compton to Hatch, NA, RG393, Part 3, Entry 439, pp.194-195; Willcox to Compton, Fort Apache, 30 May 1879, Troops in Southeastern Arizona, DoAz, NA, RG393, Part 1, Entry 232, Vol.3, 27 May, 1879-3 July, 1879, Letter No.180, p.7.

160 ? to Compton, Fort Apache, 30 May 1879, NA, RG393, Part 1, Entry 169, Vol. 9, p.168; See also Hatch to CO Fort Bayard, 8 June 1879, Telegrams Sent DoNM, Vol.2, Jan.–Dec. 1879, NA, RG393, Part 3, Entry 431, p.147.

161 Morrow to Loud AAAG Santa Fé, NA, RG393, Part 3, Entry 439, pp.187-188; Hatch to Wilcox & CO Camp Apache, 31 May 1879, Telegrams Sent DoNM, Vol.2, Jan.–Dec. 1879, NA, RG393, Part 3, Entry 431, pp.141-142; 'From the Fresco' *Grant County Herald*, 6 February 1880; *Thirty Four*, 28 May 1879.

162 Morrow, Special Order No.48, 25 May 1879 in Letters Received by HQ DoNM, September-August 1890, NA, RG393, M1088, Roll 37, April-June 1879; Morrow to Loud AAAG Santa Fé, NA, RG393, Part 3, Entry 439, p.187; See also Bi-Monthly Company Muster Rolls for Company A, 9th Cavalry, May/June 1879 in NA, RG94.

Victorio was too quick to be caught by such a clumsy manoeuvre, and on 29 May, Major Morrow reported that, at Diamond Creek, Captain Beyer had picked up the trail from Lieutenant Howard and his Apache scouts, who had been tracking Victorio trail from Arizona, and that he and C Company were in pursuit. Major Morrow estimated that the Apaches were exhausted, and that there was a good chance that they would be caught.[163] Lieutenant Emmet and his Navajo scout detachment, last reported to be in pursuit of Victorio towards San Carlos, in tandem with Lieutenant Gatewood, were also credited with maintaining a 76 mile pursuit from the Arizona border, until Captain Beyer took up the trail at Diamond Creek.[164] As a result of his efforts, Lieutenant Emmet had to return to Bayard, as his stock were unable to go any further.[165] However, Howard stated that the Apaches were also exhausted, and that there was a good chance that Beyer's command would force a fight.[166]

Captain Beyer, with Lieutenant Wright, 31 troopers from C Company and 15 men from L Company, Ninth Cavalry, one civilian and two Navajo scouts, left Fort Bayard on 25 May and picked up a two-day-old trail on 27 May, at the confluence of West Diamond Creek and the Gilita. Beyer reported that the Apaches had driven off two horses and a pony and killed some cattle from the Redmond and Halloway Ranches as they passed through the area. As the detachment followed the trail, they found the remains of several dead cattle that had obviously been slaughtered for food and had been partially or entirely consumed down to the bones.[167] By the end of the following day, Beyer had narrowed the Apaches' lead to a single day. He also reported that his quarry had set alight large areas of brush in an attempt to cover their tracks.[168]

In the meantime, the Apaches took all the horses from a corral only three miles from Fort Bayard on 27 May 1879. Morrow immediately dispatched Lieutenant Hugo with all the remaining cavalry from Fort Bayard in hot pursuit.[169]

On the morning of 29 May, Captain Beyer's detachment had followed the trail east up and over the Miembres (Mimbres) Mountains. The trail then turned to the north east and travelled up a narrow canyon. The discovery of fresh signs prompted Beyer to deploy in skirmish order. As they emerged from this defile and entered slightly more open country, they discovered Apache warriors erecting breastworks on a steep ridge. Victorio raised a white flag and attempted to parley, and in response, Beyer proposed a conference at the mid-point between the two lines. Victorio tried to persuade the captain to come alone into the Apache positions, but the latter did not trust the former's assurance of safe conduct. Victorio then let loose a verbal broadside about his treatment at the hands of the US government. Captain Beyer became convinced that this display was merely a delaying tactic to allow the women and children to escape. He also noted that throughout Victorio's harangue, the

---

163 Morrow to Loud AAAG Santa Fé, NA, RG393, Part 3, Entry 439, p.190; Willcox to AAG, Presidio, San Francisco, 31 May 1879, NA, RG393, Part 1, Entry 169, Vol. 9, pp.170-171 See also McDowell to AG of the Army, 31 May 1879 in 'Operations re Warm Springs Apaches 1877-79', Letters Rec'd by the AGO, 1871-80, NA, M666, Roll 366.

164 Compton to Hatch, NA, RG393, Part 3, Entry 439, pp.197-198.

165 Hatch to Wilcox, 21 May 1879, Telegrams Sent DoNM, Vol.2, Jan.–Dec. 1879, NA, RG393, Part 3, Entry 431, pp.141-142.

166 Hatch to CO Camp Apaches, 31 May 1879, Telegrams Sent DoNM, Vol.2, Jan.–Dec. 1879, NA, RG393, Part 3, Entry 431, pp.141-142.

167 Beyer to Post Adjutant, Fort Bayard, 16 June 1879 in Letters Received by HQ DoNM, September-August 1890, NA, RG393, M1088, Roll 37, File 658-1658, April–June 1879.

168 Beyer to Post Adjutant, Fort Bayard, 16 June 1879 in Letters Received by HQ DoNM, September-August 1890, NA, RG393, M1088, Roll 37, File 658-1658, April–June 1879.

169 Morrow to Loud AAAG Santa Fé, NA, RG393, Part 3, Entry 439, p.186; See also Loud to Hooker, 25 May 1879, Telegrams Sent DoNM, Vol.2, Jan.–Dec. 1879, NA, RG393, Part 3, Entry 431, p.138; NA, RG94, Entry 257 Vol. 896, Medical History, Fort Bayard NM May 1879 which states that "The troops of the garrison were in the field most of the month in pursuit of hostile Indians" (p.13).

Plate 6.7 West Diamond Creek runs down this canyon out of the Black Range. Captain Beyer followed Victorio up the canyon and over the continental divide before catching the Apaches somewhere beyond the ridge on the horizon. (Photo: author)

Plate 6.8 The view down West Diamond Creek Canyon from the same spot as the first photo. This shows only a fraction of the ground covered by Beyer and his men over a month. It also gives a good idea of the rough terrain which the Apaches would try to use to cripple their opponents' horses and hence their ability to maintain pursuit. (Photo: author)

rest of his warriors continued to construct rock breastworks. Beyer's concerns about treachery have to be balanced with his own admission that during the parley he had sent a civilian guide, Foster, and five men to surreptitiously round up 12 horses, two mules and two burros belonging to the Apaches. He advanced his skirmish line to within 200 yards of the Apache positions:

> At 11.50 I ordered the right skirmishers under Sergeant Delemar Benn, Company "L" Ninth Cavalry to move a little more forward and move to the right so as to flank the Indians, all of which was quietly executed. At 11.55 A.M. I gave the order to advance, the firing began, hotly returned by the Indians, the line kept advancing, the men seeking shelter from tree to tree and after about half an hours sharp fighting during which time the right skirmishers under Sergeant Benn, had gotten well around and to the rear of the position held by the Indians, the latter abandoned their works and camp, and retreated down a ridge.[170]

The Apaches quickly scattered and left, and Beyer was unable to mount a pursuit being unable to detect a clear enough trail. He stated that Victorio's position could have held off his attack had the Apaches been 'determined' enough, and claimed that they found clear evidence that some of the Apaches had been hit during the engagement and that at least two of them had possibly been mortally wounded. Beyer reported the capture of a large amount of food and utensils which were then burnt. He lost Private Frank Dorsey, killed; Private George H. Moore was badly wounded; and Private John Scott was slightly wounded. One horse was killed and another mortally wounded during the fight. Captain Beyer also mentioned the following men in his dispatch:

> The following named officers and men deserve special mention for gallantry and bravery displayed viz: 2nd Lieut. Henry H. Wright, Mr John ? Foster, citizen, Sergeant Delemar Benn Company "L" Ninth Cavalry, Sergeant George Lyman, Thomas Boyne, Corporal Isam Malry Co "C" 9' Cavalry and Private Ridgeley Company "L" 9' Cavy also Hostensoyi Navajo Scout.[171]

Beyer marched to Ojo Caliente, where he was ordered to scout down the eastern side of the Black Range, as Hatch believed that the Apaches had fled into Mexico.[172] Finding no trace of

---

170 Beyer to Post Adjutant, Fort Bayard, 16 June 1879 in Letters Received by HQ_DoNM, September-August 1890, NA, RG393, M1088, Roll 37, File 658-1658, April–June 1879; See also Hatch to CO Fort Bayard, 8 June 1879, Telegrams Sent DoNM, Vol.2, Jan.–Dec. 1879, NA, RG393, Part 3, Entry 431, p.148; Hooker to Loud AAAG Santa Fé, NA, RG393, Part 3, Entry 439, pp.200-202; various entries in NA, RG94 Entry 297 Personal File Henry H. Wright Box 334; See also Whipple to AG Washington DC, 6 June 1879, NA, RG393, Part 1, Entry 2538, p.99; Hatch to Compton, Camp Apache, 5 June 1879, Telegrams Sent DoNM, Vol.2, Jan.–Dec. 1879, NA, RG393, Part 3, Entry 431, p.146; Compton to Co Fort Bowie, 4 June 1879, Troops in Southeastern Arizona, DoAz, NA, RG393, Part 1, Entry 232, Vol.3, 27 May, 1879-3 July, 1879, Letter No.185, pp.12-13; Fort Wingate June 1879, Returns from U.S. Military Posts 1800-1916, M617, Roll 1449 in which Beyer reported that one horse was abandoned on the 28 May 1879; Hatch to AAG DoM, 6 June 1879, 'Victorio Files', NA, RG393, M1495, Roll 14; Platt to Comdg Officer DoNM, NA, RG393, Part 3, Entry 439, p.118; Medical History, Fort Bayard NM, May 1879, NA, RG94, Entry 257 Vol. 896, p.13; Whipple to AG Washington D.C., 6 June 1879 in 'Operations re Warm Springs Apaches 1877-79', Letters Rec'd by the AGO, 1871-80, NA, M666, Roll 366; Bi-Monthly Company Muster Rolls for Company I, 9th Cavalry, May/June 1879 in NA, RG94; Thrapp, 1974, p.216; Record of Engagements, p.86; Chronological List, p.47 (Chronological List of Actions &c., with Indians from 1 January 1866 to January 1891. Hereafter referred to as the 'Chronological List'.

171 Beyer to Post Adjutant, Fort Bayard, 16 June 1879 in Letters Received by HQ_DoNM, September-August 1890, NA, RG393, M1088, Roll 37, File 658-1658, April–June 1879.

172 Hatch to AAG DoM, 6 June 1879, 'Victorio Files', NA, RG393, M1495, Roll 14.

the Apaches, he continued to the Florida Mountains before returning to Fort Bayard on 12 June 1879[173] (see document file no. 5). While Hooker ordered Captain Beyer to reconnoitre the eastern side of the Black Range, he also ordered Lieutenant Merritt's company and Lieutenant Emmet's detachment of Navajo scouts to return to Fort Wingate.[174] Lieutenant Cusack, having originally been ordered to Fort Cummings, had also been sent in pursuit of Victorio, and his detachment reached Diamond Creek five days after Beyer took up the pursuit. Here, local ranchers informed him that the trail went towards Ojo Caliente. Proceeding directly to that place, he was informed of Beyer's skirmish by Captain Hooker, and he then engaged in a fruitless scout of the San Mateo Mountains. Cusack was thoroughly unimpressed with the performance of his Navajo scouts, and lobbied his superiors to employ Apache scouts, who he thought were 'better adapted'[175] for scouting this region.[176] Captain Hooker seemed confident that a telling blow had been struck against the Warm Springs Apaches: 'I anticipate more annoyance from the Mescaleros than from Southern Apaches for some time to come, it is very desirable that authority should be granted to employ & ration guides and trailers temporarily as circumstances may require.'[177] Subsequent events may have shown Captain Hooker in a very poor light, but it is clear that he understood enough about Apache warfare to appreciate the need for Indian scouts.

Hooker's instructions to Beyer also indicated an awareness that one could not necessarily assume that a single defeat would be decisive. District Headquarters, Santa Fé, were also cautious: the troops at Forts Bayard and Cummings were informed of Beyer's fight, and were instructed to keep a close watch for Apaches.[178] The lessons of Beyer's fight were not lost on his commander, Major Morrow. He thought that two factors had allowed Captain Beyer's detachment to catch up with Victorio. First, Beyer was accompanied by two Navajo scouts. Unlike Lieutenant Cusack, the major clearly thought that Indian scouts of any description were better than having no Indian scouts at all. Second, and more importantly, the Apache raiding party had been continually pursued, by successive detachments, from Ojo Caliente to Arizona, and then all the way back to the Black Range. However, Morrow also thought that such long pursuits could not guarantee success in the future, as the Apaches usually scattered into small raiding parties which were virtually impossible to track in the mountains. This led to fruitless pursuits with broken-down horses and exhausted men the only result. Without the presence of, preferably Apache, scouts, these small groups could not be tracked back to their base camp and dealt with appropriately[179] (see document file no. 6). This appreciation of the need for Apache scouts was not helped by the bureaucratic reduction, to a maximum of 10, of the official allocation of scouts to the District of New Mexico. In response, Hatch argued that Indian scouts did not work well in groups smaller than 10, and so this reduction meant that there

173 Beyer to Post Adjutant, Fort Bayard, 16 June 1879 in Letters Received by HQ DoNM, September-August 1890, NA, RG393, M1088, Roll 37, File 658-1658, April–June 1879; Hooker to Loud AAAG Santa Fé, NA, RG393, Part 3, Entry 439, p.203.

174 Hooker to Loud AAAG Santa Fé, NA, RG393, Part 3, Entry 439, pp.203-204.

175 It should be noted that Cusack is rather vague in expressing his dissatisfaction. It is fashionable to argue that the Navajo lacked the same 'fighting spirit' of the Apaches but it may also be that the employment of Navajo scouts in the heart of the Warm Springs Apaches' territory was somewhat misguided as they would not know this country as intimately.

176 Cusack to Post Adjutant, Fort Bayard, 16 June 1879 in Letters Received by HQ DoNM, September-August 1890, NA, RG393, M1088, Roll 37 April-June 1879.

177 Hooker to Loud AAAG Santa Fé, NA, RG393, Part 3, Entry 439, pp.204-205.

178 Loud to CO Fort Bayard, 8 June 1879, Telegrams Sent DoNM, Vol.2, Jan.–Dec. 1879, NA, RG393, Part 3, Entry 431, p.148.

179 Morrow to AAAG DoNM, 15 June 1879 in Letters Received by HQ DoNM, September-August 1890, NA, RG393, M1088, Roll 37, File 658-1658, April–June 1879.

could only be one column in the field that was capable of pursuing Apaches.[180] Later in the summer, Hatch also noted the effects of this campaign on the Ninth Cavalry regiment:

> The region over which the Troops are compelled to scout is exceedingly trying on their animals. All the companies require horses to replace those being lost in active service and complete their mounts. The application for horses for this regiment forwarded May 31" 1879 cannot be filled too early.[181]

Thus both Morrow and Hatch were clearly aware of the difficulties of pursuing Apache guerrillas; and yet, over the next two years, beyond requesting additional Apache scouts, they would find no apparent solution to this problem.

Elsewhere, the Tenth Cavalry maintained its scouting activities as envisioned by its commander, and during July 1879 there were six companies of the Tenth Cavalry deployed on scouting duties across western Texas between the Concho River and the New Mexican border. The western line of these operations extended from the Guadalupe Mountains in the north, and as far south as Eagle Springs, less than 20 miles from the Rio Grande and the border with Mexico.[182] In the course of their scouting, these detachments continued to pinpoint water sources, grazing and routes used by Mescalero raiding parties.[183] For the moment, these operations did not prevent Mescalero activities; but the strategy of surveying the area was to prove very successful when Grierson campaigned against the Apaches in July-August 1880.

Indians, believed to be from the Mescalero reservation, were reported to have killed a man and stolen 40 to 50 horses at a distance of 60 miles into Mexico from Presidio, Texas, on 14 June 1879.[184] The Frontier Battalion (Texas Rangers) were in action again that summer, fighting Mescalero raiders on 29 June, and capturing all the Apaches' horses, but themselves losing a couple of horses and two mules laden with five days' supplies. On 1 July, the same rangers caught up with four Mescalero Apaches, but they lost one man in the skirmish and had to leave the Apaches holding the field. A detachment of Tenth Cavalry led by Lieutenant C.R. Ward followed the trail of the raiders and buried the ranger on 4 July. Despite strenuous efforts, this detachment, aided by two of the rangers, failed to catch the raiders[185] (see document file No. 7). In the second half of July,

180 Hatch to AAG, DoM, Fort Leavenworth, 23 June 1879 in Letters Sent by the '9MD/DNM/DoNM', NA, RG393, M1072, Roll 6, Jan–Oct 1879, Letter No.303, p.218.

181 Hatch to AAG, DoM, Fort Leavenworth, 8 July 1879 in Letters Sent by the '9MD/DNM/DoNM', NA, RG393, M1072, Roll 6, Jan–Oct 1879, Letter No332. pp.236-237; Hatch to AAG, DoM, 8 July 1879 in 'Operations re Warm Springs Apaches 1877-79', Letters Rec'd by the AGO, 1871-80, NA, M666, Roll 366.

182 Grierson to AAG, DoTx, 29 July 1879, Letter No.58 in Letters Sent Jan. 31 1878–Sept 15 1879, HQ DoP 1878-1881 NA, M1381 Roll 1.

183 See for example surveying orders given to Captains Carpenter and Viele (Lt R.G. Smither to Capt. L.H. Carpenter, 4 June 1878, NA, RG393, Part 1, Entry 2546, pp.40-43; Lt. R.G. Smither Adjt. 10th Cavalry to Capt. Viele, 13 August 1878, NA, RG393, Part 1, Entry 2546, pp.43-46) and detailed reports submitted by Captains Lebo and Viele detailing such activity. (Capt. Thomas Lebo to Post Adjutant, Fort Davis, Texas, 16 February 1879, NA, RG393, Part 1, Entry 2546, pp.68-104; Capt. Viele to AAAG, DoP, Fort Concho, Texas, 24 January 1879, NA, RG393, Part 1, Entry 2546, pp.25-40) Mary L. Williams sent me a document listing not less than 67 scouting reports (368 pages) from Tenth Cavalry detachments based, mainly at Fort Davis but also at Fort Concho, carried out May 1878 to December 1879.

184 Wm. Russell, Presidio, Texas, to Lt John L. Bullis, Fort Clark, Texas, 13 July 1879, NA, RG393, Part 1, Entry 2546, p.289.

185 Ward to Post Adjutant, 15 July 1879 in Scouting Expedition Reports, Apr. 15, 1878-Dec. 9, 1880, HQ DoP 1878-1881, NA, M1381, Roll 5; 1 Lieut. C.R. Ward, 10th Cavalry to Post Adjutant, Fort Concho, Texas, 15 July 1879, NA, RG393, Part 1, Entry 2546, pp.217-221; Grierson to AAG, San Antonio, 1

another group of raiders was pursued onto the reservation by Captain Viele, who lost the trail when the raiders scattered and their diverse tracks were destroyed by heavy rain.[186] From 14 to 19 July, Lieutenant Robert D. Read, Tenth Cavalry, accompanied by some citizen volunteers, followed the trail of three Mescaleros who had killed a Mexican woman called Candelarias Frias.[187] Six ponies were also stolen. Three dead ponies were found on the trail by the pursuers, having probably been worn out in the Apaches' effort to keep ahead of any pursuit. Lieutenant Read was led into the highest section of the Apache Mountains before the trail was lost on rocky ground. It was assumed that the Apaches had crossed the border into Mexico.[188] On 27 July 1879, a small detachment of six Fourth cavalrymen and one civilian from a camp on the east fork of the Nueces River followed a party of Indians from the Mescalero reservation who had been stealing horses, only giving up the chase when their rations ran out and forced them to return, on 7 August.[189] On 25 or 27 July, a mixed patrol of Tenth cavalrymen and Twenty-Fifth infantrymen commanded by Captain M.L. Courtney clashed with Apaches at Sulphur Springs, near the Sierra Diablo, Texas. Courtney's detachment suffered two men seriously wounded and claimed to have wounded three Apaches in return, two mortally. They also captured nine ponies and a mule, plus horse furniture, a revolver and cartridge belts.[190]

As a result of these raids and skirmishes, five companies – B, D, E, F, and K, Tenth Cavalry – were deployed to the area, with orders to drive the raiders back into the mountains and protect the settlements on the rivers Concho and Pecos. They were also ordered to record the location of all water sources discovered during these scouting trips. Finally, should they discover Indians, they were to 'attack them vigorously, sparing neither horses nor men to insure their destruction, or to inflict the severest punishment which, you will not hesitate to pursue Indians to their reservation,

October 1879 in Telegrams Sent April 24, 1879-June 22, 1880, HQ DoP 1878-1881 NA, M1381 Roll 1, p.82, Letter No.199: The Record of Engagements notes that a man named Anglin was killed on the North Concho River on 30 June 1879. (p.85).

186 Capt. Viele, Fort Davis to AAG, DoTx, 3 August 1879, NA, RG393, Part 1, Entry 2546; Viele to AAAG, DoP, 2 August 1879 in Telegrams Sent April 24, 1879-June 22, 1880, HQ DoP 1878-1881 NA, M1381 Roll 1, pp.53-54, Letter No.143.

187 Carpenter to AAAG, DoP, 14 July 1879 in Register of Telegrams Rec'd Jan. 23, 1878-Feb. 4, 1881, HQ DoP 1878-1881, NA, M1381, Roll 2, p.139, Letter No.93; Smither to CO Fort Stockton & Grierson to AAG, San Antonio, Texas, 15 July 1879 in Telegrams Sent April 24, 1879-June 22, 1880, HQ DoP 1878-1881 NA, M1381 Roll 1, pp.40-41, Letter No.'s 115-116; Carpenter to AAAG, DoP, 17 September, 1879 in Register of Telegrams Rec'd Jan. 23, 1878-Feb. 4, 1881, HQ DoP 1878-1881, NA, M1381, Roll 2, pp.175-176, Letter No.178; 'Tabular Statement of Scouts, DoTx, 1880', NA, RG393, Part 1, Entry 2546, p.627; See also Record of Events July 1879 in Returns From Regular Army Cavalry Regiments 1833-1916, 10th Cavalry Regimental Returns 1873 to 1880, NA, M744, Roll 96; Grierson to AAG, San Antonio, 1 October 1879 in Telegrams Sent April 24, 1879-June 22, 1880, HQ DoP 1878-1881 NA, M1381 Roll 1, p.82, Letter No.199.

188 Grierson to AAG, San Antonio, Texas, 20 July 1879 in Telegrams Sent April 24, 1879-June 22, 1880, HQ DoP 1878-1881 NA, M1381 Roll 1, pp.43-44, Letter No.123.

189 'Tabular Statement of Scouts, DoTx, 1880', NA, RG393, Part 1, Entry 2546, p.625.

190 Carpenter to AAAG, DoP, 27 July 1879 in Telegrams Rec'd , Jan. 23-July 31, 1878 & Oct. 1, 1878–May 17, 1880, HQ DoP 1878-1881, NA, M1381, Roll 3; Grierson to AAG, San Antonio, Texas, 28 July 1880 in Telegrams Sent April 24, 1879-June 22, 1880, HQ DoP 1878-1881 NA, M1381 Roll 1, p.48, Letter No.131; Tabular Statement of Expeditions and Scouts against Indians & c., made in the Department of Texas during the Year ending 30 September, 1879, NA, RG393, Part 1, Entry 2551, Annual Reports of Departments 1879-1881, MDoM; See also Grierson to AAG, San Antonio, 28 July 1879, NA, RG393, Part 1, Entry 2546, pp.223-224; Record of Events August 1879 in Returns From Regular Army Cavalry Regiments 1833-1916, 10th Cavalry Regimental Returns 1873 to 1880, NA, M744, Roll 96; Return for August 1879 in Returns From U.S. Military Posts 1800-1916 Fort Davis, Texas, Jan 1879–June 1891, NA, M617, Roll 298Webb, 1976, p.86.

if practicable.'[191] General Ord requested that General Sheridan issue orders that would allow troops from Texas to follow Apache raiders onto their New Mexico reservation to confiscate stolen property. If such orders could not be issued, Ord argued, pursuits would be pointless.[192]

A Comanche chief reported that, while he was visiting the Fort Stanton reservation during the summer of 1879, three Mescalero Apaches had arrived driving stolen horses, and another seven had arrived claiming that they had had a skirmish with US troops or rangers.[193] The raiding continued, and on 11 August, 17 horses were stolen from a ranch on the Black River, allegedly by Mescalero warriors from the Fort Stanton reservation.[194] This party was followed onto the Mescalero reservation by a detachment led by Lieutenant John McMartin, and 29 stolen horses were recovered (at $2 per horse), though the agent would not hand over the culprits.[195] This pursuit was so close that for a while, the detachment had the raiders in sight; but they could not reduce the distance to 'carbine range.'[196] On 12 August, Lieutenant Maxon, with troops from F Company, Tenth Cavalry, also reported the discovery of a trail of approximately 12 raiders going south, presumably to raid either in Texas or even in Mexico. He alerted Forts Concho and Clark to be on the lookout for these raiders,[197] and he closed the gap between himself and the Apaches, so that the latter, at a point 20 miles from the junction of the Pecos River and the Rio Grande, were forced to scatter into the mountains. Maxon lost their trail but recovered six horses and was commended by Colonel Grierson for pursuing them so closely as to prevent them from raiding.[198]

Colonel Grierson also noted that the Mescalero Apaches did not have a monopoly on brigandage in the area. In one case, a horse-stealing episode from near Camp Charlotte on 25 July, it was not clear whether Anglo-Americans or Apaches were responsible. In another incident, Anglo-American horse thieves were apprehended near Fort Concho by Texan peace officers on 27 July.[199] On 1 August 1879, it was reported that Apaches had attacked a sheep herder and stolen 10 mules and two horses two miles from El Muerto.[200] The raiders were quickly pursued and the stock was recaptured seven miles from El Muerto from a band of Mexicans, who were deemed to have been the ones responsible for stealing it.[201]

Reports were also received from Colonel N.A.M. Dudley, commandant of Fort Stanton, on the effects of illegal liquor trading on the Mescalero reservation. The Mescalero Indian agent had complained to him that large quantities of whiskey were being sold on the reservation. While

---

191 Lt. Smither, Adjutant 10th Cavalry. To Commanding Officer, Company D, 10th Cavalry, Fort Concho, Texas, 26 July 1879, NA, RG393, Part 1, Entry 2546, pp.292-294; See also Col. Grierson's Report for Year ending 31 December 1879, NA, RG393, Part 1, Entry 2546, p.321.

192 Ord to Lieut General, 4 August 1879, NA, RG393, Part 1, Entry 2546, pp.294-295.

193 J.P. Hatch, 4th Cavalry to AAG, DoM, Fort Leavenworth, Kansas, 21 August 1879, NA, RG393, Part 1, Entry 2546, pp.225-227.

194 Capt Van Valzah, 25th Infantry, to AAG, DoTx, 12 August 1879, NA, RG393, Part 1, Entry 2546, p.290.

195 Record of Events September, 1879 in Returns From Regular Army Cavalry Regiments 1833-1916, 10th Cavalry Regimental Returns 1873 to 1880, NA, M744, Roll 96; Ord to AG, MDoM, 29 August 1879, NA, RG393, Part 1, Entry 2546, p.301; 'Tabular Statement of Scouts, DoTx, 1880', NA, RG393, Part 1, Entry 2546, p.631.

196 'Tabular Statement of Scouts, DoTx, 1880', NA, RG393, Part 1, Entry 2546, p.631.

197 Grierson to AAG, DoTx, 14 August 1879, NA, RG393, Part 1, Entry 2546, pp.298-299.

198 Grierson to AAG, San Antonio, Texas, 21 August 1879 in Telegrams Sent April 24, 1879–June 22, 1880, HQ DoP 1878-1881 NA, M1381 Roll 1, pp.62-63, Letter No.161.

199 Grierson to AAG, DoTx, 29 July 1879, NA, RG393, Part 1, Entry 2546, p.303.

200 Lt. Wilson, 25th Infantry to CO, Fort Davis 2 August 1879 in Telegrams Sent April 24, 1879–June 22, 1880, HQ DoP 1878-1881 NA, M1381 Roll 1, p.53, Letter No.142.

201 Viele to Smither, 3 August 1879 in Telegrams Sent April 24, 1879-June 22, 1880, HQ DoP 1878-1881 NA, M1381 Roll 1, p.54, Letter No.144; Viele to AAAG, DoP, 3 August 1879 in Telegrams Rec'd, Jan. 23-July 31, 1878 & Oct. 1, 1878–May 17, 1880, HQ DoP 1878-1881, NA, M1381, Roll 3.

Dudley doubted the quantity alleged, he did point out to his superiors that the nature of the rough terrain made it impossible to prevent either whiskey smugglers trying to penetrate the reservation or Mescaleros slipping out of its bounds.[202]

This on-going situation prompted Colonel Grierson and Lieutenant General Sheridan to pinpoint the Mescalero reservation as the source of most raids in New Mexico and north-western Texas, with Sheridan describing the reservation as 'a refuge for murderers and thieves.'[203] This developing reputation of the reservation, in the eyes of the US army, would form a key element in the army's operations against the Apaches in April 1880.

In Mexico, columns of troops under the command of General Trevino were in the field, probably in western Coahuila, in pursuit of Indian raiders. One of these columns, led by Colonel Pedro Valdez, pursued a band of Indians to the Rio Grande but, in compliance with orders from General Trevino, did not cross the river. Valdez's scouts detected the raiders' return and pursued them for approximately 100 miles, before catching them on 26 June, at Tinaja de los Lipanes, killing one, and capturing their possessions before they scattered. Between 18 June and 2 August 1879, a second column, commanded by Colonel Nicanor Valdez, trawled the Sierras along the Rio Grande and counted three trails of Indians laden with plunder who had crossed the Rio Grande into Texas.[204]

Indeed, a letter from General Trevino dated 11 June 1879,[205] which criticised the United States' apparent inability to prevent Apaches raiding into Mexico, was read with 'painful interest' by F.W. Seward, Acting US Secretary of State.[206] This prompted General Ord to conduct an investigation into reports of pursuits dating back to 1877, and he also concluded that the Fort Stanton reservation was the likely source of the raids, an opinion firmly endorsed by General Sheridan. Sheridan also saw direct military control of the reservations as the only means of curbing these raids.[207] General Pope, while sympathising with this sentiment, pinpointed the problems of 1) having too few troops to effectively police the Mescalero reservation, 2) having, often, quite scant evidence that the raiders had originated from the Fort Stanton reservation, and 3) having the dual involvement of the Indian and the War Departments concerning the control of the Indians.[208]

In his response to Ord's findings, Colonel Hatch pointed out that there were 'renegade' Warm Springs Chiricahuas based in Chihuahua and Sonora who were happy to raid across the Arizona, New Mexico and Texas borders.[209] His solution was cross-border cooperation between US and Mexican troops. One of the key advantages these Apaches enjoyed was an ability to slip to the

202 Dudley to AAAG Santa Fé, 9 December 1878, NA, RG393, Part 1, Entry 2546, pp.2-5.

203 Sheridan to Sherman, 9 August 1879, NA, RG393, Part 1, Entry 2546, pp.296-297; See also Col. Grierson's Report for Year ending 31 December 1879, NA, RG393, Part 1, Entry 2546, p.321.

204 Hunter to George W. McCrary, Secretary of War 6 November 1879, informing latter of communication between the Mexican Ambassador and W.M. Evarts, Secretary of State, 28 October 1879, containing copies of reports submitted by both Colonels Valdez, NA, RG393, Part 1, Entry 2546, pp.207-216.

205 Trevino to Ord, 11 June 1879, NA, RG393, Part 1, Entry 2546, pp.168-170.

206 Seward to G.W. McCrary, Secretary of War, 12 August 1879, NA, RG393, Part 1, Entry 235, pp.9-10.

207 See collection of reports attached to report submitted by Ord to HQ MDoM, 9 July 1879, NA, RG393, Part 1, Entry 2546, p.170-193.

208 Pope to Whipple, 4 September, 1879, NA, RG393, Part 1, Entry 2546, pp.198-202.

209 In response to an 1878 report from Mexico that Apaches from U.S. Reservations were raiding in Mexico. Hatch argued such reports "must be an error" and that these depredations were committed by Indians whose home territory had always been in Mexico and a few renegades from Arizona and possibly from Indian Territory. (Hatch to AAG, DoM, Fort Leavenworth, 1 October 1878 in Letters Sent by the '9MD/DNM/DoNM', NA, RG393, M1072, Roll 6, Letter No.437 pp.303-304; Hatch to AAG, DoM, 28 May 1879 in Letters Sent by the '9MD/DNM/DoNM', NA, RG393, M1072, Roll 6, Jan-Oct 1879, Letter No.257, pp.187-190.)

other side of the border when either Mexican or US troops were conducting operations against them. This advantage would be lost if the two countries arranged to act in tandem.[210]

Back in the District of New Mexico, Morrow informed District Headquarters in Santa Fé that the Department of Arizona had furnished him with some Apache scouts.[211] Thus Morrow intended to send out 'three columns' after Victorio and requested that an additional company be ordered south to the Caballo Mountains to cooperate with these detachments from Fort Bayard.[212] These columns were to set forth between 2 and 3 July, and were to converge on the Caballo Mountains from Ojo Caliente, Fort Bayard and Fort Bliss.[213] Hatch reported that after the fight with Captain Beyer, Victorio was thought to have regrouped in the Mimbres Mountains and to have been joined by other renegade Apaches from Arizona, New Mexico and Mexico. Overall, six companies of Ninth Cavalry, in five detachments, were in pursuit of Victorio during June 1879.[214] Nevertheless, *Thirty-Four* reported several raids on the Mimbres River settlements in late June, with a man named Pablo Montoya killed at Perrault's Ranch.[215] Hatch was also concerned enough about the alleged lively trade between the Apaches and the local Mexican communities near Fort Craig (including Paraje, San Jose, Palomas, and Cañada Alamosa) to contact the US attorney for the Territory of New Mexico, no doubt with a view to dealing with individuals found to be running guns and ammunition to the Apaches.[216]

In the event, Victorio pre-empted Morrow's operation by arriving at the Mescalero reservation on 30 June 1879, though Colonel Hatch claimed this was as a result of the pressure applied by the Ninth Cavalry.[217] Victorio followed his usual tactic of 'testing the water' before committing himself to face-to-face talks with the Mescalero agent. On 24 June, a Warm Springs Apache was brought into the Mescalero agency and informed Russell that Victorio was ensconced in the Black Range. Two Apaches were sent out with assurances that the Warm Springs Apaches would receive good treatment if they came in.[218] Victorio informed the agent there that he desired only 'peace and quiet.'[219] His people's main concern was that they were totally opposed to a move to San Carlos,

210 Hatch to AAG, DoM, 14 August 1879, NA, RG393, Part 1, Entry 2546, pp.202-205.

211 Letter 6 July 1879 in MacPherson Letters 1 Jan 1879 to 3 September 1880, University of Virginia at Charlottesville.

212 Morrow to Loud AAAG Santa Fé, NA, RG393, Part 3, Entry 439, p.206; Hatch to Hooker, 1 July 1879, Telegrams Sent DoNM, Vol.2, Jan.–Dec. 1879, NA, RG393, Part 3, Entry 431, p.158.

213 Loud to CO's Forts Bayard & Bliss, 2 July 1879, Telegrams Sent DoNM, Vol.2, Jan.–Dec. 1879, NA, RG393, Part 3, Entry 431, p.159; Bi-Monthly Company Muster Rolls for Company's A & L, 9th Cavalry, May/June 1879 in NA, RG94.

214 Hatch to AAG, DoM, Fort Leavenworth, 8 July 1879 in Letters Sent by the '9MD/DNM/DoNM', NA, RG393, M1072, Roll 6, Jan-Oct 1879, Letter No332. pp.236-237.

215 *Thirty Four*, 25 June 1879.

216 U.S. Attorney (requesting more detailed information concerning this trade as outlined in a letter rec'd from Hatch dated 9 June 1879) to Hatch, 11 July 1879 in Letters Received by HQ_DoNM, September-August 1890, NA, RG393, M1088, Roll 38 July–Sept. 1879.

217 Hatch to AAG, DoM, Fort Leavenworth, 8 July 1879 in Letters Sent by the '9MD/DNM/DoNM', NA, RG393, M1072, Roll 6, Jan-Oct 1879, Letter No332. pp.236-237; See also comments by Surgeon MacPherson in Letter 18 July 1879 in MacPherson Letters 1 Jan 1879 to 3 September 1880, University of Virginia at Charlottesville.

218 Russell to Hatch, 30 June 1879 in Letters Received by HQ_DoNM, September-August 1890, NA, RG393, M1088, Roll 38 July–Sept. 1879.

219 Hatch to AAG, DoM, Fort Leavenworth, 8 July 1879 in Letters Sent by the '9MD/DNM/DoNM', NA, RG393, M1072, Roll 6, Jan-Oct 1879, Letter No332. pp.236-237; Hatch to CO Fort Apache, 10 July 1879, NA, RG393, Part 1, Entry 235, p.5; Thrapp, 1974, p.217; see also (Loud to CO Fort Bayard and Hatch to AAG Fort Leavenworth, 30 June 1879, Telegrams Sent DoNM, Vol.2, Jan.–Dec. 1879, NA, RG393, Part 3, Entry 431, p.162; Gatewood to AAG DoAz, 18 July 1879, Troops in Southeastern Arizona, DoAz, NA, RG393, Part 1, Entry 232, Vol.4, 3 July, 1879–Dec. 13 1879, p.15; Reeve, p.308; Billington, 1991, p.89; Worcester, p.218.

to which Russell responded with assurances that they would be allowed to stay on the reservation so long as they kept the peace. Russell also promised to do what he could to get their families sent to them from San Carlos, predicting that if this could be accomplished it would mean 'the end of all the long and serious trouble with the Warm Spring Indians.'[220] In the meantime he 'gave those that were here a small quantity of clothing, provision enough to last them until the regular issue and they left in good spirits.'[221] Victorio and his followers were also stated as being present at an issue of rations on or just prior to 26 July 1879 by Lieutenant M.F. Goodwin, who reported that Agent Russell had promised that the troops would not attack them so long as they kept to the reservation.[222]

Indeed, by this time, the US authorities were becoming increasingly receptive to the idea of a reservation around Ojo Caliente.[223] Hatch argued that those Warm Springs Apaches still at San Carlos should be sent to the Mescalero reservation.[224] He was so encouraged by these developments that he predicted that the US army could be withdrawn from Ojo Caliente sometime in September or October 1879.[225]

This state of affairs failed to impress the editor of *Thirty-Four*, who accused the US army of preferring to 'sue for peace with him [Victorio] and reward him for his crimes than to punish him'[226] even when the troops apparently had the Apaches at their mercy.[227] He also claimed that the Mescalero Indian agent had captured the Apaches using the most deadly of weapons: 'sugar, coffee, flour, beef and beans.'[228] *Thirty-Four* would later claim that the Mescalero reservation was a base for all Indian renegades from Texas, New Mexico, Arizona and Mexico, where they could safely dispose of the proceeds of their brigandage.[229]

This newspaper had earlier fired the opening shots of what would become a major feud between much of the territorial press and the US army. It claimed that Captain Beyer had been beaten by a mere 18 Apaches in his fight against Victorio in May 1879. The original source of this story was said to be a miner from Hillsboro. It also noted that Beyer's command had passed through Las Cruces on 4 June, and that only hours after their departure, six horses were stolen by Apaches.[230] The newspaper later admitted that some of its original story might have been less than accurate; but it still maintained that Beyer had been 'ignominiously defeated.'[231] For the moment, it would remain a lone dissenting voice amongst the press. This vitriol is somewhat explained by the fact that

220 Russell to CoIA, 30 June 1879 in 'Operations re Warm Springs Apaches 1877-79', Letters Rec'd by the AGO, 1871-80, NA, M666, Roll 366.
221 Russell to CoIA, 30 June 1879 in 'Operations re Warm Springs Apaches 1877-79', Letters Rec'd by the AGO, 1871-80, NA, M666, Roll 366.
222 Goodwin to Post Adjutant, Fort Stanton, 26 July 1879 in Letters Received by HQ DoNM, September-August 1890, NA, RG393, M1088, Roll 38 July–Sept. 1879.
223 Martin AA Genl. to Gen. Willcox, Palace Hotel, San Francisco, 8 August 1879, NA, RG393, Part 1, Entry 169, Vol. 9, p.293.
224 Hatch to Wilcox, 4 August 1879, Telegrams Sent DoNM, Vol.2, Jan.–Dec. 1879, NA, RG393, Part 3, Entry 431, p.189.
225 Hatch to Hooker, 14 August 1879 in Letters Sent by the '9MD/DNM/DoNM', NA, RG393, M1072, Roll 6, Jan-Oct 1879, Letter No.392, p.279.
226 'Victorio' Editorial, *Thirty Four*, 20 August 1879.
227 'Victorio' Editorial, *Thirty Four*, 20 August 1879.
228 *Thirty Four*, 16 July 1879.
229 *Thirty Four*, 13 August 1879.
230 *Thirty Four*, 18 June 1879; it should be noted that on the 4 of June Beyer, according to his own report was moving between Las Animas Canyon and McEvers' Ranch. (Letters Received by HQ DoNM, September-August 1890, NA, RG393, M1088, Roll 37, File 658-1658, April–June 1879; See also Hatch to CO Fort Bayard, 8 June 1879, Telegrams Sent DoNM, Vol.2, Jan.–Dec. 1879, NA, RG393, Part 3, Entry 431, p.148.)
231 *Thirty Four*, 25 June 1879.

Plate 6.9 The Caballo Mountains seen from the floor of the Rio Grande valley. These mountains afford an excellent perspective to the west over the Rio Grande valley and to the east over the Jornada Del Muerto desert. Even if Major Morrow had managed to trap Victorio in these mountains, once ensconced, the Apaches would have been very difficult to overcome. (Photo: author)

Plate 6.10 The stunning view from the top of the Caballo Mountains. The Rio Grande can be seen snaking its way through the valley floor far below. This made these mountains an ideal refuge and observation post for the Apaches. (Photo: author)

this newspaper was based in the very area that the Apaches were periodically raiding and it only reflected the general feeling of the local US citizenry.

It should be noted that, just because Victorio and Nana were now on the Mescalero reservation, this did not necessarily entail a cessation of hostilities. Sometime in June, a small 'Indian' trail was discovered near Ojo Caliente. Captain Hooker sent out Lieutenant D.H. Clark, Fifteenth Infantry, and 12 men from E Company, Ninth Cavalry, to follow the trail. Later that day, around noon, Lieutenant Cusack with G Company, Ninth Cavalry, accompanied by Navajo scouts commanded by Lieutenant James Maney, Fifteenth Infantry, arrived at Ojo Caliente. Hooker, concerned that Lieutenant Clark might be too inexperienced to call for reinforcements, devised a plan whereby he and Lieutenant Cusack would attempt to cut off and trap the Apaches. The trail appeared to be making for Red Canyon in the San Mateo Mountains. It was predicted that the Apaches might then make for the San Andres Mountains, across the Rio Grande. In response, Lieutenant Cusack's detachment was to follow Clark, while Hooker, leaving a small guard at Ojo Caliente, was to take the balance of his company to Cañada Alamosa and move up the far side of the San Mateo Mountains, in an attempt to head off the Apaches.[232] There is no record of the outcome of this expedition, so it is safe to assume that no Apaches were encountered.

In Arizona, Lieutenant Gatewood with his Apache scout company had undertaken a long reconnoitre from Fort Apache through the Gila country to Silver City, setting out on 19 June, and arriving at Fort Bayard on 7 or 8 July. He was ordered to stay there until his scouts had rested and then return to Fort Apache.[233] Gatewood cabled from Bayard a rumour that 'Joronoma' [Geronimo] had left 'Hoo' [Juh] and was supposedly making for New Mexico.[234] A fresh Apache trail going east was discovered on 2 August near Fort Bowie, and Lieutenant Blocksom was sent out to follow it up. The commander of Fort Huachuca was also instructed to contact the Mexican army commander in Fronteras to alert him to the presence of Apaches raiders making for the border.[235] From San Bernadino, almost on the Mexican line, Blocksom followed the trail of four Indians and one Mexican 160 miles to where he found the remains of a camp. He estimated that as many as 60 Apaches had been in this camp, which was six days old. The trail had then turned further south into Mexico. Mexican travellers encountered on the way back to Camp Rucker informed Blocksom that approximately 200 Apaches were in the vicinity of Casas Grandes in Chihuahua.[236] In Sonora, they had allegedly killed two men, wounded a third and stolen a large number of horses

232 Capt. Hooker's rebuttal statement in Captain Charles Steelhammer, Ojo Caliente, to AAAG DoNM, 11 December 1879 (Hereafter referred to as 'Steelhammer Report'), in Letters Received by HQ DoNM, September-August 1890, NA, RG393, M1088 Roll 38, File 1664-2491, July–Sept.ember 1879.

233 Compton to Arnold, Fort Apache, 11 July 1879, Troops in Southeastern Arizona, DoAz, NA, RG393, Part 1, Entry 232, Vol.4, 3 July, 1879–Dec. 13 1879, p.6; Arnold to Gatewood, 18 July 1879, Troops in Southeastern Arizona, DoAz, NA, RG393, Part 1, Entry 232, Vol.4, 3 July, 1879–Dec. 13 1879, p.15.

234 Arnold to CO Fort Lowell, 18 July 1879, Troops in Southeastern Arizona, DoAz, NA, RG393, Part 1, Entry 232, Vol.4, 3 July, 1879–Dec. 13 1879, p.14.

235 McLellan, CO Fort Bowie to Blocksom, 3 August 1879, Troops in Southeastern Arizona, DoAz, NA, RG393, Part 1, Entry 232, Vol.4, 3 July, 1879–Dec. 13 1879, Letter No.35, p.22; Arnold to AAG Dept. Arizona, 4 August 1879, Troops in Southeastern Arizona, DoAz, NA, RG393, Part 1, Entry 232, Vol.4, 3 July, 1879–Dec. 13 1879, Letter No.30, p.18; Arnold to CO Huachuca, 10 August 1879, Troops in Southeastern Arizona, DoAz, NA, RG393, Part 1, Entry 232, Vol.4, 3 July, 1879–Dec. 13 1879, p.28; Arnold to Commander of Mexican Forces Stationed at Fronteras, 11 August 1879, Troops in Southeastern Arizona, DoAz, NA, RG393, Part 1, Entry 232, Vol.4, 3 July, 1879–Dec. 13 1879, Letter No.47, pp.29-30.

236 Blocksom to Arnold, Fort Grant, 26 August 1879, Troops in Southeastern Arizona, DoAz, NA, RG393, Part 1, Entry 232, Vol.4, 3 July, 1879–Dec. 13 1879, Letter No.75, p.49.

and mules in the vicinity of Santa Cruz.[237] This suggests that a party led by Geronimo may have been responsible for attacks in the USA, perhaps hoping to pick up ammunition, while Juh raided around Santa Cruz.

Captain Hooker reported the recovery of horses stolen by 24 Apache raiders from San Jose on the Rio Grande on or around 13 August. Lieutenant F.B. Taylor had followed the trail to a Navajo camp near Fort Wingate, where he recovered the horses, which the Apaches had traded with the Navajos. The raiders had returned to the San Jose area where they had briefly skirmished with 'citizens' before making off eastwards in the direction of the Mescalero reservation.[238] This led Hooker to assume the raiders were Mescaleros, yet it is possible that they were Warm Springs Apaches under Nana, who had set up camp in the Riconada, a remote section of the Mescalero reservation, during this period. The previous day, Hooker had reported widespread raiding to the northwest of Ojo Caliente. Moreover, in response to earlier reports of raiding in the Datil and Mogollon Mountains, he had sent a small detachment west to Tularosa (the site of the Warm Springs Apache reservation from 1872-4), and was now short of officers and men. To deal with this situation, he sought cooperation from troops stationed at Forts Bayard and Wingate. He also reported no signs of Apaches in the San Mateo and Mimbres Mountains.[239] In fact, despite his rather limited resources, Captain Hooker maintained quite a vigorous programme of patrols and escorts during July and August, 1879.

Table 6.1 Patrols from Ojo Caliente, July and August 1879

7-12 July	Lieutenant Taylor and 22 enlisted men scout through the San Mateo Mountains.
12-15 August	Lieutenant Taylor and 15 enlisted men scout through the San Mateo Mountains.
13-15 August	First Sergeant Robinson and 4 enlisted men scout the mountains to the west.
15 August	Sergeant Williams sent to scout through mountains to the north west. Returns same day. Size of detachment unknown.
16-30 August	Lieutenant Taylor and 25 enlisted men pursue raiders to Navajo Camp at Alamocito.
28 August	Sergeant Howard and 4 enlisted men with 9 days' rations sent to scout towards Tularosa.
Regularly patrolled by escorts and couriers throughout July and August	Route between Ojo Caliente and Paraje via Cañada Alamosa and San Jose. Route between Ojo Caliente and Alamocito via Monica and Pueblo Springs.

The key point about this activity between western Texas and eastern Arizona, and on both sides of the border, between 1876 and 1879, is that there was a low level of conflict between the USA and Mexico on the one side, and Mescalero and Chiricahua Apaches on the other. This was not isolated raiding by a few renegade Apaches; and certainly, where the various branches of the Chiricahua Apaches were concerned, much of this activity was a rejection of the concentration policy.

237 Arnold to AAG Dept. Arizona, 4 August 1879, Troops in Southeastern Arizona, DoAz, NA, RG393, Part 1, Entry 232, Vol.4, 3 July, 1879–Dec. 13 1879, Letter No.30, p.18.

238 Taylor to Hooker, 31 August 1879 in Letters Received by HQ DoNM, September-August 1890, NA, RG393, M1088, Roll 38, July–Sept. 1879; Hooker to Loud, AAAG Santa Fé, 30 August 1879, NA, RG393, Part 3, Entry 439, pp.216-217 & pp.223-224; See also Loud to CO Fort Bayard, Telegrams Sent DoNM, Vol.2, Jan.–Dec. 1879, NA, RG393, Part 3, Entry 431, pp.203-204; Return for August 1879 in Returns From U.S. Military Posts 1800-1916 Ojo Caliente, New Mexico, May 1879-Mar. 1882, NA, M617, Roll 877.

239 Hooker to Loud AAAG Santa Fé, NA, RG393, Part 3, Entry 439, pp.218-220 & pp.223-224.

Moreover, this low-level conflict was still intensive enough for the US Army to attempt to develop more effective ways to counter Apache guerrillas. The lessons concerning the use of Apache scouts were, appreciated by most, but not all, field officers in the Southwest. However, some other innovations were less effective. For example, as a result of the continued field operations against independent Apaches, Colonel Hatch became convinced that pack mules were not particularly effective, and he suggested that burros (donkeys) might be a more viable alternative.[240] Hatch received permission to hire a number of burros to test out their suitability in an experiment to be based at Fort Bayard.[241] As pack burro trains did not replace mule trains during the remainder of the Apache Wars, it would appear that this experiment was a failure or was never actually initiated. It is worth noting that Captain Moore, in 1868, had already reported that pack burros were a complete failure in this region.[242] The reason why mules had proved less effective than Hatch had hoped could have been due to the failure to deploy *enough* of them. Captain Moore argued that extra mules should be employed in a couple of shifts to avoid mules dying of exhaustion from being constantly loaded with supplies.

Returning to Victorio, his apparent settlement on the Mescalero reservation might have suggested that he was heading towards a period of relative peace. However, we should be very wary of assuming that Victorio had given up his goal of a reservation at Ojo Caliente; and his settlement on the reservation may just have been intended to allow him a temporary respite before he resumed his campaign. Soon, strife between the Warm Springs and Mescalero Apaches was reported in the local press.[243] The apparent lull in low-level conflict was about to be shattered.

The most popular story concerning the outbreak of hostilities is that, following earlier raiding, the legal representatives of the citizens of Grant County, New Mexico had issued three warrants against Victorio for horse thieving and murder. The Apache leader had apparently been made aware of these charges. Therefore, when a judge and prosecuting attorney entered the Mescalero reservation on a hunting and fishing trip, Victorio, fearing treachery, arrived at the conclusion that he was their target. He gathered the Warm Springs Apaches present and fled.[244] At first glance this is a bizarre event to trigger a declaration of war. Yet this may have been the case: the hunting expedition could have seemed the culmination of a long series of provocations which saw Victorio increasingly forced into opting for an all-out war.

This story surfaced in October 1879, in a report from Russell, the Mescalero Apache agent. He stated that 'Mr Fountain', one of the officials who had entered the reservation, had heard this story from the Apaches. Fountain was well known to many of the Apaches as he had lived in the area for several years.[245] It should be noted that Russell's story was dismissed in some quarters as a complete

---

240 Hatch to AAG, DoM, Fort Leavenworth, 3 September, 1879 in Letters Sent by the '9MD/DNM/DoNM', NA, RG393, M1072, Roll 6, Jan-Oct 1879, Letter No.437, pp.311-312.

241 Platt AAG, Fort Leavenworth to CO DoNM, 17 October 1879 in Letters Received by HQ DoNM, September-August 1890, NA, RG393, M1088, Roll 39, Oct-Dec 1879.

242 Capt. Moore, 38th Inf. CO Fort Cummings to Lt. E. Hunter AAAG, DoNM, 27 November 1868 in Letters sent Vol.3 June 24 1867-Jan. 20 1869 H.Q. Records, Fort Cummings, NA, RG393, M1081, Roll 1, pp.141-145.

243 *Thirty Four*, 13 August 1879.

244 See Dept of Interior (passing on letter from Russell to CoIA dated 18 October 1879) to Sec. of War, 4 November 1879 in Letters Received by HQ DoNM, September-August 1890, NA, RG393, M1088, Roll 39, Oct-Dec 1879; Thrapp, 1967, p.181 see also 1974, p.217; Thrapp, 1988, p.513; Reeve, pp.308-309; Debo, p.119; Worcester, pp.218-219; Opler & Opler, p.28; Haley, 1981, pp.320-321.

245 Russell to Commissioner for Indian Affairs, 18 October 1879 in Papers relating to military operations against Chief Victorio's band of Mescalero Apache in southern New Mexico, 1879-81 in Letters Rec'd by the AGO, 1871-80, (Hereafter referred to as 'Victorio Papers'), NA, M666, Roll 526; Same letter also contained in Letters Received, DoM 1868-98, RG 393, Entry A1-1 2601, Box 85; 'The Apache War' *Army & Navy Journal*, Vol.17, 8 November 1879, p.264.

lie. Ashenfelter, the editor of the *Grant County Herald*, angrily accused Russell of trying to throw the blame for the war onto the local settlers in his report on the breakout to the Commissioner of Indian Affairs.[246] However, Ashenfelter may have been a less than detached commentator, as he stated that, 'The editor of this paper was foreman of the Grand Jury which indicted Victorio, and, as his fellow jurymen will acknowledge, the evidence was sufficient to have convicted any white man'[247] (see document file no. 8).

That the local authorities were capable of issuing arrest warrants for Apache leaders is indisputable, as the arrest warrant for Mangus reproduced later in this chapter attests. The author has yet to see an original warrant for the arrest of Victorio, but there is a source which quotes the original arrest warrant:

> Mr Griggs also has a warrant to the sheriff of Dona Ana county for the arrest of the Apache chief Victorio, which is a source of amusement to old timers who recall that it required the armies of two countries to subdue the wily savage. On the warrant is a note by the sheriff reading: "I have sought diligently for him and have failed to find him."
>
> The warrant against Victoria[248] is signed by John Sherman, Jr., and H.J. Cuniff, United States marshals, Sept. 6, 1879.[249]

Mangus, son of Mangas Coloradas. His activities in the Victorio Campaign are obscure but there are indications that he may have led a significant number of Chihenne Apaches between 1879 and 1881. The US army were certainly convinced that he was a significant leader in the Victorio Campaign. (The National Archives)

If one examines the arrest warrant for Mangus, which was issued by the same individuals, one can discern some very interesting similarities between it and features of the Victorio arrest warrant referred to above. Sherman appears to have very sensibly ensured that his 'diligence' did not pay dividends. Had Sherman found Victorio or Mangus and attempted to serve these warrants, one can only speculate as to the marshal's probable destiny. This also explains the amused reaction to Sherman's annotated comment appended to the warrant among those who could remember those times.

Thus, while there is no doubt that an arrest warrant was issued for the Chihenne leader, it is open to question whether it provoked an

246 'Cause of the Apache Outbreak', *Grant County Herald,* 8 November 1879; Ashenfelter Editorial – *Grant County Herald*, 29 November 1880.

247 'Cause of the Apache Outbreak', *Grant County Herald*, 8 November 1879; See also comments made in 'Victorio' Editorial *Thirty Four*, 20 August 1879.

248 As spelled in the source utilised. One suspects that this is no accident and that the original arrest warrant was issued for the arrest of 'Victoria' rather than 'Victorio'.

249 Griggs, G. (1974), *History of the Old West* (Bronson Printing Co,: Las Cruces N.M.) p.104.

outright declaration of war on the USA by Victorio. The Apache version of events recounts two further possible reasons, but also contradicts actions reported by Russell himself. Eve Ball recounts how Victorio was prevented from drawing rations by the Mescalero agent, S.A. Russell, who would not issue food to the Warm Springs Apaches until given permission by Washington. Such permission would take more than three weeks to be received. While angered, Victorio merely informed Russell that a month was: 'a long time to be without food.'[250]

In the meantime, Victorio received food from a sympathetic Anglo-American trader, Dr Joseph C. Blazer, who ran a trading post near the agency.[251] It was Blazer who tipped off Victorio to the existence of the arrest warrants. The arrival of additional troops in the area prompted Victorio to visit Russell for a second time. The agent's offhand manner was, however, too much for Victorio:

> Kaytennae looked at his chief and Victorio nodded. The young man grabbed the agent's long beard and dragged him about his office, the agent all the while imploring the interpreter to "talk pretty" to Victorio. Jose Carillo was thoroughly enjoying the spectacle, and not until Kaytennae had kicked the agent out of his own office did Jose convey the message.[252]

Victorio having assaulted the agent, all that was required to provoke a breakout was the coincidental appearance of a US cavalry detachment at Blazer's store.[253]

Sherry Robinson, on reviewing Eve Ball's unpublished material, argues that it was Russell's initial refusal to issue rations which provoked the assault, this time administered by Victorio himself. The Apaches believed that Russell had then telegraphed for troops from Fort Stanton, and it was their imminent arrival which prompted Victorio's flight.[254] Certainly, Russell is on record as having recommended that Victorio and his Warm Springs Apaches would benefit from harsh chastisement from the US army.[255]

Equally, as noted earlier, Russell claimed to have issued rations and clothing to the Warm Springs Apaches on their arrival. Furthermore, in July, Lieutenant Goodwin strongly implied that the Warm Springs Apaches were drawing rations. Finally, it should be noted that Russell, on 26 April, in response to instructions from the Commissioner of Indian Affairs, stated that he was happy to accept the Warm Springs Apaches onto his reservation.[256]

The key point is that the Apache version of events highlights a combination and culmination of several short-term factors – arrest warrants, red tape and US troop movements – rather than the single appearance of an isolated hunting party,[257] as the precipitators of Victorio's breakout.[258] We

250 Ball, 1970, p.62.
251 Ball, 1962, p.23.
252 Ball, 1970, p.63; see also Ball, 1962, p.40.
253 Ball, 1962, p.40 & 1970, p.63.
254 Robinson, 2000, pp.146-147.
255 Thrapp, 1974, p.220.
256 Russell to Loud, 26 April 1879 in Letters Received by HQ DoNM, September-August 1890, NA, RG393, M1088, Roll 37 April-June 1879.
257 Which on sober reflection could have encountered more than it had bargained for by entering the Mescalero Reservation whether in search of Victorio or not.
258 There is even a remote possibility that a U.S. Army detachment had clashed with Victorio's warriors in early August 1879. Moore states that the Warm Springs Apaches had lost three warriors and some horses in a skirmish between fifty two Ninth Cavalrymen commanded by Captain H. Carroll and Lt Wright's 19 Navajo scouts. This took place to the south of the reservation along Dog Canyon in the Sacramento Mountains. (Moore, p.212) However, this skirmish actually seems to have occurred in the summer of 1878 and it is by no means certain that the Apaches involved belonged to Victorio's band. (Leckie, 1967, p.191) The Chronological List dates this skirmish to 5 August, 1878. (p.45) Lt. Wright's personal file dates this skirmish to 6 August, 1878. (NA, RG94 Entry 297 Personal File Henry H. Wright Box 334)

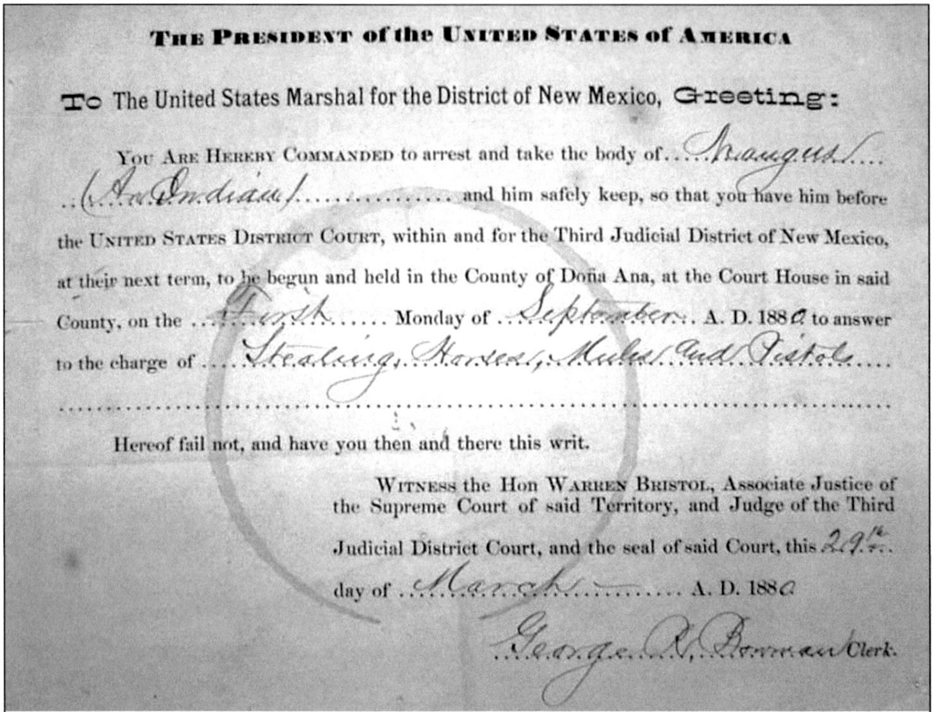

THE PRESIDENT of the UNITED STATES of AMERICA

To The United States Marshal for the District of New Mexico, Greeting:

YOU ARE HEREBY COMMANDED to arrest and take the body of ... Mangus ... (An Indian) ... and him safely keep, so that you have him before the UNITED STATES DISTRICT COURT, within and for the Third Judicial District of New Mexico, at their next term, to be begun and held in the County of Doña Ana, at the Court House in said County, on the ... First ... Monday of ... September ... A. D. 1880 to answer to the charge of ... Stealing, Horses, Mules and Pistols ...

Hereof fail not, and have you then and there this writ.

WITNESS the Hon WARREN BRISTOL, Associate Justice of the Supreme Court of said Territory, and Judge of the Third Judicial District Court, and the seal of said Court, this 29th day of ... March ... A. D. 1880

George R. Bowman Clerk.

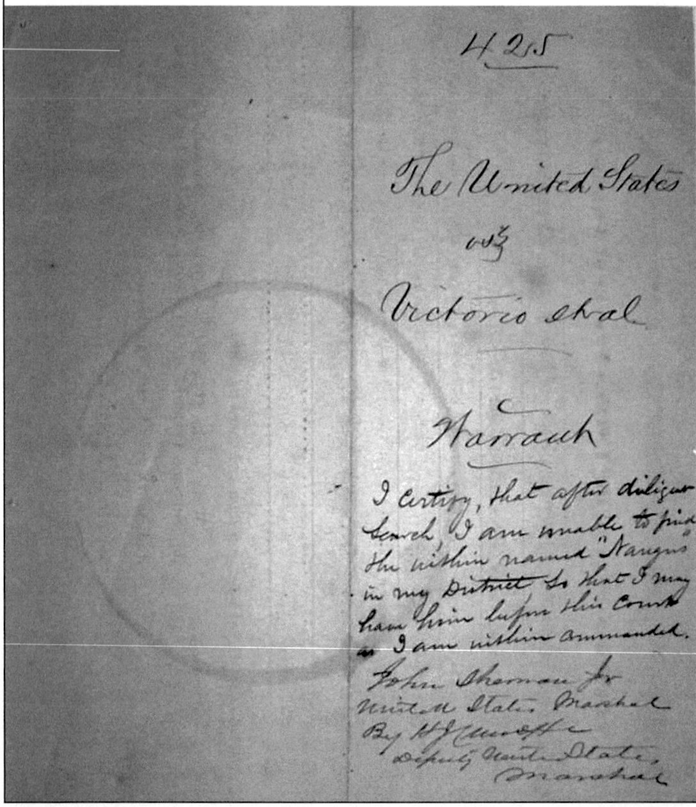

The reverse of the arrest warrant (left) reads as follows:

The United States
viz
Victorio et al

Warrant

I certify, that after diligent search, I am unable to find the within named "Mangus" in my District so that I may have him before this court as I am within commanded.

John Sherman for United States Marshal By HJ Cuniff Deputy, United States Marshal".

Figure 6.1 Arrest Warrant for Mangus, 29 March 1880.

should also not forget that there were a series of longer-term factors relating to the concentration policy which should be factored into the equation.

There is, too, the distinct possibility that Victorio had never had any intention of remaining on the Mescalero reservation. He may have viewed the reservation as a useful supply base where plunder could be sold and arms and ammunition procured. In late July to early August 1879, John Ayer, a former agent of the Warm Springs Apaches, saw 25 of these Apaches at Casas Grandes in the State of Chihuahua. He was told there were 80 Apaches in this particular group.[259] This suggests that some Warm Springs Apaches had remained in Mexico while Victorio and Nana had moved to the Mescalero reservation; yet these Apaches had also expressed the intention of fighting to the finish if they were not allowed to settle at Ojo Caliente.[260] Ayer also informed Hatch that the Warm Springs Apaches had made a raid into New Mexico sometime between July and October 1879, and that loot from that raid had been sold in the State of Chihuahua. His informant was one 'T.S. Parker, brother to the Parker who commands your scouts at Fort Bayard, and who is about to be married to the niece of the Gov. of Chihuahua.'[261] Hatch noted that the Apaches had no difficulty in obtaining firearms from 'Mexicans or Citizens of Mexican descent (Some of whom have been held Captives by the Apaches in former times) whenever they, the Indians, have property or Stolen Stock to dispose of.'[262] Hatch already suspected certain Mexican-American communities (Paraje and Palomas are named), but noted that time would be required to develop more detail as to the names of the individuals concerned.[263] He also stated that deserters in this region invariably fled south of the border to sell their arms and equipment to Mexicans, who were more than willing to trade them on to the Apaches.[264] Hatch therefore recommended joint action by both US and Mexican forces aimed at the 'capture or destruction' of the Apaches who, Hatch argued, were more than willing to play one government off against the other when it suited them.[265]

James Kaywaykla's recollections suggested that Nana at least was using the Fort Stanton reservation as a base to support continued efforts to resist the United States. If these groups of Warm Springs Apaches were acting in concert, and Kaywaykla implies that they probably were, then one wonders whether Victorio needed much encouragement to leave the reservation. However, the presence of a relatively large group of Warm Springs Apaches in Northern Mexico at the same time as Victorio and Nana were known to be on the Mescalero reservation also raises the possibility that

---

Capt. Carroll commended Corporal Baker of 'H' Company and Private Abram McDonald for their "good conduct" during the skirmish of 5 August, 1878. (Loud to CO 9th Cavalry, 30 September, 1878 in Letters Sent by the '9MD/DNM/DoNM', NA, RG393, M1072, Roll 6, Letter No.428 p.299) Moore would appear to have been mistaken in dating this skirmish to the summer of 1879.

259 Martin AA General to General Willcox, Palace Hotel, San Francisco, 8 August 1879, NA, RG393, Part 1, Entry 169, Vol. 9, p.293; See also Ayer to Hatch, 26 October 1879 in Letters Received by HQ DoNM, September-August 1890, NA, RG393, M1088, Roll 39, Oct-Dec 1879.

The Army & Navy Journal reproduced a communication from Ayers which claimed that he had met twenty to twenty-five Warm Springs Apaches at Casas Grandes in July 1879; the discrepancy in the numbers may refer to the number of fighters present with this group ('Indian Affairs' *Army & Navy Journal,* Vol.17, 17 April 1880, p.751).

260 'Indian Affairs' *Army & Navy Journal,* Vol.17, 27 March 1880, p.693.

261 Ayer to Hatch, 26 October 1879 in Letters Received by HQ DoNM, September-August 1890, NA, RG393, M1088, Roll 39, Oct-Dec 1879.

262 Hatch to AAG, DoM, Fort Leavenworth, 28 May 1879 in Letters Sent by the '9MD/DNM/DoNM', NA, RG393, M1072, Roll 6, Jan-Oct 1879, Letter No.257, pp.187-190.

263 Hatch to S.M. Baines, U.S. Attorney for New Mexico, 12 July 1879 in Letters Sent by the '9MD/DNM/DoNM', NA, RG393, M1072, Roll 6, Jan-Oct 1879, Letter No.337, pp.239-240.

264 Hatch to AAG, DoM, Fort Leavenworth, 6 September, 1879 in Letters Sent by the '9MD/DNM/DoNM', NA, RG393, M1072, Roll 6, Jan-Oct 1879, Letter No.445 pp.316-320.

265 Hatch to AAG, DoM, Fort Leavenworth, 14 August 1879 in Letters Sent by the '9MD/DNM/DoNM', NA, RG393, M1072, Roll 6, Jan-Oct 1879, Letter No.394, pp.280-282.

Victorio and Nana may not have been the only men of influence directing the Chihenne Apaches. Mangus, son of Mangas Coloradas, was another Warm Springs Apache leader whose activities during the 1877-81 period remain very elusive, but who was clearly regarded as an influential leader by the US army during this time. There are tantalising references to his leading quite a large following in Mexico during late 1880 and 1881. It is possible that Ayer may have encountered Warm Springs Apaches led by Mangus.

Colonel Hatch also claimed that he had suspected that Victorio was considering leaving the reservation, and had gone to visit him on the reservation:

> I remember that I began to suspect the outbreak just at the time I was starting for the scene of the Ute massacre. I was taking the infantry and leaving Morrow with the cavalry to hold the place while I was away. I thought I would go and see old Victoria and ask about the matter. I went alone to see the old man and told him I knew what he was thinking of doing. He replied that I was alone and that he could kill me. 'I know you could.' Said I, 'but I know you will not. You are going on the war-path and the end of it will be the destruction of yourself and your whole people. I am going away from here with some troops, but others will take our place and you will surely get the worst of it.' The old man replied that he had not made up his mind to go out, but that if he did he never intended to surrender again. 'I will not surrender the hair of a horse's tail,' was his grim remark.[266]

One should be very wary of Hatch's testimony, as this is from an *Army and Navy Journal* article of 7 January 1882, over two years after the event. In the subsequent campaign, Hatch was utterly vilified by the press and local population for his alleged shortcomings in dealing with Victorio's warriors. As we shall see, Hatch was not above distorting the facts in his reporting of progress in the campaign against Victorio. He claimed to have seen Victorio just prior to the 'Ute massacre'; yet Victorio's final breakout predated this event by almost a month. Was this a case of Hatch's memory playing him false, or of him re-writing history with a view to justifying his role in the campaign? It is also possible that Hatch, who *had* met with Warm Springs Apaches led by Nana and Tomas in May 1879, was played false by his own memory, and that he was in fact quoting either Nana or Tomas. Therefore, on balance, the above statement was probably made; and whether it was uttered by Victorio, Nana or Tomas, the sentiment reflects the feelings elsewhere attributed to both Victorio and Nana.

In the aftermath of Victorio's departure from the Mescalero reservation, the nature of the conflict changed completely. Victorio had, up until that point, engaged in what we have termed low-level conflict, in the hope of winning a return to the Ojo Caliente reservation. While there had been some raiding and a few fatalities inflicted by both sides, it was only after the period from September 1877 to August 1879, which could be termed a 'phoney war', that Victorio effectively declared war. As we shall see, during September to November 1879, the numbers killed by the Chihenne Apaches and their allies rose by at least a factor of ten in comparison to the earlier period.

Frank Clifford, whom we met earlier, came to very much the same conclusion. His account of events both prior to and after Victorio's departure from the Mescalero reservation is quite perceptive.

266 'Indian Warfare – Gen. Hatch's Opinion.' in the *Army & Navy Journal*, Vol.19, 7 January 1882, p.496; Hatch cited in Laumbach, p.110.

> At that time old Geronimo [Victorio] and his braves went through Hillsboro on their way down to old Mexico. They weren't on the warpath, just going through the country stealing horses.[267]

As we saw earlier, Clifford joined the pursuit of the Apaches who had stolen horses from the Hillsboro area and engaged in a skirmish with the raiders. It is with his concluding statement that we shall end this account of the phoney war of 1877-9. Having received advice from the commander of Fort Bayard that their stolen horses had long since vanished into Mexico, Clifford concluded:

> We knew he was right, and we gave up the chase and went back to Hillsboro, planning to get a quicker start the next time, but there wasn't any next time. When old Geronimo [Victorio] returned the next Spring[268] he came killing instead of stealing and that made the story entirely different.[269]

267 Clifford, F. & Nolan, F. (editor) 2011, *Deep Trails in the Old West: A Frontier Memory* (University of Oklahoma Press: Norman) p.47.

268 Author's note. As we shall see in the next chapter, Clifford accurately recalls that his friend Tom Hughes was killed in an ambush when Victorio returned. US army records show that Hughes was killed in September 1879.

269 Clifford, F. & Nolan, F. (editor) 2011, *Deep Trails in the Old West: A Frontier Memory* (University of Oklahoma Press: Norman) p.49.

7

Ojo Caliente and McEvers' Ranch, August-September 1879

> Had not heard of 5 men being killed and 52 horses being taken from Co. E &c. and am sorry to hear it, this is about one horse for each Indian man. Rather a joke on the Cavalry, isn't it.
> (Agent Russell, Mescalero Agency, 12 September 1879)

Initial Breakout, August-September 1879

> Warm Springs Indians have all left this reservation going west, will probably try to intercept those supposed to be on the way from San Carlos. Have informed the military.[1]

There is some dispute as to when Victorio's final breakout actually occurred.[2] A telegram to the AAAG District of New Mexico, possibly dated either 18 September or 18 October, notes that '43 Warm Springs Indians left about Aug 19 1879.'"[3] It was certainly known to the US army by 25 August that they had left.[4] Sixty horses were stolen from Tulerosa on 23 August,[5] from rancher Pat Coghlan and other citizens, and it was thought that the Warm Springs Apaches were the culprits.[6]

A detachment of Ninth cavalry troopers under Lieutenant George Washington Smith[7] attempted to pursue the fleeing Apaches, yet was unable to close with its quarry.[8] Quite what Lieutenant Smith proposed to do with his two non-commissioned officers and 12 other ranks had he caught up with

---

1 Russell to CoIA, 21 August 1879 in 'Operations re Warm Springs Apaches 1877-79', Letters Rec'd by the AGO, 1871-80, NA, M666, Roll 366; See also Russell to CoIA, 21 August 1879 in Letters Received, DoM 1868-98, RG 393, Entry A1-1 2601, Box 83.

2 Thrapp, in his earlier book (1967, p.181) states that Victorio fled the Mescalero Reservation on 4 September, 1879. Stout concurs. (p. 89) Haley implies that Victorio fled the reservation on 2 September, 1879. (p.321) However, Thrapp in his later book on Victorio himself, quotes the Reservation Agent reporting this flight on the 21st of August (1974, p.218).

19-21 August dates would appear the more convincing. Victorio's first attack occurred at Ojo Caliente on 4 September, 1879, yet he would have had to travel over 100 miles to get there from the Mescalero Reservation. With women, children and the old in tow, crossing or circling the intervening San Andres Mountains, traversing or avoiding the Jornada Del Muerto, negotiating the Rio Grande and then launching an attack on the army unit based at Ojo Caliente, appears to be a tall order for one day's travel.

3 Lt. P.T. Swaine, CO Fort Stanton to AAAG, DoNM, 15 September 1879 in Letters Received by HQ DoNM, September 1865-August 1890, NA, RG393, M1088, Roll 38, July–Sept. 1879; NA,RG393, Part 3, Entry 439, p.341.

4 Hatch to Indian Agent, San Carlos, 25 August 1879 in Telegrams Sent DoNM, Vol.2, Jan.–Dec. 1879, NA, RG393, Part 3, Entry 431, p.208.

5 *Thirty Four*, 27 August 1879.

6 *Thirty Four*, 3 September 1879.

7 Lt GW Smith was involved in both the opening and closing episodes of The Victorio Campaign being killed almost two years later in the last skirmish of Nana's Raid in Gavilan Canyon.

8 Thrapp, 1974, p.220; Thrapp, 1988, p.1326; see also Billington, 1991, p.89.

the Apaches is unclear.[9] Lieutenant Colonel Peter Swain was all too aware of the dangers faced by Lieutenant Smith in his pursuit of Victorio. In commenting on this specific case, Swain later pinpointed one of the key issues concerning the shortage of manpower when campaigning against the Apaches. He noted that a detachment of 15 men had been stationed at Tulerosa under various officers to interdict the illegal trade between the Mexicans and the Apaches. The detachment was too small to prevent traffic going onto the reservation and risked extermination if it attempted to prevent Apaches leaving the reservation. The shortage of manpower allocated to the garrison of New Mexico meant that the detachments employed were usually less than company sized and this undermined the efficiency of each company.[10] The issue of low manpower would haunt the US army throughout the campaigns of 1879, 1880 and 1881. Swain was also contacted by Agent Russell a few days later with the information that the latter was unaware of any Mescalero Apaches leaving the reservation. Nevertheless, Russell also acknowledged that the Mescaleros could regularly leave the reservation without Russell being any the wiser.[11]

Captain G.A. Purington was also ordered to march his L Company, Ninth Cavalry, minus Lieutenant Smith's detachment, from Fort Stanton to Fort Bayard.[12] These instructions no doubt anticipated forthcoming operations against Victorio in his mountain strongholds to the immediate north and east of that post.

There is a possibility that some of Victorio's warriors slipped across the Rio Grande into Mexico, as around about this time the US consul in Chihuahua noted that a party, estimated at between 40 and 50, struck a party of Mexicans, killing three and badly wounding three more at Cantoracia (probably Cantareccio or Santa Recio). A pursuing party of Mexican volunteers was subsequently ambushed, losing one man killed and another wounded. The date of the actual attack remains unclear but the US consul in Chihuahua City sent a note on the affair to the US State Department on 19 September, stating that the culprits were believed to be Apaches from the Mescalero reservation who had left that place one month earlier.[13] These raiders could also have been the Warm Springs Apaches encountered by Ayer, Mescalero Apaches acting independently of Victorio, or Juh's Chiricahua Apaches and operating out of the Sierra Madre.

However, most of Victorio's following made for their Black Range-San Mateo Mountain heartland. On 25 August, Richard Stackpole from San Jose was alerted by Francisco Gavaldon that Apaches were killing cattle on his ranch. With five men, Stackpole followed the trail into the San Mateo Mountains and confronted the Apaches:

> but finding them better armed and too many for us we had to retreat, in coming out of the mountains they attacked us again and took three animals from us, they killed one mare property of Pedro Jose Araniz Paraje and took with them two mules property of Francisco Gavaldon, we got away from them by the skin of our teeth.[14]

---

9 See information in Special Order 81, Par 1 August 23 1879 in NA, RG393, Part 3, Entry 450.

10 Swain to HQ DoNM, 22 October 1879 in Letters Received by HQ DoNM, September 1865-August 1890, NA,RG393, M1088, Roll 39, Oct-Dec 1879.

11 Russell to Swain, 25 October 1879 in Letters Received by HQ DoNM, September 1865-August 1890, NA, RG393, M1088, Roll 39, Oct-Dec 1879.

12 Special Order 81, Par 1 August 23 1879 in NA, RG393, Part 3, Entry 450; *Army & Navy Journal,* Vol.17, 6 September 1879, p.76.

13 Louis H. Scott to Hon. J.H. Seward, Department of State, 19 September 1879, NA, RG393, Part 1, Entry 2546, pp.160-161; Scott to Seward, Department of State, Washington D.C., 19 September 1879 in Consular Despatches Chihuahua Mexico 1830-1906, NA, M289, Roll 1.

14 Stackpole, San Jose to Hooker, 31 August 1879 in Letters Received by HQ DoNM, September 1865-August 1890, NA, RG393, M1088, Roll 38, July–Sept. 1879.

It was elsewhere reported that Stackpole had had his hat shot off and was slightly wounded in the leg by a second bullet, and that the rifle of one of his companions had been irreparably damaged by an Apache bullet.[15] Stackpole was not about to give up the campaign, and, returning to San Jose, he recruited 10 men and returned to the site of the first confrontation, finding one Apache burial grave, which Stackpole took to be that of a victim of their opening volley. The group trailed the Apaches out of the San Mateo Mountains to where they crossed the Rio Grande, eight miles below San Jose. The trail continued through a pass in the Fra Cristobal Mountains and on to the San Andres Mountains. Stackpole, with his horses worn out, and two days behind the raiders, gave up the pursuit but wrote to Captain Hooker at Ojo Caliente warning him that this particular raid had netted 35 horses and mules from the ranches in the vicinity of San Jose.[16] He also clearly warned Hooker that:

> the Indians did not seem to be very alarmed as from all appearances the women were living in the mountains and the bucks went stealing. The Indians are continually passing through this pass in the San [Fra] Cristobal Range – by having a picket of ten of fifteen men stationed there am satisfied they would stop their roving in or about here.[17]

US Army Deployment, August-September 1879

Before we examine the efforts of the US army to track Victorio down, it is necessary to develop a clear picture of the overall deployment of the garrisons in the Districts of New Mexico and the Pecos (western Texas) and in the Department of Arizona. The key zone is the District of New Mexico, where much of the campaign between 1879 and 1881 would occur. Yet, at various stages during this time, troops from the Department of Arizona and the District of the Pecos would become involved in the campaign against the Apaches, so it is worth our while to build a picture of the forces arrayed against Victorio. For the moment, we shall concentrate on the garrison of the District of New Mexico; but we shall also review the US army garrisons in Arizona and western Texas. The following point must be noted. The accuracy of the various monthly and bi-monthly US army returns referred to in building our picture is subject to the strengths and weaknesses of the human beings who completed the forms. Thus, we have to be aware that the figures are best viewed as approximations which combine to give us a reasonably accurate picture of the US army's garrisons in the Southwest.

Table 7.1 shows the overall strength of the four army posts within the District of New Mexico that were involved in dealing with Victorio's resistance to the United States. Of these, Fort Bayard would be most directly involved in the opening stages of the campaign.

15 Letter from Paraje *Thirty Four*, 3 September 1879.
16 Stackpole, San Jose to Hooker, 31 August 1879 in Letters Received by HQ DoNM, September 1865-August 1890, NA, RG393, M1088, Roll 38, July–Sept. 1879.
17 Stackpole, San Jose to Hooker, 31 August 1879 in Letters Received by HQ DoNM, September 1865–August 1890, NA, RG393, M1088, Roll 38, July–Sept. 1879.

Table 7.1 US Army Roster, District of New Mexico, 1879[18]

District of New Mexico				
Post	**Commanding Officer**	**Present**		**Garrison**
		Officers	**Other Ranks**	
Fort Bayard	Major A.P. Morrow 9th Cavalry	8	222	6 Companies (9th Cavalry and 15th Infantry)
Fort Bliss (Texas)	Major N.W. Osborne 15th Infantry	6	120	3 Companies (9th Cavalry and 15th Infantry)
Fort Stanton	Captain G.A. Purington 9th Cavalry	8	162	4 Companies (9th Cavalry and 15th Infantry)
Fort Wingate	Colonel G.P. Buell 15th Infantry	8	140	3 Companies (9th Cavalry and 15th Infantry)
Totals		30	644	

From Table 7.2 we can discover that Fort Bayard had a complement of three Ninth Cavalry companies, plus the company stationed at Ojo Caliente, available to take the field against the Apaches. The companies based at Forts Stanton and Bliss would be available should they be required. Table 7.2 also reveals that one of the Ninth Cavalry's companies was absent in Wyoming, then Colorado.

Table 7.2 Location of Ninth Cavalry Companies, July to October 1879[19]

Company	July–August	September–October
A	In the Field, San Augustine Plains, New Mexico	Fort Bayard, New Mexico
B	Fort Bayard, New Mexico	Fort Bayard, New Mexico
C	Fort Bayard, New Mexico	Fort Bayard, New Mexico
D	In the Field, Colorado Territory	Fort Union, New Mexico
E	In the Field, Ojo Caliente, New Mexico. Detached from Fort Union	In the Field, Ojo Caliente, New Mexico Detached from Fort Union
F	Fort Stanton, New Mexico	In the Field, Duck Creek, New Mexico Detached from Fort Stanton
G	Fort Bayard, New Mexico	Florida Springs, Florida Mountains, New Mexico
H	Fort Stanton, New Mexico	In the Field, Near the Florida Mountains, New Mexico
I	Fort Wingate, New Mexico	Fort Wingate, New Mexico
K	In the Field near Cheyenne, Wyoming Territory	In the Field, Animas City, Colorado Territory
L	Fort Bliss, Texas	Old Fort Cummings, New Mexico
M	Fort Stanton, New Mexico	In the Field, Duck Creek, New Mexico Detached from Fort Stanton

18 Derived AR-WD 1879, pp.18-19.
19 Derived Bi-Monthly Company Muster Rolls for July/Aug., & Sept.,/Oct., 1879, 9th Cavalry in NA, RG94.

Table 7.3 gives an overview of the basic manpower available to the Ninth Cavalry during 1879. What Table 7.3 does not reveal is the regiment's available manpower in relation to the number of serviceable horses.

Table 7.3 Ninth Cavalry Monthly Roster of Strength, Gains and Losses, 1879

	Jan	Feb	Mar	Apr	May	Jun	Jul	Aug	Sept	Oct	Nov	Dec
Strength	588	631	696	736	733	729	731	733	770	766	764	755
Gains												
Recruits/Re-enlistment	2	48	72	46	–	9	5	7	53	4	4	2
Return from Desertion	–	1	1	2	–	1	–	2	–	–	–	1
Losses												
Time Expiry	–	3	1	–	1	5	–	–	5	6	-	7
Disability	–	1	–	1	–	2	–	1	–	1	1	-
Court Martial	1	1	1	2	1	2	–	1	1	1	1	1
By Order	1	–	–	1	–	–	–	–	–	–	–	1
Transfer	–	1	1	–	–	3	–	4	–	–	–	–
Killed in Action	–	–	–	–	1	2	–	–	10	–	1	–
Missing in Action	–	–	–	–	–	–	–	–	–	–	–	–
Died from Disease	–	–	–	1	–	–	2	–	–	–	–	–
Deserted	–	–	5	2	–	–	1	1	–	–	3	3

Table 7.4 indicates the overall strength of the regiment after deducting those men who at the time were sick, imprisoned or had deserted and shows that the regiment usually did not have enough horses to mount the available men. Yet this situation does not reveal the clearest picture of the combat readiness of the Ninth Cavalry when Victorio broke out of the Mescalero reservation.

Table 7.4 Ninth Cavalry Roster of Men to Horses, 1879

	Total Regt. Strength	Sick	Jailed	Deserted	Available Regt. Strength	Serviceable Horses	Un-serviceable Horses	Horses Lost in Action Died etc.
Jan	588	28	24	0	536	537	30	6
Feb	631	29	21	0	581	517	35	5
Mar	696	35	22	5	634	513	32	7
Apr	736	25	16	2	693	438	53	4
May	733	19	21	0	693	481	52	8
June	729	23	22	0	684	459	49	25
July	731	19	34	1	677	447	49	16
Aug	733	28	42	1	662	445	49	3
Sept	770	25	44	0	701	423	45	78
Oct	766	20	35	0	712	313	87	69
Nov	764	44	31	3	686	362	79	14
Dec	755	34	37	3	681	509	62	6

Table 7.5, which draws on the regiment's bi-monthly company muster rolls, shows that not one of the Ninth Cavalry companies could mount its available men between July and October 1879. The four companies of the Ninth Cavalry in closest proximity to Victorio's heartland – E Company at Ojo Caliente, and B, C and G Companies at Fort Bayard – could mount 53 and 80 cavalrymen respectively for operations in the field. This was out of a total strength of 59 cavalrymen at Ojo Caliente and 155 cavalrymen at Fort Bayard available for active service.

Table 7.5 Available Men to Serviceable Horses, Ninth Cavalry, July to October 1879

Company	Available Men July–Aug	Serviceable Horses July–Aug	Available Men Sept–Oct	Serviceable Horses Sept–Oct
A	61	26	60	26
B	52	24	57	23
C	47	28	59	Data not entered
D	45	38	55	Data not entered
E	59	53	48	11
F	52	47	53	47
G	56	28	56	Data not entered
H	56	15	61	36
I	55	33	44	35
K	49	47	54	48
L	57	35	57	25
M	53	42	53	44

The situation was no better for those companies stationed at Forts Bliss and Stanton, should reinforcements be required. L Company, at Fort Bliss, could mount 35 out of 57 cavalrymen fit for field service. F, H and M Companies, based at Fort Stanton, could put 104 Ninth cavalrymen into the field out of 161 troopers. A Company, Ninth Cavalry, then in the field at San Augustin Plains, could mount 26 men out of a total of 61 fit for duty against the Apaches.

This was not a desirable situation when faced with highly mobile Apache guerrillas whose signature tactic was to target the horses of their opponents, either by firing on them in the opening moments of an ambush, or by exhausting them in drawn-out pursuits over difficult terrain. By failing to supply the Ninth Cavalry with sufficient mounts, the US army had partially dismounted the regiment before any shots were fired in this campaign.

Before we detail the deployment of the available Ninth cavalrymen, it is worth reviewing the forces available in the Department of Arizona and the District of the Pecos. (See Tables 7.6 and 7.7) For the moment, the key point to note is the way overall numbers were spread between widely dispersed garrisons.

Table 7.6 US Army Roster, Department of Arizona, 1879

Department of Arizona				
Post	**Commanding Officer**	**Present**		**Garrison**
		Officers	**Men**	
Fort Apache	Major M.A. Cochrane 12th Infantry	6	126	3 Companies (6th Cav. and 12th Inf.)
Fort Bowie	2nd Lieutenant T.A. Touey 6th Cavalry	3	82	2 Companies (6th Cav.)
Fort Grant	Major A.K. Arnold 6th Cavalry	8	110	3 Companies (6th Cav. and 12th Inf.)
Fort Lowell	Captain W.A. Rafferty 6th Cavalry	6	65	2 Companies (6th Cav.)
Fort McDowell	Captain J.M. Norvell 12th Infantry	4	90	2 Companies (6th Cav. and 12th Inf.)
Fort Verde	Captain H.C. Egbert 12th Infantry	8	191	4 Companies (6th Cav. and 12th Inf.)
Fort Mojave	2nd Lieutenant H. Johnson 8th Infantry	1	39	1 Company (8th Inf.)
Camp Thomas	Captain M.H. Stacey 12th Infantry	3	69	2 Companies (6th Cav. and 12th Inf.)
Camp Huachuca	Captain S.M. Whiteside 6th Cavalry	4	77	1 Company (6th Cav.)
Camp J.A. Rucker	1st Lieutenant J.H. Hurst 12th Infantry	1	45	1 Company (12th Inf.)
Totals		44	894	

Table 7.7 US Army Roster, District of the Pecos, 1879

District of the Pecos				
Post Fort	**Commanding Officer**	**Present**		**Garrison**
		Officers	**Men**	
Fort Concho	Major A. Mills 10th Cavalry	13	177	7 Companies (10th Cav. and 25th Inf.)
Fort Davis	Captain C.D. Viele 10th Cavalry	8	194	6 Companies (10th Cav. and 25th Inf.)
Fort Stockton	Lt Colonel M.M. Blunt 25th Infantry	10	113	5 Companies (10th Cav. and 25th Inf.)
Totals		31	484	

US Army Reaction, August-September 1879

In August 1879, Colonel Hatch was absent, fulfilling his duties as commander of the District of New Mexico.[20] In his absence, Major Albert P. Morrow, as acting commander of the Ninth Cavalry, based at Fort Bayard, ordered his cavalrymen out in pursuit of Victorio. On 1 September, he reported that a detachment under Captain Beyer had made a sweep through the Mogollons from the San Francisco River, passing through Pinos Altos before returning to Fort Bayard. Beyer saw no signs of Apaches. Morrow also reported that a detachment under Lieutenant Day was in the field around Tularosa[21] and his arrival at Fort Bayard was expected imminently.[22]

A detachment of 15 men of the Ninth Cavalry, commanded by Lieutenant W.O. Cory,[23] was ordered out of Fort Wingate in pursuit of unidentified stock thieves who had raided McCarthy's Ranch. This detachment was also ordered to scout towards 'Hot Springs' (Ojo Caliente). Departing on 25 August, they returned on 31 August, having arrived at McCarthy's Ranch to find the stolen stock recovered and no indication of who the culprits were, or indeed, if a raid had occurred at all.[24] They found no indication that Apaches had moved into the area to the north west of Ojo Caliente.

Morrow informed District Headquarters on 5 September that, in reaction to a letter received from Agent Russell and ex-Agent Godfoy reporting that Victorio had left the reservation and was believed to be in the Socorro Mountains, he had deployed his detachments as follows:

> have sent Wright with five indians & fifteen soldiers to that point Beyer out the North Star Road to cross the river and scout the Cavallo [Caballo] Mts Hugo to go into camp of observation at the point where Beyer had his fight with Victorio ordered Beyer to communicate with Hooker. Day is still out & I think must be on the trail.[25]

If we look at the main map, this deployment may have been an attempt to screen any approach to the home range of the Warm Springs Apaches from the Mescalero reservation. However, this attempt to block, or even detect the whereabouts of, Victorio failed to make any contact with, or find any trace of, the Apaches, as it had not been deployed in time. This is no fault of Morrow's; it merely reflects the time taken to transmit news in the area at that time.

In Arizona, the Sixth Cavalry had maintained its picket duty on the border with New Mexico. On 22 August 1879, Captain E.C. Hentig, with his company and Apache scouts, was absent investigating a report that 18 horses had been stolen from a ranch in Bush Valley on the upper reaches of the San Francisco Valley, 85 miles northeast of Clifton. The raiders were reported to have departed to the south west, and Hentig was well-placed to intercept them should this rumour prove accurate.[26] News of Victorio's breakout reached Arizona troops on 30 August and, somewhat

20 Thrapp, 1967, p.190.

21 Unfortunately, Morrow does not distinguish between Old Fort Tularosa some distance northwards of Fort Bayard or the Mescalero Agency well to the east of Fort Bayard. That the troops were operating out of Fort Bayard and not Fort Stanton makes it more likely that it was Old Fort Tularosa.

22 Morrow to Loud AAAG Santa Fé, 4 September 1879 in NA, RG393, Part 3, Entry 439, p.215.

23 Lt. Cory was serving with the Fifteenth Infantry Regiment but it was not unusual to find Infantry officers commanding detachments of cavalry. This was probably due to the shortage of Cavalry officers available to command such small patrols. Indeed, during the campaigns against Victorio and Nana, small detachments of Ninth and Tenth Cavalrymen were quite frequently commanded by an experienced N.C.O.

24 Fort Wingate Aug & Sept 1879, Returns from Military Posts 1800-1916, NA, M617, Roll 1449.

25 Morrow to Loud AAAG Santa Fé, 5 September 1879 in NA, RG393, Part 3, Entry 439, p.214; See also Morrow to AAAG DoNM, 5 November 1879, 'Victorio Papers', NA, M666, Roll 526; Thrapp, 1974, p.240; 1967, p.182.

26 Cochran Fort Apache to Major Arnold, CO Fort Grant, 22 August 1879, NA, RG393, Part 1, Entry 235, pp.1-2.

ominously, Major A.K. Arnold, Sixth Cavalry, stated that: 'If Warm Springs Indians come over, we will have to do the best we can.'[27] However, Victorio's escape did not appear to ring wider alarm bells in the Department of Arizona. If Victorio had left the Mescalero reservation with the explicit intention of making a raid on the San Carlos reservation, he would have almost certainly caught the Sixth Cavalry off guard. Victorio broke out on 22 August, while the Arizona troops had not completed their deployments by 7 September.

Despite his extra duties as commander of the District of New Mexico, Colonel Hatch still managed to keep track of his own regiment, and he was somewhat concerned that the Ninth Cavalry was not equipped with enough horses to deal with the Apaches. On 3 September 1879, he informed the Department of the Missouri that, with a few exceptions, the horses which had recently been supplied to the District of New Mexico were not suitable for cavalry service, being too small or too young. He also informed him that John Tempany, Veterinary Surgeon, Ninth Cavalry, had reported that 'the contractors have practiced deception and in a manner not easily detected.'[28]

Alongside these deployments, Colonel Hatch continued to enquire as to the possibility of allowing the Warm Springs Apaches to settle at Ojo Caliente and recommended that Thomas Keams[29] be appointed their agent, as he was the only available man 'in whom they will place any confidence; he speaks the Indian language and Spanish, is a man of good habits, has thorough clerical knowledge of all business pertaining to the bureau.'[30] Hatch added that the Chihenne Apaches had grown and then lost their corn crop and had had their stock confiscated when they had been deported to San Carlos for the second time in 1878. He also noted that it had been unwise to antagonise the Chihenne Apaches as they were 'very well armed, having cached all their good arms when they were taken in 1877 to San Carlos.'[31] Hatch also stated that the agency building remained in good order and that settlers had not taken possession of any part of the reservation. He estimated that the reservation could support 1,000 Indians with grazing for 200,000 sheep and 25,000 cattle.[32] Hatch's recommendations were also approved by both General Pope and General Sheridan.[33]

However, Ojo Caliente was about to become the centre of attention for a very different reason. On 4 September, Apaches ambushed a small detachment of Ninth cavalrymen near Ojo Caliente,

27 Arnold to CO Camp Thomas, 30 August 1879, Troops in Southeastern Arizona, DoAz, NA, RG393, Part 1, Entry 232, Vol.4, 3 July, 1879–Dec. 13 1879, p.53.

28 Hatch to AAG, DoM, 3 September 1879 in Letters Received by HQ DoNM, September 1865-August 1890, NA, RG393, M1088, Roll 39, Oct-Dec 1879.

29 Keams had acted as Superintendent and Interpreter at Ojo Caliente after Victorio's first breakout from San Carlos resulting in his surrender at Fort Wingate and temporary return to Ojo Caliente. Hatch had regretfully had to dismiss him as there were no funds to pay for his continued service. (Loud to Keams, 21 February 1878 & Hatch to Keams, 21 February 1878 in Letters Sent by the '9MD/DNM/DoNM', NA, RG393, M1072, Roll 6, Letter No.68 & 69.)

30 Hatch to AAG, DoM, 8 September 1879 & ColA to Hatch, 30 August 1879, in 'Operations re Warm Springs Apaches 1877-79', Letters Rec'd by the AGO, 1871-80, NA, M666, Roll 366; See also 'Victorio Files', NA, RG393, M1495, Roll 14; Hatch to AAG, DoM, Fort Leavenworth, 8 September 1879 in Letters Sent by the '9MD/DNM/DoNM', NA, RG393, M1072, Roll 6, Jan-Oct 1879, Letter No.452, pp.325-326; 'Indian Affairs' *Army & Navy Journal,* Vol.17, 27 September 1879, p.137.

31 Hatch to AAG, DoM, 8 September 1879 & ColA to Hatch, 30 August 1879, in 'Operations re Warm Springs Apaches 1877-79', Letters Rec'd by the AGO, 1871-80, NA, M666, Roll 366; See also 'Victorio Files', NA, RG393, M1495, Roll 14; Hatch to AAG, DoM, Fort Leavenworth, 8 September 1879 in Letters Sent by the '9MD/DNM/DoNM', NA, RG393, M1072, Roll 6, Jan-Oct 1879, Letter No.452, pp.325-326; 'Indian Affairs' *Army & Navy Journal,* Vol.17, 27 September 1879, p.137.

32 Hatch to ColA, Dept. of the Interior, 6 September 1879, 'Victorio Files', NA, RG393, M1495, Roll 14 & 'Operations re Warm Springs Apaches 1877-79', Letters Rec'd by the AGO, 1871-80, NA, M666, Roll 366.

33 Pope & Sheridan, 13 September 1879, 'Victorio Files', NA, RG393, M1495, Roll 14.

killing all of the guards and successfully making off with the horses and mules assigned to E Company, Ninth Cavalry, which was stationed at Ojo Caliente. It was a coincidental stroke of bureaucratic irony that, on the very day of the Ojo Caliente raid, the Chief Quartermaster of the District of New Mexico was authorised to purchase 200 lbs of horse shoes to be sent to Captain Hooker at Ojo Caliente.[34]

Most accounts[35] of the raid on Ojo Caliente are rather cryptic,[36] and merely indicate that on 4 September 1879, Victorio, Nana, Sanchez and approximately 40 Apaches[37] killed five guards (some accounts mention three additional civilians killed) and stole E Company, Ninth Cavalry's, horse herd consisting of 68-70 horses and mules.[38] E Company's bi-monthly return reported that 52 horses and 18 mules had been taken.[39] Hooker himself admitted to the loss of four horses belonging to officers at Ojo Caliente: two belonging to Lieutenant Taylor, one belonging to Acting Assistant Surgeon A. Sewell, and one belonging to him. In addition, two horses owned by private citizens were lost with the herd. Finally, 46 horses and 18 mules belonging to the US government were stolen by the Apaches.[40] The raid is widely cited as the opening attack of the Victorio Campaign,[41]

34 Hatch to Chief Quartermaster, DoNM, 4 September 1879 in Letters Sent by the '9MD/DNM/DoNM', NA, RG393, M1072, Roll 6, Jan-Oct 1879, Letter No.440 pp.313-314.

35 Notable exceptions to this rule are Billington and Kenner who give more detail of the raid but do so in the context of developing a picture of life in the 'Buffalo Soldiers' than as part of a history of the Victorio Campaign. Kenner has devoted a whole chapter of his book to the subject of Captain Hooker and his treatment of E Company from 1869-1880. (See Billington, 1991, pp.192-197; Kenner, pp.107-111) I have concentrated upon Captain Steelhammer's report for the detail of the Ojo Caliente Raid.

36 This, in itself, is rather surprising as there is a very detailed reconstruction of the raid left on record as part of the subsequent investigation of the raid undertaken by Captain Charles Steelhammer. Lt F.B. Taylor, second in command at Ojo Caliente provided his interpretation of how the Apaches had ambushed the horse guard.

37 As there was no survivors of this attack, there is no certain indication of who led the raid, or how many Apaches were involved. This figure was cited in the Army & Navy Journal, 13 September 1879 (Vol.17, p.97: See also 'Indian Affairs' *Army & Navy Journal,* Vol.17, 27 September 1879, p.137). It is also difficult to estimate the actual numbers of Warm Springs Apache warriors present. Laumbach makes a valiant attempt to name those warriors operating with Victorio and Nana in 1878-1880 but is unable to name or enumerate these warriors with certainty. (Laumbach, pp.128-133) As early as September 21, 1879, the U.S. army noted that Victorio had left the Mescalero Reservation with "about forty men" but estimated that he may be commanding as high as seventy-five by 21 September, 1879 (Pope to AG Fort Leavenworth 21 September 1879, 'Victorio Papers', NA, M666, Roll 526) Reports were received that Victorio and between thirty-five and forty Apaches had been seen on 3 September, on the headwaters of the Cuchillo Negro and this is probably the source for these numbers. ('Steelhammer Report' in Letters Received by HQ DoNM, September 1865-August 1890, NA, RG393, M1088 Roll 38, File 1664-2491, July–Sept. 1879.)

38 Pope to Townsend AG Wash. D.C. 18 September 1879, 'Victorio Papers' NA, M666, Roll 526; Pope's Annual Report Year ending 22 September 1880, NA, RG393, Part 1, Entry 2546, p.612; Report of Gen. John Pope, 22 September 1880 in AR-WD, NA, M997, Roll 35, 1880 Vol. I-II, p.86.

39 Bi-Monthly Company Muster Rolls for E Company, 9th Cavalry, Sept/Oct 1879 in NA, RG94.

40 Hooker to AAAG, DoNM, SF, 5 Oct. 1879 in Letters Received, DoM 1868-98, RG 393, Entry A1-1 2601, Box 85.

41 Stout reports that Victorio led the pursuing troops into a 'rolling rock' ambush in a ravine though no further casualties are mentioned. He also states that the cavalry unit, for obvious reasons, did not have enough horses with which to mount an effective pursuit (p.90). This story appears to be based upon James Kaywaykla's recollections of the Apache version of events. His account, dictated in the 1950's is long after the event and it is sometimes difficult to follow the chronology of events. However, he is a valuable eyewitness of some of the events, which took place, and even if he was not present would have had close contact with those who participated. According to Kaywaykla, the raid was accomplished without a shot being fired and the Cavalry's pursuit discouraged by a shortage of mounts and warriors covering the retreat by dislodging rocks from the slopes above. (Ball, 1970, pp.72-73) Having secured remounts, and no doubt the personal firearms and ammunition from the slain horse-guards, the Apaches disappeared into the Black Range. See also Thrapp, 1974, p.220, Thrapp, 1967, p.182, Record of Engagements, p.92;

yet these accounts usually only scratch the surface of a rather complex affair. To fully understand what happened at Ojo Caliente on 4 September, one must first appreciate both the long-term relationship between the captain and his men and the daily routine established at Ojo Caliente. Once this has been accomplished, the events of 4 September can then be reconstructed in some detail.

Captain Ambrose Eugene Hooker and E Company

On 29 November 1879, Hatch sent Captain Charles Steelhammer,[42] Fifteenth Infantry, to investigate the affair of the theft of the horse herd,[43] and Steelhammer arrived on 10 December 1879.[44] He made what appears to have been a thorough investigation of a range of serious charges against Captain Hooker and the circumstances surrounding the loss of the horse herd[45] (see document file no. 9). Coincidentally, Captain Steelhammer arrived at Ojo Caliente with the horses sent to replace those lost on 4 September.[46] Hatch had ordered this investigation as a result of the loss of so many horses. As we shall see, the colonel had been angered by Hooker's clumsy attempts to exonerate himself. There were also deep concerns raised by an anonymous[47] letter sent to District Headquarters by members of E Company, Ninth Cavalry, accusing Captain Hooker of being responsible for the loss of the horses and the deaths of the five guards.

According to Steelhammer, Captain Hooker stood accused of the following:

> **1st** That Captain Hooker is responsible for the death of the herd guard at Ojo Caliente, Sept 4th 1879.
>
> **2nd** That the horseguards was not sufficiently well armed and equipped at the time of its death.
>
> **3rd** That the Captain, when the horseguard was found dead, said that he wished that all the negroes had been killed, and that he would try to get as many of the worthless sons of bitches killed as he could.

Chronological List, p.47; Stout, p.94, Leckie, 1967, pp.210-211; Schubert, 1997, p.53; Billington, 1991, p.192; Utley, 1973, p.360; Utley, 1984, p.47; Worcester, p.219; Lockwood, p.230; Haley, 1981, p.321; Wellman, 1957, p.152; Longstreet, p.91; Twitchell, p.438; see also Sewall to AAAG Loud DoNM, NA, RG393, Part 3, Entry 439, p.210, Webb, 1976, p.86; See also *Thirty Four*, 17 September 1879.

42 Steelhammer, a Swede, seems to have been used by Col Hatch as a trouble-shooter in the latter part of 1879. During October 1879, Hatch had to deal with a Ute uprising as well as Victorio and his Apaches. Concerned that the Utes were lobbying other tribes for support, he sent Steelhammer, with a minimal escort, to persuade the Jicarilla Apaches to remain at peace (See Steelhammer, 1954, pp.86-88).

43 Loud to Hatch, 29 November 1879, Telegrams Sent DoNM, Vol.2, Jan.–Dec. 1879, NA, RG393, Part 3, Entry 431, p.452; Hatch to Loud AAAG, NA, RG393, Part 3, Entry 439, p.102; see also Kenner, p.110; Billington, 1991, p.193.

44 Return for December 1879 in Returns From U.S. Military Posts 1800-1916 Ojo Caliente, New Mexico, May 1879-Mar. 1882, NA, M617 Roll 877.

45 'Steelhammer Report' in Letters Received by HQ DoNM, September 1865-August 1890, NA, RG393, M1088 Roll 38, File 1664-2491, July–Sept. 1879.

46 Return for November & December 1879 in Returns From U.S. Military Posts 1800-1916 Ojo Caliente, New Mexico, May 1879-Mar. 1882, NA, M617, Roll 877; Special Order 111, par 2, November 3 1879 in NA, RG393, Part 3, Entry 450; See also Hooker to Lt F.B. Taylor, Order No.9, In the Field, Ojo Caliente, N.M. 28 November 1879, Special Orders Rec'd from Sub Commands, NA, RG393, Part 3, Entry 453.

47 Anonymous Letter Rec'd dated Ojo Caliente, 30 September 1880 in Letters Received by HQ DoNM, September 1865-August 1890, NA, RG393, M1088, Roll 38, July–Sept. 1879.

Private Booth was identified as the actual scribe of the letter but a further sixteen men of the company were found to have been involved. ('Steelhammer Report' in Letters Received by HQ DoNM, September 1865-August 1890, NA, RG393, M1088 Roll 38, File 1664-2491, July-Sept. 1879.)

4th That Captain Hooker had several times prior to September 4, 1879, been cautioned that the Indians were about to attack the Co. or the herd but failed to pay proper attention to such caution

5th That Captain Hooker's conduct towards his men has been unofficerlike.

6th That unavailing complaints have heretofore been made by enlisted men of "E" Co. Ninth Cavalry.

Upon these allegations the examination of the men has been chiefly based. The loss of the herd will, for the sake of fairness and conscience, be treated as a separate subject.[48]

As a result of his investigation, Captain Steelhammer discovered that, for years prior to the raid, Captain Hooker had had what could only be described as an appalling relationship with his company. Steelhammer ascribed this to Hooker's prejudice against 'the colored race'[49] believing that African-Americans were, at best, third rate soldiers, and this view was based on some all-too-familiar stereotypes of laziness and stupidity. Hooker plainly thought that the only solution to this problem was to resort to a mixture of constant verbal, and occasionally physical, abuse in order to improve such poor soldiers. Of the 51 men interviewed by Captain Steelhammer, all reported varying forms of verbal or physical abuse.[50]

Civil War photo of Captain Ambrose Eugene Hooker, whose appalling treatment of the men of E Company, Ninth Cavalry resulted in an anonymous letter denouncing his conduct after Victorio and his warriors stole their horse herd and killed the five guards on 4 September, 1879. The subsequent official investigation did nothing to restore the captain's reputation. (Library of Congress. Courtesy of the Massachusetts Commandery of the Military Order of the Loyal Legion)

48 'Steelhammer Report' in Letters Received by HQ DoNM, September 1865-August 1890, NA, RG393, M1088 Roll 38, File 1664-2491, July–Sept. 1879.

49 'Steelhammer Report' in Letters Received by HQ DoNM, September 1865-August 1890, NA, RG393, M1088 Roll 38, File 1664-2491, July–Sept. 1879.

50 See Appendix I: See also comments by Dobak & Phillips, 2001, pp.191-193.

Hooker rebutted all of these allegations of harsh treatment in a long counter-statement alleging a spirit of insubordination dating back to a mutinous episode prior to Hooker's command of the company. This had led, according to Hooker, to the men colluding against him. He denied using abusive language but admitted to using 'strong emphatic language' and he flatly denied having said words to the effect that he wanted all his men slain and replaced by proper soldiers.[51]

Captain Steelhammer acknowledged that Captain Hooker had:

> in every thing acted for what he believed to be the best interest of the service and with a conscientious sense of duty, whether mistaken or not and I feel it my duty therefore to state that he, in all that relates to the details of service, its systematic division, care of Government Property, the Military Instruction of his men and the Company Commissariat is unremitting and indefatigable in his personal attention and supervision and deserving of great credit.[52]

However, Steelhammer, much to his own surprise, considering his own evaluation of African American troops as 'excitable, imaginative and disposed to exaggeration,'[53] found that Captain Hooker's own testimony certainly corroborated some of his men's charges. As part of his lengthy rebuttal of his men's allegations, Hooker admitted to having made the following comment, though he attempted to pass it off as the only time he made such a comment:

> Captain Beyer of my regiment arrived here in command of two companies five or six days subsequent to the capture of my herd and, with his officers spent some time at my quarters, and previous to his departure, when about taking leave of me in the hall, expressed the hope that my horses would be recovered or that my Company would soon be remounted. I replied to him that the Company would never be remounted if higher authority should wait until I requested it, that I didn't want any more horses until I had something besides Apes and Baboons, Chimpanzees and Monkeys, Kangaroos and Ourangatangs or Gorillas for soldiers, that I had enough of it; that I had worn myself out endeavoring to make soldiers of this material and didn't want any more of it, or words to that effect.[54]

Captain Steelhammer noted that Captain Hooker's methods of attempting to instil discipline into his company had had the opposite effect to what the captain had intended and had undermined his ability to lead his company. The statements allegedly made by Hooker after the raid are also potentially significant. He was supposed to have said to a number of his men that he wished that he could send the rest out to be killed by the Apaches (see Appendix I). While Hooker emphatically denied ever having made such statements, his arrangements for guarding the company horse herd prior to the attack must have raised strong doubts in the minds of his men as to the veracity of such denials. Steelhammer also argued that Hooker's methods had not only adversely affected his men; his constant frustration at his inability to get his men to measure up to his own standards had undermined the captain's own health. By November 1879, Captain Steelhammer found it necessary to himself write down the verbal version of events offered by Hooker, as the latter was prostrated by

51 Captain Hooker's Rebuttal Statement in 'Steelhammer Report', Letters Received by HQ DoNM, September 1865-August 1890, NA, RG393, M1088, Roll 38, File 1664-2491, July–Sept. 1879.

52 'Steelhammer Report' in Letters Received by HQ DoNM, September 1865-August 1890, NA, RG393, M1088, Roll 38, File 1664-2491, July–Sept. 1879.

53 'Steelhammer Report' in Letters Received by HQ DoNM, September 1865-August 1890, NA, RG393, M1088, Roll 38, File 1664-2491, July–Sept. 1879.

54 Captain Hooker's Rebuttal Statement in 'Steelhammer Report', Letters Received by HQ DoNM, September 1865-August 1890, NA, RG393, M1088, Roll 38, File 1664-2491, July–Sept. 1879.

an attack of neuralgia.[55] Captain Steelhammer concluded that Hooker's angry and abusive efforts to improve his company would 'hardly ever become the proper agent for increasing the efficiency of our Army.'[56] He also noted that Captain Hooker's neuralgia had been further exacerbated by the loss of his horses, and he recommended that Hooker and E Company should be stationed at a post where the commanding officer would be superior to Hooker, thereby relieving 'the Captain of immeasurable little details, thus making life easier to him and perhaps more satisfactory to his men.'[57] We therefore have to take into account the distinct possibility that a less than rational, as well as prejudiced, man was in command at Ojo Caliente prior to Victorio's attack.

We also have to acknowledge a further two factors, one general and one specific, which played a significant role in the loss of the herd. The general factor is the basic daily routine to be found at any US army post, especially one that had not been directly attacked for some time; and this was combined with the specific weather conditions at Ojo Caliente, which dictated the actual routine adopted by the garrison.

All of these factors combined to play directly into the hands of the Apaches.

Ojo Caliente Raid, 4 September 1879

The basic routine concerning the grazing and watering of the horses at Ojo Caliente was straightforward. The herd was turned out early under the guard of a sergeant and four men and brought back to the post by 11 a.m. to be watered. During this break, the guard were fed and further instructions given to the sergeant in charge. The horses would be turned out from the post at about noon, and would not be expected back at Ojo Caliente until 5 p.m.[58] Due to the dry nature of the summer, Hooker reported that it had been necessary for the herd to be driven out between four and five miles from the post in order for the horses to find sufficient grass. However, 'latterly',[59] sufficient rain had fallen and there was no need for the herd to be driven very far from the post, with the guards being specifically enjoined by Hooker not to take the horses out of the main valley and into side gullies where they could be ambushed.[60] These orders were confirmed by four of Hooker's seven non-commissioned officers.[61] (See Appendix I)

On 4 September, the morning's schedule passed without incident and Sergeant Silas Chapman led the herd back out for its afternoon forage. During the afternoon, Captain Hooker was visited by a Mr Sullivan, a citizen from Cañada Alamosa, and informed that Victorio, Nana[62] and other prominent Apaches, with 35-40 warriors, had been spotted in the area of some ranches near the

55 This is described as an "intense, typically intermittent pain along the course of a nerve, especially in the head or face." Collins English Dictionary.

56 'Steelhammer Report' in Letters Received by HQ_DoNM, September 1865-August 1890, NA, RG393, M1088, Roll 38, File 1664-2491, July–Sept. 1879.

57 'Steelhammer Report' in Letters Received by HQ_DoNM, September 1865-August 1890, NA, RG393, M1088, Roll 38, File 1664-2491, July–Sept. 1879.

58 Capt. Hooker's testimony before a Board of Survey, 9 September 1879 in 'Steelhammer Report' in Letters Received by HQ_DoNM, September 1865-August 1890, NA, RG393, M1088, Roll 38, File 1664-2491, July–Sept. 1879.

59 Capt. Hooker's testimony before a Board of Survey, 9 September 1879 in 'Steelhammer Report', Letters Received by HQ_DoNM, September 1865-August 1890, NA, RG393, M1088, Roll 38, File 1664-2491, July–Sept. 1879.

60 Capt. Hooker's testimony before a Board of Survey, 9 September 1879 & Capt. Hooker interview in 'Steelhammer Report', Letters Received by HQ_DoNM, September 1865-August 1890, NA, RG393, M1088, Roll 38, File 1664-2491, July–Sept. 1879.

61 See also comments by Dobak & Phillips, 2001, pp.191-193.

62 Spelled 'Nani' in Steelhammer's Report.

Plate 7.1 View from Ojo Caliente towards the point where the horse herd was ambushed. The sound of the shots was masked by the low ridge descending from the upper right hand side of the photograph. (Photo: author)

Plate 7.2 On the other side of the ridge shown in the previous photo is a long ridgeline bisected by a series of deep ravines running down to flat ground, exactly as described by Lieutenant Taylor. One can see how low trees could have been used to conceal Apaches tasked with killing the horse guards in and around the ravine, whose mouth opens on the left of the photo. In the meantime, those mounted Chihennes who were to prevent the horses from stampeding back to Ojo Caliente could easily have hidden in the ravine, which opens on the right of the photo. This is not necessarily exactly where the ambush occurred, nor necessarily where the mounted Apaches concealed themselves; but the photo shows the nature of the terrain, which allowed the Apaches to attack the horse herd in such a manner as to give the guards no chance either to react or to alert the garrison at Ojo Caliente. (Photo: author)

headwaters of the Rio Cuchillo Negro,[63] approximately 12-18[64] miles from Ojo Caliente.[65] There had been at least one other sighting of Victorio, though whether Hooker had been made aware of this is unknown. *Thirty-Four* reported that one Antonio Garcia, on 29 August 1879, hearing that 10 Apaches had been seen to the south of Las Palomas had set out with 20 men to investigate. These men were suddenly confronted and surrounded by Victorio and approximately 50 warriors. However, Victorio on recognising Garcia, whom he had known for many years, merely advised the men to return to their homes. Garcia and his party heeded the advice and Victorio was last seen heading towards the Black Range. It was also reported that Victorio had the horses earlier reported to have been taken from Coghlan and other citizens in the vicinity of Tulerosa.[66]

Lieutenant Taylor, on sick report after his recent expedition to recover horses stolen by the Apaches and driven towards Navajo country, approached Captain Hooker at around 5 p.m. and offered to lead a detachment in search of these Apaches. Lieutenant Taylor wanted to set out at first light the following day but Hooker ordered that the expedition should depart that evening once the moon had risen.[67] As the horse herd was expected to return at any minute, both officers walked down to where the rest of the company were waiting to take in the horses and found that the herd had not returned. This did not immediately cause any alarm as the herders had sometimes been late in returning to Ojo Caliente.[68] By 6 p.m., however, it became plain that something was amiss. First Sergeant J. Robinson took a small party of men to some higher ground on the opposite side of the valley from the post,[69] and he returned to the officers and reported seeing a large dust cloud making off in the direction of the Luna Mountains[70] or Red Canyon and Luna Springs.[71] Captain Hooker later stated that the first sergeant had 'reported to me that he saw a large dust several miles off toward and to the right of a point of a mountain in the direction of Luna Springs.'[72] At the same time, Captain Hooker's brother, with the aid of a spy glass, spotted what was thought to be an Apache's pony emerging from one of the side valleys.[73] Fearing the worst, but still unsure whether

63 Lt. F.B. Taylor's testimony before a Board of Survey, 9 September 1879, Mr John Sullivan's testimony & Lt. Taylor interview in 'Steelhammer Report', Letters Received by HQ DoNM, September 1865–August 1890, NA, RG393, M1088, Roll 38, File 1664-2491, July–Sept. 1879.

64 Mr John Sullivan's interview in Capt. Hooker's Testimony before a Board of Survey, 9 September 1879 in 'Steelhammer Report', Letters Received by HQ DoNM, September 1865–August 1890, NA, RG393, M1088, Roll 38, File 1664-2491, July–Sept. 1879.

65 Capt. Hooker interview in 'Steelhammer Report', Letters Received by HQ DoNM, September 1865–August 1890, NA, RG393, M1088, Roll 38, File 1664-2491, July–Sept. 1879.

66 *Thirty-Four*, 3 September, 1879.

67 Capt. Hooker's interview & Lt. Taylor's Testimony before a Board of Survey, 9 September 1879 in 'Steelhammer Report', Letters Received by HQ DoNM, September 1865–August 1890, NA, RG393, M1088, Roll 38, File 1664-2491, July–Sept. 1879.

68 Capt. Hooker & Lt. Taylor's Testimony before a Board of Survey, 9 September 1879 & Capt. Hooker interview in 'Steelhammer Report', Letters Received by HQ DoNM, September 1865–August 1890, NA, RG393, M1088, Roll 38, File 1664-2491, July–Sept. 1879.

69 Capt. Hooker interview in 'Steelhammer Report', Letters Received by HQ DoNM, September 1865-August 1890, NA, RG393, M1088, Roll 38, File 1664-2491, July–Sept. 1879.

70 Lt. Taylor's Testimony before a Board of Survey, 9 September 1879 in 'Steelhammer Report', Letters Received by HQ DoNM, September 1865-August 1890, NA, RG393, M1088, Roll 38, File 1664-2491, July–Sept. 1879.

71 Capt. Hooker's testimony before a Board of Survey, 9 September 1879 in 'Steelhammer Report', Letters Received by HQ DoNM, September 1865-August 1890, NA, RG393, M1088, Roll 38, File 1664-2491, July–Sept. 1879.

72 Capt. Hooker interview in 'Steelhammer Report', Letters Received by HQ DoNM, September 1865-August 1890, NA, RG393, M1088, Roll 38, File 1664-2491, July–Sept. 1879.

73 Lt. Taylor's testimony before a Board of Survey, 9 September 1879 in 'Steelhammer Report', Letters Received by HQ DoNM, September 1865-August 1890, NA, RG393, M1088, Roll 38, File 1664-2491, July–Sept. 1879.

the horses had stampeded or had been ambushed, Captain Hooker sent Lieutenant Taylor, on the only remaining mount at Ojo Caliente (a partially broken down mule), with a non-commissioned officer and six troopers to investigate.[74] By the time this detachment arrived at the area where they expected to find the horse herd, it was dark, the moon being obscured by some clouds.[75] They managed to pick up the trail where the herd had entered a side valley, about a mile and a half from Ojo Caliente, by the use of lighted matches, and they discovered the point where deeper indentations in the ground indicated that the horses had commenced running. Lieutenant Taylor was also able to make out the traces of two or three moccasin tracks. He back tracked and discovered the bodies of two of the herd guard, but failed to discover the other three men. He left a guard over the bodies and returned to Ojo Caliente by 10 p.m.[76] A second detachment was sent to the area but returned around midnight with the two dead troopers, having failed to discover the fate of the other three guards. These men were finally discovered and brought in the following morning.[77] This time, Lieutenant Taylor was able to make a thorough examination of the area. He found clear signs that the herd had been carefully stalked by the Apaches and ambushed at a point where the gunfire could not have been heard at Ojo Caliente, the sound being blocked by an intervening ridge. The Apaches had also picked a spot where:

> the Horses had been quietly grazing along. Following up their tracks, they led across one or two little ridges into and across three little short Canons making out from a long Canon running parallel to a high ridge. These little Canons indent the West side of this Ridge (the side opposite or farthest from the Camp) – it was in and on the slopes of these little Canons that the Herd evidently was grazing when surprised by the Indians.
>
> On the eastern slope of the high Ridge just mentioned are two other little short Canons leading up from a long Canon extending back some distance into the Foot-hills. It was up those two little Canons that the Indians had approached the Herd, as shown by their Moccasin and Pony tracks; it was on or near the top of this high Ridge that the Indians had crawled and secreted themselves behind and under some low growing live Oaks, while preparing their Attack upon the Herd, several of the trees bearing in the trampled grass and weeds growing about their roots the marks of concealed Indians. From the crest of this Ridge the Indians could look directly upon the Herd, grazing probably not to exceed forty yards from them down the Slope.

Taylor estimated that not more than 15 Apaches had taken part in the killing of the guards, who had been taken completely by surprise, at point blank range. He thought that two of the men had been shot from their horses, while the other three had been dismounted and had been picked off while they attempted to prevent the horses from stampeding, though he implied that one of the dismounted men was probably killed in the opening volley. The rest of the Apaches had been tasked with gathering together the stampeding herd and preventing it from making back to Ojo Caliente. Some of the horses had evaded the Apaches and had made for Ojo Caliente, only to be rounded

74 Capt. Hooker & Lt. Taylor's testimony before a Board of Survey, 9 September 1879 & Capt. Hooker interview in 'Steelhammer Report', Letters Received by HQ DoNM, September 1865-August 1890, NA, RG393, M1088, Roll 38, File 1664-2491, July–Sept. 1879.

75 Lt. Taylor's testimony before a Board of Survey, 9 September 1879 'Steelhammer Report', Letters Received by HQ DoNM, September 1865-August 1890, NA, RG393, M1088, Roll 38, File 1664-2491, July–Sept. 1879.

76 Lt. Taylor's testimony before a Board of Survey, 9 September 1879 in 'Steelhammer Report', Letters Received by HQ DoNM, September 1865-August 1890, NA, RG393, M1088, Roll 38, File 1664-2491, July–Sept. 1879.

77 Capt. Hooker interview in 'Steelhammer Report', Letters Received by HQ DoNM, September 1865-August 1890, NA, RG393, M1088, Roll 38, File 1664-2491, July–Sept. 1879.

up by a small group of mounted Apaches stationed further down the ridgeline. Taylor thought that the Apaches had struck between 3 and 4 p.m. and noted that some of them had been armed with 50 calibre rifles.[78]

Lieutenant Taylor's reconstruction shows the Apaches' extremely careful approach to warfare. The only element Taylor missed is the probability that the herd's routine had almost certainly been quietly scouted for days as the Apaches sized up the target and pinpointed the ideal spot to ambush the herd without alerting the rest of the garrison at Ojo Caliente. Captain Steelhammer, having examined the ground, was more perceptive. While his interpretation of the raid largely agreed with the account offered by Lieutenant Taylor, Steelhammer was certain that the herd's routine had been closely observed by the Apaches for some days.

> The Indians had been concealed in the hills, evidently knowing that it was the custom of the herd guard going from the Post to keep in the main valley, but on their return not always to follow the same safe road...When the herd entered the hills the Indians under absolutely perfect cover swung their flanks around it until the herd was completely enveloped. Escape for either men or horses became simply impossible.[79]

The attack is a perfect example of the practical application of the Apache warfare manual. Having carefully scouted and evaluated the odds, the attackers killed five of their enemies, captured four privately owned officers' mounts, 46 troopers' horses and 18 pack mules, dismounting the one cavalry company based in the heart of their territory at no cost in warriors lost. Having examined the relationship between Hooker and his company and reconstructed the raid, Captain Steelhammer turned his attention to the allegations that Captain Hooker was directly responsible for the killing of the guard and the loss of the horses.

Aftermath

Captain Hooker, with one tired pack mule and a dismounted command, concluded that a viable pursuit of the Apaches was impractical. He despatched a courier on the same pack mule to the nearest telegraph office to relay the alarm to District Headquarters.[80] His hurried report immediately attempted to place the blame upon the herd guard[81] (see document file no. 10). Hooker stated that some of the guard had been dismounted and obviously idling, as one man had been found lying dead on his saddle blanket.[82]

78 Lt. Taylor's testimony before a Board of Survey, 9 September 1879 in 'Steelhammer Report', Letters Received by HQ DoNM, September 1865-August 1890, NA, RG393, M1088, Roll 38, File 1664-2491, July–Sept. 1879. See also Kenner, 1999, p.110.

79 'Steelhammer Report' in Letters Received by HQ DoNM, September 1865-August 1890, NA, RG393, M1088, Roll 38, File 1664-2491, July–Sept. 1879.

80 Capt. Hooker interview in 'Steelhammer Report', Letters Received by HQ DoNM, September 1865-August 1890, NA, RG393, M1088, Roll 38, File 1664-2491, July–Sept. 1879.

81 Hooker to AAAG, 5 September 1879 in NA, RG393, Part 3, Entry 439, pp.211-213; Returns From U.S. Military Posts; September 1879 Record of Events, 1800-1916 Ojo Caliente, N.M. May 1879-March 1882, NA, M617, Roll 877.
See also Loud to Gen. Willcox & CO's Fort Bayard & Bliss, 6 September 1879, Telegrams Sent DoNM, Vol.2, Jan. – Dec. 1879, NA, RG393, Part 3, Entry 431, pp.217-219; Capt. Hooker's Testimony before a Board of Survey, 9 September 1879 & Capt. Hooker interview in 'Steelhammer Report', Letters Received by HQ DoNM, September 1865-August 1890, NA, RG393, M1088, Roll 38, File 1664-2491, July-Sept. 1879; See also Appendix II.

82 Capt. Hooker's testimony before a Board of Survey, 9 September 1879 in 'Steelhammer Report', Letters Received by HQ DoNM, September 1865-August 1890, NA, RG393, M1088, Roll 38, File 1664-2491,

A board of survey was convened to establish responsibility for the loss of the herd. This investigation was commissioned by Captain Hooker 'for the purpose of ascertaining the quantity of Ordnance, and Quartermaster Stores and property, for which Captain A.E. Hooker, 9th Cavalry, is accountable, captured by Indians on the 4th of September 1879, and fix the responsibility therefore.' With Lieutenant Taylor as its only commissioned officer, 'No other officer being available under the Regulations for that duty',[83] the investigation unsurprisingly exonerated Hooker. Lieutenant Taylor was quick to echo Hooker's conclusion that, had the horse guard followed their orders, this debacle would not have occurred.[84] However, Lieutenant Taylor's general support for Captain Hooker should be considered in the light of charges preferred against him concerning a verbal and physical assault upon Trumpeter Benjamin Hockins on 21 October 1880 at Fort Cummings.[85] The assault was serious enough for Lieutenant Taylor to receive a sentence of dismissal from the army; but the sentence was commuted to suspension of rank and Taylor being confined to his post for one year on half-pay.[86]

However, Colonel Hatch ruled Hooker's own investigation to be invalid: 'You are not competent to approve a Board of Survey on property for which you are responsible.'[87] Hatch had already received instructions from General Pope that reports indicated incompetence, and that 'a thorough investigation' was required.[88] Hooker was tersely ordered to submit a report 'separate and independent from the Board of Survey in the premises.'[89] As the fighting against the Apaches died down at the end of October, Colonel Hatch was able to turn his attention to this incident. Hooker's failure to comply with these instructions and his clumsy attempt to circumvent District Headquarters probably provoked Hatch into sending Captain Steelhammer to Ojo Caliente. The following letter from District Headquarters deserves to be quoted in full:

> By direction of the District Commander I have the honor to acknowledge receipt of your Communication of Nov. 2" 1879, returning proceedings of Board of Survey convened by your orders No.5. without your having complied with instructions contained in letter from these Head Quarters dated Sept 22 1879. and to inform you in reply to so much of your Communication as states "I forwarded them through District Headqrs simply for the information of the District Commander being then as now unaware or ignorant of any law regulation or circular now in force subjecting the proceedings to his action approval or disapproval."

July–Sept. 1879.

83 Order No.5, 9 September 1879, In the Field, Ojo Caliente, Special Orders Rec'd from Sub Commands, NA, RG393, Part 3, Entry 453; Extracts of this Board of survey are reproduced in 'Steelhammer Report', Letters Received by HQ DoNM, September 1865-August 1890, NA, RG393, M1088, Roll 38, File 1664-2491, July–Sept. 1879. See also Hooker's Statement to the Board of Survey, convened at Ojo Caliente, N.M. 9 September 1879 in 'Steelhammer Report', Letters Received by HQ DoNM, September 1865-August 1890, NA, RG393, M1088, Roll 38, File 1664-2491, July–Sept. 1879.

84 Lt. Taylor's testimony before a Board of Survey, 9 September 1879 & Lt. Taylor interview in 'Steelhammer Report', Letters Received by HQ DoNM, September 1865–August 1890, NA, RG393, M1088, Roll 38, File 1664-2491, July–Sept. 1879.

85 Van Horn, Major, 13th Infantry, Specifying charges against Lt. Taylor in Letters Received by HQ DoNM, September 1865-August 1890, NA, RG393, M1088, Roll 42, Jan–Apr 1881.

86 General Court Martial Orders, No. 61. HQ of the Army, AGO, Washington, 4 November 1881 cited in Personal File Frank Beers Taylor, NA, RG94, Entry 297, Box 501.

87 Loud to Captain Hooker, 21 September 1879, Telegrams Sent DoNM, Vol.2, Jan.–Dec. 1879, NA, RG393, Part 3, Entry 431, p.238.

88 Pope to District Commander, 19 September 1879 in Letters Received by HQ DoNM, September 1865-August 1890, NA, RG393, M1088, Roll 38, July–Sept. 1879.

89 Loud to Hooker, 30 September 1879 in Letters Sent by the '9MD/DNM/DoNM', NA, RG393, M1072, Roll 6, Jan–Oct 1879, Letter No.480, p.344.

> That all Boards of Survey like other official communications are required to be forwarded through these Head Quarters and the District Commander further directs that hereafter you will strictly comply with his instructions relative to the same as given you in letter from this Office dated Sept. 22 1879.[90]

As we have seen, Captain Steelhammer, having interviewed each member of E Company, turned his investigation to the loss of the horses.

The first thing to note is that only 17 out of the 51 troopers interviewed indicated that they believed Captain Hooker to have been in some way responsible. However, of the seven E Company non-commissioned officers[91] interviewed, five, including the first sergeant, expressed a number of reservations about Captain Hooker's actions (see Appendix I). Some of these had already been expressed in the anonymous letter sent to District Headquarters. As a whole, they can be summarised as follows: that carbines and horse furniture (saddles and bridles) had not been issued to the guards; that the horse guard had been reduced from eight to five men at the beginning of August 1879; that no officer had been to inspect the ground over which the herd would be grazed; and, finally, that Captain Hooker had been explicitly warned that Apaches were active in the area.

Perhaps the most damning evidence which emerged concerned Hooker's failure to issue his guard detachment with saddles, bridles and carbines, which had meant that their only protection was their service revolvers. Hooker justified this lack of horse furniture as having been standard practice for a number of years in his company. He also argued that saddles used on this type of duty were more injurious to the horses ridden, and that the men were often better riders with just snaffle bits and blankets. Hooker had only issued the men with revolvers as they were engaged in escorting a moving herd, and he maintained that carbines were useless in a running fight.[92] When questioned, Lieutenant Taylor expressed the opinion that the troopers of the horse guard were not adequately equipped in either arms or accoutrements.[93] Steelhammer concluded that this practice was 'contrary to my personal experience.'[94]

The reduction of the horse guard from eight to five men, and the failure to raise the number of guards after a warning that Apaches were in the vicinity of Ojo Caliente, was also seen as displaying a lack of judgement. Hooker initially argued that this reduction was due to the fact that a large proportion of his men were absent on detached service in August, but was rather vague as to why this necessitated the reduction of the horse guard to five men. Hooker then revealed that he believed that if eight men were placed on horse guard duty, most would occupy their time in gambling, with any guard activity reduced to watching for the approach of an officer.[95]

---

90 Loud to Hooker, 17 November 1879 in Letters Sent by the '9MD/DNM/DoNM', NA, RG393, M1072, Roll 6, Jan-Oct 1879, Letter No.537 pp.380-381.

91 Captain Steelhammer interviewed all the remaining NCO's of E company; the First Sergeant (Robinson), three sergeants (Howard, Joanna. J. Williams) and three Corporals (Foster, Preston, R. Williams). See 'Steelhammer Report' in Letters Received by HQ DoNM, September 1865-August 1890, NA, RG393, M1088, Roll 38, File 1664-2491, July–Sept. 1879. See also Bi-Monthly Company Muster Rolls, E Company, 9th Cavalry, Sept/Oct 1879, NA, RG94.

92 Capt. Hooker interview in 'Steelhammer Report', Letters Received by HQ DoNM, September 1865-August 1890, NA, RG393, M1088, Roll 38, File 1664-2491, July–Sept. 1879.

93 Lt. Taylor interview in 'Steelhammer Report', Letters Received by HQ DoNM, September 1865-August 1890, NA, RG393, M1088, Roll 38, File 1664-2491, July–Sept. 1879.

94 'Steelhammer Report', Letters Received by HQ DoNM, September 1865-August 1890, NA, RG393, M1088, Roll 38, File 1664-2491, July–Sept. 1879.

95 Capt. Hooker interview in 'Steelhammer Report', Letters Received by HQ DoNM, September 1865-August 1890, NA, RG393, M1088, Roll 38, File 1664-2491, July–Sept. 1879.

Lieutenant Taylor acknowledged that he had not visited the grazing area,[96] nor had he been ordered to do so.[97] Captain Hooker also admitted that he had not visited the detachment, but claimed to have kept it under surveillance via his field glasses from the upper storey of his quarters. This, he felt, was a more effective method of supervision than riding out to the herd. Hooker then pointed out that he was overworked by clerical duties, due to his being short-handed that summer with his second lieutenant (Emmet) on detached service, his first lieutenant (Taylor) on periodic sick call, and he himself remaining on duty despite being sick.[98]

Hooker, as noted earlier, had given clear orders to the non-commissioned officer in charge of the herd to take the horses and mules only a short distance up the valley. They were not to go too far into the side canyons and were instructed to mount a vidette on the closest high ground.[99] Steelhammer was unimpressed with such a 'laissez faire' approach, particularly in the light of Hooker's stated contempt for the soldiers under his command. As far as Steelhammer was concerned, Captain Hooker should have taken a more direct supervisory role. It was clear that Hooker's chosen form of supervision was ineffective; and he had had no inkling of something amiss until at least an hour after the herd was due to return. Steelhammer dismissed the argument that had Hooker's orders been obeyed, the attack could have been forestalled, as the terrain precluded such a possibility. Steelhammer also argued that if Captain Hooker had been correct in his utterly negative evaluation of his troops, then he should have directly supervised the guarding of the horse herd.[100] However, Captain Steelhammer also noted that the loss of the horses could be attributed to the guards falling into an established routine which, up to the moment of the attack, had not been threatened. He also made a point of stating that had white soldiers been placed in charge of the horses, they would have fared just as badly.[101]

Hooker's culpability concerning having been forewarned is somewhat less clear, at least as far as Steelhammer's investigation was concerned. By the time Sullivan had reached Ojo Caliente, in the late afternoon, it is probable that nothing could have been done. Sullivan denied giving a specific warning that the Apaches were intending to attack the herd.[102] Hooker himself stated that earlier reports concerning the Apaches all indicated that the raiders had left the area and were making for the San Andres Mountains. The reports received from one or two of his men he either denied receiving or dismissed as garbled versions of the reports he had already received.[103] However, Hooker must have been aware that he was situated deep inside 'Victorio' territory. Not only was he based in the middle of the Warm Springs Apaches' heartland, but he was effectively

96 Corporal Williams testified that he had had a fleeting encounter with Lt. Taylor while on horse guard duty. This was the only visit by an officer to the grazing grounds during that summer but Lt. Taylor's mission that day was to track down a missing horse not to inspect the routine of the horse guards.

97 Lt. Taylor interview in 'Steelhammer Report', Letters Received by HQ_DoNM, September 1865-August 1890, NA, RG393, M1088, Roll 38, File 1664-2491, July–Sept. 1879.

98 Capt. Hooker interview in 'Steelhammer Report', Letters Received by HQ_DoNM, September 1865-August 1890, NA, RG393, M1088, Roll 38, File 1664-2491, July–Sept. 1879.

99 Capt. Hooker interview in 'Steelhammer Report', Letters Received by HQ_DoNM, September 1865-August 1890, NA, RG393, M1088, Roll 38, File 1664-2491, July–Sept. 1879.

100 'Steelhammer Report' in Letters Received by HQ_DoNM, September 1865-August 1890, NA, RG393, M1088, Roll 38, File 1664-2491, July–Sept. 1879.

101 'Steelhammer Report' in Letters Received by HQ_DoNM, September 1865-August 1890, NA, RG393, M1088, Roll 38, File 1664-2491, July–Sept. 1879.

102 John Sullivan interview in 'Steelhammer Report', Letters Received by HQ_DoNM, September 1865-August 1890, NA, RG393, M1088, Roll 38, File 1664-2491, July–Sept. 1879.

103 Capt. Hooker interview in 'Steelhammer Report', Letters Received by HQ_DoNM, September 1865-August 1890, NA, RG393, M1088, Roll 38, File 1664-2491, July–Sept. 1879.

occupying one of their most favoured camping grounds – one from which they derived at least two of their sobriquets.[104]

Indeed, it seems clear that Hooker had received other reports of Apache raiding prior to the raid. As noted in the previous chapter, F.B. Taylor had returned to Ojo Caliente after recovering stolen horses that had been taken from San Jose and driven north to the Navajo. He reported to Hooker that he had followed a trail of 25 horses southwards to Monica Springs at the northern end of the San Mateo Mountains. Taylor, being four days behind the Apaches, gave up the pursuit. He also assumed that these Apaches were Mescaleros and were returning to their reservation.[105] This report, taken on its own, might have lulled Hooker into a false sense of security; but it was not the only report received prior to the Ojo Caliente raid. Richard Stackpole wrote to Hooker from San Jose, on 31 August, recounting his adventures with Apache raiders in the San Mateo Mountains. Hooker acknowledged receipt of Stackpole's letter on 3 September 1879.[106]

Captain Steelhammer's conclusions were very critical of Hooker; but he avoided making a specific closing comment on who was responsible for the loss. One must remember that, according to the captain's remit, this judgement would be made by District Headquarters. Nevertheless, Hooker's actions in failing to properly arm or equip his detachment, his reduction of the number of guards, and his failure to keep himself apprised of the grazing routine of his horses, were not the actions of a capable field officer. For these reasons, Captain Hooker must shoulder the responsibility for the deaths of Sergeant Chapman and Privates Graddon, Hooke, Humphrey, and Percival, and for the loss of his horses and pack mules. Even given the careful preparations made by the Apaches, it was the negligence of Captain Hooker that created conditions where the attack could not fail. Not only did the Apaches employ the right tactics; their opponents were deprived of the means to mount an adequate defence.

Ultimately, no action was taken against Hooker for his failures at Ojo Caliente, and this implies that an issue of the actual, as opposed to theoretical, status of African American soldiers had not been resolved within the US army in the two decades following the American Civil War.

Captain Steelhammer's report on events at Ojo Caliente was received at District Headquarters on 2 March 1880 and sent out to Colonel Hatch on 6 March 1880.[107] Hatch finally received the report on the circumstances surrounding the September 1879 loss of E Company's horses on 10 March 1880, and he declared that he would review the case as soon as circumstances would allow. By this time, Victorio's warriors were again making their presence felt in southern New Mexico and, for the moment, no action against Hooker was taken.[108] Then, a delay in his proposed operational timetable allowed Colonel Hatch to have Hooker briefly arrested, on 15 April 1880.[109] Captain Loud contacted Captain Edwin Pollack, Ninth Infantry, Acting Assistant Inspector, District of New Mexico, with a view to gaining the latter's opinion as to whether Hooker should be court

104 Ojo Caliente literally means 'warm eye' in Spanish and approximates to 'Warm Springs' in relation to the hot water springs in the heart of Victorio's territory. They were known, among others, to the Americans under both these names.

105 Taylor to Hooker, 31 August 1879 in Letters Received by HQ_DoNM, September 1865-August 1890, NA, RG393, M1088, Roll 38, July–Sept. 1879.

106 Hooker to Stackpole, 3 September 1879 in Letters Received by HQ_DoNM, September 1865-August 1890, NA, RG393, M1088, Roll 38, July–Sept. 1879.

107 Loud to Hatch, Fort Bayard, 6 March 1880 in Letters Sent by the '9MD/DNM/DoNM', NA, RG393, M1072, Roll 6, Jan 1880-August 1881, Letter No.126 pp.96-97.

108 DoNM, General and Special Field Orders, Letters and Telegrams, (Hereafter referred to as 'DoNM/GSFO/L&T'), NA, RG393, Part 3, Entry 475, Vol. 5, p.57; Loud to AAG, DoM, Fort Leavenworth, 15 March 1880 in Letters Sent by the '9MD/DNM/DoNM', NA, RG393, M1072, Roll 6, Jan 1880-August 1881, Letter No.149, p.110.

109 Special Field Order No.22, Para. 4, 15 April 1880, NA, RG393, Part.3, Entry 450; Special Field Orders No. 22, 'DoNM/GSFO/L&T', NA, RG393, Part 3, Entry 475, Vol. 5, p.326.

martialled.[110] Hatch, having finally considered Captain Steelhammer's report, recommended that Hooker be charged on three counts, first, for neglect of duty concerning the loss of five men and the horse herd at Ojo Caliente; second, for 'conduct prejudicial to military discipline;' and finally, given the 'gross brutal language used', for 'conduct unbecoming an officer and a gentleman.'[111]

Due to the on-going nature of field operations Hatch ordered that Hooker be released from arrest and restored to the command of his battalion on 18 April 1880.[112] Hatch referred Steelhammer's report back to Captain Pollack for his opinion as to whether Hooker should be court-martialled.[113] On 18 September 1880, Hatch recommended that Hooker should not face a court-martial, even though Captain Pollack had endorsed Hatch's earlier conclusion that Hooker should be tried in front of a military court. Hatch now argued that the cost of tracking down witnesses who had subsequently been discharged would be too expensive, and therefore he foresaw an '"uncertainty of establishing the charges before a court martial'[114]. He also pointed out that Captain Hooker's company was usually very well trained, and that there was no problem in getting men to re-enlist.[115] Hooker had probably taken the opportunity to give poor references to those men who had complained and whose terms of service had subsequently expired. The rest had probably been left in no doubt as to the hazards involved in testifying against their commanding officer. However, Hooker had destroyed any chance he might have had of further promotion. Hatch might have chosen not to air a very distasteful episode in public, but he also made it abundantly clear that the captain's conduct was not appropriate. Hatch clearly felt that this incident warranted a court martial and was confident enough to record that, as far as he was concerned, Captain Hooker was 'wholly responsible' for the loss of the horse herd.[116] General Pope, in accepting the decision not to proceed with a court martial, also recorded in the clearest language his censure of Hooker's conduct[117] (see document file no. 10)

In conclusion, we must ask ourselves what it must have been like for the men of E Company to serve under an officer who was possibly as dangerous to them as their Apache opponents. Indeed, Hooker was, in many ways, a more constant and immediate threat to their wellbeing. Off the post, they would have to maintain their vigilance for ambush by adept Apache guerrillas. Yet no matter where they were, in the field or on-post, they also had to contend with a very hostile officer.

One man, however, found the raid rather amusing, though his glee was probably prompted by intergovernmental rivalry. Agent Russell, on receipt of the news that Ojo Caliente had been attacked, wrote to Lieutenant Smith and concluded, 'am sorry to hear it, this is about one horse for

110 Loud to Pollock, 23 April 1880 in Letters Sent by the '9MD/DNM/DoNM', NA, RG393, M1072, Roll 6, Jan 1880-August 1881, Letter No.215, p.146.

111 Hatch to AAG, 17 April 1880, DoNM General and Special Field Orders, Letters and Telegrams, NA, RG393, Part 3, Entry 475, Vol. 5, p.163 & p.177.

112 Special Field Order No. 24, 18 April 1880, NA, RG393, Part 3, Entry 450.

113 Loud (citing Hatch to AAAG, DoNM, 17 April 1880) to Pollack, 23 April 1880 in Letters Received by HQ DoNM, September 1865-August 1890, NA, RG393, M1088, Roll 40, Jan.–June 1880.

114 Hatch to AAG, DoM, Fort Leavenworth, 13 September 1880 in Letters Sent by the '9MD/DNM/DoNM', NA, RG393, M1072,Roll 6, Jan 1880–August 1881, Letter No.483, pp.312-313.

115 Hatch to AAG, DoM, Fort Leavenworth, 13 September 1880 in Letters Sent by the '9MD/DNM/DoNM', NA, RG393, M1072, Roll 6, Jan 1880–August 1881, Letter No.483, pp.312-313.

116 Hatch to AAG, DoM, Fort Leavenworth, 13 1880 in Letters Sent by the '9MD/DNM/DoNM', NA, RG393, M1072, Roll 6, Jan 1880–August 1881, Letter No.483, pp.312-313; See also Hatch to AAG, DoM, 13 September 1880 in Letters Received by HQ DoNM, September 1865–August 1890, NA, RG393, M1088, Roll 41, July–Dec 1880.

117 General Pope's endorsement added to Hatch to AAG, DoM, 13 September 1880 in Letters Received by HQ DoNM, September 1865-August 1890, NA, RG393, M1088, Roll 41, July–Dec 1880.

each Indian man. Rather a joke on the Cavalry, isn't it.'[118] That Russell would commit this sentiment to paper at all, let alone send it to an officer of the Ninth Cavalry, gives some measure of the man. Lieutenant Smith, who was charged with, amongst other things, guarding Russell and his employees, politely pointed out that had Russell acted in a timely fashion on the information he received that a trail of stolen animals had been seen heading towards the reservation some days previously, some of these animals might have been returned to their owners. Smith concluded:

> I desire to add that the killing of five U.S. Soldiers and the stealing of fifty two Government Animals as "A joke on the Cavalry", the light in which you regard it, is not as apparent to my mind as it is yours.[119]

McEvers' Ranch

Major Morrow received news of the Ojo Caliente raid on 6 September 1879,[120] though he later claimed that he did not hear of the raid until 11 September.[121] District Headquarters received the news on or around 7 September, and issued instructions that Morrow should 'spare no efforts' to catch the raiders, and that Hooker should resupply the major if required.[122] It was judged that the Warm Springs Apaches were becoming too 'bold', and that it was imperative that a serious reverse be inflicted on these miscreants.[123] District Headquarters also attempted to warn Lieutenant B.S. Humphrey then marching between Fort Stanton and Fort Bayard, to be on the alert for ambush and to take the closest care of his horses.[124]

On 11 September, Morrow sent couriers to Beyer ordering him to proceed from the Caballo Mountains, to take up the trail of Hooker's stolen horses in the vicinity of Luera Springs, and to follow the trail with vigour.[125] Captain Hooker reported that Beyer arrived 'five or six days' after the horses were lost.[126] Two days later, Morrow sent out Captain Byron Dawson and Lieutenant Day from Fort Bayard, with three Navajo scouts, and 17 men from A Company and five from B Company, Ninth Cavalry, to pursue Victorio from McEvers' Ranch. Dawson was also to attempt to find and join Captain Beyer's detachment. At the same time, Morrow sent instructions to Lieutenant Wright to proceed to McEvers' Ranch from Aleman and to join Captain Dawson's detachment.[127] For the second time in 1879, L Company, Ninth Cavalry was sent out from Fort Bliss to Old Fort Cummings to scout and guard the stage line that ran between the Rio Grande and Silver City.[128]

---

118 Russell to Lt. G.W. Smith, 12 September 1879 in Letters Received by HQ DoNM, September 1865-August 1890, NA, RG393, M1088, Roll 38, July–Sept. 1879.

119 Smith to Russell, 13 September 1879 in Letters Received by HQ DoNM, September 1865-August 1890, NA, RG393, M1088, Roll 38, July–Sept. 1879.

120 Morrow to Loud AAAG Santa Fé, 6 September 1879 in NA, RG393, Part 3, Entry 439, p.214.

121 Morrow to AAAG DoNM, 5 November 1879, 'Victorio Papers', NA, M666, Roll 526.

122 Loud to Hooker, 7 September 1879 in Letters Sent by the '9MD/DNM/DoNM', NA, RG393, M1072, Roll 6, Jan-Oct 1879, Letter No.447, pp.321-322.

123 Loud to CO Fort Bayard, 7 September 1879 in Letters Sent by the '9MD/DNM/DoNM', NA, RG393, M1072, Roll 6, Jan-Oct 1879, Letter No.448, pp.322-323.

124 Loud to Humphrey via hand of Lt. Emmett, 7 September 1879 in Letters Sent by the '9MD/DNM/DoNM', NA, RG393, M1072, Roll 6, Jan-Oct 1879, Letter No.449, p.323.

125 Morrow to AAAG DoNM, 5 November 1879, 'Victorio Papers', NA, M666, Roll 526.

126 Captain Hooker's Counter Statement in 'Steelhammer Report', Letters Received by HQ DoNM, September 1865-August 1890, NA, RG393, M1088, Roll 38, File 1664-2491, July–Sept. 1879.

127 Morrow to AAAG DoNM, 5 November 1879, 'Victorio Papers', NA, M666, Roll 526.

128 Hatch to CO Fort Bliss, 7 September 1879, Telegrams Sent DoNM, Vol.2, Jan.–Dec. 1879, NA, RG393, Part 3, Entry 431, p.219; *Army & Navy Journal*, Vol.17, 27 September 1879, p.136.

The raid at Ojo Caliente finally woke up the Department of Arizona to the renewed danger of an attack on San Carlos. The news was received on 7 September, and the following deployments ordered.[129] A Sixth Cavalry detachment and D Company, Apache Scouts, commanded by Lieutenant G. Howard, moved out from Camp Huachuca. Another Sixth Cavalry detachment and C Company, Apache Scouts, were activated at Fort Bowie under Lieutenant Blocksom. This detachment had orders to scout the Hatchet and Florida Mountains to investigate rumours that the Apaches were moving in that direction. A third detachment under Captain Tupper scouted west from Fort Grant towards Ash Spring near the Gila. Finally, Fort Apache sent out Second Lieutenant Gatewood with 20 White Mountain Apaches from A Company, Apache Scouts and 15 troopers from the Sixth Cavalry towards Clifton, to cover the approaches to San Carlos.[130] From the point of view of the Arizona troops, these deployments were put in place just in time, as Colonel Hatch telegraphed that it was thought the Warm Springs Apaches were in the Mogollon Mountains preparing for a strike on San Carlos.[131]

However, it was the citizens of Hillsboro and the surrounding miners' camps that would next feel Victorio's wrath. On or around 10 September 1879, the Apaches struck this area in general, attacking isolated groups of miners and ranchers. The aim of these attacks seems to have been to lure out and ambush a relief force from Hillsboro.

Here we encounter a recurring problem facing researchers: that of vague, garbled, or even inaccurate reporting. It was reported that 10 soldiers from Morrow's command had been killed in a battle with Apaches at McEvers' Ranche, south of Hillsboro,[132] on 10 September.[133] In fact, this report is a classic case of a relatively hurried telegram giving completely the wrong impression as it passed up the chain of command. There was no skirmish between the Ninth Cavalry and Apaches at McEvers' Ranch. Major Morrow was merely relaying information contained in a telegram reporting a disastrous encounter between a posse from Hillsboro and Victorio's

129 Arnold to CO Fort Bayard, 8 September 1880, Troops in Southeastern Arizona, DoAz, NA, RG393, Part 1, Entry 232, Vol.4, 3 July, 1879–Dec. 13 1879, Letter No.96, p.61.

130 Arnold to AAG Dept. Arizona, 7 September 1879, Troops in Southeastern Arizona, DoAz, NA, RG393, Part 1, Entry 232, Vol.4, 3 July, 1879–Dec. 13 1879, Letter No.59, pp.60-61; Arnold to Lt Gatewood, Fort Apache, 7 September 1879, Troops in Southeastern Arizona, DoAz, NA, RG393, Part 1, Entry 232, Vol.4, 3 July, 1879–Dec. 13 1879, Letter No.94, p.60; Arnold to CO Fort Bayard, Lt Gatewood, through CO Fort Apache, and AAG Dept. Arizona, 8 September 1880, Troops in Southeastern Arizona, DoAz, NA, RG393, Part 1, Entry 232, Vol.4, 3 July, 1879–Dec. 13 1879, Letter No.'s 96-98, pp.61-62; Field Order No. 13, 7 September 1879, NA, RG393, Part 1, Entry 238, p.6; Arnold to CO DoNM, 8 September 1879, Troops in Southeastern Arizona, DoAz, NA, RG393, Part 1, Entry 232, Vol.4, 3 July, 1879–Dec. 13 1879, p.64; Thrapp, pp.182-183; Stout, p.90 & p.94; See also *Grant County Herald*, 20 September 1879.

131 Arnold to Major Chaffee, Agent San Carlos, 11 September 1879, Troops in Southeastern Arizona, DoAz, NA, RG393, Part 1, Entry 232, Vol.4, 3 July, 1879–Dec. 13 1879, Letter No.109, p.68.

132 Hillsboro was born in 1877 when silver was discovered in the mountains around the Rio Percha (See Hillsboro webpage entry).

133 Thrapp, 1974, p.237; 'Indian Affairs' *Army & Navy Journal*, Vol.17, 27 September 1879, p.137; *Grant County Herald* of the 27 September 1879 quotes Hatch as follows: "Colonel Hatch telegraphs from Santa Fé that he had a five hours' fight near Hillsborough in which he had ten men killed and several wounded and lost all their stock. All available troops have been ordered to that point and Col. Hatch hopes shortly to overtake the Indians." ('By Telegraph', *Grant County Herald*, Sat. 27 September 1879) Stout also argues that the unfortunate Captain Hooker was once again in command of this detachment. (p.92) In view of the information gained from Kenner that Hooker did not take to the field until December 1879 when he received new mounts, Hooker himself was not present at these battles. It should be noted that O'Neal wrongly places Major Morrow in charge of this skirmish (O'Neal, p.177).

warriors.[134] This error was quickly spotted and rectified within days of its transmission.[135] (see document file no. 11) This battle would also be marked by what would be an oft repeated rumour: that Victorio had been killed in the fight.[136]

The Chronological List mentions two engagements in New Mexico on 10 September 1879. Seven 'civilians' were killed at McEvers' Ranch, and two more 'civilians' lost their lives near the Arroyo Seco.[137] Major Morrow filed a report on 17 September detailing the deaths of 10 citizens in a posse from Hillsboro and the loss of all their horses.[138] Ashenfelter, editor of the *Grant County Herald*, recorded a series of attacks on 11 September and on 20 September 1879. Seven Anglo-Americans were reported to have been slain 'in a cornfield' and 10 Mexican men, women and children were killed and 25 wounded, both attacks occurring near McEvers' Ranch. One Joe Yankie was 'mentioned in dispatches' for helping to rally the survivors of the ambush.[139]

Almost a year later, the US army carried out an investigation into the numbers of citizens killed during the Victorio 'outbreak', and it listed Refugio Alicies, Steve Hanlon, Thomas Hughes, Jose Mareno, Thornton, Perrier?,[140] Greene and Dr Williams as 'killed in action' at McEvers' Ranch on 10 September 1879[141] (see document file no. 65.3).[142] *Thirty-Four* lists seven men and 30 horses killed in a fight near McEvers' Ranch and 10 Mexicans killed at Jaralosa on 11 September.[143]

---

134 Morrow to Loud AAAG SF 13 September 1879, NA, RG393, Part 3, Entry 439, p.341; See also Arnold to Tupper & Gatewood, AAG Dept. Arizona, 13 September 1879, Troops in Southeastern Arizona, DoAz, NA, RG393, Part 1, Entry 232, Vol.4, 3 July, 1879–Dec. 13 1879, Letter No.110-112, pp.68-70; Arnold to CO Fort Thomas, Troops in Southeastern Arizona, DoAz, NA, RG393, Part 1, Entry 232, Vol.4, 3 July, 1879–Dec. 13 1879, Letter No.113, p.71; Loud to AAG Fort Leavenworth, 17 September 1879, 'Victorio Files', NA, RG393, M1495, Roll 14.

135 Loud to Hatch, Fort Garland, Col., 17 September 1879; Telegrams Sent DoNM, Vol.2, Jan.–Dec. 1879, NA, RG393, Part 3, Entry 431, p.231; See also Loud, AAA General to Major Arnold, Fort Grant, 17 September 1879, NA, RG393, Part 1, Entry 235, p.12; Loud to AAG Fort Leavenworth, 17 September 1879, 'Victorio, NA, RG393, M1495, Roll 14; Loud to Major Arnold, Fort Grant, 17 September 1879, Telegrams Sent DoNM, Vol.2, Jan.–Dec. 1879, NA, RG393, Part 3, Entry 431, p.230; Arnold to CO Fort Thomas, 15 September 1879, Troops in Southeastern Arizona, DoAz, NA, RG393, Part 1, Entry 232, Vol.4, 3 July, 1879–Dec. 13 1879, Letter No.116, pp.72-73.

136 *Thirty Four*, 17 September 1879; Loud to AAG Fort Leavenworth, 19 September 1879, Telegrams Sent DoNM, Vol.2, Jan.–Dec. 1879, NA, RG393, Part 3, Entry 431, p.234.

137 Chronological List, p.47; Webb, 1976, p.86.

138 Record of Engagements, p.92; See also Wellman, 1957, pp.152-153; Longstreet, p.91.

139 Correspondence Editorial, *Grant County Herald*, 20 September 1879.

140 The original document is sometimes hard to decipher.

141 J.J. Coppinger to AAG, DoNM, 26 July 1880 in Letters Received, DoM 1868-98, RG 393, Entry A1-1 2601, Box 91.

142 Author's note: I have tried to keep the accompanying original documents in chronological order but 65.3 was written in mid-1880 summing up the citizen fatalities from mid-1879 to mid-1880. It contains key information about the McEvers' Ranch battle but will be included in the original documents for Volume II of this history of the Victorio Campaign. If readers desire to see a copy of this report email me at r.n.watt@bham.ac.uk and title the email 'McEvers' Ranch Document' and I shall send them a copy.

143 *Thirty Four*, 17 September 1879; 'Our Indian Troubles', *Grant County Herald*, 20 September 1879; Stout, p.92.

The figures of seven Anglo-Americans and ten Mexicans killed on the same day may have led these figures to be combined into a story where seventeen or eighteen Hillsboro men being killed in the ambush. Lummis states that seventeen members of a Hillsboro posse were killed at McEvers' Ranch. (Thrapp, 1979, p.157)The El Paso Times, 1 March 1942, states that sixty men from the town of Hillsboro and the surrounding miner's camps, set forth to punish Victorio's Apaches. However, despite spotting the Apaches, before the posse could react, their enemies occupied a rocky hill and opened fire killing eighteen members of the posse. The article notes that the slain were buried in a mass, rock covered, grave that could still be seen in 1942 (See also Rakocy, 1983, pp.108-110).

The latter attack is remembered, even today, in that part of New Mexico, as being particularly savage and William Bates, recalled that they had found:

> seven men, women and children – their nude bodies mangled. A young girl, semi-conscious, lay propped up on her elbow staring at her mother. She mumbled, "Dame agua" They took her to a Hillsboro doctor where she died of lance wounds through both cheeks.[144]

Bates stated that this was at 'Jaralosa Cienega, some 5mi. from McEvers' Ranch'. He also reported that heated iron bars or drills had been used to violate the women, who were left lying on the ground 'half naked'.[145] It was reported that the victims 'were most horridly and disgustingly mutilated, iron bars being used for the purpose.'[146]

Another eyewitness account was left by Frank Clifford, who referred to the ranch as the Lake Valley Ranch rather than McEvers'. He added that the relief force from Hillsboro split into two groups. The smaller group made up of about 15 men, led by Clifford's close friend Thomas Hughes, cut through the hills making directly for McEvers' Ranch. A second, much larger, group took a more circuitous route round the hills. It was the first group which was ambushed and the second group which discovered the carnage at Jaralosa, and though Clifford implies that this was the Lake Valley Ranch, his descriptions of burnt buildings, death and mutilation agree with Bates' account.[147] Clifford notes that of the group led by Hughes, only one man escaped, and that Hughes was the first to be killed. He also noted that the ambush was sprung 'in a pocket in the hills'[148] which, if we accept that the hills referred to are no more than between 50 and 100 feet high, does fit the suspected site of this ambush. It was a sobering experience for Clifford to witness the aftermath of the attack on Jaralosa, but he also noted that 'If I had gone with Tom, as ninety-nine times out of a hundred I would have, I'd have almost certainly got mine too.'[149]

Finally, Sarah Gibson left an eyewitness account of events around McEvers' Ranch. It is this account which reveals that there were, in fact, three ranches along a lake (which Gibson describes as a swamp) 12 miles to the south of Hillsboro. McEvers lived at the upper end of the swamp, the Irwins family lived at the bottom end, and the Gibsons lived in a house between the two.[150] On the day of the attack, her son saw what he thought were Apache heads popping up and down behind rocks near the Irwins' Ranch. Mr Irwins dismissed the sighting but her son reported seeing a lot of moccasin tracks. On their return to their own ranch, they heard gunfire from McEvers' Ranch and both her husband, Bill Gibson, and Irwins grabbed their weapons and made their way towards McEvers' Ranch:

> Mrs Gibson could see Bill taking aim at an Indian who wore a very large hat and he made the remark to Irvins [Irwins] "Here hold my horse (as he dismounted and handed him the bridle),

144 William M. Bates Interview Notes c. 1940 in the Keith Humphries Collection, Geronimo Springs Museum, Truth or Consequences, New Mexico.

145 Information in the Keith Humphries interview notes with William Bates 20 Jan. 1940 (Email from Daniel D. Aranda, 8 Aug. 2014).

146 *Grant County Herald*, 20 September 1879 (Email from Daniel D. Aranda, 25 August 2014).

147 Clifford, F. & Nolan, F. (editor) 2011, *Deep Trails in the Old West: A Frontier Memory* (University of Oklahoma Press: Norman) p.49.

148 Clifford, F. & Nolan, F. (editor) 2011, *Deep Trails in the Old West: A Frontier Memory* (University of Oklahoma Press: Norman) p.50.

149 Clifford, F. & Nolan, F. (editor) 2011, *Deep Trails in the Old West: A Frontier Memory* (University of Oklahoma Press: Norman) p.50.

150 Gibson, S. *'From the Archives: Sarah Gibson's Story' Hillsboro Historical Society, February 2016, Vol. 9, No.1,* p.4.

> I want that hat" He fired and the red man fell off his horse with a loud yell, but his comrade caught him and carried him away in his arms. So Bill missed getting his hat. In the fighting one white man was wounded. A bullet hit him in the arm, tearing the flesh from it and went through his breast to the other arm. But fortunately he got all right. The Indians were after the horses and the men were shooting at the Indians to make them leave the horses alone.[151]

Gibson also recounted an incident that took place at the same time, in which the Apaches had made a Mexican family of nine members strip off their clothing and had then taunted them before leaving. One of the children, a boy, was convinced that the Apaches would return and hid in a cave. He was the only survivor when the Apaches returned and killed the rest of the family. She also mentioned that these Apaches had returned after they had killed seven men from Hillsboro.[152] These incidents are possibly a garbled version of the Jaralosa attack and the ambush of the Hillsboro posse. What this eyewitness did not realise was that she had seen the skirmishing around the eastern side of McEvers' Ranch, without realising that this was the bait to draw the Hillsboro men into the deadly ambush to the west of the ranch. Ashenfelter, editor of the *Grant County Herald*, believed that these attacks commenced with a direct attack upon McEvers' Ranch in order to revenge the loss of two warriors there 'last Spring'.[153] The Apaches took all of the horses corralled there, but nobody was killed as 'McEvers fought them hard from his yard.'[154] Ashenfelter also observed that:

> upon hearing of the attack, at least all who could raise a gun or a horse, rushed to the assistance of the ranche, going in two's and threes as fast as they could get ready; and, as the Indians occupied a position at this time, between Hillsborough a portion of the people thus scattered ran into them before they knew of their whereabouts when the battle opened.[155]

The attacks at Jaralosa and McEvers' Ranch were not the only attacks recorded at this time. The *Grant County Herald* recorded how one Stapleton,[156] though wounded, managed to hold off his attackers using a breech-loading buffalo rifle.[157] An Apache was also reported killed at the Jurado Ranch. In two other attacks, two men named Flores from Las Cruces were killed, along with an unidentified Mexican; the Armijo family, again accompanied by an unnamed Mexican, were also reported as killed by the Apaches.[158]

From the Apache point of view, since 4 September 1879, they had systematically targeted the enemy in the immediate vicinity of the Black Range and San Mateo Mountains. Victorio probably set up ambush in favourable terrain between McEvers' Ranch and Hillsboro after the attack on the Mexicans at Jaralosa. All that was left was to send a few men to harass the occupants of McEvers' Ranch. The atrocity at Jaralosa, in itself suggests an act of revenge, the Jaralosans being targeted

151 Gibson, S. *'From the Archives: Sarah Gibson's Story' Hillsboro Historical Society, February 2016, Vol. 9, No.1,* p.5.

152 Gibson, S. *'From the Archives: Sarah Gibson's Story' Hillsboro Historical Society, February 2016, Vol. 9, No.1,* p.5.

153 There appears to be no record of such an incident and it seems likely that Ashenfelter has confused an incident in May 1879 further to the west where four Apaches were killed in an attack upon a ranch in the San Fransico Valley (See Chapter Six).

154 Editorial, *Grant County Herald*, 20 September 1879.

155 Editorial, *Grant County Herald*, 20 September 1879.

156 This is probably the same individual who was involved in a skirmish with Apaches in the San Mateo Mountains just before the attack upon Hooker at Ojo Caliente.

157 'Editorial', *Grant County Herald*, 20 September 1879.

158 'Editorial', *Grant County Herald*, 20 September 1879.

for participating in earlier skirmishes and/or working for McEvers, who was an army forage agent. However, the carnage at Jaralosa was further intended to cloud the judgement of any relief force from Hillsboro, thus making the relief force even more vulnerable to an Apache ambush. While the Apaches generally had a reputation for cruelty, the events at Jaralosa seem anomalous. Though Victorio had a 'popular' image of being cruel, the reality appears to have been that he did not indulge in torture or atrocities as part of his normal routine. Therefore, if there is any truth to the Bates testimony (as we shall see, he recalls quite specific events regarding the campaign against Victorio later in September 1879), then this attack, at first glance, appears to be outside of the norm for Chihenne Apaches under the direction of Victorio and Nana. However, one possibility is that they intended their opponents' outrage to cloud any attempt at cool judgement. Could such a brutal attack have been perpetrated in this instance to provoke blind rage on the part of the relief from Hillsboro? The Chihennes would have had no hesitation in killing men, women and children when necessary;[159] but to do something like this appears beyond the pale, until one considers the intended outcome of the discovery of the bodies. Whether or not these tortures were actually committed, or were simulated post-mortem, the desired effect was probably to influence the actions of those who discovered the bodies and push them towards their own imminent destruction.

Thus, the gunfire from the direction of McEvers' Ranch was all that would have been required to precipitate these men into a headlong ride in that direction and straight into Victorio's trap.[160] In visiting this area in 2005 and 2007, we[161] discovered a likely spot for this ambush a short distance from McEvers' Ranch. This point looked quite insignificant – until it was examined more closely. If this is the correct site, it was a deadly killing ground, for the Apaches chose to picket a curve in the trail to set up a deadly crossfire from the very small bluffs to one side of the road (See Map 7.1)

From 4 September 1879, the Apaches constructed a series of 'domino' events. The attack on Ojo Caliente had crippled the only US army unit stationed in the immediate vicinity. The subsequent attack upon Jaralosa provoked a response from Hillsboro. The discovery of the bodies at Jaralosa was designed to inflame their opponents to the extent that when they detected fighting at McEvers' Ranch, they would gallop to the rescue. Killing at least 10 volunteers from Hillsboro, plus 30 horses, allowed Victorio's warriors to fan out and launch wider attacks on isolated Mexicans and Anglo-Americans without fear of interference from the only volunteer force stationed in the immediate area. It also attracted the attention of the Ninth Cavalry detachments sent out from Fort Bayard in search of the Apaches. These would be Victorio's next target.

Ninth Cavalry detachments might have been the next intended target, but the testimony of Frank Clifford states that the men from Hillsboro, realising that the women and children living at the Lake Valley Ranch were vulnerable, set out to protect the ranch from the approaching Apaches. The larger group found the carnage at Jaralosa, whilst the smaller group ran into the ambush just outside McEvers' Ranch. If Clifford's rather brief account is accurate, it would appear that Victorio's plan worked, but not in the way the Apache leader had intended. Whatever unexpected

159 After all, their enemies, American, Mexican and Apache, would have little hesitation in killing Chihenne women and children.

160 This was a tactic well known to Amerindian warriors, a good example being an ambush perpetratedby, Seneca Ottawa and Ojibway warriors at 'Devil's Hole' near Fort Niagara in September 1763, where a supply train was deliberately ambushed in order to draw out a relief force from a nearby outpost occupied by men from the 80th Regiment of Foot. The main ambush had already been prepared between the outpost and the ambushed supply column. Two companies of redcoats were caught in the trap and were virtually annihilated. The combined fatalities for both ambushes came to approximately seventy-two men. (See Parkman, pp.40-44; Anderson, 2000, pp.550-551; Brumwell, pp.173-174; Jennings, 1988 p.446.

161 I was accompanied by Dan Aranda, Emilio Tapia and Berndt Kuhn in 2005 and Dan Aranda, Emilio Tapia and Eric Fuller in 2007.

Plate 7.3 View up the road from Apache position at Point F on map 7.1. (Photo: author)

Plate 7.4 View down the road towards McEvers' Ranch from Apache position at Point D. The man just visible on the road is almost at the point where the posse was ambushed at Point A. The Apaches at Point B, who probably opened fire at point blank range, would have been based behind and above where the road passes the low tree. It is unlikely that these trees were present in 1879. The Apaches at Point F would have been just to the right and in front of the distinctive pointed dark tree. The Apache position at Point C can be partially seen on the ridge running off the upper right of the photo. (Photo: author)

Plate 7.5 View from Apache positions at Point C. If one examines the previous photo the cover looks quite sparse; but if one walks along this ridge, there are a number of spots where Apaches could have concealed themselves in good hard cover. (Photo: author)

Plate 7.6 The perspective the Hillsboro men would have had just before they turned the corner and were ambushed. Apache positions along Point C are just below the skyline across the length of the photo. Apaches hidden at Point D would be to the right and above the point from where this photograph was taken. Also note the sunflowers present at the right and in the centre of the photo. (Photo: author)

actions occurred, they did not frustrate Victorio's intention of catching a significant group of men from Hillsboro and virtually exterminating them. As Clifford himself concluded, and no doubt this was one of the intended effects of the ambush,'[s]omehow, the life there did not suit me after that, so in the late Spring[162] I pulled out again for the "wide open spaces"'.[163]

However successful the military tactics and strategies deployed by Victorio were, the damage caused by these attacks also had political effects which he probably did not foresee. These political effects would ultimately contribute to his destruction.

A key question for Ashenfelter was, where did the Apaches get their modern guns and abundant supply of ammunition? Again, he saw the reservation system as the culprit:

> Around these reservations are to be found devils, who wear human form, whose whole business is to exchange arms, ammunition and liquor, for the property stolen from the hardy pioneer.[164]

He adds that the Apaches: 'got them [arms and ammunition] in barter from blackhearted whites and Mexicans and often through the connivance of the agent and his strikers.'[165] In these press reports, we can see the seeds of a real problem for the US army embodied in the attitude to the Apaches of the majority of Anglo-American miners, ranchers and tradesmen living in New Mexico. The almost universal hostility towards the Apaches initially found its outlet in condemning the distant policies of the US federal government. As representatives of that government, the local US army units would increasingly come under fire from the majority of the local press commentators, as the Victorio Campaign dragged on with no end in sight. In other words, the very effectiveness of Victorio's resistance would ultimately undermine the possibility of a return to the Ojo Caliente reservation as a viable political solution to this conflict.

For the moment, the editor of the *Grant County Herald* was content to comment on how the US army was constrained in its ability to combat the Apaches because of federal reservation policy. In further articles, Ashenfelter faulted the reservation system for protecting 'horse thieves & brigands.'[166] He also pointed out that the long range 'needle guns', probably Springfield pattern or similar rifles, out-ranged the Winchester 73s held by most of the Hillsboro posse. Only one or two men, armed with long-range Sharps buffalo rifles, had any hope of hitting their targets.[167] It was clear that Victorio's followers were very well supplied with modern guns and ammunition. Much of this equipment was probably gathered during Nana's stay on the Mescalero reservation, but on returning to the Black Range, Victorio probably renewed his old trading links with various Mexican settlements in the area. That very month, Hatch dismissed rumours that the US Government had armed the Apaches with 'needle guns' as absurd and argued that the Apaches were able to find guns and ammunition through illegal trade networks and raiding.[168]

The ambush of the Hillsboro posse and other attacks prompted calls for the formation of at least one citizen militia at the mining camp of Shakespeare in southwestern New Mexico, for protection from the Apaches and other desperadoes. The aim of such volunteer companies was clear: the

162 As noted earlier, Clifford dates the attack in which Hughes was killed to the spring, when Hughes was killed in September 1879. Therefore, it would appear that Clifford departed Hillsboro in the fall of 1879.

163 Clifford, F. & Nolan, F. (editor) 2011, *Deep Trails in the Old West: A Frontier Memory* (University of Oklahoma Press: Norman) p.50.

164 'The Indian Question' *Grant County Herald*, 27 September 1879.

165 'Longe Range Guns' *Grant County Herald*, 27 September 1879.

166 'The Indian Question' *Grant County Herald*, 27 September 1879.

167 'Long Range Guns, *Grant County Herald*, 27 September 1879.

168 Hatch to AAG, DoM , 6 Sept. 1879 in Letters Received, DoM 1868-98, RG 393, Entry A1-1 2601, Box 83.

volunteers were to mete out summary justice to Apaches, even if the latter had retreated onto an Indian reservation.[169] Indeed, by 17 September, Governor Wallace had contacted the Secretary of War to request 'federal authority' to raise three or four companies of volunteers to serve in the field against the Apaches.[170] Having received no information as to the severity of the war, McCrary refused to grant such permission.[171] However, he did contact General Pope, asking for his opinion on the governor's request and stating that he was not inclined to accede to this request 'unless on your judgement it is absolutely necessary and then to be raised under your directions.'[172] More importantly, the Secretary of War asked that more details of the war, the number of Apaches, and an opinion as to whether the US army could deal with this problem, be sent to him as soon as possible.[173] It was at this point that Pope informed the Secretary of War of the raid on Hooker's command at Ojo Caliente and the defeat of a party near McEvers' Ranch, and gave as his opinion that there were sufficient troops to deal with the crisis.[174]

The newspapers had begun to criticise the federal government for not caring about the troubles suffered by US citizens at the hands of the Apaches. The latter, described as the federal government's 'pets', were accused of having paralysed the local economy for over a decade through their raiding and murder. The US army was not yet being heavily criticised, as its very operations were stated to have been hindered by the reservation system where 'the Indian may have "saving grace" poured into him by hypocritical psalm singers'[175].

From Victorio's point of view, his breakout had been singularly successful. As the breakout began, the aged, women and children were safely spirited into the safety of the Black Range.[176] James Kaywaykla, a child at the time, states that the Warm Springs Apaches fled from the Mescalero reservation on 21 August 1879, heading for the Black Range via the San Andres Mountains and crossing the Rio Grande. He also states that the families remained hidden, undisturbed, for several weeks, replenishing supplies from caches, while the warriors came and went, often disappearing for long periods.[177] This is a very interesting statement, as the Ninth Cavalry would record at least two major skirmishes with Victorio on 18 and 29-30 September. Kaywaykla does not indicate that he or any other women and children were nearby during these confrontations. This strongly suggests that Victorio had already adopted a tactic of focusing his opponent's attention away from the Chihenne Apache women, children and other vulnerable members of the tribe. Thus, while the Ninth Cavalry expended their efforts in a vain pursuit of unencumbered warriors, the latter's women and children, essential components in Victorio's logistic system, were left undisturbed.

Thus, by 11 September, Victorio had made a clear declaration of war by striking the two closest groups of armed opponents in his territory. But his 'domino' effect tactic was not finished; he still needed to deal with the detachments of Ninth Cavalry roaming the area in search of him. Having drawn conspicuous attention to himself at Jaralosa and McEvers' Ranch, all that was left was to leave a clear trail leading up the Animas River into the Black Range.

169 *Grant County Herald*, 20 September 1879; 'The Indian Question, *Grant County Herald*, 27 September 1879.
170 Wallace to McCrary 17 September 1879, 'Victorio Papers', NA, M666, Roll 526.
171 McCrary to Wallace, 18 September 1879, 'Victorio Papers', NA, M666, Roll 526.
172 Townsend, AG to General Pope 18 September 1879, 'Victorio Papers', NA, M666, Roll 526.
173 Townsend, AG to General Pope 18 September 1879, 'Victorio Papers', NA, M666, Roll 526.
174 Pope to Townsend AG Wash. D.C. 18 September 1879, 'Victorio Papers', NA, M666, Roll 526.
175 'The Indian Question, *Grant County Herald*, 27 September 1879; *Thirty Four* 8 October 1879.
176 Stout, p.90.
177 Ball, 1970, pp.64-67.

8

Headwaters, the Animas, 18 September 1879

> Capt Dawson & Lt Wright were attacked by Indians at head water of the animas in the black range troops were under a bluff & Indians attacked them from above shooting & throwing rocks at them. Capt Beyer & Joe Gankin [Yankie?] with force of soldiers & citizens arrived in time to prevent massacre 4 or 5 of the soldiers killed.[1]

After the events around McEvers' Ranch, the Ninth Cavalry detachments focused their attention on that ranch and Hillsboro. However, Colonel Hatch, as District Commander, was called away to deal with a crisis concerning the Utes in Colorado on or around 14 or 15 September 1879,[2] leaving the operation to trap Victorio in the hands of Major Morrow. Yet, for the moment, Morrow was unable to act, as he still did not have a clear idea of the whereabouts or the intentions of the Apaches. Morrow sent two Ninth Cavalry detachments from Fort Bayard to search for Victorio: on 13 September, Captain Dawson led out 23 cavalrymen[3] from B Company,[4] and the following day, Lieutenant Day led out 17 enlisted men from A Company.[5] Two other Ninth Cavalry detachments were already in the field searching for the Apaches. On 13 September, a detachment led by Captain Beyer passed through Hillsboro, following a trail which led towards the Mimbres River. Beyer led 28 men from C Company, accompanied by Lieutenant Hugo with 24 men from G Company.[6] Fearing that the settlements there might be in imminent danger, his command, now accompanied by some 16 citizens from Hillsboro,[7] made for the Mimbres by the most direct route. Finding no signs of Apaches, this detachment called in at Fort Bayard to replenish supplies before returning towards Hillsboro.[8] A second detachment, commanded by Lieutenant Wright, accompanied by 15 troopers and four or five Navajo scouts,[9] passed through Hillsboro late on 14 September, having marched from Aleman on the Jornada del Muerto. This detachment reached McEvers' Ranch the following morning, where its scouts attempted to pick out the main trail of the Apaches from

---

1 Undated possibly unsent telegram signed 'H' (The telegram is signed with an 'H' but this does not correspond in style with other telegrams, which are usually signed 'Hooker'. This could, of course, mean that Hooker's adjutant wrote most of these telegrams and that Hooker only wrote such missives when urgency required), NA, RG393, Part 3, Entry 439, p.348.

2 See Telegrams Sent DoNM, Vol.2, Jan.–Dec. 1879, NA, RG393, Part 3, Entry 431, pp.226-227.

3 'An Account of the Las Animas Fight' in *Thirty Four* 31 September 1879; 'Our Indian Problem' *Grant County Herald*, 20 September 1879; Thrapp, 1974, p.239.

4 Bi-Monthly Company Muster Rolls for Company B, 9th Cavalry, Sept/Oct 1879 in NA, RG94.

5 Bi-Monthly Company Muster Rolls for Company A, 9th Cavalry, Sept/Oct 1879 in NA, RG94.

6 Bi-Monthly Company Muster Rolls for Companies C & G, 9th Cavalry, Sept/Oct 1879 in NA, RG94.

7 Joe Yankie, who helped rally the survivors of the Hillsboro posse ambushed on 11 September is named as leading fifteen citizen volunteers who had joined Captain Beyer's detachment (*Grant County Herald*, 20 September 1879).

8 'An Account of the Las Animas Fight' in *Thirty Four* 31 September 1879; Thrapp, 1967, p.183

9 The typescript is too difficult to decipher ('An Account of the Las Animas Fight' in *Thirty Four* 31 September 1879).

the numerous trails leading from the site of the ambush near the ranch.[10] Here he was joined by Captain Dawson and Lieutenant Day, who must have joined forces either prior to, or on arrival at, McEvers' Ranch.

Morrow also summoned reinforcements, and Captain Purington, with H Company, Ninth Cavalry, was ordered to transfer from Fort Stanton to Fort Bayard on 7 September 1879. He arrived at Bayard on 22 September without having encountered any signs of Apaches during his march.[11] L Company, Ninth Cavalry, whom we earlier saw transferred to Old Fort Cummings, was placed at Major Morrow's disposal should he require them to pursue Victorio.[12] In the meantime, Victorio's warriors had not been idle, and two more civilians were slain in the Black Range on 17 September 1879.[13]

A clear trail was discovered by Lieutenant Wright's Navajo scouts on 16 September, going north from McEvers' Ranch. The tracks were judged to be two days old and followed the Animas River into the Black Range. The combined detachments[14] of Dawson and Wright set out in pursuit. The Animas River flows out of these mountains in a complex of steep canyons as various small creeks feed into the main river. The canyon bottoms themselves can be very steep as they descend the mountains, and they are flanked by rough, precipitous canyon walls.[15] It was in this rugged terrain that Victorio sprang his trap, as the Ninth Cavalry unit pursued the trail towards the headwaters of the river.

On the morning of 18 September, as they were ascending a canyon, with the Navajos fanning out in the lead, the cavalrymen walked straight into a prepared ambush. The trail had been littered with dead cattle, and the troops had seen what they thought might be the grave of an Apache warrior.[16] In hindsight, these signs were probably left in order to lead the pursuers into the ambush. As they neared the head of the canyon, the Navajo scouts alerted the command that they were very close

---

10 'An Account of the Las Animas Fight' in *Thirty Four* 31 September 1879.

11 Bi-Monthly Company Muster Rolls for Company H, 9th Cavalry, Sept/Oct 1879 in NA, RG94.

12 Hatch to CO Fort Bayard, 13 September 1879, Telegrams Sent DoNM, Vol.2, Jan.–Dec. 1879, NA, RG393, Part 3, Entry 431, p.225.

13 Chronological List, p.47; Webb, 1976, p.86.

14 Again, both main sources, Thrapp and Stout are very vague as to the make-up of this rapidly coalescing Ninth Cavalry battalion. Other secondary sources are difficult to reconcile. Kenner states that a small detachment under the command of Captain Dawson (B Company) and Lt Day (A Company), numbering twenty-two troopers and accompanied by three Navajo scouts were ambushed first. Captain Beyer and forty men arrived later in the day (Kenner, 1999, p.193; See also Record of Engagements, p.92). Leckie and Billington clearly state that Colonel N.A.M. Dudley commanded a group of Navajo scouts and Company B and Company E, Ninth Cavalry under Captain's Dawson and Hooker respectively. Events would subsequently suggest that there were another two Ninth Cavalry companies in the vicinity, Captain Beyer's C Company and Lt Hugo's G Company (Leckie, 1967, p.211; Billington, 1991, pp.90-91; Schubert, 1997, p.54; Beyer & Keydal v, p.413; See also Wellman, 1957, p.153; Longstreet, p.91). The Chronological List states that the column was commanded by Capt. C.D. Beyer with companies A, B, C & G (See also Webb, 1976, p.86). In the main text of his work, Burton concurs with Leckie on the Ninth Cavalry Companies, which were present and the officers in command. He gives 18 September as the date of the ambush (Burton, 1999, p.159). Yet in an appendix, he dates this battle to 16 September, and cites Company A instead of company E as being present. However, Major Morrow's own report of the battle quoted by Thrapp seems to add to the confusion. He states that a group under First Lieutenants Dawson and Wright, and Second Lieutenant Day were initially ambushed and that Hooker's and Hugo's Company's joined the fight later. (Thrapp, 1974, p.239; We must remember that Major Morrow was not present at the time. He was probably either preparing to leave Fort Bayard or was actually in the field when he wrote this report and may not have had the time to verify the details of particular events.)

15 Thrapp, 1974, p.240; See also webpages covering the ceremony commemorating the battle in the 1990s.

16 'An Account of the Las Animas Fight' in *Thirty Four* 31 September 1879.

Two photographs of a US Cavalry company on patrol in the Black Range, New Mexico a few years after the Victorio Campaign. This gives a good indication of the sort of terrain the Ninth Cavalry searched for and sometimes fought Chihenne Apaches. (The National Archives)

Kaytennae. This younger Chihenne warrior was an active participant in the war for the return of the Chihenne reservation under both Victorio 1877-1880 and Nana 1880-81. He appears to have been a very good shot and was later recorded by a US Army officer as having shot a wild pig through the head from a galloping horse. (The National Archives)

to the Apaches, and the troopers dismounted and deployed in skirmish formation.[17] Suddenly, one of the Navajo scouts was shot dead by a single rifle shot.[18] Victorio's warriors had concealed themselves along the top of the canyon walls, and held their fire until the battalion below was in the midst of their positions (see document file no. 12 for contemporary reports of this battle). The single shot was immediately followed by heavy fire from the rest of the warriors.[19] These opening volleys appear to have been aimed at the horses, as only two cavalrymen were wounded; but all three officers had their horses shot from under them.[20] Finding themselves under heavy fire from all directions, the surprised scouts and troopers tried to find adequate cover; but the Apaches had stationed themselves in hard cover from which little ground remained unexposed to their firing positions. The Ninth cavalrymen and Navajos found themselves pinned down, unable to retreat or advance under their opponent's crossfire, for almost two hours.[21] William Bates, a civilian volunteer from Hillsboro, later described the Apaches occupying bluffs hidden by thick 'manzanita' bushes.[22]

17 'An Account of the Las Animas Fight' in *Thirty Four* 31 September 1879.
18 'An Account of the Las Animas Fight' in *Thirty Four* 31 September 1879; Stout, p.96.
19 'An Account of the Las Animas Fight' in *Thirty Four* 31 September 1879; Stout, p.96.
20 'An Account of the Las Animas Fight' in *Thirty Four* 31 September 1879.
21 'An Account of the Las Animas Fight' in *Thirty Four* 31 September 1879.
22 William M. Bates Interview Notes c. 1940 in the Keith Humphries Collection, Geronimo Springs Museum, Truth or Consequences, New Mexico.

The Animas headwaters were clearly an isolated spot, and days later, when inspecting the site for himself, Morrow reported taking one hour and twenty minutes to ascend the canyon to the battle site.[23] In fact, virtually every source that mentions this site comments upon the sheer difficulty of reaching it.[24] A courier was despatched for aid[25] and the soldiers and scouts skirmished as best they could from what little cover they could find. However, Victorio's warriors had chosen their positions carefully and they proved invulnerable to either a direct assault or flanking attacks.[26] However, the noise of the battle alerted the detachment led by Captain Beyer, who attempted to relieve the trapped men. He sent a detachment under Lieutenants Emmet and Hugo to flank the Apaches' position, and they briefly overran the Apaches' camp before being driven back, losing one soldier, a civilian called Jack Hagan, and 12 horses.[27]

> The squadron galloped about three miles up the canon [canyon] to the rescue of this detachment. They found that Captain Dawson, Lieutenants Wright and Day, and a small detachment of soldiers and indian scouts were penned up under a small rocky point, unable to escape and surrounded by nearly two hundred Indians. The squadron attempted to make a direct attack, but was unable to open connection with the detachment, when the Commanding Officer directed a flank attack to be made. Lieut. Hugo – with Troop "G" – accompanied by Lieutenant Emmet moved up the canon and climbed out to attack the Indian camp in order to draw the Indians back from the ambuscade. The attack was at first successful, but the Indians returned in force from the ambuscade and slipping up through the bushes and surprised the attacking party, driving them back into the canon. Lieutenant Emmet, with five men, who had been farthest in the advance, were thus momentarily left behind and cut off from the troops. Finding that the Indians were making for a position from which they could get a direct fire on the retreating troop, the Lieutenant held this point with his party until the soldiers reached shelter in the canon; and then, noticing that a number of men including Lieutenant Hugo, had tied their horses to bushes in the indian camp and left them behind in the excitement of the sudden attack, Lieutenant Emmet and his soldiers held the indians in check until all the horses were loosened, secured together and led down the trail by one of the number, losing one of his soldiers in this gallant defense.[28]

The newcomers spent the afternoon trying in vain to dislodge Victorio's warriors. At some point during the fight, one of the Navajo scouts managed to move so close to the Apache positions that he was seen to be killed by a revolver shot.[29] Acting Assistant Surgeon Lewis Kennon, in the midst of scanning the canyon walls with his field glasses, suddenly had them blown to bits in his hands

23 Morrow to AAAG Dist. Of New Mexico, 5 November, 1879 in 'Victorio Papers', M666. Roll 526; Thrapp, 1974, p.240.

24 See Rene Romo Journal Bureau cited in Albuquerque Journal, Sept, 14, 1996; Frentzel, Albuquerque Journal, Dec 12, 1996; Associated Press cited in The Arizona Republic, June 16, 1997; Reed, The Albuquerque Tribune, cited in The Denver Post June 20, 1999; Jackson, Albuquerque Journal, Nov 16, 2000.

25 Thrapp, 1967, p.183; Ashenfelter, 'The Fight on the Animas' *Grant County Herald*, 27 September 1879.

26 'The Fight on the Animas' *Weekly New Mexican* 11 October 1879 in The Walter Lowry Finley Collection; Stout, p.96; Leckie, 1967, p.211; Schubert, 1997, p.54.

27 'An Account of the Las Animas Fight' in *Thirty Four* 31 September 1879; 'Letter from Georgetown', *Grant County Herald*, 4 October 1879.

28 Letter written by Matthias W. Day, 31 July 1898 in Personal File Robert T. Emmet, NA, RG94, Entry 297, Box 758; See also Indian War Period Medals of Honour webpage.

29 'An Account of the Las Animas Fight' in *Thirty Four* 31 September 1879.

by a bullet.[30] Many years later, aged 88, William Bates recalled that they had been trapped in the canyon bottom and that he had taken cover in some thick mountain mahogany. He was close to a Ninth cavalryman who had taken cover slightly down the canyon from him, and was talking to him 'to sorta keep up their spirits.' At that point, he heard a bullet strike what he took to be a tree and kept talking. When he got no response, he looked around to find that the soldier had been killed. He recalled that this man was the third soldier to be killed during the battle.[31] The *Phoenix Herald* and the *Arizona Citizen*, both on 4 October 1879, noted that, of the citizen volunteers, Bates 'specially distinguished himself' during the battle.[32]

The entire detachment was trapped, and the fire-fight continued until twilight. The Ninth cavalry battalion started to withdraw in the early-to-mid afternoon. However, it was only when darkness fell that they were finally to work free of the trap.[33] Beyer's troopers discharged several volleys in quick succession, intended to make the Apache warriors duck back, allowing Dawson's detachment to finally extricate itself.[34] The ground was so rough that it was impossible to remove the wounded using travois, and thus they were evacuated by mule, each wounded man astride a mule led by one of his comrades. The bodies of those killed in this fight were abandoned on the field.[35] The combined detachment retreated for 16 miles down the Animas River that night.[36] The detachment had to abandon most of the officers' baggage; and a large quantity of supplies, which probably included ammunition, were all left to Victorio's warriors, having been transported on the dead or captured horses and mules. There was no indication of any Apache casualties.[37] On 19 September, the force left the Black Range and returned to Hillsboro. Lieutenant Wright was stationed at that

30 Ashenfelter, 'The Fight on the Animas' *Grant County Herald*, 27 September 1879; 'The Fight on the Animas' *Weekly New Mexican* 11 October 1879 in The Walter Lowry Finley Collection; Thrapp, 1967, p.184; 1974, p.240.

Some modern sources indicate that a surgeon was one of the fatalities (Rene Romo Journal Southern Bureau, cited in *Albuquerque Journal*, Sept 14, 1996; Associated Press cited in *The Arizona Republic*, June 16, 1997; Reed, *The Albuquerque Tribune* cited in The Denver Post, June 20, 1999) This is unlikely as according to Special Order No 9 1880, states that Acting Assistant Surgeon Lewis Kennon's contract had been annulled. (Special Order 9, Par 1, Jan 19 1880 in NA, RG393, Part 3, Entry 450); Kennon was also noted as setting up practice in Silver City in February 1880. ('Town & County, *Grant County Herald*, 14 February 1880) Two years earlier, Hatch had received reports that Kennon on a trip to New York with Captain Oscar Hagan of the Ninth Cavalry had been unofficially reported to be "intoxicated" several times. (Hatch to Hagan, 24 September 1878 in Letters Sent by the '9MD/DNM/DoNM', NA, RG393, M1072, Roll 6, Letter No.417 p.292) Kennon was not the only army medical officer with a fondness for alcohol. Hatch recommended that the contract of AA Surgeon W.B. Lyon be terminated "He is a person of dissipated habits, and therefore not fitted for the position of Surgeon in the U.S. Army" (Hatch to AAG, DoM, Fort Leavenworth, 19 March 1879 in Letters Sent by the '9MD/DNM/DoNM', NA, RG393, M1072, Roll 6, Jan-Oct 1879, Letter No.135 p.97) The contract reported terminated by 13 May 1879 (Hatch to AAG, DoM, Fort Leavenworth, 13 May 1879 in Letters Sent by the '9MD/DNM/DoNM', NA, RG393, M1072, Roll 6, Jan-Oct 1879, Letter No.236, p.169).

31 William M. Bates Interview Notes c. 1940 in the Keith Humphries Collection, Geronimo Springs Museum, Truth or Consequences, New Mexico.

32 In Library of Congress 'Chronicling America' website (http://chroniclingamerica.loc.gov/).

33 'The Fight on the Animas' *Weekly New Mexican* 11 October 1879 in The Walter Lowry Finley Collection; *Weekly New Mexican* 27 September 1879 in The Walter Lowry Finley Collection; Thrapp, 1974, p.239; Thrapp, 1967, p.184; Thrapp, 1988, pp.383-384; Billington, 1991, p.91; Leckie, 1967, p.211.

34 Ashenfelter, 'The Fight on the Animas' *Grant County Herald*, 27 September 1879; 'The Fight on the Animas' *Weekly New Mexican* 11 October 1879 in The Walter Lowry Finley Collection.

35 Morrow to Loud AAAG 26 September 1879, NA, RG393, Part 3, Entry 439, pp.361-362; See also Hatch to AAG Fort Leavenworth, 30 September 1879, Telegrams Sent DoNM, Vol.2, Jan.–Dec. 1879, NA, RG393, Part 3, Entry 431, p.259.

36 Report of Acting Assist. Surgeon Lewis Kennon, in AR-WD, NA, M997, Roll 35, 1880 Vol. I, p.519.

37 'The Fight on the Animas' *Weekly New Mexican* 11 October 1879 in The Walter Lowry Finley Collection; Thrapp, 1974, p.239.

point, with 25 troops from C Company, while the remainder of the troops retreated to Fort Bayard, arriving at that post on 22 September 1879.[38]

The only published Apache version of this engagement is given by James Kaywaykla, who thought that Lieutenant Colonel N.A.M. Dudley[39] had commanded the troops. He stated that that the detachment was lured into a trap by a small number of Apache warriors. These were standard tactics aimed at leading Dawson's command into a trap and crippling it by targeting the horses.[40] Thus, no matter what the outcome of the ambush, it would prevent further pursuit of the Apaches. Finding themselves in an unassailable position, the Apaches then inflicted as many casualties as possible with the minimum of risk.

Three soldiers were ultimately awarded the Congressional Medal of Honor for their actions that day: Sergeant John Denny, Second Lieutenant Day and Second Lieutenant Emmet. Sergeant Denny went to the rescue of Private Alfred Freeland, B Company, carrying him to safety under intense fire.[41] Freeland was described as shot through the leg, trying to use his arms to drag himself towards his comrades, and under constant fire from the Apaches. Seeing Freeland's predicament, Sergeant Denny charged forward and carried him to cover.[42] Similarly, Lieutenant Day refused to abandon his wounded on being instructed to retire. He charged forward approximately 200 yards under sustained fire to carry off a wounded cavalryman. Despite these efforts, the trooper rescued, Jeremiah Crump (Caump in some sources) B Company, died two days later.[43] Lieutenant Day was eventually awarded the Medal of Honor for his exploit, but not before Captain Beyer allegedly tried to have him court-martialled for disobeying orders.[44] Finally, as noted earlier,[45] Lieutenant Emmet had been part of Beyer's relief effort and had bravely covered the withdrawal.

---

38 Personal File Henry H. Wright, NA, RG94, Entry 297, Box 334; 'An Account of the Las Animas Fight' in *Thirty Four* 31 September 1879; Record of Events September 1879 in Returns From Regular Army Cavalry Regiments 1833-1916, 9th Cavalry Regimental Returns 1873-1880, NA, M744, Roll 88; Bi-Monthly Company Muster Rolls for Company C, 9th Cavalry, Sept/Oct 1879 in NA, RG94.

39 It should be noted that Lt. Col. Dudley was nowhere near the Las Animas River in Sept 1879. There is clear evidence in the National Archives that Dudley had been ordered to Fort Union in March 1879. Moreover, Dudley places himself at Fort Union on 18 September 1879 as he wrote to District HQ from that post requesting transportation for witnesses at his trial concerning his conduct during the Lincoln County War (Dudley, Fort Union, N.M. to AAG, DoNM, 18 September 1879 in Letters Received by HQ DoNM, September 1865-August 1890, NA, RG393, M1088, Roll 38 July–Sept. 1879).

40 Ball, 1970, p.72.

41 Schubert, 1995; Schubert, 1997, pp.54-55; Kenner, 1999, p.194; Burton p.159; O'Neal, pp.32-33; Personal File Matthias W. Day, NA, RG94, Entry 297, Box 1; Bi-Monthly Company Muster Rolls for Company B, 9th Cavalry, Sept/Oct 1879 in NA, RG94.

42 Beyer & Keydal, pp.413-414. Freeland was shot in the thigh (Kennon to Barnes, 22 September, 1879 in Kennon L.W.C., Personal Papers of Medical Officers and Physicians (Medical Officers Files) RG 94, Entry 561).

43 Bi-Monthly Company Muster Rolls for Company B, 9th Cavalry, Sept/Oct 1879 in NA, RG94; 'The Fight on the Animas' *Weekly New Mexican* 11 October 1879 in the Walter Lowry Finley Collection; Report of Acting Assist. Surgeon Lewis Kennon, in AR-WD, NA, M997, Roll 35, 1880 Vol. I, p.519; Kenner, 1999, p.194; Schubert 1995; Schubert, 1997, p.56.

44 Thrapp, 1974, p.240; 1967, Thrapp, 1988, pp.384-385; p.184; Stout, p.97.

45 Lt Emmet is not mentioned in the original reports of this fight. In a report by Morrow, Emmet is listed as commanding Navajo scouts despatched to the area after news of the Las Animas Canyon defeat reached him. (Thrapp, 1974, p.239) Lt RT Emmet had arrived at Fort Bayard on the 27 June 1879 with ten Navajo scouts. It seems that he and his small detachment joined the pursuit of Victorio after the events in Las Animas Canyon. (Moore, pp.211-212) However, it is clear that the force involved in the Las Animas Canyon fight returned to Fort Bayard so it is perfectly possible for Emmet's Navajos to have been involved in the earlier battle and then joined in subsequent operations against the Apaches. They could have joined Beyer's command. It also should be noted that both Dawson and Wright backed

Casualty List Discrepancies

The casualty list for this engagement is rather mysterious, and the figures difficult to reconcile.[46] Some of the primary sources can be variously read to suggest that five troopers, two Navajo scouts and an American civilian were killed; two troopers were seriously wounded; 53 horses and mules were lost, many being killed in the fire fight;[47] and the citizen volunteers lost all of their horses in the engagement.[48] Against this estimate, a careful reading of telegrams sent at the time suggests that the casualty list *might* be as low as two soldiers, two Navajo scouts and one civilian scout killed[49] (see Appendix II). Yet an article published in 1993 by the writer Gene Ballinger claims that 32 soldiers, two Navajos and one Anglo-American guide were killed.[50] This last version of events is not supported by the post return for Fort Bayard, the regimental monthly return, or the bi-monthly muster rolls for the Ninth Cavalry (see Tables 8.1-8.3); and the only discrepancy concerning human fatalities the present author has come across is the statement in the monthly regimental return that one soldier from C Company, Ninth Cavalry, had been killed.

Table 8.1 Ninth Cavalry Casualties, 18 September 1879[51]

Company	Men	Horses/Mules
A	None	4 Horses killed in action
B	1 Man killed in action and 1 man wounded in action	13 Horses killed in action
C	1 Man killed in action[1]	None
G	1 Man killed in action	12 Horses killed in action

Note

1 The *Arizona Citizen*, 11 October 1879 states that 'One of the two colored soldiers wounded in the Indian battle died at McEvers and was buried with the other victims of the Indian massacre. This makes sixteen bodies in the new graveyard on the hill. We have since learned that the other wounded soldier died at Fort Bayard' in Library of Congress 'Chronicling America' website (http://chroniclingamerica.loc.gov/)

his application for a Medal of Honor in 1899 (Personal File Robert T. Emmet, NA, RG94, Entry 297, Box 758).

46 This is before we even attempt to make sense of the secondary sources. Webb notes that four soldiers and a citizen slain with a further two soldiers wounded (Webb, 1976, p.86); Schubert implies an even lower casualty list than the official one. He names Peter Haines (G Company) as being killed outright and Jeremiah Caump (B Company) as mortally wounded (Schubert, 1997, p.56; see also Schubert, 1995). The Chronological List gives the casualties as four 'enlisted' men and one 'civilian' killed and two more 'enlisted' men wounded (Chronological List, p.47). See also Thrapp, 1974, p.239; 1967, p.184; Stout p.98; Leckie, 1967, p.211; Worcester, p.220; Burton, p.159; Moore, p.212;; Wellman, 1957, p.153; Longstreet, p.91.

47 Loud to Hooker, 29 September 1879, Telegrams Sent DoNM, Vol.2, Jan.–Dec. 1879, NA, RG393, Part 3, Entry 431, pp.255-256; 'The Fight on the Animas' *Weekly New Mexican* 11 October 1879 in The Walter Lowry Finley Collection; See also Hatch to AAG, DoM, Fort Leavenworth, 14 February 1880 in Letters Sent by the '9MD/DNM/DoNM', NA, RG393, M1072, Roll 6, Jan 1880-August 1881, Letter No.82, pp58-65.

48 *Thirty Four* 31 September 1879.

49 Morrow to Loud AAAG 23 September 1879, NA, RG393, Part 3, Entry 439, pp.344-347; Loud to Hatch, 23 September 1879, Telegrams Sent DoNM, Vol.2, Jan.–Dec. 1879, NA, RG393, Part 3, Entry 431, p.241; See also McDowell to Commanding General, MDoM, 25 September 1879, 'Victorio, NA, RG393, M1495, Roll 14; Loud AAA General to AA General Fort Leavenworth 23 September 1879, 'Victorio Papers', NA, M666, Roll 526; Pope to AAG MDoM, 24 September 1879, 'Victorio Files', NA, RG393, M1495, Roll 14; McDowell to AG, Washington D.C., 25 September 1879 & Pope to Townsend AG Wash. D.C., 18 September 1879, 'Victorio Papers', NA, M666, Roll 526.

50 Ballinger, G. 'Ambush in Massacre Canyon' *The Courier*, July 29, 1993.

51 Return for Sept. 1879 in Returns From US Military Posts, 1800-1916, Fort Bayard, New Mexico 1866-Dec. 1879, NA, M617, Roll 87.

Freeland survived to be medically discharged in May 1880. So a conundrum remains: was there also a Company C soldier wounded who later died?

Table 8.2 Ninth Cavalry Casualties, 18 September 1879[52]

Company	Left Post	Men	Horses/Mules
A (Lieutenant Day)	Left Fort Bayard September 14 1879	None	5 Horses killed in action
B(Captain Dawson)	Left Fort Bayard September 13 1879	Private Daniel Caump died of wounds 20 September Private Freeland wounded	10 Horses killed in action
C[1] (Captain Beyer)	Left Fort Bayard September 5 1879	None	1 Horse killed in action
G (Lieutenant Hugo)	Left Fort Bayard September 5 1879	Private Peter Haines killed in action	12 Horses killed in action 'or escaped'

Note

1 See identical info in Bi-Monthly Company Muster Rolls for Company C, 9th Cavalry, Sept.–Oct. 1879, NA, RG94.

Table 8.3 Ninth Cavalry Casualties, 18 September 1879[53]

Company	Men	Horses/Mules
A (Lieutenant Day)		4 Horses killed in action
B (Captain Dawson)	Private Daniel Caump died of wounds 20 September Private Freeland wounded	10 Horses killed in action
C (Captain Beyer)	None	1 Horse killed in Action
G (Lieutenant Hugo)	Private Peter Haines killed in action	12 Horses killed in action or 'escaped'

Acting Assistant Surgeon Kennon stated that three men were killed and two wounded: one mortally.[54] Other accounts imply that four or five soldiers were killed.

'Telegraphic reports from the CO Ft Bayard show that on the 18th of Sept in an engagement with the Indians, 5 men were killed and 1 wounded, 2 Navajos Scouts & 1 citizen killed."[55] An officer, either Hooker or Hugo, stated that 'Capt Beyer & Joe Gankin [Yankie] with force of soldiers & citizens arrived in time to prevent massacre 4 or 5 of the soldiers killed.'[56]

The US army was not above distorting, or at the very least glossing over, either their casualties or the numbers of their opponents. Thrapp notes that the army sometimes acknowledged those killed during skirmishes with Apaches, whilst those who subsequently succumbed to their wounds

52 Record of Events Sept. 1879 in Returns from Regular Army Cavalry Regiments, 1833-1916, 9th Cavalry Regimental Returns 1873-1880, NA, M744, Roll 88.

53 Bi-Monthly Company Muster Rolls for Company C, 9th Cavalry, Sept/Oct 1879 in NA, RG94.

54 Report of Acting Assist. Surgeon Lewis Kennon, in AR-WD, NA, M997, Roll 35, 1880 Vol. I, p.519.

55 Loud, 20 November 1879 endorsed by Col. Hatch 25 November 1879, Letters & Endorsements Sent 1877-1887, NA, RG393, Part 3, Entry 477.

56 Undated possibly unsent telegram signed 'H' (The telegram is signed with an 'H' but this does not correspond in style with other telegrams, which are usually signed 'Hooker'. This could, of course, mean that Hooker's adjutant wrote most of these telegrams and that Hooker only wrote such missives when urgency required), NA, RG393, Part 3, Entry 439, p.348.

somehow never appeared on the casualty lists.[57] The only record of anyone wounded in this battle concerns Private Caump, who expired the following day, and Private Freeland, who survived after being rescued by Sergeant Denny. If the Ninth cavalrymen were pinned down with scant cover for several hours, then, by the law of averages, they must have suffered both wounded and killed. After being trapped until dusk, some of the wounded might not have received even rudimentary treatment until rescued. This increased the risk that wounded men rescued and removed from the site might succumb to their injuries at a later date.

The ambush site was remote, and this, as well as the terrain, made the removal of wounded troopers very difficult, further decreasing their chances of survival. As we shall see below, Acting Assistant Surgeon Kennon outlined the difficulties of removing the wounded, and he also admitted that all of his medical supplies and equipment had been lost. If the US army was only recording those troopers killed outright in the ambush, and failing to record those who died subsequently, then there is a distinct possibility that the actual US army losses were higher. Hence the small discrepancies mentioned above.

Bearing this factor in mind, what can be made of Ballinger's article? He is quite emphatic that the official casualty rate is erroneous. The reason for this is that there appear to be 32 graves in two rows near three other graves assumed to be the graves of the Navajo and citizen scouts.[58] However, 35 graves is almost certainly a significant overestimate, for two reasons.

First, the regimental returns and bi-monthly muster rolls do not support such a high casualty rate. Nor are these losses being hidden by recording fatalities as 'deserted' or 'discharged': the combined desertions and discharges for September to December 1879 come to three desertions and eight discharges from Companies A, B, C, and G.[59]

Second, there were civilian volunteers present, and these witnesses reported their experiences to the *Grant County Herald* and *Thirty-Four* shortly after the event. Had there been 32 fatalities, one cannot see how this could have been kept out of the local press. As we have already seen, *Thirty-Four* was quite hostile towards the officers and men of the Ninth Cavalry. The loss of 32 men in a single ambush would have been almost unprecedented in the history of the US army's campaigns against Apaches. It is to be doubted that such an occurrence could have been covered up.

Nevertheless, there *is* a whiff of a possible cover-up concerning the reporting of this ambush. Major Morrow wrote a detailed report of his September-October 1879 campaign against Victorio and stated that reports on the Animas battle from Captains Dawson and Beyer were attached as appendices. There are several copies of this report in the archives, but there are no appendices filed with his report.[60] Most of the copies are on microfilm, but at least one hard copy exists in the archives, and this too has no such appendices.[61] Morrow wrote this report on 5 November 1879; yet on 14 February 1880, Colonel Hatch claimed that 'No full Reports have reached this Office'[62]

57 Thrapp, 1967, p.366 See also Leonard, 1974, p.178.

58 Ballinger, The Courier, July 29 1993 See website article.

59 Bi-Monthly Company Muster Rolls for Companies A, B, C & G, 9th Cavalry, Sept/Oct & Nov/Dec 1879 in NA, RG94.

60 Morrow to AAAG, DoNM, 5 November 1879 in Letters Received by HQ_DoNM, September 1865-August 1890, NA, RG393, M1088, Roll 37 (Oct-Dec 1879); See also Pope to AAG HQ_MDoM, 4 November 1879, 'Victorio Files', NA, RG393, M1495, Roll 14 & Humphreys to AAAG, DoNM, 5 January 1880, 'Victorio Files', NA, RG393, M1495, Roll 14; Morrow to AAAG DoNM, 5 November 1879, 'Victorio Papers', NA, M666, Roll 526.

61 Morrow to AAAG, DoNM, 5 November 1879 in Letters Received, DoM 1868-98, RG 393, Entry A1-1 2601, Box 87.

62 Hatch to AAG, DoM, Fort Leavenworth, 14 February 1880 in Letters Sent by the '9MD/DNM/DoNM', NA, RG393, M1072, Roll 6, Jan 1880-August 1881, Letter No.82, pp58-65; same letter in Letters Received, DoM 1868-98, RG 393, Entry A1-1 2601, Box 87.

concerning the Animas canyon fight. Our knowledge of the close relationship between these two officers makes Hatch's claim very hard to believe. Hatch also stated that 'it is understood however, that Beyer in the fight lost 8 men killed and same wounded.'[63] It is these last pieces of information which suggest that something had happened in the Animas canyon which the Ninth Cavalry did not want to become public knowledge. Is one to believe that, by Valentine's Day 1880, Hatch had not been given precise reports as to the exact number of casualties sustained on 18 September 1879?

The relatively large casualty figure given by Ballinger assumes that the time and circumstances of this battle must have resulted in far higher casualties. The tardy award of the three medals of honor for gallantry in this fight may also reinforce this impression. This is probably a 'red herring', as a small casualty rate in such a situation is not as improbable as it seems. For example, on 16 August 1881, the Ninth Cavalry engaged in a fierce skirmish with Nana in the Cuchillo Negro Mountains. A number of horses were killed; yet despite the large amounts of ammunition expended by both sides, the Apaches did not kill a single Ninth Cavalryman, and there is no clear evidence, either, that any fatalities were inflicted on the Apaches. Such a low level of marksmanship on the part of the Ninth Cavalry can be put down to the failure of the US army to set aside enough ammunition to allow regular target practice. The Apaches, too, often did not have the necessary supplies of ammunition to allow them to improve their marksmanship through practice. Even when they did have enough ammunition, such activity might give away their location to their enemies. (See Appendix II)

A clue as to what exactly might have been covered up may lie in the fact that some bodies were abandoned and not recovered until several days later. Moreover, Lieutenant Day was cited for running 600 feet up the canyon and back to rescue Private Caump. If the troops had held their ground when ambushed, why had Lieutenant Day had to run so far back up the canyon to rescue one of the wounded men? What may have happened is that, in the opening moments of the ambush, the command panicked and ran some way down the canyon before finding their retreat blocked and rallying. In doing so, they abandoned not only several dead and live horses and mules, but also their dead. It is even possible that those men were abandoned while they were still alive. A letter published in the *Grant County Herald* on 4 October 1879 reported that Jack Hagan was left alive on the Animas battlefield. He had been carried, when first hit, to a safer spot, but was believed to have been left behind when the troops and citizens withdrew. He was later found shot through the head and minus an ear. The Navajo scouts were also reported to have been badly mutilated.[64] *Thirty-Four* reported an interview with one of the miners:

> Poor Jack Higgins [Hagan] fell and cried out to the boys to take him out or shoot him through the head, but the boys were running for their lives and the poor fellow was left in the hands of the Indians and nobody knows what become of him.[65]

This article also accuses Captain Beyer of directing the attack from a safe distance, and it states that he was put under arrest for cowardice on his return to Fort Bayard. However, the interview with the miner clearly implies that both miners and soldiers were under heavy gunfire and were equally relieved (and hence equally culpable for anybody being left behind) to get clear of the trap as quickly as possible (see document file no. 12.3ii).

---

63 Hatch to AAG, DoM, 14 February 1880 in Letters Received, DoM 1868–98, RG 393, Entry A1-1 2601, Box 87.

64 'Letter from Georgetown', *Grant County Herald*, 4 October 1879.

65 'Victorio's Victory in the Black Range' published in *Thirty Four* 31 September, 1879 in the Lee C. Myers Papers, NMSU Archives, Las Cruces, New Mexico.

The possibility that some men were left behind alive when the soldiers and volunteers retreated was seen as reprehensible in 1879, as it would be today. Therefore, from the Ninth Cavalry's point of view, this information needed to be suppressed, or at least to receive minimal circulation. The regiment was probably assisted in this matter by the fact that at least one of the civilian volunteers not only admitted fleeing but also admitted to leaving Hagan/Higgins behind. The US army later reported 'Jack Hagan and Hunt killed in action in Black Range,' which strongly implies that a second citizen volunteer was killed or more likely died from wounds received.[66]

Thus, two very local newspapers acknowledge men to have been abandoned, alive or dead, to the enemy; Morrow's report hints at such an event; and one branch of the US army is quite explicit about it. Yet this admission was clearly suppressed by the high command of the army. In a letter to the Surgeon General, Lewis Kennon openly admits to the fact that Private Peter Haines was 'left on field' and two Navajo scouts were 'left dead on field.'[67] This implies that it was not known whether Haines was alive or dead when he was left behind. Assistant Surgeon R.E. Smith, stationed at Fort Bayard, was even more explicit, reporting, in a letter to the Surgeon General dated 25 September 1879, that he was unable to give exact details as to the causes of death for those killed in the battle:

> I have the honor in transmitting this list of killed and wounded to say that the unknown character of these wounds results from the men being abandoned on the field by the troops.
>
> One man a private was gallantly brought away by a young Officer of the 9th Cavalry Lieut Day in the face of a steady fire of fifty rifles. The others were *left to their fate*. [My italics][68]

An extract from Kennon's letter to the Surgeon General is quoted in the *Annual Report of the Secretary of War to the President*, as follows:

> On September 5, 1879, Companies C and G, Ninth Cavalry, under command of Capt. C.D. Beyer, left Fort Bayard, New Mexico, on a scout against the Apache Indians. Acting Assist. Surg. Lewis Kennon gives the following account of the expedition: "We marched in a south-eastern direction until the morning of the 18th, when we came up to Captain Dawson, Ninth Cavalry, with Companies A and B engaged and nearly surrounded by Indians, near the head of the Rio de los Animas. One wounded man, a private, was gallantly brought away by a young officer of the Ninth Cavalry, Lieut. M.W. Day, in the face of a steady fire of 50 rifles. During the retreat in the darkness for some sixteen miles, the wounded were carried astride of pack mules, each one led by a soldier. It was impossible to adopt any other method less painful. It was out of the question to improvise any form of travois, and carrying a man in a blanket at the rate of speed we found necessary was excluded from consideration." The casualties in this engagement consisted of 3 killed and 2 wounded: one of the latter died two days after the injury.[69]

---

66 J.J. Coppinger to AAG, DoNM, 26 July 1880 in Letters Received, DoM 1868-98, RG 393, Entry A1-1 2601, Box 91 J.J. Coppinger to AAG, DoNM, 26 July 1880 in Letters Received, DoM 1868-98, RG 393, Entry A1-1 2601, Box 91.

67 Kennon to Barnes, 22 September, 1879 in Kennon L.W.C., Personal Papers of Medical Officers and Physicians (Medical Officers Files) RG 94, Entry 561.

68 Asst. Surgeon R.E. Smith?, Fort Bayard, Letter to Surgeon General of the Army, 25 September, 1879 in RG 98 Fort Bayard Interrement Record NMRA-902(8888). Microfilm held in NMSU archives, Las Cruces, New Mexico.

69 Report of Acting Assist. Surgeon Lewis Kennon, in AR-WD, NA, M997, Roll 35, 1880 Vol. I, p.519.

However this bears little relation to the letter to be found in Lewis Kennon's personnel file:

Fort Bayard New Mexico
September, 22d 1879

Brigadier General Barnes
Surgeon General USA

General
I have the honour to report my arrival at my post this day on my return from a scout against the Apache indians.

I left this Post on 5th Septr with companies C and G 9th Cav. Captain Beyer commanding scouting in a south easterly direction until the 18th.

On that day being near the head of the Rio de los Animas we saw the indians.

They were in front of and had nearly surrounded Capt Dawson 9th Cav with Companies A and B of that regiment and a few Navajoes.

We remained in front of them all day endeavouring to extricate Capt Dawson's command from its position.

Finally night came on and under cover of darkness he retreated to us and we all together left the field – Travelling about fifteen miles to a safe position.

The loss of the Command was Haines Peter, G Comp 9th Cav: killed and left on field – Crump Jeremiah B Comp 9th Cav. Shot in stomach, brought off field but died next day. Freeland Alfred B Comp 9th Cav shot in thigh now under treatment and two Navajo scouts Sam and Barrajo left dead on field.

The medicines and instruments were captured by the indians the pack mules bearing them having been shot.

I have the honour to be
Very Respectfully
Your Obedient Servant
Lewis Kennon
Acting Assistant Surgeon.[70]

One could conclude that Kennon wrote two letters. However, it is noteworthy that the comment that, as far as Kennon was aware, three men had been left behind[71] is not mentioned in the War Department's report. Unsurprisingly Smith's letter is not mentioned at all in the annual report.

There is another possible explanation as to why the US army might want to minimize the attention paid to this battle. The last sentence of Kennon's letter also states that he lost all his medical equipment. Yet the War Department also makes no mention of this in the Secretary of War's annual report. Moreover, as noted above, the monthly regimental return and bi-monthly muster rolls state respectively that 28 and 27 horses were killed. Other reports mention 32 horses lost by the Ninth Cavalry in this engagement (see Appendix II) It was acknowledged that 53 horses and mules were lost in this battle. If this is the case, then between 21 and 26 mules were lost, which implies that the Apaches might have captured a significant amount of ammunition after the battle. The *Daily Globe* of 19 October 1879 states that Beyer lost his horses, pack mules and 8,000 rounds

70 Kennon to Barnes, 22 September, 1879 in Kennon L.W.C., Personal Papers of Medical Officers and Physicians (Medical Officers Files) RG 94, Entry 561.

71 Kennon did not appear to have been aware of Hagan/Higgin's fate. Kennon may have been pinned down elsewhere and been unaware of this event.

of ammunition.[72] The civilian volunteers also lost all their horse.[73] The miner interviewed by *Thirty-Four* also admitted that:

> the Indians turned their attention to us (we were the flanking party in a deep rocky canon) and the bullets came whizzing so thick that we were compelled to dismount and seek refuge behind rocks – and sir, we had not more than dismounted before the Indians came right up and took our horses...about 50 of our horses and mules were missing. They got all of our pack mules with our provisions, ammunition, medicines and the surgeon's implements.[74]

The fact that the miner's account corroborates Kennon's account of losing his equipment lends some weight to the account from a newspaper which was often very hostile towards the Ninth Cavalry and some of its officers. However, it also points to a final reason why the army might have wished to suppress the particulars of this engagement. Had the supplies and instruments not been lost, would Private Crump/Caump have succumbed to his wounds? Moreover, would Private Freeland have avoided being medically discharged from the service on 4 May 1880 due to wounds received on 18 September 1879?[75]

The key to this mystery probably lies in the missing reports known to have been submitted by Captains Dawson and Beyer. The controversy surrounding this battle almost certainly involves the combination of a small number of possibly live casualties being abandoned and the loss of a considerable amount of ammunition, with both falling into the hands of the Apaches. The former would, if 'fortunate', would have been summarily executed by the Apaches. The capture of a large amount of military and private ammunition would have been of enormous value to the Apaches. If the army did lose approximately 8,000 rounds, and Victorio was leading between 50 and 100 warriors, this would have meant 80 to 160 cartridges per warrior.

Whatever the truth about the engagement in or near the headwaters of the Animas River, Victorio had, for the moment inflicted a disastrous defeat, in terms of lost ammunition and humiliation, upon a large detachment of Ninth cavalrymen and others supporting them.

---

72 A search on the Library of Congress' 'Chronicling America' website (http://chroniclingamerica.loc.gov/ using the search terms 'Beyer' and 'Apache' threw up several accounts of the Animas battle but all bar the *Daily Globe* source tended to be verbatim or edited versions of the army correspondence.

73 *Thirty Four,* 31 September 1879.

74 'Victorio's Victory in the Black Range' published in *Thirty Four* 31 September, 1879 in the Lee C. Myers Papers, NMSU Archives, Las Cruces, New Mexico.

75 Post Surgeon, Fort Bayard to AAG, DoM, 21 April, 1880 & Special Order 58, 4 May, 1880, AAG, HQ, DoM, in Letters Received, DoM 1868-98, RG 393, Entry A1-1 2601, Box 94.

Please see pages vii–xii for detailed notes and captions relating to the maps.

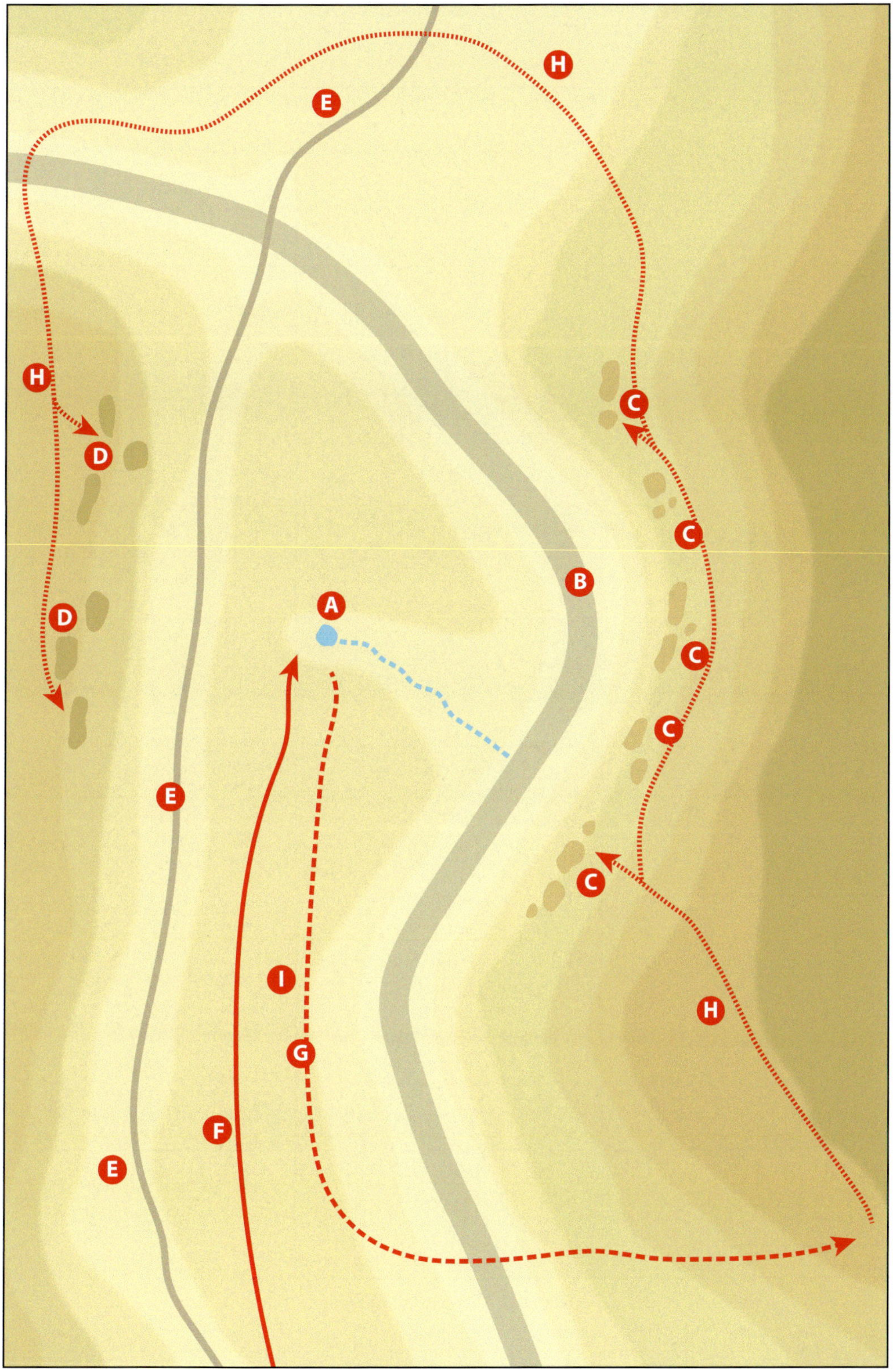

Map 2.1 Horseshoe Canyon.

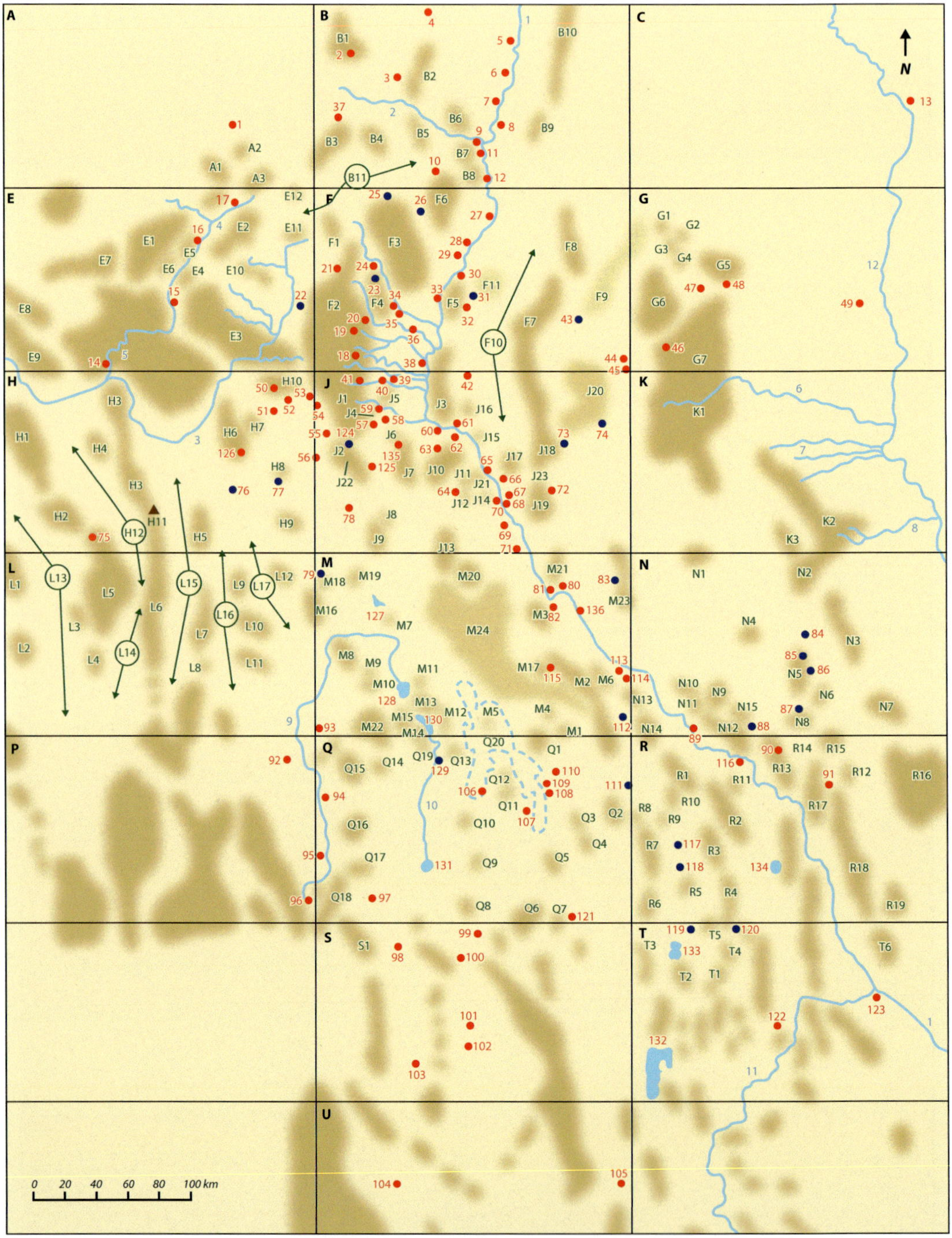

Map 4.1 Victorio Campaign.

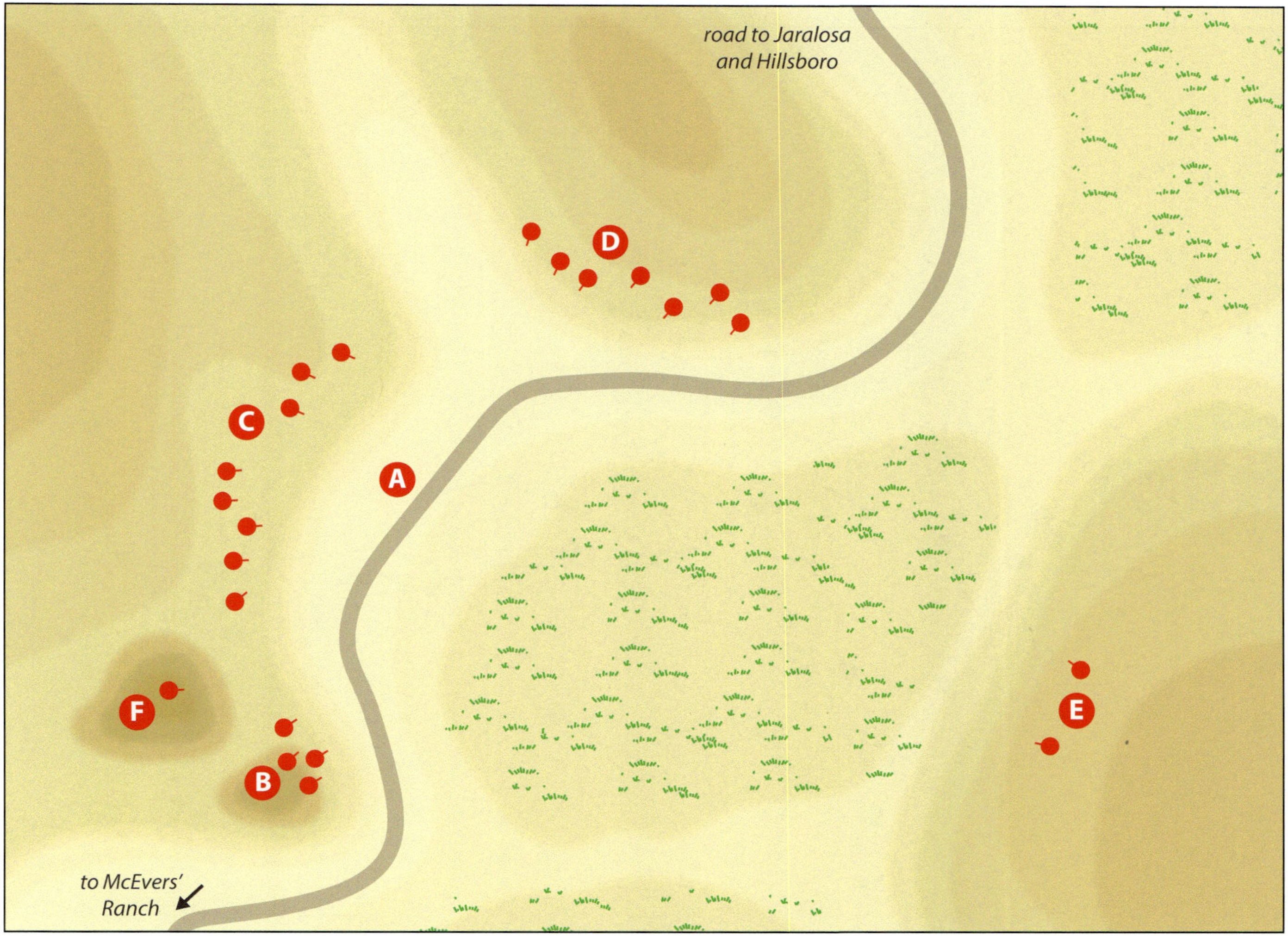

Map 7.1 McEvers' Ranch.

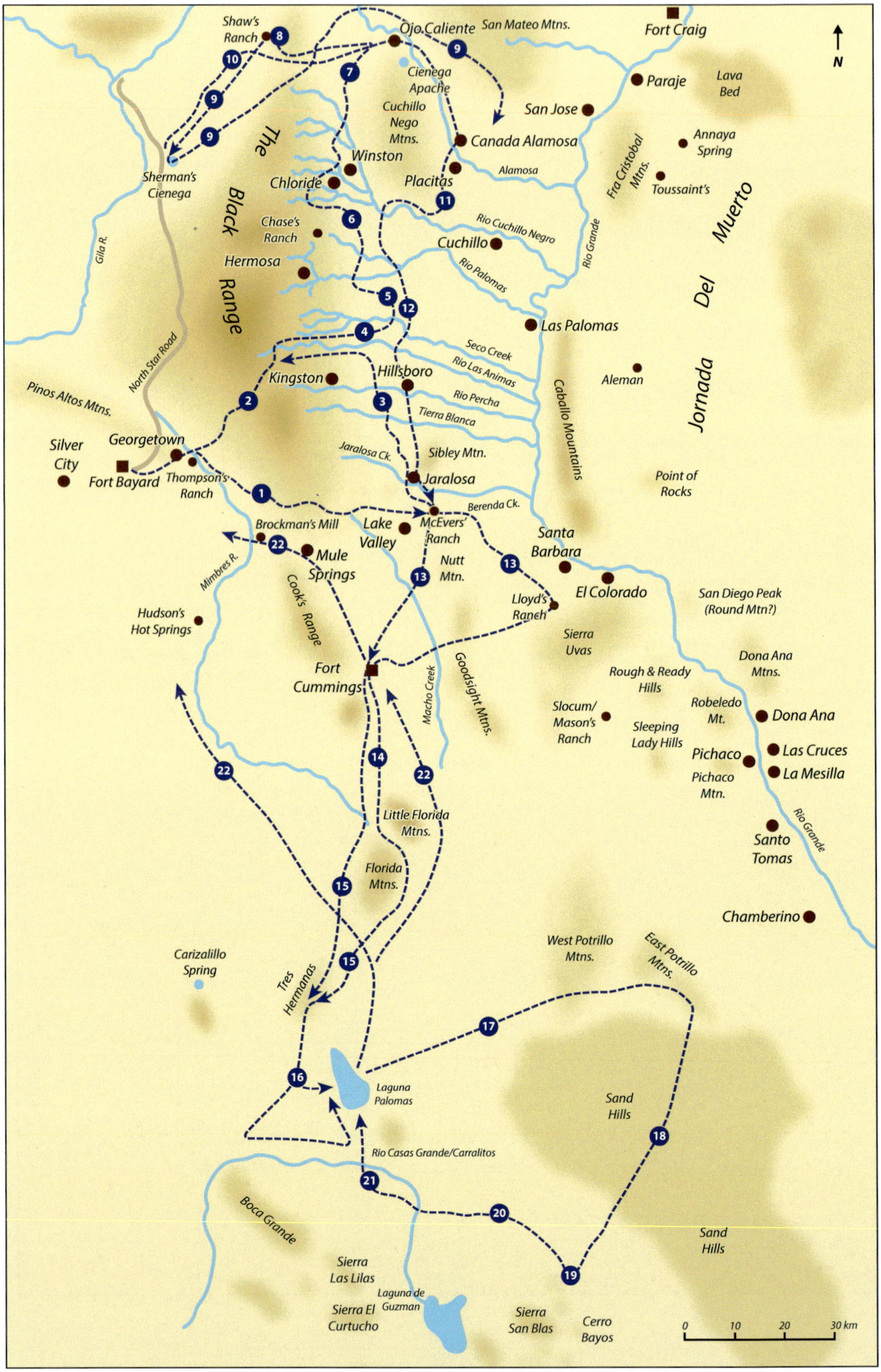

Map 9.1 Morrow's Campaign – September–October 1879 Campaign.

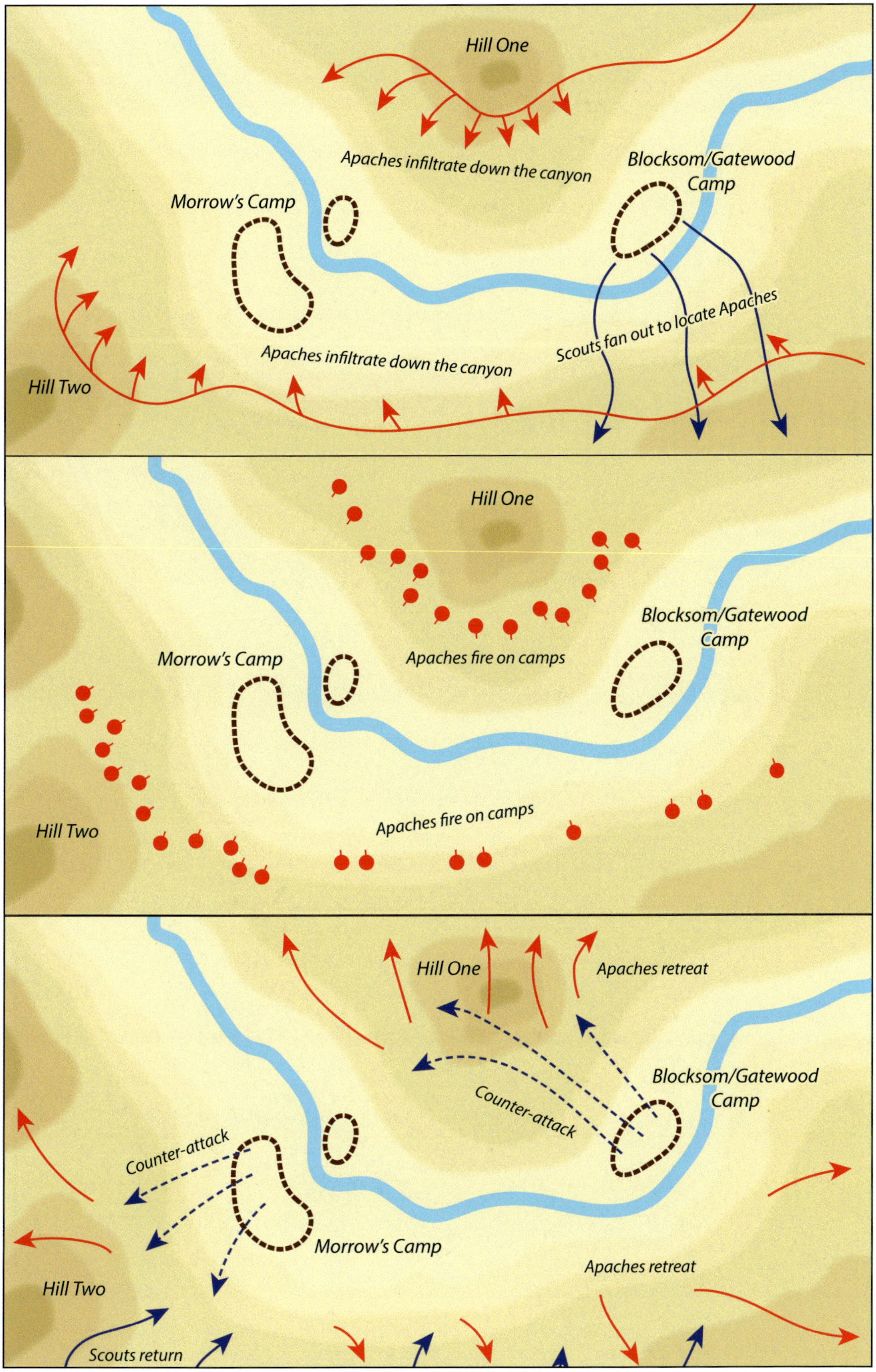

Map 9.2 Cuchillo Negro.

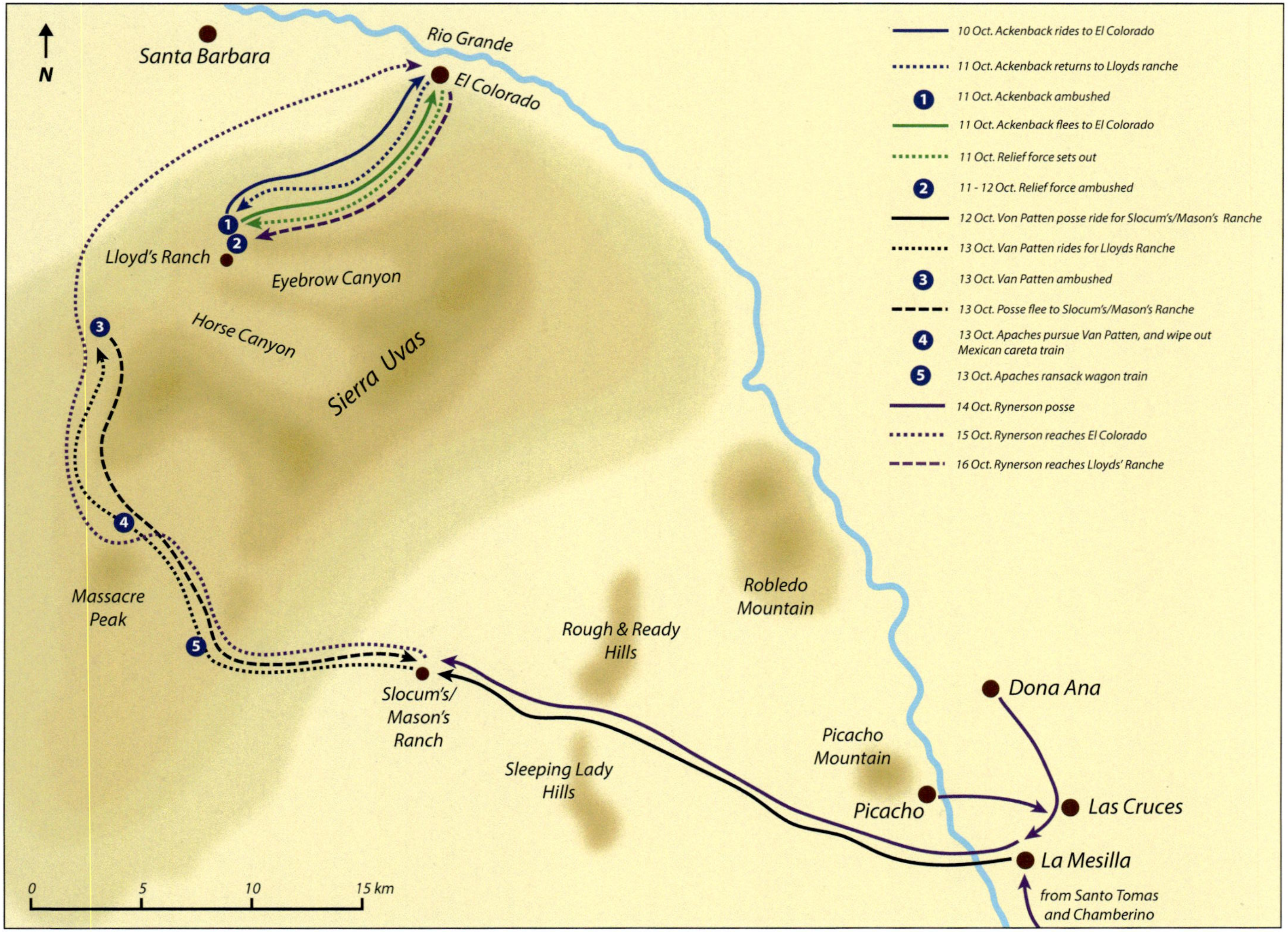

Map 10.1 Lloyd's Ranch.

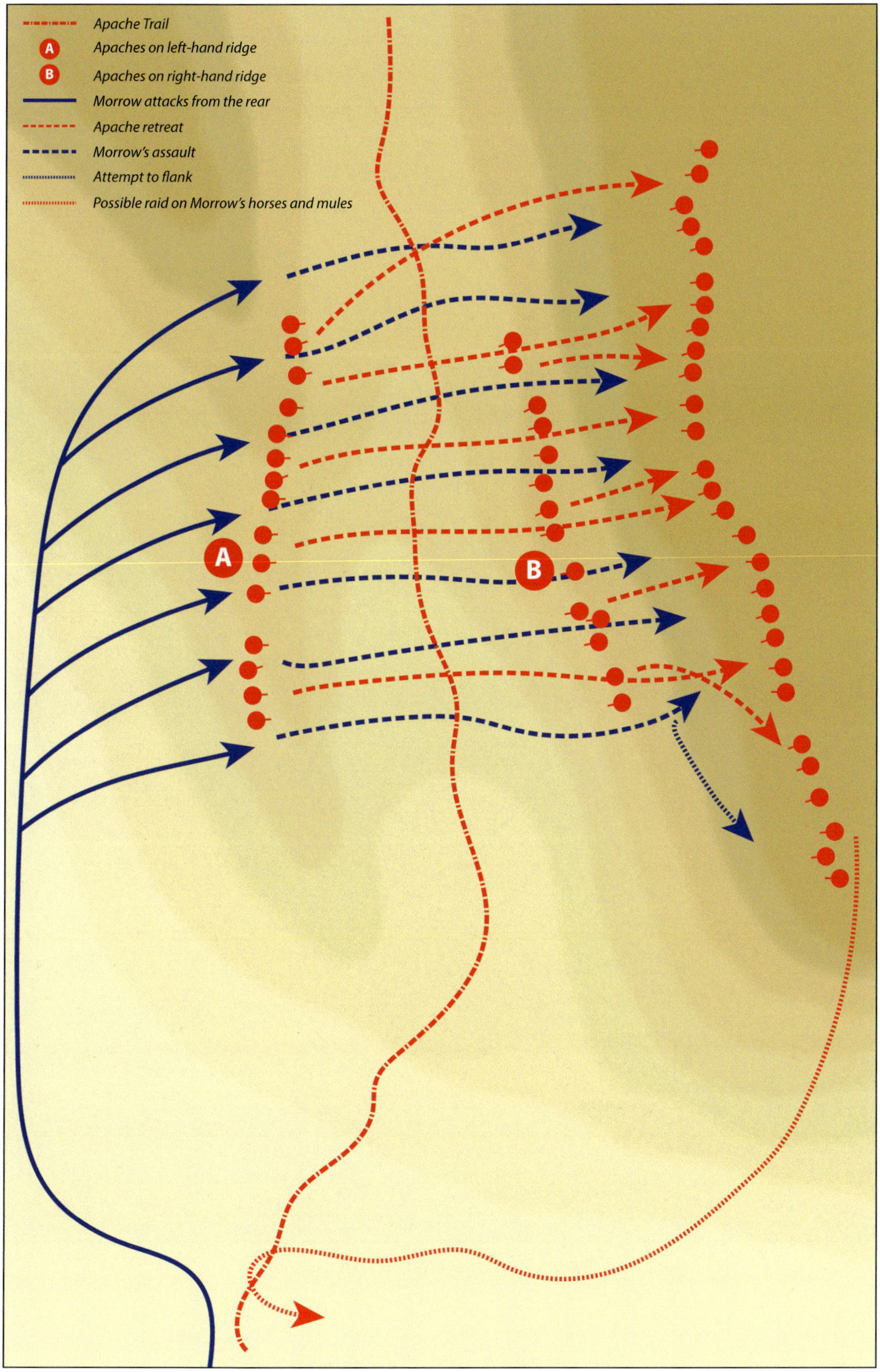

Map 11.1 Guzman Mountains.

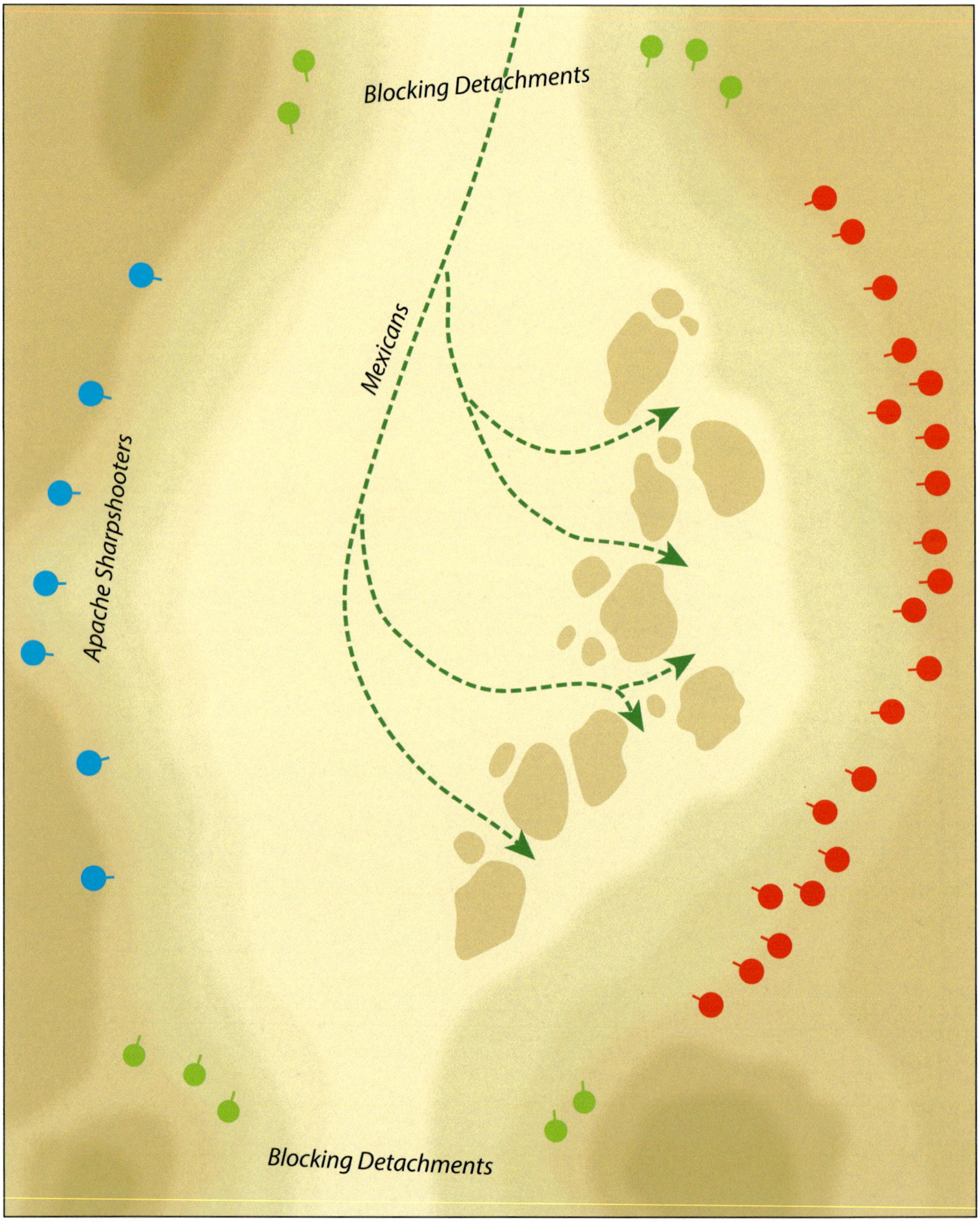

Map 12.1 Candelaraia Mountains.

9

Cuchillo Negro Fight, 29-30 September 1879

> Early next morning, as we had just finished breakfast, a single shot rang out down the canyon, then a volley, suddenly increasing into more shots and more volleys, with sounds of command, all doubled and trebled in reverberations up the valley, until it was one roar of pandemonium that was enough to set a nervous man wild. I didn't believe there was a sane man in the country, except the Corporal, who coolly informed me after awhile that I was sitting on the wrong side of a rock and pointed out to me the folly of protecting a rock.
>
> (Lieutenant Charles B. Gatewood, 30 September 1879, Cuchillo Negro)[1]

Major Morrow was informed of the clash in the Animas canyon by 20 September, and reported that Victorio was now estimated to have approximately 75 warriors[2] (see also document file no. 13). The major delayed his field operation until the arrival of Gatewood's and Blocksom's Apache scout detachments, with the former arriving at Fort Bayard on 20 September[3] and the latter on 22 September.[4] Gatewood had 19[5] Apache scouts and was accompanied by a detachment of 26[6] Sixth

1 Gatewood, p.102.

2 Morrow to Loud AAAG 20 & 22 September 1879, NA, RG393, Part 3, Entry 439, p.342; Pope to Secretary of War 22 September 1879, 'Victorio Papers', NA, M666, Roll 526; General Pope to AAG MDoM, 22 September 1879, 'Victorio Files', NA, RG393, M1495, Roll 14.

3 Gatewood, Fort Bayard to Arnold, Fort Grant, 21 September 1879, Troops in Southeastern Arizona, DoAz, NA, RG393, Part 1, Entry 232, Vol.4, 3 July, 1879–Dec. 13 1879, Letter No.129, p.82.

4 Lt Gatewood's Report on Field Service between 8 September to 4 November 1879, written 20 December 1879, (Hereafter referred to as 'Gatewood's Report 1879', NA, RG393, Part 1, Entry 240.

5 In May 1879, a proposal to reduce the numbers of Apache scouts in was raised in the Department of Arizona. (Willcox to AG Presidio, San Francisco, 2 May 1879, NA, RG393, Part 1, Entry 169, Vol. 9, p.141) Lieut Blocksom was instructed to reduce his company to twenty scouts in line with the decision to reduce all companies from 25 to 20 scouts each. (Compton to Blocksom, 15 May 1879, Field Records – Troops in Southeastern Arizona, DoAz, NA, RG393, Part 1, Entry 232, Vol.2, Sept 1 1878-27 May, 1879, Letter No. 149) This attempt was, in the short term, unsuccessfully resisted. (AAG to CO Dept. Arizona, 24 May 1879, NA, RG393 Part 1, Entry 169, Vol. 9, p.160) and Co's A and B, Indian Scouts were reduced from twenty-five to fifteen scouts per company. (Willcox to C.O.'s Companies A & B Indian Scouts (No Date Given) NA, RG393, Part 1, Entry 169, Vol.9, p.194 & p.195) It was not until November 1879, no doubt due to the outbreak of hostilities with Victorio in New Mexico, that the four scout companies in the DoAz were officially returned to twenty-five men each, (AAG to Carr, Col. Comd. Ops. In Field, 18 November 1879, NA, RG393, Part 1, Entry 169, p.428) though it is clear that in the interim both Gatewood and Blocksom's companies of scouts had slightly exceeded their official numbers.

6 In 1879 there appear to have been no formal guide as to the number of cavalrymen who should accompany Apache scout companies. By 1881 orders were issued stating that: "The Commanding Officer of Posts, at which Indian companies are stationed, will hereafter, whenever such companies are ordered out on field duty, detail, at least two non-commissioned Officers and fourteen privates of their command to accompany the pack train, to act as guard and such other duty as may be required of them." (Field Orders

cavalrymen, while Blocksom had 18 Apache scouts and 35 Sixth cavalrymen in his detachment.[7] These were intended to be Morrow's 'eyes and ears', and the major clearly felt that any attempt to attack Victorio would be wasted without their assistance.[8] Once the Department of Arizona realised that Victorio had not moved towards San Carlos, and received news of the deteriorating situation in New Mexico, Gatewood and Blocksom had been ordered to Fort Bayard in support of Morrow's command.[9]

Morrow prepared to take the field. Whilst his subsequent reports show that he remained optimistic concerning his encounters with Victorio, he had warned District Headquarters, possibly as early as 13 September 1879, that it could take two months of campaigning to finish Victorio off.[10] He had six officers and 191 soldiers (73 dismounted) and 37 Apache scouts[11] (see also document file no. 14). In addition to the two Apache scout detachments, the core of Morrow's detachment was made up of elements of A, B and C Companies, Ninth Cavalry, with L Company, Ninth Cavalry due to join the battalion from Fort Cummings.[12]

Nevertheless, District Headquarters remained confident that Victorio's days were numbered, stating that Morrow had enough troops and that they expected 'to hear good news from Troops in pursuit soon.'[13] In the same spirit, clear instructions were passed to Morrow that he should keep on the trail of the Apaches until they were killed, captured or surrendered. He was also instructed to keep District Headquarters regularly informed of events.[14] Such instructions would present officers in the field throughout this campaign with some difficulty, particularly once their operations passed outside areas within easy reach of telegraph lines.

Colonel Hatch used the reports that Victorio had had 150 men with him at the Animas canyon, to argue that a large number of Apaches from Mexico were now with Victorio, and were well

No.17 Hd Qrs Scouting Operations in S.E. Arizona, Ft Grant, A.T., 10 June 1881, NA, RG393, Part 1, Entry 185.)

7 Return for September 1879 in Returns From U.S. Military Posts 1800-1916, Fort Bayard, New Mexico 1866-Dec. 1879, NA, M617, Roll 87.

8 Morrow to Loud AAAG 20 & 22 September 1879, NA, RG393, Part 3, Entry 439, p.342; Morrow to Arnold, Fort Grant, 22 September 1879, Troops in Southeastern Arizona, DoAz, NA, RG393, Part 1, Entry 232, Vol.4, 3 July, 1879–Dec. 13 1879, Letter No.131, p.84.

9 Arnold to Tupper & Gatewood, AAG Dept. Arizona, 13 September 1879, Troops in Southeastern Arizona, DoAz, NA, RG393, Part 1, Entry 232, Vol.4, 3 July, 1879–Dec. 13 1879, Letter No.110-112, pp.68-70; Arnold to CO Fort Bowie, 13 September 1879, Troops in Southeastern Arizona, DoAz, NA, RG393, Part 1, Entry 232, Vol.4, 3 July, 1879–Dec. 13 1879, Letter No.114, p.71; Thrapp, 1967, p.184; Haley, 1981, p.322; 'Gatewood's Report 1879' NA, RG393, Part 1, Entry 240.

10 Morrow to Loud AAAG, NA, RG393, Part 3, Entry 439, p.340; This telegram is dated '13'. As it was discovered amongst telegrams dealing with events of Sept/Oct 1879 it is reasonably safe to argue that this telegram is probably 13 September 1879 as Morrow repeated this information citing an earlier telegram, on October 5, 1879. (Morrow & Hooker to Loud AAG 5 October 1879, NA, RG393, Part 3, Entry 439, pp.320-324; See also Loud to Hatch, 6 October 1879, Telegrams Sent DoNM, Vol.2, Jan.–Dec. 1879, NA, RG393, Part 3, Entry 431, pp.288-289) Morrow is quoted in the 'Indian War in the Southwest' *Weekly New Mexican*, 11 October 1879, in The Walter Finley Collection as having enough men but "it will take two months to do it".

11 Morrow to AAAG DoNM, 5 November 1879, 'Victorio Papers', NA, M666, Roll 526; Thrapp, 1974, p.241; See also Record of Engagements, p.92. The *Daily New Mexican* added that the Navajo scouts were also sent out with the Apache scouts (*Weekly New Mexican* 27 September 1879 in The Walter Lowry Finley Collection).

12 Bi-Monthly Company Muster Rolls for Company's A, B, C, & L, 9th Cavalry Sept/Oct 1879 in NA, RG94.

13 Loud to Hatch, AAG Fort Leavenworth & Gen. Willcox, 22 September 1879, Telegrams Sent DoNM, Vol.2, Jan.–Dec. 1879, NA, RG393, Part 3, Entry 431, pp.239-240 & pp.242-244.

14 Loud to Morrow, 23 September 1879, Telegrams Sent DoNM, Vol.2, Jan.–Dec. 1879, NA, RG393, Part 3, Entry 431, p.244.

Major Albert P. Morrow. This officer directed the main effort against Victorio's followers in 1879 using Fort Bayard as his headquarters. This included an epic pursuit of the Apaches between 20 September to 3 November 1879. (The National Archives)

supplied with weapons and ammunition from illegal trade south of the border. He used this information to request 'three hundred horses, fifty pack-mules and fifty good Indian Scouts'[15] from the Department of the Missouri.

Morrow left Fort Bayard with his battalion (see document file no. 15 for several documents relating to Morrow's expedition between 23 September and 3 November 1879) at 12 noon on 23 September 1879.[16] The expedition passed through Georgetown on 24 September 1879, and here they were joined by 15 citizens eager to avenge Hagan's death in the Animas canyon.[17] Morrow then proceeded by road round the south end of the mountains with his troops, and on the morning of 24 September, in the vicinity of Thompson's Ranch on the Mimbres, he split this force. Lieutenants Blocksom and Gatewood were to lead their Apache scouts directly into the Black Range,[18] with Blocksom, as the senior officer, taking command of this combined Apache scout detachment.[19] The

15 Hatch to AAG Fort Leavenworth, 28 September 1879, Telegrams Sent DoNM, Vol.2, Jan.–Dec. 1879, NA, RG393, Part 3, Entry 431, p.252; Hatch to Pope, 30 September 1879, Telegrams Sent DoNM, Vol.2, Jan.–Dec. 1879, NA, RG393, Part 3, Entry 431, p.257.

16 Purington to AAAG SF 23 September 1879, NA, RG393, Part 3, Entry 439, p.349; See also Morrow to Arnold, Fort Grant, 23 September 1879, Troops in Southeastern Arizona, DoAz, NA, RG393, Part 1, Entry 232, Vol.4, 3 July, 1879–Dec. 13 1879, Letter No.140, p.89.

17 'Correspondence', *Grant County Herald*, 4 October 1879. Schubert notes that during the Cuchillo Negro Fight, Major Morrow was leading approximately 200 men in pursuit of the Apaches (1997), p.57.

18 Morrow to AAAG DoNM, 5 November 1879, 'Victorio Papers', NA, M666, Roll 526.

19 'Gatewood's Report 1879', NA, RG393, Part 1, Entry 240.

plan was for the Apache scout companies to attack Victorio's camp from approximately the west, while the rest of Morrow's force would attack from the east.[20] As the Apache scouts were accompanied by mule trains, they could easily traverse the mountains, whereas Morrow's cavalry had to rely on a wagon train to carry their supplies, and so they marched by wagon road.[21] Morrow and his force proceeded through the Mimbres Mountains,[22] via the Gavilan Pass, to McEvers' Ranch, where they established a base camp.[23] There, on 24 September, they were joined by L Company, Ninth Cavalry,[24] and this enlarged force followed Dawson's trail into the Animas canyon to complete their attempt to catch Victorio between the two forces.[25]

Table 9.1 Morrow's Campaign, 23 September to 11 October 1879 (See Map 9.1 for overview of Morrow's Sept.-Nov. 1879 Campaign)

1.	23-24 September	Morrow marches his battalion from Fort Bayard to McEvers' Ranch. They are joined by some civilian volunteers from Georgetown.
2.	24 September	At Thompson's Ranch on the Mimbres River, Morrow sends Lieutenants Blocksom and Gatewood with their Apache scout companies into the Black Range in the direction of the Animas River.
3.	25-26 September	Morrow moves his battalion up to the Animas Canyon in the hope of trapping Victorio between his battalion and the Apache scouts.
4.	26 September	Morrow receives news of the discovery of a large trail left by the Apaches in the Arroyo Seco Creek from Lieutenant Blocksom's Apache scouts.
5.	28 September	Morrow catches up with his Apache scouts 12 miles north of the Arroyo Seco Creek, probably in the vicinity of the Palomas River. The scouts had discovered Victorio's camp but failed to surround it during the night of 28-29 September.
6.	29-30 September	Morrow's battalion engages Victorio's Apaches approximately 8 miles north of the camp on the Palomas River. This probably places it somewhere along the South Fork of the Rio Cuchillo Negro.
	1-2 October	Morrow's forces again attempt to surround Victorio's camp, located less than 4 miles from the camp assaulted on 29 October. No directions have survived, so the camp could be either north or west of this location. The Apache scouts capture a Warm Springs Apache woman and child who state that Victorio is intending to move west into the Mogollon Mountains.
	3 October	Morrow's Apache scouts reconnoitre the area and confirm that Victorio appears to be making west towards the Mogollon Mountains.
7.	4 October	Morrow's troops arrive at Ojo Caliente.
8.	5 October	Morrow arrives at Shaw's Ranch on the North Star Road.
9.	6 October	Morrow's force reaches Sherman's Cienega and is joined by reinforcements from Fort Bayard led by Captain Purington. Neither force has seen any sign of Apaches and Apache scouts are sent back into the Black Range. The scouts eventually discover that Victorio has moved into the San Mateo Mountains.

20 Morrow to AAAG DoNM, 5 November 1879, 'Victorio Papers', NA, M666, Roll 526.

21 Gatewood, p.102; See also Loud to AAG Fort Leavenworth, 24 September 1879, Telegrams Sent DoNM, Vol.2, Jan.–Dec. 1879, NA, RG393, Part 3, Entry 431, p.246.

22 The southern section of the Black Range is also known as the Mimbres Mountains.

23 Martin to Arnold, 24 September 1879, NA, RG393, Part 1, Entry 235, p.13; Ashenfelter, 'The Fight on the Animas' *Grant County Herald*, 27 September 1879; 'The Fight on the Animas' *Weekly New Mexican* 11 October 1879 in The Walter Lowry Finley Collection.

24 Loud to AAG Fort Leavenworth, 24 September 1879, 'Victorio Papers', NA, RG393, M1495, Roll 14; Bi-Monthly Company Muster Rolls for Company L, 9th Cavalry, Sept/Oct 1879 in NA, RG94.

25 Morrow to AAAG DoNM, 5 November 1879, 'Victorio Papers', NA, M666, Roll 526.

9.	10 October	Lieutenant Gatewood's scouts discover Victorio's trail as it leaves the San Mateo Mountains.
10.	11 October	Morrow returns to Ojo Caliente and spends the next day replenishing his supplies.

The manoeuvre was carried out successfully. The only problem with this plan was that, much to Morrow's disappointment, Victorio had departed the area at least three days previously, leaving behind only a few scouts to monitor the movements of any force sent out after him.[26] This implies that Morrow had assumed that Victorio, having successfully defended his 'camp' in the Animas canyon, would remain in the vicinity. This appears to be based on the erroneous assumption that Victorio was directly defending his dependants. In fact, Victorio appears to have been deliberately leading the US cavalry away from his families and attempting to wear them down in the process.[27]

Other small parties of raiders may have continued to cause havoc *independently* of Victorio. Indeed, the *Grant County Herald* reported the receipt of a telegram from Las Lunas stating that 'five men were killed between Rita Quemada and the Datil Mountains on Monday last' [22 September 1879].[28] The report was judged to be reliable by the paper, but estimating the number of Apaches at 60 warriors was probably an exaggeration.

Historian Frank N. Schubert also reports a clash of sorts between Victorio's warriors and troops belonging to Morrow's battalion on 24 September, on the Cuchillo Negro River. The account is tantalisingly vague:

> The Indians surprised Lieutenant Wright while he and some of his troopers were bringing in a wounded man. Wright's horse fell dead under a hail of bullets, and the Apaches were closing in when Sergeant Boyne and a detachment came to the officer's assistance, flanked the Indians, charged, and drove them off.[29]

If the wounded man had been attacked by the Apaches, then this suggests an earlier skirmish or the conclusion to a running battle.[30] The fact that Lieutenant Wright was involved suggests that this involved the detachment left at Hillsboro after the Animas battle. There is no indication that the wounded man was even a soldier: he could equally have been a civilian wounded in a skirmish with Apaches who had been picked up by a patrol led by Wright. In an interview with *Thirty-Four* on 19 November 1879, Lieutenant C.M. Schaeffer, Ninth Cavalry, claimed that troops from his regiment

26 Morrow to Loud AAAG 26 September 1879, NA, RG393, Part 3, Entry 439, pp.361-362; See also Hatch to AAG Fort Leavenworth, 30 September 1879, Telegrams Sent DoNM, Vol.2, Jan.–Dec. 1879, NA, RG393, Part 3, Entry 431, p.259; Morrow to AAAG DoNM, 5 November 1879, 'Victorio Papers', NA, M666, Roll 526; Thrapp, 1974, p.241.

27 I will deal with this point later in this chapter.

28 'By Telegraph Section' *Grant County Herald*, 27 September 1879.

29 Schubert, 1997, p.57.

30 This is another example of the lack of detail in the source material on this campaign. Sergeant Boyne was, in fact, awarded a Medal of Honor for his "bravery in action at Mimbres Mountain N.M., May 29th 1879 and at Cuchillo Negro, N.M., September 27th 1879." Schubert, 1997, p.58; According to Schubert, Boyne actually wrote to his officer requesting that his services against Victorio merited some recognition. This may explain why he received his medal so quickly. Lt Wright and Major Morrow gave glowing endorsements to his application and the Medal of Honor was awarded on 6 January, 1882. The award is dated 27 September, rather than 24 September, 1879. See also Burton, pp.158-159 & p.262; Beyer & Keydal (v), p.411 gives a very garbled account of this skirmish. They state that Lt Wright was escorting a wounded trooper to Fort Stanton in May 1879 when ambushed by Victorio in the Membres Mountains. Not only is the date wrong but both Forts Craig and Bayard were far closer to the Membres mountains than Fort Stanton.

had fought and defeated the Apaches on 23 September.[31] In the last chapter, we left Lieutenant Wright in command of a detachment of men at McEvers' Ranch. If a skirmish occurred on 23 or 24 September, then it probably occurred prior to the arrival of Morrow's force and thus missed inclusion in the major's report of his campaign.[32]

What was becoming clear was that the pursuit of Victorio was gravitating northwards into that portion of the Black Range drained by the Cuchillo Negro River and its tributaries. A large trail was discovered by Blocksom's Apache scouts at the Arroyo Seco Creek late on 26 September.[33] This was estimated to have been made by a group consisting of about 150 animals and 75-100 Apaches, most of whom were warriors.[34] At this point Morrow and his force reached the head of the Animas River, where Morrow sent back to Fort Bayard all the dismounted men he had with him.[35] He also took the opportunity to bury four dead abandoned after the Animas canyon ambush.[36] Having moved north from the Animas creek, he caught up with Blocksom in the early hours of 28 September, 12 miles north-east of the Arroyo Seco, as the lieutenant and his scouts were making their way into the Black Range to surround Victorio's camp. Once again, to the great chagrin of the army, their presence was detected and the Apaches melted into the mountains without a shot being fired, although approximately 20-30 horses were abandoned in the process.[37] The location of this camp, reported as 12 miles north east of the Arroyo Seco, was probably sited somewhere along the Palomas River.[38]

While Morrow was prowling the southern Cuchillo Negro Mountains, the Apaches once again targeted members of the Ojo Caliente garrison. On the morning of 28 September, a five-man mail escort detail from E Company, led by Sergeant Henry Robinson, was returning to Camp

31 *Thirty Four*, 19 November 1879.

32 The Chronological List also notes a series of clashes between 26 and 30 September, 1879 in which one trooper was killed (Chronological List, p.47). The Record of Engagements mentions two skirmishes on the 26 and 30 September, 1879 (Record of Engagements, p.92). However, it is possible that these refer to clashes between Morrow's battalion and Victorio, which occurred on 29-30 September, in the Cuchillo Negro Mountains. However, Webb's version of the Chronological List clearly states that one soldier was killed between 26 and 30 September, "near Ojo Caliente", adding that two soldiers were killed at the Cuchillo Negro River on 29/30 September, 1879 (Webb, 1976, p.87).

33 Morrow to AAAG DoNM, 5 November 1879, 'Victorio Papers', NA, M666, Roll 526.

34 Morrow to Loud AAAG 26 September 1879, NA, RG393, Part 3, Entry 439, pp.361-362; See also Hatch to AAG Fort Leavenworth, 30 September 1879, Telegrams Sent DoNM, Vol.2, Jan.–Dec. 1879, NA, RG393, Part 3, Entry 431, p.259.

35 Morrow to Loud AAAG 26 September 1879, NA, RG393, Part 3, Entry 439, pp.361-362; Morrow to AAAG DoNM, 5 November 1879, 'Victorio Papers', NA, M666, Roll 526.

The Ninth Cavalry Regimental Return stated that those dismounted men from L Company were sent back to McEvers' Ranche but they do not appear to have been present when Apaches attacked and burned that place in mid-October 1879 (Record of Events September 1879 in Returns From Regular Army Cavalry Regiments 1833-1916, 9th Cavalry Regimental Returns 1873-1880, NA, M744, Roll 88).

36 Morrow to Loud AAAG 26 September 1879, NA, RG393, Part 3, Entry 439, pp.361-362; See also Hatch to AAG Fort Leavenworth, 30 September 1879, Telegrams Sent DoNM, Vol.2, Jan.–Dec. 1879, NA, RG393, Part 3, Entry 431, p.259.

The one Ninth Cavalryman clearly identified as being killed during the fight, Peter Haines of Company G, was recovered and buried at this point (Bi-Monthly Company Muster Rolls for Company G, 9th Cavalry, Sept/Oct 1879 in NA, RG94).

37 Morrow to AAAG DoNM, 5 November 1879, 'Victorio Papers', NA, M666, Roll 526; Thrapp, 1974, pp.241-242; Lt Gatewood left a detailed account of his participation in the pursuit of Victorio during September and October 1879 in 1894. He makes no mention of this operation. This suggests that Gatewood and Blocksom's detachments had separated and were operating independently despite Gatewood acting under the command of Blocksom during this period.

38 Morrow to AAAG DoNM, 5 November 1879, 'Victorio Papers', NA, M666, Roll 526.

Gatewood with his scouts. (The National Archives)

The original caption give the following information:
Co. A Apache Indian Scouts (White Mount.) taken in 1880, just after a protracted campaign after Victoria and his band , in which US Troops fought several stiff engagements with the hostiles in Mexico and New Mexico #1 Lt CB Gatewood commanding #2 Sam Bowman interpreter and chief of scouts, #3 Lt Thomas Cruse, # Dr McPherson #5 Alchesay, 1st Sgt. Of the CO, and Chief of the White Mount. Apaches.

"Taken on the day Co. A was discharged at Fort Apache about Oct 30th 1880. This band had been in three hard fights – August [September 29-30, 1879] *Black Range and thence to Hillsboro and finally after a long and tedious trail after hostiles (under Victorio and Nana) had wound up about Oct 2nd* [27/28 October, 1879] *in a big fight down in Old Mexico at Lake Guzman where Gatewood said they came near defeating him and two troops 9th Cavalry under Col. Morrow. Co. A came home to Apache to be discharged as their six months expired about Nov 1st 1880. Alchesay and several others did not intend to re-enlist" (General Thomas Cruse)*

The original caption states that this is an Oct/Nov 1880 photograph but the detail given suggested that this is more likely to be an 1879 photograph. However, the informant appears to have been Thomas Cruse, whose memory for dates and events, is not always exactly accurate, I have added the correct months/dates within square brackets above. If Cruse is in the photograph this cannot be an 1879 photograph as Cruse did not join Gatewood's scout company till early 1880. I suspect that this is an 1880 photograph with an 1879 caption telling a more exciting story than that experienced in Sept/Oct 1880 when this company did enter Mexico in pursuit of Victorio but did not encounter any of their opponents. Whatever the case the photograph gives a good idea of what Apache scouts would have looked like in 1879 and 1880.

Ojo Caliente when it was ambushed in a canyon barely two miles from the post.[39] The detail was pursued by between 50 and 70 Apache warriors, led by Victorio, and many of the warriors were riding captured US army mounts.[40] It was fortunate for the mail detail that Sergeant James Williams, E Company, Ninth Cavalry, had left the Camp Ojo Caliente leading a small hunting expedition. Hearing the firing, Williams and his group rushed to the scene and joined their comrades in holding off the Apaches, who kept up their pursuit until the troopers were almost at Ojo Caliente. Hooker turned out the guard and remained on the alert for the rest of the day.[41] It was also fortunate for the detachment that the upper reaches of the canyon were very narrow and twisted, making it impossible for the Apaches to overtake and surround the retreating troopers.[42] The mail detachment probably represented a relatively easy target for the Apaches. The unexpected arrival of the other group of men , and the nature of the terrain, saved E Company from sustaining further casualties (see document file no. 10).

Captain Hooker became a prisoner in his own post, convinced that this attack was intended to draw him into pursuing the Apaches so that he could be ambushed, or so that he would find the post ransacked on his return. He thought that there were not enough troops to defend the post *and* pursue the Apaches. 'Extravagant rumours' of defeated Ninth Cavalry detachments also plagued the captain, reducing him to sending out couriers during the night.[43] Hooker was also concerned that the Apaches, if they failed to draw him out from Ojo Caliente, would then attempt to lift his remaining herd. He was advised to keep the Apaches in check by 'light skirmishing' and that Major Morrow was moving towards him with a substantial command.[44] While Sergeant Robinson had succeeded in delivering the mail, it was clear that, for the foreseeable future, getting mail details in and out of Ojo Caliente would be fraught with danger. Hooker adopted the tactic of sending these details out at night, which was good in principle, but did not prevent encounters with Apaches. On the night of 28 September, Hooker sent Sergeant William Howard, with four mounted men, to take the mail to Paraje.[45] On their outward journey, they encountered, but managed to evade, a

---

39 Returns From U.S. Military Posts; September 1879 Record of Events, 1800-1916, Ojo Caliente, N.M. May 1879-March 1882, NA, M617, Roll 877; Record of Events September 1879 in Returns From Regular Army Cavalry Regiments 1833-1916, 9th Cavalry Regimental Returns 1873-1880, NA, M744, Roll 88; Schubert, 1995, p.357; Billington, 1991, p.91; Webb, 1976, p.87.

40 Returns From U.S. Military Posts; September 1879 Record of Events, 1800-1916, Ojo Caliente, N.M. May 1879-March 1882, NA, M617, Roll 877; Billington, 1991, p.91; see Hooker to Loud AAAG 29 September 1879, NA, RG393, Part 3, Entry 439, pp.358-359.

41 Hatch to Pope, 30 September 1879, Telegrams Sent DoNM, Vol.2, Jan.–Dec. 1879, NA, RG393, Part 3, Entry 431, p.257; Arnold to AAG Dept. Arizona, 1 October 1879, Troops in Southeastern Arizona, DoAz, NA, RG393, Part 1, Entry 232, Vol.4, 3 July, 1879–Dec. 13 1879, Letter No.166, p.106; Record of Events September 1879 in Returns From Regular Army Cavalry Regiments 1833-1916, 9th Cavalry Regimental Returns 1873-1880, NA, M744, Roll 88; Billington, 1991, p.91; Kenner, 1999, p.109; Schubert, 1995, p.357.

42 Personal observation of Canyon by author September 2005.

43 Hooker to Loud AAAG 29 September 1879, NA, RG393, Part 3, Entry 439, pp.359-360 & Bi-Monthly Company Muster Rolls for E Company, 9th Cavalry, Sept/Oct 1879 in NA, RG94; See also comments in 'Indian War in the Southwest' *Weekly New Mexican*, 11 October 1879 in The Walter Lowry Finley Collection; Returns From U.S. Military Posts; September 1879 Record of Events, 1800-1916, Ojo Caliente, N.M. May 1879-March 1882, NA, M617, Roll 877.

44 Loud to Hooker, 29 September 1879, Telegrams Sent DoNM, Vol.2, Jan.–Dec. 1879, NA, RG393, Part 3, Entry 431, pp.255-256; Hatch to Pope, 30 September 1879, Telegrams Sent DoNM, Vol.2, Jan.–Dec. 1879, NA, RG393, Part 3, Entry 431, p.257; Loud to CO Fort Bayard, 30 September 1879, Telegrams Sent DoNM, Vol.2, Jan.–Dec. 1879, NA, RG393, Part 3, Entry 431, pp.257-258; Pope to Col. Whipple, Chicago, 1 October 1879, 'Victorio Files', NA, RG393, M1495, Roll 14.

45 Morrow & Hooker to AAAG SF 1 October 1879, NA, RG393, Part 3, Entry 439, pp.326-333; Loud to Willcox, 4 October 1879, Telegrams Sent DoNM, Vol.2, Jan.–Dec. 1879, NA, RG393, Part 3, Entry 431, pp.280-281; See also Arnold to AAG Dept. Arizona, 4 October 1879, Troops in Southeastern

small party of Apaches in the canyon above Cañada Alamosa. The return trip proved more difficult. Two days later, and two miles from Cañada Alamosa, they were attacked by 20 mounted Apaches, and after a long running skirmish they broke contact and returned to Paraje.[46] Hooker sent out Lieutenant F.B. Taylor with 20 dismounted men to look for Sergeant Howard's missing detachment, which he feared had been killed by Apaches.[47] Taylor reached Cañada Alamosa and sent on a detachment of four men with the mail buckboard. This detachment returned on 3 October, with Howard's detachment. Taylor also noted a fresh trail of eight to 10 Apaches between Ojo Caliente and Cañada Alamosa, and numerous older indications that Apaches had been active in the area. On 1 October, Taylor spotted eight Apaches in the hills surrounding Cañada Alamosa, and a further two were seen in the canyon above the hamlet. Finally, Taylor reported that there was a spur of the San Mateo Mountains which overlooked the route between Cañada Alamosa and San Jose which was a favoured site for ambushes, due to its excellent cover and superb view of the surrounding land.[48] It was at this point that Sergeant Howard had been attacked on his return trip, although 'the bright moonlight and his being mounted on better or faster horses than the Indians, saved him and his party from being killed or captured'[49] (see document files nos.10 and 16).

On the night of 28 September, Fort Craig went on the alert, as it was suspected that Apaches were in close proximity to the post.[50]

In the meantime, there were also ominous reports that Mescalero warriors were leaving the reservation, either to join Victorio or to raid independently. It was noted that Lieutenant G.W. Smith had done an unofficial headcount of Mescaleros on the reservation and could only find 33 men over 20 years old. He was ordered to contact the Indian agent to find out if any Mescaleros had left the reservation.[51] At least one press report warned that the root cause of this exodus was the manner in which their agent treated the Mescalero Apaches, particularly with reference to how the latter reacted to his piety:

> GORGONIO their medicine chief said in conversation a few days ago "the Tata (Agent) is all the time on his knees pretending to talk to God, he tries to make the Indians think that he knows God, but I guess God don't want to know him." This is not written irreverently, but in

Arizona, DoAz, NA, RG393, Part 1, Entry 232, Vol.4, 3 July, 1879–Dec. 13 1879, Letter No.179, pp.114-115; Hatch to Willcox, 7 October 1879, 'Victorio Papers', NA, M666, Roll 526.

46 Lt F.B. Taylor to Hooker, 4 October 1879 in Letters Received by HQ DoNM, September 1865-August 1890, NA, RG393, M1088, Roll 39, Oct-Dec 1879; Returns From U.S. Military Posts; September 1879 Record of Events, 1800-1916, Ojo Caliente, N.M. May 1879-March 1882, NA, M617, Roll 877; Howard to Hatch, 1 October 1879, NA, RG393, Part 3, Entry 439, p.364; Record of Events September 1879 in Returns From Regular Army Cavalry Regiments 1833-1916, 9th Cavalry Regimental Returns 1873-1880, NA, M744, Roll 88; See also Kenner, 1999, p.109.

47 Morrow & Hooker to AAAG SF, 1 October 1879, NA, RG393, Part 3, Entry 439, pp.326-333; Loud to Willcox, 4 October 1879, Telegrams Sent DoNM, Vol.2, Jan.–Dec. 1879, NA, RG393, Part 3, Entry 431, pp.280-281; See also Arnold to AAG Dept. Arizona, 4 October 1879, Troops in Southeastern Arizona, DoAz, NA, RG393, Part 1, Entry 232, Vol.4, 3 July, 1879–Dec. 13 1879, Letter No.179, pp.114-115; Hatch to Willcox, 7 October 1879, 'Victorio Papers', NA, M666, Roll 526; Morrow & Hooker to Loud AAG 5 October 1879, NA, RG393, Part 3, Entry 439, pp.320-324; See also Loud to Hatch, 6 October 1879, Telegrams Sent DoNM, Vol.2, Jan.–Dec. 1879, NA, RG393, Part 3, Entry 431, pp.288-289.

48 Lt F.B. Taylor to Hooker, 4 October 1879 in Letters Received by HQ DoNM, September 1865-August 1890, NA, RG393, M1088, Roll 39, Oct-Dec 1879.

49 Lt F.B. Taylor to Hooker, 4 October 1879 in Letters Received by HQ DoNM, September 1865-August 1890, NA, RG393, M1088, Roll 39, Oct-Dec 1879.

50 'Territorial News', *Grant County Herald*, 4 October 1879.

51 Loud to CO Fort Stanton, 18 October 1879 in Letters Sent by the '9MD/DNM/DoNM', NA, RG393, M1072, Roll 6, Jan-Oct 1879, Letter No.506, pp.361-362.

> order to show precisely how the Indians regard their Agent. I predict that the incapacity of this man to deal with Indians, and his criminal blunders, will result in the loss of many lives and much property in Southern New Mexico, before many weeks elapse.[52]

His piety was not, perhaps, the real problem. Two months later, Lieutenant Smith,[53] whilst commanding a small detachment of Ninth cavalrymen at Tulerosa, reported that the agent had forbidden the brewing of tiswin; had refused to give them beef for a feast; and had attempted to forbid trade on and off the reservation. This situation was dangerous, as the agent had singularly failed to win the respect of the Mescalero Apaches, the latter regarding him as an 'old woman'. Their reaction to such rules was to challenge the agent to stop them from following their traditional ways. General Crook had instituted, and would again institute, some of these very rules on Apache reservations in Arizona. However, Crook had earned the respect of the Apaches and could challenge such traditional practices. The issue of trade on and off the reservation was expressed to Lieutenant Smith as involving trade in such items as vegetables, coffee and sugar.[54] However, we should not be blind to the possibility that the Mescaleros' hostility towards their agent might have been born of a perceived threat to their illicit trade in liquor, guns and ammunition.

Cuchillo Negro Fight, 29-30 September 1879

Around 25 or 26 September, Lieutenant Gatewood's Apache scouts discovered another trail some miles to the north of the Animas canyon. He and his scouts left their mule train behind and, with each man carrying his own supplies and equipment, they set out after the Apaches. They trekked for four days in conditions of continual rain and travelling mostly at night to avoid detection:

> We laid over in the daytime, concealing ourselves in the narrow gorges and canons. It rained every minute of the time, and we dared to build only very small fires to do our cooking by, there was no chance to dry our clothing and the few blankets in the party. The only part of the little food we had to eat not spoiled by the rain was the bacon. Bread and tobacco fell into a pulpy mixture that could neither be eaten nor smoked. Shortage of rations was made up somewhat the second day with some jerked horse meat we found in a deserted camp, and the third day an old abandoned government mule filled the long-felt want. The soldiers some time before had "packed" him until he could go no further, and was left to die. Then the hostiles used him till he was not quite dead, and left him to live if he could. It was not difficult to see every bone in his body, and his back was a mass of-what you might expect to see on a mule so much abused. From the time his throat was cut by a scout till the stew of bacon and mule was simmering on the little fire in a frying pan picked up on the trail, a very few minutes elapsed. The meat was too tough for mastication and had to be swallowed whole, and, as the mule lay with his back towards the fire, the sight of him was not appetizing. However, it was better than nothing.[55]

Sometime on 29 September, the mule train and Morrow's column, complete with supply wagons, caught up with the scouts.[56] Apart from the immediate relief this provided, the reinforcement

52 'The Mescalero Apaches', Letter to *Thirty Four*, 9 October 1879.
53 This is the same officer who attempted to pursue Victorio after he left the Mescalero Reservation in August 1879.
54 Smith to Post Adjutant, Fort Stanton, 17 November 1879, 'Victorio Papers', NA, M666, Roll 527.
55 Gatewood, p.102.
56 Gatewood, p.102.

Plate 9.1 Looking down Cañada Alamosa Canyon. Sergeant Robinson's mail detachment would have been pursued towards the camera. (Photo: author)

Plate 9.2 Another photo of Cañada Alamosa Canyon taken from above the canyon floor. This is further up the canyon, towards Ojo Caliente. It shows how the canyon progressively narrows as it approaches Ojo Caliente. If the Apaches had managed to get in front of the Ninth cavalrymen, then this could easily have become a death-trap. Yet the canyon acted as a barrier to the pursuing Apaches. (Photo: author)

proved fortuitous. Blocksom and Gatewood's[57] scouts took the lead and once more entered the mountains with the Ninth Cavalry battalion close behind. Towards the end of 29 September, they stumbled upon Victorio's camp, both sides spotting each other virtually instantaneously. At first, the Warm Springs Apaches, failing to detect US troops in support, became in Gatewood's words: 'saucy and facetious, daring them to come closer and even inviting them to supper.'[58] The initial skirmish attracted the main body of troops and scouts, and when Blocksom's detachment of Sixth Cavalrymen joined the engagement, the camp was taken and Victorio's people slipped away into the mountains. In the gathering dusk, the Apache scouts lost the trail.[59] Gatewood stated that the Apaches had had time to get their animals away, and that what remained would be 'not worth much after we got it.'[60] However, both Blocksom and Morrow claimed three 'hostiles' killed and 60 horses and mules recaptured, including 12 horses from Captain Hooker's company[61] and all the mules lost in the Animas canyon.[62] Morrow stated that 15 heavily laden horses were part of the captured stock.[63] Blocksom and Gatewood qualified this statement to acknowledge that two warriors and a woman, and possibly a child, were killed, with no fatalities being sustained by the US force.[64] The Apache scouts then went into camp half a mile further up the canyon from the

57 It was with a great deal of interest that I discovered both Blocksom and Gatewood's original reports in the archives. However, instead of providing separate and concurrent reports, Blocksom's report covers the period that he was in the field alongside Gatewood. Gatewood's report then concentrates upon the period after Blocksom left Morrow's command. Obviously, on being asked to produce reports both officers, to save time, produced, in effect, a composite report. The only problem with this is that Blocksom's report appears to give a slightly different version of elements of the story than Gatewood's 1894 article, and Gatewood's original report does not provide a comparison point. I am inclined to take Blocksom's version as it was produced within three months of the actual events and as there seems to be enough evidence to suggest that both officers cooperated to produce their reports (See Document File No.15).

58 Lt Blocksom's Report on Field Service between 24 September & Early October 1879, (Hereafter referred to as 'Blocksom's Report 1879', NA, RG393, Part 1, Entry 240; Gatewood, p.102; Thrapp, 1967, p.185; see also Stout, p.99; Thrapp, 1974, p.242; Haley, 1981, p.322.

59 'Blocksom's Report 1879', NA, RG393, Part 1, Entry 240.

60 Thrapp, 1974, p.243.

61 'Blocksom's Report 1879', NA, RG393, Part 1, Entry 240; See also 'Indian Affairs' *Army & Navy Journal*, Vol.17, 11 October 1879, p.178.

Another possible sighting of some of Hooker's lost horses was a trail of approximately thirty large and shod horses reported going south from the San Francisco River towards Mexico running close to the Arizona line in late October 1879. Carr alerted Lt. Howard to look out for this trail as he returned with Company D, Indian Scouts from Fort Bayard. (Carr to Howard, Fort Bayard, 28 October 1879, Troops in Southeastern Arizona, DoAz, NA, RG393, Part 1, Entry 232, Vol.4, 3 July, 1879–Dec. 13 1879, Letter No.216, p.151.)

62 Morrow to Purington 30 September 1879, NA, RG393, Part 3, Entry 439, p.336; Hatch to Pope, 3 October 1879, Telegrams Sent DoNM, Vol.2, Jan.–Dec. 1879, NA, RG393, Part 3, Entry 431, p.277; Morrow & Hooker to AAAG SF 1 October 1879, NA, RG393, Part 3, Entry 439, pp.326-333; Loud to Willcox, 4 October 1879, Telegrams Sent DoNM, Vol.2, Jan.–Dec. 1879, NA, RG393, Part 3, Entry 431, pp.280-281; See also Arnold to AAG Dept. Arizona, 4 October 1879, Troops in Southeastern Arizona, DoAz, NA, RG393, Part 1, Entry 232, Vol.4, 3 July, 1879–Dec. 13 1879, Letter No.179, pp.114-115; Hatch to Willcox, 7 October 1879, 'Victorio Papers', NA, M666, Roll 526; See also 'Indian War in the Southwest' *Weekly New Mexican*, 11 October 1879 in The Walter Lowry Finley Collection; Thrapp, 1974, p.242.

63 Morrow to AAAG DoNM, 5 November 1879, 'Victorio Papers', NA, M666, Roll 526; Billington, 1991, p.91.

64 'Blocksom's Report 1879', NA, RG393, Part 1, Entry 240; Thrapp, 1974, p.242; Stout p.99; see also Chronological List, p.47; O'Neal, p.177.

camp set up by the Ninth Cavalry detachment. Both camps were out of sight of each other, hidden by a curve in the canyon.[65]

Early the following morning, the Apache scouts picked up the trail of Victorio's fleeing warriors, leaving Gatewood and Blocksom and their Sixth Cavalry trooper escort in camp.[66] The Apache scouts were accompanied by two civilian guides called Dunn and Borman.[67] The Apaches either failed to detect this movement, or more likely, deliberately let the Apache scouts follow the trails out for a distance of four to five miles before moving in behind the scouts to occupy the heights above Morrow's camp. As the battalion prepared breakfast, a distinct rifle shot rang out, immediately followed by heavy firing from the surrounding heights. The first shot killed Private John Johnson of L Company,[68] Ninth Cavalry, the trooper on guard high above the camps.[69] Gatewood described the canyon as '800 feet deep, with steep rocky sides covered with pine, oak and heavy underbrush.'[70] Victorio's warriors occupied the top of the cliffs and rained a heavy fire down into the canyon.[71] Morrow's camp, and any attempt to reach it, was caught in a vicious crossfire.[72] (See Map 9.2.) Morrow had stationed 12 men above the camp on picket duty, and that the Apaches struck when 11 of these men came down from the surrounding bluffs to take breakfast. The sentry left on duty was shot from behind. The Apaches then turned their attention to the camp below, and for some time there was utter confusion as they sent shot after shot into the canyon.[73] This fire also killed the cook who 'was standing by the fire drinking coffee. One 45-70 ball tore the cup out of his hand and another struck him between the eyes.'[74] Later the Surgeon General would report '2 privates of the Ninth Cavalry, shot through the brain and instantly killed.'[75] The timing of the dawn attack is was significant. It was standard practice for Morrow to mount a strong guard above or around his camp on the march, but the flaw in this procedure was that most of these pickets returned to camp for breakfast. For Victorio to strike at the one point when this system was at its most vulnerable strongly suggests that Major Morrow's command had been carefully watched for some days.

Once the troops had gathered their wits, they tried to mount a counter-attack. Blocksom directed Gatewood and some of his men to move down the canyon to contact Major Morrow. The sheer volume of Apache fire was such that Gatewood found himself unable to advance towards the Ninth Cavalrymen. Once again, while surprised, the US cavalry troopers did not panic. Finding what

65 Thrapp, 1974, p.242.
66 'Blocksom's Report 1879', NA, RG393, Part 1, Entry 240; Gatewood, p.102.
67 'Blocksom's Report 1879', NA, RG393, Part 1, Entry 240.
68 Return for October 1879 in Returns From U.S. Military Posts 1800-1916, Fort Bliss, Texas Jan. 1872-Dec. 1885, NA, M617, Roll 117; Bi-Monthly Company Muster Rolls for Company L, 9th Cavalry, Sept/Oct 1879 in NA, RG94.
69 Morrow to AAAG DoNM, 5 November 1879, 'Victorio Papers', NA, M666, Roll 526; Gatewood, p.103; 'Indian War in the Southwest' *Weekly New Mexican*, 11 October 1879 in The Walter Lowry Finley Collection; William M. Bates Interview Notes c. 1940 in the Keith Humphries Collection, Geronimo Springs Museum, Truth or Consequences, New Mexico; Thrapp, 1974, p.243; Record of Engagements, p.92; Leckie, 1967, p.212; Schubert, 1997, p.57; Billington, 1991, p.91.
70 Gatewood, p.102; Thrapp, 1974, p.243.
71 Morrow to AAAG DoNM, 5 November 1879, 'Victorio Papers', NA, M666, Roll 526.
72 Gatewood, p.102; Thrapp, 1974, p.243; It should be noted that Gatewood's article gives the impression that both camps came under fire but Blocksom's report makes it clear that Morrow's camp was attacked and that Gatewood came under fire when trying to reach Morrow ('Blocksom's Report 1879', NA, RG393, Part 1, Entry 240).
73 William M. Bates Interview Notes c. 1940 in the Keith Humphries Collection, Geronimo Springs Museum, Truth or Consequences, New Mexico.
74 William M. Bates Interview Notes c. 1940 in the Keith Humphries Collection, Geronimo Springs Museum, Truth or Consequences, New Mexico.
75 Report of The Surgeon General in AR-WD 1880, NA, M997, Roll 35, 1880 Vol. I, p.520.

cover they could, they returned fire. Gatewood noted that the level of gunfire was intense and that, at first, he thought complete confusion prevailed. However, when he took cover behind a rock, his corporal informed him that he had taken cover on the wrong side of the boulder 'and pointed out to me the folly of protecting a rock.'[76] Gatewood then noted how calm his men were under such a heavy fire:

> Up to that time, it seemed to me, we would all be killed for every man had lost his head, and was yelling with all his might and shooting in the air. But once anchored on the right side of the rock, I was astonished to see how cool they were, and how steady was their aim, some even laughing and joking.[77]

This deadlock was broken approximately one hour later, when the Apache scouts were summoned back by the sound of the gunfire. They launched a flank attack on the Ojo Caliente Apaches, announcing their presence with a loud volley.[78] This was supported by a frontal assault, led by Major Morrow himself, up the slope of the canyon, towards the point where the sentry had been killed.[79] Though of the 30 men started the charge with Morrow, only eight appear to have followed him all the way to the top.[80] Indeed, Morrow mentioned seven enlisted men[81] in his overall report on his pursuit of the Apaches in September-October 1879, citing them for gallantry during the Cuchillo Negro battle. These must have been the men who remained with him to the top of the hill:[82]

> I would have to mention the names of some enlisted men of the 9th Cavalry, who behaved exceptionally well during the affair of the 29th of September, other men doubtless behaved as well, but these happened to come under my immediate observation.

Sergt. Thomas F. Fredericks	Co "H", 9th Cav.
Sergt. David Badie	Co "B", 9th Cav.
Corporal Charles A. Parker	Co "G", 9th Cav.
Sergt. Nathaniel Howard	Co "L", 9th Cav.
Trumpeter Louis T. Green	Co "H", 9th Cav.
Pvt. Issac Holbrook	Co "H", 9th Cav.
Pvt. Wm. Jones	Co "L", 9th Cav.[83]

Captain Hooker, when he was informed of the fight a couple of days later, was contemptuous:

> I remember distinctly of expressing myself somewhat strongly at that time, when informed by some of Major Morrow's officers, that on the morning of a day or two previous to the arrival of Major Morrow's Command, a camp of his battalion had been attacked by the hostiles when the command was at break-fast, the camp was fired upon from a high point

76 Gatewood, p.102; 'Blocksom's Report 1879', NA, RG393, Part 1, Entry 240; Thrapp, 1967, p.185.
77 Gatewood, p.102; Thrapp, 1974, p243.
78 'Blocksom's Report 1879', NA, RG393, Part 1, Entry 240.
79 Morrow to AAAG DoNM, 5 November 1879, 'Victorio Papers', NA, M666, Roll 526.
80 'Blocksom's Report 1879', NA, RG393, Part 1, Entry 240.
81 Morrow to AAAG DoNM, 5 November 1879, 'Victorio Papers', NA, M666, Roll 526; See also Schubert, 1995.
82 Morrow to AAAG DoNM, 5 November 1879, 'Victorio Papers', NA, M666, Roll 526.
83 Morrow to AAAG Dist. Of New Mexico, 5 November 1879 in Papers relating to military operations against Chief Victorio's band of Mescalero Apache in southern New Mexico, 1879-81 in Letters Rec'd by the Office of the Adjutant General (Main series). 1871-80, NA, M666, Roll 526.

> in the immediate vicinity covering the camp and some men killed and wounded. Major Morrow immediately gathered together thirty non-commissioned officers and men and stormed the height in person, arriving upon the height with six men, the remainder of the storming party having skulked and deserted him during the charge, the Major and his small party, principally non-commissioned officers only being saved from destruction by the opportune arrival from an opposite direction of Lieutenant Gatewood's Arizona Apache Scouts who, being camped at some distance from the main force, had rushed to the combat on hearing the firing.[84]

It is clear from Hooker's statement that he had been given an accurate account of the battle itself, even though his interpretation of events may be challenged. Thirty men may have participated in the opening movement up the ridge, but Major Morrow may well have chosen a specific point on the ridge at which to aim the charge. If he adopted a rough wedge-shaped attack, he would drop off men to either side of the charge in an effort to pin down the Chihenne firing line pinned down along the top of the ridge. In working their way towards the top of the ridge, these men would prevent any effort by the Apaches to infiltrate behind the major and cut him off from his camp.

Morrow's assault was supported by Gatewood's detachment of Sixth cavalrymen, who had, by that time, cleared and occupied a peak on the opposite side of the canyon and pinned down the Apaches with 'such a continuous firing that the hostiles could do no more damage on the camp below.'[85] However, the flank attack seems to have been detected by Victorio's warriors before it could do any damage, though Gatewood claimed that the signs showed that some of the Apaches had been hit.[86] Blocksom stated that Victorio's men had had time enough to remove their wounded,[87] suggesting that they had been keeping an eye out for the returning scouts. Once again, the Chihennes disappeared into the mountains where, as Gatewood put it, the 'impertinent rascals'[88] loudly mocked their enemies. Blocksom estimated that Victorio had between 40 and 50 warriors, and after a pursuit of about three miles, the Apaches took up positions on a large rocky outcrop. This position was too well defended for an assault,[89] and Morrow ordered a withdrawal towards the Cuchillo Negro River to seek water and to save his horses, which were being actively targeted by the Apaches[90] (see document file no. 16). Here, the rugged terrain intervened: while the canyon in which Victorio had camped was open to ascent by the cavalrymen's horses and mules, it was far too steep for them to descend safely with their animals. A new way out had to be found.[91] While the scouts acted as videttes, this was achieved under a renewed attack by Victorio's warriors

---

84 Captain Hooker's Counter Statement in Captain Charles Steelhammer, Ojo Caliente, to AAAG Dist. of New Mexico, Santa Fe, 11 December 1879, in Letters Received by Headquarters District of New Mexico September 1865-August 1890, NA, RG393, M1088, Roll 38, File 1664-2491, July–Sept. 1879.

85 'Blocksom's Report 1879', NA, RG393, Part 1, Entry 240; Gatewood, p.102; Morrow to AAAG DoNM, 5 November 1879, 'Victorio Papers', NA, M666, Roll 526; Thrapp, 1974, pp.243-244; Stout, p.90

86 Gatewood, p.103.

87 'Blocksom's Report 1879', NA, RG393, Part 1, Entry 240.

88 Gatewood, p.102; Thrapp, 1967, p.185.

89 'Blocksom's Report 1879', NA, RG393, Part 1, Entry 240.

90 Morrow & Hooker to AAAG SF, 1 October 1879, NA, RG393, Part 3, Entry 439, pp.326-333; Loud to Willcox, 4 October 1879, Telegrams Sent DoNM, Vol.2, Jan.–Dec. 1879, NA, RG393, Part 3, Entry 431, pp.280-281; See also 'Blocksom's Report 1879', NA, RG393, Part 1, Entry 240; Morrow to AAAG DoNM, 5 November 1879, 'Victorio Papers', NA, M666, Roll 526; Arnold to AAG Dept. Arizona, 4 October 1879, Troops in Southeastern Arizona, DoAz, NA, RG393, Part 1, Entry 232, Vol.4, 3 July, 1879–Dec. 13 1879, Letter No.179, pp.114-115; Hatch to Willcox, 7 October 1879, 'Victorio Papers', NA, M666, Roll 526.

91 Thrapp, 1974, p.244.

Plate 9.3 The opening of Cañada Alamosa canyon at Ojo Caliente. The last quarter of a mile is dominated by sheer high cliffs and the riverbed is the trail for most of that distance, so there could be an additional threat posed to travellers by flash flooding. Again, the narrow nature of the terrain in this case saved the Ninth cavalrymen from disaster, but travel through the canyon was a dangerous duty for the small detachments of cavalry tasked with maintaining communication with the outside world. (Photo: author)

who, according to Gatewood, harassed their withdrawal and at varying points opened fire on the front, middle and rear of the column as it descended out of the mountains. They continued to fire on the unit until it reached the Cuchillo Negro.[92]

Two Ninth cavalrymen had been killed in the fighting: troopers John Johnson and Private Major[93] Woodward of L Company.[94] Johnson was named as the 'vidette' killed, so presumably Woodward was the unfortunate chef.[95] Gatewood notes that 'several soldiers had been killed'[96] but gives no further details.

92 Gatewood, p.103.

93 This is a first name not a rank.

94 Bi-Monthly Company Muster Rolls for Company L, 9th Cavalry, Sept/Oct 1879 in NA, RG94; See also Morrow to Purington 30 September 1879, NA, RG393, Part 3, Entry 439, pp.335-336; Morrow & Hooker to AAAG SF, 1 October 1879, NA, RG393, Part 3, Entry 439, pp.326-333; Loud to Willcox, 4 October 1879, Telegrams Sent DoNM, Vol.2, Jan.–Dec. 1879, NA, RG393, Part 3, Entry 431, pp.280-281; Leckie, 1967, p.212; Schubert, 1995; Schubert, 1997, p.57; See also Chronological List, p.47; Kenner p.188; Billington, 1991, p.91; O'Neal, p.177.

95 Tabular Statement of Expeditions and Scouts sent out from the Posts in the District of New Mexico against Hostile Indians during the Fourth Quarter ending December 31st 1879 in Letters Received, DoM 1868-98, RG 393, Entry A1-1 2601, Box 90.

96 Gatewood, p.103; Thrapp, 1967, p.185.

Plates 9.4 and 9.5 It is not clear from Morrow's report where along the Rio Cuchillo Negro he pursued and fought the Apaches. These two photos give a sample of the sort of terrain to be encountered along the river to the west of the small town of Winston. (Both photos: author)

While the Apaches had once again forced the Ninth Cavalry to withdraw, this time they had definitely suffered casualties. Two Warm Springs Apache warriors and a woman had been killed, and any such loss was a serious blow to them. Kaywaykla thought that it was common for wives to accompany their husbands on raids. It seems plausible to argue that the woman killed on 29 September was accompanying the warriors in this capacity rather than concluding that the army had come close to threatening the Apache warriors' families, who were hidden deep within the Black Range.[97] If we look again at Kaywaykla's account of the flight to the Black Range, we find that he recalls a period of peace and tranquillity. Yet, as we have seen, September 1879 was punctuated by several hard battles between the Ninth Cavalry and the Warm Springs Apaches. Kaywaykla provided accounts of several battles later in the campaign, often as an eyewitness; yet his versions of these skirmishes in September 1879 were written with the detachment of a historian.

While the Ninth Cavalry had several fierce encounters with the Apaches in this period, it was quite possible that they came nowhere near to finding the warriors' families secreted deep within the Black Range. If we examine the map, we find that these battles were concentrated on the eastern face of the Black Range and the Cuchillo Negro Mountains, and they rarely penetrated the mountains. Throughout September, the Apache warriors, acting independently of their families, consistently kept the Ninth Cavalry focused on their activities. When the Ninth Cavalry battalion did move into the mountains, the soldiers either assaulted what they found to be deserted camps or were driven out by the Apaches. Victorio may have been caught out on 29 September, yet he rapidly rallied his men, and on the following day he effectively drove Morrow's unit out of the Cuchillo Negro Mountains. Accounts describe the US army as constantly 'attacking Victorio's camp', implying that the cavalry had come near to defeating their opponent, or were forcing the band as a whole to be constantly on the move. In actual fact, the Apaches seem to have split into two broad groupings: families hidden deep in the mountains with some of the older warriors providing a guard; and the rest of the warriors acting either as one or several guerrilla groups, constantly decoying and harassing their opponents far away from their dependants. While Morrow claimed that he had inflicted 'severe punishment'[98] on the Apaches, it is clear from the account above that he had had to withdraw from the field for lack of water and to save his horses. Morrow's assertion that he had defeated Victorio was somewhat undermined by the assertion, in the same dispatch, that Victorio was 'evidently determined to fight it out on this line.'[99]

The major was also running short of ammunition. Immediately after the Cuchillo Negro fight, sent out word via Hooker at Ojo Caliente that he was short of men, ammunition and food. Hooker could supply ammunition and rations, but not men. Hooker informed District Headquarters of the need for additional support for Morrow, because the dismounted patrol, under Lieutenant Taylor, had been sent towards Paraje in search of Sergeant Howard's missing mail detachment.[100] From the

97 Ball, 1970, p.8.

98 Morrow & Hooker to AAAG SF, 1 October 1879, NA, RG393, Part 3, Entry 439, pp.326-333; Loud to Willcox, 4 October 1879, Telegrams Sent DoNM, Vol.2, Jan.–Dec. 1879, NA, RG393, Part 3, Entry 431, pp.280-281; See also Arnold to AAG Dept. Arizona, 4 October 1879, Troops in Southeastern Arizona, DoAz, NA, RG393, Part 1, Entry 232, Vol.4, 3 July, 1879–Dec. 13 1879, Letter No.179, pp.114-115; Hatch to Willcox, 7 October 1879, 'Victorio Papers', NA, M666, Roll 526.

99 Morrow & Hooker to AAAG SF, 1 October 1879, NA, RG393, Part 3, Entry 439, pp.326-333; Loud to Willcox, 4 October 1879, Telegrams Sent DoNM, Vol.2, Jan.–Dec. 1879, NA, RG393, Part 3, Entry 431, pp.280-281; See also Arnold to AAG Dept. Arizona, 4 October 1879, Troops in Southeastern Arizona, DoAz, NA, RG393, Part 1, Entry 232, Vol.4, 3 July, 1879–Dec. 13 1879, Letter No.179, pp.114-115; Hatch to Willcox, 7 October 1879, 'Victorio Papers', NA, M666, Roll 526.

100 Morrow & Hooker to AAAG SF, 1 October 1879, NA, RG393, Part 3, Entry 439, pp.326-333; Loud to Willcox, 4 October 1879, Telegrams Sent DoNM, Vol.2, Jan.–Dec. 1879, NA, RG393, Part 3, Entry 431, pp.280-281; See also Arnold to AAG Dept. Arizona, 4 October 1879, Troops in Southeastern Arizona, DoAz, NA, RG393, Part 1, Entry 232, Vol.4, 3 July, 1879–Dec. 13 1879, Letter No.179,

army's point of view, the campaign so far had been a complete failure, though that did not prevent them claiming that the Apaches had been soundly defeated by the end of September.[101] Even if we accept only acknowledged fatalities, the Ninth Cavalry had lost 10 men killed in action. In other words, the deaths registered for this one month amounted to just under a quarter of the fatalities sustained by the regiment between 1866 and 1898.[102] They had also failed to destroy or force the surrender of Victorio's band.

The local press rejected the army's version of events, with one newspaper stating that, in 30 years of service in New Mexico, the army had not lost so heavily to 'seventy or eighty raiders.'[103] *Thirty-Four* went so far as to call for the Ninth Cavalry to be converted into a minstrel troup.[104] Moreover, some very critical correspondence reached the *Grant County Herald*, in which it was stated that 'those who were with the soldiers in the last fight,[105] are ashamed – not for themselves, but for the company they were in.'[106] The press also criticised the failure of Washington DC to react to the trouble in southern New Mexico, and the federal government was condemned as the 'harborer of our enemies.'[107] The *Grant County Herald* and *Thirty-Four* may have been guilty of exaggerating the situation; and they were certainly guilty of condemning the soldiers involved with little justification. Nevertheless, they may have had a valid point concerning the lack of priority given to the Apache troubles in southern New Mexico. For example, in a telegram sent on 29 September, General Pope refused Colonel Hatch's request for additional Apache scouts. In fact, Pope's instructions to Hatch between 29 September and 2 October were contradictory to say the least. The telegram went on to suggest to Hatch that surely he had enough troops to deal with the situation, but that if he did not, he could use the troops based at Forts Bliss and Wingate.[108] Pope reversed his decision the following day, as on 30 September he authorised Hatch to recruit 24 Apache scouts for one month.[109] Pope also informed Hatch that additional horses and mules would be supplied as soon as possible.[110] Pope, in no uncertain terms, instructed Hatch to make bringing the war to a successful conclusion his top priority;[111] but a day later, he instructed Hatch to concentrate on dealing with the uprising by the Utes and to leave Morrow to pursue the war against Victorio.[112] The attention this caused Hatch to give to the Ute conflict did not endear him to the citizens of southern New Mexico, who felt that he had abandoned them in the face of the enemy. In an age when emails from the United Kingdom to the United States can be answered in minutes, if not seconds, it is easy to

---

pp.114-115; Hatch to Willcox, 7 October 1879, 'Victorio Papers', NA, M666, Roll 526; Morrow & Hooker to Loud AAG, 5 October 1879, NA, RG393, Part 3, Entry 439, pp.320-324; See also Loud to Hatch, 6 October 1879, Telegrams Sent DoNM, Vol.2, Jan.–Dec. 1879, NA, RG393, Part 3, Entry 431, pp.288-289.

101 Hatch to Willcox, 4 October 1879, 'Victorio Papers', NA, M666, Roll 526; AG to Gen. Sherman, 4 October 1879, NA, RG393, Part 1, Entry 2539, Press Copies of Letters and Endorsements Sent, MDoM, Vol. 11, p.864; See also Sheridan to Sherman, 4 October 1879, 'Victorio Papers', NA, M666, Roll 526; Arnold to CO Fort Apache, 8 October 1879, Troops in Southeastern Arizona, DoAz, NA, RG393, Part 1, Entry 232, Vol.4, 3 July, 1879–Dec. 13 1879, p.118; Pope to Col. Whipple AAG MDoM, Victorio Files', NA, RG393, M1495, Roll 14.

102 Schubert, 1995, p.514; 1997, p.58.

103 'Correspondence', *Grant County Herald*, 4 October 1879.

104 *Thirty Four*, 24 September 1879.

105 It is unclear whether the correspondent is referring to the Las Animas or Cuchillo Negro fights.

106 'Correspondence', *Grant County Herald*, 11 October 1879.

107 'Ashenfelter Editorial', *Grant County Herald*, 4 October 1879.

108 Pope to Hatch, 29 September 1879 in NA, RG393, Part 3, Entry 439, p.93.

109 Dunn to Hatch, 30 September 1879 in NA, RG393, Part 3, Entry 439, p.94.

110 Pope to Hatch, 30 September 1879, NA, RG393, Part 3, Entry 439, p.93 & Pope to Hatch, 1 October 1879, NA, RG393, Part 3, Entry 439, p.94.

111 Pope to Hatch, 1 October 1879, NA, RG393, Part 3, Entry 439, p.94.

112 Pope to Hatch, 2 October 1879, NA, RG393, Part 3, Entry 439, p.95.

forget that both General Pope and Colonel Hatch were trying to deploy their meagre resources without the benefit of genuinely portable field telecommunications.[113] The best they could hope for was information transmitted by telegraph; but even this medium of communication had to be reached before it could be utilised. Information received could be hours, if not days, old and was not a particularly effective way of keeping track of the highly mobile Apaches. The telegraph lines could also be used by outraged citizens to report actual or rumoured atrocities and demand an immediate US army response. Sorting out the reliable from the unreliable information at headquarters level cannot have been easy. The added pressure for information and effective action, in relation to both the Apaches and the Utes, from Hatch's superiors cannot have been helpful.

Hatch did his best, ordering Morrow to continue campaigning against the Chihennes, and indicating that such troops and supplies as were available at Santa Fé and Fort Bayard were to be used as the major saw fit.[114] Hatch also made enquiries, on the basis of a request from Morrow, as to the availability of 'Jackass' Howitzers[115] (see document file no. 17). Morrow thought that artillery, broken down and packed on mules, was an essential element of any assault on the inaccessible spots in which Victorio routinely chose to site his camps.[116] Fort Mims replied to this request with the following:

> In reply to your dispatch of this date [7 October 1879] asking after Jackass Howitzers, never heard of such a thing. We have mountain howitzers but no carriages or mountings for them plenty of ammunition.[117]

For Victorio, his war with the United States had progressed well. He had successfully secreted his families away in the Black Range, where they laboured to produce extra supplies for their commissary, while his warriors had prevented the US army from entering the mountains. They had also inflicted several defeats on their enemies, causing casualties and taking booty each time with minimal fatalities. In effect, under Victorio's leadership, the Apaches had, so far, completely outmanoeuvred the Ninth Cavalry.

Continuing Pursuit and Skirmishes, 1-20 October 1879

On 1 October 1879, the Apache scouts caught a Chihenne Apache woman and child who indicated that Victorio planned to make for the Mogollon Mountains, to the west of the Black Range, on the other side of the Gila River. She also informed Morrow that Victorio had had a number of men wounded, including his son Washington, during the recent fighting.[118] This woman reported that some 30 of Victorio's warriors had gone into Cañada Alamosa to replenish their ammunition and

113 Though as we shall see, in 1880, portable means of tapping into the telegraph line was deployed by the U.S. army against Victorio.

114 Guilfoyle AAAG in field to AAAG Santa Fé, NA, RG393, Part 3, Entry 439, p.98.

115 See Telegrams Sent DoNM, Vol.2, Jan.–Dec. 1879, NA, RG393, Part 3, Entry 431, p.292; On 4 October, 1879, *Grant County Herald* "hoped that Maj. Morrow has taken a couple of mountain howitzers with him" arguing that such equipment would swiftly deal with the Apaches (*Grant County Herald*, 4 October 1879).

116 Morrow & Hooker to Loud AAG 5 October 1879, NA, RG393, Part 3, Entry 439, pp.320-324; See also Loud to Hatch, 6 October 1879, Telegrams Sent DoNM, Vol.2, Jan.–Dec. 1879, NA, RG393, Part 3, Entry 431, pp.288-289.

117 Shoemaker to Loud AAAG Santa Fé 7 October 1879, NA, RG393, Part 3, Entry 439, p.98.

118 Morrow & Hooker to Loud AAG, 5 October 1879, NA, RG393, Part 3, Entry 439, pp.320-324; See also Loud to Hatch, 6 October 1879, Telegrams Sent DoNM, Vol.2, Jan.–Dec. 1879, NA, RG393, Part 3, Entry 431, pp.288-289; Morrow to AAAG DoNM, 5 November 1879, 'Victorio Papers', NA, M666, Roll 526; Record of Engagements, p.92; 'Indian War in the Southwest' *Weekly New Mexican,* 11 October

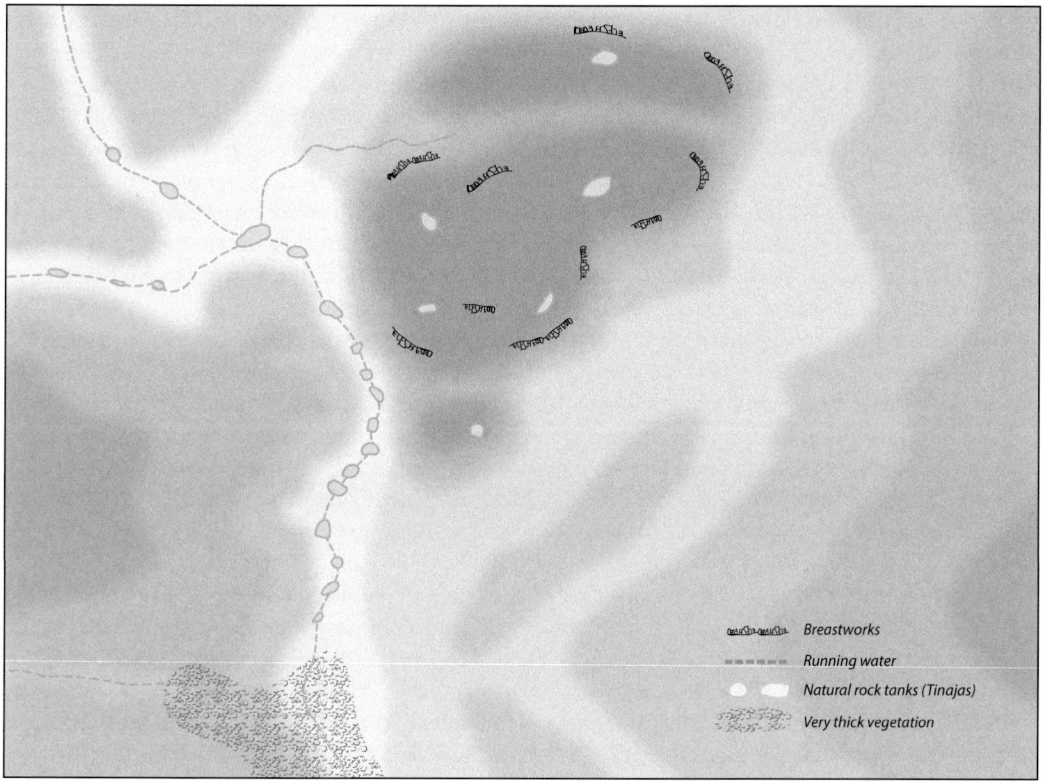

Map 9.3 Fortified Apache Camp in the Black Range Mountains.

other items.[119] This reached the ears of Captain Hooker, who immediately accused the citizens of Cañada Alamosa of outright collaboration with the Apaches, to the extent that they 'prevented the citizens of Cuchillo Negro (on the morning of Sept. 4. 79) from bringing me information of the near approach of Victorio and 40 of his band.'[120] Whatever Hooker's personal motives were, it is clear that it was widely believed by the military that a great deal of unwelcome collaboration existed between certain US citizens, both Anglo-American and Mexican, and the Apaches.

Major Morrow, having regrouped, despatched his scouts to find Victorio. They located him only four miles 'as the crow flies' from the location of the camp that had been attacked on 29 September. On the night of 1 October, Morrow ordered the scouts to move into position on the further side of the camp, while he moved in from the front. Victorio was not to be caught this time, and an empty camp was assaulted at dawn on 2 October, though the scouts found the fires still lit and 'meat cooking.'[121] Morrow concluded that this was probably fortunate, as the location of the encampment would have made a 'hot' assault very dangerous, due to the difficult terrain, which was made

1879 in The Walter Lowry Finley Collection; Thrapp, 1974, p.244: Wellman, 1957, p.155; Longstreet, p.91.

119 Hooker to DoNM, 4 October 1879 in Letters Received by HQ DoNM, September 1865-August 1890, NA, RG393, M1088, Roll 39, Oct–Dec 1879.

120 Hooker to DoNM, 4 October 1879 in Letters Received by HQ DoNM, September 1865-August 1890, NA, RG393, M1088, Roll 39, Oct–Dec 1879.

121 'Blocksom's Report 1879', NA, RG393, Part 1, Entry 240; Morrow to AAAG DoNM, 5 November 1879, 'Victorio Papers', NA, M666, Roll 526; Thrapp, 1974, p.244; Billington, 1991, pp.91-92; Record of Engagements, p.92.

even more suitable for defence by rock parapets constructed to protect the Apache warriors from enemy fire.[122] A surviving example of one such camp can still be seen in the Black Range (see Map 9.3). Not only was this camp well-defended, but it had a number of escape routes in place, their utility depending upon the line-of-march of the enemy. Even if the enemy had managed to trap the Apaches, they would have suffered serious casualties in attempting to storm this position. It was also well provided with water, both outside, with water running through numerous tinajas, and inside, where tinajas within the main defences could provide good water during a siege, should it ever come to that. This camp was deep within Chihenne Apache territory. If this camp was not the one chosen and developed by Victorio, it would have been the work of the ancestors who had taught him his craft by passing such knowledge down the generations.

The next day Morrow once more sent out his scouts, who confirmed their captive's suggestion that Victorio appeared to be making for the Mogollon Mountains. It was assumed that Victorio would then head for Mexico via the Burro Mountains.[123] Lieutenant Howard, operating out of Fort Huachuca with D Company, Indian Scouts, was alerted and ordered to move east to the Hatchet Mountains to intercept Victorio should he go that way.[124] In fact, Howard, finding no signs of Apaches, but hearing rumours that they had turned north again, scouted all the way to Fort Bayard, but again found no trace of his quarry.[125] This was welcome news to General Sheridan, who feared an alliance between the Utes and the Apaches.[126]

Morrow arrived at Ojo Caliente on 4 October, to take on supplies and re-shoe his horses. He left the following day, marching down the western side of the Black Range, looking for signs of the Apaches and making camp at Shaw's Ranch.[127] He had earlier sent for more troops from Fort Bayard to rendezvous with him for a projected pursuit of Victorio into the Mogollons.[128] Accordingly, Captain Purington proceeded towards Shaw's Ranch along the North Star Road, with 30 days' supplies and 2,000 rounds of ammunition. Morrow had also requested, if possible, that 15 days'

122 Morrow to AAAG DoNM, 5 November 1879, 'Victorio Papers', NA, M666, Roll 526; Thrapp, 1974, p.244; Billington, 1991, pp.91-92; Record of Engagements, p.92.

123 Morrow & Hooker to Loud AAG, 5 October 1879, NA, RG393, Part 3, Entry 439, pp.320-324; See also Loud to Hatch, 6 October 1879, Telegrams Sent DoNM, Vol.2, Jan.–Dec. 1879, NA, RG393, Part 3, Entry 431, pp.288-289; Morrow to AAAG DoNM, 5 November 1879, 'Victorio Papers', NA, M666, Roll 526; Sheridan to AG Wash. D.C., 'Victorio Papers', NA, M666, Roll 526; Sheridan to AG, 8 October 1879, NA, RG393, Part 1, Entry 2539, Press Copies of Letters and Endorsements Sent, MDoM, Vol. 11, p.896 & p.897; Arnold to CO Fort Bowie, 10 October 1879, Troops in Southeastern Arizona, DoAz, NA, RG393, Part 1, Entry 232, Vol.4, 3 July, 1879–Dec. 13 1879, p.119; Pope to AAG HQ MDoM, 8 October 1879, 'Victorio Files', NA, RG393, M1495, Roll 14.

124 Arnold to Lt Howard through CO Fort Huachuca & AAG Dept. Arizona, 10 October 1879, Troops in Southeastern Arizona, DoAz, NA, RG393, Part 1, Entry 232, Vol.4, 3 July, 1879–Dec. 13 1879, pp.120-121; See also Carr to Howard, 22 October 1879, Troops in Southeastern Arizona, DoAz, NA, RG393, Part 1, Entry 232, Vol.4, 3 July, 1879–Dec. 13 1879, p.134.

125 Carr to AG Dept Arizona, 24 October 1879, Troops in Southeastern Arizona, DoAz, NA, RG393, Part 1, Entry 232, Vol.4, 3 July, 1879–Dec. 13 1879, Letter No.209, pp.136-137.

126 Sheridan to Sherman, 8 October 1879, NA, RG393, Part 1, Entry 2539, Press Copies of Letters and Endorsements Sent, MDoM, Vol. 11, p.898; Sheridan to Sherman, 8 October 1879, NA, RG393, Part 1, Entry 2538, p.183.

127 Morrow & Hooker to Loud AAG, 5 October 1879, NA, RG393, Part 3, Entry 439, pp.320-324; See also Loud to Hatch, 6 October 1879, Telegrams Sent DoNM, Vol.2, Jan.–Dec. 1879, NA, RG393, Part 3, Entry 431, pp.288-289; Loud to Hatch, 7 October 1879, Telegrams Sent DoNM, Vol.2, Jan.–Dec. 1879, NA, RG393, Part 3, Entry 431, p.292; Morrow to AAAG DoNM, 5 November 1879, 'Victorio Papers', NA, M666, Roll 526; Return for October 1879 in Returns From U.S. Military Posts 1800-1916, Ojo Caliente, New Mexico, May 1879-Mar. 1882, NA, M617, Roll 877.

128 Morrow, Chaves Ranche, Cuchillo Negro to Purington 30 September 1879, NA, RG393, Part 3, Entry 439, pp.334-335.

supplies be brought for the detachment from Fort Bayard led by Lieutenant Eugene Dimmick.[129] The troops from Fort Bayard linked up with Morrow's force on 6 October, at Sherman's Cienega. This reinforcement numbered 113 troops made up from detachments from C and H Companies, Ninth Cavalry under Captains Purington and Beyer, plus a detachment from A Company, Sixth Cavalry and a company of Apache scouts.[130] The Sixth Cavalryman and Apache scouts had arrived at Fort Bayard on 28 September, from San Carlos, and were unassigned to any scout duty. Captain Purington immediately put in a request to recruit them and this was granted on 1 October. The Apache scouts were commanded by Lieutenant Maney of the Fifteenth Infantry,[131] and there may also have been a detachment from the Fifteenth Infantry Regiment.[132] Hatch hoped that these fresh troops from Fort Bayard would finish the campaign, stating that he 'now [had] no doubt of final result. This relieves me so I can attend to Ute country.'[133] It should be noted that this does not square with his later claim that he saw Victorio just prior to the breakout in August. This confidence, transmitted to his superior, General Pope, was in distinct contrast to the orders issued to Captain Purington by Hatch prior to the former's departure from Fort Bayard:

> Have troops take every possible round of ammunition you can give them even if you reduce amount left at post to twenty rounds per man left. It must be distinctly understood that the troops going to Morrow is to include every available man mentioned and that they must make forced marches to reach Morrow as soon as possible, the necessity of this you will understand from Morrow's dispatch to you. Morrow will be given every available man and every facility to enable him to exterminate Victorio.[134]

Captain Purington's response, that he would reach Morrow in three and a half days, was rejected as suggesting he would move too slowly, and Hatch reminded Purington of the urgency of the situation and ordered him to make a forced march to meet Morrow no later than 6 October 1879.[135]

Other troops were ordered into the field in an attempt to aid Morrow. On 29 September, two Ninth Cavalry companies (F and M), led by Captain Carroll, were ordered from Fort Stanton to Tulerosa to watch the Mescalero reservation for any signs of Apaches moving into that area from Ojo Caliente.[136] This detachment was also warned to be cautious, as it was thought that they might be facing a strong force of Apaches.[137] On 2 October, Carroll was ordered to proceed from Tulerosa

---

129 Morrow, Chaves Ranche, Cuchillo Negro to Purington 30 September 1879, NA, RG393, Part 3, Entry 439, pp.334-335; Loud to CO Fort Bayard, 3 October 1879, Telegrams Sent DoNM, Vol.2, Jan.–Dec. 1879, NA, RG393, Part 3, Entry 431, p.274.

130 Morrow to AAAG DoNM, 5 November 1879, 'Victorio Papers', NA, M666, Roll 526.

131 Hatch to AAG Fort Leavenworth, 29 September 1879, Telegrams Sent DoNM, Vol.2, Jan.–Dec. 1879, NA, RG393, Part 3, Entry 431, p.253; Loud to CO Fort Bayard, 3 October 1879, Telegrams Sent DoNM, Vol.2, Jan.–Dec. 1879, NA, RG393, Part 3, Entry 431, p.276; Loud to CO Fort Bayard, 29 September & 1 October 1879, Telegrams Sent DoNM, Vol.2, Jan.–Dec. 1879, NA, RG393, Part 3, Entry 431, p.253 & pp.259-260; Hatch to AAG MDoM, 30 September 1879, & Pope to Col. Whipple, AAG MDOM, 1 October 1879, 'Victorio Files', NA, RG393, M1495, Roll 14.

132 Leckie, 1967, p.212; Thrapp, 1974, p.245; Billington, 1991, p.92.

133 Hatch to Pope, 3 October 1879, Telegrams Sent DoNM, Vol.2, Jan.–Dec. 1879, NA, RG393, Part 3, Entry 431, p.277.

134 Loud to CO Fort Bayard, 3 October 1879, Telegrams Sent DoNM, Vol.2, Jan.–Dec. 1879, NA, RG393, Part 3, Entry 431, p.278.

135 Loud to CO Fort Bayard, 4 October 1879,Telegrams Sent DoNM, Vol.2, Jan.–Dec. 1879, NA, RG393, Part 3, Entry 431, p.281.

136 Loud to Morrow, Ojo Caliente, 13 October 1879, Telegrams Sent DoNM, Vol.2, Jan.–Dec. 1879, NA, RG393, Part 3, Entry 431, p.314.

137 Loud to CO Fort Stanton 29 September 1879, Telegrams Sent DoNM, Vol.2, Jan.–Dec. 1879, NA, RG393, Part 3, Entry 431, p.255; Hatch to Pope, 30 September 1879, Telegrams Sent DoNM. of

Plate 9.6 As Morrow marched westwards across the northern reaches of the Black Range, he crossed the continental divide into territory where he would traverse thick pine forests and mountains. (Photo: author)

Plate 9.7 Morrow would also encounter open areas of grass meadow surrounded by more open pinewoods. This terrain does not fit the popular image of 'Apache country', and US troops found it a stiff challenge to detect, let alone track, Apaches through such terrain, especially when those Apaches had laid a false trail towards this country but had not actually entered it. (Photo: author)

to Ojo Caliente.[138] That same day, his troops' orders were changed, sending them to Paraje to await further instructions.[139] As this information had to be carried from La Mesilla to Tulerosa by courier, Carroll's detachment did not start this move until 4 October. Being aware of the risk to lone couriers, and the time and distance involved, the same instructions were also sent from District Headquarters. to Lieutenant Taylor[140] at Paraje, with orders to send couriers from that point to Carroll's command at Tulerosa.[141]

Failures in communication were not only the result of interception by Apaches. Couriers to troops active in the field sometimes could not locate these columns. On 26 September, Pope informed Sheridan that he had had no news of Morrow, though he repeated his assertion that Victorio would soon be hunted down.[142] By 30 September, Captain Purington informed District Headquarters that his couriers had failed to contact Morrow, but that A Company, Sixth Cavalry, had arrived at Fort Bayard: did District Headquarters have any orders for their deployment?[143] Hatch also reported that between 23 and 30 September, he had no news of the progress of Major Morrow's campaign.[144] In fact Hatch would not know of Morrow's progress until 3 October, when he was informed that the major had clashed with Victorio in the Cuchillo Negro Mountains three days earlier.[145]

Predicting what the Apaches were going to do was also a problem where deploying troops was concerned. Captain Carroll, with two officers, one surgeon, 83 enlisted men and three teamsters, very well armed and mounted but with very poor transportation, had left Fort Stanton to pursue the Apaches. There were three problems with this deployment. First, District Headquarters did not know where Morrow's command was, so they first instructed Carroll to proceed to Tulerosa, on the assumption that the Apaches would attempt to return to the Mescalero reservation. The aim was for Carroll's detachment to hold them in check until Morrow's command could fall on them from the rear. Carroll was also warned that he should not mistake Morrow's Apache scouts for the 'hostiles', but instructions as to how he should avoid such a 'disastrous' event were not forthcoming. It is clear that District Headquarters had become somewhat rattled at the recent success of the Apaches, as Carroll was instructed to employ a 'well organized system of pickets and flankers and avoid being

New Mexico, Vol.2, Jan.–Dec. 1879, NA, RG393, Part 3, Entry 431, p.257; Loud to CO Fort Bayard, 30 September 1879, Telegrams Sent DoNM, Vol.2, Jan.–Dec. 1879, NA, RG393, Part 3, Entry 431, pp.257-258; Loud to Major Arnold, Camp Grant& CO Fort Bayard, 30 September 1879, Telegrams Sent DoNM, Vol.2, Jan.–Dec. 1879, NA, RG393, Part 3, Entry 431, pp.257-258.

138 Loud to CO 9th Cav. at Tulerosa, 2 October 1879, Telegrams Sent DoNM, Vol.2, Jan.–Dec. 1879, NA, RG393, Part 3, Entry 431, p.266.

139 Loud to CO 9th Cav. at Tulerosa, 2 October 1879, Telegrams Sent DoNM, Vol.2, Jan.–Dec. 1879, NA, RG393, Part 3, Entry 431, p.267.

140 Whose dismounted patrol from Ojo Caliente must have reached Paraje in search of Sgt. Howard's missing detachment.

141 Loud to F.B. Taylor, 3 October 1879, Telegrams Sent DoNM, Vol.2, Jan.–Dec. 1879, NA, RG393, Part 3, Entry 431, pp.274-275.

142 Pope to Sheridan 26 September 1879, 'Victorio Papers', NA, M666, Roll 526.

143 Purington to AAAG DoNM, 30 September 1879, NA, RG393, Part 3, Entry 439, p.364; Arnold to AAG Dept. Arizona, 1 October 1879, Troops in Southeastern Arizona, DoAz, NA, RG393, Part 1, Entry 232, Vol.4, 3 July, 1879–Dec. 13 1879, Letter No.166, p.106; See also *Grant County Herald*, 4 October 1879, which noted that forty-one men with Capt. C.H. Campbell and Lt. Glass passed through Silver City on the 30 September 1879 ('Town and County', *Grant County Herald*, 4 October 1879

144 Loud to CO Fort Bayard, 30 September 1879, Telegrams Sent DoNM, Vol.2, Jan.–Dec. 1879, NA, RG393, Part 3, Entry 431, pp.257-258.

145 Loud to CO Fort Bayard, 3 October 1879, Telegrams Sent DoNM, Vol.2, Jan.–Dec. 1879, NA, RG393, Part 3, Entry 431, p.274.

surprised and ambushed yourself.'[146] However, the lack of information at District Headquarters led them to station Carroll's force at too great a distance to support Morrow when the Apaches did not act as predicted. An attempt had to be made to coordinate troops against the Apaches; but there was just too little information available to do this effectively beyond relying upon a healthy serving of blind luck. Secondly, the telegram instructing Carroll's command to take the field was issued by District Headquarters on 29 September, but did not arrive until 9 a.m. on 3 October. The men were sent out from Fort Stanton by 2 p.m. of the same day, but this aptly illustrates the difficulty, if not impossibility, for those in Santa Fé of coordinating a campaign against such fast-moving guerrillas as the Apaches. Finally, these orders left Lieutenant Colonel Swain, Commanding Officer, Fort Stanton, very short of troops to protect the area around the fort.[147] Already, a relatively small group of Apache guerrillas was straining the resources of the District of New Mexico, at the same time as the latter was being asked to help confront the Utes in southern Colorado.

Therefore, the Department of Arizona also sent further aid, though it should be noted that despite their willingness to support their comrades in New Mexico, Major A.K. Arnold, Sixth Cavalry, had to submit a request for maps of New Mexico, as none were available in Arizona.[148] In addition to Blocksom and Gatewood's Apache scout companies, on 14 September 1879, General Willcox issued instructions to Major Arnold that the latter should picket 'Ralston & St Simon Valley, Clifton, Pueblo Viejo and Ash Springs' And that he should 'Keep in communication with Hatch.'[149] The day after Morrow's battalion had left Fort Bayard, Hatch contacted Willcox to request that, in addition to the Apache scout detachments already with Morrow, could the Department of Arizona spare any troops for service in New Mexico?[150]

As it became clear that Victorio had chosen to make a stand in the Black Range, the troops in Arizona Territory remained on standby. There remained the ever-present threat that the Warm Springs Apaches might launch a rescue bid on behalf of their relatives living at San Carlos. In fact, rumours that Victorio had been seen near San Carlos[151] were investigated by a company of Sixth Cavalry and a detachment of Apache scouts, despite the general opinion that these rumours were groundless. Nevertheless, Major Arnold also informed the District of New Mexico that if these rumours were proved to be false, he would (and subsequently he did) order A Company, Sixth Cavalry, to march to Fort Bayard to assist Morrow.[152] As noted earlier, A Company, Sixth

---

146 1st Lt. Goodwin, Post Adjutant, Fort Stanton to Capt Carroll, 3 October 1879 in Letters Received by HQ DoNM, September 1865-August 1890, NA, RG393, M1088, Roll 39, Oct-Dec 1879.

147 CO Fort Stanton to AAAG, Santa Fé, 4 October 1879 in Letters Received by HQ DoNM, September 1865-August 1890, NA, RG393, M1088, Roll 39, Oct–Dec 1879.

148 Arnold to Hatch 22 September? 1879, NA, RG393, Part 3, Entry 439, p.343.

149 Willcox to Major Arnold in Command Scouting Operations, 16 September 1879, NA, RG393, Part 1, Entry 169, Vol. 9, p.351.

150 Loud to Willcox, 24 September 1879, Telegrams Sent DoNM, Vol.2, Jan.–Dec. 1879, NA, RG393, Part 3, Entry 431, p.247.

151 Chaffee to Stacey, Fort Thomas, No Date, Troops in Southeastern Arizona, DoAz, NA, RG393, Part 1, Entry 232, Vol.4, 3 July, 1879–Dec. 13 1879, Letter No.143, p.91; Stacey Comdg Camp Thomas to Major Arnold Comdg Grant, 24 September 1879, 1PM, NA, RG393, Part 1, Entry 235, p.15; Arnold to CO Fort Apache, 24 September 1879, Troops in Southeastern Arizona, DoAz, NA, RG393, Part 1, Entry 232, Vol.4, 3 July, 1879–Dec. 13 1879, Letter No.146, p.93; Martin AAG to Arnold, Camp Grant, 24 September 1879, NA, RG393, Part 1, Entry 235, pp.13-14.

152 Arnold to AAAG, Santa Fé, 25 September 1879, NA, RG393, Part 3, Entry 439, pp.350-351, 352 & p.354; Arnold to AAG Dept. Arizona, AAG DoNM & CO Fort Bayard, 25 September 1879, Troops in Southeastern Arizona, DoAz, NA, RG393, Part 1, Entry 232, Vol.4, 3 July, 1879–Dec. 13 1879, Letter No.'s 150, 151, 152 & 153, pp.96-98; Field Order No.14, 25 September 1879, NA, RG393, Part 1, Entry 238, p.7; Martin to Arnold, 24 September 1879, NA, RG393, Part 1, Entry 169, Vol. 9, p.360; Arnold to CO Fort Thomas, 25 September 1879, Troops in Southeastern Arizona, DoAz, NA, RG393, Part 1, Entry 232, Vol.4, 3 July, 1879–Dec. 13 1879, Letter No.145, p.92; Loud to CO Fort Bayard, 26

Cavalry, under Captain Charles H. Campbell, with Lieutenant Glass and 38 enlisted men,[153] joined Morrow's battalion as part of the detachment led by Captain Purington to rendezvous with Morrow on 6 October. Further detachments from Fort Thomas (Captain W.L. Foulk) and Fort Grant (Captain Adam Kramer) were sent into the field to search for signs of Apaches. Major Arnold, Sixth Cavalry, also informed Hatch that he had already sent out detachments from Fort Bowie and Fort Apache to scout the Florida Mountains and the area around Clifton respectively for signs of Apaches.[154] These were probably D and G Companies, Sixth Cavalry, commanded by Captain E.C. Hentig and Captain Tupper, who were sent into the field on 22 August and 8 September respectively.[155]

The main worry for the Arizona command[156] was that, if Victorio eluded Morrow and made a run for San Carlos, two of their Apache scout companies were already with Morrow in New Mexico. Should such an event materialise, these scouts would immediately be ordered to march *poste haste* to San Carlos.[157] This was indeed a worrying possibility, as the AAAG of the District of New Mexico admitted that the troops in New Mexico had lost contact with Victorio for the week that had passed since the fight in the Animas canyon on 18 September.[158] Despite having lost touch with the Apaches, General Pope was confident that Victorio would soon be caught, there being no reports of any raiding and 'plenty of troops for the work now out.'[159] Indeed, Morrow was sent a telegram instructing him that if Victorio did make a move towards San Carlos, he was to send Gatewood and Blocksom ahead and follow them up without delay.[160] A small foray onto the San Carlos reservation was reported on 26 September, with four horses, two colts and two mules being stolen from Apaches living on the San Carlos reservation. The culprits were described as

---

September 1879, Telegrams Sent DoNM, Vol.2, Jan.–Dec. 1879, NA, RG393, Part 3, Entry 431, p.251; Major General McDowell to Commanding General MDoM, 25 September 1879, 'Victorio Files', NA, RG393, M1495, Roll 14.

153 Record of Events September 1879 in Returns From Regular Army Cavalry Regiments 1833-1916, 6th Cavalry Regimental Returns 1875 to 1880, NA, M744, Roll 63.

154 Arnold to CO Fort Bayard, 25 September 1879, Troops in Southeastern Arizona, DoAz, NA, RG393, Part 1, Entry 232, Vol.4, 3 July, 1879–Dec. 13 1879, Letter No.419, pp.94-95; Arnold to CO DoNM, 8 October 1879, NA, RG393, Part 3, Entry 439, p.339; See also Press Copies of Letters and Endorsements Sent, MDoM, NA, RG393, Part 1, Entry 2539, Vol. 11, pp.800-801; See also Loud AAA General to Major Arnold, Camp Grant, NA, RG393, Part 1, Entry 235, p.16; Loud to CO Fort Bayard, 25 September 1879, Telegrams Sent DoNM, Vol.2, Jan.–Dec. 1879, NA, RG393, Part 3, Entry 431, pp.247-248.

155 Record of Events September 1879 in Returns From Regular Army Cavalry Regiments 1833-1916, 6th Cavalry Regimental Returns 1875 to 1880, NA, M744, Roll 63.

156 Other worries would include the horse thieving activities by Mexicans and Anglo-Americans. On 1 October, 1879, the "Quartermasters herd" (14 mules), eight Company horses and three private horses were stolen from Fort Huachuca by "masked men." (Arnold to CO Fort Lowell, CO Fort Bowie, AAG Dept. Arizona, 1 October 1879, Troops in Southeastern Arizona, DoAz, NA, RG393, Part 1, Entry 232, Vol.4, 3 July, 1879–Dec. 13 1879, Letter No.'s162-164, pp.104-105) Unluckily for these horse thieves, the various detachments in the field on the lookout for Victorio were alerted. Within 24 Hours all but six of the horses stolen had been recovered and two Mexicans detained. The rest of the thieves were being looked for. (Arnold to CO Fort Bowie, 2 October 1879, Troops in Southeastern Arizona, DoAz, NA, RG393, Part 1, Entry 232, Vol.4, 3 July, 1879–Dec. 13 1879, p.110.)

157 Martin to Loud, 24 September 1879, NA, RG393, Part 1, Entry 169, Vol. 9, pp.360-361; Martin AAG Arizona to Loud AAAG 25 September 1879, NA, RG393, Part 3, Entry 439, pp.353-355.

158 Loud AAA General to Major Arnold, Camp Grant, 25 September 1879, NA, RG393, Part 1, Entry 235, p.16.

159 Pope to Gen. P.H. Sheridan, 26 September 1879, 'Victorio Files', NA, RG393, M1495, Roll 14.

160 Loud to CO Fort Bayard (to be sent to Morrow by courier), 25 September 1879, Telegrams Sent DoNM, Vol.2, Jan.–Dec. 1879, NA, RG393, Part 3, Entry 431, p.249.

nine 'renegades' from Victorio's band who had subsequently returned to New Mexico.[161] It was predicted that this raid would not presage a descent into the use of force against San Carlos by Victorio.[162] After a thorough scout, no traces of any Apaches were found, and it was concluded that the whole report was a false alarm.[163] Nevertheless, on 27 September, it was decided that a close watch should be maintained on the Arizona-New Mexico border, in view of the possible risk of the Chihennes mounting an attack to release their relatives at San Carlos. Two companies of Sixth Cavalry were tasked with watching the approaches to San Carlos.[164] By 18 October, Colonel Carr, on viewing events in New Mexico, came to the conclusion that further Arizona troops, beyond those already sent to New Mexico, would not be required, though he maintained the watch on the border between Arizona and New Mexico.[165] Carr evidently did some investigating concerning the numbers of Warm Springs families at San Carlos:

> The stories about the number of families there of Indians now hostile seem to be ridiculously exaggerated – In village of the Warm Springs by count there are 14 families, i.e. wives and children of bucks at [Fort] Stanton when Victorio was asking [July-August 1879] to have their families sent there
>
> It is fair to suppose that not more than 10 or 15 men would come to San Carlos after their families.[166]

While one can see Carr's line of reasoning, he forgot the other Chihenne families living at San Carlos under the leadership of Loco. Throughout the Victorio and Nana war of 1879-81 and beyond, Loco would make it clear that he desired a return to Ojo Caliente. If the independent Chihennes had managed to get to their people at San Carlos, they might well have persuaded or forced the San Carlos Chihennes to depart *en masse*. As the events of 1882 would show, one of the reasons the Chiricahua Apaches living in the Sierra Madre, Mexico, wanted Loco's following was because it would significantly add to their warrior count.

At Sherman's Cienega, Captain Purington informed Morrow that he had seen no signs of Apaches crossing the road on his passage from Fort Bayard. Morrow immediately sent his scouts back over the Black Range to pick up the trail, spending all of 8 October, and till noon on the following day, in camp before his scouts reported back.[167] Victorio, ever the wily guerrilla, was

161 Stacey CO Camp Thomas to Major Arnold, Grant, 27 September 1879, NA, RG393, Part 1, Entry 235, p.18.

162 Stacey to Arnold, Fort Grant, 25 September 1879, Troops in Southeastern Arizona, DoAz, NA, RG393, Part 1, Entry 232, Vol.4, 3 July, 1879–Dec. 13 1879, Letter No.150, pp.95-96; Arnold to AAG Dept. Arizona, 30 September 1879, Troops in Southeastern Arizona, DoAz, NA, RG393, Part 1, Entry 232, Vol.4, 3 July, 1879–Dec. 13 1879, Letter No.161, p.103.

163 Stacey Comdg to Major Arnold, Camp Grant, 28 September 1879, NA, RG393, Part 1, Entry 235, p.20.

164 Arnold to Tupper, 27 September 1879, Troops in Southeastern Arizona, DoAz, NA, RG393, Part 1, Entry 232, Vol.4, 3 July, 1879–Dec. 13 1879, Letter No.160, pp.102-103; Arnold to Rafferty through CO Fort Thomas, 3 October 1879, Troops in Southeastern Arizona, DoAz, NA, RG393, Part 1, Entry 232, Vol.4, 3 July, 1879–Dec. 13 1879, Letter No.175, p.112; See also Arnold to Rafferty, 14 October 1879, Troops in Southeastern Arizona, DoAz, NA, RG393, Part 1, Entry 232, Vol.4, 3 July, 1879–Dec. 13 1879, Letter No.193, pp.123-124; Arnold to CO Fort Apache, 4 October 1879, Troops in Southeastern Arizona, DoAz, NA, RG393, Part 1, Entry 232, Vol.4, 3 July, 1879–Dec. 13 1879, Letter No.176, pp.112-113.

165 Carr to AAG Dept. Arizona, 18 October 1879, Troops in Southeastern Arizona, DoAz, NA, RG393, Part 1, Entry 232, Vol.4, 3 July, 1879–Dec. 13 1879, Letter No.196, pp.126-127.

166 Carr to AG Dept. Arizona, 26 October 1879, Troops in Southeastern Arizona, DoAz, NA, RG393, Part 1, Entry 232, Vol.4, 3 July, 1879–Dec. 13 1879, Letter No.213, pp.139-141.

167 Morrow to AAAG DoNM, 5 November 1879, 'Victorio Papers', NA, M666, Roll 526.

subsequently found to have moved north from the Black Range, behind Morrow, into the San Mateo Mountains.[168] The frustrated major regrouped his force, sending some of the most exhausted troops back to Fort Bayard and disbanding Blocksom's scout detachment, whose service was time-expired.[169] Morrow also suspected the latter of leading him west, nearer to their Arizona homes, to take advantage of the imminent ending of their term of service, instead of following Victorio. Whether this is true, or whether one Apache woman completely fooled Morrow, is open to question. His battalion backtracked to Ojo Caliente, and between 11 and 12 October again replenished its provisions,[170] to the tune of '1,000 rations of Bacon, Flour, Rice (or its equivalent) Coffee, sugar, soap, salt, Candles, Pepper and yeast Powder.'[171]

In the meantime, the prolonged pursuit of Victorio was already beginning to wear out a number of horses and men. On 9 October 1879, Morrow instructed Captain Beyer to lead a detachment back to Fort Bayard. This included L Company, Ninth Cavalry and Blocksom's time-expired scout company. The detachment also included Lieutenants Dimmick, Emmet, Wright and a number of dismounted men. The detachment arrived back at Fort Bayard on 12 October. Morrow instructed Beyer, once the latter had reached Fort Bayard, to send L Company on to Fort Cummings where they were to operate against Apaches.[172] This made sense. If Morrow, knowing that Victorio was now in the San Mateo Mountains, returned to the pursuit, there would be a good chance that the Apaches would try to make their way down to Mexico in the broad vicinity of that post.

A further problem arose. Despite Morrow having twice replenished his supplies from Ojo Caliente, fresh supplies of food and ammunition had to be authorised and sent to his troops in the field. District Headquarters had not been idle, sending additional ammunition (15,000 rounds) and food for Morrow's command from Santa Fé and the Fort Union arsenal. In the short term, it was also decided that it would be impracticable to obtain the mountain howitzers requested by Morrow.[173] These supplies were to be escorted to Ojo Caliente by Captain Carroll's command, which had been previously directed to Paraje. These supplies did not reach Fort Craig until approx-

168 Loud to Carroll, 13 October 1879, Telegrams Sent DoNM, Vol.2, Jan.–Dec. 1879, NA, RG393, Part 3, Entry 431, p.311; Thrapp, 1974, p.245.

169 Gatewood dates the departure of Blocksom and his scout company to the 8 October 1879 ('Gatewood's Report 1879', NA, RG393, Part 1, Entry 240).

170 Return for October 1879 in Returns From U.S. Military Posts 1800-1916, Ojo Caliente, New Mexico, May 1879-Mar. 1882, NA, M617, Roll 877.

171 Hooker to Taylor, 16 October 1879, Special Orders Rec'd from Sub Commands, NA, RG393, Part 3, Entry 453.

172 Beyer to AAAG 13 October 1879, NA, RG393, Part 3, Entry 439, p.315; Loud to Carroll, 13 October 1879, Telegrams Sent DoNM, Vol.2, Jan.–Dec. 1879, NA, RG393, Part 3, Entry 431, p.311; Arnold to Blocksom, through CO Fort Bayard, 14 October 1879, Troops in Southeastern Arizona, DoAz, NA, RG393, Part 1, Entry 232, Vol.4, 3 July, 1879–Dec. 13 1879, Letter No.194, p.124; Personal File Eugene D. Dimmick, NA, RG94, Entry 297, Box 1496; See also Morrow to AAAG DoNM, 5 November 1879, 'Victorio Papers', NA, M666, Roll 526; Loud to Pope, 14 October 1879, 'Victorio Papers', NA, M666, Roll 526; Loud AAAG to Pope copied to Gen. Sherman, 16 of October 1879, NA, RG393, Part 1, Entry 2539, Press Copies of Letters and Endorsements Sent, MDoM, Vol. 12, p.33; Sheridan to Sherman, 16 October 1879, NA, RG393, Part 1, Entry 2538, pp.198-199; Carr to AAG Dept. Arizona, 22 October 1879, Troops in Southeastern Arizona, DoAz, NA, RG393, Part 1, Entry 232, Vol.4, 3 July, 1879–Dec. 13 1879, Letter No.203, pp.131-132; Loud to AAG Fort Leavenworth, 14 October 1879, 'Victorio Files', NA, RG393, M1495, Roll 14.

173 Loud to Lt Delany, Fort Union, and Lt F.B. Taylor, Paraje, 3 October 1879, Telegrams Sent DoNM, Vol.2, Jan.–Dec. 1879, NA, RG393, Part 3, Entry 431, pp.274-275; Loud to Hooker, 4 October 1879, Telegrams Sent DoNM, Vol.2, Jan.–Dec. 1879, NA, RG393, Part 3, Entry 431, p.284; Loud to Hooker, 6 October 1879, Telegrams Sent DoNM, Vol.2, Jan.–Dec. 1879, NA, RG393, Part 3, Entry 431, pp.289-290); Hooker to Taylor, 16 October 1879, Special Orders Rec'd from Sub Commands, NA, RG393, Part 3, Entry 453; Loud to Stedman, 9 October 1879 in Letters Sent by the '9MD/DNM/DoNM', NA, RG393, M1072, Roll 6, Jan-Oct 1879, Letter No.496, pp.355-356.

imately 11 October, because Captain Carroll was ordered to wait for the supply wagons, which were to be escorted to Paraje by the E Company mail detachment that had been unable to return to Ojo Caliente. The latter had been ordered up to Fort Craig from Paraje, and would escort the supply train back down to Paraje. Carroll was ordered to provide an escort for the supply train between Paraje and Ojo Caliente, as Hooker's command had already lost its horses to the Apaches. Thus, it would be impracticable to expect E Company to escort the wagons from Paraje to Ojo Caliente. Carroll was also informed that his detachment was to be regarded as completely independent of Hooker.[174]

While Carroll was waiting for the supplies to arrive, he was ordered to scout the region between Paraje and Ojo Caliente, in order to drive off any Apaches lurking in that vicinity.[175] On 12 October, Carroll was instructed to include the Hillsboro region in his scouting operations, in response to the sacking of McEvers' Ranch (see next chapter).[176] Carroll, having detached 21 men to escort the wagons through to Ojo Caliente, pointed out that this accounted for approximately one quarter of his men and would undermine his ability to scout effectively.

Carroll also informed District Headquarters that he had been experiencing difficulties with telegraph operators 'who are scarcely civil, much less willing to advance the interests of the service by employing one minute of his time, not strictly belonging to his official duty.'[177] This astonishing information also underlined a further 'human' obstacle to the effective use of the telegraph lines by the US army. Unfortunately, this would not be the last occasion on which operators would fail to prioritise, or would even hinder, military communications during this conflict.

Carroll spent some time scouting the area near Ojo Caliente, and his detachment passed through Ojo Caliente twice, on 15-16 and 22-23 October.[178] In fact, Carroll's command would cover 507 miles during October 1879, and not only scouted the San Andres, San Mateo and Mimbres Mountains, but also further west into the Mogollon Mountains.[179] He did not encounter any Apaches, which is perhaps unsurprising, as he commenced his scout of the area north of McEvers' Ranch, after both Victorio and Morrow's forces had left the area (see next chapter).

Morrow's intended move into the San Mateo Mountains was, unknown to the major, already based upon antiquated information, as the Apaches had started to move south from the San Mateo Mountains. As the Apaches moved south out of the San Mateos, the mail run to Ojo Caliente was once again briefly disrupted.[180] Gatewood's Apache scout detachment re-discovered Victorio's trail

174 Loud to Carroll, Paraje, 13 October 1879, Telegrams Sent DoNM, Vol.2, Jan.–Dec. 1879, NA, RG393, Part 3, Entry 431, p.309; Loud to AAG Fort Leavenworth, 14 October 1879, 'Victorio Files', NA, RG393, M1495, Roll 14.

175 Loud to Capt. Carroll & Hatch, 10 October 1879, Telegrams Sent DoNM, Vol.2, Jan.–Dec. 1879, NA, RG393, Part 3, Entry 431, pp.301-302.

176 Loud to Capt Carroll, Paraje, 12 October 1879, Telegrams Sent DoNM, Vol.2, Jan.–Dec. 1879, NA, RG393, Part 3, Entry 431, pp.307-308.

177 Capt Carroll, Fort Craig to AG DoNM, 12 October 1879 in Letters Received by HQ DoNM, September1865-August 1890, NA, RG393, M1088, Roll 39, Oct-Dec 1879.

178 Return for October 1879 in Returns From U.S. Military Posts 1800-1916, Ojo Caliente, New Mexico, May 1879-Mar. 1882, NA, M617, Roll 877; Loud to AAG Fort Leavenworth, 19 October 1879, Telegrams Sent DoNM, Vol.2, Jan.–Dec. 1879, NA, RG393, Part 3, Entry 431, pp.335-336; Loud AAAG to Pope copied to Gen. Sherman, 16 of October 1879, NA, RG393, Part 1, Entry 2539, Press Copies of Letters and Endorsements Sent, MDoM, Vol. 12, p.35; Sheridan to Sherman, 16 October 1879, NA, RG393, Part 1, Entry 2538, pp.198-199.

179 Bi-Monthly Company Muster Rolls for Company F, 9th Cavalry, Sept/Oct 1879 in NA, RG94.

180 In two undated telegrams, Sergeant Robinson, Ninth Cavalry, in charge of a three-man mail detail, made enquiries as to the safest means to deliver mail to Ojo Caliente from Socorro. (Robinson to AAAG SF, possibly 7 or 9 October 1879, NA, RG393, Part 3, Entry 439, p.325.)

leading out of the San Mateo Mountains on or around 10 October 1879.[181] The tracks repaired southwards over the very same territory that Morrow had pursued the Apaches across between 23 September and 3 October.[182] Morrow alerted his superiors that Victorio was making for Mexico, and they warned the Mexican authorities to be prepared to intercept the Apaches.[183]

As these two telegrams were found amongst a tranche of telegrams dealing with events from late September to mid-October 1879, it seems reasonable to argue that these telegrams coincide with Victorio's movement southwards from the San Mateo Mountains.

181 'Gatewood's Report 1879', NA, RG393, Part 1, Entry 240; Morrow to AAAG DoNM, 5 November 1879, 'Victorio Papers', NA, M666, Roll 526.

182 Thrapp, 1974, pp. 245-246.

183 Haskell to Willcox, 13 October 1879, 'Victorio Papers', NA, M666, Roll 526.

10

Massacre Peak: Victorio Strikes the Rio Grande Valley, October 1879

Morrow and his force commenced pursuit of Victorio on 11 October, from Ojo Caliente and passing through Cañada Alamosa; and by the following day they had reached Chase's Ranch on the Cuchillo Negro River. The next day, the battalion followed the trail southwards, in torrential rain, to the Palomas River. There they discovered an old camp that enabled the Apache scouts to estimate that they were four days behind Victorio. The following morning, the march took a south-easterly direction 'over fearfully rough trail through drenching rain', and in the process five horses and one mule were lost.[1] On 15 October, Morrow was overtaken by Mr Chase, who informed him that there was a 'squaw trail' running parallel to, and two miles to the left of, the trail Morrow was following. Chase also told Morrow that McEvers' Ranch had been burned by the Apaches.[2] On the same day, the battalion arrived back at McEvers' Ranch,[3] which they found had indeed been sacked by Victorio's warriors, possibly in retaliation for McEvers' cooperation with the US army.[4] In the early hours of the following morning, a citizen courier reached Morrow's camp and gave him news of an attack upon Lloyd's Ranch. This was the first indication that Victorio had launched a number of attacks on settlements to the south. At dawn, Morrow sent out Gatewood with his scouts and a small detachment of Sixth Cavalry under Lieutenant J.N. Glass, Sixth Cavalry, to investigate these reports.[5] The Apache scouts, who had joined Morrow's command from Fort Bayard, and were commanded by Lieutenant Maney, also went with Gatewood.[6]

The information concerning a 'squaw trail' would seem to confirm Kaywaykla's account of some weeks of peaceful existence in the mountains, and indicate that the warriors were operating as a separate group. By raiding as they moved south, they kept the pursuing US army units hot on their trail, while their families moved southwards separately. But why were their dependants also on the move? It would appear that, sometime in early October, Victorio had decided to move his whole following southwards, towards Mexico. Perhaps the loss of two valued warriors on 29 September, and the sheer persistence of Morrow's pursuit, had convinced him that it was not possible for his Black Range strongholds to hold out indefinitely against the Ninth Cavalry and its Apache scouts. This change in strategy required a diversionary manoeuvre to give the families time to move southwards. Victorio may, or may not, have 'planted' the woman who had sent Morrow on a wild goose chase towards the Mogollon Mountains. However, for the moment, he had evaded Morrow's

1 Morrow to AAAG DoNM, 5 November 1879, 'Victorio Papers', NA, M666, Roll 526.
2 Morrow to AAAG DoNM, 5 November, 1879, 'Victorio Papers', NA, M666, Roll 526; Thrapp, p. 246.
3 'Gatewood's Report 1879', NA, RG393, Part 1, Entry 240; Thrapp, 1974, p.246.
4 There may be some truth in this, as from 21 July 1879, R. D. McEvers was the US army Forage Agent within the "Fort Bayard Forage District" (Special Order 67, par 3, July 21 1879, NA, RG393, Part 3, Entry 450).
5 Morrow to AAAG DoNM, 5 November 1879, 'Victorio Papers', NA, M666, Roll 526; Thrapp, 1974, p.246.
6 'Gatewood's Report 1879', NA, RG393, Part 1, Entry 240; Morrow to AAAG DoNM, 5 November 1879, 'Victorio Papers', NA, M666, Roll 526.

pursuit. This gained the Apaches a breathing space while the pursuing US army units floundered around trying to re-establish contact.

Table 10.1 Morrow's Campaign, 12 October to 21 October 1879 (See Map 9.1 for overview of Morrow's Sept.-Nov. 1879 Campaign)

11.	12 October	Morrow reaches the Chase Ranch on the Cuchillo Negro River.
12.	15 October	Morrow's forces arrive at the recently burned McEvers' Ranch.
13.	16-18 October	Apache scouts, sent out from McEvers' Ranch arrive at Lloyd's Ranch to discover the trail of the Apaches going into the Goodsight Mountains. They leave the trail and make for Fort Cummings, where they are joined by the rest of Morrow's battalion, who have marched directly from McEvers' Ranch.
14.	19-20 October	Gatewood's Apache scouts are sent south to the Florida Mountains and spend the following day searching this range.
15.	21 October	Gatewood moves on to the Tres Hermanas Mountains, where he is joined by the rest of Morrow's battalion.

There may have been a second reason for Victorio's move south – one which involved the annual subsistence cycle of the Chihenne Apaches. By October, most, though not necessarily all, the Chihennes would move south for the winter months and would hunt and gather in the southern part of their range, which by 1879 was centred on the Laguna (Lake) de Guzman and other lagunas further south of that point in Chihuahua, Mexico.[7]

McEvers himself reported the sacking of his ranch in a letter to the *Grant County Herald* of Saturday 18 October 1879 (see document file no. 18). He and a companion were loading his wagon next to his corn field when two men passed by on the road to Hillsboro in another wagon. They were hardly out of sight when McEvers heard a number of shots. He was in the act of jumping down from his wagon when there came a blistering volley from the edge of the cornfield and he and his companion were lucky to make it unscathed to a large thicket of sunflowers. The Apaches surrounded them, and kept them pinned down for twelve hours, whilst McEvers' Ranch was ransacked and burned. McEvers claimed that the Apaches captured 1400 rounds of government ammunition and 100 rounds of ammunition that was his property.[8] McEvers did not record the fate of the two men who had just passed on the road to Hillsboro.

The attack on McEvers' Ranch was first reported by an escaped herder, who brought the news to Fort Cummings that McEvers and three others had been attacked and were presumed killed by Apaches.[9] McEvers himself managed to get word to Fort Cummings by 12 October, and his request for soldiers was passed on to Fort Bayard.[10] District Headquarters endorsed McEvers' plea for protection, but this pushed Fort Bayard's manpower to the limits. On 11 October, there

7 See: Stephen H. Lekson, 1992, *Warm Spring Apache Subsistence*, Cortez CO, Crow Canyon Archaeological Center.

8 Letter to *Grant County Herald* published 18 October 1879; see also Beyer to AAAG SF, 13 October 1879, NA, RG393, Part 3, Entry 439, p.314; Loud to Hatch, 11 October 1879, Telegrams Sent DoNM, Vol.2, Jan.–Dec. 1879, NA, RG393, Part 3, Entry 431, p.305; Loud to Carroll, 13 October 1879, Telegrams Sent DoNM, Vol.2, Jan.–Dec. 1879, NA, RG393, Part 3, Entry 431, p.311; Loud to Pope, 14 October 1879, 'Victorio Papers', NA, M666, Roll 526; Sheridan to Sherman, 16 October 1879, NA, RG393, Part 1, Entry 2538, pp.198-199; see also 'By Telegraph', *Grant County Herald*, 11 October 1879.

9 Burnham to AAAG SF 11 October 1879, NA, RG393, Part 3, Entry 439, pp.318-319; 'Town and County', *Grant County Herald*, 11 October 1879; *Thirty Four*, 15 October 1879.

10 Beyer to AAAG, 13 October 1879, NA, RG393, Part 3, Entry 439, p.314.

were 53 troops fit for active service.[11] The return of Beyer's detachment on 12 October failed to improve the situation, as L Company, Ninth Cavalry, was to return to Old Fort Cummings to refit, and Blocksom's time-expired Apache scouts were set to leave for Fort Grant on 14 October.[12] This would leave Fort Bayard with a total of 14 mounted troops. However, something had to be done in response to McEvers' plea, and on the morning of 15 October, Captain Beyer ordered 12 dismounted troopers to march to McEvers' Ranch.[13]

From McEvers' Ranch, Morrow informed District Headquarters that Victorio seemed to be making for Mexico, but that he could not rule out the possibility that the Apaches might swing east to make for Fort Stanton. Morrow also stated that 'owing to the disaffection of one of the Indian companies whose term of enlistment had expired several days were lost in following blind trails.'[14] Morrow designated McEvers' Ranch as his supply depot and sent instructions that days' supplies be sent there from Fort Bayard.[15] This was easier said than done. To fulfil Morrow's requisition, some supplies had to be bought locally and there was no transportation immediately available at Fort Bayard for conveying these supplies to Morrow. However, a supply train from Santa Fé was expected to arrive on 16 October, and it was planned to utilise this once it made its appearance.[16] District Headquarters also expected Fort Bayard to furnish supplies to re-stock those stores earlier requisitioned from Ojo Caliente. On 14 October, a projected detachment of one non-commissioned officer and 16 men, with three wagons, were given the helpful advice by District Headquarters, unaware that the wagons were not forthcoming, to be very cautious on its way going into and out of Ojo Caliente.[17] As early as 30 September, Captain Purington informed District Headquarters that the troops at Fort Bayard were short of horses and ammunition, with some weapons unserviceable, and requested that 'ordnance stores due to this post on requisition should be forwarded at once.'[18] Army 'red tape' also intervened at this point when the commander of the Fort Union arsenal refused to supply carbine and rifle ammunition requisitioned by Morrow as it was 'contrary to existing orders.' General Pope had to ask General Sheridan to order the Fort Union arsenal to comply with this requisition.[19]

As noted above, it was as he was approaching McEvers' Ranch that news reached Morrow of widespread attacks by Apaches between Cooke's Range and Rodey on the Rio Grande.[20] The

11 Burnham to AAAG SF 11 October 1879, NA, RG393, Part 3, Entry 439, pp.316-317; Loud to CO Fort Bayard, 13 October 1879, Telegrams Sent DoNM, Mexico, Vol.2, Jan.–Dec. 1879, NA, RG393, Part 3, Entry 431, p.313.

12 Beyer to AAAG SF, 13 October 1879, NA, RG393, Part 3, Entry 439, pp.311-312.

13 Beyer to AAAG SF, 14 October 1879, NA, RG393, Part 3, Entry 439, p.310 & p.312; see also Loud AAAG to Pope copied to Gen. Sherman, 16 October 1879, NA, RG393, Part 1, Entry 2539, Press Copies of Letters and Endorsements Sent, MDoM, Vol. 12, pp.34-35.

14 Morrow to Loud AAAG, 15 October 1879, NA, RG393, Part 3, Entry 439, p.305; Loud to AAG Fort Leavenworth, 17 October 1879, Telegrams Sent DoNM, Vol.2, Jan.–Dec. 1879, NA, RG393, Part 3, Entry 431, p.325; See also Morrow to Pope, 15 October 1879, 'Victorio Papers', NA, M666, Roll 526; Loud to Major Arnold, Fort Grant, NA, RG393, Part 1, Entry 235, p.23; Sheridan to Townsend, 18 of October 1879, NA, RG393, Part 1, Entry 2539, Press Copies of Letters and Endorsements Sent, MDoM, Vol. 12, pp.55-56.

15 Morrow to Loud AAAG 15 October 1879, NA, RG393, Part 3, Entry 439, pp.305-306; Loud to AAG Fort Leavenworth, 16 October 1879, Telegrams Sent DoNM, Vol.2, Jan.–Dec. 1879, NA, RG393, Part 3, Entry 431, p.321.

16 Beyer to AAAG SF, 16 October 1879, NA, RG393, Part 3, Entry 439, pp.308-309.

17 Loud to CO Fort Bayard, 14 October 1879, Telegrams Sent DoNM, Vol.2, Jan.–Dec. 1879, NA, RG393, Part 3, Entry 431, p.317.

18 Purington to Loud AAAG 30 September, 1879, NA, RG393, Part 3, Entry 439, pp.356-357.

19 Pope to Sheridan, 17 October 1879, 'Victorio Files', NA, RG393, M1495, Roll 14.

20 Beyer to AAAG SF 13 October 1879, NA, RG393, Part 3, Entry 439, p.314; 'Gatewood's Report 1879', NA, RG393, Part 1, Entry 240.

Apaches had taken full advantage of their head start on Morrow to strike the area to the west of La Mesilla with a number of raids.

Victorio Raids the Settlements between Lloyd's Ranch and El Colorado[21]

A posse of 20 men from Mesilla on the Rio Grande, out hunting the Apaches, was ambushed on 12 October, near the abandoned Fort Cummings, and five Mexicans and an American were killed. Near Slocum's Ranch, on 13 October, a wagon train was destroyed and all 11 teamsters were slain, some with extreme cruelty. Other attacks were reported near El Colorado, but the actual details are unclear.[22] The *Grant County Herald* listed a number near Santa Barbara: at Mason's Ranch, Slocum's Ranch and El Colorado. The paper also noted that a large party of 75-100 volunteers was gathering, drawn from La Mesilla, Las Cruces and other settlements. Finally, mail couriers in the area were travelling at night in view of the presence of Apaches.[23] This included a report of four men killed and a wagon train captured at Grape Springs.[24] As Lloyd's Ranch was located in the Sierra Uvas, named for the grapes growing in the vicinity of that ranch, this would appear to refer to the report Morrow had received about an attack on this ranch. However, the reports of these attacks were garbled, and have made it difficult for the historian, let alone Morrow, to decipher what exactly happened when the Apaches attacked the area.

Daniel D. Aranda[25] provides a much clearer picture of events (see Map 10.1 and document file no. 19 for a number of contemporary reports concerning this episode). Lloyd's Ranch was attacked and presumably burned, with a number of cattle being slaughtered, on 10 October 1879. The alarm was raised by one of a group of citizens camped to the east of the ranch, while the remainder tried to remain concealed. The courier, George Ackenback, reached El Colorado and persuaded five local men to return to Lloyd's Ranch. The following morning, this group was ambushed less than a mile from the ranch. Of the six,[26] only Ackenback and one Julian Torres[27] survived, and they fled back to El Colorado to renew the alarm. A much larger party of El Colorado citizens responded to the two survivors, but this 35-man posse was also ambushed and trapped, not escaping until the morning of 12 October. Aranda reports that 'several'[28] of this party were killed, with the survivors being pursued almost all the way back to El Colorado. A series of news notes from *Thirty-Four* state that nine citizens of El Colorado were killed in this attack,[29] though it is not quite clear if this included the four killed on the previous day. Small groups of Apaches haunted the area, occasion-

21 Now Rodey N.M.

22 Loud AAAG to Pope copied to Gen. Sherman, 16 October 1879, NA, RG393, Part 1, Entry 2539, Press Copies of Letters and Endorsements Sent, MDoM, Vol. 12, pp.33-34; Telegrams Sent DoNM, Vol.2, Jan.–Dec. 1879, NA, RG393, Part 3, Entry 431, p.315-317; Loud to Pope, 14 October 1879, 'Victorio Papers', NA, M666, Roll 526; Loud to AAG Fort Leavenworth, 17 October 1879, Telegrams Sent DoNM, Vol.2, Jan.–Dec. 1879, NA, RG393, Part 3, Entry 431, p.326; See also Sheridan to Sherman, 16 October 1879, NA, RG393, Part 1, Entry 2538, pp.198-199; Thrapp, 1974, p.246; See also Thrapp, 1973, p.12; Chronological List, p.48; Haley, 1981, p.323.

23 'By Telegraph', *Grant County Herald*, 18 October 1879.

24 'By Telegraph' Section, *Grant County Herald*, 18 October 1879.

25 In two articles from 1984 & 1995 (see bibliography) Aranda gives a very clear account of the raids in mid-October and his work is the main source for the account that follows on the attacks made by Apaches in or around the Sierra Uvas in mid-October 1879.

26 Those killed were named as Nestor Garcia, Cosmo de la O., Victor de la O. and Malendes (*Thirty Four*, 15 October 1879).

27 Nestor Garcia, Cosme and Victor De La O and a Mr Melendes were all killed in the opening volley.

28 Aranda, 1984, p.15; See also Beyer to AAAG SF, 13 October 1879, NA, RG393, Part 3, Entry 439, p.314.

29 *Thirty Four*, 15 October 1879; Misc.4 Document.

Two Photos: Fort Bayard and Fort Stanton: Both illustrate the 'open plan' nature of military bases on the American frontier. These two forts were at the centre of the efforts to engage those Apaches resisting the US in New Mexico. Nevertheless, it was extremely rare for Apaches to launch direct attacks upon such forts. (The National Archives)

ally harassing the local inhabitants with sniping fire. This would have been easily accomplished, as the cultivated area around El Colorado is dominated by high bluffs to the north-west and south. The Rio Grande flows past the village to the east. On the same day, though the population in the area were short of guns and mounts, a small group of 12 volunteers, led by Eugene van Patten, set out from Las Cruces and were joined by five more men from La Mesilla.[30] The posse sheltered overnight from a heavy rainstorm at Mason's Ranch,[31] and returned to the trail on 13 October, apparently having moved north on the old Fort Fillmore-Fort Thorn road. At approximately 1 p.m. they ran into a classic Apache ambush. Three unattended horses were spotted standing out in the open. While some of the posse members were eager for spoils, others were more cautious. A halt was called, weapons were readied and girths tightened.[32] Thus it was that the Apaches did not catch Van Patten's posse completely unawares. As the men closed with the loose horses, they were ambushed by Apache warriors, hidden behind some innocuous humps close to the road. Some of the Apaches are reported as waving blankets to scare the horses.[33] The standard tactic of targeting the horses doesn't seem to have been used, suggesting that the Apaches might have been looking to capture horses in this ambush. One man seems to have been killed outright in the opening attack. Another four men were killed in a fighting retreat before the posse broke contact.[34] Van Patten claimed to have killed one Apache warrior at point blank range and seriously wounded another in an attempt to support one Cleto Sanches. The latter, already shot, continued to fire at the Apaches, before being wounded in the thigh and then finally killed by a shot in the chest. Some of the survivors reported that, as the fight progressed, the Apaches were not only to their front but had worked round both flanks in an attempt to surround the posse.[35] Lieutenant Gatewood reported a rumour that sometime around this time an Apache named Torribo was killed.[36] This *might* be 'Turevia', one of the Pajarito brothers badly wounded in a fight with Nana and Loco in 1873 (see chapter 4).

There are two versions of what happened next. Fleeing members of the posse managed to warn a party of pioneers and freighters, and a stagecoach, of the immediate danger. The latter immediately turned back and made good its escape; the former initially circled their wagons, but wiser counsel prevailed and they decided to make a run for it in the lighter wagons, abandoning the rest to the Apaches.[37] The pursuing Apaches spotted the abandoned wagon circle and closed in carefully.

30 *Thirty Four*, 15 October 1879.

31 "also known as Slocum's, was a popular rest stop on the road from La Mesilla to Fort Cummings. John D. Slocum bought the buildings at this site in the spring of 1870. He ran and developed the place and then leased it to Richard "Kit" Mason in the spring of 1877. The ranch was comprised of eighteen buildings facing an inner court, two large corrals, and high loop-holed walls. Of great importance to this place were the natural water tanks that furnished the only dependable water between La Mesilla and Fort Cummings." (Aranda, p.16) The site was heavily eroded in 2006 but one can still see the broad outline of this ranch.

32 See also Misc.4 Document.

33 See also Misc.4 Document.

34 Beyer to AAAG SF, 14 October 1879, NA, RG393, Part 3, Entry 439, p.313; Frost to Lt Allen, 14 October 1879, NA, RG393, Part 3, Entry 439, p.313; Beyer to AAAG SF, 16 October 1879, NA, RG393, Part 3, Entry 439, p.303; See also Misc.4 Document.

Thirty Four, 15 October 1879, states that WT Jones, Nepurnuseno Barragan, Cleto Sanches, Venceslado Lara and Pancho Beltran were cut down in the opening volley and that Van Patten's party engaged in a two-hour fight with the Apaches.

35 Misc.4 Document.

36 Gatewood, 1894, p.102. The *Arizona Sentinel*, 7 June, 1879 reported that 'Terrivio' was killed in the battle between Victorio and Capt. Beyer on 29 May, 1880 See Library of Congress 'Chronicling America' website (http://chroniclingamerica.loc.gov/) Use combined search terms 'Beyer' and 'Apache'.

37 *Grant County Herald* notes the recent arrival of the Parks and Flory families in Silver City having lost all to the Apaches "near Slocum's." The paper asked for provisions and old clothing to be donated for their relief ('Town and County', *Grant County Herald*, 25 October 1879).

Plate 10.1 The remains of Slocum's Ranch, also known as Mason's Ranch. (Photo: author)

Plate 10.2 Looking south-eastwards through Magdalena Gap. Van Patten's volunteers rode through this pass, coming towards the camera, on their way to Lloyd's Ranch, and retreated through it after they had been ambushed. (Photo: author)

When their fire drew no response, they sacked the wagon train, carrying off a large quantity of loot and destroying the rest. There was a large amount of flour stored in strong cloth bags. The Apache warriors dumped the contents and kept the bags, leaving the ground around the abandoned wagons white with loose flour.

Having abandoned their pursuit of the posse to ransack the wagon train, the Apaches turned westwards to intercept an approaching Mexican carreta train.[38] Passing through Magdalena Gap and underneath the shadow of a flat-topped hill later named 'Massacre Peak' they ambushed and quickly slaughtered the Mexican teamsters[39] whose muzzle-loading weapons were totally outmatched by the Apache's breech-loaders. A single Anglo-American was with the caravan who:

> made a dash for safety before he was forced to stop and fight for his life. He fought his way to a large yucca about a hundred and fifty yards off the road. He dug a small pit with his knife for added protection. He fired over a hundred rounds from his .44 Winchester before he was riddled with bullets.[40]

The Mexican's muzzle-loaders were found smashed up at the scene of the ambush. This suggests that by this stage of the Apache Wars, the Apaches had no use for such weapons, but also followed the principle that any weapons, no matter how obsolete, should be denied to the enemy.

The second version of the incident[41] has the Apaches spotting the carreta train first, as they pursued Van Patten and breaking off to destroy it. This allowed a breathing space for both the posse and the wagon train coming from Mason's Ranch to flee. The Mexican party was coming from the west and the pursuit of Van Patten was coming broadly from the north, so the carreta train may have failed to spot the fleeing posse as their view would have been obscured by a low ridge that they would have had to climb before turning around the northern flank of Massacre Peak and heading southeast towards Magdalena Gap. Both versions appear to have equal plausibility and so are both recorded here.

In the meantime, the survivors of van Patten's posse had reached Mason's Ranch and sent out couriers to the local settlements. One of the survivors 'stopped a short time at Mason's, then reached La Mesilla, about 45 miles from the battlefield, in six hours.'[42] This man reported that he was the only survivor of Van Patten's party, though this was not believed from the outset.[43] More accurate news was received at Mesilla on the same day, and this stated that five men, including Jones, had been killed.[44] Word was also sent to the military, including a message from R.S. Mason himself pleading for the army to give him protection and stating that there had been at least 16 people killed, including his partner at Mason's stock ranch (probably Lloyd's Ranch)[45] (see document file no. 19.6).

38 These were: "two wheeled vehicles...pulled by oxen and had large spokeless wooden wheels that produced a loud screeching noise that could be heard a long ways off" (Aranda, p.17).

39 A Mr Solomon reported coming across twelve bodies and a number of carretas "four miles the other side of Magdalena Canon." (*Thirty Four*, 15 October 1879).

40 Aranda, 1984, p.17; See also Misc.4 Document.

41 Berndt Kuhn was so strongly in favour of this second version that he convinced me that I should consider both versions. Having done so, for the moment, I find both versions equally plausible.

42 Misc.4 Document.

43 Carr to AAG Dept. Arizona, 18 October 1879, Troops in Southeastern Arizona, DoAz, NA, RG393, Part 1, Entry 232, Vol.4, 3 July, 1879–Dec. 13 1879, Letter No.196, pp.126-127.

44 Mesilla Operator to Lt Allen 14 October 1879, NA, RG393, Part 3, Entry 439, p.313.

45 Mason to Hatch, 18 October 1879 in Letters Received by HQ DoNM, September 1865-August 1890, NA, RG393, M1088, Roll 39, Oct-Dec 1879.

Plate 10.3 The entrance to Horse Canyon, Sierra Uvas. Van Patten's party was ambushed in this canyon. (Photo: author)

Plate 10.4 Massacre Peak. Somewhere on the flat ground below this mountain, Victorio's warriors wiped out the Mexican carreta train. (Photo: author)

Almost 80 men from La Mesilla, Las Cruces, Dona Ana, Picacho, Santo Tomas and Chamberino responded to the call. This force congregated at La Mesilla on 14 October, and left for Mason's Ranch at noon. They elected William Logan Rynerson, a civil war veteran of the California Column, as their leader.[46] They joined the survivors of Van Patten's posse at Mason's Ranch that evening. Some of the survivors joined Rynerson, but Van Patten and most of his party returned to their homes.[47] With the news of the loss of five men to the Apaches, confirmed at Mason's Ranch, some of Rynerson's men found their ardour thoroughly dampened and considered returning to their homes. Rynerson called his posse together and made it clear that they might have to engage Apaches, but they had a duty to recover their dead. He requested that those who wished to return to their homes should do so before he led his men out the following morning. By the following morning all had elected to remain with Rynerson and see the expedition through to the end.

Rynerson had enough men to send out ten in advance, and two further groups of ten acted as flank guards. In the event, they encountered no Apaches but followed the trail of devastation, recovering or burying the bodies. At the site of the carreta ambush, they were confronted by what appeared to be one of the Mexicans meandering around in his ox-drawn carreta. He had in fact been shot dead in that position and his oxen left to wander by the Apaches.[48] The caravan had been returning to El Paso, the Mexicans having sold their cargoes of dried fruit in Silver City, and the attack had yielded little plunder to the Apaches. One can imagine Apache warriors making a cursory check on the contents of this particular carreta and searching the driver before moving on. The posse buried the remains of the dead in a mass grave. The expedition moved on and recovered the bodies of those killed when Van Patten was ambushed. Four were buried near the site of the ambush, the fifth was returned to La Mesilla for burial.[49]

On 16 October, Rynerson and his men reached El Colorado, and here a further 20 volunteers signed up for the advance on Lloyd's Ranch. When they arrived, there were more bodies to be buried. They also found more than 100 dead cattle and chickens scattered around the ranch.[50] Rynerson led his expedition back, and they reached La Mesilla by 17 October 1879, having exhausted their rations.[51] Rynerson reported that 17 bodies had been recovered, which meant that seven men remained missing.[52] *Thirty-Four* noted that the posse had buried 20 men, but had failed to find the bodies of four more known to have been killed. It also stated that three dead Apaches, wrapped in blankets lost by Jacinto Armijo in the Van Patten fight, had been discovered by Apache scouts on 19 October.[53] The paper also reported that a party of eight poorly armed miners had been attacked near Fort Cummings on 15 October, and that six had been killed. This party had been

46 Mesilla Operator to Lt Allen 14 October 1879, NA, RG393, Part 3, Entry 439, p.307; See also Misc.4 Document; Frost to Loud, NA, RG393, Part 3, Entry 439, p.310; Anon Mesilla to Loud AAAG 14 October 1879, NA, RG393, Part 3, Entry 439, p.307 & 310; Loud to AAG Fort Leavenworth, 16 October 1879, Telegrams Sent DoNM, Vol.2, Jan.–Dec. 1879, NA, RG393, Part 3, Entry 431, p.321.

47 See also Misc.4 Document.

48 See also Misc.4 Document.

49 Aranda states that most of the bodies were in a poor state of preservation and/or mutilated and were buried in situ for that reason. (p.18; See also Rynerson to Lt Allen 17 October 1879, NA, RG393, Part 3, Entry 439, p.300; Beyer to AAAG SF, 16 October 1879, NA, RG393, Part 3, Entry 439, pp.303-304.)

50 Aranda, 1984, p.18; See also 'Home Again'. *Thirty Four,* 22 October 1879.

51 Misc.4 Document.

52 Mesilla Operator to Lt Allen 17 October 1879, NA, RG393, Part 3, Entry 439, pp. 300-302; Loud to AAG Fort Leavenworth, 17 October 1879, Telegrams Sent DoNM, Vol.2, Jan.–Dec. 1879, NA, RG393, Part 3, Entry 431, pp.330-331; see also 'Indian News' *The New Mexican* 18 October 1879 in The Walter Lowry Finley Collection.

53 *Thirty Four,* 22 October 1879.

en-route to the Shakespeare Mines from Las Cruces and included 'Thos. Godfrey, 'Sand' Joslyn, Thos. Grady, Thos. Petty, Mr Hartley and James Lannen.'[54]

A rather cryptic note by Rynerson concerning Morrow's arrival at Lloyd's Ranch[55] inferred that this was a case of 'too little too late'. Morrow had responded to the news of these raids, received on 15 October at McEvers' Ranch, by dispatching Apache scouts and some troops to the area; but unfortunately, for whatever, reason, Gatewood was misinformed about the distance from McEvers' to Lloyd's Ranch. He thought it was 12 miles, when, in fact, it was 30. This meant his party took only two days' rations. They picked up the trail of the Apaches and followed it towards the Goodsight Mountains, but were forced to move off the trail and put into Fort Cummings to await Morrow's battalion and to get fresh supplies.[56] Morrow's own force had to remain in camp until dawn on 18 October, replacing horseshoes, awaiting some concrete information from their scouts, and being bombarded with unconfirmed reports of many citizens killed and Santa Barbara destroyed. That same day, Morrow marched his battalion to Fort Cummings to join Gatewood's detachment.[57]

Even as Rynerson's force set out in pursuit of the Apaches, reports of these attacks had reached the attention of the citizens of Santa Fé, including the governor. A committee of concerned citizens fronted by the governor offered to put 500 volunteers in the field if the US government could bear the expense of rationing them.[58] General Pope recommended that this request be complied with in the short-term in order to help calm the citizens of New Mexico.[59] Privately, he stated that Morrow had in the field 500 men, including over 100 Indian scouts, and that the panic among the citizens was caused by wildly exaggerated reports of Apache atrocities.[60] His public request was briskly turned down by General Sherman, who chose to interpret it as requesting help to protect Santa Fé itself, which he rightly judged to be threatened by neither Utes or Apaches:[61]

> We have no lawful right to issue rations to allay the excitement of the people of Santa Fé – Who is threatening the safety of the people there! Has Col. Morrow asked for help – if so he must be reinforced by every soldier subject to our joint Command.[62]

Nevertheless, Governor Wallace issued new rifles to many of the areas raided by Victorio and his warriors in September-October 1879.[63]

---

54 *Thirty Four*, 5 November, 1879. It should be noted that my colleague Berndt Kuhn believes that this attack is one of the many erroneous reports which routinely appeared.

55 This probably refers to a detachment from Morrow's battalion of Gatewood and Maney's scouts accompanied by a detachment of Sixth Cavalrymen. Morrow himself did not visit Lloyds Ranch.

56 'Gatewood's Report 1879', NA, RG393, Part 1, Entry 240; see also Loud to AAG MDoM, 20 October 1879, 'Victorio Papers', NA, M666, Roll 526; Loud to Major Arnold, Fort Grant, NA, RG393, Part 1, Entry 235, pp.21-22; Beyer to AAAG, 18 October 1879, NA, RG393, Part 3, Entry 439, p.298; Thrapp, 1974, p.247.

57 Morrow to AAAG DoNM, 5 November, 1879, 'Victorio Papers', NA, M666, Roll 526.

58 Lew Wallace to Pope passed on to Sherman, 16 of October 1879, NA, RG393, Part 1, Entry 2539, Press Copies of Letters and Endorsements Sent, MDoM, Vol. 12, pp.28-30.

59 Pope to AAG HQ MDoM, 15 October 1879, 'Victorio Files', NA, RG393, M1495, Roll 14.

60 Pope to Sheridan, 17 October 1879, 'Victorio Files', NA, RG393, M1495, Roll 14.

61 Sherman to Sheridan, 17 October 1879, NA, RG393, Part 1, Entry 2539, Press Copies of Letters and Endorsements Sent, MDoM, Vol. 12, pp.36-37; Sherman to Sheridan, 16 October 1879, 'Victorio Files', NA, RG393, M1495, Roll 14.

62 Sherman to Sheridan, 16 October 1879, 'Victorio Papers', NA, M666, Roll 526.

63 Lt. Walter Finley noted that he reached his first posting at Fort Bayard escorting a load of rifles and ammunition issued to the Governor of the territory of New Mexico. (Letter dated Toussaints Ranch, 9 October 1879 in The Walter Lowry Finley Collection.)

The destruction wreaked by the Apaches may seem indiscriminate, but one must remember the Apache principles of war, which were in many respects similar to those used by the US army when combating American Indians. The destruction of livestock and merchandise at Lloyd's Ranch and the abandoned wagon train illustrate aspects of the Apache use of total warfare techniques to target enemy resources, whilst simultaneously supplementing their own logistics. What they could not use immediately was destroyed to deny its use to the enemy. These attacks had wreaked havoc on the local economy, where a significant amount of resources had been appropriated or destroyed, and at least 25 members of the local community had been killed; and over and above these tangible effects came the psychological effects on those people left to carry on in the wake of the Apache raiders.

As the campaign against Victorio continued, the territorial press would become increasingly critical of the US army's efforts. Major Morrow was blamed for some of the attacks, on the basis that he had earlier claimed to have defeated the Apaches and 'was holding them in check at 80 miles north.'[64] He was also criticised for not warning the citizens that Victorio was moving south into their area. Why could he not have sent a courier to Fort Bayard and then telegraphed Fort Cummings with instructions to raise the alarm?[65] The answer was that Morrow could not have predicted the movement of Victorio's warriors, and to raise the alarm across the entirety of southern New Mexico would simply have played into the Apaches' hands. The paralysis of commerce across the territory would have been equally, if not more, censured by the same press.

Captain Carroll also came under fire in a short clip:

> LOST. Captain Carroll and 80 men. He was ordered to join Morrow immediately Oct. 4th, he didn't stop over 2 weeks at Paraje. After the Indians have killed 100 and been gone 4 weeks he will probably start on their trail.[66]

As noted earlier, it is quite clear that Carroll had not been ordered to join Morrow's command, and that there had been good reason for his apparent stay at Paraje. Around the same time, Captain Beyer had to request that District Headquarters quash a rumour that I am in arrest or under cloud for cowardice as published in the *Rocky Mountain Sentinel* of 9 October, 1879.'[67]

The negative reporting continued. *Thirty-Four* stated that, by 15 October, 75 citizens had been slaughtered by the Apaches since Victorio left the Mescalero reservation in August 1879.[68] Issues of the *Grant County Herald* for 18 and 25 October 1879 contained a number of accusations and proposed solutions concerning the warfare with the Apaches. These accusations were varied: the Apaches were being supplied with recruits and ammunition by Quaker Indian agents;[69] Major Morrow was delaying pursuit of the Apaches and exaggerating the extent of the victory over the Apaches at Cuchillo Negro; the large number of horses and mules recaptured at Cuchillo Negro were mostly broken down and abandoned by the Apaches. This apparently led to the volunteers from Georgetown leaving Morrow's command in disgust.[70] The federal government was lambasted for being more concerned about costs than protecting citizens. It was also accused of actively obstructing Governor Wallace's efforts to turn out a militia force.[71] The solution advocated came

64 See Misc.4 Document.
65 Misc.4 Document.
66 Misc.4 Document.
67 Beyer to Loud SF, 14 October 1879, NA, RG393, Part 3, Entry 439, p.299.
68 *Thirty Four*, 15 October 1879.
69 'From Georgetown', *Grant County Herald*, 25 October 1879.
70 'From Georgetown', *Grant County Herald*, 25 October 1879; See also extract published in *Thirty Four*, 29 October 1879.
71 *Grant County Herald*, 18 October 1879.

Plate 10.5 The remains of Lloyd's Ranch. (Photo: author)

Plate 10.6 Another view of Lloyd's Ranch with La Ceja ('the eyebrow') Canyon in the background. The distinctive rock formations from which this name is derived can be clearly seen. It is believed that the second party which left El Colorado on 11 October 1879, was ambushed and pinned down in this canyon. (Photo: author)

from a criticism that the reservation system must be flawed if Apaches were motivated to break out. Corrupt practices were identified as the cause of such break outs. The solution was, for the territorial press of the time, quite surprisingly progressive from a territorial Anglo-American perspective. First, the Apaches should not be recognised as a national unit but as family units; and each should be given a farm and assistance to develop their farming skills. Second, Apache children should be provided with good schooling to erase their former warlike culture. Third, disarm the Apaches and have sufficient troops on hand to keep the peace.[72]

However, the paper concluded that:

> The facts are these. Victorio is not yet subdued and if no better headway is made in that direction in the future, than has been during this last campaign he never will be. He [Victorio] knows and has said "that he and his party will all be killed in the end but that he will get many a one before they go up.[73]

General Pope telegraphed District Headquarters at Santa Fé on 15 October, stating that all available troops should be put at Morrow's disposal and that District Headquarters must not interfere with these operations.[74] Yet Pope also confirmed that Morrow had not asked for additional aid and, as far as Pope was aware, Morrow had 500 men, and the major felt that this number was sufficient for the task.[75] General Pope also demanded that he be kept informed of events in southern New Mexico twice daily in response to the news that 19 people had been killed.[76] Given the general's concern about the public impact of the raids around Slocum's and Lloyd's Ranches, District Headquarters contacted Morrow to inform him that a victory over Victorio was urgently required.[77] The major thus found himself caught between angry citizens and supportive but anxious and interfering superiors, few of whom had any understanding of the difficulties of prosecuting operations against Apaches with very limited resources.

Over and above negative reporting, false stories of Apache activity were published. There was an alleged, and if true, quite disastrous, clash between Lieutenant Blocksom's Apache scouts and the Warm Springs Apaches. Seventeen scouts and two soldiers were supposedly slain.[78] We should remember that Lieutenant Blocksom's Apache scouts had been disbanded, and while not impossible, there appears to be no hard evidence for such a heavy defeat of a company of Apache scouts by Victorio's warriors. This may reflect the tendency of the local newspapers to exaggerate or even fabricate atrocity stories to embarrass the US army. *Thirty-Four* stated that Morrow's Apache scouts'

---

72 'Correspondence', *Grant County Herald*, 18 October 1879.

73 'Correspondence', *Grant County Herald*, 25 October 1879.

74 Pope to Loud AAAG Santa Fé, 16 Oct 1879, NA, RG393, Part 3, Entry 439, p.100 see also Pope to Loud AAAG Santa Fé, 24 October 1879, NA, RG393, Part 3, Entry 439, p.101; Loud to Morrow, 17 October 1879, Telegrams Sent DoNM, Vol.2, Jan.–Dec. 1879, NA, RG393, Part 3, Entry 431, p.329.

75 Pope to Sheridan, 17 October 1879, 'Victorio Papers', NA, M666, Roll 526.

76 Pope to Loud AAAG Santa Fé, 15 Oct 1879, NA, RG393, Part 3, Entry 439, p.99; see also Lew Wallace to Gen. Pope copied to Gen. Sherman, 16 October 1879, NA, RG393, Part 1, Entry 2539, Press Copies of Letters and Endorsements Sent, MDoM, Vol. 12, pp.28-30.

77 Loud to Morrow, 16 October 1879, Telegrams Sent DoNM, Vol.2, Jan.–Dec. 1879, NA, RG393, Part 3, Entry 431, pp.322-323.

78 Thrapp notes that this battle is not mentioned in the Chronological List and may be exaggerated. After all, the source is the *Arizona Star.* Yet he does not discount the possibility that Victorio had rebuffed a scout detachment, and inflicting casualties in the process, though not to the magnitude described in the press. (Thrapp, 1967, p.186; Stout, p.102) Nolan notes that the Star reported the slaying of seventeen Apache scouts and two soldiers from Lt Blocksom's detachment but also acknowledges Thrapp's doubts over the accuracy of the report. (Nolan, 1997, p.167) Haley reports that on 22 October, 1879, Victorio's Apaches slaughtered an Indian scout detachment killing nineteen people (Haley, p.323).

enlistment had expired and they had returned to Arizona because 'they didn't want any more of it.'[79] The absence of a skirmish from the 'Chronological List' does not necessarily undermine the veracity of the story. This source records six 'enlisted men' killed on 13 October, at, or near, Lloyd's Ranch.[80] There was a similar rumour circulating that Morrow had clashed again with Victorio 'near Colorado on Saturday and Sunday'[81] According to the Cambridge Encyclopaedia, this would have been 11 and 12 October 1879. It is clear from both Blocksom's and Gatewood's reports (see document file no. 15) that the former had already returned to Arizona Territory with his time-expired scouts and the latter did not recall any such encounter. This only leaves Maney's detachment of scouts. It should be noted that the Chronological List routinely put Apache scout casualties under 'enlisted men' with a separate entry for civilian casualties. This incident is most probably a garbled account of the ambush of Van Patten's party. However, the possibility that some Apache scouts may have been ambushed and killed around this time cannot be completely ruled out.

This issue highlights the continuing problem of exaggerated and false reports of Apache activity. A stagecoach driver was dismissed for spreading false reports of Apaches raiding to the north of the Mogollon Mountains near Fort Wingate on or around 19 October.[82] Another report, of a Mexican killed and a train attacked by Apaches near Fort Craig, was investigated by Lieutenant Taylor, who had just arrived to escort some wagons to Ojo Caliente. The attack upon the supply train proved to be fictitious or, as Taylor put it a 'canard', and the Mexican had been shot dead by citizens.[83] There were even rumours that the officers' families had fled Fort Wingate in a convoy of ambulances.[84]

To make matters worse for the army, it is during this period of the campaign that Juh, the Southern Chiricahua leader, enters the picture. Louis Scott, the US Consul in Chihuahua, referred to Juh having 'a terribly bad reputation.'[85] Juh was widely believed to torture captives, and these deaths may have been ascribed to Victorio, who was seen, by the Americans, as their principal enemy at that juncture.[86] Morrow was not sure whether Victorio's warriors or Juh, (with approximately 50 Southern Chiricahua warriors from Mexico), might have been involved in some of these

79 *Thirty Four*, 22 October 1879.

80 Chronological List, p.48; Webb, 1976, p.87; this may be an error on the part of those compiling the list. There may be no coincidence that the Mesilla posse lost six men on the very previous day. The Chronological List usually gives the unit involved if the U.S. army is involved. In this case no unit is cited. However, the Chronological List appears to class Indian scouts as 'enlisted men', so it is possible that Lt Blocksom was also ambushed in the area, losing some scouts. The newspapers may have subsumed the casualties from several attacks into a single unconfirmed ambush.

81 Loud to Hatch, 13 October 1879, Telegrams Sent DoNM, Vol.2, Jan.–Dec. 1879, NA, RG393, Part 3, Entry 431, p.314; Loud to Pope, 14 October 1879, 'Victorio Papers', NA, M666, Roll 526; Loud AAAG to Pope copied to Gen. Sherman, 16 October 1879, NA, RG393, Part 1, Entry 2539, Press Copies of Letters and Endorsements Sent, MDoM, Vol. 12, pp.33-34; Sheridan to Sherman, 16 October 1879, NA, RG393, Part 1, Entry 2538, pp.198-199; Loud to AAG Fort Leavenworth, 14 October 1879, 'Victorio Files', NA, RG393, M1495, Roll 14; 'Other Indian Operations' *Army & Navy Journal*, Vol.17, 25 October 1879, p.219.

82 Telegrams Sent DoNM, Vol.2, Jan.–Dec. 1879, NA, RG393, Part 3, Entry 431, p.336 &pp.346-348; Carr to AAG Dept. Arizona, 22 October 1879, Troops in Southeastern Arizona, DoAz, NA, RG393, Part 1, Entry 232, Vol.4, 3 July, 1879–Dec. 13 1879, Letter No.203, pp.131-132.

83 Loud to AAG Fort Leavenworth, 28 October 1879, Telegrams Sent DoNM, Vol.2, Jan.–Dec. 1879, NA, RG393, Part 3, Entry 431, p.381.

84 Lt. Tyler, 9th Cavalry to DoNM, 20 October 1879 in Letters Received by HQ_DoNM, September 1865-August 1890, NA, RG393, M1088, Roll 39, Oct-Dec 1879.

85 Louis H. Scott to Hon. J.H. Seward, Department of State, 19 September, 1879, NA, RG393, Part 1, Entry 2546, p.162; Scott to Seward, Department of State, Washington D.C., 19 September, 1879 in Consular Despatches Chihuahua Mexico 1830-1906, NA, M289, Roll 1; See also Willcox to Francisco L. Prieto, Mexican Consul, Tucson, 8 November, 1879, 'Victorio Papers', NA, M666, Roll 527.

86 Thrapp, 1973, p.11; Thrapp, 1974, p.xvii; Thrapp, 1988, p.753; See also Collins, 1994, pp.74-75; Haley, 1981, p.279 & p.352.

attacks. As early as 24 September, there came a report of a horse raid in Mexico where 12 men set out in pursuit of horse thieves and ran into an ambush, with only two, mortally wounded, survivors making it back to their homes. The other ten men were presumed to have been slain.[87]

On 29 September, a warning was sent to District Headquarters that a large group of Apaches from Mexico had crossed the border and passed between Hudson's Hot Springs and Mason's Ranch going to the north.[88] Soon afterwards, reports that Humo's (Juh's)[89] warriors had joined with Victorio were being circulated.[90] This was based on the information gathered by the pursuers of three Apaches who had stolen a horse from some Mexicans on the lower Mimbres River. This horse, despite being tethered within yards of Jose Trujillo's house, had been spirited off by the Apaches on the night of 27 September 1879. Pancho Solis and five men pursued the Apaches into Cooke's Range. At 'Len's' Springs, they found that their quarry had joined a very fresh trail of 60 Apaches who were moving north. The Mexicans estimated that the trail was less than half-an-hour old. The Mexicans promptly withdrew to raise both the alarm and a larger posse.[91] A report was also received from one citizen, Rudden, stating that he had spotted approximately 100 Apaches moving north from Mexico 'just after the first fight Major Morrow had with Victoria.'[92] Captain H.H. Humphreys, who was commanding officer at Fort Bayard in Morrow's absence, sent in information that 'Hooes band of Indians numbering fifty from Mexico, passed in vicinity of Cummings October second or third.'[93] If true, this would put Juh moving north around the beginning of October 1879.

On 18 October 1879, Morrow noted that the trail left by the Apaches was much larger than previously noted.[94] This certainly allows for the possibility that Victorio had been joined by Juh before or during the attacks in and around Mason's and Lloyd's Ranches and the village of El Colorado. It could also mean that the Chihenne women and children had joined the warriors. On the same day, probably in response to such reports, Sheridan stated that the recent raids in the El Colorado area were perpetrated by Apaches from Mexico.[95] Morrow himself subsequently reported that, in his opinion, Juh's warriors only became involved in the fighting on or around 27 October 1879, though he gave no indication as to why he reached this conclusion.[96] As subsequent events

87 *Thirty Four*, 24 September, 1879.

88 Messrs William G. Boyle & James E. Carroll to HQ DoNM, 29 September, 1879 in Letters Received by HQ DoNM, September 1865-August 1890, NA, RG393, M1088, Roll 38, July–Sept. 1879.

89 The name 'Juh' is pronounced 'Whoo' so written sources of the time record various phonetic versions of his name.

90 'Correspondence', *Grant County Herald*, 4 October 1879.

91 'Town and County', *Grant County Herald*, 4 October 1879.

92 Rudden to Hatch 17 October 1879, NA, RG393, Part 3, Entry 439, p.299; Loud to AAG Fort Leavenworth, 18 October 1879, Telegrams Sent DoNM, Vol.2, Jan.–Dec. 1879, NA, RG393, Part 3, Entry 431, p.334; Loud to Willcox, 5 November, 1879, Telegrams Sent DoNM, Vol.2, Jan.–Dec. 1879, NA, RG393, Part 3, Entry 431, pp.403-404.

93 Loud citing Rudden's report, to AAG Fort Leavenworth, 17 October 1879, Telegrams Sent DoNM, Vol.2, Jan.–Dec. 1879, NA, RG393, Part 3, Entry 431, p.326; See also 'Indian News' *The New Mexican*, 18 October 1879, in The Walter Lowry Finley Collection.

94 Morrow to Loud AAAG SF via Bayard, 18 October 1879, NA, RG393, Part 3, Entry 439, p.295; Sheridan to Townsend AG Washington D.C., 18 October 1879, 'Victorio Papers', NA, M666, Roll 526; Loud to AAG Fort Leavenworth, Gen. Willcox & Major Arnold, 19 October 1879, Telegrams Sent DoNM, Vol.2, Jan.–Dec. 1879, NA, RG393, Part 3, Entry 431, p.335& pp.337-338; Pope to AAG MDoM, 20 October 1879, 'Victorio Files', NA, RG393, M1495, Roll 14.

95 Sheridan to Townsend, 18 October 1879, NA, RG393, Part 1, Entry 2539, Press Copies of Letters and Endorsements Sent, MDoM, Vol. 12, pp.55-56.

96 Loud to Hatch, 3 November, 1879, Telegrams Sent DoNM, Vol.2, Jan.–Dec. 1879, NA, RG393, Part 3, Entry 431, p.393; Morrow, Bayard to Carr, Grant, 5 November, (October is actually stated but this is a mistake) 1879, NA, RG393, Part 1, Entry 235, p.26.

unfolded, it appeared that Juh and Victorio had joined forces from sometime around mid-October and remained together until early November 1879.

An argument has been made to the effect that Juh came to Victorio's rescue. However, the idea that Juh charged into south-western New Mexico with the specific intent of causing enough chaos to allow Victorio to escape is hard to believe.[97] What is more plausible is that news of the major confrontation between Victorio and the Ninth Cavalry from 4 September 1879 onwards would have travelled. This renewed turmoil may have encouraged Juh to take advantage of the situation and return across the border in October 1879 to raid in southern New Mexico. As there were family ties between members of Juh's and Victorio's bands (Nana was married to Geronimo's sister),[98] then it would not be at all surprising if they formed an alliance for a time, though there was some doubt as to whether Victorio and Juh were on friendly terms. Equally, while the two leaders may have had personal differences, both were leaders of high standing among the Chiricahua Apaches. Neither would have been inclined to endanger their standing by starting a fight that would benefit neither faction and bring only relief to a common enemy. Finally, we should recall the Warm Springs Apaches, possibly led by Mangus, had been spotted in Mexico at the same time as both Nana and Victorio were on the Mescalero reservation during August 1879. It is not beyond the bounds of possibility that they may have moved north to reinforce Victorio.

By 8 November 1879, the *Weekly New Mexican* reported that Victorio had been joined by 'Hooey's' Apaches and Fort Stanton Mescaleros.[99] The reference to Mescalero Apaches highlighted further concerns that other Apaches might be tempted to throw their lot in with Victorio, and, in doing so, would widen the scope of the conflict. As we have seen in earlier chapters, other Apaches were continuing to maintain their independent way of life, and merely by doing so represented an obstacle to US economic development (dare we say exploitation) of the Southwest. The army was well aware that there were other Apaches, independent of Victorio's following, who could be drawn into the conflict. The fear was that these would gravitate towards a successful leader, thus focusing Apache resistance to the US government. The many rivalries, clans and tribes among the people whom outsiders termed Apaches meant that this was less of a threat than was feared; but it must be understood that to dismiss such fears now is done with the confidence of hindsight. What must be realised is that, as events unfolded in September and October 1879, the army suspected that other

97 See Thrapp, 1974, pp. 246-247; Thrapp, 1973, p.12; While having great admiration for Thrapp, who as a historian has made a huge contribution to our knowledge of the Apache Wars in general, and the Victorio Campaign in particular, he does have a tendency to indulge in 'hero-worship' concerning Juh and Victorio. His argument that:

> In 1879 when the hard-pressed Victorio was trying to escape into Mexico from the Black range with his people, Juh stormed to his assistance. Juh-led warriors rushed up from Mexico, slammed into the ranches and communities along the Rio Grande and created such confusion and panic among Anglo-Americans that Victorio could save himself and his followers. (Thrapp, 1973, p.ii; See also Thrapp, 1988, pp.548-549)

Debo rightly points out that Kaywaykla did not mention meeting with Juh until late 1881 and argues that the story which allies Juh/Geronimo with Victorio appears to be "untenable." (Debo, pp.119-120) In fact both accounts bear re-examination. Victorio was not as hard-pressed as Thrapp nor the US army would have us believe, even Thrapp's account of the Victorio Campaign implies as much. Moreover, the decision to leave the Mescalero reservation in August was a spontaneous reaction to perceived treachery on the part of the US authorities. It does not seem to have been specifically planned in advance though this does not preclude the possibility that the Warm Springs Apaches had contingency plans in case of sudden emergencies. Equally, Debo too easily dismisses the possibility that they temporarily joined forces at this point. The probability that the warriors were regularly acting independently of their families would explain why James Kaywaykla failed to mention this alliance.

98 Debo, p.27.

99 The Latest Indian News' *Weekly New Mexican,* 8 November, 1879 in The Walter Lowry Finley Collection.

Chiricahua Apaches had joined Victorio. If some, or all, of the Mescaleros decided to ally with the Warm Springs Apache leader, the situation could become unmanageable without considerable reinforcement by the US army. If we look briefly eastwards into Texas, there were clear signs that there were many independent Mescalero Apaches who had not given up their hunting and raiding lifestyle, and might be inclined to join Victorio.

Mexican Militia and Texas Rangers Versus Mescalero Apaches

As noted earlier, Lieutenant G.W. Smith had drawn attention to 'savage bands of well armed Apaches reported going south from Mescalero reservation 19th ulto' [September][100] *Thirty-Four* later repeated this information but added, significantly, that these Mescalero Apaches were travelling to the south or east and, by implication, were not going to join Victorio.[101] In the light of Smith's intelligence, on 3 October 1879, Hatch informed his colleagues in the District of the Pecos that large bands of well-armed Apaches were reported to be leaving the Fort Stanton reservation and moving south. He added that the Ute crisis left him with his 'hands full.'[102] General Pope also reported that a survey of the Mescaleros present on the Fort Stanton reservation revealed only 33 males. He advised moving some of the Tenth Cavalry to the Pecos to counter Mescalero raiding parties.[103] Colonel Grierson ordered his troops in the field to be extra vigilant,[104] but was left speculating as to whether the Apaches reportedly moving into his district were Mescaleros or were Apaches from the borders between New Mexico and Arizona. He also had no idea of how well mounted and armed they might be, and asked Hatch if he could furnish more details.[105]

While it was clear to Grierson that Victorio was not expected to move south, other parties of Apaches might pass through western Texas, and he feared that these would arrive in greater strength than those Apaches previously trailed or encountered in the area. Detachments of the Tenth Cavalry were sent instructions that scouting detachments should be made up of no less than 20 other ranks commanded by an officer. Company commanders were also warned that they might have to remain in the field for longer than was expected.[106] The news that a recent head count at the Mescalero reservation found only 33 men raised further concern that a major raid might materialise in western Texas, and General Pope recommended that additional companies from the Tenth Cavalry be sent west to the Pecos to counter this threat.[107] Captain Louis H. Carpenter and

100 Smith to AAAG SF, 1 October 1879? NA, RG393, Part 3, Entry 439, p.365; Loud to AAG San Antonio, DoTx, 17 October 1879, Telegrams Sent DoNM, Vol.2, Jan.–Dec. 1879, NA, RG393, Part 3, Entry 431, p.330.

101 *Thirty Four*, 15 October 1879.

102 Hatch to CO, DoP, 3 October 1879 in Telegrams Sent, 24 April 1879–22 June, 1880, HQ DoP 1878-1881, NA, RG393, M1381, Roll 1, pp.84-85, Letter No.204.

103 Pope to Whipple AAG, Chicago, 18 October 1879, NA, RG393, Part 1, Entry 2546, p.229.

104 Smither to CO, Grierson Spring, 3 October 1879 in Telegrams Sent 24 April 1879-22 June, 1880, HQ DoP 1878-1881, NA, RG393, M1381, Roll 1, pp.85-86, Letter No.206; Grierson to AAG, San Antonio, Texas, 13 October 1879 in Telegrams Sent 24 April 1879-22 June, 1880, HQ DoP 1878-1881, NA, RG393, M1381, Roll 1, p.92, Letter No.217; See also 'Indian Movements in New Mexico' *Army & Navy Journal*, Vol.17, 18 October 1879, p.198.

105 Grierson to CO, DoNM, 3 October 1879 in Telegrams Sent 24 April 1879-22 June, 1880, HQ DoP 1878-1881, NA, RG393, M1381, Roll 1, p.85, Letter No.205.

106 Smither to CO Company D, 10th Cavalry, 8 October 1879 in Letters Sent September, 19, 1879–August 11, 1880, HQ DoP 1878-1881, NA, RG393, M1381, Roll 1, Letter No.9.

107 Maxon AAG, to District Commander, Fort Concho, 19 October 1879 in Register of Telegrams Rec'd October 11, 1879-October 8, 1880, HQ 1878-1881, NA, RG393, M1381, Roll 2, pp.16-17, Letter No.11; Pope cited in Smither to CO's Co. D, F & M, 10th Cavalry & CO's Grierson's Springs & Camp-Charlotte, 20 October 1879 in Letters Sent September, 19, 1879–August 11, 1880, HQ DoP 1878-1881, NA, RG393, M1381, Roll 1, Letter No.'s 16-18 & 20-22; See also Smither to CO's, Forts Stockton &

his company of Tenth cavalrymen were also ordered to march to Eagle Springs to watch for any Apaches.[108] By the end of October, the detachments listed in Table 10.2 were in the field.[109]

Table 10.2 Tenth Cavalry Deployment – Western Texas, October 1879

Post	Unit	Location
Fort Concho	Company D, 10th Cavalry	Head of N. Concho River, Texas
	Company E, 10th Cavalry	Grierson's Springs, Texas
	Company A, 25th Infantry (Det)	Camp Charlotte, Texas
	Company A, 25th Infantry (Det)	Pecos Hills, Texas
	Company G, 25th Infantry	Pena Colorado, Texas
Fort Stockton	Company B, 10th Cavalry	Frazier's Ranch, Texas
	Company L, 10th Cavalry (Det)	Pena Colorado, Texas
	Company L, 10th Cavalry (Det)	Escondido, Texas
	Company F, 25th Infantry	Pena Colorado, Texas
Fort Davis	Company H, 10th Cavalry	Eagle Springs, Texas
	Company K, 10th Cavalry	Guadalupe Mountains, Texas
	Company E, 25th Infantry	Mesquis Canon, Texas
	Company H, 25th Infantry (Det)	Eagle Springs, Texas
	Company H, 25th Infantry (Det)	Seven Springs, Texas
	Company H, 25th Infantry (Det)	Guadalupe Mountains, Texas

The mass movement of Mescaleros into the District of the Pecos failed to materialise, but small parties were detected passing through the area in mid-October. Lieutenant Bigelow, with a detachment of 22 soldiers, found himself ordered out to pursue five Apaches who had been spotted near Pecos Falls, Texas. Captain J.M. Kelley was ordered out in an attempt to intercept this party.[110] Grierson also requested that, as the Fourth Cavalry had been ordered into the Department of the Missouri from the Department of Texas, the three companies of the Tenth Cavalry based at Fort Sill (in the Department of the Missouri) be sent to the Department of Texas.[111]

In response to these raiding parties, and a report from Fort Bliss of a large party of Indians moving south along the Rio Grande, on the Mexican side, and predicted to be going to cross into the United States around Old Fort Quitman, Grierson mobilised his forces. He facilitated their intended operations by sending supplies to strategic points, in case active field operations should be undertaken. As Grierson prepared to take control personally, the threat from both north and south

Davis, 20 October 1879 in Telegrams Sent 24 April 1879-22 June, 1880, HQ_DoP 1878-1881, NA, RG393, M1381, Roll 1, pp.97-98, Letter No.'s 226 & 227.

108 Smither to Capt. Keyes, 10th Cavalry, 25 October 1879 in Letters Sent 19 September, 1879–11 August 1880, HQ_DoP 1878-1881, NA, RG393, M1381, Roll 1, Letter No.22; Smiher to CO Fort Davis, 21 October 1879 in Telegrams Sent April 24, 1879-June 22, 1880, HQ_DoP 1878-1881, NA, RG393, M1381, Roll 1, pp.101-102, Letter No.230.

109 Smither to AAG, San Antonio, Texas (Date not included) in Telegrams Sent 24 April 1879–22 June, 1880, HQ_DoP 1878-1881, NA, RG393, M1381, Roll 1, pp.113-114, Letter No.249.

110 Smither to CO, Grierson's Spring, 11 October 1879 in Telegrams Sent April 24, 1879-June 22, 1880, HQ_DoP 1878-1881, NA, RG393, M1381, Roll 1, p.90, Letter No.214; Grierson to AAG, San Antonio, Texas, 13 October 1879 in Telegrams Sent April 24, 1879-June 22, 1880, HQ_DoP 1878-1881, NA, RG393, M1381, Roll 1, p.92, Letter No.217.

111 Grierson to AAG, San Antonio, Texas, 13 October 1879 in Telegrams Sent April 24, 1879-June 22, 1880, HQ_DoP 1878-1881, NA, RG393, M1381, Roll 1, p.92, Letter No.217.

simply failed to materialise, and the colonel concluded that the Apaches had turned aside and made for Mexico.[112] His commanding officer, General Ord, later argued that the only solution to this raiding was either to remove the Apaches from the area or to 'feed them sufficiently well, thus to make it unnecessary for them to plunder for food, whether in Texas or in Mexico.'[113]

Texas Rangers[114] were also stationed in the region, and in early October 1879 a detachment of these had pursued a well-armed band of Mescaleros across the border into Mexico. These Apaches had attacked some hay cutters near San Elizario, thereby alerting the Rangers to their presence.[115] In alliance with some Mexican militia, the Rangers had fought a brisk skirmish with the Apaches in the Sierra Ventanas approximately 30 miles southwest of Old Fort Quitman, quite close to the El Paso-Chihuahua Road.[116]

As the Rangers and Mexicans started out in pursuit of the Apaches, Captain George Baylor, commanding the Ranger detachment, estimated that they were pursuing 18 Mescaleros, well-armed with Winchesters and Sharps Rifles. James Gillett, his sergeant, reckoned that there were 16 Apaches in the raiding party.[117] There were 11 rangers and 23 Mexican militiamen in the pursuing group.[118] As the pursuers approached a pass through a canyon in the Sierra Ventana which they suspected was being held by the Mescaleros, and after a debate over tactics,[119] they decided to avoid the pass and attack their would-be ambushers by climbing the reverse slopes of the canyon. Leaving some of their men to guard the horses, they began their manoeuvre, but were spotted by the Apaches, who managed to reach the top of the ridgeline before them. There ensued a brisk gun battle in which both Sergeant Gillett and Captain Baylor were lucky not to have been killed. The former was targeted by a large Apache whose first bullet struck the ground immediately in front of the prone ranger[120] and filled his mouth with plant debris. A second bullet ripped part of Gillett's hat brim off, before the sergeant shot the Mescalero dead. Captain Baylor also had a narrow escape when an Apache bullet hit his hat, missing his face by about six inches. Gillett noted that the Apache he had killed was armed with an older model Winchester Rifle with an octagonal barrel and was carrying a makeshift bag with 250 rounds of ammunition made out of a tied-off shirt sleeve.[121]

As the skirmish continued, the Apaches started to shoot at their pursuers' horses, killing at least one, and Baylor despatched a courier to get their stock moved out of range.[122] Later in the day, the Apaches withdrew higher up into the pass and during this movement one of the Mexican militiamen shot dead another Apache.[123] The pursuers now took up positions on the edge of the canyon and were able to observe the deeper reaches of the pass. They immediately spotted the Apaches' mounts and stolen horses, hobbled by some water-holes a distance away; but the Mescalero warriors had redeployed to cover both the water and their horses. After some discussion, Baylor and the Mexican leader decided that, while they could probably take the water-holes and the Apache stock,

112 Col. Grierson's Report for Year ending 31 December 1879, NA, RG393, Part 1, Entry 2546, pp.322-324.

113 Ord to AG, Washington D.C., 1 December 1879, NA, RG393, Part 1, Entry 2546, p.258.

114 Referred to as 'State Troops' by the U.S. Army (Brinkerhoff to AAA General Santa Fé NM 18 April 1881 NA, RG393, Part.3, Entry 440, pp.8-9).

115 *Thirty Four*, 15 October 1879.

116 Baylor, 1996, p.282 note 13.

117 Baylor, 1996, p.277:Gillett, 1976, p.155.

118 Baylor, 1996, p.278.

119 Gillett notes that Baylor informed him just before this fight that Apaches fought differently from the Plains Indians (Gillett, 1926, pp.7-8, & p.46).

120 My apologies to the reader but I could not resist this play on words.

121 Gillett, 1976, pp.157-158; Baylor, 1996, p.279.

122 Gillett, 1976 pp.158-159.

123 Gillett, 1976, p.159.

this would leave the men guarding their own horses extremely vulnerable to attack. The rest of the skirmish involved long range and completely ineffective sniping by both sides.[124] The pursuers withdrew at nightfall leaving the pass in the possession of the Apaches.

From the Texan-Mexican point of view, they had killed two Apache warriors; yet they had failed to either dislodge the Apaches from the pass or to recapture their booty; so, they could not claim a victory. Nevertheless, the Apaches would not have regarded this as a clear victory either, two of their warriors having been killed.

In terms of the relevance of this incident to the Victorio Campaign, it serves to illustrate the point that, while Victorio might have become the focal point of Apache independence, the Chihennes were not the only Apaches resisting American efforts to confine them on reservations. In immediate terms, the raiders who fought the Mexican militia and Texas Rangers were almost certainly Mescaleros who had left their reservation to hunt and raid down into Mexico. If the Mescalero Apaches had been satisfied with the reservation life being thrust upon them, why leave in the first place?

The longer-term implications of this willingness to raid were that some Mescaleros might be attracted to Victorio's success and provide him with fresh recruits. Furthermore, the Mescaleros' reservation had already been used by Nana to replenish his food and ammunition stocks. This reservation would become the most important location for illicit trading of raided booty for arms and ammunition with the Warm Springs Apaches. Had the US government ensured that what they had promised the Apaches in general had been delivered, then Victorio might not have declared war. If he had broken out, he might have found much less support amongst neighbouring Apaches. The US army was having enough difficulty with Victorio as things were. This spread of dissatisfaction amongst the Mescaleros did not bode well for the future.

However, we must store these implications for future chapters and return to southern New Mexico, where we left Victorio moving towards the Mexican border, with Morrow's battalion approaching Fort Cummings in pursuit.

Morrow caught up with Gatewood's detachment, encamped at Fort Cummings, on 18 October, and the entire command was re-supplied from Fort Bayard that night. The Apaches were thought to be moving towards the Mexican border via the Florida Mountains.[125] A number of Major Morrow's mules were found to be worn out on arrival at Fort Cummings. These were replaced when Morrow requisitioned six serviceable mules from Lieutenant Wright's command.[126]

However, Morrow, having been deceived once before, believed that the trail leading towards the Florida Mountains was intended to mislead him. He expected that instead of taking this direction, Victorio would turn northwards towards the Mogollon or the San Francisco Mountains.[127] Therefore, he ordered Captain Carroll to cross the Black Range with his detachment and attempt to cut Victorio off should he attempt to double back for a second time during Morrow's pursuit. Carroll was instructed to proceed down the North Star Road and, at the same time, the company

---

124 Baylor, 1996, p.280.

125 Loud to AAG MDoM, 20 October 1879, 'Victorio Papers', NA, M666, Roll 526; Loud to Major Arnold, Fort Grant, NA, RG393, Part 1, Entry 235, pp.21-22; Beyer to AAAG 18 October 1879, NA, RG393, Part 3, Entry 439, p.298; Thrapp, 1974, p.247.

126 Special Field Orders No.2, 19 October 1879, Miscellaneous Records 1868-1889, NA, RG393, Part 3, Entry 453; Morrow to AAAG DoNM, 5 November, 1879, 'Victorio Papers', NA, M666, Roll 526.

127 Beyer to AAAG SF, 24 October 1879 (Morrow sent original telegram to Beyer at Ft Bayard on 20 October 1879) NA, RG393, Part 3, Entry 439, pp.291-292; See also p295 & pp.296-297; Loud to AAG MDoM, 20 October 1879, 'Victorio Papers', NA, M666, Roll 526; Loud to Major Arnold, Fort Grant, NA, RG393, Part 1, Entry 235, pp.21-22; Morrow to AAAG DoNM, 5 November, 1879, 'Victorio Papers', NA, M666, Roll 526; Thrapp, 1974, p.248; Pope to AAG MDoM, 21 October 1879, 'Victorio Files', NA, RG393, M1495, Roll 14.

of Indian scouts under Lieutenant Maney which was with Morrow at Fort Cummings was to march to Diamond Creek up the North Star Road. Captain Louis H. Rucker, commanding M Company, Ninth Cavalry, part of Carroll's detachment, reported a seven-day scout from Ojo Caliente which returned on 26 October 1879 having seen nothing. While he dutifully prepared to lead a detachment into the Mogollon Mountains, he was pessimistic, for he did not believe that 'we will accomplish much out here except to wear out horses and men.'[128]

While, at first glance, such operations seem fruitless, if Morrow wished to defeat the Apaches, this required more than a dogged pursuit of these seasoned guerrilla fighters. He also had to try to predict Victorio's future actions and direct his other detachments to positions where they might act decisively. However, and this implies no criticism of Major Morrow, accurately predicting the activities of these fundamentally unpredictable guerrilla warriors was not easy. Less than a week before, Morrow had been unsure as to whether Victorio was going to Mexico or turning eastwards and making for the Mescalero reservation.[129] Now he was unsure as to whether Victorio was going to Mexico or intending to swing west and north to the Mogollon Mountains. The difficulty was that prediction, which was being used with limited military resources, was a less than reliable method of combating Apaches. In fact, when facing guerrillas led by the likes of Victorio, Nana or Juh, there might have been no reliable method of predicting their movements. Thus, Morrow's countermeasures were in vain. Instead of turning north, as predicted, Victorio had turned south. The question was: had he travelled to the Florida Mountains, as assumed by Gatewood's Apache scouts when they broke off their pursuit in the Goodsight Mountains?

Gatewood and his scouts, accompanied by Lieutenant Glass and his detachment of Sixth cavalrymen, were ordered into the Florida Mountains on 19 October.[130] As much of the ground between Fort Cummings and the Floridas was relatively flat, the approach march was made at night, in an effort to foil any early warning the Apaches' sentinels might pick up of their approach.[131] The following day, the Apache scouts scoured the Florida Mountains, while Gatewood and the rest of the detachment encamped at the southern end of the Floridas. There was no trace of any Apaches to be found, and the detachment moved on to the Tres Hermanas Mountains. Meanwhile, at Fort Cummings, Morrow once again refitted his battalion as best he could 'dividing rations, shoeing horses, culling out the unserviceable, owing to limited number and poor condition of pack mules – could only carry fifteen days rations.'[132] Morrow's column joined Gatewood's detachment at the Tres Hermanas late on 21 October.[133] On 22 October, Morrow and Gatewood carried their pursuit of Victorio into Mexico, sending out Gatewood's scouts with a detachment of Ninth Cavalry under Lieutenant Schaeffer at dawn, and with the balance of Morrow's command following at 9 a.m.[134] From the army's point of view, Morrow's command would disappear for almost two weeks before returning to the United States in early November. This caused much anxiety, with the commanding officer at Fort Bayard, in response to requests for information as to Morrow's whereabouts, reporting that he had had no contact with Morrow since 20 October.[135]

128 Rucker to Loud 26 October 1879, NA, RG393, Part 3, Entry 439, p.287.
129 Sheridan to Townsend, 18 October 1879, NA, RG393, Part 1, Entry 2539, Press Copies of Letters and Endorsements Sent, MDoM, Vol. 12, pp.55-56.
130 Morrow to AAAG DoNM, 5 November, 1879, 'Victorio Papers', NA, M666, Roll 526.
131 'Gatewood's Report 1879', NA, RG393, Part 1, Entry 240.
132 Morrow to AAAG DoNM, 5 November, 1879, 'Victorio Papers', NA, M666, Roll 526.
133 'Gatewood's Report 1879', NA, RG393, Part 1, Entry 240; Morrow to AAAG DoNM, 5 November, 1879, 'Victorio Papers', NA, M666, Roll 526.
134 Morrow to AAAG DoNM, 5 November, 1879, 'Victorio Papers', NA, M666, Roll 526; Thrapp, 1974, p.248.
135 Loud to Pope, 25 October 1879, 'Victorio Files', NA, RG393, M1495, Roll 14.

Nevertheless, the higher echelons of the US army were quietly confident that the Apaches would soon be dealt with, and relative easily (see document file no. 20).[136] This was the sort of confident reporting that would come back to haunt the US army, particularly Colonel Hatch after he took over the direction of field operations against Victorio in early 1880. The report was inaccurate; and it played down the number of citizens killed. Such optimistic reporting was quickly perceived by an already sceptical, if not already hostile, territorial press as a deliberate attempt to mislead the federal authorities as to the seriousness of the situation in southern New Mexico.

136 Sheridan to Townsend, AG Army 22 October 1879, (Excerpt from summary of operations against hostile Indians in MDoM since 25 October 1878) NA, RG393, Part 1, Entry 2538, p.213; *Army & Navy Journal,* Vol.17, 8 November, 1879, p.258.

11

Pursuit into Mexico, October 1879

Morrow was accompanied into Mexico by an unusually cosmopolitan force of African American troopers from the Ninth Cavalry, Anglo-American troopers from the Sixth plus Apache scouts.[1] Captain Beyer also believed that two Navajo scouts were present with Morrow's battalion.[2] A civilian scout, a miner called John or Jack Dunn, also accompanied them.[3] If these numbers are accurate, it implies that Morrow's battalion had been substantially reduced in number since its reinforcement on 6 October 1879 by troops from Fort Bayard. On 23 October, Captain Beyer *estimated* that Morrow's battalion was made up as shown in Table 11.1.

Table 11.1 Morrow's Battalion, October 23 1879[4]

Number of Men	Company	Regiment
28	A	Ninth Cavalry
23	B	Ninth Cavalry
25	C	Ninth Cavalry
32	G	Ninth Cavalry
15	H	Ninth Cavalry
123 (sub-total)		
34[1]	A	Sixth Cavalry
36		Sixth Cavalry and Apache Scouts
193 (sub-total)		
9	Officers	

Note

1 The Tabular Statement of Scouts and Expeditions of Companies 6th Cavalry from July 1st 1879 to July 31st 1880. (NA, RG393, Part 1, Entry 240) lists Campbell's command as consisting of 2 Officers and 38 enlisted men.

On the other hand, the further removed and higher up the army chain of command was the source of the estimate, the higher it put the number of the troops under Morrow's command. District Headquarters, while acknowledging that this did not account for casualties or sick or dismounted men, estimated the numbers of Morrow's battalion at 300 troops, with 10 Navajo and

1 Beyer to AAAG SF, 24 October 1879, NA, RG393, Part 3, Entry 439, p.292; Thrapp, 1973, p12-13; Billington, 1991, p.93.
2 Beyer to AAAG SF, 24 October 1879, NA, RG393, Part 3, Entry 439, p.292.
3 Thrapp, 1988, p.432.
4 Beyer to AAAG, 23 Oct., 1879, NA, RG393, Part 3, Entry 439, p.294.

24 Apache scouts,[5] while Sheridan thought that Morrow commanded 557 men.[6] While Morrow may have nominally commanded such totals, far fewer were under his direct command. As we have seen, his force fluctuated in numbers as detachments joined and left it. There was also an assumption at the higher level of army command that a simple numbers game could be played against Apache guerrillas. If one outnumbered the enemy approximately four to one, how could one not prevail?

Table 11.2 Morrow's Campaign, 22 October to 3 November 1879 (See Map 9.1 for overview of Morrow's Sept.-Nov. 1879 Campaign)

16.	22 October	The command moves to a camp next to Palomas Lake. Gatewood's scouts are sent to scout along the Corralitos River.
17.	23 October	During Gatewood's absence Morrow, from his camp at Palomas Lake, spots smoke in the Potrillo Mountains.
	24 October	Gatewood is sent to scout the Potrillo Mountains but returns to report no sign of the Apaches.
	25 October	Morrow returns to the Potrillo Mountains with his command and discovers a four-day-old camp.
	26 October	Further scouting in the Potrillo Mountains reveals a second abandoned campsite.
18.	27 October	Victorio's trail is pursued south through the Sand Hills in Northern Chihuahua.
19.	27-28 October	Morrow engages Victorio and Juh, probably in the hills in front of the Sierra San Blas.
20.	28 October	Morrow breaks off and makes for the Corralitos River for water.
21.	30 October	Morrow arrives back at Palomas Lake.
22.	2-3 November	Morrow's battalion returns to Fort Bayard.

As we have seen, Morrow had attempted to remain on the trail of Victorio, but had lost track of the Apache leader twice since leaving Fort Bayard on 23 September 1879. Also, he could not afford to simply follow the trail of the Apaches; he had to try and outmanoeuvre them by guessing where Victorio was going and directing troops to points where they might intercept him; but the fact was the he did not have nearly enough troops to cover a fraction of the territory traversed by the Apaches. Moreover, the speed at which instructions were transmitted was dependent upon how close the troops were to telegraph lines; otherwise mounted couriers had to be used. The latter were all too vulnerable if there were Apaches in the area. So, Morrow's overall fighting capacity was below what it might appear in several ways. First, some of his troops were never with his battalion: for example, Carroll's two companies, having performed their escort and patrol duties at Paraje, had been directed west over the Black Range to intercept Victorio should he double back towards the Mogollons. Second, men had dropped out due to sickness, exhaustion and loss of mounts. This second point demonstrates the effectiveness of the avoidance strategies employed by the Apaches, where an opponent's numbers were whittled down by evasion and attrition, as opposed to direct confrontation. Third, Morrow was forced to leave 'penny-packet' detachments to protect specific locations from the Apaches. While dismounted cavalrymen and infantry could perform this duty perfectly well, they became, of necessity, static combatants. Thus, Morrow left Captain Dawson in charge of his base camp at McEvers' Ranch. A further 12 dismounted troopers had been left

5 Loud to Pope, 22 October 1879, Telegrams Sent DoNM, Vol.2, Jan.–Dec. 1879, NA, RG393, Part 3, Entry 431, p.353.

6 Pope to Sheridan & Sheridan to Sherman, 24 October 1879, 'Victorio Papers', NA, M666, Roll 526.

to guard Chase's Ranch 'on the Animas.'[7] Some of the dismounted men who had returned to Fort Bayard, and some infantry, had been sent out to provide picket posts at Knight's Ranch, Burro Springs, Hot Springs and Mason's Ranch.[8] Unless these guard details dropped their guard and become an easy target, any Apaches in the area would simply avoid them. Unfortunately, the local press was quick to condemn any perceived army inactivity.

Thus, on paper, while Morrow had the numbers to prevail, the Apache response to these odds, which was to use the vast range of their home territory to evade their foes, simply negated any advantage in numbers possessed by the US army.

Into Mexico

From the Tres Hermanas Mountains, the command moved south to Palomas Lake,[9] five miles inside Mexico. Morrow established a base camp and sent Gatewood, with his scouts, on to the Corralitos River. Here the scouts spent the day reconnoitring to the east, but again found no sign of Apaches.[10] The earlier miscalculation of the mileage between McEvers' and Lloyd's Ranches, which had forced Gatewood's detachment to abandon the trail near the Goodsight Mountains, had allowed Victorio to evade his pursuers. It had been assumed that the Apaches were making for the Florida Mountains and it was now plain that they had not done so. Morrow was once again faced with the possibility that Victorio might have doubled back into New Mexico. However, it was Morrow himself who discovered the first sign of their quarry. On or around 23 October, from his camp at Palomas Lake, he spotted smoke in the nearby Potrillo Mountains.[11] The Potrillo Mountains are situated to the east of the Florida Mountains, but are still just within the United States. Gatewood makes it quite clear that the Potrillo Mountains were 'an extension of the Good Sight' Mountains.[12] If one examines Map 9.1, this is not strictly true; but the Potrillos offered Victorio just as likely a route into Mexico as the Florida Mountains. Indeed, in late 1881, a well-defended watering hole was discovered hidden in the Goodsight Mountains, about three miles south of the stage road which ran through these mountains:

> after winding around the canon's, whose general direction is east for about three miles & entered a box canon with perpendicular rock walls, about 60-80 feet high, which at a point about one hundred yards up it becomes seemingly impassable at this point, I found four rock water tanks with enough water for four companies for two or three days. I should judge this Canon is only about 2 yards wide at this point, ascending almost perpendicularly near these water tanks, I found the tops on both sides strongly fortified.[13]

7 Morrow to Loud via Bayard, 18 October 1879, NA, RG393, Part 3, Entry 439, pp.295-296.
8 Loud to Pope, 24 October 1879, Telegrams Sent DoNM, Vol.2, Jan.–Dec. 1879, NA, RG393, Part 3, Entry 431, p.361.
9 Rasch states that Palomas Lake is 12 miles south of Columbus. (1960, p.9) On modern maps the Laguna would appear to be approximately ten to fifteen kilometres south of Columbus. See NH 13-1 – El Paso (USGS) & H13-1 – Cuidad Juarez (INEGI).
10 'Gatewood's Report 1879', NA, RG393, Part 1, Entry 240; See also Morrow to AAAG DoNM, 5 November 1879, 'Victorio Papers', NA, M666, Roll 526; Thrapp, 1974, p.248; This estimate seems to be broadly accurate the author having passed Palomas Lake in Sept. 2005.
11 Morrow to AAAG DoNM, 5 November 1879, 'Victorio Papers', NA, M666, Roll 526; Thrapp, 1974, p.248.
12 'Gatewood's Report 1879', NA, RG393, Part 1, Entry 240.
13 McDonald to Post Adjutant, Fort Cummings, 25 December 1881 in Reports of Scouts, Nov 2nd 1880 to Aug 1st 1882 HQ Records of Fort Cummings, New Mexico, 1863-1873 & 1880-1884, NA, RG393, M1081, Roll 8.

Victorio had probably made for this point in the Goodsight Mountains, after the attacks on Lloyd's Ranch, El Colorado and the area near Mason's Ranch, before moving on to the Potrillo Mountains. If Gatewood had had enough supplies, this camp in the Goodsight Mountains might have been discovered two years earlier. A hidden campsite, it would play an important role in Victorio's activities in January 1880 (see Chapter One – Victorio Campaign 1880).[14]

Morrow immediately sent gallopers ahead to Gatewood's scouts to direct them east to the Potrillo Mountains. The latter returned to Palomas Lake on 25 October, to report that their subsequent search of the Potrillos had shown no trace of the Apaches.[15] However, Morrow was convinced of his sighting, and he moved his battalion into the mountains later that same day.[16] A deserted four-day-old camp was discovered; and on 26 October, they stumbled across a second camp, three miles from the first.[17] The trail of the Apaches was discovered leading southwards towards the Guzman Mountains;[18] but an immediate problem facing Morrow was the general lack of water in the Potrillo Mountains. Gatewood noted that there was no sure supply of water for 75 miles south of the Goodsight Mountains 'except what may accumulate in holes from rains & these tanks do not last long.'[19] The Apaches had clearly used up what water was available before moving on.

Morrow's decision to pursue Victorio into Mexico was a bold move for several reasons. Apart from the obvious shortage of water and the political ramifications for both republics, he was also isolating himself and his command by losing contact with the Military District of New Mexico. Captain Beyer, at Fort Bayard, contacted District Headquarters asking for any information they might have regarding the whereabouts of Morrow's battalion. Beyer wanted to try to establish a courier service between Fort Bayard and Major Morrow. However, he also stated that even if such a link was established, it would be less than reliable as there were no 'public horses at this post able to carry riders over 20 miles a day.'[20]

Lieutenant Gatewood left a vivid[21] account (see document file no. 21), written over a decade after the event, of the killing heat and lack of water that affected Morrow's command as they trudged over the desert towards the Guzman Mountains. Several horses and mules had to be shot as they succumbed to the heat and thirst. The Apaches had also made every effort to hinder their progress by muddying the first waterhole and poisoning a large natural tank of water by dumping a disembowelled coyote in it. The Apache scouts discovered several sites where the Apaches had deployed ready for an ambush, before moving on when their pursuers failed to materialise. The command

14 This refers to the first chapter of volume two of this history of the Victorio Campaign.
15 Morrow to AAAG DoNM, 5 November 1879, 'Victorio Papers', NA, M666, Roll 526.
16 Morrow to AAAG DoNM, 5 November 1879, 'Victorio Papers', NA, M666, Roll 526.
Morrow's conviction may have been reinforced if Captain Beyer at Ft Bayard had managed to transmit Lt Howard's news that no signs of Apaches moving north had been discovered. This news had been received on the 24 October 1879. This also has to be balanced with the fact that Beyer had also reported that he did not have a clear idea as to Morrow's exact location nor were there any horses left at Ft Bayard fit to perform effective courier duties.
17 Morrow to AAAG DoNM, 5 November 1879, 'Victorio Papers', NA, M666, Roll 526; Thrapp, 1974, p.248.
18 'Gatewood's Report 1879', NA, RG393, Part 1, Entry 240; Morrow to AAAG DoNM, 5 November 1879, 'Victorio Papers', NA, M666, Roll 526.
19 'Gatewood's Report 1879', NA, RG393, Part 1, Entry 240.
20 Beyer to AAAG SF, 24 October 1879, NA, RG393, Part 3, Entry 439, p.287.
21 This is in marked contrast to his original field report where he sums up the march as "a long march over a sandy country." ('Gatewood's Report 1879', NA, RG393, Part 1, Entry 240.)
For another account of the geographical conditions facing a scouting expedition in the American Southwest see Remington's description of his trip with the Tenth Cavalry in the late 1880s (See Remington, 1888/1889, particularly p.907).

Plate 11.1 The Florida Mountains. Gatewood's Apache scouts searched these mountains as they reconnoitred southwards in search of Victorio. (Photo: author)

Plate 11.2 Gatewood's scouts then moved on to the Tres Hermanas Mountains near the Mexican Border. (Photo: author)

Plate 11.3 The terrain around Palomas Lake. The lake is visible as a thin strip below the horizon at the top left of this photo. (Photo: author)

Plate 11.4 The Potrillo Mountains, on the far horizon, from the region to the south of Palomas Lake. It was from his camp near the lake that Morrow spotted smoke in these distant mountains and thus managed to re-locate the trail left by the Apaches. (Photo: author)

Plate 11.5 One reason that Victorio chose to enter Mexico via the Potrillo Mountains in mid-October 1879, instead of via the Florida Mountains, may have been the temporary availability of water in small lakes known as 'playas'. The author encountered several such playas on 6 October 2015, when visiting the Potrillo Mountains. The presence of semi-aquatic plants suggests that, though temporary, these lakes fill regularly enough to support such vegetation, and that the Apaches would have known these cycles. Most importantly, the Apaches had used up most of the water and moved on by the time the soldiers arrived in the area. (Photo: author)

Plate 11.6 The perspective looking southwest into Mexico from the southern edge of the western Potrillo Mountains. Morrow's detachment was already short of water when confronted with a 25-30-mile march across this desert to the next range of mountains in Northern Chihuahua in pursuit of Victorio. (Photo: author)

was thus very much on its guard when it drew near to the Guzman Mountains.[22] Lieutenant Walter L. Finley noted the usual cheerful endurance of the Ninth Cavalry on this march,[23] though he did note, in terms that would come across today as, at best, paternalistic, that he had heard some grumbling over food that was quickly countered by one of the sergeants:

> he yelled out, "you niggers shut up. Dahs dey ain't one ob you ever had a square meal in your life befo you come into de army an' you knows it."[24]

Towards the end of 27 October, dust had been spotted in some foothills by the scouts, and Gatewood estimated that they had caught up with their quarry.[25] Morrow did not identify the foothills as belonging to the Guzman Mountains,[26] though looking at Map 9.1 we can see that they were either the Cerros Bayos or the Sierra San Blas to the east of the Laguna de Guzman. Morrow sent his Apache scouts ahead to check the ground, but waited until dusk before attempting to move the rest of his force to the mountains. As they neared their objective, his scouts returned and warned Morrow that they had detected an ambush laid along two sets of converging ridges.[27] Victorio and Juh obviously intended to catch the US force between them in a deadly crossfire. Morrow clearly described the ambush site as a canyon,[28] yet Gatewood's account suggested that the left-hand ridge, from Morrow's point of view, was an outlier of the Guzman Range, whereas the right-hand ridge appeared to be higher and deeper in the mountains.

Moonlit Battle in the Guzman Mountains, 27-28 October 1879

As night fell, Morrow attempted to move into a flanking position by wheeling his battalion to the left.[29] His original plan was to launch a surprise flanking attack on the Apaches, on foot, the next morning, sending out his scouts again to discover the Apache positions in detail. Unfortunately, the thirsty horses and mules made such a din that this manoeuvre was spotted by the Apaches.[30] Morrow claimed that almost half his troopers were left behind to guard the horses and mules. In effect, he was attacking between 60 and possibly as many as 120 Apache warriors with 18 Apache scouts and approximately 40 troopers.[31]

At first glance, the assault may appear foolhardy; yet Major Morrow was taking a calculated risk which, in the event, partially succeeded. An experienced officer such as Morrow would have been aware that Apache warriors were reluctant night fighters. Also, Gatewood was certainly aware that the Apaches were unlikely to engage in set-piece hand-to-hand encounters. The calculated risk was to put on a bold front and take the battle to the Apaches. If the Apaches were placed in a situation

22 Gatewood, 1894, p.103; See also Lt. Finley, Letter dated Fort Bayard, 4 November 1879, in The Walter Lowry Finley Collection.
23 Lt. Finley, Letter dated Fort Bayard, 11 November 1879 in The Walter Lowry Finley Collection.
24 Ibid.
25 'Gatewood's Report 1879', NA, RG393, Part 1, Entry 240; Gatewood, 1894, p.103.
26 Morrow to AAAG DoNM, 5 November 1879, 'Victorio Papers', NA, M666, Roll 526; Thrapp tentatively suggests that Gatewood may have been mistaken as to the location of the battle. Based upon Gatewood's own estimation of the distances travelled, the battle may have taken place in the Cerros de la Cal, approximately 20 miles to the north of Janos (Thrapp, 1974, p.364 Note 46).
27 Morrow to AAAG DoNM, 5 November 1879, 'Victorio Papers', NA, M666, Roll 526.
28 Morrow to AAAG DoNM, 5 November 1879, 'Victorio Papers', NA, M666, Roll 526.
29 Morrow to AAAG DoNM, 5 November 1879, 'Victorio Papers', NA, M666, Roll 526; Thrapp, 1974, p.249.
30 Morrow to AAAG DoNM, 5 November 1879, 'Victorio Papers', NA, M666, Roll 526; Thrapp, 1974, p.249; Utley, 1984ii, p.48.
31 Morrow to AAAG DoNM, 5 November 1879, 'Victorio Papers', NA, M666, Roll 526.

Gatewood's pack mule train. Listed as taken in 1880 this is an interesting photograph given the second-hand information given by Lt Cruse to Gatewood's son concerning two white mules during the moonlit battle in northern Mexico on 27/28 October, 1879. (The National Archives)

where they felt that fatalities would be incurred, unless they were cornered, they would retreat. Nevertheless, if the Apaches felt secure and stood their ground, an assault could become untenable, potentially making the attackers vulnerable to heavy casualties.

Under a bright moon, the attack was launched. The scouts and cavalrymen were, in effect, attacking from the opposite direction from that intended by Victorio and Juh. The Apache warriors turned around and opened fire, but swiftly withdrew to the opposite ridge. They were driven off this second ridge, and withdrew to a higher ridge.[32] Here their fortune changed, as the US detachment now launched a frontal assault on prepared Apaches who had clear targets in the bright moonlight.[33] A prodigious fire was directed against the attackers (see document files nos. 21 and 15).

> the moment our Indians reached the crest of the first hill they were fired upon. I immediately advanced with the Command leaving a sufficient guard for the Horses. We had no trouble in dislodging the enemy from the two hills which they then occupied, as we took them in rear and their Breastworks were made to face the trail which led through the Canon. They leaped over the works, across the Canon trail, and into the works on the opposite hills. We kept up a lively fire and followed at a run until we commenced to ascend the hills upon which they

32 'Gatewood's Report 1879', NA, RG393, Part 1, Entry 240; Morrow notes that they dislodged the Apaches from two hills and gives the impression that the Apaches withdrew from one ridge and occupied and defended the other ridge. (Morrow to AAAG DoNM, 5 November 1879, 'Victorio Papers', NA, M666, Roll 526.)

33 Lt. Finley, Letter dated Fort Bayard, 4 November 1879 in The Walter Lowry Finley Collection; Morrow to AAAG DoNM, 5 November 1879, 'Victorio Papers', NA, M666, Roll 526; Gatewood, 1894, pp.103-104.

West Point Class of 1877 as noted in the photo taken in 1879. In this group there are four cadets who would be destined to lead Apache scout companies against Victorio in 1879 and 1880. Charles B. Gatewood, Robert T. Emmet, Augustus P. Blocksom, and Stephen C. Mills. A fifth member of this group Matthias W. Day, along with Emmet would ultimately be awarded Medals of Honor for gallantry in Las Animas Canyon on 18 September 1879. (Photo courtesy of U.S. Army Military History Institute, RG126S-W.C. Brown Coll. 169)

were fortified and in strong force, where we had to take it slowly owing to the difficulty of climbing.[34]

The assault was suddenly stalled when the attackers encountered a 20 foot cliff blocking their ascent that had been hidden in the shadows cast by the moonlight.[35] According to Morrow, the Apache fire was largely aimed too high, only killing one scout and wounding two others.[36] Gatewood described the ridgeline above him as being marked out by the continuous muzzle flashes of the Apaches' Winchester rifles, which were met with the answering flashes of the Apache scouts and soldier's Springfields, and he described the noise as a 'continuous roar.'[37] Morrow sent Gatewood and some scouts to the right in an attempt to flank this position. Though they worked their way to within approximately 10 yards of some of the Apache positions, Gatewood and his scouts found themselves pinned down by heavy gunfire. They also had to avoid large rocks rolled down at them from above.[38]

As the Apaches started to close in on Gatewood's advance party, the latter had to keep up a rapid fire and move from cover to cover to give a false impression of the size of the advance party.[39] Gatewood was expecting a detachment of Sixth Cavalry troopers led by Captain Campbell to follow up the advance, the Ninth Cavalrymen having borne the brunt of the earlier fighting.[40] However, for reasons unknown, the Sixth cavalrymen were moved into position further out to the left of Gatewood's position. Captain Campbell was to subsequently claim he had advanced to the spot indicated to him.[41] Gatewood was utterly unimpressed with this excuse and noted that Captain Campbell had 'since resigned.'[42] In the meantime, the Apaches infiltrated around Gatewood until he was in danger of being cut off, at which point the detachment was ordered to retreat.[43] They were also running dangerously low on ammunition.[44]

34 Morrow to AAAG DoNM, 5 November 1879, 'Victorio Papers', NA, M666, Roll 526; Thrapp, 1973, p.14.
35 Gatewood, 1894, pp.103-104; Thrapp, 1974, p.250; Kenner, 1999, p.196.
36 Morrow to AAAG DoNM, 5 November 1879, 'Victorio Papers', NA, M666, Roll 526; Thrapp, 1973, p.14; See also 'Gatewood's Report 1879', NA, RG393, Part 1, Entry 240; Thrapp, 1974, pp.249-250; Record of Engagements, p.92; See also Report of E.A. Carr, 29 Aug 1880; Billington, 1991, p.92.
37 Gatewood, 1894 pp.103-104.
38 Morrow to AAAG DoNM, 5 November 1879, 'Victorio Papers', NA, M666, Roll 526; Thrapp, 1973, p.14; See also 'Gatewood's Report 1879', NA, RG393, Part 1, Entry 240; Thrapp, 1974, pp.249-250; Record of Engagements, p.92; See also Report of E.A. Carr, 29 Aug 1880; Billington, 1991, p.92.
39 Gatewood, p.104.
40 Gatewood, p.104.
41 Gatewood, p.104.
42 Gatewood, p.104; Thrapp, 1974, p.366 Note 48; Various papers in NA, RG393 Part 1, Entry 204 Miscellaneous Records, Department of Arizona 1879-80 state that on 17 and 18 September, 1880, Captain Charles H. Campbell was found to be drunk at Fort Bowie prior to departing with a battalion of Sixth Cavalry for service with General Buell's expedition against Victorio (See Chapter 28 in volume two of this history of the Victorio Campaign) He was even accused of absenting himself from parade in order that he could partake of a bottle of liquor behind the officers quarters. He was drunk throughout the first day's march to the extent that he was seen "swaying" in his saddle. He remained intoxicated when in camp that night to the extent that he was found to be "puking" (subsequently changed to "vomiting" on the charge record) in Lt. Touey's tent. When finally sent back to Fort Bowie under arrest on 20 September, he remained drunk and gave his guards "much trouble to take care of him." He resigned his commission on 15 February, 1881. Thrapp hints that Campbell's alcoholism may have influenced his actions during the battle. (Thrapp, 1988, p.215 & p.565.)
43 Gatewood, p.104.
44 Morrow to AAAG DoNM, 5 November 1879, 'Victorio Papers', NA, M666, Roll 526; Thrapp, 1973, p.14; See also 'Gatewood's Report 1879', NA, RG393, Part 1, Entry 240; Thrapp, 1974, pp.249-250; Record of Engagements, p.92; See also Report of E.A. Carr, 29 Aug 1880; Billington, 1991, p.92.

Morrow simply did not have the numbers to force Victorio's position, and in the early hours of the morning he ordered his men to withdraw.[45] Gatewood noted that the initial disengagement was accomplished by withdrawing behind a ridge.[46] This is likely to have been the ridge assaulted and cleared of Apaches in the first stage of the attack. As the fighting died down and the US troops regrouped, an Apache, said to be Victorio himself, accompanied by a single drum, sang out, apparently encouraging the Apache scouts to desert and turn on the hated pony soldiers.[47]

During the fight, the Apaches had enough men to detach a force directed by Nana, and these men launched an attack on the troops guarding the horses and mules. Lieutenant Cruse makes passing reference to a fight near Guzman Lake, south of the border, stating that Nana's flanking movement managed to net two or three mules packed with bedding and Gatewood's own personal mount, but failed to garner any ammunition.[48] In a letter to Gatewood's son, Cruse gave a much more detailed account, in which he claimed that 'Cherko', the white mule carrying the cooking utensils, and another white mule that carried the ammunition, were central to thwarting Nana's attempt to run off Morrow's mule train:

> It was at night when the Indian Scouts struck Vic after a hard march from the Tres Hermanos. Vic let the 9th Cav. And Scouts get committed to the frontal attack, to reach water, and then sent Nana with six or eight men clear around the flank to jump the pack train and get the ammunition mule if possible. But the Mexican cook-Old Tom-had dismounted from the Bell Mare, and the ammunition mule, as always, was right by her. Of course when they opened in the darkness things became mixed, and I have heard your father (Lt. Gatewood) say many times afterwards that the occasion was one when he had a feeling of "goneness" and felt uncomfortable. He knew Vic was after the ammunition; and if he got it, the hunted became the hunter at once. The packers and men of the herd guard put up a swift fight, but the hostiles got away with three or four pack mules with their loads and incidentally with your father's horse, "Bob"… In the meantime the ammunition mule had maintained his proper post right next to the Bell mare, and as she didn't move, neither did he; and your father and Col. Morrow breathed freely once more.[49]

45 Morrow to AAAG DoNM, 5 November 1879, 'Victorio Papers', NA, M666, Roll 526; Thrapp, 1973, p.14; See also 'Gatewood's Report 1879', NA, RG393, Part 1, Entry 240; Thrapp, 1974, pp.249-250; Record of Engagements, p.92; See also Report of E.A. Carr, 29 Aug 1880; Billington, 1991, p.92.

46 Gatewood, p.104; Thrapp, 1967, p.188.

47 Thrapp, 1974, p.250; Roberts, p.181.

48 Cruse, 1987, p.56.

49 Cruse, 1987, Letter to Gatewood, 26 March 1926 cited in Laumbach, p.118; there are times when Cruse gets the dating of events wrong. For example he dates the finale of Nana's raid of 1881, an ambush in Gavilan Canyon, in which an officer and three troopers were among those slain, to February 1880. However, this passing remark has a ring of truth about it. Cruse served with Gatewood for several months in 1880 and must have got to know him well. The only battle in which Gatewood participated in south of the border in this period was this very engagement in October 1879. Kraft states that Gatewood lost some horses including Lt Gatewood's personal mount. He apparently went as far as to request $125 from the U.S. Government in compensation for his loss but his claim was rejected. (pp.26-27) The reason for this may have been related to a Court of Claims judgement that claims made against Indians would not stand if a particular grouping within the tribe was at war with the United States. (Skogen, pp.145-147) Thus the attacks by Victorio's warriors would not leave the Chiricahua's in general, liable for subsequent compensation claims. It has to be noted that these legal decisions were ratified by the Supreme Court in 1901. However, a genuine act of war may have been the reason for rejecting Gatewood's claim upon the US government.

This makes a stirring story, but given Nana's power to commandeer ammunition, the storyteller appears particularly anxious to emphasise that no ammunition was lost, which makes one wonder whether some ammunition was taken by the Apaches. Morrow may have left fewer guards than was usual in charge of his horses and mules because of the number of Apaches facing him. Once the troops and Apache scouts were fully committed to the assault on the ridge, his opponents were given the opportunity to detach some of their number to attack the major's horses and mules.

Victorio, Nana and Juh had chosen their ground with care. They had been given the time to organize an ambush, and took up positions that would enable them to fire down on their pursuers, catching them in a deadly crossfire without creating a situation in which their fire risked hitting Apache warriors on the opposite ridge. Moreover, it was the Apaches' calculation of the risk involved which ultimately led to success. It was the combination of drawing Morrow into a long pursuit, over difficult terrain, plus the selection of a strong, even impregnable, fall-back position when Victorio eventually decided to ambush his pursuers that won the battle. Gatewood came to a very similar conclusion, arguing that a combination of the good position occupied by the Apaches and the lack of water and exhaustion among Morrow's command accounted for their withdrawal.[50] During the battle some of the troopers were so tired that they fell asleep during the fighting and had to be woken by their officers.[51]

There may have been gallant conduct on the part of the battalion; but while citations for gallantry can be used to reward victory, they can also be used to disguise defeat. Major Morrow's battalion had spent five weeks in a pursuit of Victorio that had ended in failure many miles inside Mexico. It was now in the early hours of 28 October, and the troops had been in action from 7 p.m. until approximately 1 a.m.[52] Morrow, with an exhausted and thirsty command that had no permission to be where it was, faced by an entrenched enemy who had plentiful ammunition and who, at this stage, may have outnumbered the US force, withdrew in search of desperately-needed water.[53] The retreat was covered by a rearguard action commanded by Lieutenant Day.[54] After participating in the first charge, Day had been ordered to gather up the sick, wounded and stragglers and established a position on a hill above their picket lines to the rear.[55]

The fact that Morrow had fought the Apaches in Mexico without the permission of the Mexican authorities was another good reason for this retreat. It was not simply that this battle had occurred in Mexico; it was the fact that the US troops had failed to visit defeat on Victorio. While a victory against a common enemy might be easily tolerated, a defeat, if it became common knowledge, could present the Mexican federal authorities with domestic political difficulties. This could translate into diplomatic issues between the US and Mexico. It was now expedient for the major to lead his battalion, whether fit for action, or not, back into US territory.

In the immediate aftermath of the fight, Gatewood clearly acknowledged one scout killed and one wounded.[56] He later recalled 'several soldiers killed and six or seven wounded',[57] but he made no mention of such casualties in his original report.[58] Captain Adam Kramer, Sixth Cavalry, reported

50 Gatewood, p.104.
51 Gatewood, p.104.
52 Record of Events October 1879 in Returns From Regular Army Cavalry Regiments 1833-1916, 6th Cavalry Regimental Returns 1875 to 1880, NA, M744, Roll 63.
53 'Gatewood's Report 1879', NA, RG393, Part 1, Entry 240.
54 Personal File Matthias W. Day, NA, RG94, Entry 297, Box 1.
55 Personal File Matthias W. Day, NA, RG94, Entry 297, Box 1.
56 'Gatewood's Report 1879', NA, RG393, Part 1, Entry 240; See Carr to AG Dept. Arizona, 11 November 1879, Troops in Southeastern Arizona, DoAz, NA, RG393, Part 1, Entry 232, Vol.4, 3 July, 1879–Dec. 13 1879, Letter No.227, pp.151-152.
57 Gatewood, p.104; Thrapp, 1974, p.250; see also O'Neal, p.177.
58 'Gatewood's Report 1879', NA, RG393, Part 1, Entry 240.

that he could not be sure of the casualties sustained by the corporal and 11 enlisted men of E Company who had been attached to Gatewood's Apache scout company since September 8 1879, by reason of 'the Officer in Command[59] not belonging to the company and he not furnishing the Company Commander any data.'[60] Morrow claimed to have lost two killed and two wounded.[61] The 'Tabular Statement of Expeditions and Scouts sent out from Posts in the District of New Mexico against Hostile Indians during the Fourth Quarter ending December 31st, 1879' stated that one Apache scout was killed and two scouts were wounded.[62] A telegram from Colonel Carr hints at the possibility that two soldiers from the Sixth Cavalry were killed. '[H]e [Morrow] says he had two men killed and two wounded[63] in his fight on 27th Thus almost all the losses are from our troops.'[64] Private Reinhold Cochlovins, A Company, Sixth Cavalry, was listed as killed in action.[65] 'On October 26 and 27, at Grozman Mountain, an Apache scout was wounded. Another Apache scout and a private of Company A, Sixth Cavalry, reported missing by Acting Assist. Surg. William M. Handy, are supposed to have been killed.'[66] Cochlovins' body was not found until the following year, when an Apache scout company visited the battlefield as part of the Buell Expedition into Mexico in September and October 1880.[67]

Gatewood estimated that the battalion had faced approximately 150 warriors, including 'renegade' Mescaleros, Lipan Apaches, Navajos and Comanches.[68] Thrapp suggests that it was much more likely to be a combination of Victorio's Chihennes and Juh's Southern Chiricahuas,[69] plus no more than one or two, if any at all, from each of the above tribes. Morrow was convinced that Victorio had been heavily reinforced by both Mescalero and Southern Chiricahua Apaches and stated that:

> Victorio's force consists of his own people and Nanas band about 40 warriors well armed with breech loaders and plenty of ammunition during his retreat to Mexico he was joined by about the same number of Mescalero Apaches and just before I struck him on the night of the 27th

59 It is not clear whether Kramer was referring to Gatewood or Campbell.

60 Tabular Statement of Scouts and Expeditions of Company "E" 6th Cavalry during the 4th Quarter 1879, NA, RG393, Part 1, Entry 240.

Being very familiar with the Bi-Monthly returns company officers were supposed to complete, this statement does not reflect particularly well upon Captain Kramer, suggesting he was less than efficient in maintaining his own company records in the first place.

61 Loud to Hatch, 3 November 1879, Telegrams Sent DoNM, Vol.2, Jan.–Dec. 1879, NA, RG393, Part 3, Entry 431, p.393; See also web article The Ninth Regiment of Cavalry by Lt G. Hutcheson.

62 See in Letters Received, DoM 1868-98, RG 393, Entry A1-1 2601, Box 90.

63 The *Grant County Herald* notes that Major Morrow lost two killed and two wounded in action in Mexico ('Ashenfelter Editorial', *Grant County Herald*, 8 November 1879).

64 Carr to Adjt Gen'l Whipple Barracks A.T. undated telegram, NA, RG393, Part 1, Entry 240.

65 Carr to AG Dept. Arizona, 11 November 1879, Troops in Southeastern Arizona, DoAz, NA, RG393, Part 1, Entry 232, Vol.4, 3 July, 1879–Dec. 13 1879, Letter No.227, pp.151-152; 'Fighting on Mexican Soil' *Army & Navy Journal,* Vol.17, 15 November 1879, p.278; Tabular Statement of Scouts and Expeditions of Companies 6th Cavalry from July 1st 1879 to July 31st 1880, NA, RG393, Part 1, Entry 240; Record of Events October 1879 in Returns From Regular Army Cavalry Regiments 1833-1916, 6th Cavalry Regimental Returns 1875 to 1880, NA, M744, Roll 63.

66 Report of The Surgeon General in AR-WD 1880: NA, M997, Roll 35, 1880 Vol. I, p.520.

67 Lt. Stephen C. Mills Report to AAAG Troops in the Field in S.E. Arizona, 11 October 1880 in Reports & Tabular Statements of Scouting Expeditions 1867-91, NA, RG391, Entry 841.

68 Gatewood, p.104; Thrapp, 1974, p.250.

69 Thrapp, 1973, pp.13-15.

> ult. Was re-inforced by about one hundred Indians apparently Hooes band of Chirichuca from the Sierra Madre.[70]

Finally, as noted in chapter 2, the Apaches were very reluctant to fight at night, and their success in holding off the army in such a fierce night skirmish was very unusual, and should be ascribed to the exceptional leadership of both Victorio and Juh.

The desperately needed water turned out to be almost 12 miles away, at a source which Morrow identified as the Corralitos River.[71] This was reached at 5 a.m., much to the relief of both the men and the surviving horses and mules. Morrow had intended to return to the attack, but on inspection of his men and horses, concluded that a combination of exhausted men and animals and a shortage of ammunition precluded such an option.[72] He then drew a rather surprising conclusion:

> I knew it would take a whole days hard fighting to dislodge him from his present position and then we would have to repeat the operation indefinitely suffering loss all the time, whilst we were inflicting none. I had accomplished my object so far as the means at my disposal would permit, had punished Victorio severely and had driven him from the Country which he declared he would never leave.[73]

Morrow and his battalion had certainly maintained a dogged pursuit of Victorio; but the notion that his campaign between 23 September and 28 October had driven Victorio out of the territory he laid claim to is nonsense. It should also be noted that the Chihenne Apaches had not actually been driven from what they viewed as their country. They had merely moved into the southern segment of, as Lekson puts it, their 'subsistence range in northern Chihuahua.'[74]

Morrow's claim that the Apaches had been heavily damaged after his campaign also seems somewhat over-optimistic.[75] Colonel Carr expressed himself somewhat sceptical of Morrow's claims, arguing that Victorio was more likely to be basking in the glow of his recent successes.[76] The claim to have inflicted severe punishment on the Apaches is simply not sustainable. If Victorio had sustained heavy losses, he would almost certainly have lost his position of leadership among the Chihenne Apaches. Almost a year later, General Pope praised Morrow's efforts and claimed that their lack of success was 'due to the utter desolation of the country, and not to the prowess of the Indians.'[77] This completely failed to appreciate that one of Victorio's primary weapons was the use of that very desolation to wear down his pursuers. Moreover, whilst Morrow's pursuit was dogged and determined, one cannot shake off the strong suspicion that this resolve merely suited Victorio's

---

70 Morrow, Bayard to Carr, Grant, 5 November 1879 (October is stated in the original telegram but this is a mistake.) NA, RG393, Part 1, Entry 235, p.24.

71 Morrow to AAAG DoNM, 5 November 1879, 'Victorio Papers', NA, M666, Roll 526.
Thrapp suggests this to be the Casas Grandes River (Thrapp, 1974, p.366 Note 46) Utley states that the engagement occurred near the Corralitos River. (Utley, 1973, p.360; See also Leckie, 1967, p.212) This merely helps to clarify the position as the river, which passes near the settlement of Corralitos, is, in fact, the Casas Grandes River.

72 Morrow to AAAG DoNM, 5 November 1879, 'Victorio Papers', NA, M666, Roll 526.

73 Morrow to AAAG DoNM, 5 November 1879, 'Victorio Papers', NA, M666, Roll 526.

74 See Lekson, S.H., (1992,) 'Warm Spring Apache Subsistence', Crow Canyon Archaeological Center. Unpublished manuscript in the author's possession.

75 Morrow, Bayard to Carr, Grant, 5 November 1879 (October is stated in the original telegram but this is a mistake.) NA, RG393, Part 1, Entry 235, p.24.

76 Carr to AG Dept Arizona, 6 November 1879, Troops in Southeastern Arizona, DoAz, NA, RG393, Part 1, Entry 232, Vol.4, 3 July, 1879–Dec. 13 1879, Letter No.229, pp.156-157.

77 Report of General John Pope, 22 September 1880 in AR-WD: NA, M997, Roll 35, 1880 Vol. I-II, p.86.

purposes. After all, the end result was the complete exhaustion of the majority of the Ninth cavalry companies deployed against the Apaches in September and October 1879.

Major Morrow's force returned to Palomas Lake by 30 October. The following day, Gatewood and Campbell's commands were sent to Fort Cummings, while Morrow proceeded towards Bayard, arriving at that post on 2 November. Those troops sent via Fort Cummings arrived at Fort Bayard the following day.[78] The army would endure much media criticism during the Victorio Campaign. Yet, on balance, faced with incredibly rough terrain and Apache warriors armed with an intimate knowledge of this, as well as with modern weaponry, the Ninth Cavalry and other army detachments had managed to keep on Victorio's trail. As noted above, this may well have played directly into their opponent's hands; but the physical endurance displayed by the US troops should also not be dismissed. Much of this was thanks to their Apache scouts.[79] Morrow gave full credit to the Apache scouts,[80] under Lieutenants Gatewood and Blocksom, for their role in driving Victorio and his warriors from the USA.[81] He even went so far as to predict that Victorio would avoid Arizona in the future, as he 'fears your San Carlos Indians.'[82] He seemed convinced that Victorio had been so severely dealt with that he would not be able 'to raid anywhere for the next two months.'[83] Events in Mexico would soon prove that prediction to be completely wrong.

While the media had previously been highly critical of Morrow, on his return to Fort Bayard, the major found himself suddenly rehabilitated in the eyes of the *Grant County Herald* as the 'right man in the right place,'[84] though *Thirty-Four* was initially quick to point out that the major had been defeated by Victorio and Juh 50 miles below the border.[85] The paper later retracted its criticism of Morrow, after an interview with Lieutenant Schaeffer. Schaeffer claimed that troops had fought and beaten the Apaches on 23,[86] 29 and 30[87] September. The same newspaper initially dismissed the Ninth Cavalry as obviously unfit to fight Indians, claiming they had been defeated in every skirmish. If more troops were to be sent, they should be white troops led by competent officers of the calibre of 'Crook and McKenzie and Custer.'[88] After the interview with Schaeffer, the paper still expressed a sceptical attitude towards the Ninth Cavalry, arguing that 1,000 white troops would quickly deal with the Apaches. In a grudging article, it was argued that 'the African race is lacking in that best substitute for bravery – Pride' but the article concluded: 'we have neither a disposition to underrate them nor give them credit they do not deserve: Give the Ninth another

78 Morrow to AAAG DoNM, 5 November 1879, 'Victorio Papers', NA, M666, Roll 526; Thrapp, 1974, p.251; Record of Engagements, p.92; Haley, 1981, p.323; Wellman, 1957, p.154; Longstreet, p.91.

79 A fact that Morrow explicitly acknowledged. (Morrow to AAAG DoNM, 5 November 1879, 'Victorio Papers', NA, M666, Roll 526.)

80 Surgeon MacPherson reported that on their return to San Carlos, the Apaches scouts had a tiswin drinking session at which a fight broke out and some were killed. (Letter 9 December 1879 in MacPherson Letters 1st Jan 1879 to 3rd Sept. 1880, University of Virginia at Charlottesville.)

81 Morrow to AAAG DoNM, 5 November 1879, 'Victorio Papers', NA, M666, Roll 526; Willcox to AG, Presidio, San Francisco, 5 November 1879, NA, RG393, Part 1, Entry 169, Vol. 9, pp.411-412; Se also Carr to AG Dept. Arizona, 11 November 1879, Troops in Southeastern Arizona, DoAz, NA, RG393, Part 1, Entry 232, Vol.4, July 3 1879–Dec. 13 1879, Letter No.227, pp.151-152; Thrapp, 1988, p.128.

82 Morrow, Bayard to Carr, Grant, 5 November 1879, (October stated in original telegram but this is a mistake) NA, RG393, Part 1, Entry 235, p.24.

83 Morrow, Bayard to Carr, Grant, 5 November 1879, (October stated in original telegram but this is a mistake) NA, RG393, Part 1, Entry 235, p.24.

84 'Ashenfelter Editorial', *Grant County Herald*, 8 November 1879.

85 *Thirty-Four*, 5 November 1879.

86 The author has discovered no clear record of any clash between the Army and Apaches on 23 September 1879.

87 *Thirty-Four*, 19 November 1879.

88 *Thirty-Four*, 12 November 1879; the last choice of candidate could be seen, even then, as a somewhat ironic choice.

chance.'[89] The editor of the *Grant County Herald* also fired off a salvo, this time at the citizens of Silver City for failing to provide a single volunteer to fight the Apaches.[90]

However, *Thirty-Four* remained very hostile towards Hatch, claiming that in May and June 1879, Hatch had had the chance to finish off the Apaches, whom he had surrounded in the San Andres Mountains. The paper reached this conclusion on the basis that there were troops in the Caballo Mountains in that period, at Aleman and at Tulerosa, who could easily have finished off the Apaches. By failing to destroy Victorio then, Hatch had given him the breathing space he needed to wage war in September and October. They also accused Hatch of abandoning New Mexico to deal with the Ute War and failing to supply the troops with sufficient ammunition.[91] *Thirty-Four* demanded Hatch's removal[92] and a congressional investigation of his performance as commander of the District of New Mexico.[93] If one is at all familiar with the terrain, one can see that the presence of US troops at three points around the San Andres Mountains did not mean that Victorio was in any way trapped. Moreover, Hatch's departure to fight the Utes in Colorado Territory had been ordered by his superiors. The charges made by *Thirty-Four* were clearly unreasonable, though they do give us a flavour of the sort of hyperbolic attacks Hatch would face in 1880.

To summarise the campaign so far, the army had, between 4 September and 28 October, officially lost 14 soldiers and scouts killed. Dozens of US citizens had also been killed. In return, the army claimed to have killed and wounded Apaches on various occasions, yet could only confirm two dead warriors. Human body counts alone do not give us an accurate picture of the effect of two months' campaigning against Victorio sustained by the Ninth Cavalry. If we examine the casualties amongst the Ninth Cavalry's horses we see that those companies involved in Morrow's direct pursuit of the Apaches, (Companies A, B, C, G, H & L), suffered the majority of the increase in unserviceable horses. Company E lost most of its horses when the horse herd was attacked at Ojo Caliente on 4 September 1879. (See Table 11.3). The only Ninth Cavalry company which suffered major horse fatalities was D Company, which had gone to the relief of US forces trapped by Utes in Colorado and had lost most of their horses in the fighting. Captain Carroll's two companies (F and M), by contrast, had suffered relatively low horse losses, having been on lighter, scouting duties, on which they made no contact with Apaches and were thus not tempted into self-punishing pursuits, and on picket duty during late September and October 1879. Finally, the remaining two companies (I and K), stationed at Fort Wingate, had not been committed to the campaign (see black type). Yet it should be noted that these last two companies were still chronically short of horses to mount available men. As noted before, the Apache tactic of targeting horses was clearly effective; but they were exacerbating an existing difficulty rather than creating the problem in the first place.

89 *Thirty-Four*, 19 November 1879.
90 'Ashenfelter Editorial', *Grant County Herald*, 8 November 1879.
91 *Thirty-Four*, 26 November 1879.
92 *Thirty-Four*, 19 November 1879.
93 *Thirty-Four*, 26 November 1879.

Table 11.3 Serviceable, Unserviceable and Lost Horses to Available Men, Ninth Cavalry, August to November 1879[94]

Company	Month	Serviceable Horses	Unserviceable Horses	Horses Lost	Available Men
A	August	26	5	0	55
	September	12	11	5	59
	October	26	8	0	59
	November	7	18	9	54
B	August	24	3	0	52
	September	19	1	11	57
	October	19	7	0	59
	November	22	8	0	56
C	August	28	4	0	47
	September	39	7	2	59
	October	30	9	7	59
	November	19	16	4	55
D	August	38	5	0	45
	September	39	4	0	57
	October	0	1	42	55
	November	53	2	1	57
E	August	53	3	0	60
	September	11	0	46	55
	October	11	0	0	55
	November	11	0	0	50
F	August	47	0	0	52
	September	47	0	0	54
	October	47	0	0	56
	November	46	1	0	56
G	August	28	4	0	55
	September	37	12	0	57
	October	3	16	8	59
	November	18	11	0	57
H	August	37	7	2	56
	September	37	6	0	60
	October	15	18	10	61
	November	23	10	0	56
I	August	33	6	0	55
	September	33	5	0	51
	October	35	3	0	50
	November	35	3	0	47

94 Derived from Returns From Regular Army Cavalry Regiments 1833-1916, 9th Cavalry 1873-1880, NA, M744, Roll 88.

Company	Month	Serviceable Horses	Unserviceable Horses	Horses Lost	Available Men
K	August	47	3	1	46
	September	45	2	0	57
	October	47	3	0	55
	November	47	3	0	57
L	August	35	6	0	57
	September	31	7	2	56
	October	25	11	2	60
	November	30	6	0	57
M	August	42	3	0	54
	September	43	2	0	52
	October	44	1	0	55
	November	44	1	0	56

It was the Apaches who had, so far, emerged as clear military victors. Whether this success could be translated into a political victory with a return to Ojo Caliente remained to be seen. For the moment, having demonstrated that he could defeat any force sent against him, Victorio and his followers disappeared into Mexico.

12

Ambush in the Candelaria Mountains, November 1879

After repulsing Morrow's pursuit in the Guzman Mountains, Victorio, appears to have camped for a few days in the region of the Lagunas de Guzman and Santa Maria, before moving to the east to camp in the Candelaria Mountains.[1] Here his warriors could rest: the wounded could recuperate, while the fit warriors fanned out into the surrounding countryside in search of food, horses and ammunition by both raiding and trading in Mexican towns. A report was filed by Louis Scott, US Consul in Chihuahua, on 7 November 1879 in which he wrote that he had received 'positive and correct' reports that Juh had been raiding into the United States during October, 'had just returned', and 'had killed a great many white people and some negroes.'[2] He also reported that 'a reliable gentleman informed me today that he had met a Mexican gentleman who had seen and talked with Victoria a few days before at Cases Grandes.'[3] Juh was reported as having recently been seen with his men at Janos, presumably having stopped to trade on his way back to his people in the Sierra Madre. They were said to be both well mounted and armed.[4] Scott warned that a large number of 'renegade' warriors had made peace with the local Mexican authorities. These men would thus be poised to launch raids into the United States.[5] Such a situation was not new: Captain Alexander Moore in 1868 stated that the Apaches had arranged a peace with the northern Mexican town of Janos, and therefore had a market for goods stolen in the United States.[6] However, it was the Mexican inhabitants of Carrizal, Chihuahua, whose experience at the hands of the Chihenne Apaches, would thoroughly disprove Morrow's statement that the latter would be incapable of mounting a another campaign for at least two months.

1 Thrapp, 1973, pp.15-16; Thrapp, 1974, p.257.

2 Scott to W. Hunter, 2nd Asst. Secretary of State, 7 November 1879, NA, RG393, Part 1, Entry 2546, p.264: & in Consular Despatches Chihuahua Mexico 1830-1906, M289 Roll 1; See also Scott to Hunter 28 November 1879 in Evarts, Dept. of State to Alexander Ramsey, Secretary of War, 16 December 1879, 'Victorio Files', NA, RG393, M1495, Roll 14 see same letter in Papers relating to the Frelinghuysen-Romero Agreement of July 29, 1882, providing for reciprocal crossings of the international boundary by troops of the United States and Mexico in pursuit of hostile Indians, Feb. 1862-June 1867(Hereafter referred to 'Frelinghuysen-Romero Papers'), Letters Rec'd by the AGO, 1881-1889. NA, M689, Roll 81.

3 Scott to W. Hunter, 2nd Asst. Secretary of State, 7 November 1879, NA, RG393, Part 1, Entry 2546, p.264 & in Consular Despatches Chihuahua Mexico 1830-1906 M289 Roll 1.

4 *Thirty Four*, 5 November 1879.

5 Scott to W. Hunter, 2nd Asst. Secretary of State, 7 November 1879, NA, RG393, Part 1, Entry 2546, p.264.

6 Capt. Moore, 38th Inf. CO Fort Cummings to Lt. E. Hunter AAAG, DoNM, 27 November 1868 in Letters sent Vol. 3 June 24 1867–Jan 20 1869, HQ Records of Fort Cummings, New Mexico, 1863-1873 & 1880-1884, NA, RG393, M1081, Roll 1, pp.141-145.

Ambush in the Candelaria Mountains, November 1879

Both the background to, and the dates of, Victorio's devastating twin ambushes of Mexican irregulars in the Candelaria Mountains are somewhat obscure. The American version has a small party of warriors running off some horses in the Carrizal area, but does not offer a precise date or an indication of the numbers involved.[7] A party of Carrizal men set off in pursuit.

The Apache version, as told by James Kaywaykla, makes no mention of a provocative horse raid. Instead, Kaywaykla relates how the Apaches noted an unusual amount of activity in and around the village of Carrizal. Sanchez, a warrior who had spent some years as a captive of the Mexicans and knew their ways, was despatched to the settlement. Using the clothes of a slain Mexican vaquero, he scouted Carrizal undetected. A plot was afoot to lure the Apaches into town, ply them with strong liquor and then exterminate them, a tactic used before on unwary Apaches.[8] However, Victorio was not one to fall for this sort of trap. He is known to have expressly forbidden the use of strong spirits among his people precisely because of this danger.[9] Apparently, an emissary was sent to the Apaches inviting them to the town, and was politely treated, lulling the people of Carrizal into a false sense of security. This envoy saw few warriors present in the Apaches' camp, many being absent raiding. Kaywaykla reports that Victorio hoped that this apparent weakness would provoke an attack, and he carefully planned an ambush.

At first glance, neither of the versions is no more, or less, plausible. However, one wonders whether the Apaches had been based in the Candelaria Mountains for long enough for their presence to become known to the town of Carrizal. For this reason, this work will adopt the horse-raid version of events.

For whatever reason, a party of 18 Mexican citizens from Carrizal entered the Candelaria Mountains, and was ambushed and annihilated on or around 7 November (see map 12.1)[10] – an ambush that James Kaywaykla witnessed (see document file no. 22). Lookouts stationed high in the Candelarias had alerted Victorio to the approach of this party, which was following the tracks of the small raiding party. If this party of Mexicans continued into the Candelaria Mountains, they would discover evidence alerting them to the presence of a much larger party of Apaches. Realising this, Victorio set his ambush before the point where the Mexicans would realise their peril. Captain Baylor of the Texas Rangers later described the location as 'a low place between and commanded by, three rocky peaks.'[11] Some of the better shots among Victorio's warriors hid on the northern side of the canyon. Other warriors stationed themselves to block the Mexicans' advance and retreat once

7 Gillett states that the horses were taken from the small hamlet of San Jose and a party from Carrizal set out in pursuit. As the tracks revealed no more than six raiders, a group of between 15 and 18 Mexicans varyingly described as 'citizens' (Thrapp, 1974, p254; Gillett, 1976, p.162) and 'frontiersmen' (Stout p112; Thrapp, 1967, p.189) Wellman describes this party as being drawn from the more prosperous families of the district and headed by one Don Jose Rodriguez (Wellman, p.158) Following the trail into the Candelaria Mountains, they were ambushed and all killed on 9 November, (From the '*New York Sun*' clearly states that the ambush occurred "on Sunday last in an article titled 'An American Battle in Mexico' 12 November 1879, 'Victorio Papers', NA, M666, Roll 527) Sonnichsen and Wellman argue that the attack took place on 7 November (Sonnichsen, p.188; See also Wellman, 1957, p.158).

8 Ball, 1970, p.12.

9 Ball, 1970, p.74.

10 Scott (citing letter from Martinez, Carrizal, 9 November 1879) to Hunter, 2nd Assistant Secretary of State, 4 December 1879 in NA, RG393, Letters Received by HQ_DoNM, September 1865-August 1890, NA, RG393, M1088, Roll 37 (Oct-Dec 1879); See also 'Frelinghuysen-Romero Papers', Letters Rec'd by the AGO, 1881-1889, NA, M689, Roll 81.

11 Lt Baylor to Gen. J.B. Jones, AG, Austin, Texas, 3 December 1879, 'Victorio Files', NA, RG393, M1495, Roll 14; As above in 'Victorio Papers', NA, M666, Roll 526; See also Thrapp, 1974, p254, see also Baylor, 1996, pp.287-288.

Frijole – member of Nana's following. This would mean that the photo almost certainly shows a Chihenne Apache veteran warrior who took part in the Victorio Campaign. Of particular note is his US army belt and Springfield carbine. They might have been taken from a slain US soldier but more likely obtained through trading. Original guidance places this photograph to 1886-7 but Allan Radbourne, UK states that this photograph was taken earlier around the time Nana returned to the San Carlos reservation in 1883/84. (Smithsonian Institution)

the latter had entered the trap, while the rest hid higher up on the southern side of the canyon. The signal to open fire was flashed by mirrors. The first group and the two blocking parties opened fire, and the surviving Mexicans were given no option but to take cover among boulders strewn along the southern side of the canyon. While this afforded good cover from the Apache marksmen to the north, it offered little cover from the majority of the Apache warriors, who were stationed on the south side of the canyon overlooking these boulders.[12] Kaywaykla also emphasised that the positions chosen by the Apaches not only created the best killing ground, but were also judged excellent because they afforded an easy retreat should anything go wrong. Lookouts were also stationed at points where they could watch the surrounding country and warn of the approach of additional enemies.[13]

12 Ball, 1970, pp.13-14 & p.15.
13 Ball, 1970, pp.13-14 & p.15.

Most accounts state that the 18 Mexicans from Carrizal were annihilated. Another group of 35 Mexicans departed from Carrizal in search of their companions. This group was also ambushed in the same spot, with a further 15 men being killed and most others being wounded.[14] There are discrepancies over the numbers killed, but a Mexican source, written on 9 November, (see document file no. 22) clearly states that 18 men were killed in the first ambush, with a further 15 slain in the second, with 20 survivors of the second group returning to Carrizal minus their horses.[15] This source indicates that two prominent citizens of Carrizal, Josi Rodriguez and Jesus Dominguez, were killed in the second ambush, and that there was at least one wounded survivor from the first ambush, though it is possible that he subsequently died from his wounds.

Kaywaykla challenged some of the stories surrounding the waging of war by the Apaches. They might not have taken any prisoners; but equally, in this case, they did not, according to Kaywaykla, indulge in some of the more lurid activities routinely ascribed to them by their opponents.[16] It is also worth noting that, just after Victorio inflicted such a bloody defeat on his enemies, Major Morrow reiterated his view that the Apache leader was, for the moment, neutralised. 'I think he is not in condition to raid and before he is recuperated I will strike him again.'[17]

The citizens of Carrizal raised the general alarm by sending a message to the surrounding towns of El Carmen and San Lorenzo. The dead were left where they had fallen, as the Apaches were judged to be too well positioned in the Candelarias. It was estimated that a force of at least 200 men would be required to assail the Apaches.[18] The rural judge of the town of El Carmen sent this news to Chihuahua City, appealing both for an end to political dissension (of which more later) and for aid. He also stated that he had written to the towns of San Buenaventura and Galeana for additional volunteers, and that when the men from San Lorenzo arrived, he would proceed to Carrizal to aid in the campaign.[19]

The news also reached the Mexican border towns, with more garbled versions of the alarm reaching the United States.[20] The *Army and Navy Journal* used these muddled reports as evidence

---

14 Gillett, 1976, pp.162-163; Thrapp, 1974, pp.253-255; Wellman, 1957, pp158-161.

15 Scott (citing letter from Martinez, Carrizal, 9 November 1879) to Hunter, 2nd Assistant Secretary of State, 4 December 1879, Letters Received by HQ_DoNM, September 1865-August 1890, NA, RG393, M1088, Roll 37 (Oct-Dec 1879); See also 'Frelinghuysen-Romero Papers', Letters Rec'd by the AGO, 1881-1889, NA, M689, Roll 81; *Thirty Four*, 19 November 1879, reported that the first party was ambushed on 9 November, with all but two men killed and the second party ambushed on 11 November, of which only two out of thirty escaped. This appears to be a garbled version of events as the Mexican source notes the ambush of both parties and is dated 9 November.

16 Ball, 1970, pp.13-14 & p.15.

17 Morrow, Bayard to Carr, Grant, 11 November 1879, NA, RG393, Part 1, Entry 235, p.27.

18 Scott (citing letter from Martinez, Carrizal, 9 November 1879) to Hunter, 2nd Assistant Secretary of State, 4 December 1879, Letters Received by HQ_DoNM, September 1865-August 1890, NA, RG393, M1088, Roll 37 (Oct-Dec 1879); See also 'Frelinghuysen-Romero Papers', Letters Rec'd by the AGO, 1881-1889, NA, M689, Roll 81.

19 Scott (citing letter from Jaquez, Rural Judge, El Carmen 11 P.M., 9 November 1879) to Hunter, 2nd Assistant Secretary of State, 4 December 1879, Letters Received by HQ_DoNM, September 1865-August 1890, NA, RG393, M1088, Roll 37 (Oct-Dec 1879); See also 'Frelinghuysen-Romero Papers', Letters Rec'd by the AGO, 1881-1889, NA, M689, Roll 81.

20 The *Grant County Herald* stating that thirty-eight Mexicans had been killed and that Carrizal had been captured. It also warned that the Apaches were moving north and predicted renewed raiding in the United States ('By Telegraph', *Grant County Herald*, 15 November 1879); Captain Carpenter, Tenth Cavalry, led his company along the Rio Grande to search for a large party of Mescaleros who had been raiding around Mesilla and were moving south along the Mexican side of the Rio Grande and who had recently wiped out two parties of Mexican militia. This expedition from Eagle Springs, from 23 October, to 30 November, found an old trail but no other sign of Apaches ('Tabular Statement of Scouts, DoTx, 1880', NA, RG393, Part 1, Entry 2546, p.627).

for rejecting the notion that 'frontiersmen' knew more about Indian fighting than the professional army, and it pontificated that citizens should instead appeal for more troops for their protection.[21] News reached Dr Mariano Samaniego, at his San Jose ranch, on 9 November, that the Carrizal men were trapped. It appears that the men from Carrizal had been joined by some men from San Jose. One of these volunteers, though wounded managed to return to San Jose to raise the alarm. Samaniego dispatched a messenger to El Paso del Norte and Guadalupe asking for aid. This message reached El Paso that afternoon and Guadalupe the following morning. Much to Samaniego's dismay, the response from these towns was that there was nothing they could do as they had no weapons to hand.[22] Thus, according to Samaniego, a further force did not take the field until 20 November, when 30 to 40 better-armed volunteers arrived from the United States.[23] One Senor Ramos organised a large, well-armed posse recruited from towns along the Rio Grande between El Paso and Guadalupe to search for the missing men from Carrizal. This was placed under the command of Don Fransisco Escajeda from Guadalupe.[24] A group of Texas Rangers, including Captain Baylor and Sergeant Gillett, were unofficially invited to join this larger expedition of over 100 Mexicans to search the Candelaria Mountains.[25] By this time, a large force had been gathered from the Mexican communities on both sides of the international border:

> Our command consisted of 42 men from El Paso under Jesus Varga, 25 from Guadaloupe under Francisco Escajera; 18 from San Ignacio, 13 from Saragossa; the rangers and 4 volunteers from this side. Near the Candelaria Mts. we were joined by 11 men from Carrizal; 15 from Lucero and 41 Infantry from Carmel making about 179 mostly armed with breech-loading arms. So if "Victoria" had been there we could have made a pretty good fight, but the sign showed they had only remained there about two days after the slaughter of the Mexicans.
>
> We found 10 saddles of the dead men, hid in the rocks. The muzzle loading guns and swords were all broken,[26] showing that Victoria is well supplied with arms.[27]

Despite their number, the posse approached the Candelaria Mountains from the north with a great deal of caution. Their scouts discovered a fresh trail leading towards the Laguna de Santa Maria to the north west. All the indications argued for Victorio's departure; but they still proceeded with due care and attention. Advance detachments occupied the high ground before the rest of the posse entered the mountains, and thus it was that they soon discovered the carnage.[28]

From the evidence they observed, Baylor and Gillett gave the same account of the first ambush as was later recorded by the Apaches (see document file no. 22). While he was aware of the second ambush, Kaywaykla was clearly not present, and mentioned it only in passing. However, the Texas Rangers were able to reconstruct what happened to the second group of men. Baylor thought that

21 *Army & Navy Journal*, Vol.17, 15 November 1879, p.285.

22 Samaniego letter dated 21 November 1879 in Scott to Hunter 2nd Assistant Secretary of State, Washington D.C., 10 December 1879 in Consular Despatches Chihuahua Mexico 1830-1906, M289, Roll 1.

23 Samaniego letter dated 21 November 1879 in Scott to Hunter, 2nd Assistant Secretary of State, Washington D.C., 10 December 1879 in Consular Despatches Chihuahua Mexico 1830-1906, M289, Roll 1.

24 Baylor, 1996, p.286; Wellman, 1957, p.161.

25 Baylor, 1996, p.286; Gillett, 1976, pp.164-165.

26 The fact that the swords were broken may indicate that the Apaches had taken the blades to make lance heads.

27 Lt Baylor to Gen. J.B. Jones, AG, Austin, Texas, 3 December 1879 'Victorio Files', NA, RG393, M1495, Roll 14; Baylor cited in Thrapp, 1974, p254; Baylor, 1996, p.290.

28 Wellman, 1957, pp.161-162.

the rescue party had gathered up the bodies of the first party, and were in the process of burying them in a crevice, when the Apaches opened fire. Baylor suspected them of being there all the time, toying with their victims before they went for the kill.[29] However, while probably deriving a grim sense of satisfaction that their plan had worked, they were merely taking advantage of their knowledge of how their opponents would act when they found the bodies of their companions. The Apaches must have known that there was a strong likelihood that they would bury their dead in a common grave. What better target than a closely bunched group of men in the process of covering the grave? Even the poorest shot amongst the Apaches would have had a very good chance of hitting somebody in a close-packed group.

From our point of view, the second ambush may appear inordinately callous; yet once again we are seeing the Apache ethos of maximum damage with minimum loss fulfilled to the letter. It also gives an indication of the basic discipline common among the Apaches. Not one of the younger warriors had opened fire prematurely. In fact, Gillett in particular noted the deadly patience with which the Apaches stalked the trapped Mexicans whilst exposing themselves to the minimum of risk:

> I saw where one Mexican had got into a crevice from which he could shoot anyone coming at him from east or west. He was hidden also from the Indians in the cliffs above him, but his legs were exposed to the warriors on the north side and they had literally shot them off up to his knees. I also found seven dead Mexicans in a small gully, and on a little peak above them I discovered the lair of one old Indian who had fired twenty seven shots at the tiny group until he had killed them all, for I found that number of .45-70 cartridge shells in one pile.[30]

According to Gillett, the rescue party had managed to break out of the trap and a running fight had developed, leaving bodies scattered over a much wider area. One man had managed to get approximately 600 yards out from the hills before he was trapped, and despite putting up a desperate fight, he had eventually been killed. Gillett noted that this man's right hand had been cut off by the Apaches.[31] Baylor later recorded that the man's arm had been severed, and that this signified that the Apaches thought that he had made a valiant stand, and by taking off the right arm, they would absorb his bravery themselves.[32]

Many uncertainties remain concerning this incident; such as whether Juh and his warriors were present. The Chihuahua City US Consul, Scott, sent information that Victorio and Juh had been allied and that, as far as he was concerned, both had perpetrated the massacre:

> I had a call this morning from Thos. Parker, whose brother is an officer in the Arizona Indian Scouts. Mr Parker has just passed through Casas Grandes (on 27th inst.) and reports only two Indians there, Juh and the others have gone, most probably to join Victoria, who I now learn for a certainty, is in the State at the head of forty-five warriors, all well armed. Juh's Indians are not well armed, but Victoria has plenty of ammunition and needle-guns in abundance.
>
> Morrow ran Victoria sixty miles this side of the line, and fought him at La Laguna Busman [Guzman?] about the first of this month
>
> About this time, or before, he was joined by Juh, who in reality belongs to the same tribe of Indians as Victoria, but these two worthy cut-throats have not been able to agree for years, and personally are not friends.

29 Baylor, 1996, pp.287-288; Gillett, p.166-167.
30 Gillett, 1976, pp.162-163.
31 Gillett, 1976, pp.163-164.
32 Baylor 1996, p.301.

> After their fight with Morrow, they crossed to the Candelaria Mountains, where they got in their terribly bloody work on the Carrizal party – where they killed over thirty Mexicans and some splendid citizens.[33]

Scott also added that he had received information from a reliable source who had spoken to a third party who had recently met and spoken with Victorio in Casas Grandes. This source also confirmed that Juh and Victorio had joined forces during the recent fighting in New Mexico.[34] However, the witness did not confirm Juh's presence at the Candelaria Mountains ambush; Scott assumed it to be the case. Kaywaykla, the Apache eyewitness to the ambush, made no mention of Juh or any other strangers among the warriors at the time. He also strongly implied that he first met Juh in late 1880-81 in the Sierra Madre.[35] Kaywaykla would surely have noticed a large number of strange warriors present, which suggests that Juh was not present. It is also worth noting that a somewhat garbled version of events published in *Thirty-Four* is adamant that Victorio was in command of this fight and that Juh was not present.[36]

Some details of these incidents remain elusive. For instance, did both ambushes take place on the same day or was the second party of Mexicans ambushed the next day? There is also some question as to how well-equipped the men killed in the Candelaria Mountains were. As noted above, Samaniego was unable to drum up immediate support due to a lack of available weapons. Nevertheless, Baylor reported that it was possible for a well-armed group of men to set out two weeks later, presumably having had enough time to organize sufficient equipment. Some of the Carrizal militia must have carried breech-loading weapons, as Kaywaykla clearly mentioned the gathering up of rifles and cartridge belts by the victorious warriors.

Britton Davis, an officer of the Apache Scouts during the pursuit of Geronimo in 1885, gave a description of the arms of a village militia in Mexico:

> When I entered Oputo all the able bodied men of the town, some thirty-five or forty in number, were lined up in front of the principal *cantina* (saloon) ready to take the warpath. They were armed with every conceivable type of antiquated firearm, aged cap and ball horse pistols, muzzle-loading, single barrel shotguns; these, with a few Sharps rifles that had seen better days, made up the major part of the arsenal. Here and there I noted an aged Winchester, but as the ammunition I saw for this arm appeared to be mostly refilled shells I had my doubts of the efficacy even of this, the most promising of their weapons for offense.[37]

South of the border the response to the Apaches was varied, often hampered by limited resources and political in-fighting. The federal infantry seems to have been armed with rifled muskets, though some of the federal troops may have been armed with Remington breech-loading rifles. The more unofficial state and local militia and volunteer units, if they were raised at all, seem to have been

---

33 Scott to Hunter, 2nd Assistant Secretary of State, Washington D.C. 28 November 1879 in Consular Despatches Chihuahua Mexico 1830-1906, M289, Roll 1; Scott to Hunter, 2nd Assistant Secretary of State, Washington D.C. 28 November 1879 in Consular Despatches Chihuahua Mexico 1830-1906, M289, Roll 1; Scott to Hunter 28 November 1879 cited in Evarts, Dept. of State to Alexander Ramsey, Secretary of War, 16 December 1879, 'Victorio Files', NA, RG393, M1495, Roll 14 see same letter in 'Frelinghuysen-Romero Papers', Letters Rec'd by the AGO, 1881-1889, NA, M689, Roll 81; See also Thrapp, 1974, p.258.

34 U.S. Consul to 2nd Asst. Secretary of State, 7 November 1879 in Letters Received by HQ DoNM, September 1865-August 1890, NA, RG393, M1088, Roll 39, Oct-Dec 1879.

35 Ball, 1970, pp.123-124.

36 *Thirty Four*, 19 November 1879.

37 Davis, 1976, p.165; Faulk, 1969, p.66.

equipped with a variety of weapons. At one end of the scale, some seem to have been very well armed, whilst others were supplied with thoroughly antiquated weaponry. The force with the Texas Ranger detachment seems to have been well provisioned with breech-loading weapons.

The political situation was also less than stable. For example, before joining forces with Victorio, Juh was reported to have been at Casas Grandes with over 40 warriors. He demanded food and other goods from Governor Trias of Chihuahua, who had no troops with which to challenge him and was thus forced to play along with these demands.[38] This state of affairs was exacerbated when the Chihuahuan state troops were merged with the federal troops and then withdrawn to the neighbouring state of Durango. In the meantime, the government of Chihuahua was faced with regular raids by well-equipped Apaches nominally based on reservations in Arizona and New Mexico, which resulted in heavy loss of life and cattle, and effectively 'depopulated the mining district of Dolores.'[39] Luis Terrazas sent a petition to the US State Department informing them that in recent years the Apaches were better armed than the ranchers who, without troops to back them up, were finding it increasingly difficult to combat these raiders.[40] In July 1879, Louis Scott reported that over 20 Mexicans had been killed near Temocachic. He also reported that some of the plunder from raids dating back to 1876 had turned up on the Mescalero reservation.[41] This state of affairs had been worsened by the more recent activity of American citizens rustling cattle in Mexico and selling their plunder in the United States[42]

Another problem faced by Governor Trias was caused by his political rivals.[43] The governor was charged with corruption, and faced an internal revolution headed by one G. Casavantes, who was based in Guerrero.[44] This revolt appears to have been sparked off in response to efforts to balance the state books by levying additional 'complimentary contributions' on the Chihuahuan people.[45] It was then reported that Governor Trias was spending this money to raise and arm a force to oppose the rebels, said to be well equipped and numbering approximately 400 men.[46] In September and October 1879, there were a number of skirmishes between the factions without resolving the issue, but Trias did not have the men and equipment to prevail against the rebels, and by the end of

38 Louis H. Scott to Hon. J.H. Seward, Department of State, 19 September 1879, NA, RG393, Part 1, Entry 2546, pp.161-162; See also Stacy to A.A.G., Camp Thomas, 9 August 1879, NA, RG393, Part 1, Entry 2546, pp.205-206; Scott to Seward, Department of State, Washington D.C., 19 September 1879 in Consular Despatches Chihuahua Mexico 1830-1906, M289, Roll 1; Thrapp, 1973, pp.10-11.

39 Scott to Second Assistant Secretary of State, Washington D.C., 20 July 1879 & Scott's Commercial Report from U.S. Consulate Chihuahua for year ending 30 September 1879 in Consular Despatches Chihuahua Mexico 1830-1906, NA, M289, Roll 1.

40 Scott to Seward, Department of State, Washington D.C., 19 September 1879 in Consular Despatches Chihuahua Mexico 1830-1906, NA, M289, Roll 1.

41 Scott to Second Assistant Secretary of State, Washington D.C., 20 July 1879 in Consular Despatches Chihuahua Mexico 1830-1906, NA, M289, Roll 1.

42 Scott to Second Assistant Secretary of State, Washington D.C., 20 July 1879 in Consular Despatches Chihuahua Mexico 1830-1906, NA, M289, Roll 1.

43 Governor Trias seems to have also had a fondness for the bottle. During 1864, while entertaining the fugitive President Juarez in Chihuahua City, the U.S. Consul reported that Trias got so inebriated as to be almost unable to stand. (Creel to the Secretary of State, Washington D.C. 16 October 1864 & similar comment in Scott to John Foster, 8 March 1877 in Consular Despatches Chihuahua Mexico 1830-1906, NA, M289, Roll 1.)

44 Scott to Hunter, 2nd Assistant Secretary of State, Washington D.C., 7 November 1879 in Consular Despatches Chihuahua Mexico 1830-1906, NA, M289, Roll 1.

45 Scott to Second Assistant Secretary of State, Washington D.C., 12 September 1879 in Consular Despatches Chihuahua Mexico 1830-1906, NA, M289, Roll 1.

46 Scott to Acting Secretary of State, Washington D.C., 18 September 1879 in Consular Despatches Chihuahua Mexico 1830-1906, NA, M289, Roll 1.

October both Governor Trias and Chihuahua City were in the hands of the rebels.[47] During 1879, Trias purchased 125 Remington breech-loading carbines with 80,000 rounds of ammunition in Texas. This shipment of arms was ambushed by his political rivals and stolen.[48] Thus, the situation below the border was much less politically stable than in the United States. Moreover, if the US army felt that it was under-funded and under-equipped, then one wonders what they would have made of the resources available to the Mexican federal army and state troops. The US army was at least routinely armed with modern breech-loading rifles and carbines.

There remains one final point to make on the disaster in the Candelaria Mountains. As noted above, there appeared to be a long-standing trade in stolen stock and other contraband on the Mescalero reservation. Some horses and saddles from the Candelaria victims turned up on the Mescalero reservation, which seems to confirm that Victorio had trading links with that reservation. It may also indicate that, by this time, some Mescalero Apaches had joined Victorio's following. Dr Mariano Samaniego reported that he had received word from a Mexican citizen in Tulerosa that a party of Apaches had arrived on 13 November, with the horses, saddles and guns captured from the Carrizal party. Samaniego also reported that the Apaches were able to sell their loot to traders at Tulerosa, and that the reservations in the United States were little more than safe havens for these raiders.[49] Dr Blazer had also been to see Samaniego, who had empowered him to recover any stolen stock he spotted. Blazer had reported seeing more than 100 horses with Luis Terrazas' brand, but 'that he declined to claim them for fear of his life.'[50] Samaniego concluded that only strong military action would solve this problem and noted that 'this is the only recourse left us, to get rid of them. I believe it could be done, since the US forces have recently crossed over and have been repulsed by the same Indians.'[51] At the very least, the Mescalero reservation was being used to launder loot taken in Mexico, a fact that was already known to the Department of the Interior. Agent Russell had been instructed to ascertain where this trade was conducted and to curtail it by enlisting the aid of the army.[52] Apaches riding stolen horses were reported as having been seen on the Mescalero reservation in the territorial press.[53] The skirmish fought with the Apaches by the Mexican militia and the Texas Rangers in October 1879, in Mexico, demonstrates that Mescaleros were actively involved in this trade on their own account. Russell himself, on 9 November 1879, requested additional troops from Fort Stanton, through Lieutenant Smith at Tulerosa, stating that he feared a return of Victorio's warriors to the Mescalero reservation. The commander of Fort Stanton, Lieutenant Colonel Swain, 15th Infantry, tersely informed the agent

47 Scott to Seward, Department of State, Washington D.C., 26 September & 3 October 1879 and Scott to Hunter, 2nd Assistant Secretary of State, Washington D.C., 31 October & 7 November 1879 in Consular Despatches Chihuahua Mexico 1830-1906, NA, M289, Roll1; See also article in *Thirty Four*, 19 November 1879. The latter stated that Governor Trias was guilty of tyranny by mob rule and that on 31 October, Jose Casavantes had captured Chihuahua City without any fighting. "Our Neighbors across the line are improving in the art of revolution and may yet learn to govern themselves".

48 Stout p.104.

49 Samaniego letter dated 21 November 1879 in Scott to Hunter, 2nd Assistant Secretary of State, Washington D.C., 10 December 1879 in Consular Despatches Chihuahua Mexico 1830-1906, NA, M289, Roll 1.

50 Samaniego letter dated 21 November 1879 in Scott to Hunter, 2nd Assistant Secretary of State, Washington D.C., 10 December 1879 in Consular Despatches Chihuahua Mexico 1830-1906, NA, M289, Roll 1.

51 Samaniego letter dated 21 November 1879 in Scott to Hunter, 2nd Assistant Secretary of State, Washington D.C., 10 December 1879 in Consular Despatches Chihuahua Mexico 1830-1906, NA, M289, Roll 1.

52 Acting Secretary, Dept of the Interior to the Secretary of War, 25 September 1879 in Letters Received by HQ DoNM, September 1865-August 1890, NA, RG393, M1088, Roll 39, Oct-Dec 1879.

53 *Thirty Four*, 29 October 1879.

that the available troops were all absent, chasing the Apaches who had originally left his reservation. Russell was advised that, if Lieutenant Smith's small detachment at Tulerosa was insufficient to defend the reservation, he should evacuate and proceed to Fort Stanton or Tulerosa for protection.[54] This implies that Russell was aware of the above trade and knew that Chihenne and allied Mescalero Apaches were a frequent danger on his reservation, even though he could not admit this publicly, let alone deal with the activity. Swain's response revealed his lack of sympathy for Russell by offering a solution he knew the Indian agent could not effectively accept: the subordination of the Department of the Interior to the War Department.

It is also useful to review the tactics used by the US army during September and October 1879 in the light of the deadly ambush in the Candelaria Mountains. As we have seen, the Ninth Cavalry suffered some losses in the process of concentrating their forces in reaction to Victorio's decision to wage war. However, they came nowhere near the defeat suffered by the Mexican militia in the Candelaria Mountains. The closest they came to such a defeat was the ambush in the maze of canyons at the head of the Animas River. In that case, they were lucky to have another unit following them up so closely. Yet once the Ninth Cavalry had regrouped under the command of Major Morrow, with the addition of Apache scouts, the US forces changed tack. They adopted formations made up of Apache scouts who ranged out ahead, backed up by small detachments of US troops protecting their mule-borne supplies. These were supported by a much stronger detachment of US cavalry. The decisive edge was provided by the presence of Apache scouts. Once these detachments had joined with the Ninth Cavalry, their superior skills in tracking and detecting ambushes proved their worth.

Two points spring to mind in relation to the Apache scouts. First, their presence on the US side did not prevent Victorio from drawing the army into pursuits that would kill their horses. Second, the presence of Apache scout companies clearly gave Victorio pause for thought where direct military action was concerned. Between 4 and 18 September, he gave every indication of being prepared to strike his enemies hard. In particular, he was not afraid to stand his ground against a large number of Ninth cavalrymen with Navajo scouts and some citizen volunteers, and he emerged victorious. Once he realised that Apache scouts were involved, however, he appears to have changed his tactics. It is possible that he might not have been aware of the presence of the scouts until he lost two warriors and a woman to them, on 29 September. The following morning his warriors waited until the Apache scouts had left the camp before moving in to attack the soldiers left behind. From 30 September to 27 October, Victorio switched from direct to indirect action to deal with Morrow's battalion. It was only when the US expedition had been appreciably whittled down as a result of such indirect tactics, combined with the fact that Victorio had been significantly reinforced by Juh, that the Apaches chose to drive Morrow off completely. By that time the odds, on every conceivable measure, were so in their favour that the risks to their own warriors were minimal. Yet they still only won the battle by taking account of the possibility of failure.

In fact, Victorio and his warriors had used classic Apache tactics. Since leaving the Mescalero reservation in August 1879, they had, on several occasions, held their ground against, or successfully ambushed, American and Mexican forces. They were clearly aware of the potential of breech-loading weaponry in the art of ambush, particularly the use of crossfire to disrupt, disorient and ultimately destroy their opponents. They had set up deadly crossfire ambushes several times between September and November 1879. Of particular note are the ambushes near McEvers' Ranch, at the headwaters of the Animas River, and in the Candelaria Mountains. Recent archaeological evidence would suggest that the Apaches swiftly adapted their traditional tactics to a most effective

54 Lt. Smith to Post Adjutant, Fort Stanton, 9 November 1879 & Swain to Russell, 10 November, 1879 in Letters Received, DoM 1868-98, RG 393, Entry A1-1 2601, Box 85.

employment of modern single-shot and repeating breech-loaders, with deadly effect. This point will be expanded on when we discuss the Hembrillo Canyon battle, which occurred in April 1880. (See Volume II of the Victorio Campaign) .

We should also not draw incorrect conclusions about the disastrous defeat of the Carrizal militiamen. These men were facing one of the most accomplished Apache military leaders of the later Apache wars. Testimony provided by the Texas Rangers supports the notion that, despite a lack of resources and continuing political instability, Mexican armed units were by no means ineffective. When the authorities did manage to muster local militias, these appear to have been quite well equipped and efficiently led. The men from Carrizal faced formidable odds. They were completely unprepared for the presence of such a large number of Apaches, on ground of the latter's choosing, and well supplied with both modern weapons and ammunition.

The Mexican response to the Apaches was largely devolved to the individual state governments. The overall policy of the federal government of Mexico, under Porfirio Diaz, was threefold, 'extermination, deportation and colonization.'[55] According to Spicer, if sustained resistance was encountered by the Mexican federal and state governments, force was, if possible, the preferred option. However, much of the actual implementation of these broad policy goals, designed to strengthen the concept of a unified Mexican political entity,[56] was left to the individual states. In Diaz's case, these operations were supported by federal subsidy.[57] The federal government would also mediate in local political disputes by sending in federal troops. Hatfield argues that while the federal government did not use extermination policies, it was quite happy to allow both Sonora and Chihuahua the discretion to adopt such policies.[58] Chihuahua maintained a military census of all 'able bodied'[59] men between 18 and 50 from the 1830s to the 1870s, and these were organised into local militia units.[60] Chihuahua state was divided into 17 districts, each headed by a prefect who answered to the state prefect in Chihuahua.[61] However, this policy was not always effective. In 1867, Moye, the US consul in Chihuahua, noted that the state had detachments of troops scattered across the territory, but these detachments, usually of about a dozen men, were too small to be effective on their own.[62] The members were usually drawn from the poorer classes, the peasants and the hacienda vaqueros. More wealthy nominees could contribute money to the state to avoid actual service.[63] This may have provided the money with which the state of Chihuahua could buy arms for its local defence force. In 1867, their agent, one Mr Aldrede 'from Texas', purchased 1,500 Enfield rifles and 60 Spencer repeating rifles.[64] So the state of Chihuahua was capable of supplying a significant force for

55 Hatfield, p.9.
56 Spicer, 338.
57 Hatfield, p.9.
58 Hatfield p.9; see also Spicer, p.240; Moye, U.S. Consul in Chihuahua reported that in 1867 there was a clear system of bounties for Apache scalps and prisoners; $200 for a Male scalp; $250 for a female scalp; $250 for a male captive and $150 for a female or child captive. This strongly suggests a policy of extermination as it would appear that the greatest incentive was to collect female scalps with its attendant negative effect upon population growth. (Moye to Secretary of State, 3 June 1867 in Consular Despatches Chihuahua Mexico 1830-1906, NA, M289, Roll 1.)
59 Almada, cited in Alonso, p.40.
60 Alonso, p.40.
61 Moye to Secretary of State, 3 June 1867 in Consular Despatches Chihuahua Mexico 1830-1906, NA, M289, Roll 1.
62 Moye to Secretary of State, 3 June 1867 in Consular Despatches Chihuahua Mexico 1830-1906, NA, M289, Roll 1.
63 Alonso p.40 & p.43.
64 Moye to Secretary of State, 10 October 1867 in Consular Despatches Chihuahua Mexico 1830-1906, NA, M289, Roll 1.

a defence against Apaches. As seen above, it was internal political divisions in Chihuahua which often served to undermine the state's efforts to defend itself against the Apaches.

Historian A.M. Alonso argues that leadership of forces by the Mexican states was based on the status and charisma of participants at four different levels: villagers, regional personalities, people from the towns, and Chihuahua state officials.[65] This structure worked as follows:

> Simultaneously "sons of the pueblo" and government functionaries, municipal and district authorities were military brokers who mediated between the state and local warriors and charismatic military leaders... On the one hand, they supplied peasant warriors and their leaders with the authorization and the resources to conduct campaigns. On the other hand, they regulated the social use of violence and kept higher-level functionaries informed about who was waging war, when, and how. On the whole, in the conduct of warfare, municipal, and district authorities were a source of organization, leadership and resources. It was through them that the state managed to gain knowledge about and a measure of control over the use of violence against *indigenes.*
>
> By regulating the supply of arms and munitions and by providing warriors with needed resources, the state was able to gain a measure of control over the management of warfare. Peasants were often too poor to buy the arms and ammunition, the horses and mules they needed for community defense. Even though the peasant-warriors of Namiquipa were unusually well-armed, in 1849 about 50 percent of them lacked their own weapons, and all were dependent on the state for ammunition. Peasant fighters were unable to equip themselves fully and relied on the state to supply them with some of the means of warfare. These arms were doled out to volunteers when they went out on campaigns and subsequently retrieved by municipal and district authorities, who kept them on deposit. Not only was the state usually informed about campaigns, but by controlling the supply of arms and munitions, it had the power to determine which campaigns would be waged and thus regulate and legitimate the use of violence.[66]

Frederic Remington later described this feudal organisation in Chihuahua during his travels in the region.[67] Daly notes that the 'Seguridad Publica' had been raised by General Terrazas and consisted of: 'two companies of irregulars, made up from volunteers from the various hamlets of Ascencion, Janos, Casas Grandes, etc. For scouts and trailers, a company of Tarahumari Indians was enlisted.'[68] Bourke noted that the Sonorans:

> are armed to resist the Apaches; they work in their fields with arms in their hands and have organized into patrols, which in bands of twenty-five or thirty each day explore the country, looking for trails or other signs of the hostiles.[69]

Bourke also reported that the Sonorans called their militia the 'Guardia Nacional.'[70] The Chihuahuan state also maintained a measure of control by monopolising the distribution of rewards

For the record it was found that all the Enfield rifles were in such bad condition that the State of Chihuahua refused to purchase them.

65 Alonso, pp.40-42.
66 Alonso, pp.42-43.
67 McCracken, p.140.
68 Daly, 2001, p.462.
69 Bourke, 2001ii, p.353.
70 Bourke, 2001ii, p.354 & p.356.

for outstanding military service.[71] Don Jesus Tarin later recalled that the levels of pay were also relatively attractive, and so he joined Terrazas' militia.[72]

Therefore, while the Mexican state militia may not necessarily have been as well-equipped and formally trained as the US army, it was better organised than it was given credit for north of the border. Indeed, the New Mexican civilian militias and posses called out during the Victorio Campaign could be defined by their singularly ineffective and disastrous encounters with Apaches. While the Mexican state militia had their disasters, they were also capable of inflicting the severest of defeats on the Apaches. The Mexican state authorities' claim to their federal colleagues that they were powerless in the face of Apache attacks was a clear attempt to divert federal funding to the afflicted states.[73] Nevertheless, ex-governor of the District of Columbia, Alexander Robey Shepherd, who subsequently operated several silver mines in Northern Mexico, described the devastating effect of Apache depredations in Chihuahua. He also stated that, in general, he felt that the local populace was out-gunned and at a psychological disadvantage when faced with the far more aggressive Apaches.[74] He added that:

> It is not possible for the Mexicans to make any stand against them, as they [the Apaches] can easily pick off with their needle guns and Winchester rifles, the poorly armed settlers, who are thus kept in continual apprehension of personal damage and great pecuniary loss.[75]

The attack in the Candelaria Mountains drew an unequivocal response from Louis Scott, US consul in Chihuahua, concerning how the United States and Mexico should deal with the Apaches. Both republics must set aside their political differences and cooperate wholeheartedly in the complete destruction of the Apaches. This should involve the drawing up of a reciprocal agreement that, when in pursuit of Apaches, troops from the United States should be free to enter Mexico, and vice versa. He noted that there was a lot of support for such an arrangement from the landowners in Chihuahua and Sonora, and these men would happily render direct assistance to US forces if requested.[76] As we shall see, this diplomat had rather undiplomatically outlined what ultimately became the very subtle political solution that was, at least unofficially, adopted by both Republics to deal with Victorio's resistance. Yet many months were to pass, and a number of political obstacles had to be tackled, before any such action could be taken.

---

71 Alonso, p.43.

72 Aceves, p.25.

73 See for example Original Reports numbered 1-7 forwarded by Angel Trias (7 Feb., 1879) to Mr Ruelas, Minister for Foreign Affairs, Mexico, who submitted them (13 March 1879) to John W. Foster, Minister of the United States to Mexico, who in turn passed them on (15 March 1879) to William M. Evarts, U.S. Secretary of State who finally passed them on to George W. McCrary, Secretary of War on 7 April 1879, NA, RG393, Part 1, Entry 2546, pp.119-149.

74 Shepherd to Whipple, AAG, MDoM, 30 October 1879, NA, RG393, Part 1, Entry 2546, pp.163-167.

75 Shepherd to Whipple, AAG, MDoM, 30 October 1879, NA, RG393, Part 1, Entry 2546, p.164.

76 Scott to Hunter, 2nd Assistant Secretary of State, 4 December 1879, Letters Received by HQ DoNM, September 1865-August 1890, NA, RG393, M1088, Roll 37 (Oct-Dec 1879); See also Scott to Hunter, 2nd Assistant Secretary of State, Washington D.C. 28 November 1879 in Consular Despatches Chihuahua Mexico 1830-1906, NA, M289, Roll1; Scott to Hunter 28 November 1879 in Evarts, Dept. of State to Alexander Ramsey, Secretary of War, 16 December 1879, 'Victorio Files', NA, RG393, M1495, Roll 14 see same letter in 'Frelinghuysen-Romero Papers', Letters Rec'd by the AGO, 1881-1889, NA, M689, Roll 81.

Further Raiding in Mexico, November-December 1879

Widespread raiding continued (see document file no. 23). A 'train' (it is unclear whether this was a mule or wagon train) and its 11-man escort was looted and destroyed at Salada some days after the Carrizal men were killed.[77] Two Mexicans were slaughtered and one badly wounded when between 60 and 70 horses were stolen at Galeana on 23 November 1879.[78] On the following day, 300 horses, which had been concentrated at San Lorenzo in order to keep them further south and avoid the Apache raiders, were driven off, with a further three Mexican guards killed.[79] The Apaches then moved towards Santa Clara in two groups, one herding their loot, the other continuing their raids. Scott stated that the Apaches had, by 29 November: 'killed one hundred and fifty persons within the past six weeks.'[80] Raiding continued deep into December. Roman Aranda's ranch, 20 miles from Guadalupe and 60 miles from El Paso, was attacked on Christmas Day. The Apaches lifted Aranda's entire stock of horses and mules.[81] Thirty-nine men with a wagon train were alleged to have been wiped out.[82] *Thirty-Four* published news from Janos that 23 men had been killed at Galeana, three at Los Mosquitos and 12 on the El Paso road.[83] Many such reports were false or exaggerated; but it is clear that during November and December northern Chihuahua was hit hard by the Apaches. Indeed, by the end of December, the *Grant County Herald* alleged that 300 people had been killed by Apaches in the State of Chihuahua, and that its government was now offering a bounty of $100 per Apache scalp.[84] Whatever the truth, the perceived effects of such attacks were causing economic chaos in complete disproportion to the actual numbers of Apaches involved and the number of attacks perpetrated.

An Apache raid in the vicinity of Georgetown at this time may be taken as a further indication that members of Victorio's following were passing back and forth between Mexico and the United States. Four horses and one mule were taken from Eulogia Lopez on the Mimbres River. Lopez and 12 others pursued the raiders, originally thought to be Mexicans, towards Cooke's Peak and the Florida Mountains.[85] Apaches were also reported to have been seen between Las Cruces and El Colorado in early November,[86] and near Cooke's Peak on 18 November.[87] One Charley Bottom and his party lost 17 horses to Apaches near the Mexican border to the south of Silver

77 Scott to Hunter, 2nd Assistant Secretary of State, Washington D.C. 28 November 1879 in Consular Despatches Chihuahua Mexico 1830-1906, NA, M289, Roll1; Scott to Hunter 28 November 1879 in Evarts, Dept. of State to Alexander Ramsey, Secretary of War, 16 December 1879, 'Victorio Files', NA, RG393, M1495, Roll 14 see same letter in 'Frelinghuysen-Romero Papers', Letters Rec'd by the AGO, 1881-1889, NA, M689, Roll 81; See also Thrapp, 1974, p.367 Note 14.

78 Scott to Hunter, 2nd Assistant Secretary of State, Washington D.C. 28 November 1879 in Consular Despatches Chihuahua Mexico 1830-1906, NA, M289, Roll1; Scott to Hunter 28 November 1879 in Evarts, Dept. of State to Alexander Ramsey, Secretary of War, 16 December 1879, 'Victorio Files', NA, RG393, M1495, Roll 14 see same letter in 'Frelinghuysen-Romero Papers', Letters Rec'd by the AGO, 1881-1889, NA, M689, Roll 81; See also Thrapp, 1974, p.257.

79 Scott to Hunter, 2nd Assistant Secretary of State, Washington D.C. 28 November 1879 in Consular Despatches Chihuahua Mexico 1830-1906, NA, M289, Roll1; Scott to Hunter 28 November 1879 in Evarts, Dept. of State to Alexander Ramsey, Secretary of War, 16 December 1879, 'Victorio Files', NA, RG393, M1495, Roll 14 see same letter in 'Frelinghuysen-Romero Papers', Letters Rec'd by the AGO, 1881-1889, NA, M689, Roll 81; See also Thrapp, 1974, p.257.

80 Thrapp, 1974, p.257.

81 'From El Paso', *Grant County Herald*, 27 December 1879.

82 Letter dated 2 January 1880 published in 'Town and County', *Grant County Herald*, 10 January 1880.

83 *Thirty Four*, 3 December 1879.

84 'News and Notes', *Grant County Herald*, 3 January 1880.

85 'From Georgetown', *Grant County Herald*, 15 November 1879.

86 *Thirty Four*, 5 November 1879.

87 'Town and County', *Grant County Herald*, 22 November 1879.

Plates 12.1and 12.2 Two shots of the stable complex at El Carmen, Chihuahua, dating back to the Apache wars. Had the Chihuahua ranchers managed to get their horses to a complex of this nature, then the Apaches would probably not have attacked. This stable building is about 20 km north of San Lorenzo. (Photos: author)

City. No casualties were inflicted on either side, though 'the red devils were within about 500 yards of them.'[88] If these were Apaches, it suggests another careful theft where the Apaches were not detected until they were well away. By the beginning of December, *Thirty-Four* was noting that sightings of Apaches were being reported daily, along with discoveries of small trails going north to the Black Range, though the newspaper could not track down reliable sources for this information.[89] As late as 20 December, a small party of Apaches was reported to have stolen horses at San Isidoro near Georgetown. As the victims were not armed, the raiders were not challenged and made off with three horses.[90] On or around the same date, a herder was said to have been killed and 100 cattle stolen from the vicinity of Slocum's and Shedd's Ranches.[91] It should be noted that the latter ranch is located just to the east of the juncture of the Organ and San Andres Mountains and is thus some distance from the former, suggesting one or more parties of Apache raiders operating between the Mescalero reservation and Mexico. There was also some indication that provisions were leaving the Mescalero reservation, though whether bound for Victorio's adherents is open to question. Lieutenant Smith sent intelligence that a party of Mescaleros had left the reservation carrying a large amount of meat. This was assumed to be destined for a substantial party of Apaches.[92] Lieutenant Maney was reported as tracking a small band of Apaches in the Animas River area in the Black Range on 4 December,[93] and Captain Dawson was noted as being absent from Fort Bayard with 18 enlisted men in pursuit of Apaches in the Florida Mountains.[94] All of which indicated regular traffic between independent Apaches in Mexico and the Mescalero reservation or hamlets such as Cañada Alamosa and Las Palomas where the Apaches knew they could trade their plunder with no questions asked.

This traffic also suggested that a significant number of Mescalero Apaches were becoming dissatisfied with life on the reservation. In November, Lieutenant Smith sent in a report to Fort Stanton stating that he had spoken to some Mescalero Apache warriors who openly expressed their contempt for Russell. While not necessarily a neutral observer, Smith reported that the dissatisfaction stemmed from a perception that the agent was not a military man and made no effort to understand the Mescalero Apaches. In other words, Russell did not deserve to be obeyed as he had not earned the respect of the Apaches. The agent made no effort to understand the language, let alone the culture, of the Mescaleros. having failed to gain their respect, he was quick to issue orders, for example, forbidding the brewing of tiswin, refusing hunting passes, declining to issue extra beef rations for a feast, and even refusing to allow the Mescaleros to trade for vegetables.[95] The irony of issuing edicts to stop the public trading of vegetables at the same time as completely failing to act on the trade in stolen goods on the reservation cannot have escaped the Apaches. In their culture, if a leadership figure was found to be inadequate he would lose followers. In this case, lack of respect for Russell would lead to Mescalero Apaches leaving the reservation and engaging in activities which would bring them to the attention of the War Department.

88 'Town and County' *Grant County Herald*, 22 November 1879.
89 *Thirty Four*, 3 December 1879.
90 'From Georgetown', *Grant County Herald*, 20 December 1879.
91 'From El Paso', *Grant County Herald*, 27 December 1879.
92 Loud to AAG Fort Leavenworth, 29 November 1879, Telegrams Sent DoNM, Vol.2, Jan.–Dec. 1879, NA, RG393, Part 3, Entry 431, pp.450-451.
93 Loud to AAG Fort Leavenworth, 4 December 1879, Telegrams Sent DoNM, Vol.2, Jan.–Dec. 1879, NA, RG393, Part 3, Entry 431, p.463
94 Return for December 1879 in Returns From U.S. Military Posts 1800-1916, Fort Bayard, New Mexico 1866-Dec. 1879, NA, M617, Roll 87
95 Smith to Post Adjutant, Fort Stanton, 17 November 1879, in Letters Received, DoM 1868-98, RG 393, Entry A1-1 2601, Box 85

News of the activities of Apache raiders eventually reached the Secretary of War with the reporting of several deaths of Mexican citizens at the hands of 'American Indians'[96] during August and September 1879.[97] In response to these reports, Sheridan, while acknowledging that some of these raiders were certainly from the Fort Stanton reservation, indicated that he firmly believed that most of the raids troubling Chihuahua were perpetrated by Indians from Mexico,[98] who were also not averse to raiding in the United States.

> The band of the Apache Chief Victoria, by whom a score of murders have within a short time been committed, much valuable property destroyed and with whom we have been at hostilities for several months, is made up largely of Indians from Mexico. I am also of the opinion that much of the damage attributed to Indians from the United States, is done by those belonging to Mexico. It is not improbable that a few Indians from Arizona may cross the line into Mexico.[99]

More than 500 federales under General Trevino were sent to Chihuahua.[100] However, the primary reason for this deployment seems to have been to deal with the fighting between Governor Angel Trias and political rival Gabriel Casavantes. The latter and the men he led in the revolt against Trias, eventually succeeded in occupying Chihuahua City and imprisoning the governor.[101] When General Trevino arrived in Chihuahua, Casavantes immediately surrendered. The revolt was almost immediately vindicated with the impeachment of Governor Trias, who was replaced by Luis Terrazas, possibly the richest landowner in Chihuahua. In all probability, Terrazas had used Casavantes as a front for his own political ambition, as he had already served as governor of Chihuahua as early as 1858. Having lost much property to the Apaches, Terrazas was determined to defeat the Apache raiders once political stability had been restored.[102] His cousin, Joaquin Terrazas, who had been leading scalp-hunting expeditions of state troops against the Apaches since the 1850s, was placed in charge of the Chihuahua state troops.

Having re-established political order within Chihuahua, General Trevino turned his attention to Victorio and Juh and their Apaches. Yet, before he had even arrived in Chihuahua from campaigning against Indians in the neighbouring state of Coahuila, he had noted that the federal force at his disposal was insufficient for the task. In fact, he had contacted General Ord, commander of the Department of Texas, requesting companies from the Tenth Cavalry and Twenty-Second

96 By 'American Indians' he was referring to Indians from the USA entering Mexico

97 W. Hunter to Geo W. McCrary, Secretary of War, 7 October 1879, NA, RG393, Part 1, Entry 2546, p.157; Full text of Consul's letter of 19 September 1879 see NA, RG393, Part 1, Entry 2546, pp.159-162

98 This is probably a reference to Juh's Chiricahuas who were reported by Scott as appearing at Casas Grandes to open negotiations with Governor Trias. This incident was in the same letter that reported the above raid.

99 Sheridan endorsement added to the Consul's letter, 4 November 1879, NA, RG393, Part 1, Entry 2546, p.159

100 Luis Terrazas to AAA Genl SF, 2 January 1880? NA, RG393, Part 3, Entry 439, p.472; Scott to Hunter 28 November 1879 in Evarts, Dept. of State to Alexander Ramsey, Secretary of War, 16 December 1879, 'Victorio Files', NA, RG393, M1495, Roll 14 see same letter in 'Frelinghuysen-Romero Papers', Letters Rec'd by the AGO, 1881-1889, NA, M689, Roll 81; See also Thrapp, 1967, p.190; Dinges, 1987, p.85 & p.86; Haley, 1981, p.324.

101 Scott to Hunter, 2nd Assistant Secretary of State, Washington D.C. 28 November 1879 in Consular Despatches Chihuahua Mexico 1830-1906, NA, M289, Roll1; Bancroft, 1889, p.625; See also ???? to Ord, 12 January 1880, NA, RG393, Part 1, Entry 2546, pp.306-309; The *Grant County Herald* notes a revolution in Chihuahua resulting in the capture of all the major figures in Trias' administration. It also stated that General Trevino had been sent with Federal forces to suppress this unrest.

102 Bancroft, 1889, p.625; See also ???? to Ord, 12 January 1880, NA, RG393, Part 1, Entry 2546, pp.306-309; Thrapp, 1974, p.257.

Infantry to picket the border to aid his campaign.[103] Trevino needed all the support Chihuahua could muster. Given this, Joaquin Terrazas raised some of his militia in December 1879, subordinating his command to Colonel Ponciano Cisneros, who was leading a 100-man detachment of General Trevino's federales. Operating out of the town of San Andres, they scoured Northern Chihuahua, but without result, and returned to Chihuahua City on 5 February, 1880.[104] Overall, it was reported that Trevino had sent two strong columns into action against Victorio's Apaches.[105] It was also rumoured that, at dawn on 5 December, Mexican troops, both federales and Sonoran militia, had surprised 'Hoo' and inflicted heavy casualties on the Apaches.[106]

103 Ord to Whipple, 11 December 1879, NA, RG393, Part 1, Entry 2546, pp.265-266; Col. Grierson's Report for Year ending 31 December 1879, NA, RG393, Part 1, Entry 2546, p.330.

104 Stout, pp.172-173; *Thirty Four*, 7 January 1880 states that Mexican troops in pursuit of Victorio were commanded by Col.'s Casavantes and Joaquin Terrazas.

105 ???? to Ord, 12 January 1880, NA, RG393, Part 1, Entry 2546, pp.306-309.

106 Loud to AAG Fort Leavenworth, 10 December 1879, Telegrams Sent DoNM, Vol.2, Jan.–Dec. 1879, NA, RG393, Part 3, Entry 431, p.476; *Thirty Four*, 10 December 1879; 'Town and County', *Grant County Herald*, 13 December 1879; See also Willcox to Haskell, Camp Rucker, 15 December 1879, NA, RG393, Part 1, Entry 169, Vol. 9, p.467.

13

Unfinished Business: Major Morrow Prepares for the 1880 Indian Campaign, November–December 1879

The US army had not been idle during Victorio's absence, but had been anticipating a return by the Warm Springs Apaches and making every effort to counter this threat. It was now believed that a significant number of Mescalero Apaches had joined Victorio and were still with him. General Pope requested that the Mescalero agent ascertain the numbers missing, and that a list of names be supplied to the commanding officer at Fort Stanton, in order that these individuals could be arrested on their return to the reservation. He felt that such action would make it far easier to control the Mescalero Apaches in future. Equally, if nothing was done, this could only reinforce a feeling of contempt for the United States among the Mescaleros.[1] Pope assumed that the Apaches would attempt to slip back onto the reservations in order to be fed during the winter, and that such arrests would be possible.[2]

On his return to Fort Bayard in early November, Major Morrow made every effort to refit and prepare his command for the return of the Warm Springs Apaches. In the short term, he retained the services of two companies from Carroll's command, F and M Companies, and also L Company, in order to deal with any immediate return to New Mexico by Victorio and his warriors.[3] However, L Company was quickly relieved of this duty and ordered to its station, Fort Bliss, to refit and prepare itself for future field service.[4]

As part of his preparations, Morrow requested two mountain howitzers, more horses, and 50 pack mules.[5] He was given permission to purchase 50 mules for his command, and these had largely been acquired by 18 November.[6] However, his endeavour to obtain the mountain howitzers turned

1 Pope to Sheridan, 4 November 1879, 'Victorio Files', NA, RG393, M1495, Roll 14; Pope to Sheridan, 4 November 1879, 'Victorio Papers', NA, M666, Roll 526.

2 Pope to Col. Whipple, AAG MDoM, 6 November 1879, 'Victorio Files', NA, RG393, M1495, Roll 14.

3 Loud to AAG Fort Leavenworth, 7 November 1879, Telegrams Sent DoNM, Vol.2, Jan.–Dec. 1879, NA, RG393, Part 3, Entry 431, p.408; Loud to Hatch, 8 November 1879, Telegrams Sent DoNM, Vol.2, Jan.–Dec. 1879, NA, RG393, Part 3, Entry 431, p.413; Loud to CO Fort Bliss, 12 November 1879, Telegrams Sent DoNM, Vol.2, Jan.–Dec. 1879, NA, RG393, Part 3, Entry 431, p.425.

4 Loud to CO Fort Bayard, 13 November 1879, Telegrams Sent DoNM, Vol.2, Jan.–Dec. 1879, NA, RG393, Part 3, Entry 431, p.427; Loud to CO Fort Bliss, 7 December 1879, Telegrams Sent DoNM, Vol.2, Jan.–Dec. 1879, NA, RG393, Part 3, Entry 431, p.469.

5 Loud to Hatch, 3 November 1879, Telegrams Sent DoNM, Vol.2, Jan.–Dec. 1879, NA, RG393, Part 3, Entry 431, p.393; Loud to AA General Fort Leavenworth, 4 November 1879, 'Victorio Papers', NA, M666, Roll 526.

6 Loud to Hatch, 18 November 1879, Telegrams Sent DoNM, Vol.2, Jan.–Dec. 1879, NA, RG393, Part 3, Entry 431, p.438; Pope to Whipple, 4 November 1879, Whipple to Pope, 7 November 1879, 'Victorio Files', NA, RG393, M1495, Roll 14; Whipple to Gen. Pope, 7 November 1879, NA, RG393, Part 1, Entry 2539, Press Copies of Letters and Endorsements Sent, MDoM, Vol. 12, p.158; Hatch to Loud, 6 November 1879 in Letters Sent by the '9MD/DNM/DoNM', NA, RG393, M1072, Roll 6, Jan-Oct 1879, Letter No.631, p.436.

into something of an epic manoeuvre. First, there was some confusion as to what he meant by 'Jackass' guns. Once this was clarified to mean small howitzers that were packed on mules, rather than dragged on wheels by a team,[7] a manual for the use and transportation of mountain howitzers was quickly sent from the Cheyenne ordnance depot to Las Vegas, NM.[8] Obtaining the howitzers themselves, however, was far more difficult. The Department of the Missouri had 26 mountain howitzers, but it was thought that none of these guns 'could be depended on for field service, owing to the condition of carriages and harness.'[9]

Table 13.1 Availability of Field Howitzers in the Department of the Missouri, November 1879[10]

Posts	Howitzers	Carriages	Condition	Remarks
Fort Garland	2	2	Serviceable	2 Sets of harnesses for wheel horses; no ammunition
Fort Bliss	2	2	Good	No harnesses; sufficient ammunition
Fort Wallace	1	1	Serviceable	No harnesses; sufficient ammunition
Fort Dodge	4	4	Seats badly worn	3 Sets of harnesses, badly worn; plenty of ammunition
Fort Hays	5	4	All old and worn	2 Sets of harnesses for wheel horses; sufficient ammunition
Fort Sill	4	4	Serviceable	No harnesses; sufficient ammunition
Fort Elliott	1	1	Bad wheels	4 Sets of harnesses, all worn
Fort Stanton	2	1	Bad carriage	No harnesses; sufficient amin[1]
Fort Supply	5	5	Serviceable	12 Sets of harnesses; sufficient amin

Note

1 By 'Amin' I presume this means 'Ammunition'.

It emerged that various depots and forts had various elements of this equipment, but none had a full set, and the individual parts had to be tracked down and ordered separately.[11] The US army had purchased 30 Hotchkiss mountain rifles in 1877. When accompanying cavalry units, these small

7 Loud to Hatch, 5 November 1879, Telegrams Sent DoNM, Vol.2, Jan.–Dec. 1879, NA, RG393, Part 3, Entry 431, p.402.

8 Cheyenne Ordnance Depot to AAAG, DoNM, 8 November 1879 in Letters Received by HQ DoNM, September 1865-August 1890, NA, RG393, M1088, Roll 39, Oct-Dec 1879.

9 Reilly, Capt. of Ordnance, to AAG, MDoM, 6 November 1879, 'Victorio Files', NA, RG393, M1495, Roll 14.

10 Reilly, Capt. of Ordnance, to AAG, MDoM, 6 Nov., 1879, 'Victorio Files', NA, RG393, M1495, Roll 14.

11 Loud to Morrow, 3 November 1879, Telegrams Sent DoNM, Vol.2, Jan.–Dec. 1879, NA, RG393, Part 3, Entry 431, p.395; Hatch to CO Fort Bliss, 5 November 1879,Telegrams Sent DoNM, Vol.2, Jan.–Dec. 1879, NA, RG393, Part 3, Entry 431, p.400; See also Letter from Loud to Capt. Shoemaker at Fort Union, 10 November 1879 "The District Commander directs that you ship at once to Santa Fé N.M., two (2) Mountain Howitzers, with or without carriages. If they have the limbers without axles and wheels they will answer." in Letters Sent by the '9MD/DNM/DoNM', NA, RG393, M1072, Roll 6, Jan-Oct 1879, Letter No.533 p.378.

A few days later, probably on realisation that carriages and wheels were still required if one wanted to fire the howitzer, Capt. Shoemaker was ordered to collect the required 'bits' but if this looked like exceeding a "reasonable time" he was to ship what he had. (Loud to Shoemaker, 17 November 1879 in Letters Sent by the '9MD/DNM/DoNM', NA, RG393, M1072, Roll 6, Jan-Oct 1879, Letter No.536, p.380.)

artillery pieces could be dismantled and transported on pack mules.[12] On 7 November 1879, General Pope informed District Headquarters in Santa Fé that a Hotchkiss mountain howitzer would be sent from Departmental Headquarters, Fort Leavenworth, Kansas, to Las Vegas and should be sent to on to Morrow, at Fort Bayard, immediately.[13] In fact, two mountain howitzers with 3,400 rounds of ammunition were reported to be en route in late November 1879, despite a delay in delivering pack saddles designed to carry the howitzers.[14] Morrow was delighted to be offered the two howitzers ; but he prophetically stated that he would not wait for them should the Apaches return before they were delivered.[15] This was just as well, as one howitzer seems to have been 'lost in the post.'[16] Just how effective a weapon the mountain howitzer would be against the Apaches was open to question. Indeed, in April 1880, a request was sent down from Division Headquarters that any reports on the performance of Hotchkiss guns in the field should be forwarded to them.[17] One of the howitzers despatched was tested on arrival at Fort Marcy in early December 1879. Five shots were fired at a ridge 1,400 yards away, and Table 13.2 shows the results obtained.

Table 13.2 Test Firing Results for the Hotchkiss Mountain Howitzer, Fort Marcy, December 1879[18]

Shot	Elevation	Result
1	No Elevation	Shell range 300 yards
2	5° Elevation	Passed over target ridge
3	3° Elevation	Passed over target ridge
4	1° Elevation	Shell range 550 yards. Fragmentation of shell poor as it buried itself in soft earth.
5	1° Elevation	Shell range 575 yards. Fragments scattered up to 40 yards from impact.

It was soon realised that the time required to range the weapon properly would give the Apaches ample time to withdraw. Also, the mountain howitzers did not come with a trained crew. One Corporal Robert Benjamin of M Company, Ninth Cavalry, was noted as an acting battery sergeant major in the company's bi-monthly return for March and April 1880.[19]

A telegram concerning the final shipping of the howitzer from Santa Fé also reveals that, during November, Morrow may have become seriously ill as a result of the campaign he had waged against Victorio. Hatch designated Captain Carroll as field commander should a replacement commander

12 Steffen, p.157.

13 Pope to Loud AAAG Santa Fé, NA, RG393, Part 3, Entry 439, p.101 see also Pope to Whipple, AAG, Chicago, 7 November 1879, NA, RG393, Part 1, Entry 2546, p.238.

14 Bloomfield to Loud AAAG Santa Fé, NA, RG393, Part 3, Entry 439, p.104; See also Whipple AAG to Col. Williams, Fort Omaha, 17? November 1879?, NA, RG393, Part 1, Entry 2539, Press Copies of Letters and Endorsements Sent, MDoM, Vol. 12, p.159.

15 Morrow to Loud AAAG, NA, RG393, Part 3, Entry 439 pp.10-11; (Loud to Hatch 5 November 1879, Telegrams Sent DoNM, Vol.2, Jan.–Dec. 1879, NA, RG393, Part 3, Entry 431, p.413; From Silver City it was reported that "a Gattling Gun intended for an interview with Victorio was sent south Wednesday." ('Territorial News', *Grant County Herald*, 13 December 1879.)

16 Loud to AAG Fort Leavenworth, 24 November 1879, Telegrams Sent DoNM, Vol.2, Jan.–Dec. 1879, NA, RG393, Part 3, Entry 431, p.444.

17 Chief Ordnance Officer, MDoM to AAG MDoM, 19 April 1880 in Letters Received by HQ_DoNM, September 1865-August 1890, NA, RG393, M1088, Roll 40, Jan-June 1880.

18 Lt Bradley to AAAG, DoNM, 8 Dec., 1879 in Letters Received by HQ_DoNM, September 1865-August 1890, NA, RG393, M1088, Roll 39, Oct-Dec 1879; Same letter in Letters Received, DoM 1868-98, RG 393, Entry A1-1 2601, Box 86.

19 Bi-Monthly Company Muster Rolls for Company M, 9th Cavalry, March/April 1880 in NA, RG94.

be needed. Hatch also suggested that the field command might be split into two columns, with Captain Carroll in command of one column and Captain Dodge in command of the other.[20]

Hatch continued to demand additional scouts, requesting that the 24 Apache scouts authorised earlier be employed for an additional three months from 1 January 1880. These were the Apache scouts originally recruited by Captain Purington on 1 October 1879 at Fort Bayard, and who were commanded by Lieutenant Maney. The extension of their service was finally authorised on 5 December 1879,[21] and Hatch approved scouts 'Mississippi' and 'Clenniwoody' to be made sergeants, and 'Dick Sweeny' and 'Chicken' to be made corporals of the company.[22] However, all that could be authorised in the meantime was the recruitment of 12 Navajo scouts.[23] By 29 November, Lieutenant Maney, with 25 troops and 25 Apache scouts, was stationed at Old Fort Cummings for the purpose of scouting the surrounding country for signs of Apaches.[24]

Lieutenant James[25] Allen, in charge of the military telegraph lines in New Mexico, requested the use of a detachment of one sergeant and 10 enlisted men from either Fort Bliss or Fort Bayard to help install approximately 1,500 new poles. This would allow Allen to put the telegraph lines 'in first class condition for the ensuing year.'[26] The work was completed on or around 13 April 1880.[27]

Two hundred replacement horses were urgently required, and were requested on 29 October 1879[28] (see Table 13.3). By 18 November, these replacements had arrived at Santa Fé and would be sent out under the command of Captain Dodge to their designated companies.[29]

Table 13.3 Replacement Horses for the Ninth Cavalry by Company, November 1879[30]

Company	A	B	C	D	E	F	G	H	L	M
Number of horses required	18	14	12	55	42	10	16	13	10	10

20 Hatch to Loud AAAG Santa Fé 24 November 1879, NA, RG393, Part 3, Entry 439, p.103; See also Loud to Hatch, 18 November 1879, Telegrams Sent DoNM, Vol.2, Jan.–Dec. 1879, NA, RG393, Part 3, Entry 431, p.438.

21 Loud to CO Fort Bayard, 5 & 6 December 1879, Telegrams Sent DoNM, Vol.2, Jan.–Dec. 1879, NA, RG393, Part 3, Entry 431, p.464 & p.466; Platt AAG Fort Leavenworth to Loud AAAG Santa Fé DoNM, 5 December 1879, NA, RG393, Part 3, Entry 439, p.105; Pope to Whipple, AAG, 8 November 1879, & Pope to Whipple, HQ_MDoM, 4 December 1879, 'Victorio Files', NA, RG393, M1495, Roll 14.

22 Special Order 121, par 2, December 6, 1879 in NA, RG393, Part 3, Entry 450.

23 Loud to CO Fort Bayard, 5 December 1879, Telegrams Sent DoNM, Vol.2, Jan.–Dec. 1879, NA, RG393, Part 3, Entry 431, pp.464-465; Loud to AAG Fort Leavenworth, 3 December 1880, Telegrams Sent DoNM, Vol.2, Jan.–Dec. 1879, NA, RG393, Part 3, Entry 431, p.458; Platt AAG Fort Leavenworth to AAAG DoNM, 4 December 1879, NA, RG393, Part 3, Entry 439, p.104.

24 Loud to AAG Fort Leavenworth, 24 November 1879, Telegrams Sent DoNM, Vol.2, Jan.–Dec. 1879, NA, RG393, Part 3, Entry 431, p.445; *Grant County Herald*, 29 November 1879; See also *Thirty Four*, 3 December 1879.

25 Having checked through Heitman's Historical Dictionary of U.S. Army Officers I am reasonably sure that this officer's first name is James.

26 Lt. Allen to AAAG DoNM, 2 December 1879 in Letters Received by HQ_DoNM, September 1865-August 1890, NA, RG393, M1088, Roll 39, Oct-Dec 1879.

27 Allen, Signals Officer, New Mexico Division to AAAG, DoNM, 13 April 1880 in Letters Received by HQ_DoNM, September 1865–August 1890, NA, RG393, M1088, Roll 40, Jan.–June 1880.

28 AAAG DoNM, 29 October 1879 in Letters Received by HQ_DoNM, September 1865–August 1890, NA, RG393, M1088, Roll 39, Oct-Dec 1879.

29 Loud to AAG Fort Leavenworth, 18 November 1879, Telegrams Sent DoNM, Vol.2, Jan.–Dec. 1879, NA, RG393, Part 3, Entry 431, pp.438-439.

30 AAAG DoNM, 29 Oct., 1879 in Letters Received by HQ_DoNM, Sept.–Aug., 1890, NA, RG393, M1088, Roll 39, Oct-Dec 1879.

Colonel Hatch organised the replacement of horses for the following companies from Fort Union. Rather than 200 replacement horses, the District of New Mexico appears to have been given 210 new mounts. A veterinary surgeon was posted to Fort Union with specific instructions to facilitate the resupply of horses.[31] Captain Dodge, with D Company, was to escort these replacement mounts to Fort Craig, where an escort detail from Ojo Caliente would receive E Company's horses. These were collected by Lieutenant F.B. Taylor with 22 enlisted men, and this party left Ojo Caliente on 29 November and returned with the remounts on 10 December. Dodge would continue with the balance of the horses to Fort Bayard, where they would be distributed to their respective companies. Captain Dodge, with his company, was then to place himself and his company under Major Morrow 'for duty in the field.'[32] The replacement horses for L Company were to be sent with an escort to Fort Selden, where they would be turned over to a detachment from Fort Bliss, Texas, and delivered to that company.[33] An Acting Assistant Surgeon was also directed to report to Fort Bayard.[34] Captain Hooker's newly remounted E Company was also instructed to place itself under Morrow's command, ready for field service should Morrow require its services.[35] On or around 6 December, two Ninth Cavalry companies, A and G, moved to Fort Stanton, swapping their station posting for that of F and M companies, who remained at Fort Bayard,[36] as Morrow had decided that Victorio was 'no longer within reach and not likely to be this winter.'[37] The latter two companies had left Fort Stanton with Captain Carroll, and since they had not engaged in any direct pursuits of the Apaches likely to affect the number and condition of their horses, or their own well-being. Therefore, both horses and men were almost certainly in better physical shape than at the height of the 1879 campaign. This strongly suggests that the replacement horses for these companies had also arrived, allowing Hatch to re-deploy two of the six companies currently based in or around Fort Bayard. After all, there was no guarantee that Victorio would return from Mexico to the vicinity of Fort Bayard. As we have seen, the army was convinced that a substantial number of Mescalero Apaches had joined Victorio. The return of two companies of cavalry to Fort Stanton was imperative. It would also relieve pressure on the army's logistical arrangements if two companies could be removed from the Fort Bayard garrison. Nevertheless it was clear that these replacement horses had still not completely remounted the regiment.

Thus, even with the arrival of 210 replacement horses, only two companies, E and K, now had enough horses to mount their available men, though D Company was only two horses short. As late as 19 December, Headquarters, Department of the Missouri contacted the District of New Mexico asking, 'how many horses required to mount Ninth Cavalry and to what points should they

31 Special Order 111, par 1, November 3 1879 in NA, RG393, Part 3, Entry 450.

32 Special Order 111, par 2, November 3 1879 in NA, RG393, Part 3, Entry 450; See also Hooker to Lt F.B. Taylor, Order No.9, In the Field, Ojo Caliente, N.M. 28 November 1879, Special Orders Rec'd from Sub Commands, NA, RG393, Part 3, Entry 453.

33 Special Order 111, par 3, November 3 1879 in NA, RG393, Part 3, Entry 450; Captain Dodge with 45 men of Company D, Ninth Cavalry passed near Santa Fé on November 26, 1879 with 10 horses for Fort Bliss, 42 for Ojo Caliente and 98 for Fort Bayard. ('By Telegraph', *Grant County Herald*, 29 November 1879.)

34 Special Order 120, December 3, 1879 in NA, RG393, Part 3, Entry 450.

35 Loud to Hooker, Ojo Caliente, 22 December 1879, Telegrams Sent DoNM, Vol.2, Jan.–Dec. 1879, NA, RG393, Part 3, Entry 431, p.486.

36 Loud to CO Fort Bayard, 6 December 1879, Telegrams Sent DoNM, Vol.2, Jan.–Dec. 1879, NA, RG393, Part 3, Entry 431, p.467.

37 Loud to AAG Fort Leavenworth and Hatch 2 December 1880, Telegrams Sent DoNM, Vol.2, Jan.–Dec. 1879, NA, RG393, Part 3, Entry 431, pp.456-457; See also Special Order 121, par 3 & 4, December 6, 1879 in NA, RG393, Part 3, Entry 450; See also 'Town and County, *Grant County Herald*, 13 December 1879.

be sent?'[38] As Table 13.4 shows, even a substantial delivery of replacement mounts only resulted in 496 serviceable horses to 642 available men, and this is if we assume that I Company had enough horses for their available men. This left the Ninth Cavalry at least 146 horses short to mount the available troops.[39] The bi-monthly muster rolls also reveal that the Ninth Cavalry also possessed 59 unserviceable horses at that period. Even if those horses recovered, it meant that the regiment was still 87 horses short of mounting the available men.[40]

Table 13.4 Available Men to Serviceable Horses, Ninth Cavalry, November to December 1879[41]

Company	Available Men Nov-Dec	Serviceable Horses Nov–Dec	Company	Available Men Nov–Dec	Serviceable Horses Nov–Dec
A	57	31	G	55	35
B	55	32	H	57	36
C	53	33	I	48	No entry
D	55	53	K	47	47
E	48	51	L	54	39
F	56	47	M	57	44

Morrow was aware of another factor contributing to the 'red peril' he faced, and this appeared in the form of US army bureaucracy. He complained that 'I cannot draw ammunition as post commander but must get it from my Co[mpany] Commander.'[42] However, bureaucratic 'red tape' could sometimes be mobilised positively and it was reported that the Division of the Missouri was trying to limit the number of Indian scouts raised by other Departments, thereby allowing the District of New Mexico to recruit its own Indian scouts without exceeding the US army's authorised strength. Hence the following instructions issued to the commander of the Department of Dakota.

> The recent field operations, and those contemplated, having made it necessary to increase the number of Indian scouts heretofore allowed the Department of the Missouri, I am directed by the Lieut. General comd'g to inform you that not more than (100) Indian scouts can be allowed to your Department for the present.[43]

On 3 December 1879, General Pope put Morrow directly in command of operations against Apaches in southern New Mexico. He argued that Morrow now commanded nine cavalry companies and was supported by a substantial number of infantry. He had been sent replacement horses and a mountain howitzer, and had been furnished with a pack train of 50 mules. Pope stated that 'sufficient' Apache and Navajo scouts had been allocated to Morrow's command. In addition, Morrow had been granted authorization to refit his command from any post in southern New

38 Platt AAG Fort Leavenworth to AAAG DoNM, 19 December 1879, NA, RG393, Part 3, Entry 439, p.105.
39 There are no figures entered in the bi-monthly muster rolls for Company I, but as they were not committed to the campaign along with Company K, I think it is reasonable to assume that they probably had the requisite number of serviceable horses to available men.
40 Derived Bi-Monthly Company Muster Rolls for November/December 1879, 9th Cavalry, NA, RG94.
41 Derived Bi-Monthly Company Muster Rolls for Nov.,/Dec., 1879, 9th Cavalry, NA, RG94.
42 Morrow to Loud AAAG, NA, RG393, Part 3, Entry 439 p.10.
43 NA, RG393, Part 1, Entry 2539, Press Copies of Letters and Endorsements Sent, MDoM, Vol. 12, p.184.

Mexico.[44] Whether Morrow had received enough scouts, or horses, is open to question; and, so far, the mountain howitzer had not arrived. However, it was clear that General Pope thought that there were more than enough men and materials in place to deal with Victorio. In giving the major complete control of operations, Pope also placed responsibility for the success of future operations squarely on Morrow's shoulders:

> I simply desire to impress upon you that in my judgement you have sufficient force to accomplish the duty assigned you, and that it is well equipped for field service in every respect. If you need anything more it will be furnished you but you are to understand that I rely upon you to keep the peace in that region. That your force is sufficient for the purpose so far as the Indians at any of the Agencies in New Mexico are concerned appears to me clear and I am equally sure, that by judicious management of the force and the requisite authority, this result can be entirely secured.[45]

Finally, Pope made it clear that a major show of force should be visited on the Mescalero Apaches on their reservation. Pope stated that he had contacted the Department of the Interior to 'order' their agent to discover the identities of those Apaches engaged in raiding, so that they could be arrested and punished.[46]

Not only did Morrow have to cope with Pope's assumption that a 'superiority in numbers' approach would deal with Apache guerrillas; the major also had to contend with false allegations that Victorio had immediately doubled back into New Mexico and was slaying citizens in the vicinity of Hillsboro and McEvers' Ranch. To be fair, District Headquarters made it quite clear that they did not believe these reports, but had to make enquiries.[47] For example, Lieutenant Emmet was sent to McEvers' Ranch to investigate a rumour that nine men had been killed near that point and returned to inform Morrow that there was no truth in this story.[48] In an exasperated telegram to Santa Fé, Morrow stated that:

> The report that Indians are in this country committing depredations and that I was followed back by Victorio and that men have been killed by Victorio at or near Hillsboro or McEvers' Ranch is absolutely false there is not an Indian in the country except our scouts nor has there been since I drove Victorio out of NM mendacious citizens to the contrary not withstanding. Maney with his scouts is at Cummings scouting the country. Wright has detach of 30 Cav and ten Navahoes at McEvers. Twelve men at Chases[49] on the Animas. I receive reports every day from my own posts and these rumours I heard were too ridiculous and too baseless to merit attention.[50]

---

44 Pope to Morrow, 3 December 1879 in Letters Received by HQ DoNM, September 1865-August 1890, NA, RG393, M1088, Roll 39, Oct-Dec 1879.

45 Pope to Morrow, 3 December 1879 in Letters Received by HQ DoNM, September 1865-August 1890, NA, RG393, M1088, Roll 39, Oct-Dec 1879.

46 Pope to Morrow, 3 December 1879 in Letters Received by HQ DoNM, September 1865-August 1890, NA, RG393, M1088, Roll 39, Oct-Dec 1879.

47 Loud to Morrow, 26 November 1879, Telegrams Sent DoNM, Vol.2, Jan.–Dec. 1879, NA, RG393, Part 3, Entry 431, p.449.

48 Emmett to Post Adjutant, Fort Bayard, 30 November 1879 in Letters Received by HQ DoNM, September 1865-August 1890, NA, RG393, M1088, Roll 39, Oct–Dec 1879.

49 Swain, to AAG DoNM, 10 November 1879 in Letters Received by HQ DoNM, September 1865-August 1890, NA, RG393, M1088, Roll 39, Oct–Dec 1879.

50 Morrow to Loud AAAG, 26 November? 1879, NA, RG393, Part 3, Entry 439 pp.14-15; Same letter in Letters Received, DoM 1868-98, RG 393, Entry A1-1 2601, Box 85; See also Morrow to Loud & Loud to Morrow, 16 November 1879, 'Victorio Files', NA, RG393, M1495, Roll 14; Morrow to

Other rumours circulating insisted that Victorio had been identified as having led an attack on miners in the Sacramento Mountains. This attack was investigated by Lieutenant Smith, who concluded that Victorio was nowhere near the Sacramento Mountains and that the raid in question had been made by Comanches and Kiowas.[51] If an attack by Apaches had occurred at all, it was far more likely the work of Mescalero Apaches. Furthermore, large numbers of Apaches had been seen heading west from the Mescalero reservation towards the Rio Grande.[52] Smith's main concern was that, at this time, he did not have enough troops to protect the Indian agency, let alone patrol the area between La Luz and the Seven Rivers in an attempt to provide as early a warning of Victorio's return as possible. In the meantime, Smith had asked some Mexican-American citizens to keep an eye on the country. In a further investigation by Lieutenant Schaeffer, these reports were found to be at best exaggerated, and at worst completely fabricated.[53] Rumours also drifted north from Mexico suggesting that General Trevino, with 900 troops, had Victorio corralled in the Guzman Mountains. Morrow sent this information to District Headquarters on 8 December 1879, stating that Lieutenant Maney and his scouts were already in a good position to patrol the international line should any Apaches break free and make for the United States.[54] As with many other reports, this one turned out to be false.

As the campaign progressed, relations between the army and the local citizenry, particularly the press, again deteriorated rapidly. For the moment, the *Grant County Herald* confined itself to promoting the re-establishment of Fort Cummings as the most advantageous point from which to combat Apaches and other desperadoes.[55] However, the paper also reported a number of rumours concerning Victorio's whereabouts. Victorio was said to have returned to the United States via Fort Quitman and western Texas, and the road to Chihuahua City from El Paso was said to be blocked by the Apaches.[56] Despite these additional pressures, Major Morrow made every effort to deploy his forces so as to give as early a warning as possible of a return to the US by Victorio. Small detachments of troops were stationed at Chase's Ranch on the Animas River, at Brockman's Ranch on the Mimbres River, at Slocum's Ranch, at Parson William's Ranch in the San Francisco Valley, at Burro Springs, and at Knight's Ranch. A company of cavalry with Navajo scouts under Lieutenant Wright was stationed at McEvers' Ranch.[57] This won a cautious welcome from the *Grant County Herald*.[58]

Loud AAAG 26 November 1879 (See also Bennett to Post Adjutant Fort Bayard, 30 November 1879), 'Victorio Papers', NA, M666, Roll 526.

51 This is unlikely. Photographs of Mescalero Apaches show a Plains Indian influenced appearance and suggests that if any raid had been made it was by Mescalero Apaches. Loud to AAG Fort Leavenworth, 13 December 1879, Telegrams Sent DoNM, Vol.2, Jan.–Dec. 1879, NA, RG393, Part 3, Entry 431, p.478.

52 Loud to CO Fort Bayard, 4 December 1879, Telegrams Sent DoNM, Vol.2, Jan.–Dec. 1879, NA, RG393, Part 3, Entry 431, p.461.

53 Loud to CO Fort Bayard, 4 December 1879, Telegrams Sent DoNM, Vol.2, Jan.–Dec. 1879, NA, RG393, Part 3, Entry 431, p.460.

54 Loud to AAG Fort Leavenworth, 8 December 1879, Telegrams Sent DoNM, Vol.2, Jan.–Dec. 1879, NA, RG393, Part 3, Entry 431.

55 'Town and County', *Grant County Herald*, 15 November 1879; 'Editorial', *Grant County Herald*, 22 November 1879.

56 'Territorial News', *Grant County Herald*, 22 November 1879; *Thirty Four*, 19 November 1879.

57 Loud to AAG MDoM, 5 November 1879, 'Victorio Files', NA, RG393, M1495, Roll 14; Loud to AAG Fort Leavenworth, 4 November 1879, 'Victorio Papers', NA, M666, Roll 526); Returns for November & December 1879 in Returns From U.S. Military Posts 1800-1916 Fort Bayard, New Mexico 1866-Dec. 1879, M617 Roll 87; 'Ashenfelter Editorial', *Grant County Herald*, 22 November 1879; See also *Thirty Four*, 26 November 1879.

58 'Ashenfelter Editorial', *Grant County Herald*, 22 November 1879.

General Ord, commanding the Military Department of Texas, had also contacted Colonel Grierson, with a view to preventing Apaches passing through western Texas. As part of this effort, Grierson was instructed to cooperate with the Mexican military authorities, by sending and receiving information through Mariano Samaniego in El Paso del Norte. The Tenth Cavalry were well placed to perform this task and picket the Rio Grande frontier, having actively surveyed the area in response to General Ord's earlier instructions to carefully map western Texas in order to limit the activities of Apache raiders.[59] On receipt of information that the Mexican federal army was preparing an offensive against the Apaches, Grierson placed the troops based at Forts Davis and Stockton on the alert to be ready to move immediately into the field should any Apaches attempt to move into the District of the Pecos.[60]

In the Department of Arizona, it was clear that Colonel Carr was anxious about the Warm Springs Apaches returning to the United States, and about the possibility that they might do so via southeastern Arizona. As noted earlier, Carr did not believe that Victorio had been beaten, and he thought that the Warm Springs Apaches could make trouble in southern Arizona. He telegraphed Morrow on 11 November 1879, asking for information on the size and location of, and the general direction taken by, Victorio's following.[61] On the same day, Lieutenant Blocksom, in charge of a newly recruited C Company, Indian Scouts and 20 Sixth cavalrymen, was sent to scout south-eastern Arizona.[62] Blocksom was instructed to report to Lieutenant Harry L. Haskell, at Camp Rucker, in order that attempts to persuade Juh to settle on the San Carlos reservation were not jeopardised by Blocksom's scouting activities However, Blocksom was also ordered to be vigilant for any activity by Apaches. Carr estimated the Warm Springs Apaches to be within 90 miles of the Arizona border and 18 miles south-east of Ascuncion. This placed Blocksom in a rather awkward position, as Juh was widely, and probably rightly, believed to have been allied with Victorio.[63] Lieutenant Howard was ordered to move his Apache scout company to Fort Bowie and place himself ready to act upon any instructions issued by Lieutenant Haskell.[64] Later in December, Carr had to sharply remind Lieutenant Blocksom to move east, as was stipulated in his original orders, so as to avoid any clash with any of Juh's Chiricahuas moving north to surrender.[65] The following day, Lieutenant Howard was ordered to move to Camp Huachuca again, with strict instructions to proceed with care in order to preclude any incident which might imperil Lieutenant Haskell's activities.[66]

59 See for example Vincent to CO, DoP, 30 April 1878 in Register of Telegrams Rec'd Jan. 23, 1878-Feb. 4, 1881, HQ DoP 1878-1881, NA, RG393, M1381, Roll 2, Page.19, Letter No. 40, ; Vincent, AAG, DoTx, to CO, DoP, 11 March 1879 in Letters Rec'd File Mar. 19, 1878-Feb. 14, 1881, HQ DoP 1878-1881, NA, RG393, M1381, Roll 2; McChristian, 1982, p.49; Temple, 1962, pp.86-87.

60 Grierson to AAG, DoTx, 31 December 1879 in Letters Sent September 19, 1879–August 11, 1880, HQ DoP 1878-1881, NA, RG393, M1381 Roll 1, Letter No. 27.

61 Carr to Morrow, 11 November 1879, Troops in Southeastern Arizona, DoAz, NA, RG393, Part 1, Entry 232, Vol.4, July 3, 1879–Dec. 13 1879, Letter No.225, p.151.

62 Carr to CO Fort Grant & Lt. Blocksom (through CO Fort Bowie), 11 November 1879, Troops in Southeastern Arizona, DoAz, NA, RG393, Part 1, Entry 232, Vol.4, July 3, 1879–Dec. 13 1879, Letter No.'s 234 & 235, pp.160-161.

63 Carr to Blocksom, 11 November 1879, Troops in Southeastern Arizona, DoAz, NA, RG393, Part 1, Entry 232, Vol.4, July 3, 1879–Dec. 13, 1879, Letter No.236, pp.161-163.

64 AAAG to Howard, 17 November 1879, Troops in Southeastern Arizona, DoAz, NA, RG393, Part 1, Entry 232, Vol.4, July 3, 1879–Dec. 13, 1879, Letter No.249, pp.171-172.

65 Carr to Blocksom, 16 December 1879, Troops in Southeastern Arizona, DoAz, NA, RG393, Part 1, Entry 232, Vol.5, Dec. 13, 1879–May 7, 1880, Letter No.290, pp.6-7.

66 Carr to Howard, 17 December 1879, Troops in Southeastern Arizona, DoAz, NA, RG393, Part 1, Entry 232, Vol.5, Dec. 13, 1879–May 7, 1880, Letter No.291, pp.7-8.

General Willcox, in charge of the Military Department of Arizona, issued similar orders concerning the guarding of the Arizona-New Mexico border. Lieutenant John Brown Kerr, at Fort Lowell, was warned to be extra vigilant when scout companies were rotated in south-eastern Arizona. He was also told that 'if anything requires attention, act without further instructions.'[67] On the last day of 1879, Lieutenant Gatewood, with his Apache scout company plus seven non-commissioned officers and 27 privates, Sixth Cavalry, was ordered out to scout the area between the Gila River and the San Francisco River. Gatewood's comments about the lack of medical personnel assigned to Indian Scout companies must have registered with his superiors, as a medical officer was ordered to join Gatewood's detachment, as was one Second Lieutenant Cruse.[68] In fact, Carr had recommended that each Apache scout company should have two elements – Apache scouts and a detachment of US cavalry – with the mule train. He also recommended that two officers should be assigned to each scout company: one to remain with the mule train while the other ranged ahead with the Apache scouts.[69]

Carr also drew attention to the shortage of stores, mules and officers, which was impeding the efficient scouting of the territory for Apaches. This situation was leading to considerable 'overwork' of mules and concomitant mule losses. He also recommended 'a more liberal supply even at the risk of some spoiling as Officers in the country are so dependent upon the commissary.'[70]

However, Colonel Carr, in matters where cooperation between the Department of Arizona and the District of New Mexico were concerned, was utterly tactless. He suggested that Arizona troops had taken the brunt of the losses in the Guzman Mountains fighting, and that, based on this fact, it was only right that the District of New Mexico should be 'attached to our Department.'[71] If one examines the progress of the campaign so far, it is clear that the Sixth Cavalry and, in particular, the Apache scout detachments from Arizona, had played a significant role in the campaign; but to claim they had borne the lion's share of the fighting was a significant exaggeration. On the one hand, it may have made perfect sense to put operations against the Apaches under one command structure. On the other hand, to place the District of New Mexico under the command of the Department of Arizona, thus shifting it from the Military Division of the Missouri to the Military Division of the Pacific, implied a failure on the part of Colonel Hatch, General Pope and, indeed, General Sheridan. While the smooth co-ordination of plans between the three military departments – Arizona, Missouri and Texas – and the Mexicans could be very difficult, the basic problem was the lack of enough troops and logistical support to decisively combat Apache guerrilla techniques. While the Apaches were respected as opponents by many officers, at many levels of the army, there was still a basic lack of understanding of the sheer sophistication of the Apache principles of warfare. As we have seen, and shall see again, the Apaches did not make the same mistake, and their techniques were designed to take maximum advantage of the weaknesses of their foes.

67 Carter, Acting ADC, HQ Troops in the Field, Camp on the Black River to Lieut. Kerr, Lowell 25 November/December? 1879, NA, RG393, Part 1, Entry 235, p.29.

68 Carr Special Orders No 12, 31 December 1879, NA, RG393, Part 1, Entry 240; Carr to CO Fort Apache, 14 December 1879, Troops in Southeastern Arizona, DoAz, NA, RG393, Part 1, Entry 232, Vol.5, Dec. 13, 1879–May 7, 1880, p.2.

69 Carr to AAG DoAz, 18 November 1879, Troops in Southeastern Arizona, DoAz, NA, RG393, Part 1, Entry 232, Vol.4, July 3, 1879–Dec. 13, 1879, Letter No.252, pp.173-174.

70 Carr to Chief Quartermaster through AG Dept. Arizona, 25 November 1879, Troops in Southeastern Arizona, DoAz, NA, RG393, Part 1, Entry 232, Vol.4, July 3, 1879–Dec. 13, 1879, Letter No.259, p.178.

71 Carr to AG, Whipple Barracks A.T. undated telegram, NA, RG393, Part 1, Entry 240; Carr to AD DoAz, 6 November 1879, Troops in Southeastern Arizona, DoAz, NA, RG393, Part 1, Entry 232, Vol.4, July 3, 1879–Dec. 13, 1879, Letter No.229, pp.156-157.

For them, success could only be accomplished by a keen interest in understanding how their enemy operated. The Apaches could simply not afford to take their enemies for granted.

Finally, Lew Wallace, Governor of the Territory of New Mexico, considered raising a territorial militia to combat the Apaches. He inspected the area in December 1879 and viewed concrete evidence of Apache raids that had resulted in 'sixteen mutilated corpses of men women and children.'[72] His inspection tour seems to have been undertaken in response to citizens lobbying for the state to provide them with the means to defend themselves.[73] There were protests in at least one editorial that if arms and ammunition were not to be forthcoming, communities should organise 'volunteer companies' and 'take the Indian question in their own hands and deal to the Indians the justice they justly deserve.'[74] When Victorio's raids intensified, in 1880, the legislature voted the sum of $100,000 to equip a volunteer militia of no more than 1,000 members.[75] However, in marked contrast to the state militia of Chihuahua, US citizen posses and militias could be defined by their ineffectiveness throughout this campaign.

Having prepared themselves as best they could, US forces faced the coming year and a fresh round of campaigning against the Apaches. With Mexican forces in the field as well, it was only a matter of time before the US army once again crossed swords with Victorio. Thus, as 1879 closed, Major Morrow's command was as prepared as could be expected for a return to New Mexico by Victorio. However, it would be both those Mescalero Apaches who were unaffiliated with Victorio and his former allies, the southern Chiricahua Apaches, led by Juh, who would first attract the attention of the United States authorities.

Mescalero Apaches Raid the Pecos Valley Settlements

In late December, a number of raids by Mescalero Apaches were reported from Roswell down to the Delaware and Black Rivers. Several ranches were struck, with cattle killed and horses stolen. After one ranch, Ashby's near Seven Rivers, was raided, the owner, Ashby, gathered a posse of 10 men and followed the raiders into the Guadalupe Mountains, where they were ambushed, although they managed to withdraw after half an hour's fighting.[76] This information was passed to the US Army with appeals for protection. It was assumed that the Mescaleros involved were based, in force, in the Sacramento and Guadalupe Mountains, and that any response by the US army should involve a well-organised command.[77] Some Mescaleros had clearly drifted down into Texas, for in the first

72 Jones, 1985, p.138.

73 Jones, 1985, p.138: See also Town & County Section *Grant County Herald* 20 September 1879; Territorial News Section, *Grant County Herald*, 27 September 1879.

74 Territorial News Section, *Grant County Herald*, 27 September 1879.

75 Jones, 1985, p.138.

76 Ashby to Swain, 27 December 1879 in Letters Received by HQ DoNM, September 1865-August 1890, NA, , RG393, M1088, Roll 39, Oct-Dec 1879; Same letter in Letters Received, DoM 1868-98, RG 393, Entry A1-1 2601, Box 86; Loud to Co Fort Bayard, 2 January 1880 on receipt of a letter dated Roswell N.M. 27 December 1879, Telegrams Sent DoNM, Vol.3, Jan.–Nov. 1880 NA, RG393, Part 3, Entry 431, pp.2-3 See also p.4; Pope to AAG HQ MDoM, 3 January 1880, 'Victorio Files', NA, RG393, M1495, Roll 14; See also Smither to CO's Forts Stockton & Davis, 10 January 1880 in Telegrams Sent 24 April 1879-22 June, 1880, HQ DoP 1878-1881, NA, RG393, M1381, Roll 1, pp.170-171, Letter No.18.

77 Swain to AAAG, DoNM, 29 December 1879 in Letters Received by HQ DoNM, September 1865-August 1890, NA, RG393, M1088, Roll 39, Oct-Dec 1879; Loud to Co Fort Bayard, 2 January 1880 on receipt of a letter dated Roswell N.M. 27 December 1879, Telegrams Sent DoNM, Vol.3, Jan.–Nov. 1880 NA, RG393, Part 3, Entry 431, pp.2-3 see also p.4; Pope to AAG HQ MDoM, 3 January 1880, 'Victorio Files', NA, RG393, M1495, Roll 14; 'Indian Affairs' *Army & Navy Journal*, Vol.17, 17 January 1880, p.465.

days of January, the mail carrier between Pecan Springs and Howard's Well was chased by eight Apaches and was only able to complete his journey by retreating to a cow-camp and persuading three cow-boys to escort him.[78] This news prompted Grierson to order both Fort Davis and Fort Stockton to each put on alert at their garrison one company of cavalry and infantry which would respond to further threats should materialise. Scouts from both posts were ordered to reconnoitre towards the Black and Delaware Rivers to confirm whether these attacks presaged a general attack on the Pecos Valley.[79] The scout detachment from Fort Stockton could only discover the week-old signs of four Apaches, with stolen horses, who were heading back towards their reservation.[80] This group had passed a ranch owned by a Mr Richards and stolen some horses before escaping towards the Mescalero reservation.[81]

Juh and Geronimo Negotiate their Way into the San Carlos Reservation

By mid-December 1879, with Chihuahua State thoroughly stirred up and threatening to become too hot for them, Juh and his followers – 90 persons in all – were slipping northwards to negotiate their way onto the San Carlos reservation in Arizona.[82] It was reported that 84 previously hostile Apaches had surrendered at Camp Rucker, Arizona Territory, and it was at first assumed that this was Victorio's following.[83] The illusion was quickly banished. Juh and Geronimo were said to have acknowledged that they had been raiding on their own account, but had denied an alliance with Victorio.[84]

This was the last round of intermittent attempts to induce those Chiricahuas who had left, or had never accepted the move to, the San Carlos reservation, to come in from their strongholds in Mexico. As early as February 1879, Major Compton suggested that the groups led by Geronimo, Juh and Nolgee could be persuaded to return to the reservation through the assistance of friends and relatives who had moved to the reservation in 1876.[85] It is known that, in the following month, four Chiricahuas from San Carlos were preparing to go into Chihuahua in an attempt

---

78 Blunt, CO Fort Stockton to AAG, DoP, 4 January 1880 in Register of Telegrams Rec'd 11 October 1879-8 October 1880, HQ DoP 1878-1881, NA, RG393, M1381, Roll 2, p.59, Letter No.3; Smither to CO, Grierson's Spring, 5 January 1880 in Telegrams Sent 24 April 1879–22 June, 1880, HQ DoP 1878-1881 NA, RG393, M1381, Roll 1, p.164, Letter No.7.

79 Smither to CO's Forts Stockton & Davis, 10 January 1880 in Telegrams Sent 24 April 1879-22 June, 1880, HQ DoP 1878-1881, NA, RG393, M1381 Roll 1, pp.170-171, Letter No.18.

80 Grierson to CO DoNM, 18 January 1880 in Telegrams Sent 24 April 1879-22 June, 1880, HQ DoP 1878-1881, NA, RG393, M1381 Roll 1, pp.175-176, Letter No.24.

81 Blunt to AAAG, Fort Concho, 16 January 1880 in Register of Telegrams Rec'd 11 October 1879-8 October 1880, HQ DoP 1878-1881, NA, RG393, M1381, Roll 2, p.68, Letter No.26.

82 Haskell to Willcox, 21 December 1879, in 'Frelinghuysen-Romero Papers', Letters Rec'd by the AGO, 1881-1889, NA, M689, Roll 81; See also Thrapp, 1974, p.259; See also 'Town and County', *Grant County Herald*, 20 December 1879.

83 Loud to AAG Fort Leavenworth, 20 December 1879, Telegrams Sent DoNM, Vol.2, Jan.–Dec. 1879, NA, RG393, Part 3, Entry 431, p.483; 'Ashenfelter Editorial', *Grant County Herald*, 20 December 1879; 'From Georgetown', *Grant County Herald*, 27 December 1879; This prompted some wishful but also prophetic thinking. "Old Vic has probably committed suicide, as he has sworn to die rather than to surrender. We hope so at least." ('From Georgetown', *Grant County Herald*, 27 December 1879.)

84 Haskell to Willcox, 14 December 1879, in 'Frelinghuysen-Romero Papers', Letters Rec'd by the AGO, 1881-1889, NA, M689, Roll 81; Report sent by Van C. Smith, Camp Bowie, 16 December 1879 in *Thirty Four*, 24 December 1879; 'By Telegraph', *Grant County Herald*, 24 January 1880.

85 Compton to Hart, U.S. Indian Agent, San Carlos, 13 February 1879, Field Records – Troops in Southeastern Arizona, DoAz, NA, RG393, Part 1, Entry 232, Vol.2, Sept 1 1878–May 27, 1879, Letter No. 51.

to contact and open negotiations with the independent Chiricahuas.[86] It is not clear what the result of this embassy was, but in August 1879, General Willcox expressed an interest in trying to induce 'renegades' in Chihuahua to return to their reservations.[87] On 5 September 1879, he reported that the Chiricahua leaders on the San Carlos reservation had let it be known that the independent Chiricahuas 'may now be prevailed upon to join the agency at San Carlos.'[88] Again, the Chiricahuas at San Carlos offered to help facilitate the return. Willcox stated that he had information that 25 families were known to be at Casas Grandes, with a number of other families ranging through northern Chihuahua.[89] On 4 September 1879, Willcox had sent his aide-de-camp, Lieutenant Haskell, to investigate this development. He also requested that 'during this movement the Government be requested not to interpose any diplomatic obstacles to its success.'[90] Haskell's mission was temporarily suspended on 13 September, pending further instructions from Washington DC.[91] The main obstacle to this initiative was how to send a US army officer, plus several leading Chiricahua Apaches, into Mexico without causing a diplomatic incident.[92] This was quickly resolved the following day, when it was decided that 'officially' the US authorities were to make no formal contact with the Chiricahuas in Mexico. However, 'informal' contact could be attempted, but only with the cooperation of the local Mexican authorities. On this basis, Haskell was informed that he could continue with his mission.[93]

Thus, even as open warfare flared up in New Mexico, during September and October 1879, a diplomatic initiative aimed at persuading the Chiricahuas in Mexico to return to Arizona was in progress. Once it was clear that Victorio was making for Mexico, Lieutenant Haskell was asked to contact the local Mexican authorities 'either direct or through Major Arnold, with a view to securing the arrest of Victoria's people,'[94] provided that such negotiations did not jeopardise his ongoing efforts to secure the surrender of Juh's Chiricahuas: this despite the fact that some of the latter were strongly suspected of having joined Victorio. Willcox emphatically identified Hoo [Juh] as leading the Chiricahuas in Mexico, and described him as 'a bad Indian' who 'is continually raiding and creating disturbance.'[95] Just over a week after Morrow's clash with Victorio in Mexico, an Indian policeman named Atzebee, who had been sent into Mexico by Lieutenant Haskell, returned with two Chiricahua men, two women and three children. These reported that the rest of their number would be arriving in the next 30 or 40 days, and that Mexican troops were in the field

86 Compton to CB McLellan, 24 March 1879, Field Records – Troops in Southeastern Arizona, DoAz, NA, RG393, Part 1, Entry 232, Vol.2, Sept 1, 1878-May 27, 1879, Letter No. 86.

87 Willcox to Hatch, 25 August 1879, NA, RG393, Part 1, Entry 169, Vol. 9., p.308; See also Report of Gen. Willcox in AR-WD, NA, M997, Roll 33, 1879 Vol. I-II, p.166.

88 Willcox to AAG, Presidio, San Francisco, 5 September 1879, NA, RG393, Part 1, Entry 169, Vol. 9, p.328; Willcox to Fremont, Governor of Arizona Territory, 3 April 1880, NA, RG393, Part 1, Entry 169, Vol. 10, pp.137-140; See also Report of General O.B. Willcox, 11 September 1880, in AR-WD 1880, NA, M997, Roll 35, 1880 Vol. I, p.207; See also 'Frelinghuysen-Romero Papers', Letters Rec'd by the AGO, 1881-1889, NA, M689, Roll 81.

89 Willcox to AAG, Presidio, San Francisco, 5 September 1879, NA, RG393, Part 1, Entry 169, Vol. 9, pp.328-329.

90 Willcox to AAG, Presidio, San Francisco, 5 September 1879, NA, RG393, Part 1, Entry 169, Vol. 9, p.329.

91 Martin to AG Presidio, San Francisco, 13 September 1879, NA, RG393, Part 1, Entry 169, Vol. 9, p.342; Martin to Haskell, San Carlos, NA, RG393, Part 1, Entry 169, Vol. 9, p.341; See also 'Frelinghuysen-Romero Papers', Letters Rec'd by the AGO, 1881-1889, NA, M689, Roll 81.

92 Martin to AG Presidio, San Francisco, 13 September 1879, NA, RG393, Part 1, Entry 169, Vol. 9, p.342.

93 Martin AAG to Haskell ADC, Thomas, 14 September 1879, NA, RG393, Part 1, Entry 169, Vol. 9, p.344.

94 Martin to Haskell, 11 October 1879, NA, RG393, Part 1, Entry 169, Vol. 9, pp.382-383.

95 Willcox to Mexican Consul, Tucson, 8 November 1879, NA, RG393, Part 1, Entry 169, Vol. 9, p.417.

hunting for the Apaches.[96] Rumours had been circulating that Juh's followers had sustained heavy casualties on or around 5 December 1879 when Mexican troops launched a surprise attack upon his camp. On hearing these rumours, Willcox telegraphed Lieutenant Haskell suggesting that if the information was true, his mission ought to be aborted.[97] However, Haskell informed the general that Juh and his followers were on the point of accepting settlement on the San Carlos reservation, prompting Willcox to express grave doubts as to the veracity of the rumour that Juh had been badly defeated.[98] By 16 December, Captain Adna Chaffee, Sixth Cavalry, acting as Indian agent at San Carlos, had been instructed to settle the Chiricahuas on the reservation.[99]

There might have been an element of truth in the reports of a defeat sustained by Juh. The event might have been grossly exaggerated; but an attack upon his camp might have shaken him into seeking a quieter haven in the USA. Haskell also noted, that in from his first contact with Juh's people, that they were 'very wild and poorly clothed, even for Southern Indians, they have but little plunder.'[100] This is an interesting statement when weighed against the observations made by Van C. Smith at Camp Bowie, where he described the affluence of Juh's following, which he acknowledges might have been traded as opposed to raided, but which suggested that they were not as heavily defeated as rumour would have it.[101] What might reconcile the two reports is the possibility that Juh and his followers gave Haskell the impression of poverty as a negotiating ploy and, more importantly, to deflect awkward questions about recent raiding in both the USA and Mexico. Once negotiations were concluded and the Apaches were safely across the border, this pretence could be dropped. Having successfully pulled off a major diplomatic coup, Haskell was hardly going to draw attention to such issues.

On 20 December 1879, Haskell was authorised to draw rations at army posts on the route from Camp Rucker to San Carlos to feed Juh's 'surrendered' Chiricahuas.[102] To finalise this arrangement, on 30 December, a council was held between Haskell, and representatives of 102 Chiricahuas from Mexico, with Tom Jeffords also present.[103] Haskell and Jeffords were subsequently noted for their courage, skill and patience in persuading Juh's following to settle at San Carlos.[104] By 13 January 1880, the Chiricahuas from Mexico were reported to be happily settled on the San Carlos reservation.[105]

It is only fair to record that this arrangement did not receive much approbation in the State of Chihuahua. US Consul Scott noted that both he and Governor Terrazas could derive but 'poor satisfaction' that these individuals had been allowed to settle on the San Carlos reservation. Scott was frustrated both by the apparent lack of questions asked of the Apaches and by the lack of

---

96 Willcox to AG, Presidio, San Francisco, 5 November 1879, NA, RG393, Part 1, Entry 169, Vol. 9, p.411.

97 Willcox to Haskell, Camp Rucker, 15 December 1879, NA, RG393, Part 1, Entry 169, Vol. 9, p.467.

98 Willcox to AG, Presidio, San Francisco, 16 December 1879, NA, RG393, Part 1, Entry 169, Vol. 9, pp.469-470; Haskell to Willcox, 14 December 1879, in See also 'Frelinghuysen-Romero Papers', Letters Rec'd by the AGO, 1881-1889, NA, M689, Roll 81.

99 Martin to Chaffee, 16 December 1879, NA, RG393, Part 1, Entry 169, Vol. 9, p.469.

100 Haskell to Willcox, 21 December 1879, in 'Frelinghuysen-Romero Papers', Letters Rec'd by the AGO, 1881-1889, NA, M689, Roll 81.

101 *Thirty Four*, 7 January 1880.

102 Martin to Haskell, 20 December 1879, NA, RG393, Part 1, Entry 169, Vol. 9, p.475.

103 Willcox to AAG, Presidio, San Francisco, 6 January 1880, NA, RG393, Part 1, Entry 169, Vol. 10, p.6; Report of General O.B. Willcox, 11 September 1880, in AR-WD, NA, M997, Roll 35, 1880 Vol. I, p.207.

104 Martin to AG MDoP, Presidio, San Francisco, 11 September 1880, NA, RG393, Part 1, Entry 169, Vol. 10, p.419; Report of General O.B. Willcox, 11 September 1880, in AR-WD, NA, M997, Roll 35, 1880 Vol. I, p.207.

105 Chaffee to Willcox, 13 January 1880, in 'Frelinghuysen-Romero Papers', Letters Rec'd by the AGO, 1881-1889, NA, M689, Roll 81.

retribution exacted for their earlier activities in both the United States and Mexico.[106] However, Willcox (see document file no. 24) was certain that he had done the right thing in allowing the Chiricahuas to settle at San Carlos. He argued that these Apaches had surrendered in good faith; they were also 'American' Indians and therefore the responsibility of the United States. Moreover, their raiding on both sides of the border had been neutralized – something the Mexican authorities had singularly failed to accomplish. Finally:

> we have effected the separation of Juh and Jeronimo from Victoria; and by the use of the very Indians in question, we are assisting Gen'l Hatch to operate against Victoria in New Mexico; therefore military policy will not allow their being given up, even if there were doubts as to the justice of the case; and this military policy is as much for the benefit of our Mexican neighbors as for ourselves against a common enemy.[107]

That common enemy, Victorio and his Chihenne Apaches with their Mescalero Apache allies, were now poised to return to the United States, where, at first glance, Major Morrow's forces appeared to be fully prepared for their return.

106 Scott to Hunter, 2nd Assistant Secretary of State, Washington D.C., 7 April 1880 in Consular Despatches Chihuahua Mexico 1830-1906, NA, M289, Roll 1.

107 Willcox to Fremont, Governor of Arizona Territory, 3 April 1880, NA, RG393, Part 1, Entry 169, Vol. 10, pp.137-140; See also Report of General O.B. Willcox, 11 September 1880, in AR-WD 1880, NA, M997, Roll 35, 1880 Vol. I, p.207; Martin to AG, MDoP, Presidio San Francisco, 11 September 1880, where he notes that no more was heard of this application to return Juh and his followers to the Republic of Mexico. (NA, RG393, Part 1, Entry 169, Vol. 10, p.419).

Appendix I

Material relating to Chapter 7

Capt. Steelhammer's Summary of E Company, Ninth Cavalry's Abuse Allegations.

Key:

A. General Abuse of Company as a whole.
B. Personal Verbal Abuse.
C. Personal Punishment.
D. Personal Assault.
E. Statements made to the effect that Captain Hooker wished to send the rest of his company out to be killed by the Apaches
F. Company Members who stated that Hooker had not personally abused them.

Name	Rank	A	B	C	D	E	F
Beale, *Henry*	Private	X					
Bledsoe, *Daniel*	Private	X	X	X[1]		X	
Booth, *Abraham H.*	Private	X	X	X[2]		X	
Corker, *William*	Private	X		X[3]			
Craven, *Luther*	Private	X					X
Crawford, *Heartley*	Private	X	X	X[4]		X	
Downing, *Daniel*	Private	X	X		X[5]		
Fields, *John M.*	Private	X				X	
Foster, *Allen*	Corporal	X				X	X
Gillem, *Taylor*	Private		X				
Green, *Isom*	Private	X	X			X	
Hails, *Daniel*	Saddler	X				X	
Haines, *David*	Farrier		X			X	
Hawkins, *Benjamin*	Trumpeter	X					
Howard, *John*	Private		X	X[6]			
Howard, *William*	Sergeant						X
Irwin, *Samuel*	Private	X					X
Jackson, *Thornton*	Private	X	X	X[7]	X[8]		
Joanna, *Redmond*	Sergeant	X	X				
Johnson, *Josiah*	Private	X					
Johnson, *Noah*	Private	X					
Kibbey, *Wesley*	Private	X					
Koerl, *Arthur*	Private		X				

Name	Rank	A	B	C	D	E	F
Lockman, *George*	Private					X	X
Loge, *John*	Private	X				X	
Lyons, *Joseph*	Private	X	X				
McGill, *McElroy*	Private			X[9]	X[10]		
Miner, *William*	Private		X				
Peters, *David*	Private			X[11]			
Preston, *Willis*	Corporal	X					
Quarle, *John W.*	Private	X	X				
Riley, *Henry*	Private	X	X				
Robinson, *Henry*	1st Sergeant	X	X				
Roundtree, *George*	Private	X		X[12]			
Scott, *Richard*	Blacksmith	X	X				
Shanklin, *Evan*	Private	X					
Smith, *Frank*	Private			X[13]			
Smith, *Jerry K.*	Private	X				X	
Sykes, *Siegel*	Private	X					
Thomas, *William*	Private	X	X				
Timbers, *Robert*	Private	X		X[14]		X	
Turner, *Willis*	Private			X[15]			
Vance, *George, W.*	Private	X	X			X	
Walters, *Joseph*	Trumpeter	X				X	
Williams, *James*	Sergeant					X	X
Williams, *Richard*	Corporal	X	X			X	
Willis, *Robert*	Private	X				X	
Wilson, *Lawrence*	Private	X	X			X	
Wilson, *Royal*	Private	X				X	
Wise, *Washington*	Private	X	X	X[16]			
Woods, *Jacob*	Private	X					X

Notes

1 Made to walk on scout after failure to control his horse on a scout.
2 Made to carry Log for 6 days after horse herd stampeded.
3 Made to carry Log for not shouting loudly enough during guard duty.
4 Made to carry Log – no apparent reason given.
5 Assault with riding whip.
6 Made to carry Log and 'Bucked' and 'Gagged' and 'Chained' for shooting at Squirrels.
7 'Bucked' and 'Gagged' for alleged insolence after failing to pack Captain Hooker's Tent. Chained to wagon. Alleged that he was dragged 30 yards when he fell over from fatigue.
8 Struck wih fist and kicked and then kicked when lying down.
9 Tied to Pack Mule 'Bucked' and 'Gagged'.
10 Assault with lariat and riding whip.
11 Made to carry dead turkey after his detachment opened fire on turkeys contrary to standing orders.
12 Made to carry log for 3 days. No apparent reason given.
13 Made to carry a Log for 7 days after horse herd stampeded.
14 Made to carry Log for 6 days after horse herd stampeded.
15 Made to carry log for 3 days. No apparent reason given.
16 Made to carry Log after horse herd stampeded.

Capt. Steelhammer's Summary of E Company, Ninth Cavalry's Attribution of Blame for the loss of the Horse Herd and Guards.

Key:

A. Troops who noted the failure to issue carbines or horse furniture as a factor.
B. Troops who claimed that Captain Hooker had been forewarned about the presence of Apaches.
C. Troops who stated that no Officer had inspected the grazing area.
D. Troops who indicated that the horse guard had been reduced from eight to five men.
E. Troops who stated that Captain Hooker had issued orders that the guard were not to go too far from the post and that a mounted lookout keeping to the high ground should be maintained.

Name	Rank	A	B	C	D	E
Beale, *Henry*	Private					
Bledsoe, *Daniel*	Private	X	X	X	X[17]	
Booth, *Abraham H.*	Private					
Corker, *William*	Private					
Craven, *Luther*	Private	X	X	X		
Crawford, *Heartley*	Private					
Downing, *Daniel*	Private					
Fields, *John M.*	Private	X				
Foster, *Allen*	Corporal	X		X	X	X
Gillem, *Taylor*	Private					
Green, *Isom*	Private	X				
Hails, *Daniel*	Saddler					
Haines, *David*	Farrier					
Hawkins, *Benjamin*	Trumpeter					
Howard, *John*	Private	X	X	X		
Howard, *William*	Sergeant	X		X		X
Irwin, *Samuel*	Private					
Jackson, *Thornton*	Private					
Joanna, *Redmond*	Sergeant					X
Johnson, *Josiah*	Private					
Johnson, *Noah*	Private					
Kibbey, *Wesley*	Private					
Koerl, *Arthur*	Private					
Lockman, *George*	Private					
Loge, *John*	Private					
Lyons, *Joseph*	Private					
McGill, *McElroy*	Private					
Miner, *William*	Private		X[18]			
Peters, *David*	Private	X	X	X	X	X
Preston, *Willis*	Corporal					
Quarle, *John W.*	Private					
Riley, *Henry*	Private					
Robinson, *Henry*	1st Sergeant	X			X	

Name	Rank	A	B	C	D	E
Roundtree, *George*	Private					
Scott, *Richard*	Blacksmith					
Shanklin, *Evan*	Private	X				
Smith, *Frank*	Private					
Smith, *Jerry K.*	Private					
Sykes, *Siegel*	Private					
Thomas, *William*	Private					
Timbers, *Robert*	Private					
Turner, *Willis*	Private					
Vance, *George, W.*	Private	X	X[19]		X	
Walters, *Joseph*	Trumpeter					
Williams, *James*	Sergeant	X				
Williams, *Richard*	Corporal	X		X[20]		X
Willis, *Robert*	Private		X[21]			
Wilson, *Lawrence*	Private					
Wilson, *Royal*	Private	X				
Wise, *Washington*	Private					
Woods, *Jacob*	Private	X	X[22]			

Notes

17 Bledsoe stated that this was done the day before the attack. Other testimony clearly states that this change was affected at the beginning of August. Considering the relationship between Bledsoe and Hooker one suspects an attempt to gain revenge upon his commanding officer.

18 Miner reported that while Sullivan delivered his warning Hooker ordered him to escort Sullivan off the post as Hooker suspected that Sullivan was in league with the Apaches. Miner's testimony does not make it clear if Hooker made this opinion known to Mr Sullivan.

19 Vance reported bringing in news of the presence of Apaches and also cites the letter from Stackpole concerning his skirmish in the San Mateos prior to the raid.

20 Williams testified that the only visit by an officer to the grazing grounds had been a fleeting encounter with Lt. Taylor, the latter in search of a missing horse.

21 Overheard Sullivan warning Hooker of the presence of thirty Apaches in the area and that Sullivan stated that the report was from a reliable source.

22 Woods personally reported seeing Apache signs between Ojo Caliente and Paraje plus receiving a warning from the Paraje Postmaster that Apaches were operating in the area prior to the attack.

Appendix II

Material relating to Chapter 8

Casualty Discrepancies or Misinterpretation of Loss in Reports of the Ambush in Las Animas Canyon 18 September, 1879.

The first two reports are ambiguous concerning the number of fatalities sustained in Las Animas Canyon. The third clearly states that the two Navajo scouts and one civilian scout were in addition to the five soldiers killed. However, we cannot rule out this correction as a case of an ambiguity solved by an **assumption** that these must be in addition to those killed

Date: Ft Bayard 23
Rec'd: SF 23
To: Loud SF

Dawson Wright & Day struck Victorio's trail at Head of the Tierra Blanca Canon two days old on 16th, followed it to head of Las Animas River where on the 18th they ran upon the Indians who held a strong position troops were virtually caught in a trap Capt Beyer with his Co and Hugo's came up & took part in fight after fighting all day the troops were compelled to withdraw under cover of darkness with a loss of five men killed & one wounded & 32 horses killed & six wounded. I have sent Blocksoms & Gatewood with their Apache Scouts & Emmet with his Navajos to the scene of the action and follow immediately with all available men of the post my cavy will be principally dismounted Wright with 22 men of C Co is at Hillsboro & will join me. I have ordered Dimmick to meet me at McEvers' Ranch. Purington is here and his Co goes with me. Victorio is said to to [the two 'to's' are in original telegram] have about 140 men, two Navajo Indians & one citizen were killed in the fight. I will make my base of operations at McEvers' Ranch.
Morrow
Maj Comd.[1]

Compare with the following two reports

Dawson Wright & Day struck Victorio's trail at Head of the Tierra Blanca Canon two days old on the sixteenth followed it to head of Las Animas River where on the eighteenth they ran upon the Indians who held a strong position. Troops were virtually caught in a trap Capt Hooker [Beyer] with his company and Hugo's came up and took part in fight. After fighting all day, the troops were compelled to withdraw under cover of darkness with a loss of five men killed & one wounded and

---

1 Morrow to Loud AAAG 23 Sept., 1879, NA, RG393, Part 3, Entry 439, pp.344-347; Loud to Hatch, 23 Sept., 1879, Telegrams Sent DoNM, Vol.2, Jan.–Dec. 1879, NA, RG393, Part 3, Entry 431, p.241; See also McDowell to Commanding General, MDoM, 25 Sept., 1879, 'Victorio Files', NA, RG393, M1495, Roll 14.

thirty two horses killed & six wounded. I have sent Blocksoms & Gatewood with their Apache Scouts and Emmet with his Navajos to the scene of the action and follow immediately myself with all the available men of the post. My Cavalry will be principally dismounted. Wright with 22 men of "C" company is at Hillsboro and will join me. I have ordered Dimmick to meet me at McEvers' Ranch. Purington is here and his company goes with me. Victoria is said to have about 140 men. Two Navajo Indians & one citizen were killed in the fight. I will make my base of operations at McEvers' Ranch.

(Signed) Morrow Comd.[2]

Following telegram received yesterday from Commdg officer Dept Arizona. Major Morrow reports following just received from Col. Hatch ?????? Sept Twenty Third Seventy Nine. Lieuts Dawson Wright and Day struck Victoria trail at head of Serco Blancia Canon two days old on sixteenth followed it to hd of Las animas River where on the eighteenth they ran upon the Indians who held a strong position. Capt Beyer with his company and Hugo came up & took part in fight. After fighting all day the troops were compelled to withdraw under cover of Darkness with a loss of five men & one wounded & thirty two horses killed & six wounded. Morrow has sent Lieut Blocksom & Gatewood Sixth Cavalry with their Apache Scouts & Emmet with Navajoes which arrived at Bayard yesterday to the scene of action & will follow immediately with all available men of Post. Company L Ninth Cavalry & Lt Wright with twenty two men Company C will join tomorrow. Victoria is said to have about one hundred & forty Indians. Two Navajoes & One Citizen were also killed in fight. Morrow will make base operations at McEvers' Ranche.[3]

Emotional and Technical Factors influencing Apache and U.S. Army target Practice Proficiency

We may be taken aback by an all day long battle in which the net loss to the U.S. Cavalry is five killed, two wounded, and approximately fifty-five horses and mules killed or captured. However, battles in the Old West seem to feature prodigious expenditure of ammunition for often minuscule casualty lists. This is not a Hollywood movie, and several important factors need to be noted:

Emotional/Psychological Factors

While ambushed and trapped in the canyon, the soldiers and civilians appear to have become trapped in a situation where the Apaches could dominate the area through long-range fire. However, the Apaches appear not to have had the cover necessary to safely infiltrate to close quarters. Therefore, to inflict more damage, the Apaches would have had to close in upon an enemy 'on the rocks' which was probably thoroughly stirred yet not shaken enough to rout. Thus this would almost certainly entail fatalities on their side. As noted earlier, a war leader who sustained unnecessary casualties would lose respect and position. Apache warriors saw suicidal bravery as pointless unless this was the only option available. To the Apaches, the best result was the maximum booty gained from, and damage inflicted upon the enemy, with the absolute minimum damage (ideally none) sustained.[4] In this case the Chihenne Apache warriors had their enemies pinned down exactly where they wanted them, with little cover in a situation where the follow up relief

2 Loud AAA General to AA General Fort Leavenworth 23 Sept., 1879, 'Victorio Papers', NA, M666, Roll 526; Pope to AAG MDoM, 24 Sept., 1879, 'Victorio Files', NA, RG393, M1495, Roll 14.

3 McDowell to AG, Washington D.C. 25 Sept., 1879 & Pope to Townsend AG Wash. D.C. 18 Sept., 1879, 'Victorio Papers', NA, M666, Roll 526; See also *Army & Navy Journal*, Vol.17, 4 Oct., 1879, p.158.

4 See Bourke, 1987, p.34.

forces had no scope to effect a flanking attack. The only realistic option for the U.S. unit was retreat leaving behind a good haul of booty, including ammunition, to the Apaches.

Equally, how many of us would remain cool enough once both sides were firing at each other to take our time over their aim. To do so would increase the risk of injury or worse to oneself. Moreover, once the firing had commenced, then gun-smoke and dust flung up by bullets and panicked stock would obscure targets.

Another factor that requires our consideration is the difficulty of judging aim when shooting down or up at targets. In such instances it is more difficult to accurately judge ones aim than if the firer and target are on the same level.[5] Indeed, this last factor could be argued to straddle the psychological/technical divide.

Technical Factors

Over and above the emotional/psychological factors, we must also consider two related technical factors: First, could the available weapons, in the hands of fully trained marksmen, be reasonably be expected to produce pinpoint accuracy over relatively long ranges? Second, were their users in receipt of such training?

In all honesty the author is not qualified to answer the first question, though the second question can be addressed. To be an accurate shot requires practice. To zero in one's sights then it is necessary to fire off a few practice rounds.

We also have to wean ourselves away from the Hollywood western 'weapons which work perfectly at all times' myth. The weapons used were not necessarily as reliable, nor accurate, as legend would suggest. For example, several of the artefacts unearthed at the Hembrillo Canyon battle site were cartridge cases fired from Henry repeating rifles:

> The Henry cartridges provide mute testimony that the Apache remained in this position for most of the night. Most of the Henry cartridges had misfired several times before finally firing. This would have required manually extracting the cartridge, rotating it slightly, replacing it in the chamber, and firing again. One of the Henry's has twenty-seven sets of strike marks.[6]

Nor were both sides proficient in the use of these weapons. The warriors, even if they had adequate supplies of cartridges, rarely felt secure enough to expend ammunition in practice shooting fearing detection by their enemies.[7] The army was often unwilling to expend dollars for live ammunition target practice for its own troops. Upham recounts the complete failure of the Camp Apache garrison to hit a bear trotting past the camp buildings at approximately 50 yards distance.[8] During January 1879, *Thirty Four* recorded the results of two 'Chicken Shooting' competitions where in the first contest 116 shots were fired with 13 chickens killed (11.2%).[9] The second competition recorded 281 shots 22 Chickens Killed (7.8%)[10] and these are presumably the better shots in this community. The shooting accuracy on both sides varied widely. Kaytennae, one of Victorio's warriors was acknowledged as a superb marksman and it is tempting, but pure speculation, to suggest that the

5 See Sweeney, 1998, p.433 & 435. I would like some feedback on this; I have come across a couple of references to the difficulty in judging one's aim when firing downhill. Is this so and more importantly why does this occur?
6 Laumbach, p.215.
7 Ball, 1970, p.159.
8 Upham, 2001, pp.88-89.
9 *Thirty Four*, 1 Jan., 1879.
10 *Thirty Four*, 8 Jan., 1879.

single shot which killed the Navajo scout came from this warrior. In the later Geronimo Campaign of 1885-1886, Kaytennae was observed shooting dead a wild pig from a running horse.[11] It was around this period when the U.S. army started to institute fairly regular target practice. However, even where regular weekly or even twice-weekly target practice was held the results were variable: "In all the companies there are a number of men who attain to nearly the greatest proficiency. As a rule however, the average for a company is about 50 per cent."[12] On 18 February, 1880, the Secretary of War authorised the stop-gap measure of allowing troops in the Military Divisions of the Missouri and Pacific to utilise cartridges manufactured before 1 January, 1877, for target practice.[13]

Even, if the Apache warrior or Ninth Cavalryman overcame the above emotional factors, they would still have to deal with some technical factors. No matter how cool and collected they were, if their sights are misaligned along the horizontal and/or vertical plane, they may believe that, by lining up the back sight, foresight and target, they are likely to hit the latter. If we assume that the distance between the front and rear sights is equal to one metre. An error of 1mm over that metre can have a surprising margin of error over long distances. For example, if an Apache warrior whose rifle sights misaligned by 1mm over 1m, spots a soldier two hundred metres away. He may ignore all the potential emotional turmoil and coldly aim at the head of the U.S. cavalryman (presuming of course that the trooper is going to stay still for long enough). At 200 metres, this small margin of error translates into a 20cm error i.e. the bullet will actually strike twenty cm away from the warrior's intended mark. This may still result in a hit if the rifle's vertical range settings result in a hit below the intended point. If the error is to the right, left or above the target, then even a millimetre's error may result in a missed shot. Farrow was particularly unimpressed with the quality of sights fitted to Springfield service rifles and carbines, which he thought would militate against accurate shooting.[14]

Do we know how robust the sights were on the breech-loading weapons at the time? However, all the motion of horse riding and moving across rough terrain, the U.S. Cavalry carrying their carbines on slings may have had an effect. All this constant motion may have had the effect of gradually knocking their sighting mechanisms out of trim. Many of the U.S. troops and Apaches may not have known how to adjust their sights accurately. An experienced person can learn to mentally adjust their aim and home their shots on to their opponents. To be able to do so successfully the person has to rely upon spotting where his shot falls. This also requires the target to remain still for long enough. If there are several persons firing at the same target, there is a chance that he may spot the bullet strike of one of his comrades. A failure to spot any bullet strike at all means that all the firer knows is that he has missed the target; the margin of error remains a mystery.

Thus there are a myriad of factors[15] which may combine to suggest that these low casualty figures are not necessarily abnormal.

11 Bourke, 1980, p473; See also Lekson, 1987, p.5; Debo, 1993, p.254; Faulk, 1969, p.86.

12 Annual Report for year ending July 31, 1881, Maj. Arnold to AAG Dept. Arizona, 5 Aug., 1881, NA, RG393 Part 1, Entry 181, pp.99-100.

13 Chief Ordinance Officer, War Dept., Wash. D.C. to Chief Ordinance Officer, MDoM, 18 Feb., 1880 in Letters Received, DoM 1868-98, RG 393, Entry A1-1 2601, Box 88.

14 Farrow, p.30.

15 I have only scratched the surface of these factors. I would refer interested readers to ES Farrow's 'Mountain Scouting' Chapter II particularly points 1-15, pp.28-36.

Annex: Original Documents

Contents

Note: Documents written in ***italics*** refer to handwritten sources. Normal text indicates printed sources.

Document 1.1

Survey Orders issued to Capt. Carpenter, Tenth Cavalry, 4 June, 1878

Headquarters District of the Pecos
In the field Fresno, Cariso Mountains, Texas
June 4th 1878

Captain L.H. Carpenter, 10th Cavalry,
Commanding Company H, 10th Cavalry
Fresno, Cariso Mountains, Texas.

Sir:
The District Commander directs that you scout and explore the country thoroughly in all directions within fifty miles of your present camp: It is desired that the positions of all springs, permanent waters, tanks, pools, & c. be carefully noted, that the hiding places and runways of depredating Indians become known not only to yourself, but to your entire command. You will examine carefully and report such places as in your judgement is most suitable for Infantry or Cavalry camps, also select the best locations that can be found within the compass designated, for a military post, noting carefully all matters in the way of information that may hereafter be of value to the Government, as to the supply of wood, water, grazing, building material & c.

The importance of discovering permanent or living water heretofore unknown, can hardly be over estimated, and it can only be accomplished if at all, by hard work, continued scouting and explorations; In case the supply of water should give out where your present camp is located you are authorized to change its location to the most available place that can be found, so situated as to enable you to accomplish the work desired.

The greatest care possible will be taken of public animals and other government property placed in your care, and all due precautions taken at all times, in case you come upon Indians you will attack them vigorously at all hazards and spare neither horses nor men to secure the desired results, which is the destruction of the Indians, or the severest punishment that can be inflicted upon them, to accomplish which, you will not hesitate to follow Indians even to their reservations. Captain Nowell with his Company and Detachment of Infantry is camped near Guadalupe peak of the Guadalupe Mountains with supplies to July 31st. He will have similar instructions to those given you, and although it is desired that the commands operate separately, yet in case of emergency they can be brought together to meet any combination in force on the part of the Indians, too large for the commands to deal with separately. The positions of the camp must be maintained and such instructions will be given by the District Commander that additional troops will in case necessity be promptly furnished from Fort Davis or elsewhere

Any information of importance will be communicated to these Headquarters through Commanding Officer Fort Davis, Texas, and any additional instructions that may be deemed necessary will be furnished to you by the District Commander either direct or through the Commanding Officer Fort Davis, Texas.

Very Respectfully,
Your Obedient Servant
(signed) Robert G. Smither
1st Lieut. And Adjutant 10th Cavalry[1]

1 Lt R.G. Smither to Capt. L.H. Carpenter, 4 June, 1878, RG393, Part 1, Entry 2546, pp.40-43.

Document 1.2

Survey Orders issued to Capt. Viele, Tenth Cavalry, 13 August, 1878

Headquarters District of the Pecos
Fort Concho, Texas, August 13th 1878

Captain C.D. Viele, 10th Cavalry,
Commanding Company "C", 10th Cavalry
Fort Davis, Texas.

Sir:
In addition to the orders, which you receive from the Commanding Officer of Fort Davis, The Colonel Commanding directs me to say, that, he desires you upon relieving Captain Carpenter at Eagle Springs, to obtain from that Officer all the information possible, with reference to the country in which you are expected to scout, and exploring the country from the Rio Grande to the Salt Plains, north of the Cariso and Smoke Mountains, covering a belt of country fully fifty miles wide, scouting as far West as Fort Quitman, and south well on towards Presidio, Texas.

In continuing the work of scouting, it is desired that you avoid travelling (as far as practicable) over routes taken by Carpenter, and others, in order that a still more thorough knowledge of the entire country can be obtained.

It is also desired that the positions of all springs, permanent water, Pools, etc, be carefully noted, including those heretofore known, as well as any that may hereafter be discovered by your command.

It is desired to discover, if possible permanent or living water heretofore unknown to troops and important that the hiding places and runways of Indians, become known not only to yourself, but to your entire command, and the knowledge can only be obtained, if at all, by hard and persistent work in scouting and exploring the country minutely and thoroughly in all directions within the limits indicated.

The occupation of that portion of the country by troops, to which you are sent, has already had the effect to drive Indians off, and to keep them out of the country, and it is believed that continued activity on the part of the troops, will go far towards preventing them from returning to commit depredations within that portion of the District.

You will endeavour to gain all the information possible of the country, which may hereafter be of value to the Government, as to the supply of wood, water, grazing, etc, and the best location that can be found in that section of the country for a Military Post, in case one should be ordered to be built as is now contemplated.

If the supply of water should again become sufficient as Fresno (Captain Carpenter's former camp in the Cariso Mountains) you can if practicable change your camp to that place, as it is deemed more suitable as a point from which to accomplish the desired work, than Eagle Springs.

All due precautions will be taken at all times, and proper care of animals. In case however you come upon Indians, you will attack them vigorously at all hazards, sparing neither horses nor men to insure their destruction, or the infliction of the severest punishment possible upon them, to accomplish which you will not hesitate to follow Indians to their reservation to the northward, but only in the event of being in hot pursuit, on a fresh trail, or in sight of raiding Indians whom have been raiding in Texas, and in the act of returning from Texas to Mexico from their marauding expeditions, will you be authorized to cross the Rio Grande in pursuit.

Any information of importance will be communicated through the Commanding Officer of Fort Davis, to these Headquarters, and any additional instructions that may be deemed necessary, will be furnished you either direct, or through Post Commander of Fort Davis

Very respectfully
Your Obedient Servant,
(Signed) Robert G. Smither
1st Lieut. And Adjt. 10th Cavalry.[2]

2 Lt. R.G. Smither Adjt. Tenth Cavalry to Capt. Viele, 13 August, 1878, RG393, Part 1, Entry 2546, pp.43-46.

Document 1.3

Detailed Report of Scouts by Captain Viele, commanding Company C, Tenth Cavalry, during August-November 1878

Fort Davis, Texas
January 24th 1879

Acting Assistant Adjutant General,
District of the Pecos,
Fort Concho, Texas.

Sir:
I have the honor to submit the following report of scouts made by "C" Company, 10th Cavalry, in obedience to orders received from Headquarters Fort Davis, Texas, and Headquarters District of the Pecos.

Appended and marked "A" "B" "C" and "D".

The company left Fort Davis, Texas, August 22nd in compliance with S.O. No. 125,[3] Headquarters Fort Davis, Texas, August 19th 1878. The command consisted of two Commissioned Officers, Captain C.D. Viele, and 2nd Lieutenant R.E. Safford, A.[4] Assistant Surgeon P. Brumond, and fifty nine enlisted men. Reached Eagle Springs, Texas on the 25th of August, after a march of 94 miles, and relieved "H" Company 10th Cavalry, Captain L.H. Carpenter, Commanding.

Eagle Springs is situated on the El Paso stage road, at Eagle Mountain, the stage company have a station there, and it furnishes sufficient water for one hundred and fifty head of stock.

Sept. 3rd Left camp with 2nd Lieutenant R.E. Safford, and forty enlisted men, to scout the country north of Eagle Springs, marched over to, and went into camp on the Fresno, found water by digging in bed of stream.

Grass and wood in abundance. Distance 23 miles.

Sept. 4th Marched to Rattle Snake Springs, water very abundant and very good although slightly impregnated with sulphur. Grass poor and wood scarce. Distance 16 miles.

Sept. 5th Marched back to Fresno and struck off N. West into the Diablo Mountains and camped at some water holes in rocks. Grass very good, wood scarce, and water only to be obtained after rains. Distance 25 miles.

Sept. 6th Marched to La Prieta and went into camp on east side of mountains, the tanks on east side are very large, but at this time were perfectly dry, grass good, wood scarce, Distance 24 miles.

Sept. 7th Marched 12 miles over to Sulphur water holes on east side of Diablo Mountains, watered stock and started for Tinaja Pinta, marched about twelve miles and made dry camp. Distance 24 miles.

Sept. 8th Marched 21 miles to Tinaja Pinta, watered and went into camp, the water is up a ravine on east side of south peak, and cannot be relied upon, as it is only rain water caught in rocks. Broke camp in afternoon, took back trail 15 miles and made dry camp. Distance 36 miles.

Sept. 9th Started at sunrise, marched eighteen miles and made noon camp at Sulphur water holes. Marched to Apache Springs in Diablo Mountains in afternoon and went into camp, after a hard march of 22

3 See RG393, Part 1, Entry 2546, pp.47-48.

4 This, at first glance, looks to be rather ungrammatical. However, the 'A' probably refers to 'Acting Assistant Surgeon'.

miles, the water is some distance up the mountain and very hard to get at with stock, grass very good, wood scarce. Distance 40 miles.

Sept. 10th Marched 10 miles to Rattle Snake Springs, watered, 17 miles to camp, and moved over to Fresno, grass good and water abundant, water only after rains.

Distance 25 miles.

Sept. 11th Marched 22miles back to camp at Eagle Springs arriving therein afternoon.

Total distance marched on scout two hundred and eighty four (284) miles. I have not seen any signs of Indians, having recently been in the country passed over, in fact none have been there since the scouts made by Captain Carpenter.

The Guide furnished me, Bernado Leguin, although he may know the trails and water holes in this section of the country, is entirely unfit for his position, as he can speak very little English, and understands less. He seems to know nothing about the names of mountains and water holes, besides being old he is nearly blind.

Sept. 17th Left Camp in morning with 2nd Lieutenant R.E. Safford, A. Assistant Surgeon P. Brumond, and forty enlisted men, for a short scout up the Rio Grande, marched west on the stage road until we had passed the Eagle range when we struck off the south west, reached the river after a march of 30 miles, the last ten miles of which was over a very rough country, camped just above the Ojo Caliente. The Springs are two in number situated in the river bottom and quite salt, with a temperature of about 160 degrees; one of them that I sounded, was fully twenty five feet deep. The ground about them is covered with a deposit of very good salt, grass very poor.

Sept. 18th Marched about eighteen miles up the river and went into camp, the country passed over is very rough. The river is very narrow with little or no bottom band, all the trails along the river are very old and much worn, but nothing of late date.

Sept. 19th Marched thirteen miles up the river to Fort Quitman, watered stock and struck off in direction of La Blanca, went into camp after a march of thirteen miles, in Quitman mountains. Water may be found here after rains but it is dry at present, grass good and wood abundant.

Sept. 20th Reached Eagle Spring after a march of thirty four miles.

Total distance marched on scout One hundred and eight miles.

October. 3rd Left camp in morning with 2nd Lieutenant R.E. Safford, A. Assistant Surgeon P. Brumond, and forty enlisted men, for a scout down the Rio Grande, marched twenty one miles, course almost due south, on east side of Eagle mountains camping at Tinaja Vieja, fair grass, but very little wood.

October 4th Marched 22 miles camping at some rain water holes in ravine, very poor grass, and but little wood.

October 5th Reached the Rio Grande after a march of sixteen miles, marched nine miles down the river and went into camp, grass very poor.

October 6th Marched eight miles down river when we were obliged to cross, as the mountains ran up to the river and it was almost impossible to get over the bluffs. Recrossed the river twenty five miles below, and camped one mile below crossing, grass very poor.

October 7th Marched five miles down the river camping at Russells Ranche, could learn nothing of Indians crossing in the vicinity none having been seen since last winter.

October 8th Marched eleven miles up river to Caporta Canyon, marched up canyon about five miles and made camp, good grass and water.

October 9th Marched up to head of canyon, over a very rough trail camping at springs, good grass and water. The canyon breaks off very abruptly forming a cascade of some 150 feet, with a large pool of water at the bottom, it is evidently a favourite camping place of the Indians, as there is evidence of their camps all about the springs. The signs are all old however. Distance marched fourteen miles.

October 10th Started for Barrel Springs on El Paso road, marched over a beautiful grazing country, reaching the springs after a march of thirty four miles, good grass and water.

October 11th Went into Fort Davis. Distance twenty two miles.

Oct. 12" 13" 14" 15" Remained at Fort Davis having animals shod &c.

October 16th Left Fort Davis and marched to Barrel Springs, distance twenty two miles, good grass and water.

October 17th Marched out three miles on my trail of October 10th and then took a course a little north of west, marched fifteen miles and camped at rain water holes, in bottom, grass good, wood scarce.

October 18th Marched seven miles to Vieja Pass, crossed the mountain over a very steep and rough trail reaching canon on west side after a hard climb of three miles, marched south about five miles and camped at Tinaja, grass good, wood abundant.

October 19th Marched seventeen miles over very rough country camping at Tinaja Borego.

October 20th Marched 14 miles camping near camp of the 3rd at Tinaja Vieja.

October 21st Marched twenty one miles reaching camp at Eagle Spring in afternoon. Have not seen any signs of Indians having been in the country since last winter.

Total distance marched in scout three hundred and five miles.

November 5th Left camp in morning with 2nd Lieutenant R.E. Safford and thirty five enlisted men for a scout on the Rio Grande, marched out fifteen miles on our old trail east of Eagle mountains, then followed an old Indian trail bearing to the south west. After a march of five miles into the mountains we reached a large Tinaja of very good water, but very little wood.

November 6th Took westerly course for the Rio Grande reaching it after a hard march of twelve miles over very rough country, marched up the river five miles in vain search for good grass, and went into camp.

November 7th Marched down the river thirteen miles and went into camp. The grass is miserable along the river and I am obliged to make short marches in order that the stock can get time to pick up a little to eat.

November 8th Marched eleven miles down the river over a very rough country, and went into camp, the Rio Grande is very narrow at this point, passing through a gorge about sixty feet wide, the mountains rising almost perpendicularly from the water to a height of 200 feet on either side, grass good and wood abundant.

November 9th Marched eleven miles down the river and went into camp, grass good.

November 10th Started in morning for Tinaja Vieja, found a small spring about eight miles from the river, it might be made serviceable with a little work, but is too near the river to be of any importance. Followed up an old creek bed until we reached our old trail of October 20th which we struck about a mile from our old camp, went into camp having marched twenty one and a half miles.

November 11th Took our old trail for Eagle Springs arriving in afternoon after a march of twenty two miles.

Total distance marched on scout One hundred and seventeen miles.

November 13th 2nd Lieutenant R.E. Safford, left camp in the morning with a detachment of twenty five men for a short scout over to Nariz Mountain to prove previous compass readings, returned on the 14th having marched forty eight miles. The water holes found there in September are now perfectly dry, and Lieutenant Safford was unable to find any water in the country.

November 17th Left camp in morning with 2nd Lieutenant R.E. Safford, and 30 enlisted men, rationed for five days, to explore that portion of the Rio Grande between the Ojo Calienta and my camp of November 6th, marched nine miles due west through the Eagle mountains, when I struck an Indian trail going north, the trail was about thirty-six hours old, and between forty and fifty head of stock on trail. Immediately sent detachment back to camp for five days more rations, with orders to follow me as rapidly as possible, and started at once upon trail with the balance of the command. After a march of fifteen miles we reached the camp evidently made by the indians on the 15th, marched twelve miles further on trail when it became too dark to trail, and we were obliged to make dry camp.

November 18th Started in morning as soon as it was light enough to trail, reaching Tanke Colorado after a march of seven miles. This seems to be a favourite camping place for Indians, as old signs were numerous, but the Tanks are now dry. The trail was joined here by another small party coming from the south with some ten head of stock, and led north through the Sierra Diablo over the roughest country I have ever seen, in fact it was impossible to keep the men in the saddle more than a quarter of the time, consequently our march was slow and very laborious. After marching thirty-seven miles we came upon the camp left by the Indians this morning. They had evidently camped here on the 16th and 17th and had been joined by another small party coming in from the south-east, with some fifteen head of stock, we were delayed here a long time in finding the trail, upon which they had left, as they had been grazing their stock all over the mountains, and driving up the ravines in search of water, making trails leading in every direction. The trail was at last found, and after following it for seven miles it became too dark to trail and I was obliged to camp. I sent out my guide and some men on foot to see if they could discover any signs of the camp ahead, as it was my opinion that they were only moving about in search of water. These men returned after midnight and reported that they had been unable to discover the camp, my party with pack train and additional rations came up during the night.

November 19th Started on trail as soon as it was light enough for travel, reached La Prieta after a march of fourteen miles and found that the Indians had camped there the night before and that they were undoubtedly making for Tinaja Pinta. As there was no water at La Prieta I was obliged to leave the trail and strike over to the Sulphur water holes, as my horses were showing signs of weakness for want of water, reached the water holes after a march of twelve miles and watered my stock for the first time in fifty-two hours. As the country is very open south of Tinaja Pinta I waited here until dark, in fact it took until sundown to water, as we were obliged to dip up the water in camp kettles, and the horses had been so long without water, great care was necessary to see that they did not get too much at once. Started for Tinaja Pinta at dark, marched until 3 A.M., having marched thirty three miles, and halted about a mile from water holes and waited for day to break.

November 20th Found at daybreak that there was no water in the Tinaja and that the Indians had not made camp. Sent Lieutenant Safford to east of mountain with 2nd Platoon, while I went to the west side with the balance of the command, to look for the trail. Lieutenant Safford struck trail about one mile from our resting place, the Indians had camped here, and from signs on the trail, evidently had heard us come in, and had at once started at a gallop, as the Indians were undoubtedly aware that troops were after them. My only chance now was to crowd them as fast as possible. The trail was very plain and I followed at brisk trot and gallop for twenty miles reaching San Antonio Springs where the Indians had watered their stock, using up all of the water. We at once pushed on reaching the Corrudas late in afternoon, watered stock and followed trail until dark when I was obliged to stop, and for the first time in twenty-four hours my horses were unsaddled.

Distance marched by command seventy seven miles.

The hard riding and want of water had told very severely on my stock during the last ten hours, in fact I had but twelve men with me when I went into camp.

November 21st The conditions of my horses convinced me that it was foolishness to pursue this party any further, so I started back for the Corrudas reaching that place in afternoon, meeting on the way back Lieutenant Safford with my pack train, and the men whose horses had played out the day before.

November 22nd Started back to Eagle Springs, marched twenty-one miles and made dry camp just N.W. of mountain north of Tinaja Pinta, watered at noon at San Antonio Springs, the water runs quite freely and if the tanks in ????? were cleaned out quite a large supply of water could be obtained. As it was I watered fifty head of stock, and filled eighty canteens in about two hours. The tanks are some distance up the mountain.

November 23rd Was obliged to march to Sulphur water holes to camp, as it was the nearest water, arrived there about sundown after a march of thirty-nine miles.

November 24th Marched twenty-four miles to Rattlesnake Springs, a severe norther blowing all day, with a snow storm in evening that kept up all night.

November 25th The snow is so deep that my animals cannot graze, marched sixteen miles camping at the Fresno, snowed almost all day, with a cold wind from the north.

November 26th Marched twenty-one miles arriving at Eagle Springs in afternoon.

I immediately started out my wagon with water kegs and forage to meet the detachment left on trail in charge of weak animals.

This detachment arrived in evening bringing up all the animals that we had been able to get as far as the Fresno.

Total distance marched on scout Three hundred and forty-six miles.

Received orders November 27th to return to Fort Davis

Broke camp on morning of the 28th and arrived at Fort Davis, December 1st after a march of ninety-four miles.

In all the country passed over by my command, I have not found any locality that is at all suitable for a military Post.

The map accompanying this report, drawn by 2nd Lieutenant R.E. Safford, has been made with a great deal of care, and this Officer deserves credit, for the careful manner in which he has performed this, as well as other duties required of him.

Respectfully submitted
(sgd) Chas. D. Viele
Captain 10th Cavalry
Commanding "C" Company[5]

5 Capt. Viele to Acting Assistant Adjutant General, District of the Pecos, Fort Concho, Texas, 24 January, 1879, RG393, Part 1, Entry 2546, pp.25-40.

Document 1.4

Detailed Report of Scouts by Captain Lebo, commanding Company K, Tenth Cavalry during September-November 1878

Fort Davis, Texas
February 16th 1879.

Post Adjutant,
Fort Davis, Texas:

Sir:

I have the honor to submit the following report and itinerary of the operations of Company "K", 10th Cavalry in the field from September 4th to November 30th 1878, pursuant to Orders No. 131. dated Headquarters Fort Davis, Texas, September 2nd 1878 and also in accordance with telegraphic instructions for Commanding Officer of the District of the Pecos, Fort Concho, Texas, August 29th, 1878.

September 4th In accordance with the order and instructions mentioned above, I left Fort Davis at 1.30 P.M. with my Command and proceeded down the stage road (N.E.) through the Limpia Canon to a place known as the "Brig Hill" and pitched camp at 5.30 P.M. Distance marched today 13 miles.

September 5th Broke camp and started the wagon train at 7.40 A.M. Started with the Company at 9A.M. marched down the stage Road (N) 6 miles to the "Point of Rocks", thence by the Vitoria road W. 5 miles to the camp of Company "H", 25th Infantry (Captain Courtney's) at "Seven Springs" Thence by road leaving W. 9 miles to Vitoria – a small Mexican settlement near the head of Toyah Creek – pitched camp at 3.45 P.M. –Grazing in the immediate vicinity is very poor – being kept down by the cattle here – Toyah Creek runs a very large stream of water for several miles below this point.
The water is slightly brackish.
Distance marched to-day 20 miles.

September 6th Broke camp and started the wagon train at 7.30 A.M. started with the company at 8.10 A.M. marched W-18-N along an old wagon trail towards the point of the foot hills off Gomez Peak – followed this trail over rolling prairie covered with thin chaparral of Sage and Mesquite for a distance of 15 miles from Vitoria; left the trail in order to go by way of "San Martin Spring"; proceeded thence up a narrow ravine towards Gomez Peak S.W. 5 miles to top of low divide; thence about due W. 2½ to lower end of level valley extending N.W. thence due N. 2 miles to San Martin Spring which is situated about N-14-W from Gomez Peak – the Company reached San Martin Spring and unsaddled at 6.30 P.M. – the capacity of this spring averages about 140 gallons of water per hour, by actual experiment, the water runs but a short distance below the spring as it is rapidly absorbed by the soil; but by constructing a small dam, an ample supply was easily obtained for the whole command, in which there are 120 head of stock including mules and horses – the water is of excellent quality – Wood, in the vicinity, is very scarce – the grazing here is very good – the progress of the wagon train was impeded by the heavy roads and the unfavourable character of the ground – (being pretty rough and stony between here and Gomez Peak) – that it was overtaken while en route by night-fall; and it being impracticable to proceed, although several men were sent back at different points to point out the best and shortest route to the spring, bivouac was made for the night and consequently the wagons did not arrive at the spring till about 6 A.M. on the 7th instant. Distance marched on the 6th. 27½ miles

September 7th The distance from this point to the next known water (the "Salado")on our course being too great for a single day's march, remained in Camp at San Martin Spring until evening, to allow the

animals to graze and rest after the long march of yesterday – broke camp and started the wagons at 4.15 P.M.; followed with the Company at 5.50 P.M., down wagon trail in narrow ravine through low hills nearly due N. 4½ Miles to level open prairie, thence bearing gradually to left 3½ miles to intersection with the wagon trail direct from Vitoria – thence by this road (N.W.) over smooth level prairie 10 miles crossed deep arroyo and pitched camp at 11.30 P.M. – Wood along the arroyo plentiful – Grass is pretty good in low depressions near the arroyo – found a very small quantity of water in arroyo East of road – (subsequently informed by Mr Peck, of the Texas and Pacific Railroad Engineering party, that he had recently discovered a spring of excellent water in this arroyo about 2 miles west of the road at this point – it is indicated on the accompanying map as "Peck's Spring".)
Distance marched today 18 miles.

September 8th Broke camp and started wagons at 6.50 A.M.; followed with Company at 7.30 A.M. and marched along the road towards Guadalupe Peak (N.W.) over rolling prairie about 10 miles, thence winding through low hills (spur of the "Pesuno de Caballo" Range a few miles west of the road) 2 miles – thence resuming the general direction N.W. the road descends a very gradual slope about 5 miles to a deep arroyo running nearly due East – pitched camp at 12 M. near the crossing of the road here there is a very large pool of permanent water known as the "Saladillo" (little Salado) or "Lower Salado" – it is strongly impregnated with gypsum and other mineral substances together with decayed vegetable matter and is not very palatable – there are other pools of the same character about 2 miles above this one (W.) in the same arroyo the watering place above is known as the "Salado', simply, or the "Upper Salado" – there is an abundance of cedar wood in this vicinity – it is the beginning of the extensive "Cedar Breaks" between here and the valley of Delaware Creek there are also a few cottonwoods along the arroyo here – grazing here is not very good, too much alkali in the soil – Distance marched today 15 miles.

September 9th The distance being too great for a single day's march to the next known water, the head of Delaware Creek, remained in camp until the afternoon, in order to divide the distance by making a night march to a dry camp and thence to the Delaware as soon as possible tomorrow morning.

Broke camp and started the wagons at 3 P.M. left with the Company at 3.45 P.M. marched along road N.W. over rolling prairie – proceeded about 19 miles in this direction to a point where road makes an abrupt turn to left – deep arroyo in front (Leoncita, unknown to one then) thence about 1 mile to left, thence gradually curving to right 5 miles over high rolling prairie and made dry camp in slight depression at 11 P.M. When a very cold norther commenced blowing with a slight drizzle which continued all night – Grass here is very poor – Wood is not very plentiful, only a few dead cedars – this point seems to be the limit in this direction of the extensive "Cedar Brakes" between here and the "Salado".

Distance marched to-day 25½ miles.

September 10th Broke camp and started wagons at 6.30 A.M. followed with Company a little later – the road here leaves the alkali prairie and winds to left through low range of hills gradually descending about 1½ miles into low sandy valley – thence down the valley N 4½ miles to the "Wild Horse Tanks" which are large pools of water in the sandstone bed of the south fork of Delaware Creek – they are said to be not permanent but there is almost always water in them – marched thence down low sandy flat about N-15-E 6½ mile to the old Mail Station at the head of Delaware Creek and pitched camp at 10.45 A.M. Near the old station there is a large spring of excellent fresh water – and a few hundred yards above (W) there is another large spring having a strong taste of sulphur – this is the head of the running water in Delaware Creek there are also several small springs in the bed of the stream; the water from them is black and is strongly impregnated with sulphur – Wood is very scarce in this vicinity – there being only a small quantity of small brush along the creek and a few mesquite roots exposed in the adjacent sand flats – the grazing here is not very good.

Distance marched to-day 12½ miles.

September 11th Broke camp and started the wagons at 6.40 A.M. left with the Company a few minutes later – proceeded up the old stage road nearly due West about 6 miles towards Guadalupe Peak which is the highest point of the Guadalupe Range and is situated at its extreme southern limit – Met the guide (Briggs) who was ordered to report for duty with my command, and being informed by him that a better road to Captain Norvell's Camp (our present destination) lay about two miles to the north of this one, left the road here and proceeded in a northwesterly direction about 2 miles to the other road; thence by this road nearly due west 6 miles to Marr's Sheep Ranche; thence followed old wagon road, (being very crooked and having several bad places for wagons due W. 8 miles to Camp of Company "M", 10th Cavalry (Captain Norvell's) at "Ojo Toro" or "Bull Spring" near the base of the "Sierra Guadalupe" – the Company arrived here at 4.30 P.M. but the wagons being delayed by the bad road did not reach camp until 11.30 P.M. – pitched camp near that of "M" Company.

Distance marched to-day 24 miles.

Relieved Captain Norvell's command and obtained from him all the information that it was deemed important to know, of this section of Country, and received the tentage from Captain Norvell as directed.

September 12th Captain Norvell's Command left at 8 A.M. for Fort Concho.

Having decided to locate my permanent Camp at Pine Spring about 3 miles west from Bull Spring, broke camp at 9 A.M. and started the wagons around by the road to Pine Spring – left with the Company a few minutes later; followed an old Indian trail along the base of the Mountains nearly due west 3 miles to Pine Spring – selected a suitable site and pitched camp at 11 A.M. the camp is situated about 500 yards East of Pine Spring – the spring branch however runs within 100 yards of Camp – the site is a narrow tract of pretty smooth ground between two deep gullies – at a high elevation on the slope at the base of the mountains; it commands an unobstructed view of the valley included between the Eastern Range of the Guadalupes and the low chain of the "Sierra del Presuno de Caballo" within a radius of 30 miles from camp: besides Pine Springs on the west, there is another spring (nearly as large as Pine Spring,) about 100 feet above and about 200 yards to the East of Camp – Both of these springs afford an abundant supply of water – Pine Spring alone being sufficient for supplying four or five Companies of Cavalry – All of the water which flows from the mountains is impregnated with Carbonate of Lime, but is very good; Grazing in the vicinity of camp is very fine indeed – there being an abundance of grass of the finest quality – Wood is plentiful here – in the valley are found juniper, oak and mansanita there are also a great many pines in the gullies along the base of the mountains and a few also out in the open valley. Upon the tops of the mountains and in the deep canons penetrating them, there is a great quantity of heavy timber (pine and pinon) many of the pines are of very large size, measuring from 10 to 30 inches in diameter and from 25 to 60 feet in height – by means of shoots a great quantity of excellent timber for making lumber could be collected here – there is also an abundance of stone (Sandstones and Limestones) suitable for building purposes, which could be easily quarried at different places in the valley.

September 13th The transportation which was to return to Fort Davis, left camp to-day under charge of 2nd Lieutenant W.S. Scott, 25th Infantry.

Remained in camp from September 13th to September 19th.

September 19th Left camp at Pine Springs at 10.30 A.M. with 2nd Lieutenant R.D. Read Jr, 10th cavalry, Acting Assistant Surgeon Ward, and the Scout Briggs and 40 enlisted men of my Company, with 100 rounds of ammunition per man, rationed for ten days – my intention being to make a scout west as far as the Corrudas – took an old Indian trail a short distance below camp and followed it S.W. 3 miles to Guadalupe Spring near the pass of the same name – proceeded thence by old trail circling to the right met a succession of very rough ridges at the base of the high Guadalupe bluff – (the extreme southern point of the Guadalupe Range) about 6¼ miles to "Bowen Spring" situated at the head of a very deep and narrow canon, immediately under Guadalupe Peak on the west side – thence down the Canon (trail exceedingly rough) ¾ mile to the east side of wide level valley in which are situated the extensive Salt Lakes of El Paso County – pitched camp near mouth of canon at 2.15 P.M. Grass pretty good – Water, large and permanent spring of same character as Pine Spring – Distance marched 10 miles.

Had been in camp but a few minutes when a large dust was discovered off the Sierra Prieta (S.W.) on the opposite side of the Salt Lakes – it arose continuously and seemed to be made by a body of horsemen moving in the direction of Cow Spring (N.W.) struck camp and proceeded down into the valley, behind a range of low hills, S.W. 1½ miles Crossed old stage road – thence same direction 1½ miles to base of hills – ascended to the top of ridge and then discovered that the party making the dust were moving in the direction of the "Sulphur Spring" which is situated near the Quitman Salt Road on opposite side of Lakes – moved back to the old stage road 1½ miles, marched thence on this road in a southeasterly direction 7½ miles to its junction with old road running S.W. to "Sulphur Spring" – thence by this road S.E. [This doesn't appear to make sense] *9 miles and bivouacked at 12.10 A.M. behind a low hillock which stands alone in the open prairie about 5 miles from the Salt Lakes – Distance marched from Camp near Bowen Spring 22 miles.*

September 20th Resumed the march at 4.15 A.M. and proceeded down road 5½ miles to the west side of Salt Lakes when we observed a Mexican Salt train a short distance up the Lake being loaded with salt – ascertaining that it had arrived the evening before, from the direction in which the dust was observed – and consequently came to the conclusion that it had been made by the salt train – proceeded thence 2½ miles to "Sulphur Spring" and pitched camp at 7.10 A.M. Distance marched to-day 8 miles.

Remained in camp to-day to allow the animals to graze and rest after long and tiresome march of yesterday and last night – the grass here is pretty good – wood very scarce – water is not very good – being brackish and having a strong taste of sulphur – it is obtained by digging in soft boggy soil on the border of an extensive salt marsh, covered with a dense growth of tule and Carrizo grass.

September 21st Being now far off our course to the "Corrudas", decided to make a scout southwards from this point and return to camp by crossing the "Presuno de Caballo " Range – Broke camp at 6.30 A.M. and proceeded down west side of Salt Lake Valley over level alkali prairie in a south easterly direction; having proceeded about 7 miles, crossed narrow arm connecting two groups of Salt Lakes which seem to be detached from main body of Lakes, which extends from a point a few miles north of Crow Spring in a southeasterly direction about 35 miles to a point a short distance below the Quitman Road from Guadalupe Pass – Continued in the same direction gradually approaching the extreme N.E. point of the Sierra Diablo, marched 12 miles and halted near the base of the Sierra Diablo, just opposite "Apache Spring" which is situated at a considerable elevation up the steep slope of the mountains – the Guide visited the spring and reported the supply of water insufficient for the Command – proceeded thence in same direction 3 miles down into a wide cienaga or meadow, known as the Cavallada, near the centre of which there is a marsh similar to the one at Sulphur Spring left this morning – finding the watering place dry marched nearly due S. 5¼ miles down the valley to Rattlesnake Spring, which is situated near the border of one of a small group of Salt Lakes – the water, although having a saline and sulphurous taste is very good – the animals are watered by means of Camp Kettle from holes dug in the soft marshy soil, which become filled nearly as fast as the water is dipped out; Grazing here is not very good and wood is exceedingly scarce.

Distance marched to-day 28 miles.

September 22nd Broke camp at 7.25 A.M. and marched back up valley N. about 2 miles, thence across the valley passing between two small Lakes and over rolling prairie nearly due N.E. 3 miles, thence in same direction over level sandy flat 6½ miles to edge of low foot hills of "Pesuno de Caballo" Range thence through foot hills (a succession of low rocky ridges)same direction 3½ miles to entrance of Canon (leading up into "Pesuno de Caballo" Range) thence by an old Indian trail due N. up Canon (narrow and very rough) 4½ miles to three large pools of rain water in the solid yellow sandstone bed of the arroyo, containing about 500 gallons each – these are known as the "Tinajas Amasillas" (Yellow tanks) proceeded thence same direction 2¼ to summit of the divide of the "Pesuno de Caballo" Range thence same direction 3¼ miles down another ravine running towards the Delaware – pitched camp in ravine at 4 P.M. near a large pool of rain water in the arroyo – sufficient for the command – Grazing very good – wood plentiful, oak and cedar.

Country very rough – broken on all sides.

Distance marched to-day 25 miles.

September 23rd Broke camp at 7.10 A.M. and proceeded down the arroyo in a north easterly direction passing several pools of rain water (not permanent) 1¼ miles to a large tank supplied by a spring, this tank is said to be permanent and is known as "The Cottonwoods" (marked on map) thence same direction 1¼ miles where the ravine becomes wider and is not as rough as it is above – thence down narrow valley same direction about 6 miles out of the broken country of the Pesuno de Caballo Range – Changed direction about 90° to left and marched thence N.W. 7 miles up wide sandy flat lying between Pesuno de Caballo Range on W. and a number of prominent mesas on East – pitched camp at 12.40 P.M. near two large tanks of rain water (not permanent) the tanks are in a deep arroyo running East across our course – Grazing is very good here – wood is very scarce.

Distance marched to-day 15 miles.

September 24th Broke camp at 7.30 A.M. and marched on up same flat N.W. 2 miles – thence across low level flat due north 2 miles – thence over rough broken ground north 4 miles to Independence Spring – thence by old stage road W. 6 miles to Camp at Pine Spring – Distance 15 miles.

September 25th Remained in camp at pine Spring till October 2nd

October 2nd Left Infantry Detachment in charge of camp took same command as on previous scout (September 19th) with rations for about 18 days – left camp at 9.40 A.M. and marched down wagon road (see September 11.) nearly due East about 8 miles to Marr's Sheep Ranche thence by wagon trail N.E. 3 miles through low hills to open prairie – thence by road over rolling prairie N.E. 6 miles – left road and proceeded thence down shallow ravine in prairie due E. 3 miles to "Grape Spring" which is situated about ½ mile north of the Texas and New Mexico boundary line – pitched camp near Grape Spring at 4.10 P.M. found four cattle men encamped here – taking refuge from the Lincoln County, New Mexico feud – these men had in charge about 200 head of cattle and were engaged in constructing a stockade corral – Grape Spring flows a very large body of water which sinks again within a mile and a half of the sources – the grazing about here is pretty good – considerable quantity of wood in the ravine near spring.

Distance marched to-day 19½ miles.

October 3rd Broke camp at 7.10 A.M. and marched by an old trail N.E. 3 miles to crossing of deep arroyo – thence nearly due North 5 miles to junction with road from Marr's Ranche; thence by road N.E. about 3½ miles and pitched camp at 10.30 A.M. a short distance below "Rattlesnake Spring". Distance marched to-day 11½ miles. Grazing here is very good – wood is very scarce – the spring flows a very large stream of water which runs about one mile due E. and empties into Black River – which at this point is a very large stream – (an abundance of small fish) – Black River has its source in the interior of the Guadalupe Mountains a few miles north of the Peak and flows nearly due north in a very deep and picturesque canon about 5 miles to a point near the New Mexico line thence East about 4 miles and sinks near the mouth of the canon on the East side of the Guadalupe Range about 8 miles northeast of Pine Spring – thence for a distance of about 20 miles its bed is dry to a point about 5 miles south of Rattlesnake Spring N.M. where it rises again, flows north about 6 miles and sinks again about one mile east of Rattlesnake Spring, its bed is dry again for a distance of about 10 or 12 miles – it rises again a few miles south – west of Brigg's Ranche and flows continuously 16 miles and empties into the Pecos.

October 4th Broke camp at 7.30 A.M. and marched on wagon road in a northeasterly direction 15 miles to Brigg's Ranche on Black River – pitched camp near the river at 12.40 P.M. about 1¼ miles below the ranche. Wood is very scarce in the immediate vicinity – there is very fine grazing in the flats adjacent to the river – also very good on the higher ground towards the mountains – the "Guadalupes" are quite low just opposite the ranche (N.W. 5 miles) they gradually increase in height towards the Peak (S.W.) where they are highest – the west range does not fall off so rapidly as the east – at Brigg's Ranche there is an abundance of water on all sides – there being a very large spring about 200 yards west of the ranche and another a short distance below our camp (E.) the river here is a very large stream, it contains an abundance of fish.

October 5th Broke camp at 7.30 A.M. marched nearly due north 14 miles, over rolling prairie, to the junction of road from Brigg's Ranche with the old road along the Pecos – proceeded thence about a mile up the river to a place known as "Loven's Bend" and pitched camp at 12.15 P.M. Wood is very scarce here – only a few mesquite root exposed in the sandy flats along the river besides a little drift wood along its banks – the grazing here is pretty good – the watering place is easy of access and the river can be easily forded – being shoaly for a considerable distance.

October 6th Broke camp at 7.10 A.M. marched across prairie S.W. 4 miles to mouth of wide ravine thence up this ravine bearing gradually towards the south 6 miles to entrance to deep and narrow canon thence up this canon S.W. 2 miles – thence south 2 miles – where course of main canon is nearly due west – the guide says that this is the canon of Guadalupe Creek (our objective point) but he believes the canon to be impossible for Cavalry at several places within a few miles of this point – proceeded thence up branch of canon (left) south 1½ miles and pitched camp at 12.40 P.M. near large pool of water supplied by a small spring, this spring we called "Ojo Nogal" (Walnut Spring) Wood here is very scarce – grazing is pretty good – the water is perhaps permanent.
Distance marched to-day 15½ miles.

October 7th Broke camp at 6.50 A.M. proceeded up right hand branch of canon S.W. 1½ miles and discovered another spring larger than "Ojo Nogal", thence up arroyo ¼ mile and ascended to high ground (the general level) – thence across this high ground S.W. 2 miles descended into ravine thence ¼ mile up this ravine and discovered a very long deep pool of water supplied by a spring (marked on map <u>Lebo's Spring</u>.) there is a considerable quantity of level ground at the turns in this ravine, grazing is very good – wood plentiful in and adjacent to ravine – oak and juniper. From "Lebo's Spring" marched up ravine due west 5 miles to its head – thence ½ mile over a narrow <u>divide</u> and descended into what appeared to be the head of a deep canon running S.E. out of the mountains – crossed this deep basin and ascended to high ground again – and marched in a northwesterly direction 4 miles to the summit of a very high ridge on the edge of the Canon of Guadalupe Creek – thence descended a long rough slope south 1½ miles into wide canon which runs S.E. out of the mountains just opposite to "Rattlesnake Spring Canon" – thence marched up this canon along an old Indian trail west one mile – thence over a very high and rough ridge N.W. 1½ mile and descended into great canon of Guadalupe Creek – the descent here is very steep and difficult – thence marched up this canon following its course in a northwesterly direction 10 miles and pitched camp about 4.30 P.M. (sunset) found a little water here in holes in the rocks – just sufficient for the Command night and morning – the grazing here is excellent – wood is plentiful scrub-oak and juniper, and a quantity of drift wood (pine &c.) in the arroyo; at this point the canon is about ¼ mile wide and has considerable level area – by ascending a hill on the north side of the canon observed that the country opens into a wide level prairie enclosed on the south and west by the Guadalupe Mountains and on the East by a range of high hills along the Pecos – there seems to be an easy outlet from Guadalupe Creek in this direction – Distance marched to-day 22½ miles.

October 8th Having sent the guide in advance to reconnoitre, he returned and reported that the lower end of the running water in the Creek was only a short distance above our camp – Broke camp at 9.10 A.M.

moved 1¼ miles up the canon and pitched camp near an old corral constructed of poles in a small recess on the north side of the canon – there is an abundance of wood about here and the grazing is excellent.

Guadalupe Creek rises about 3 miles above this point and is a very large body of water for that distance – it sinks in the arroyo about 50 yards from the old corral – the guide (Briggs) who has lived for several years in this part of New Mexico, says that this corral was constructed by a band of cattle thieves who infested this section of country a few years ago, and that it was used by them for penning cattle to change their brands or marks. No signs of any persons having been here recently.

October 9th Broke camp at 6.40 A.M. proceeded up the canon (west) 3 miles to the head of the Creek passing at intervals very long deep holes of water and at several places where the trail crosses the creek, it is from 20 to 40 yards in width and 2 to 3 feet in depth – with a very strong current – at head of creek made a very sharp turn to left ¾ miles thence followed the course of the canon S.W. 5 miles to two or three large pools of rain water in the arroyo – probably permanent – thence same direction up canon 7¼ miles and pitched camp at 1.55 P.M. in a grove of heavy pine timber near several small pools of rain water in the arroyo – for the last six miles back passed through groves of very heavy pine timber – for several miles in every direction from camp there is a dense growth of pine and pinon – also a great quantity of oak and juniper throughout this canon and some mansanita trees.

The mountains from this point south to Guadalupe Peak are heavily timbered, the country is broken up by canons and ravines and is exceedingly rough – the grazing here is very good – there is enough water at this place to supply a Company of Cavalry for a week perhaps, but it is not permanent water – there are signs about here of an old camp – an old camp kettle, tin cups, an old powder can &c. were found – also a human skull lying on top of the ground and a number of old graves in the vicinity – there are other large pools of rain water in this canon at intervals for several miles above this place (south).

Distance marched to-day 16 miles.

October 10th Broke camp at 7.25 A.M. and marched up the canon (southwest) 3 miles – left the main canon and marched up a narrow ravine nearly due west about 3 miles to the high crest of the western range of the Sierra Guadalupe, discovered here that our course direct to the Corrudas (W.) was intercepted by a detached range of very high hills, diverging from the "Guadalupes" near the Peak and ranging in a northwesterly direction and are almost as high as the "Guadalupes" themselves – there seemed to be an easy passage around the point of this range (Northwest). Made the descent of the western slope of the Guadalupe by an old zig-zag Indian trail – the descent is very steep and difficult – marched thence west through a short canon 2½ miles down into the level sandy valley included between the detached range and the Guadalupes proper – thence down this valley northwest 8 miles to entrance of narrow canon (exceedingly rough) through low hills; thence down this canon N.W. 5 miles and pitched camp in canon at 5.35 P.M. about an hour after sunset – having found a few small pools of rain water just sufficient for cooking purposes, filling the canteens and watering the animals night and morning – Wood very scarce and grass very poor.

Distance marched to-day 21 miles.

October 11th Broke camp at 7.15 A.M. followed an old Indian trail out of canon to left (West) over low ridge about one mile and a quarter to edge of wide level valley – thence leaving to left (S.W.) marched around foot hills 4½ miles – from this point there seemed to be a pass or canon through range of foot hills on opposite side of valley in a direct line with the "Corrudas" – about W-30°-S – proceeded in this direction 5 miles to opposite side of level flat – thence marched in same direction up narrow valley through low hills 8 miles and ascended a short rocky slope to open prairie – thence same direction over rolling prairie 12 miles – thence over rough rocky ridges 5 miles to level flat – thence towards the "Corrudas" 1½ miles to old stage road near the base of the mountains thence by road around its base 2 miles and pitched camp at 8 o'clock P.M. a short distance above old mail station on west side – Wood here is pretty scarce – there being only mesquite brush and a few scrub oaks among the boulders on the sides of the mountain – Grazing here is very good, there are several large pools of rain water in the solid granite on the western slope of the mountain at different elevations – these tanks will probably hold about five or six thousand gallons of water; they have been known to become dry, but almost always contain water – at present they are pretty well filled with good water – this is the only watering place on the old stage road that can be relied upon, between Crow Spring and the Hueco Tanks a distance of about 70 miles – there is sometimes water at the Alamo Spring about 9 miles west of this place – but it is very uncertain – it is dry at present. The mountain called "the Corrudas" is conspicuously situated in open prairie country about 45 miles from Guadalupe Peak about W-20-N – and about 9 miles (it is said) nearly due north from the "Sierra del Aire" a prominent group of three or four conical peaks a little north of the 32nd parallel (the boundary line between Texas and New Mexico) the mountain is a very curious formation – and is unlike any other geological formation in this section of country, being of volcanic origin, whereas the prevalent formation is of aqueous origin – being mainly limestones, sandstones and shales – the top of this isolated granite peak presents unmistakeably the appearance of a crater of an extinct volcano; having a circular rim varying from 10 to 100 feet in height, enclosing an interior space of nearly 40 acres which is nearly level and is covered with a thick growth of very fine grass – the mountain is made up of large boulders of feldspathic granite of various sizes and shapes loosely piled together forming crevices through which a man might easily pass from the top to the bottom of the mountain without being seen from the outside – it presents a very bold bluff-like appearance on all sides except the west, where the slope is pretty gradual but is exceedingly rough – Distance marched the 11th instant about 39 miles.

October 12th Remained in camp to-day to allow the animals to graze and rest after the very long and tiresome march of yesterday.

October 13th Broke camp at 7 A.M. and followed the old stage road around to east side of the mountain – thence marched along road through broken and rolling country about 18 miles in a southeasterly direction – thence same direction over level sandy flat adjacent to the Salt Lakes 11 miles to "Crow Spring" an old mail station – about ½ mile south of the New Mexico line – pitched camp about sunset (4.35 P.M. – the grass here is very poor – wood is exceedingly scarce – there is an abundance of water, but it is brackish and has an unpleasant taste of sulphur – Distance marched 29 miles.

October 14th Broke camp at 6.30 A.M. and marched along old stage road over rolling sandy prairie in a southwesterly direction 6 miles to the point of a remarkably isolated group of dazzling white sand hills – thence same direction 6 miles – left the road and proceeded thence nearly due East up gradual slope about 2½ miles to the mouth of the "Bowen Spring" Canon thence up canon ¾ mile to "Bowen Spring" thence followed trail (of September 19th) around southern point of the Guadalupes 9¼ miles to camp at Pine Spring Distance marched to-day 26 miles – Arrived at camp at 3.45 P.M. a few minutes ahead of the supply train from Fort Davis bringing supplies for the Command for the month of November.

October 15th Remained in camp until October 21st.

October 19th Gen. Grierson, Commanding Officer of the District of the Pecos arrived from Fort Concho.

October 21st The General desiring to visit and explore the canon of Black River – I took 2nd Lieutenant R.D. Read Jr. 10th Cavalry, Acting Assistant Surgeon Ward and a detachment of ten men, as an escort, with two days rations: left 1st Sergeant Helm in charge of camp; followed an old Indian trail northeast along the base of the mountains over rough broken country – to the mouth of the canon, a distance of about 8 miles from Pine Spring – proceeded thence (west) about three miles up the canon and pitched camp under a clump of maples near the stream – the grass here is very good – but the supply is limited – there being but little ground in the canon on which it can grow – Distance marched to-day 11 miles, left the detachment encamped here – took the orderlies and proceeded mounted up the canon about 1½ miles – finding it impracticable to proceed further with the horses – left them here and proceeded up the canon on foot bearing well to the south – explored it for a distance of about 3½ miles from where the horses were left – this being as far as it was practicable to go – the canon at this point has two branches, one coming from the south, the other from the west – both being very narrow gorges in the solid rock – about 10 feet in width and having almost perpendicular walls about 150 feet in height – there is a great quantity of water in both forks – forming deep pools at the bottom of the gorge – about a mile below this point the canon becomes wider and the scenery is of the grandest character – the sides of the canon in some places stand out bold vertical bluffs nearly a thousand feet in altitude – along the bed of the canon and in many places extending to the tops of the mountains, there is a dense growth of trees and shrubs of many varieties – which produces a very picturesque effect – the natural scenery of this canon is perhaps excelled by none in the state in beauty and grandeur. In some places the timber is very heavy and comprises the following species: viz – Pine, pinon, juniper, oak, maple, walnut, cedar, ash, wild cherry, elm, mansanita &c. The stream is not continuous throughout, but rises and sinks in its bed of gravel at short intervals – it sinks at the mouth of the canon and does not rise again for a distance of about 20 miles (near Rattlesnake Spring, New Mexico.)

October 22nd Returned by our trail, of yesterday, to camp at Pine Spring, Distance 11 miles.

October 23rd Remained in camp till November 10th.

October 25th Shannon's train arrived from Fort Concho bringing 30,000 lbs. of forage (corn and oats) for month of November.

October 26th Forage train started for Concho to-day. Gen. Grierson started about noon for Eagle Springs, taking a small detachment as escort, as far as the "Sulphur Springs", on west side of Salt Lake Valley.

October 30th Lieutenant Read, while engaged in obtaining data for map, fell from a stone-wall (the ruins of an old mail station about 800 yards below camp) sustaining very serious injuries about the head.

November 10th Left camp at Pine Spring at 8.30 A.M. with a detachment of 25 men, rationed for 10 days leaving Lieutenant Read (sick) and Acting Assistant Surgeon Ward in camp – marched down old stage road by way of Independence Spring 16 miles: below Independence Spring several very bad places in road, left road 8 miles from head of Delaware Creek – marched over level sandy valley through scattered low hills (sandstone buttes) – southeast about 8 miles to "Wild Horse Tanks" for wood water and grass see journal of November 22nd.

November 11th Left camp at 7.30 A.M. – marched down road to the "Leoncita" 10½ miles – (See journal November 23rd)

November 12th Left camp at 7.45 A.M. marched down road to the "Saladillo" or "Lower Salado" – 14½ miles (see journal September 8th)

November 13th Left Camp at 7.30 A.M. marched up the arroyo west 2 miles and pitched camp at the "Upper Salado" (November 24th) – left wagon here with a guard – and marched up the arroyo west 3 miles – thence southwest 6 miles to "Horse Tanks" – finding them dry, marched back to the Upper Salado about 9 miles.

Distance marched to-day 20 miles.

November 14th Left camp at 7.45 A.M. and marched in a northwesterly direction about 14½ miles over rolling prairie through scattered low hills and mesas – pitched camp near large pool of rain water in rocks – (not permanent) – a little wood, sufficient for camp – grass very good – named this place "Rabbit Tanks" – (marked on map) – Distance 14½ miles.

November 15th Left camp at 8 A.M. – marched in a northwesterly direction 15½ miles to my trail of September 23rd, thence N.W. by this trail 7 miles to old camp of September 23rd about 9 miles south of Independence Spring – found the tanks there dry – Very bad crossing for wagons over arroyo at this place – grass very good – wood rather scarce.

Distance marched to-day 22 miles.

November 16th Broke camp at 7.40 A.M. and followed my trail of September 24th to camp at Pine Spring. Distance 15 miles.

November 17th Remained in camp till November 22nd.

November 21st Made preparations to start for Fort Davis tomorrow morning.

November 22nd Struck camp at Pine Spring at Pine Spring at 8 P.M. [A.M.?] *marched down old stage road nearly due E. 6miles to Independence Spring – thence same direction ¾ mile and left road – marched thence across level sandy valley southeast 3½ miles passed over low ridge into narrow ravine – soil loose and sandy – thence down this ravine through low hills nearly due east 1½ miles – thence across level open prairie East 2 miles; thence down narrow sand flat through scattered hills same direction 2 miles; thence curving gradually to right over low stony ridges 1½ miles – thence over open rolling prairie east 3½ miles to point of low sandstone ridge thence south one mile to "Wild Horse Tanks" and pitched camp at 3.25 P.M. – there are several large pools of rain water in the sandstone bed of the South Fork of Delaware Creek – there is almost always water in them – grazing here is pretty good.*

Our new trail from the Independence Spring road to this point almost direct is a very good natural road – there is only one bad place (in loose sandy ravine at crossing of a small arroyo) and this could be easily remedied by a little work – it is <u>much better</u> than the old road by way of the head of Delaware Creek and is shorter by five or six miles.

Distance marched to-day 21 miles.

November 23rd Broke camp and started the wagons at 8 A.M. – left with the Company at 8.40 A.M. – marched along wagon road as described in journal of September 9th to a place known as the "Leoncita" – in the open alkali prairie – the water here has a peculiar brackish taste – there is apparently but a small quantity of water here, but the little pool is kept constantly supplied by a spring and is permanent – there is an abundance of Cedar wood here, grazing is pretty good – Distance marched to-day 10½ miles.

November 24th Broke camp and started wagons at 8 A.M. followed with Company at 8.30 A.M. – marched along the road over rolling alkali prairie (September 8th) to a point about 4 miles from the "Saladillo" – left the road and proceeded down gentle slope 2 miles to the Upper Salado – an abundance of Cedar wood here, also a few cottonwoods – grazing is pretty good, the water has an unpleasant brackish taste, being highly impregnated with gypsum and other mineral substances but it is perhaps a little better than that of the Lower Salado.

Distance marched to-day 14½ miles.

November 25th Snow fell during the night covering the ground to a depth of about 3 inches, a very cold day – remained in camp to-day.

November 26th Broke camp and started the wagons at 7.30 A.M. left with Company at 8.10 A.M. followed an old Indian and Cavalry trail (Captain Chilson's) over rolling prairie about S-30°-E 5½ miles – passed over low ridge (in spur of the "Presuno de Cavallo" Range) thence down level sandy flat towards Gomez Peak 3 miles – thence over broken and rolling country 3 miles to very large arroyo running east – thence same direction (S.E.) over level prairie 6½ miles – thence over rough broken ground same direction 1¾ miles to top of low rocky ridge thence across level flat S.E. 3½ miles – Made dry camp at 3.45 P.M. Wood very scarce – grazing very good.

Distance marched to-day 23¾ miles.

November 27th Broke camp at 8 A.M. and proceeded through low scattered hills southeast 3½ miles to ravine running N.E. from "San Martin Spring" – thence by trail of September 7th south 2 miles to San Martin Spring found the Texas and Pacific Railroad Surveying party here – with a detachment of ten men from the 10th Infantry – they had been encamped here about two weeks – grazed 3½ hours – watered and moved on at 1.30 P.M. marched over rolling ground through scattered foot-hills off Gomez Peak southeast 4½ miles to intersection with my trail of September 6th thence down this trail east ½ mile – left trail and marched over smooth rolling ground through low hills – southeast about 2 miles and made dry camp at 4.05 P.M. wood very scarce – grazing very good – Distance marched to-day 14 miles.

November 28th Broke camp at 8 A.M. marched southeast 12½ miles almost direct to "Phantom Lake" – country of same character as passed over yesterday, as noted in journal – pitched camp at 1.15 P.M. – Wood very scarce – the grazing is pretty good – the "lake" is situated in open rolling prairie – the water flows out in a very large volume from a limestone cave in the side of a low ridge – and empties into the "lake" which is about 50 yards in length – 10 or 12 yards in width and varying from 2 to 4 feet in depth – the water sinks at the lower end as fast as it runs in at the upper end. Distance marched to-day 12½ miles.

November 29th Broke camp at 8 A.M. and marched across level sandy prairie, crossing the rough gravel beds of two or three shallow arroyos – nearly due south 4 miles to the Vitoria and Fort Davis road – about 8 miles south of vitoria thence by road southeast 1½ miles to "Seven Springs" thence by road 5½ miles to the Stage Road near the "Point of Rocks" – thence by stage road up Limpia Canon to a place known as "the Cottonwoods" about 4½ miles below Fort Davis – pitched camp at 4,25 P.M.

Distance marched to-day 25 miles.

November 30th Broke camp at 8.30 A.M. and marched up the Stage Road 4½ miles to Fort Davis; arrived 10.15 A.M.

Discovered no trail or recent signs of Indians in the section of Country covered by my operations during the time mentioned in the foregoing report.

I am, Sir very respectfully
Your obedient servant
(Signed) Thos. C. Lebo
Captain 10th Cavalry
Commanding Company "K".[6]

6 Capt. Thomas Lebo to Post Adjutant, Fort Davis, Texas, 16 February, 1879, RG393, Part 1, Entry 2546, pp.68-104.

Document 2

Governor Angel Trias' Report to Mr Ruelas, Minister for Foreign Affairs, Mexico on Apache Raids in Chihuahua January 1879

Department of Government.

Executive Power of the free and sovereign State of Chihuahua.
Section of Government No 41

By the copies which numbered 1,2,3,4,5,6, and 7, I have the honor to enclose to you, your Department will be informed of the different events which have taken place in various cantons of the State on account of the incursions of savage Indians, whose frequency may be estimated by the cases which have occurred in the short period of one month, as stated by the said copies.

The continual threat suffered by the inhabitants of said cantons has caused them to solicit increasingly of this Government arms and the other necessary auxiliaries in order to defend their lives and property, without, not withstanding their just petitions, it being possible to attend to their needs on account of the almost absolute want of all these elements, and especially of ammunition and arms, the great urgency of which compels one to beg you to be pleased to interest yourself to the end, and that the state may be given the arms and ammunition necessary to defend itself against the savages who, being perfectly armed, kill with the greatest impunity in their ruthless attacks the unfortunate persons who having no arms can oppose no resistance whatever.

Only on account of the great necessity, which appears from the simple reading of the enclosed copies, can I bring myself to intrude upon your attention, repeating the request which I have often made.

It may be said that this necessity cannot be so extreme, relying, as should be done, upon the forces of the Colonies destined to the pursuit of the common enemy; but they being in my opinion absolutely unequal to their task, as much on account of their organization as their present reduced number, such an assertion is immediately destroyed, the more completely if we remember that during the time said force has been in the State, its only act has been to capture the Indians who were living in peace in Presidio del Norte, while the State in three campaigns has obtained good results in all.

To conclude, I venture to assure you, Mr Secretary, that if the State enjoyed the subvention given in times past for these expenses, or that demanded for the support of the Colonies, it would never again molest the general Government by asking for arms, or for anything else.

Liberty and Constitution
Chihuahua, Feby 7, 1879
(Sgd) Angel Trias

To the Secretary of the Department of Government
Mexico

No.1
Executive Power of the free and sovereign State of Chihuahua

About four O'clock in the afternoon of today, a message was received from the President (municipal) of Temochic that on the 1st inst. Savage Indians attacked Vacente Antillon's muleteers at the point called "La Viega" on the road to the mining district of Jesus Maria, killing two men, driving off the mules, and there still being three men missing.

This office immediately ordered that the interested party, Antillon, should go with twenty men in pursuit of the savages.

Of which I inform you in order that you may be pleased to advise the Governor of the State.

Liberty in the Constitution
Jany 3, 1879
(Sgd) Janquin Chavez
To the Secretary of the Government of the State
Chihuahua
A true copy of the original to which I certify.
Chihuahua, Feby 7, 1879
(Sgd) F. Hemera
1st Official

No. 2

Executive Power of the free and sovereign State of Chihuahua Prefecture of the Canton of Guerrero.

Vicente Antillon, a pursuer of the savage Indian says the following:

Headqrs of the National Guard of Palmiria-chic

In the expedition made against the savage Indians who robbed my property and that of Mr Juano Pareja at the point called "La Viega for which purpose, by order of your office, I was furnished the auxiliaries which I asked in the towns of Palmiria-Chic and Tomachic, with which I made my expedition with a body of twenty-one men, immediately commencing my march into the mountain of Tosanachic, where the savage Indians left six mules, of which four were alive, and two dead, and some other objects of the robbery they committed belonging to me – So soon as I arrived at said point of Tosanachic, I presented myself to the political authority, who placed me in possession of the property stated, with the exception of a little flour and a little salt, which said authority had seen fit to divide among the inhabitants, considering the property as booty, although those who gathered it did not see a single Indian: at the same time I received opportune notice from that authority of the trail of four Indians – three afoot and one on horseback, at the point called Talagotes, very close to where the robbery took place – We went to said point, taking as a guide one of the persons who saw the trail, but we did not find it on account of a heavy rain that fell on the previous day, and gave notice to the authority of Tomochic of the expedition. I have in unvarying terms extolled the conduct of the citizens who accompanied me on account of their bravery and good will.

Of which I inform you for your intelligence and other ends.

Liberty and Constitution
San Ignacio de Palmiria-chic, Jany 14, 1879
(Sgd) Vicente Antillon.
Cuidas Guerrero, Jany 24. 1879
(Sgd) Juan ?????????? Vargas
A true copy of the original to which I certify
Chihuahua, Feby 7, 1879
(Sgd) F. Hemera
1st Official

No.3

R.M. Municipal Presidency of Carizal.

This section being constantly persecuted by the Indians, as appears from the communications that have been sent to the Chief Officer the district of Bravos on the 13th instant: they have again returned and have driven off 25 animals belonging to residents of this place, an official account of which is given under date of today, and as aforesaid, the population being very poor and absolutely without arms, it is not possible to pursue the savages; therefore I beg you to be pleased to furnish 15 or 20 guns so that we can ourselves pursue the Indians who are constantly ruining us, for which important service this town will be deeply grateful, as it does not possess a single gun, and perhaps this is the reason the citizens are refusing to follow the Indians – Hoping you will be pleased to resolve what you think proper upon the subject.

Liberty and Constitution
Carizal, Jany 25, 1879.
(Sgd) Estaban Martinez
To the Secretary of the Supreme Government of the State of Chihuahua.
A true copy of the original, to which I certify
Chihuahua, Feby 7, 1879
(Sgd) F. Hemera
1st Official
From the Diaris Official, March 11, 1879
Concluded

No.4

Executive power of the free and sovereign State of Chihuahua Political prefecture of the District of Iturbide.

Today I have received through the mountains a communication from the rural judge of Carmen, the contents of which are as follows:

"At eight O'Clock this morning information was received from the presidency of Carizal of sixty Indians having passed in the direction of the '"Fierro", who committed some depredations in Guadalupe, to wit: six persons being killed and six missing. Of which I hasten to inform you for your intelligence.

A true copy of the original, to which I certify
Chihuahua, Feby 7, 1879
(Sgd) F. Hemera
1st Official

No. 5

Political prefecture of the Canton of Bravos

The president of the Municipality of Guadalupe says to this prefecture under date of the 27th inst. The following:-

The incursions of barbarous Indians into this vicinity within the last month have been very frequent – On the 18th of this month, a few men skirmishing with two Indians who were taking off two animals belonging to Mr Ramon Aranda of the watering place "Canta Ricio", and forced them to leave two others which they had stolen, and which have been delivered to their owners.

On the 18th of the same month, some explorers reported that on the left bank of the Rio Grande was the trail of nine Indians afoot and one horse, and that they went up from the river to the hills to the east of the town – I immediately dictated my measures to prevent a surprise, and for the same purpose I communicated with the municipal President of San Ignacio. On the 21st the municipal President of San Ignacio informs me that he was told that below "Presidio Viejo" fifteen Indians went down to the river from the Mexican side with two loaded asses and a scalp, and as requested I sent ten mounted men to pursue said Indians, and to give aid to the different rancheros who live in that region.

The commander of said party sent to me about 4O'Clock P.M. of that day a message by one of his veterans that a trail, as if of ten Indians, crossed the Rio Grande into Mexico in the direction of "Canta Ricio" – I hastened to give notice with all speed to those rancheros and to issue orders for safety.

About 8 O'Clock on the morning of the 22nd Miguel Otero sent me a message from the place where he lives asking aid in order to go and recover some corpses of persons and companions who had been taking care of his cattle, and of some other persons which were lying in the mountains, and to enable him to collect his scattered cattle.

I immediately ordered out fourteen men with instructions to aid Mr Otero.

The day before yesterday the two parties out returned, reporting to me having found in the ranch of the said Mr Otero, the bodies of four persons killed by Indians, and that the Indians had also killed a part of the sheep: that these people were heading (as I infer is communicated to you by the municipal President of San Ignacio) and that the trail of about twenty Indians crossed the Rio Grande, entering our territory over the mountain called "Presidio Viejo", and thus keep us in continual alarm. The murdered persons are Antonio Silva, Ramon and his little son and a servant of Mr Miguel Otero whose name I do not remember. All of the Indians who annoy us proceed from the territory of the United States of North America, where they return with their plunder and are freed from pursuit by merely crossing the river. If there is no other way for the interested parties to recover their property which has been stolen, which only within the last few days amounts to more than a hundred beeves and forty horses belonging to different owners; it would be to their advantage to permit them to follow the Indians and thieves into that territory as far as possible, and I wait to learn whether this can be done without compromising the peace of Mexico, as our situation as may be seen is critical. One of the greatest obstacles in this municipality to the pursuit of savages who pass the line from the United States, armed with needle guns and sufficient ammunition, which are furnished them by that Government, as if for the purpose, is the want of arms, owing to the fact that these inhabitants gave those that they had to the Nation, to the number of one hundred, during the time of the intervention, as appears published in the list in the Periodico Oficial (Official Newspaper) of the State of that date, with the loan made in grain, cattle and money to the general government when it returned from Paso del Norte to the Capital of the State, which amounted to more than one hundred thousand dollars ($100,000), and which sum is still due. This class of honourable, patriotic and tried citizens are now left to their own resources, and invaded at every step by savages, without security, for this reason, to their person and property. I find myself obliged in their name to raise my voice in an appeal for protection and security, confining myself to asking of the Government through the respectable channel of your Prefecture, for a considerable number of arms and ammunition in order that these inhabitants may personally make war on or pursue the savages and outlaws, which being permitted, will not be left undone, for they will be defending their property – Further, if this should not be possible, I ask that we are protected by the Federal force having this duty in the State, for the necessity is pressing, and the protection needed, if it is intended to comply with duty.

For some time the Government of the State has had allotted to us, as is known to your Prefecture, fifteen Remingtons, and it is to the public interests that they be delivered without delay, as such protection is as useful to us as necessary.

Yesterday I called together these inhabitants in a popular meeting in accord with the municipal Board, and demonstrated to them the situation, urging them to prepare for the defense of our persons and property, inasmuch as we have nothing to depend upon for our protection but what we furnish ourselves. And the organization of twenty men was agreed to by my worthy fellow citizens who being mounted and armed at their own expense, would be ready and prepared to pursue the savages and outlaws whenever the authorities should order it, making daily scouts to the banks of the Rio Grande and along the foot of the mountains to the west of this town, being exempt from all the other common services to which the other inhabitants are liable.

This organization has given good results here in former years – This Presidency would desire that the Government of the State aid such squads of Cavalry at least with arms and ammunition, and that the towns composing the canton of Brazos should establish the same kind of force for mutual aid when the necessity arises and if it seems proper to you, I beg you to initiate the movement, using your influence in order that this communication which is based on truth and zeal for the general welfare, may be published in the official paper – "United we shall be string". He will work to realize it.

And I have the honor to trans-cribe it to you in order that you may be pleased to report it to the superior government of the State, not hesitating in recommending that the Presidency be furnished with the fifteen Remingtons which are asked, for defense against savage Indians and other outlaws: it is very little that is asked, it being in the opinion of this Prefecture more economical to aid that municipality with the said arms than with the Federal force, as is manifested in the enclosed communication, as this being more costly and paid by the Federation, it is better to locate it at some of the uninhabited watering places, like that of the Candelaria Mountain, the "Ojo" at the end of the mountain northeast of this town, and near the dividing line between Mexico and the United States and other watering places in the State, as it is neither proper nor convenient that in protecting rural property the said Federal force be stationed in the towns and less in the municipality of Guadalupe and San Ignacio of this Canton, as by arming the inhabitants they can defend themselves as there are men among those citizens zealous in the punishment of the said enemies, voluntarily giving their services for that object, as they are giving them and have given them in past times with no other compensation than exemption from fatigue service, which can be rendered by those who do not render the other service.

Liberty and Constitution
Paso del Norte, Jan 30, 1879
(Sgd) Jesue Padilla
Rafael Barron, Secretary
For the Secretary of Government of the Sate
Chihuahua.
A true copy of the original, to which I certify
Chihuahua, Feby 7, 1879
(Sgd) F. Hemera
1st Official

No 6

Under date of the 24th instant, the Municipal President of San Ignacio says to this prefecture the following:

On the 23rd inst. I was informed by Romnaldo Gazaldon that he had gone through the mountains in front of "Presidio Viego" in search of a herd of sheep belonging to his brother-in-law, Antonio Silva, who according to the signs he saw, had been killed by the savages: immediately the personnel of this Presidency with all the neighbors it was possible to get ready started out, and as on account of the repeated notices of incursions of Indians these were already out a party from this town and another from the municipality of Guadalupe – These noticed the fire in the said mountain, and also went there with promptness; but although the efforts made were sufficient and rendered with activity, it was not possible to prevent the misfortune which took place at "Ojo del Venado" the murder of Antonio Silva, Antonio Evora, Ramon Apertis and his son Pilar Apertis, a child eight years old, all killed with bullets, who were brought and buried in this municipality; there having also been killed and wounded, a large number of sheep, and four asses, with some clothes and arms were carried off – Nine Indians committed the said depredations.

Such a misfortune on the part of persons who devoted their time to working for the support of their families, is deserving of compassion, as they leave small orphans.

At the time it was impossible to drive the Indians out of the mountains, on account of their lurking in the roughest part, and the many times that such services have been demanded, this Presidency having to contend with the scarcity of arms among the inhabitants.

And I improve this opportunity to request the Governor of the State through your Prefecture to be pleased to furnish this municipality with 15 rifles with which to meet necessities like the present, while the Indians from foreign reservations are constantly preying upon the people.

And I have the honor to enclose it to you for the superior information of the Governor of the State, recommending that 25 Remingtons be that Presidency, which can be bought for this object with the direct contributions paid by those citizens as I have manifested in another communication; and this is the greatest benefit that can be conferred upon these inhabitants – better than except them from the payment of said contribution as having been solicited, as the arms they use at present are inferior to those carried by the savage Indians, and it would be a source of shame for the savages to triumph on this account, in case of a battle.

Liberty and Constitution
Paso del Norte, January 30, 1879
(Sgd) Jesus Padilla
Rafael Barron, Secretary
To the Secretary of Government of the State
Chihuahua
A true copy of the original, to which I certify
Chihuahua, Feby 7, 1879
(Sgd) F. Hemera
1st Official

No 7
Executive Power of the free and sovereign State of Chihuahua
The Municipal President of Carrizal says to the Prefecture under date of the 25th instant the following:

On the 13th, at 8 o'clock in the morning this Presidency received information through the Judge (de campo) of Moctezuma that at daybreak that morning the Indians had carried off nine horses cutting the ropes with which they were tied at the doors of the house: fifteen men appointed by this Presidency went out, but did not succeed in overtaking them – The Indians left a horse and an ass, which are deposited in this Presidency – The pursuers report that the Indians went out towards the river, passing up the "Fierro"

Of which I inform you that you may advise the superior authorities, and I have the honor to trans-cribe it to you that you may be pleased to make it known to the Governor of the State, starting in addition that the Indians referred to in the enclosed note proceed from the United States, where they are armed, perhaps in order that they may annoy us, thus making war indirectly on Mexico.

Liberty and Constitution
Paso del Norte, January 30, 1879
(Sgd) Jesus Padilla
Rafael Barron, Secretary
To the Secretary of Government of the State
Chihuahua
A true copy of the original, to which I certify
Chihuahua, Feby 7, 1879
(Sgd) F. Hemera
1st Official[7]

7 Original Reports numbered 1-7 forwarded by Angel Trias (7 February, 1879) to Mr Ruelas, Minister for Foreign Affairs, Mexico, who submitted them (13 March, 1879) to John W. Foster, Minister of the United States to Mexico, who in turn passed them on (15 March, 1879) to William M. Evarts, U.S. Secretary of State who finally passed them on to George W. McCrary, Secretary of War on 7 April, 1879, RG393, Part 1, Entry 2546, pp.119-149.

Document 3

Merritt's Report on the Surrender of Victorio at Ojo Caliente on the 8 February, 1879

Ojo Caliente, N.M.
Febr'y, 20. 1879

The Act. Ass't Adjutant General,
District of New Mexico,
Santa Fe, N.M.

Sir.
In reply to your telegram of the 18th inst. I have the honor to make the following report.

On the evening of the 7th inst. Victorio and twenty two other Warm Spring Apache Indians came near Ojo Caliente and alarmed the camp by their hallooing. I immediately ordered the Company to hold itself in readiness and sent for an interpreter, (by name of Kelley). I went out to where Victorio was, and he said he wanted to have a talk with me. I appointed the next day, saying it was too late then. He assented and said all right. On the following day I went out, I should judge, at least one half mile and sent up my interpreter to tell him I was ready for a talk, to come down.

He said he would not come down, for me to come up where he was. At that time he was on the highest mountain on the right as you leave Ojo Caliente. I debated some time and asked the interpreter what was best to do, as he was well acquainted with these Indians; after some deliberation he concluded it was best for us to go up, for if we did not, that the Indians would leave and we could not catch them. (I would here state that Victorio would not allow us to carry any arms, or take any soldiers with us.) I went up on this mountain and had a talk with him, and told him what I would do if he came in and gave himself up as a prisoner of war. (I would here state that it would have taken a regiment of cavalry to have captured him and his band for there were only a few present, the remainder of his band and horses, were some eight or ten miles away at that time.) After the talk was over and I had told him what was expected of him, he asked me if he could be sent to Stanton Reservation and tell his other people to come in. I asked him how many he wanted to go and for how long. He said two for fifteen days. I said I would give him a pass, but did not want the Indians to be over the time specified in the pass and that they should not molest any one while away. They left and were away the time specified and were very prompt to return at the very hour. I enclose pass for the information of the District Commander.

The depredations which have been committed on the River and the surrounding country has been done by Nanna and his band which escaped from Capt. Bennett last fall, for I have information from a man by the name of Green who lost fifteen horses and followed their trail into the camp of Nanna, who is on the Stanton Reservation, and recaptured them. He says that Victorio was never there but went direct from here to Old Mexico with the twenty two who came in with him, and I am convinced myself from the appearance of Victorio and his party, and from the stock &c they have in their possession, they have been to Old Mexico.

The letter of instructions turned over to me by Lieut. Wright, it would seem that I was to use my own judgement to bring these Indians in and stop all depredations if possible. Victorio would not have staid [stayed] *here one hour if I had not given him permission to send to Stanton for Nanna and his band, for it was understood by Nanna and his party that Victorio had gone to Old Mexico to get horses and ammunition for the whole party, for a summers campaign.*

Nanna was only waiting for Victorio from Stanton Reservation. Victorio has come direct from Old Mexico and has not been near Stanton Reservation and in my opinion if these Indians are allowed to come here from Stanton Reservation there will be no trouble in future and less in moving them.

If they are not allowed to come in here openly and surrender as prisoners of war, there is nothing to prevent them visiting Victorio secretly, and in going and coming committing depredations and thereby making the Indians here restless and uneasy. It is the wish of the majority to come in here and not stop or stay at Stanton Reservation. In my opinion they cannot be controlled with a part of them here and a part there.

Victorio or any of his band are not allowed to leave Camp without a pass. I have done what my judgement prompted me to do for the best, and I am very sorry if I have committed an error in misinterpreting the letter of instructions.

Very respectfully,
your obedient servant,
(signed) C.W. Merritt
2nd Lieut. 9th Cavalry
Comd'g[8]

8 Merritt, Ojo Caliente to AAAG Dist. of N.M. in 'Victorio Campaign, Feb. 1879-Nov. 1880' in "Special Files" Created by the Military Division of the Missouri. Records of US Army Continental Commands, 1821-1920 Record Group 393 M1495, Roll 14.

Document 4

Account of the Apache Raid in the San Francisco Valley, May 1879, published in the *Grant County Herald* 6 February, 1880

On the 22nd of May [1879], Mr J. Keller started to hunt cattle and when four miles from home was fired at by Indians. He rode back to the Robert's ranche and notified Messrs Roberts, who arrived at the ranche in time to protect their wives and little ones. Mr Keller then rode up the valley and alarmed the residents, and returning, reached the Roberts ranche in time to aid them in the fight. A fine horse valued at $300, was shot under him. No one was hurt in the settlement, but one red skin was badly wounded, if not fatally. He saw him kicking in the cornfield. Mr Keller then called on volunteers to go with him to alarm the lower settlement, John Morris and Robert Coulter accompanied him. They reached the next settlement about twenty minutes before the Indians. They notified Messrs Foster and Harrington of the attack on their ranches, and that the reds had been driven off, with the loss of one of their number, and were coming that way. A horse tied to a corn crib was allowed to remain there as a decoy. Five minutes afterwards the Indians appeared on the hill above the house. Silence was the order and wait the result. These brave, determined men knew not how many they had to contend with. They had seen six in the first fight and five retreated down the valley, but the tracks showed they had been joined by others. How many redskins attacked them is not known but the result was that four Indians were killed and the remainder retreated down the valley. After the fight Mr Keller and John Roberts rode to Parson Williams and Mr Robert Site? Sire? Started for Dry Creek to give the alarm. The latter arrived at the farm of Ogden and Irwin before dark and found everything destroyed or stolen. Two watches, shot gun, ammunition and one years provisions were taken. Four cows killed, the crops destroyed by Indian horses, the dairy utensils, harness, clothing, and every thing these men possessed were also destroyed. Mr Ogden was wounded in the hip and Mr Irwin slightly wounded in the arm. The poor fellows managed to reach Parson Williams farm but in a pitiable condition.[9]

9 From the Fresco' *Grant County Herald*, 6 February, 1880.

Document 5

Captain Beyer's Report of his Scout after Victorio 25 May to the 12 June, 1879

Fort Bayard N.M.
June 16th 1879

To the
Post Adjutant
Fort Bayard N.M.

Sir

I have the honor to report that in compliance with requirements of Special Order No. 58 per Hdqrs Post of Fort Bayard N.M. dated May 25' 79. I left this post at 1 o'clock P.M. May 25' 1879, with 2' Lieut. Henry H. Wright, 9' Cavy, and thirty one (31) enlisted men "C?" 9'Cav (all that could be mounted) also a detachment of fifteen enlisted men of Company "L" 9' Cavalry and two Navajo scouts. Mr Foster, a citizen, accompanied my command as volunteer guide. The Scouts and detachment of Company "L" were to be sent to their station, Ojo Caliente N.M., should I find that I could dispense with their services.

Marched to Rio Miembres arriving at 5 o'clock P.M. Distance marched 15 miles.

My 26' 1879. Left Camp at 6.30 A.M. marched up the Miembres across the divide to the Sapio, along Sapio, to trail across to the Gila River at junction of West Diamond Creek (Known as the Rio San Juan on the old maps of New Mexico) arrived in camp at 6 o'clock P.M. found little grass. The entire country through which we marched from time of leaving the Sapio to Gila River was burning and it was with some difficulty that we succeeded in getting through to camp.

Wood and Water plenty – distance marched 30 miles

May 27' 1879 Left camp at 5 A.M. marched up West Diamond Creek to Redmond's and Halloway's Ranche, situated 7 miles from junction of W. Diamond Creek and Gila River. Learned here that the Indians were seen on the Mesa north of the ranche on the afternoon of May 25' 1879, that the Indians had killed four or five cows and ran off two horses and a pony. Continued our march up the creek to mouth of the Gilita and there struck trail, (two days old) of about 20 Indians. Mr Foster pronounced the trail from signs that he recognized to be made by the party of Indians I was ordered to intercept, followed trail to Gila River – crossed and continued to East Diamond Creek. On the trail found seven dead cattle, the last three entirely consumed – also found a one year old stallion, dead, recognized by Mr Foster as the property of Irwin and Oppen on the San Francisco. At 3.30 P.M. found deserted Indian Camp, which the Indians had abandoned early in the morning, found a cow and a mare, partly consumed followed ?????? **(word too blotted)** *up E. Diamond Creek bottom for about two miles, to where it left the Creek and led up the divide between the Gila River and the Creek, made a temporary halt of two hours and a half to enable the command to get something to eat and graze the horses & c. left at sunset and marched until 11.15 P.M. and camped near crossing of North Star Road and Diamond Creek, on the trail. Distance marched 24 miles.*

May 28' 79 Left camp at 5.15 A.M. followed trail east along Diamond Creek. Halted at 8.30 A.M. for breakfast and grazing, distance marched 10 miles. Moved on again on the trail at 11.30 A.M. marched up Diamond Creek about 15 or 16 miles to near its head – thence crossed over a very steep mountain into a Canon running parallel with Diamond Creek. Marched up this Canon about 2 miles and struck the Indian camp made the night previous. Our march during the day having been a very hard one, most of the time on foot and through burning forest and underbrush (set on fire by the Indians to cover their trail) went into camp at 4.30 P.M. good water and grass plenty of wood, distance marched, between 25 and 28 miles.

May 29' '79. Left camp at 6.30 A.M. continued up canon until 7.30 A.M. ascended the Miembres Mountains, reached the summit at 9 o'clock crossed and continued down ridge of mountain spur going N. and N.E., left ridge at 10 A.M. and entered canon having on its left high ridges or rather mountains, found small pools of water and fresh Indian signs, deployed skirmish line and left the canon, taking to an open ridge to our right and front, at 10.50 discovered two horses about half a mile distant, grazing and a few moments afterwards discovered the Indians on a rock peak about 400 yards to our left and front (very high and steep) busily engaged building up breastworks, at same instant an Indian on the peak, whom I afterwards learned was Victorio, called out in Apache "Hoca-Hoca" – (which Hostensoyi one of the Navajo Scouts who understood Apache, said was – Come Here – Come Here) at the same time raising a white flag, and crying out in Apache (and interpreted by Hostensoyi) that I should also raise a flag as he, Victorio, wanted to have a talk with the officer commanding the troops. I ordered a halt, and advancing about 50 yards in front of my skirmishers, I placed a white handkerchief on a stick, told the Navajo Indian to tell Victorio I was ready for a talk with him. Victorio would not consent to have a talk, unless I came up to his camp and breastworks (which we could see and count 16 warriors) which I refused to do not trusting to his promise that I should not be harmed, I tried to get him to meet me half way which he declined to do. He then made a harangue, and all that could be gathered from it was, to the effect that he, Victorio and his people were poor, that they did not want to fight my soldiers, and all they wanted was to be let alone. Victorio finally wound up his harangue by waving a lance around and over his head and taking down his flag of truce. Not having any faith in Victorio, and convinced that he only made use of his flag to get the women and children out of the way, and as during all the time that the parley lasted his men continued to erect new breast-works, I did not hesitate to move my skirmishers under Lieut. Wright, half way up the mountain and within 200 yards of Victorio's works, where the line halted waiting for the orders to advance to the attack. When the Indians were first discovered I placed a small detachment of skirmishers between the Indians and their herd, and during the parley, Mr Foster and a detail of 5 mounted men quietly captured the herd consisting of 12 horses, 2 mules and 2 burros, without the Indians perceiving the movement. At 11.50 I ordered the right skirmishers under Sergeant Delemar Benn, Company "L" Ninth Cavalry to move a little more forward and move to the right so as to flank the Indians, all of which was quietly executed. At 11.55 A.M. I gave the order to advance, the firing began, hotly returned by the Indians, the line kept advancing, the men seeking shelter from tree to tree and after about half an hours sharp fighting during which time the right skirmishers under Sergeant Benn, had gotten well around and to the rear of the position held by the Indians, the latter abandoned their works and camp, and retreated down a ridge that ????? ????? in rear of their camp, and scattered, my men gaining the position from which they had driven the Indians a few minutes after they had retreated. The Indians being afoot, they left no trail and consequently they could not be pursued. In the works occupied by the Indians (and which a determined body of men could have held against five times the strength of my command) sufficient evidence was found to indicate that a number were wounded and in two places, signs that at least two were seriously if not mortally wounded. All the plunder, which was considerable, found in the camp, consisting of blankets, skins, hides, baskets, meat and mescal and such other plunder as is usually found in an Indian camp, I had destroyed by fire. My loss during the affair was, Private Frank Dorsey, Company "C?" 9th Cavalry, killed and Private George H. Moore Company "C?" seriously and John Scott, Company "L" 9th Cavalry slightly wounded. One horse killed and one wounded (since died). The following named officers and men deserve special mention for gallantry and bravery displayed viz: 2nd Lieut. Henry H. Wright, Mr John ? Foster, citizen, Sergeant Delemar Benn Company "L" 9th Cavalry, Sergeant George Lyman, Thomas Boyne, Corporal Isam Malry Co "C" 9' Cavalry and Private Ridgeley Company "L" 9' Cavy also Hostensoyi Navajo Scout.

Private Frank Dorsey, Company "C", 9' Cavy was buried near to where he fell and his grave marked.

Finding that the Indians had scattered, leaving no trail, I moved south about mile and a half and made camp at 6 P.M. Distance marched today 10 miles.

May 30' '79 Left camp at 8 A.M. crossed over three spurs on ridges of the Miembres Mountains and struck the Cuchillo Negro, at about a mile east of Victorio's old camp (the one jumped by Lieut. Wright, 9' Cavalry in September '76) Halted from 11 o'clock A.M. to 1. o'clock P.M. for our breakfast and grazing, renewed the march at 1. P.M. and arrived at Ojo Caliente N.M. at 7.30 P.M. Private Moore Company

"C?" who was seriously wounded was turned over to Dr Sewall, Acting Assistant Surgeon at Ojo Caliente for treatment. Distance marched 30 miles.

May 31' 1879 Remained at Ojo Caliente this day, reshoeing horses &c.

June 1' 1879 Left Ojo Caliente at 10 A.M. marched to Cañada Alamosa and camped at Forage Agency, no grain, poor hay, no grass, little wood, plenty of water. Distance marched 19 miles.

June 2' '79 Left Camp at 6. A.M. via Cuchillo Negro to Palomas River and camped at 2,30 P.M. at Spring about ???? below crossing of trail at Palomas River. Distance marched 22 miles

June 3' 1879 Left Camp at 6 A.M., marched 10 miles to Rio Las Animas and camped on the mesa, were[10] *good grass was found. Being without meat for my men I traded off one of the captured burros for a beef. One of the captured horses being unable to travel was shot to death.*

Learned from a Mr Harvey residing on the Las Animas, that two dismounted Indians were seen yesterday evening going south

June 4' '79. Left camp at 6 A.M. marched via Hillsborough to McEvers' Ranch at Laguna Las Basenos and camped Distance marched 25 miles.

June 5' 1879 Left camp at 7A.M. marched 12 miles to Mule Springs, Camped until evening, continued the march until 8 P.M. and camped on mesa on Fort Cummings Road and 6 miles from Fort Cummings. Distance marched today 24 miles. June 6' '79 Left camp at 5.30 A.M. and arrived at Fort Cummings N.M. at 7.30 remained at Cummings until 4 o'clock P.M. when accompanied by 23 men of Company "A" 9' Cavalry, under Lieut. Day 9' Cavy. I left for the Florida Mountains and Carizullio Springs in compliance with telegraphic instructions received whilst at Cummings, from Major A.P. Morrow, 9' Cavalry, Commanding Fort Bayard N.M. marched until 11 o'clock P.M. and made a dry camp in the plain near Florida Mountains. Distance marched 18 miles.

June 7' 1879 Left camp at day-break, marched to Florida Mountains, visited Black Rock Tanks and Kettle Springs, found no water, at 10 A.M. arrived at Beyer's Springs (In middle of range of mountains east side) were[11] *water was found, rested there during the day and at night marched via the Tinajas at S.E. point of mountains to plain south of Floridas and made a dry camp. Distance marched 20 miles.*

June 8' '79 Left camp at 5 A.M. marched to Spring in Tres Hermanas Mountains, found but little water, remained there until evening and then continued the march to plain near Carazillo Springs and made dry camp. Distance marched 26 miles.

June 9' '79 Left camp at daybreak, marched 6 miles and arrived at Carazillo Springs at 6 A.M. remained in camp at Springs until 5 P.M. and marched north on road to Cow Springs, until 12 midnight when dry camp was made. Distance marched this day 36 miles.

June 10' Left camp at daybreak, continued march to Cow Springs; arriving at 11 A.M. Distance marched 14 miles.

June 11' '79 Left camp at 8 A.M. and marched to Hudson's Hot Springs arriving at 11:30 A.M. Distance marched 14 miles.

June 12' '79 Left Hot Springs at 7 A.M. and marched through by trail to Fort Bayard and arriving at 12 M. Distance marched 18 miles

10 As spelled in original document.
11 As spelled in original document.

Total number of days absent from post	*19*
Number of miles travelled during scout	*369*
Number of horses captured	*12*
Number of mules captured	*2*
Number of Burros captured	*2*

Loss

One Private killed in action May 29' '79

One Private wounded seriously in action May 29' '79

One Private wounded slightly in action May 29' '79

One horse killed Co C 9 Cavy

One Horse wounded Died June 2' 79

One Horse Company ? 9' Cavalry, broke down on march and shot to prevent falling in hands of Indians

Respectfully Submitted
(Signed) Chas D. Beyer
Capt 9' Cavalry
For route pursued &c. see notes, kept by Lieut. Wright, 9' Cavy. And herewith submitted.
(Signed) Chas D. Beyer
Capt 9' Cavalry.[12]

12 Beyer to Post Adjutant, Fort Bayard, 16 June, 1879 in Letters Received by Headquarters District of New Mexico September 1865-August 1890 Microfilm 1088 from Record Group 393, Roll 37, File 658-1658, April–June 1879.

Document 6

Morrow's Request for Additional Indian Scouts, 15 June, 1879

Fort Bayard N.M.
June 15th 1879

To the:
Actins Assistant Adjutant General
Dist N.M.
Santa Fe N.M.

Sir:
In view of the recent extensive depredations committed by hostile Indians in this vicinity, I have the honor to request that as large a number of Indian scouts, as can be obtained, may be ordered for duty at this post.

It has been demonstrated to my entire satisfaction that without their assistance troops can do no more than protect, by their immediate presence, the isolated ranches, and render the roads comparatively safe by constant patrols.

All of the Cavalry (three companies) of this command have been in the field constantly for the past month, each party accompanied by one, or more, citizens, who have lost stock, and who were generally good trailers and certainly eager in the pursuit. In some instances – notably one in which I was in command, the Indians had only an hours start of us and yet they succeeded in eluding me.

The only success, so far, was accomplished by Capt. Beyer and he had the assistance of two Navajo Indians and the Indians found by him had been chased uninterruptedly from Ojo Caliente into Arizona and back again, and were worn out. As soon as one of the following parties would lose or quit the trail another would take it up; therefore it by no means follows that because the Troops found the Indians in this instance, they may do it again.

Yesterday a small party (say ten Indians) attacked a ranche on the Miembres, resulting in one Indian and one Ranchman being killed, the Indians getting away with stock. This occurred thirty miles from here. Say the news comes today at noon and I mount a company and start it at once for the scene of action. Citizens in the mean time have found a trail and volunteer to accompany the troops, the trail then taken is forty eight hours old. The indians are certain to go over the roughest country possible (and all of this country is so rough that it is next to impossible for mounted men to get through it) but will probably give the pursuers a good trail for one or two days and then they scatter, leaving no more sign than if they had taken wings, and I will defy the best troops or frontiersmen living to follow them further.

The troops must then resort to guesswork or return, worn out and disgusted with, in all probability, a broken down lot of horses, which will not be fit for use for a week or two. This kind of business can be stopped if we had but about twenty good foot Indians, such as they have in Arizona.

Victoria has but about forty men, divided probably into eight or ten stealing and murdering bands, and it is simply impossible for a troop, or fifty troops of Cavalry to catch three or four foot Indians in these almost inaccessible mountains: but with the Indian scouts it would be possible to follow some of them to their permanent camp and then give them their quietus.

The Indians are even now reported within ????? miles of this Post at McKie's Ranche, I have sent a detachment with rations in haversacks, to make all haste and endeavour to punish them; but I have not the slightest hope of accomplishing anything. I therefore most earnestly entreat that some Indian scouts be sent me to enable me to follow these hostiles until the last one perishes or surrenders.

Very Respectfully
Your obedient servant
AP Morrow
Major 9th Cavalry
Commanding Post.[13]

13 Morrow to AAAG, Santa Fe, 15 June, 1879 in Letters Received by Headquarters District of New Mexico September 1865-August 1890 M1088 from Record Group 393, Roll 37, File 658-1658, April–June 1879.

Document 7

Lt. Ward's, Report concerning pursuit of Mescalero Raiders June/July 1879 (Includes account of two skirmishes between these raiders and the Texas Rangers)

Fort Concho, Texas
July 15th 1879

To the
Post Adjutant
Fort Concho, Texas

Sir
I have the honor to state, that in compliance with the verbal instructions of the Commanding Officer, I left the Post at 11 P.M. on June 29th in pursuit of Indians reported to have stolen stock on the North Concho River. Marched up the stream 2 miles and camped; grass good, wood and water in abundance.

June 30th Broke camp at daylight and marched on old military road up the stream 25 miles and camped. Grass good – wood and water in abundance.

July 1st Broke camp at daylight and marched on road up the Concho 28 miles and camped; grass good, wood and water in abundance.

July 2nd Broke camp at daylight and marched on road to "Head of Concho (Holland's Ranche) and camped, distance travelled 5 miles; Grass good – wood and water in abundance. As I learned at this place that the Rangers were hunting for the trail of the Indians that they had the fight with on the 29th June 1879, and that they had said they would return as soon as they had found it, I concluded to remain at this point till the afternoon, as I received no word by 3 P.M. I broke camp and marched on Col. Shafter's trail to Mustang Springs 17 miles when I met four Rangers who reported that they had had a fight on the —— July and lost one (1) man. I went into camp at this place, no water, grass good, wood in abundance.

July 3rd Broke camp at daylight, and marched on same trail to Mustang Springs and camped distance travelled 43 miles; grass good, wood scarce. Water in abundance.

July 4th Broke camp at daylight, and marched in a N. of W. direction 25 miles, when I struck the trail of the Rangers and Indians, then on the trail 4 miles when I found a small pool of rain water; I formed my camp at this place, and took fifteen men and marched six miles farther on when I found the body of the Ranger; I buried him and returned to camp; distance travelled 41 miles, grass good, wood and water (temporary) scarce.

July 5th Broke camp at daylight and marched in an Easterly direction 9 miles when I found a rain water hole and camped; grass good wood and water in abundance.

July 6th Marched in an Easterly direction to Baldwin Springs and camped; grass fair, wood and water in abundance; distance travelled 12 miles.

July 7th Marched in a Northerly direction to Sulphur Springs and camped; grass poor, wood and water in abundance, distance travelled 19 miles.

July 8th I sent a detachment to Soda Springs, they reported no signs on their return; distance marched 8 miles.

Broke Camp about 10 A.M. and marched to Wild Horse Springs and camped, distance travelled 28 miles; grass good, wood and water in abundance.

July 9th Remained in camp.

July 10th Marched on road to Big Springs and camped; distance travelled 14 miles; grass poor, wood and water in abundance.

July 11th Marched to Day's (Map) Springs and camped; distance travelled 9 miles; grass excellent, wood and water in abundance.

July 12th Marched in a Southerly direction to Col. Shafter's old trail, then on trail to head of North Concho and camped; distance travelled 25 miles; grass good, wood and water in abundance.

July 13th Marched down road to my camp of June 30th and camped; distance travelled 32 miles.

July 14th Marched on Road to the Post; distance travelled 28 miles.

I would state that on the evening of the 29 of June, seven (7) Rangers struck a party of Indians near the Head of the North Concho, they captured all the horses of the Indian's, and lost two (2) horses, two pack mules, and five days rations; the engagement lasted until dark when the Rangers retired; No loss of life on either side.

The next day the Rangers and six (6) men, thirteen (13 in all) took the trail of the two mules, and after following it one day and a half, came in sight of the Indians, and after a chase of about 12 miles, compelled the Indians, four in number, to abandon the mules and dig two (2) rifle pits; An engagement took place for a time, one Ranger named Anglin being killed at the first fire of the Indians; The Indians were left in possession of the field and the two mules. We buried Anglin on the 4th July.

I was joined by two Rangers named Burton, and Patti on the 3rd of July, I am indebted to them for great assistance, which was cheerfully given in every instance.

About 25 miles from the head of the North Concho near the place marked on the enclosed map, as the Russell water hole, in a thicket, six saddles were found by the Rangers which were left by the Indians.

As there had been ten Indians at first, and only four had been overtaken, and as they had left six saddles on the trail, and as they had been dismounted, my marches from the place of the last fight were made with the hope of striking the Indians on their return from the settlements.

Several blankets, nearly new, marked U.S.I.D. were found on the trail

Total distance marched 345 miles.

Very Respectfully
Your Obt. Servant
(Sgd) C.R. Ward
1st Lieut. 10th Cavalry
Commanding Co. D.[14]

14 1st Lieut. C.R. Ward, Tenth Cavalry to Post Adjutant, Fort Concho, Texas, 15 July, 1879, RG393, Part 1, Entry 2546, pp.217-221.

Document 8.1

'Cause of the Apache Outbreak' Article Published in the *Grant County Herald*, 8 November, 1879

CAUSE OF THE APACHE OUTBREAK

Washington, Oct. 30 – Agent Russell writes to the Commissioner of Indian Affairs from the Mescalero Agency in regard to the Apache outbreak in New Mexico, as follows: Victorio heard of indictment against him in Grant county or as they say "a paper" was out against him. Three days after, Judge Bristol, Fountain Prosecuting Attorney and others passed through the reservation to a point some eighteen miles east of the agency on a pleasure excursion, hunting and fishing. The Indians were acquainted with these persons, knew their official positions and connected their visit here with "the papers" referred to and believed that Victorio and perhaps his people were to be arrested. Fountain who has been in the country for eighteen years is personally acquainted with many of the Indians and learned from them that this circumstance induced Victorio to leave at the time he did.

The responsibility for the above is so intermingled, that it is difficult to decide whether Agent Russell or A.J. Fountain is the liar.

The editor of this paper was foreman of the Grand Jury which indicted Victorio, and, as his fellow jurymen will acknowledge, the evidence was sufficient to have convicted any white man.

Document 8.2

'Victorio' Editorial 20 August, 1879 in *Thirty Four*

VICTORIO

The people of this portion of New Mexico, who have been the principal sufferers from the marauding and murdering raids of this notorious renegade, would like to know what right Gen. Hatch, or an Indian Agent , or any one else, has to offer immunity to thieves and assassins. We are reliably informed that at the very time Victorio's band were depredating in this and Grant counties, Gen. Hatch sent a message to him to induce him to come to the Mescalero Agency, promising him protection if he would do so. Victorio was not found by the messenger at that time but has since accepted the proffered amnesty and is to-day quietly drawing rations from the Agent instead of from the Sheriff of Grant County. The troops that were ostensibly scouting the whole country for him could easily have captured or killed the entire band: but it seems to have been considered cheaper to sue for peace with him and reward him for his crimes than to punish him. We stated, at the time such a show was being made by moving the troops hither and thither, that they appeared to have orders not to find the renegade. Whether such orders were actually issued or not, it is certain that the troops were managed in just such a way as though they had been issued.

By a recent decision, Indians are responsible under the law just as any other class of citizens; and as there are several indictments against Victorio in Grant County, it is to be hoped that sheriff Whitehill or his deputy will proceed to the Mescalero Agency, arrest the red rascal, and hold him in jail to await his trial.

Document 9.1

Captain Steelhammer's Report on Captain Hooker's Conduct at Ojo Caliente. November 1879

Ojo Caliente, New Mexico
December 11th 1879

To the
Actg. Asst. Adjt.General
District of New Mexico
Santa Fe N.M.

Sir:
I have the honor to report that, in obedience to instructions received, I left Santa Fe, December 1st and arrived here yesterday. The letter of complaint against Captain A.E. Hooker 9th Cavy, being anonymous, and not very specific in its allegations, I shall, in justice to both 'E' Co. 9th Cavy and its Commander, give every enlisted man in the Co. an opportunity to be heard.

They now speak for themselves, and in the order in which they are called.

Sergeant James Williams

Says that he had been well enough treated individually, but that Capt. Hooker at the time the herd guard was found killed, made use of the expression "that he wished that all the negro son's of bitches had been killed were dead and in hell – that he liked to get a company, of decent soldiers to command – the one he had was not fit to have horses".

This was said in the presence of the assembled Co. the day after the herd had been jumped. Sergeant Williams further says that he would feel more secure while on horse guard with his horse saddled and his carbine along, but that the carbine would be but an incumbrance[15] *if he was not allowed the use of a saddle. Sergt. Williams complained once before while the Co. was stationed at Ft. Wingate, N.M.*

The complaint was made to the Post Commander, but no action was ever taken thereon so far as the complainant knows.

Private Henry Beale

States that Captain Hooker has more than once while in front of his Co. called his men collectively "damned sons of bitches as fit to be soldiers as cur dogs to be saints". This happened in September last, but he cannot recollect the date. He does not know what reason the Captain has for speaking thus to his men. Priv. Beal has complained once before while the Co. was stationed at Ft. Wingate but no action was taken thereon by the Post Commander.

Private Daniel Downing

States that his only complaint is that the Captain is constantly calling the members of his Co. "sons of bitches" and that he was individually so called along in the Spring of 1878 about the time the Co. left this

15 As spelled in the original document.

place. The horses were being watered when the Captain told me to keep my horse better in line, I was trying to do so, when the Captain rode up and hit me with his riding whip, and when I asked him not to strike me, he called me a son of a bitch.

Private Luther Craven

Says that he wants to complain against his Captain, because he knows that the captain was warned of the presence of Indians before 12 n. on the day the herd was captured – that he heard Mr Sullivan, in the Store of Captain Hooker's brother, at this place, tell a Mr Kelly that the Indians were around for the purpose of capturing the herd. This conversation took place, to the best of his knowledge, about 10 o'clock A.M. as the herd was then in sight being watered.

He does not know from personal knowledge that the Captain was warned, but has been told that he had been so warned, before dinner, by said Sullivan. The herd guard was not properly armed and equipped. They had neither saddles nor carbines, only saddle blankets, pistols and twelve rounds of ammunition.

The morning after the herd guard had been killed the Captain came into the Co. Street. When the Co. was in line, cursed and swore, calling us "damned negro sons of bitches – not one of us fit to be a soldier" – adding, that he would send us out in small squads so as to have us all killed. He has never called me individually by a hard name. I have been on horse guard many times during this Summer, and in no instance has a Commissioned Officer visited or inspected the grazing herd.

Private Daniel Bledsoe

Believes that Captain Hooker was responsible for the killing of the herd guard, because on the day previous to the killing of the guard we were eight men on guard, the Captain got mad at us, and only sent five men on the next day, which was not a sufficient number to guard so large a herd, besides – the guard had only six shooters to defend themselves with. The morning after the herd guard had been killed and the men had been formed into line with a view of having a detachment picked to go in search of the missing bodies, the captain said to us " that a parcel of idiotical damned sons of bitches drove the horses up in that Canon for the purpose of getting killed, and that he wished that all the rest of us would get killed"; and when we were digging the grave (I was one of the party) he again cussed us calling us "damned sons of bitches", adding that if any of us spoke he would have another funeral. Sometime before the herd was taken, when I was about going on a scout with the Capt., I complained that my horse was used up, when the Captain called me a "damned monkey son of a bitch" and while on the scout because I did not understand one of his Commands he made me walk.

Mr Sullivan was here during the forenoon of the day the herd was captured and told me that he had informed the Captain that the Indians were around trying to capture his herd. Have always been badly used and called by bad names by my Captain, he has scarcely spoken to me, without at the same time Cursing me. Have frequently been on herd guard during the last Summer the men had nothing to defend themselves with except six [pistols][16] *shooters, and rode without saddles. No Officer has ever come out to visit and inspect the grazing herd, while we have been at this place.*

16 Steelhammer seems to have added the term 'pistols' suggesting that his superiors may not have been familiar with the term 'six-shooter'.

Private John Howard

Complains that the Captain Curses and Calls him names, all the same, whether he does his duty or not. About three months ago he was out with a party and, as there were no orders to the contrary, he fired at some squirrels jointly with another man of his party. On their return the Captain Cursed them Calling them "sons of bitches" and ordered them to carry logs.

They threw the logs down after a while and asked the sergt. to permit them to see the Captain. He refused – they broke and ran to see the Captain. The Captain had him (Howard) bucked and gagged, a forty pound log put on his shoulder and a heavy bearing Chain fastened to his wrist and wound around his neck telling the sergeant to keep Howard walking in that state until further orders, and that he (the Captain) would go to sleep and not mind any complaints even if he (Howard) was dying. The Captain was warned by Mr Sullivan, on the very day the herd was taken, that the Indians would attempt to capture it. I heard Sullivan tell the Capt., this was between three and four O'Clock in the afternoon. The Captain did nothing but walk up and down on his porch for some time after. Sullivan got mad at something the Captain said and mounted his horse and rode off. T

The herd guard was not sufficiently well armed. The Capt. told Corporal Williams Sept. 5th 79 who was in charge of the party digging a grave to make it large enough for five, and that if there was any talking or nonsense among the party, to dig the grave large enough for six, as he would in that case have the Corporal shot. I have been on horse guard during that time have never seen an officer visit the herd.

Private Arthur Koerl

Thinks the Captain treats him badly because he curses him for a damned black son of a bitch very often – the last time only a couple of weeks ago because at dinner call he did not fall in and go to dinner. He did not want any dinner that day

Private Isom Green

Says that on the morning of Sept. 5. 79. the Captain came to him and said "You god damned black son of a bitch, if you don't hurry hitching up that cart, I will buck and gag you, god damn you, within an inch of your life"; and on the morning of the sixth of September 1879, the Captain ordered him and four others to go after the mail saying that they were the very five god damned sons of bitches that he wanted to go down after the mail, as he wanted the Indians to kill them – god damn the dirty niggers. He said that he would send the Co. off four and five at a time until the Indians had killed every god damned one of them.

During October or November following, the day that Sergeant Shanklin was reduced the Capt. walked up and down before the Company saying that "if there was any damned son of a bitch in it wishing to make a complaint let him step out now, and I will put him in irons, god damn him". The herd guard was in no condition to protect either the herd or itself. They had only six shooters [pistols] and their horses were not saddled.

Have often been on herd guard and wished to tell the captain that I did not consider myself sufficiently well armed and equipped, but I was too afraid as he never allowed anyone to tell him anything about what he ought to do

Private Jacob Woods

I complain of no direct personal illtreatment,[17] *but indirectly I have time and time again been called a black son of a bitch, for it is the Captain's habit when addressing the Co. to call us by the hardest names imaginable.*

I consider the Captain responsible for the killing of the herd guard, because the men were only armed with six [pistols] shooters and their horses had no saddles. Besides I had been used as an escort to the mail and five or six days before the Indians jumped the herd had reported to the Captain that the Indians were around. My information was partly obtained from the Postmaster at Paraje but I had seen distinct signs of Indians myself. About four days before our herd was run off I told the Captain that the Indians had driven off a sheepherder in the vicinity and killed some sheep.

Private Willis? Turner

I like to make complaint against my Captain for making me carry a log, two hours on and one hour off, for three days, during august last. I don't know why I was so punished as I had done nothing nor could I see the Captain. I sent word to him but he refused to see me.

Private Samuel Irwin

I have no other complaint than that the Capt. Has called me "a damned idiot" and "a black son of a bitch" along with the rest of the Company, when I have been in the ranks.

Private Royal Wilson

Wishes to say that had the herd guard been sufficiently well armed, all of them would not have been killed. They had no show the way they were armed. I heard the Captain say when the grave for the dead guard was being dug "dig the grave deep and wide may be we will have to put some other son of a bitch in there". About two months ago, as near as I can tell, The Captain told us, when the Company was in line, "If any of you damned sons of bitches has a complaint to make, make it now – step out and make it and I will have him put in irons".

Private George Lockman

The Captain has never cursed me individually, but frequently together with the rest of the Company, calling me "black sons of bitches" "puppies" "dogs" and "idiots" this happened in May last.

After the herd guard had been killed the Captain said in my presence, that he wished to God that the Indians would kill us all.

Trumpeter Benjamin Hawkins

The Captain told us on the morning after the herd guard had been killed, that we were not soldiers but "damned niggers" "sons of bitches" and "idiots" these expressions have been frequently used.

17 As spelled in original document.

Private David Peters

In the middle of September last I, as lance Corporal was sent with a party of recruits to drive some cattle through the Canon.

While performing this duty we ran across a flock of Turkeys, and some of my party fired into them, contrary to my orders. On my return the captain called me a "damned idiot" and said that I was like the rest of the god damned fools, he then ordered the Sergeant to cut my Chevrons off, and said "the damned dog shall carry the turkey until it rots on his back". I was then hand cuffed, the turkey tied on my back. I carried it from two P.M. until taps and again from reveille until 9 O'clock, A.M. when I was released. I turned over the herd to Sergeant Chapman on the morning of the day he was killed

I turned over to him the number of horses and mules in the herd and the instructions were not to take the herd too far from Camp, and to bring it in at 10 O'Clock, A.M. for water, and to bring the herd in at 5 O'Clock P.M. Stables. The nearest good grass was from one mile to one mile and a half from the post. Sometime before this it had been the custom to herd with eight men, but it had been reduced to five. The orders I received from the Captain were to take charge of the herd, not to go too far from the Camp, and to keep a strict lookout for the Indians. You have only four men besides yourself and you have to do the best you can with them, bring the herd in for water at 10 O'Clock A.M., the men to get their dinners at the same time, and to report to me again for further orders" – I did so – He told me to take the herd back.

I did not consider that I was sufficiently well armed or mounted, in case I had been attacked. The reason I did not tell the Captain of this was that ever since I came to the Company it has been standing orders that the guard over the herd should only carry their pistols and ride their horses without saddles. No officer has ever visited the herd while I have been on guard since we came to Ojo Caliente. I saw Mr Sullivan when he came to the post September 4th 1879, it was then about ten o'clock A.M.

1st Sergeant Henry Robertson (Robinson?)

On the 29th day of November last the Captain cursed me for making the mistake of calling a "detail" a "layout". It is the only time that I have been cursed individually.

The Company is frequently called sons of bitches. On the morning of the 5th of last September when I was fixing to go out after the dead men, the Captain cursed the Company for a pack of sons of bitches.

The men on herd guard were armed with revolving pistols only, and their horses had no saddles. We usually had eight men on herd guard but the number was reduced to five sometime in August 1879. The Company is well fed, well instructed and well cared for.

Sergeant William Howard

I have no individual complaint to make against my Captain. I have frequently been on herd guard while at Ojo Caliente. My orders have always been "To take the herd out a good way from Camp where there was plenty of grass – to have one man mounted and posted upon the highest point in the vicinity as vidette – to keep a good watch around the country and if he sees any party of men coming from any direction he calls the sergeant in charge. The sergeant then advances with a file of men in order to identify the approaching party. If Indians, the sergt, will send a man back to drive the herd to Camp, and with the rest of his men keep the Indians off until the herd get a sufficient start, then the sergt. with his men, starts after the herd and drives it into Camp as quickly as possible. The moment Indians are discovered one man is sent in to the post to report to the Captain. We herd with six shooters, saddle blankets and curcingles on our horses, using watering bits.

I have always considered it difficult to stand off Indians should they attack us, mounted as we were. The horses cannot be guided with watering bits and the pistols are serviceable only at short range.

No officer has ever visited the grazing herd, while I have been in charge of it since we came here.

Sergeant Redmond Joanna?

My Captain curses and abuses us. He has always done so, but more especially since the herd was stolen by the Indians.

The week after the herd was lost, he called me a damned idiot. The day after the capture of the herd, he cursed and abused the whole Company. He said that we were not fit to be soldiers; called us damned monkeys and apes – He said much more but I cannot recall it all now.

Have been acting Quartermaster Sergeant and therefore but seldom on horse guard.

Was on such duty however one day about a week before the herd was run off.

My orders then were to keep a strict lookout, and to keep one man as vidette on the nearest highest hill to keep the rest of the men a round the herd – to lookout for the Indians so that they could not slip up on the herd unawares, and if any suspicious characters, Indians or otherwise, were seen to run the herd in.

Corporal Allen Foster

The Complaint I wish to make against the Captain is that he curses and damns the Company and as I am a member of it I consider, although he does not single me out individually, that I get my full share of it. He has done the most of this Cursing since September last. He curses us for "damned black sons of bitches", calls us "damned niggers", and says that "a nigger has as much business to be a soldier as a cur dog has to be a saint". This happened I think in the latter part of September 1879 at the time we were signing the payroll. He frequently calls us "damned dogs "monkeys" and "idiots" and I do not think it is quite the thing for an Officer to call his men by such names. I have heard him say that he wished that the Indians would kill the last one of us. He said this between the 7th and the last day of September 1879.

I have frequently been on horse guard while at Ojo Caliente. My orders have been "Take the herd where the horses can have good grass and where such a place is found to put a man on the lookout and watch closely for an approaching enemy and if any is seen to try to get the herd in". We never were allowed any other weapons, while on herd, than six shooters, with twelve rounds of ammunition, nor were we allowed the use of saddles. The horses had on them only saddle blankets, curcingles watering bits, and lariats. When we first came here we herded with eight men. Later we herded with five men only

No commissioned officer has ever visited the herd, while I have been in charge of it since we came here.

Corporal Richard Williams

I want to enter complaint against my Capt. For cursing me, with the rest of the Company, as a "damned black son of a bitch". This has occurred frequently after the herd was taken. On the 6th of September last he gave me four men to go to Canada to meet Private Reiley whom he had sent after the mail the day before. The Captain asked of me the names of the men to go with me. I told him – when he said "I hope, god damn you, that the Indians will kill you all before you get through the Canon" – "no damned black sons of bitches of niggers were fitted to be soldiers anyway". Last Summer I was on herd guard in charge most every four days. My orders were "to take the herd out a mile or a mile and a half, where the best grass could be found; to keep a man as vidette on the nearest highest hill' to keep one man mounted going around the herd while it was grazing, the rest of the horses picketed so that they would be handy on the approach of danger, and to bring in the herd in time for stables about four o'clock P.M.

We had but pistols and (12) twelve rounds of ammunition to defend ourselves with. No officer has ever visited the herd while I have been in charge of it, at this post. Lieutenant Taylor lost a horse one evening and trying to hunt him up, passed by the herd next morning.

That is the only visit any officer ever made.

Private Washington Wise

I wish to say that I have been abused ever since I came here, cursed as "a son of a bitch" and "a damned idiot" by my Captain. Shortly after the horses had been stolen, the Co. was in line one day, one man had gotten himself into trouble for being drunk, when Captain Hooker stepped up to me and said "You god damned son of a bitch what have you to do with it – have you any complaint to make – if you have and want to go in irons now in your time". Sometime in August last when I was on herd, the herd ran in. I was taken and put on the ring with a fifty pound log and made to carry it. I asked permission to see the Captain. Corporal Shanklin brought word that when the Captain got ready for me he would send for me, and that I should carry that log until hell froze over. The Captain has never sent for me since and I have never had an opportunity to explain or to find out why I was punished.

Private George W. Vance

I wish to say that my Captain is responsible for the killing of the herd guard on the 4th day of September last, because the guard was neither large enough or sufficiently well armed. On the morning of the 5th day of September last, the Captain came out at reveille Cursing and called us, as we were standing in the ranks, "a parcel of cowards" and "sons of bitches". Shortly after when the detail went to dig the mens grave he told the detail to dig the grave of a size, that permitted five more of them to be buried in it. On or about the 22nd day of August last I brought in reports to the Captain that Indians were around. I knew also that along in August last the Captain got a letter from a Mr Stackpole reporting Indian depredations somewhere around San Jose I believe. I know this because I had to copy the letter myself. I have complained once before at Fort Wingate, when the Company was stationed there, but so far as I know no investigation was ever made. I have been trying to do my duty, but when I have done my best, I have been reprimanded as freely as if the reverse had been the case.

Instead of elevating us, the effort seems to have been made to keep us in ignorance and we are constantly being told that we are brutes.

Farrier David Haines

I have this complaint to make against my Captain, that I have been cursed and abused by him before, and especially after the herd was lost. He cursed me for a "damned nigger" and a "damned dog" and called me a "son of a bitch" sometime in September last, when I had to report to him with reference to getting mule shoes. During November last he called me a "damned black son of a bitch" for not being ready to go with a detail, when I had not been previously been notified. The morning the dead herd guard was brought in, the Capt. Said that he wished "that every god damned nigger was in hell and that the Indians would kill every god damned one of them", and called us a "pack of god damned sons of bitches".

Private Robert Willis

The Captain calls us "Baboons" "Arabs" "Monkeys" "Kangaroos" and "damned worthless sons of bitches". These expressions have been very frequent especially during the last six months. About two months ago I heard him use words towards us in effect as above. The morning the herd guard was brought in, I heard him say that he "wished that every god damned son of a bitch of us had been killed by the Indians". A few days previous to September 4th 1879 I had asked the Captain to let me go to Paraje along with the mail. On the morning of September 4th 1879, the Captain told me that he could not spare me as the Indians were raising hell around here and people were complaining. About four O'Clock P.M. September 4th 1879 as I was calling the Captain to dinner I met Mr Sullivan coming out of the Captain's Office door and heard him say to the Captain: "These are facts that I am telling you, the man is reliable – he slipped off from the spring and said that there were some thirty or forty Indians". The Captain replied "very well I will see about it".

Private Siegel Sykes

I have the complaint to make that the Captain cursed us, while in the ranks, for "god damned black sons of bitches". It has been a regular thing since the herd was taken. It happened on the morning of September 5th 1879 and after since.

Private Evan Shanklin

I consider my Captain largely responsible for the killing of the herd guard on Sept. 4th 1879, as the guard was neither properly armed nor mounted. I have complained three times before against the Captain, but nothing has ever come of it so far as I know. I have complained to General ??????? Colonel Buell and Commanding Officer at Fort Wingate. The Captain has cursed us as monkeys and dogs ever since we left Fort Union. In the beginning of September last, the day I was reduced, he fell the Company in and cursed us for niggers and sons of bitches, and wanted to know if any one had any report to make and if they had to stepout.

Private John W. Quarle

In August last, when I was reduced, the Captain cursed me for a black son of a bitch. In May last he cursed me, along with the other men, in the ranks, calling us damned monkeys.

Private McElroy McGill

About the 9th of June, in the Canada Canon the Captain tied me to a pack mule, bucked and gagged me and drove me through the water to Canada. He lariated me the same evening out on herd, with the horses as if I had been one of them. He struck me over my head with his riding whip after I had been tied and bucked. It cut my eye and injured it.

Private Frank Smith

On the 16th of August last I was on herd. The herd was stampeded and came into the post on a run. The rest of the men also came on a run guiding the horses. I came in on a walk behind the herd. I remained behind in order to keep the straggling stock together as well as I could. When I got into the post I was disarmed, with the rest of the guard and put into the guard house. I was made to carry a log seven days and seven nights, two hours on and two hours off. I asked the sergeant of the guard for permission to see my Company Commander. He brought me to him. When I asked the Captain what I was punished for, he replied: "Stay there until you find out. I will keep you carrying a log until hell freezes over". In September last my hat became unserviceable so that I was compelled to wear a government cap, for this offense the Captain called me a god damned son of a bitch.

Private Thornton Jackson

On or about the 26th day of April last, when we left Fort Union, the Captain cursed me with the rest of the Company as a damned black son of a bitch and on or about the 6th day of May 1879, when I, as old? Guard and on fatigue as such for the first time, and occupied with taking down the Captain's tent and loading his wagon, was putting the tent pins away – the Captain came up and said that he never saw a nigger who could put anything in straight. I then looked up when he said, "god damn you when I speak I don't want you to look up at me." I replied, "Captain, what do you take me for? I am a soldier and want to be treated as such". He then ran on to me, struck and kicked me and told me to shut up my god damned mouth. When I tried to protect myself against his blows, he called a corporal and told him to buck and gag me, as he wanted to teach a god damned dog like me how to speak to his Captain. The Corporal bucked me and started off after a gag when the Captain said "Corporal you need not get a gag, my foot is a good enough gag for the god damned dog". I replied that I was no more of a dog than he was, whereupon, bound as I was, he came up and kicked me three times in the neck saying that if I uttered another word he would kick every god damned tooth in my head down my throat.

When we pulled out from Camp, he hand cuffed me behind a wagon. Being weak from the previous day's march and was dragged behind the wagon about thirty feet. At night when we came in Camp, he got a large fifth Chain and put on me, chaining me to a wagon and made me walk five days, hand cuffed to that wagon. On September last he caused us all to face in line, and asked us if we had any reports to make, and he came to me and made me step out, saying, – "step out here, god damn you, I want to hear what report you are going to make, so I can put you in irons".

Saddler Daniel Hails

Captain Hooker has frequently cursed me along with the rest of his Company, for nigger sons of bitches. This occurred once on the morning of September 5th 1879. On the same day the captain said that he wished to god that the Indians would kill every god damned one of us – at the same time he called us thieves.

Private Noah Johnson

I want to enter complaint against my Captain. He is in the habit of cursing me with the rest of his Company for a damned nigger and son of a bitch. He did this on the 5th day of September last.

Private John M. Fields

The herd guard is not sent out properly armed and equipped. On the morning of September 5th last the Captain cursed us for being damned idiots and sons of bitches and said that he wished that the Indians had killed us all. About ten or twelve days after the herd was taken, the captain had us in line and cursed us, calling us black sons of bitches, saying that if we had any complaints to make we should step out and he would put us in irons.

Private Abraham H. Booth

On the morning of the 5th of September 1879 the Captain said to me, as I stood among the other men, after I had just come in with the five bodies of the herd guard. – "You god damned black sons of bitches, I wish the Indians had killed the last one of you, I would not have regretted it a god damned bit". After the firing party, of which I was one, had fired over the grave the Captain said, "the Indians did not think enough of the god damned black sons of bitches to even take their scalps".

On the following day I was ordered to go to Canada, as one of a party to escort the mail. The Captain asked the Corporal our several names. The Corporal told him, the Captain replied: "it is the very crowd I want the Indians to get and kill". On or about the 17th day of August last I was on herd guard, when the herd came into camp on a run. I was ordered by the Corporal to remain in front of the herd while it was running towards Camp. For obeying this order, I was compelled to carry a log six days, the log weighing about fifty pounds. I asked permission to speak to the Captain for the purpose of asking him what I was being punished for. The only satisfaction I got was, "that I could carry that log until I found out, even if I had to wait until the expiration of my term of service".

When I asked to be released from the log and stated that I had done nothing that I was aware of except obeying orders I was ordered off. After this I was not permitted to see the Captain for anything, right or wrong, and like a ?????? brute I had to suffer as long as it pleased him. In the month of August 1879 while I was on target practice, he told the Company Clerk to tell me to report he ordered the trumpeter to sound "Commence firing". After the trumpeter had blown the signal the Captain ordered me back to the pit saying, that he did not give a god damned if the top of my head was blown off.

Private Robert Timbers

I like to report that during August last when I was on herd guard, I had orders from the Corporal in charge to keep in front of the herd, as it was by some accident stampeded into the post on our return in the evening. After we got in the Captain ordered me to carry a log until further orders. I did so until 9 O'Clock P.M. that day when I asked permission to see the Captain. It was refused. I heard nothing more for six days during which time I had to carry the log. On the morning of September 5th 1879, I heard the Captain say, that he wished the Indians had killed us all. I made a complaint in 1876 at Fort Wingate but obtained no satisfaction.

Private Henry Riley

Would like to complain against my Captain for the manner in which he has abused and cursed me. In the beginning of November last he called me a damned fool and an idiot, without any cause, and the morning after the herd was taken he stood on his porch and cursed me, together with the rest of his men, calling us damned black sons of bitches. I complained at Wingate in 1876 but nothing resulted from it.

Blacksmith Richard Scott

The Captain abuses me and the rest of us, calling us dogs, idiots and damned sons of bitches. In February last, at Fort Union, he cursed me calling me a dog.

On the morning of September 5th 1879, he cursed me, among the rest of the Company, saying that we were damned sons of bitches and that he wished every damned nigger was dead and in hell.

Private Joseph Lyons

The Captain cursed me with the rest of the Company, on the morning of September 5th 1879, calling us "damned black sons of bitches". Shortly after we left Fort Union, the Captain accused me of having spilled some corn, and when I replied that I had not he said, "shut up, you god damned black son of a bitch".

Private Taylor Gillem

I like to state that my Captain cursed me for a black son of a bitch one evening when I was on post. This happened some time in the month of September last some days after the herd had been captured, and I had not done anything except obeying orders received from my Corporal.

Private Wesley Kibbey

On the morning after the herd had been taken the Captain cursed me, along with the rest of the Company, calling us "damned sons of bitches" and "idiots".

Private William Miner

I wish to complain of my Captain for having called me a son of a bitch, while I was on post. This happened shortly after the herd had been taken. When Sullivan was at the post reporting the presence of Indians, on the very day that the herd was captured, I was on guard – the Captain sent for me and told me to put Sullivan out through the Canon as he believes him to be in with the Indians. This happened about four o'clock P.M.

Private George Roundtree

I wish to complain of my Captain for calling me and the rest of the men "damned idiots" and "sons of bitches". He did this about the 15th day of last month. He made me carry a log three days and nights in June last, when I had done nothing. I asked to see him but he would not permit me.

Private Josiah Johnson

I have this complaint to make against my Captain, that he frequently curses me along with the rest of the Company Calling us "damned sons of bitches" and "idiots". He did this day before yesterday December 10th 1879 because No. 1 of the guard did not hear the call of No. 2 I was present.

Private Lawrence Wilson

I have been illtreated by my Captain, cursed as a "nigger" a "damned son of a bitch" and most every thing else.

Next morning after the herd had been taken he said that he wished the Indians could get the last damned one of us and scalp us. In October last he met me going to target practice. He said to me "go and get your gun – you look as if you could sight a gun! You god damned dog, you – go and get your gun and bring it here to me".

Private Heartley Crawford

I want to state how I have been abused by my Captain, on the way out here from Fort Union, and after my arrival at this post. Four miles this side of Las Vegas, on our way here I was assisting to put up his tent, and he made me carry a log because some other man had taken my ax, to drive a tent pin with. He cursed me at the time and called me a "worthless dog". I carried the log two hours. On or about the 7th day of September last, he sent me with a party under Corporal Williams, to meet the mail. The Captain put me on the detail saying, "these are the very scoundrels I want to get killed". On the morning after the killing of the herd guard the captain said to us: "the god damned cowardly sons of bitches they were all asleep; I wish the Indians would get the last god damned one of you.

Private William Corker

The day after the herd was taken he, the Captain told me, along with the rest of the men, that we were "god damned idiots" and "sons of bitches", and of no account. Some days after the herd had been taken I was on guard on post no.1, and because I did not sing out loud enough, although I yelled as hard as I could, for the guard to turn out for the Commanding Officer, the captain made me carry a log from 11 O'Clock, A.M. until retreat of the same day.

Private John Loge

Directly after the herd had been taken, and the dead men buried, the Captain called me and the others "damned dogs" saying that he wished that we were all dead, and that he would try and have us all killed off.

Corporal Willis Preston

On the morning of the 5th day of September 1879, the Captain cursed me along with the rest of the Company, calling us "damned black sons of bitches".

Private Jerry K. Smith

The morning after the day the herd had been run off, the captain cursed us calling us "damned black sons of bitches". About a day after this he spoke to the 1st sergeant saying, that he would not care if the last one of the damned niggers was killed. I was present.

Trumpeter Joseph Walters

I have not been treated right by my Captain, but cursed and abused. On the 4th day of September last, when the two first bodies had been brought in, he cursed me along with the rest of the men, saying "I wish that the whole of you had been killed, god damn you. When you get instructions you don't carry them out; they go in one ear and out through the other".

Private William Thomas

I complain of being always called a "damned idiot" a "damned nigger" or a "damned fool" by my Captain. I am always being cursed, individually and with the rest of the men. On the morning of September 5th 1879 after the herd guard had been killed, the Captain said that he wished that all the damned niggers had been killed the same way

There are now at Ojo Caliente 51 enlisted men, present with "E" CO. 9th Cavy. Each and every one of these men made his statement while alone with me and, except occasional necessary changes in the phraseology and exclusion of matters foreign to the subject under investigation, each individual statement was at once reduced to writing, read to the man and pronounced correct.

Seventeen men were concerned in writing the anonymous letter. Its actual writer was Priv. A.B. Booth. Of these seventeen men two are serving their 2nd Enlistment: seven have nearly completed their first: Three have served more than four years; one more than three years and one more than two years. The remaining three men are recruits.

The allegations contained in the anonymous letter are as follows:

1st *That Captain Hooker is responsible for the death of the herd guard at Ojo Caliente, Sept 4th 1879.*

2nd *That the horseguards was not sufficiently well armed and equipped at the time of its death.*

3rd *That the Captain, when the horseguard was found dead, said that he wished that all the negroes had been killed, and that he would try to get as many of the worthless sons of bitches killed as he could.*

4th *That Captain Hooker had several times prior to September 4th 1879, been cautioned that the Indians were about to attack the Co. or the herd but failed to pay proper attention to such caution*

5th *That Captain Hooker's conduct towards his me has been unofficerlike.*

6th *That unavailing complaints have heretofore been made by enlisted men of "E" Co. 9th Cavalry.*

Upon these allegations the examination of the men has been chiefly based.

The loss of the herd will, for the sake of fairness and conscience, be treated as a separate subject.

The statements made by the enlisted men were all referred to Captain Hooker who, declining any cross examination, makes the following:

Counter Statement

In reply to the statements made by the men of my Company, I wish to say 1st that the reference so generally made by them, to the fact that they are being armed with pistols only, and mounted without saddles, is manifestly the result of an afterthought on their part and no doubt suggested by Private Vance, an agitate and malcontent of long standing in the Company, he having been reduced from Sergeant nearly four years since for insubordinate conduct and who, in the capacity of Company Clerk was employed by Lieut. Taylor to copy proceedings of a Board of Survey in the matter of the capture of the horses, wherein the Lieut. Says, after recording his opinion, "that neither Captain Hooker nor any living person can be held for said capture and loss," " the Board after long and conscientious deliberation upon the whole affair finds nothing that requires condemnation in Captain Hooker's arrangements for the herding of his horses, and at the time of the herd's capture it was guarded so far as the detail of men and their instructions were concerned practically the same as the Board would have made it guarded had Captain Hooker been about or not in command. There is a difference of opinion between Captain Hooker and the Board as to the most proper manner of mounting and arming the herdguards when out with horses, the preference of the Board being that the "men should use their saddles and carry their carbines, but there being matters of opinion and individual practice the Board will not discuss them, nor does the Board allow them to influence it in making up its judgement in the premise as might be the case were the Board to give away to its prejudices, particularly against the pistol, which the Board does not consider either an efficient or a necessary weapon for our Colored Cavalry as at present organized and equipped."[18]

18 This Board of Survey was commissioned by Captain Hooker "for the purpose of ascertaining the quantity of Ordnance, and Quartermaster Stores and property, for which Captain A.E. Hooker, 9th Cavalry, is accountable, captured by Indians on the 4th of September 1879, and fix the responsibility therefore."

Now I wish to say here in passing, that much older and perhaps better Cavalry Officers than either Lieut. Taylor or myself favor the use of the pistol as a mounted arm in a running, hand to hand, fight, the Carbine under these circumstances being held a useless weapon. This portion of the proceedings of the Board was doubtless communicated to the Company by Private Vance, who is esteemed to be something of an oracle in the Company as a Champion of his race and extensively engaged in, what he deems to be, the amelioration of its present condition, more particularly in the service and more especially in my Company. This I think is plainly evidenced in the combined statements of fifty one men, the total enlisted present, wherein collusion on their part is most manifest throughout. As a further evidence of this I can state that almost invariably when men have lost or sold their pistols, and for a time deprived of them in consequence, as a punishment, they have, when permitted, borrowed pistols for use on herds, thereby showing their preference for their pistols, and the same may be said with reference to the saddle, as but a few days previous to the capture of the horses I gave instructions that two goodsized pony horses, the property of Citizens, which were in fine condition, round and fat, which were running with the Company herd, should be ridden on herd daily by such of the herders whose horses were in poor condition. These horses not being so gentle and tractable as the troop horses, I gave instructions that the men should ride them with their saddles and curb bridles if they preferred to do so, I observed after the first day or two, that the men discontinued, in their own accord, the use of the saddle. This fact may be equally significant as the facts stated in connection with the pistol.

Now, as to the very general assertion that I have been in the habit of addressing the Company as "black sons of bitches," I deny it in tote. I am the original Captain of my Company, "E," 9th, Cav'y and I trust that it will not be deemed egoism on my part to say that when I came to the 9th Cav'y, after some years service elsewhere, I was not considered either a profane or a coarse man, but I do not deny that after some years experience with these troops, that my limited supply of refined english became exhausted and worn out, and that from constant association with men who seemed to have no proper comprehension of refined english I found myself gradually adopting language better comprehended and appreciated and much more effective with men to whom choice English expressions were much the same as ***????**.*

I plead guilty, at times, to the use of strong emphatic language in individual cases. I have been due to express my opinion of thieves, shirks and malingerers as contemptible dogs, unfit to be soldiers and that a Co, that would harbor thieves and not expose them to justice, might well be considered no better than the guilty parties.

I have endeavoured for years to cultivate in the Company a distinction between the better class of privates and the worthless portion of the same grade, but without avail.

To that portion of the anonymous letter setting forth that complaints have heretofore been made and no attention been paid, particular reference being made in the statements of the men bearing upon that point to complaints made to General Schuier, to General Buell and at Fort Wingate, I will say that in each and every instance, due investigation was made. In the first instance, the complaints made to General Schuier were found to be frivolous, groundless and unworthy of further notice. The complaints made to General Buell in 1874 were thoroughly investigated by him, and pronounced the result of a spirit of insubordination bordering on mutiny; so thoroughly was General Buell convinced of this that he informed the Company that any further manifestation of that spirit, while under his command, would meet with the prompt action the circumstances might demand, the Company then being a portion of Gen'l Buell's column operating against hostile Indians in the Indian Territory – Court Martial being impracticable under the circumstances, non-commissioned officers taking a leading part were summarily reduced to the ranks, and rigid discipline enforced.

The complaints made at Fort Wingate, in the spring of 1876, in which privates Vance, Frank Smith and Shanklin, then non-commissioned officers, were leading spirits, were duly investigated by the District

---

with Lt. Taylor as it's only commissioned officer "No other officer being available under the Regulations for that duty." (Order No.5, 9th September 1879, In the Field, Ojo Caliente, Special Orders Rec'd from Sub Commands, RG393, Part 3, Entry 453.)

Commander, the Colonel of my Regiment, and were found to be frivolous and the result of a spirit of insubordination and rebellion against the rigid discipline which I have always aimed to maintain in my Company. It is a significant fact that notwithstanding the grievous complaints made against me at that time that, on the return from field service in the fall of that year when fourteen men of my Company were discharged by expiration of service, eleven of them re-enlisted in the Company, notwithstanding the fact that they at that time could have taken their choice of the Companies of the Regiment, some of them however delaying their re-enlistment from fifteen to forty days and having ample time to look about them and decide their preference. Of the three men that did not re-enlist, one was discharged without character, one was physically disabled, the third went east to visit his friends. It may not be out of place for me here to state the fact that there has always been a spirit of insubordination in my Company from its organization, which has required the most rigid discipline, with a firm and unwavering hand, to suppress and keep down. In the spring of 1867, shortly after the Company was organized and before I had joined it, being then on detached service, the Regiment then being at San Antonio, Texas, enroute to the occupancy of the various posts to which the Regiment was assigned, the Company then were under the command of the Lieutenant, now a Captain of the 4th Cavalry, broke out in open mutiny, seriously wounded the Lieut. And killed the officer of the Day, who was assisting in an attempt to quell the mutiny. When I joined the Company, nearly two years afterwards, I found a number of those who were engaged in this mutiny, among them one of the ringleaders who had with his sabre split open the skull of the Officer of the Day. I had not been with my Company twenty four hours when I was informed by a Private servant whom I had brought with me, a perfect stranger to the Company and utterly ignorant of the mutiny referred to, that one of the men, whose name she gave me, and who had been a leading spirit in the mutiny had boastingly informed her of the facts connected with the mutiny and saying that the Captain had better go very slow or words to that effect, as he had a hard crowd to deal with, and if he did not look out they would get away with him.

I might say that there are still three men with the Company who were in the Company at that time, several others who enlisted shortly afterwards, and this spirit of insubordination would appear to have been handed down with the traditions of the Company. During the summer of 1876 while encamped on the Headwaters of the Gila with my Company where I was ordered from Wingate shortly after the investigation of the complaints made there and previously referred to, I being alone with my Company at that time, I received a notice in the shape of a written postal on a tree near my tent to the effect "that it had been the intention to get away with me between Wingate and that point and that I had better go very slow or they would get away with me before the Company would get back to its post."

It may not be improper for me to say in this connection that, although these manifestations of insubordination have not had the effect to intimidate me in the proper discharge of what I deemed to be my duty in the enforcement of strict discipline, the result has probably been an increased vigilance and possibly more rigid discipline.

Now as to the individual statements of the men, in so far as I have not covered in my forgoing statement, Sergeant Williams and others state that I express myself in presence of the assembled Company and to the Company in line, as some have it, that I wished all of the negro sons of bitches had been killed; were dead and in here, that I would like a company of decent soldiers to command, the one I have not being fit to have horses &c.

I deny making use of such expressions or any other expressions of a similar character to or in the presence of the assembled Company or the Company in line on this day after the herd was jumped or on any subsequent day. I did however after having fully satisfied myself as to the manner of the capture from having visited the grounds and seen sufficient evidence to satisfy myself and others that the surprise and capture were owing to a total disregard of my instructions, first in taking the herd into a perfect trap when it could be easily surprised and cut off and secondly, in the failure to post a vidette to watch all the approaches to the herd, the Indians, having crawled within forty yards of where three of the guards were lounging upon the ground, one of them lying upon his saddle blanket, which he had removed from his horse for that purpose. (even in the unfavorable locality had a vidette been posted and properly performed his duty it is improbable that the

Indians could have approached sufficiently near to have surprised and captured the herd before it could have been run out of danger) Naturally feel very much incensed and did express myself to the Lieut. Afterwards to the 1st Sergeant, afterwards to others, on hearing some expressions of sympathy for the dead men to the effect that I had no sympathy whatever for men who lost their lives through an utter disregard of or failure to comply with instructions which had been so constantly reiterated. I did also frequently say that I hoped that any and all other men who failed to obey their orders under similar circumstances would pay the forfeit of their lives. I did further say that such men were not fit to have horses, and that they never would again be mounted at my request, that I had worn myself out by constant application and endeavor to make soldiers of them, and that such men were as fit to be soldiers as our dogs to be saints.

On some of these occasions some of the men of the Company were doubtless within earshot. In talking to the 1st Sergeant I gave him to understand that I wished what I said to be **?? ?????** *to the Company. I wished them to know the estimation in which I held them, and that I should make no concealment of my sentiments to higher authority. I deny the use of the expressions attributed to me or any similar expressions as being made to the grave diggers or subsequently at the funeral.*

Lieut. Taylor was present with me on both occasions and superintended the funeral with my direction, and will be able to testify whether or no I made use of the expressions attributed to me. Private Vance and Wilson who gave evidence as to my language to the grave diggers, were neither of them present, Vance being on daily duty as Company Clerk and Wilson as Company Cook and not on the roster for fatigue duty. None were present beside the Lieutenant, myself and the fatigue detail. I deny the language attributed to me in presence of the Company in line on the day Sergeant Shanklin was reduced. The circumstances were these, the 1st Sergeant was absent in command of a detachment, Sergeant Williams, Senior duty Sergeant, was in charge of the Company as acting 1st Sergeant and under my instruction was daily drilling the Company, under my supervision, more especially for the benefit of several recruits who joined the Company just previous to leaving post for field service. Sergeant Williams a most thorough drill sergeant, is much disliked in the Company, and there was a spirit of rebellion against his authority cropping out, more particularly on drill. On the day in question, Sergt. Shanklin grumbled, talked back and cursed Sgt. Williams on drill. After drill Sergeant Shanklin and some others became intoxicated, presumably on some vile whiskey, smuggled into the command by a citizen teamster, which I discovered, after making search, in his possession and had thrown out. This spirit of insubordination which at first cropped out on drill was renewed subsequently in the Company quarters and Company street. I was busily engaged that day in writing, Sergt. Williams reported to me at my quarters what had transpired on drill and was transpiring in the Company. I directed him to bring Sergeant Shanklin before me, which he did, he was flushed, excited and insubordinate in my presence, claiming that Sergeant Williams was no better than he was and that he would not take orders from him or words to that effect. He failed to desist from his insubordinate language and when I informed him that I would be compelled to reduce him to the ranks if he persisted he replied defiantly that I could do so. The Corporal of the Guard at the same time reported that there was a disturbance in the Company street, that he had arrested two men in accordance with my instructions, for disorderly conduct, and that he thought that they were drunk or had been drinking. I immediately caused the assembly to be sounded, sent my compliments to Lieutenant Taylor, and directed him to put on his sabre in the capacity of temporary officer of the day, to publish a verbal order reducing Sergeant Shanklin to the ranks for insubordinate conduct, subject to the approval of the Regimental Commander, to have his stripes and Chevrons removed and confine him under guard, which orders he executed.

Sergeant Shanklin being marched off by the Corporal and a file of the guard, I then went before the Company, the Lieutenant still being present and in charge of it, with a view to ascertain if there were others present which required my attention, and inquired if there were others in the Company who had complaints to make or words to that effect. I informed the Company, if there was any further disposition to rebel against the authority of the 1st Sergeant or the Sergeant acting as 1st Sergeant under my orders, that I would put the offenders in irons. I remember distinctly that I did order Privates Wise and Jackson, the expression of whose countenances were particularly defiant, to step two paces to the front, and asked them what they had to say, they replied "nothing." I remember distinctly that I was very particular with them as to the manner in which they again took their places in ranks when so directed, causing them to repeat the movement and to make an about face in a soldierly manner and step through the ranks, one pace to the rear of the line, again face about and step up to their places in ranks. I did not address them as black sons of bitches or use any similar opprobrious epithets. I undoubtedly was stern, perhaps harsh, being initiated by a repetition of such demonstrations in the Company. Lieut. Taylor being present, can verify the truthfulness of my statement in this connection. As to the statement of Private Frank Smith to the effect that I called him a son of a bitch for wearing a government cap, the Company being in ranks at target practice, and with the exception of Smith, wearing the Company field hat, I did take him to task for appearing in ranks with a different head cover from the rest of the Company. As I do not permit men of my Company, even in the field, to wear all sorts and shades of headgear and clothing generally. It was the first and only instance of that nature that has come to my notice since the Company left post. I directed the 1st Sergeant to put Private Smith in the awkward squad until he should find his hat, which he claims was worn out. I observed subsequently that Private Smith wore his hat which to the best of my knowledge and belief was the same which he claimed to have worn out. Lieut. Taylor was in immediate charge of the Company at the time, and Dr Sewell was present. Both will probably remember the circumstances and will be able to state whether I used the language alleged or any similar opprobrious epithets.

Another instance in which I will be able to disprove the language alleged against me is that referred to by Corporal Williams and Privates Crawford, Booth and others on the 6th or 7th of September, on the occasion of giving instructions to a dismounted detachment sent to Canada to meet Private Riley, who had been sent into Paraje with dispatches on a condemned pack mule, as before stated. Lieutenant Taylor was within hearing, and will be able to state whether I made use of the language ascribed to me on that occasion, which language I most emphatically deny. With reference to Private Crawford one of the allegations in this instance, although he is hardly worth the time, I will state that he has been from the time he joined the Company early in 1875, a professional dead beat and malingerer of the worst character, which statement will be contradicted by the hospital records of Forts Clark, Wingate and Union, and the Surgeon in Charge here has reported him to me as a malingerer and suggested the propriety of charges in his case. My Company sick book would show, if present, frequent entries of "dead beat" and "malingerer" opposite to his name, entered by Surgeons Middleton and ***??????***

Notwithstanding this he is considered an oracle in the Company, can read and write and talk well. He is looked up to even by the 1st Sergt., who, together with many others in the Company, consider Crawford a much abused man at the hands of the Doctors and of his Captain.

Among other troops he would long since have been kicked out of the Company as a dead beat and a disgrace. He is not the only instance of this kind.

I cannot ***?turn?*** *the negative of the other statements, except as above referred to, by other than my own denial which may or may not be taken into consideration against the combined statements of fifty one men who have been led on and probably in some instances coerced by a few leading insubordinate spirits in the Company.*

First Sergeant Robinson truthfully states that I on one occasion cursed him (No one being present), for reporting a detail to me as a "lay out," informing him that I did not wish him to come to me with any of his barrack gambling nigger slang. He could have said more to the effect that I would not allow him to report details to me by name, calling private Timbers, "Bob" Timbers, Private Samuel Irwin as "Bones" Irwin. Pvt McGill and "Monkey" McGill. I do not permit the men of my Company to be spoken of in my presence in that manner, nor the Pvts to address the non-commissioned officers in my presence as John Williams or Dick Williams, but have endeavored to impress upon them that there was a great difference between soldiers of the United States Army and Cornfield Niggers. I do not permit my men to lounge about my quarters or tent or smoke my pipe, nor do I address them familiarly as "Bol" or "Pete", nor do I permit them to lounge against the doorposts when reporting to me, and I do not deny that familiarity of that nature are met on my part, with curses and strong expression of my appreciation of that style of things, and as

Private ***????*** *truly says, (the only truthful portion of his entire statement) I am indisposed to allow my men to dictate to me what I ought to do or how they should be armed or mounted or perform their various duties assigned them. There are doubtless sources of* ***?serious?*** *grievance on the part of some of the men, although not specifically referred to in their statements. It will be noted however that 1st Sergt. is truthful enough to state "the Company is well led and instructed and well cared for." This statement perhaps, with equal regard for truth, might have been corroborated by the entire Company, it being susceptible of proof even were*[19] *they do state the contrary. I do not deny having made use of some of the expressions, attributed to me as having been made to and in the presence of the Company in ranks, in my private quarters, since the capture of my herd. These expressions have been overheard doubtless, by eavesdroppers and carried to the Company and canvassed over from time to time until they have almost unanimously adopted the idea that each individual has heard the language in person and that it was made to and in the presence of the Company in ranks. For instance, in the case of Private Willis, who had been employed, since the Company has been in the field, as cook for my mess. Captain Beyer of my regiment arrived here in command of two companies five or six days subsequent to the capture of my herd and, with his officers spent some time at my quarters, and previous to his departure, when about taking leave of me in the hall, expressed the hope that my horses would be recovered or that my Company would soon be remounted. I replied to him that the Company would never be remounted if higher authority should wait until I requested it, that I didn't want any more horses until I had something besides Apes and Baboons, Chimpanzees and Monkeys, Kangaroos and Ourangatangs or Gorillas for soldiers, that I had enough of it; that I had worn myself out endeavoring to make soldiers of this material and didn't want any more of it, or words to that effect. I remember this conversation as the only instance of the kind and Private Willis was doubtless listening, to gather what information he could, to carry to the Company, as there was evidently some curiosity to know my sentiment in that connection. Some time subsequently Major Morrow of my regiment arrived here with a battalion including ten officers besides himself, all of whom were my guests. I have no doubt matters were freely discussed during their stay here. I remember distinctly of expressing myself somewhat strongly at that time, when informed by some of Major Morrow's officers, that on the morning of a day or two previous to the arrival of Major Morrow's Command, a camp of his battalion had been attacked by the hostiles when the command was at break-fast, the camp was fired upon from a high point in the immediate vicinity covering the camp and some men killed and wounded. Major Morrow immediately gathered together thirty non-commissioned officers and men and stormed the height in person, arriving upon the height with six men, the remainder of the storming party having skulked and deserted him during the charge, the Major and his small party, principally non commissioned officers only being saved from destruction by the opportune arrival from an opposite direction of Lieutenant Gatewood's Arizona Apache Scouts who, being camped at some distance from the main force, had rushed to the combat on hearing the firing. I did on this occasion express myself somewhat freely as to the merits of such soldiers, and the chances taken by officers who led them into danger.*

My ***?culinary?*** *department is some distance to the rear of my private quarters and conversation in my quarters would not be overheard except by systematic eavesdropping. Parts of sentences have doubtless been overheard in this way and forwarded and put together to suit the taste and convenience of listeners and those who have made use of the information thus gained, all of which is perhaps a suitable material for an anonymous communication.*

In the case of Private Downing. Who alleges illtreatment, the circumstances were as follows; the Company left this place on the seventeenth or eighteenth of March 1878 en route to the Ute Country in Colorado, on arrival at Fort Craig, where the Company camped two nights, the second in great part owing to the fact that many of the men were absent without leave during the first night and the morning of the next day and many of the men drunk and unfit for duty including the 1st Sergeant and other non-commissioned officers.

19 As spelled in original document.

The march was delayed until the next day when the Company moved out with the 1st Sergeant under arrest and several men under guard and the Company to some extent demoralized by their spice the result in part of having been a long time at this place without opportunity of indulgence. After marching some distance, arriving at a convenient place to water, water call was sounded and the horses watered, the Company being directed after watering their horses to resume their places in column of fours on the road ready for the march.

Private Downing's place was in the second set of fours from the head of the column. In taking his place as number four he placed his horse diagonally across, thereby preventing No. three from coming into his proper position. I directed him to straighten his horse in his position in order to permit number three to ride into his place. Downing who is a half breed Cherokee, and of a rather sulky and ugly disposition simply looked at me in a manner as much as to say "what are you going to do about it if I aren't" he had evidently been drinking. I repeated the command – straighten your horse in column to his proper position that number three may ride into his place – he barely made a pretence of changing the position of his horse saying impudently, "He can get in if he wants to," I rode upon him and cut him over the head with my riding whip, when he drew his carbine upon me, and Lieut. Emmet, who rode up at this moment, assisted me in disarming him. He was taken to the rear and if I remember, put in irons under guard, he remained in confinement some days , when, showing signs of penitence, as the Company was under orders for active field service in the Ute Country, I released him subject to further action in his case, and informed him, as he was a recruit, but a little over a year in the service, that further action in his case, would depend largely upon his subsequent conduct. I withheld the charges and as his conduct since that time has been exceptionally good, he being one of the best behaved and most cleanly soldiers in the Company, almost invariably taking orderly when at post, as the cleanest man on guard, I have never forwarded them. Without going into detail I will say that the case of Private Jackson is much of the same character, as that of Downing. Jackson taking it upon himself to resent the reprimand I gave a man working in the same party with him and when told to attend to his duties and not speak until he was spoken to he persisted in his insolence, and when I advanced upon him, he drew his pistol on me. I had him disarmed, put him in irons and marched him from Sabinal to this place, five days march, with a handcuff upon one of his hands and during the march the other handcuff was attached to the rear of one of the wagons, this to prevent his escape and any further mischief at his hands. He remained in confinement some days after the arrival the Company at this place, in May last, as the Company was ordered out for only sixty days field service I withheld charges until the Company should return to post, it being thought impracticable to bring him before a Court Martial while the Company remained in the field. There being no guards house or proper place for confinement of prisoners here, and the man evidencing some degree of penitence, I took into consideration that he was but a recruit, who had just joined the Company, not a month before the Company left post, and released him from confinement subject to further action in his case, which he was also informed might depend largely upon his future good conduct. I have delayed to forward charges in his case until the Company should return to post, where he could be placed in confinement and brought before a General Court Martial for trial. His conduct has been uniformly good since he was restored to duty. With reference to his statement that he was dragged thirty feet, I know nothing of it, I inspected him frequently on the march, saw him hand cuffed to the wagon in the morning before the team started out, and released there from on going into camp about noon. I heard no complaint of his being sick or unable to walk, he experienced no injury and has not to my knowledge been to the Doctor since he has been in the service.

With the use of handcuffs there is no danger of an undue pressure or stoppage of circulation as might be the case when restraining dangerous men, by the use of cords or ropes. I did not as he asserts strike or kick him but, when the Corporal had him down upon the ground and was about to gag him, for his continuing insolent and insulting language to myself, I did tell the Corporal he need not wait to gag him, that my boot heel would just fit his mouth and that he might rest assured that I should place it there if he opened his mouth again to me. Jackson seeing that I would probably be as good as my word, desisted from further talk. I did curse him as a dog, saying that he was a fine soldier, who hadn't been in the service a month and the first use he proposed to make of his pistol was upon his Captain. I would defy a saint from the realms above, or a pious representative of the Indian Department, to serve any length of command of my Company, if he had the least soldierly qualifications, without becoming as profane as a trooper.

In the case of Private John Howard, in which he complains of illtreatment, the circumstances were as follows. Private Howard was one of a detail sent out to cut and haul wood for the command under charge of a non-commissioned officer, the party was armed, for protection of themselves and the train in case of attack by Indians which was not improbable at that time, positive orders were given that there should be no firing except the party was attacked by Indians, these orders had been constantly repeated on all occasions to prevent unnecessary alarm. Not long after the party went out, the Corporal of the Guard reported to me, that several shots had been fired in the direction in which the wood party had gone. I at once sent out a detachment to see what the occasion of the firing was and learned that Private Howard and another man had been shooting at rabbits or squirrels. On return of the wood party I questioned the non-commissioned Officer in Charge and he confirmed the statement of the Non-Commissioned Officer who had been sent out. I took him to task for permitting the firing. He stated that he had forbidden the men to fire, and endeavored to prevent them without avail, I therefore ordered the men into Confinement to pack logs, weighing forty pounds (the heaviest I have ordered in such cases) on number one post, in front of the Guards, until further orders, it being deemed necessary to make an example of the men in such cases, in order that the command should not be constantly and unnecessarily alarmed by promiscuous firing in the vicinity of the Camp, as I had held myself, with the rest of the Command, in readiness for action in case this firing had been the result of an attack by Indians. After packing the logs a short time, Private Howard threw down his log, refusing to pack it, saying that he was going to see the captain, to which the Sergeant of the Guard objected and endeavoring to prevent him from coming to me without permission, Howard broke and ran, followed by the Sergeant with a view to restrain him. Howard ran to the woodpile, seized an ax and stood the Sergeant off, threatening to split his head open or to cut him down if he attempted to further restrain him, and from the statement made to me by the Sergeant, at the time, would probably have done so but for the assistance of other men of the guard who closed on Howard from the rear and seized him. Howard is under charge for this latter offence, the punishment having been ordered for his former offence in firing contrary to orders when out with the wood party. I then had him ironed by placing handcuffs on one wrist, the other side of the handcuff attached to a log chain to prevent further attempt at escape and dangerous mischief. His statement that I called him a son of a bitch, or caused the chain to be wound around his neck are deliberately and wilfully false and of a piece with all similar statements made by men of the Company which are evidently the result of Conspiracy and Collusion.

The circumstances referred to by Private Quarle (at the time a Corporal) Frank Smith, Turner, Timbers, Booth, Wise and others in which they complain of having been punished on the day that Quarle was reduced from Corporal the circumstances were as follows: it was on the 1st day of August, Quarle and seven Pvt's. were on herd guard, the herd was taken up the main valley or canon in the afternoon a long distance, the herd not being in sight at recall, water and stable. I was looking with my glass to discover the whereabouts if possible and the cause of the delay. The Company fell in at water call, under orders of the 1st Sergeant, and marched out side the bottom near the water, where the herd was usually caught up and waited nearby, if not a quite an hour for the approach of the herd. At last I discovered a cloud of dust coming in from a side Canon about three miles up the valley and coming down at a dead run, as it approached closer I discovered Corp. Quarle and five or six of the men of the guard running all of half a mile ahead of the herd engaged in a spirited horse race, the herd following more quietly at an easy gallop, (having doubtless had a sufficient run) followed by one or two of the herders who were endeavoring, apparently to force the herd to a faster gait. The party in front, from their antics were evidently whooping and yelling amusing themselves in Indian fashion, doubtless thinking that they were still too far distant to be observed from Camp. I directed on the arrival of the herd in Camp, the Corporal of the Camp Guard to arrest Corporal Quarle and his entire party, have them turn in their arms in to the 1st Sergeant, take the Privates into confinement and report the Corporal to the 1st Sergeant under arrest. At retreat I reduced the Corporal to the ranks, subject to the approval of the Colonel of the Regiment, ordered him into confinement and caused the whole party to pack forty pound logs. I had reason to believe that the Corporal and his party had taken the herd out of the main Canon, where it served to be out of sight and that he and this party had been engaged in gambling for their tobacco, which had been issued to them for the month the night previous; this being an invariable custom in the Company. The plugs of tobacco, or a portion of the plugs being cut for that purpose into eight or two ounce pieces and Corporal Quarle being one of the leading and one of the most inveterate gamblers. In this view of the case I was confirmed by my Lieut. who was present when the herds came in, and said to me " they have probably been gambling for their tobacco and the time had slipped away unawares" which he thought accounted for the delay. I asked neither Corporal Quarle nor any of his party for any explanation, preferring to save them the trouble of telling me, as usual, a string of preconcerted lies, the universal result in such cases. It is doubtless well known that these men are from force of circumstances and education (for which they are perhaps not entirely to blame) natural born thieves and liars, at all events, if occasion should offer, the preponderance of evidence will amply sustain this assertion.

For the same reason that I declined to examine the Corporal and his party, I declined to permit individuals to be brought to me for that purpose, when they so requested, I remember distinctly that I said to the Sergeant of the Guard, when he reported to me, that some of the party wished to see me with reference to the matter, that I would save them the trouble and myself the annoyance and disgust of listening to their preconcerted and concocted lies, with reference to the matter or words to that effect. I had seen enough myself, through my glass , of the proceedings independent of the suspicion that the party had been gambling on herd, to warrant me in making an example of the Corporal and his party for the benefit of the Company.

In the case of Private Peters the circumstances were as follows: he, as Lance Corporal, with a detail (not of recruits as he states, there being old soldiers in the party) was sent to drive a small herd of cattle, which was encroaching upon the only grazing grounds in the immediate vicinity of Camp, down the Canon, the party being fully armed instructed to keep a sharp lookout for Indians to prevent surprise and under no circumstance to do any firing, except attacked, as it would cause an alarm in Camp and a force would be sent to their support, (this occurring but a few days after the capture of the herd.) After the party had been gone some time, firing was heard down the Canon. The alarm was sounded, the Company fell in under arms, the herd of ten horses, grazing in the immediate vicinity of the Camp was promptly brought in by the Non-Commissioned Officer in Charge, in accordance with instructions which he had received. I sent Lieut. Taylor with ten mounted men at once down the Canon to ascertain the occasion of the firing. He was closely followed by Sergt. Williams, with a detachment of dismounted men; they had barely reached the Canon when they came upon Peters and his party returning, one of the party with a turkey slung across his shoulders. The Lieutenant immediately reported back with his mounted detachment, followed in due time by the dismounted detachment and the turkey which the Lieutenant had directed to be brought in. Peters and his party were marched up to my Quarters and an explanation demanded. Peters explained that some of his party had fired upon turkeys without permission, and contrary to his orders, but failed to inform me, who the guilty parties were, as usual in such cases, and neither of the party would inform me who the guilty parties were, each in turn denying for himself that he had done any firing, and the Corporal being equally disposed with the others, to screen the guilty parties.

Of course I was naturally under the circumstance highly incensed, as well as much disappointed in the Corporal to whom I said "I am much disappointed in you, I had hoped better things of you, but you are like all the rest of the god damned idiots." He being only a Lance Corporal I had the Chevrons removed and ordered him into confinement with a pair of handcuffs on, the turkey lashed to his back, with instructions that he should walk to the post, in front of the guards, saying "that he should carry the turkey until it rotted on his back," the next day the turkey beginning to smell badly, I had it removed from his back and he, in the mean time having regretted not reporting to me the true facts in the first place as he should have done and thereby preventing his punishment and disgrace, informed me who the offenders were.

I placed them also in confinement, caused them to be furnished with tools, picks and spades, and directed that Peters and the two offenders should dig a large and deep hole, in number one post, in front of the guard, bury the turkey at the bottom of it, refill the hole, level and police the ground.

In the case of Private McGill, the circumstances were as follows: Early in June last, about the third I think, a small trail of moccasin and pony tracks being discovered in the vicinity, I sent Lieut. Clark, 15th Inf. The only officer with me, and who was very desirous of going, with twelve mounted men to take up and follow the trail, with instructions to send back a courier if he discovered anything of importance, that I might follow up and support him with a stronger detachment of my Company if that course should be deemed advisable.

The same day, about noon, Lieut. Cusack, with Company "G" 9th Cav'y, accompanied by Lieutenant Maney, 15th Inf, arrived here on a scout from Fort Bayard. I informed Lieut. Cusack of the scout sent out under Lieut. Clark that morning, stating my apprehensions to Lieutenant Cusack that Lieut. Clark even should he come upon a trail of Indians might feel a matter of pride about sending back for support and perhaps take too great chances in endeavoring to ???? with a large hostile party, with his small detachment, and it was arranged between lieut. Cusack and myself that he, who had some Navajoe trailers with him, should move out with his Company early the next day, take up and follow Lieutenant Clark's trail which, it was thought would lead by way of the head of the Red Canon into the San Mateo Mountains and I, with the remains of my Company, leaving a small guard here at the same time, to proceed down the Canon Cañada Alamosa thence into the San Mateo Mountains, which programme was carried out with a view to intercepting the hostile party, if any, pursued by Lieutenants Clark and Cusack and cutting off their retreat across the Rio Grande, in the direction of San Andreas Mountains and Fort Stanton Reservation, a point having been designated where the different commands would meet with a view to further operations should neither of us fall in with any hostile Indians.

On the second days march, having been obliged, owing to the impossibility of getting through the San Mateo Mountains, to the opposite side, to return to the Cañada Alamosa, for the purpose of passing around the San Mateo Mountains as well as to get water, at that time not found in the mountains, Private McGill was reported to me by the Sergeant of the Guard, in charge of the pack mules, as refusing to lead one of the mules. I directed the Sergeant to dismount McGill and cause him to lead the mule dismounted, until he was willing to obey orders promptly and without grumbling and to see that the pack mules were kept closed up to the Command.

Directly the sergeant reported to me again that he could do nothing with McGill, he would not walk and he would not lead a packmule, and the pack train was falling to the rear. Under the circumstances I could not afford to be delayed by the persistent obstreperousness and obstinacy of such a man. I halted my Company and rode back to assist the Sergeant in bringing McGill to a proper sense of his duty: McGill still refusing to walk up and lead the mule. I directed the Sergeant to take his lariat, having no hand cuffs with me, tie McGill by the hands and fasten him be side of one of the packmules, a lariat being attached for that purpose to the breeching harness of the pack saddle. McGill persisting in the use of violent and insulting language, both to the Sergeant and myself, I caused him to be gagged, to prevent a further repetition which was not to be endured. This being done, I ordered "forwards" sounded and remained in rear to observe McGill's conduct and assist the Sergeant in keeping him up. He was very violent and threatening in his demonstrations and when the Command moved forwards persistently threw his weight back with all his force, thereby breaking the pack harness, when I warned him, being immediately in his rear, that if he persisted in that course I should be compelled to use my whip on him, he persisted and I used the whip one or two energetic application however suffered so long as I remained immediately in the rear.

The saying As his eye complained of is a myth and a subterfuge. He has had no trouble or treatment on that account. His complaint that that he was taken out with the herd, amounts to simply this, the only guard I had was the herd guard, and he was under charge of that guard and necessarily out with the herd when the herd was out. McGill finally relates under this treatment promised obedience, was returned to duty and his conduct since been exceptionally good and, in this connection, I wish to say of those making complaints, there are quite a number who have always been obedient soldiers, never to my knowledge in confinement and never by me harshly reprimanded or addressed among whom I will name Privates Beal Craven, Ward, Lockman, Willis Corporal Foster and others who in exceptional cases have perhaps been taken to task for their stupidity and want of comprehension but have never been seriously punished. It will be observed that a number of the complainants disclaim any illtreatment experienced by themselves but feel called upon, doubtless at the dictation of the leading malcontents and agitators for the benefit of the race in my Company, to join in the General Complaint the burden being "the black sons of bitches" an expression I have never used. I have ever carefully avoided, from my first service with these troops, the use of any expression, calculating or tending to originate, cultivate or foster, any question as to distinction on account of race or color and have formerly endeavored to prevent the use of the vile epithets and beastly obscene expressions so commonly used among them of which "black son of a bitch" and other expressions too vile for utterance, are the most common, even in "fun" as they term it, among themselves. I have long since however abandoned the idea of effecting any improvement or change for the better in that respect

I have found at times that ridicule has a greater effect upon these men that severity, as in the case of an awkward seat in the saddle and unsoldierly manner of mounting and dismounting the horse, a remark which causes a delinquent to be ridiculed by his comrades, after the ranks have been broken and the Company dismissed, often times having a most salutary effect in the way of improvement, as for instance I have told awkward men that they mounted and dismounted their horse more like an Indian squaw, or a Texas Cowboy or a Cornfield Nigger than like a soldier, or perhaps that he sat his horse more like a baboon than a well drilled soldier

On the case of Private Rowntree, I don't recall the circumstance of which he refers. I can however well imagine from the character of the man that he has on more than one occasion been packed with a log for offences committed in the field, when the Company was away from Guard House and Court Martial facilities. Although I cannot now recall any special instance, he doubtless could more truthfully state that he has been packed with a log at least a half a dozen times during his service of nearly five years, as he is considered by me one of the most worthless and trifling soldiers in the Company, although never detected in any very aggravated or serious offences.

In this connection I will ask that it be borne in mind that since my return from sick leave, nearly six years since, I have not been on leave of absence or detached service from my Company a day, and knowing the material I have to deal with, I have avoided detached service, and even requested the Colonel of my Regiment, the present District Commander, not to cause me to be detached from my Company and although much of the time during the last year, I have been barely able to do my duty, I have from choice remained in command of my Company well knowing, from a former experience, that it is much easier to keep a company in hand, than to reduce it to subjection after relaxed discipline. I think it must be apparent to my superiors in authority that the position of an Officer situated as I am and have been, much of the time alone in the field, away from the advantages derived from guard house and Court Martial, in command of a treacherous, conspiring race, utterly devoid of anything like honorable or truthful instincts, must be anything but agreeable or safe, and although my sense of duty and utter repugnance to serving with a demoralized mob, will cause me to assume the necessary responsibilities in maintaining a rigid discipline, while serving under such circumstances, the duty is at the same time a most unpleasant and undesirable one.

Service with a mixed Command under a superior Officer with guard house and Court martial facilities would certainly be far preferable and more to my taste and, whatever may be the result of the investigation, either in the effect upon the discipline of my Company or the welfare and safety of it's Captain I feel well assured that the Departmental Commander must have held the class of men of which my Company is composed in something the same estimation I do myself, as a similar sneaking anonymous communication from a Company of white soldiers, would doubtless have received the treatment it merited, either silent contempt and indifference or perhaps a reference to the Company Commander for his information and a report of facts.

First Lieut. F.B. Taylor, 9th Cav'y being called and questioned replied as follows:

Question	*State your name, rank, regiment and the Company with which you are serving.*
Ans.	*F.B. Taylor, 1. Lieut. 9th Cav'y, Comp. "E"*
Question	*Where have you been stationed during the past six months?*
Answer	*At this place, Ojo Caliente, since June 8th 1879*
Question	*Who was your immediate commanding officer during that time?*
Answer	*Captain A.E. Hooker, 9th Cav.*
Quest.	*How long have you served under Capt. Hooker?*
Ans.	*Since the Summer of 1876*
Quest.	*Were you present with the Captain at the selection of a suitable place for a grave and at the subsequent funeral of the herdguard Killed at Ojo Caliente, N.M. by the Indians September 4th 1879?*
Ans.	*I was.*
Quest.	*Did you on any of those occasions hear the Captain use any abusive, coarse or profane language towards his men or to you with reference to the men?*
Ans.	*I do not remember of any and I don't think that he used any as his manner was very quiet that day.*
Quest.	*If the Captain had used abusive, coarse or profane language on those occasions, could it have escaped your observation?*
A.	*Yes, I might have been out of hearing or paying no attention. I was not within hearing of the Captain all the time on those occasions.*
Q.	*Do you remember the occasion when Sergeant Shanklin was reduced?*
A.	*I do.*
Q.	*Please relate as near as you can what Captain Hooker said to any or all of his men, on the occasion referred to.*
A.	*I cannot. I only distinctly remember of Captain Hooker walking up to one of the men in the ranks ordering him to step out two paces to the front and asking him if he had anything to say or any complaint to make, or words of like import. The circumstance attracted my attention, because the man in question was a recruit not long joined to the Company and of whom I had never heard any complaint made that I remembered of – The man's name was Thornton Jackson.*
Q.	*Did you hear the Captain, at the time referred to, use any coarse, profane or abusive language to any of his men?*
A.	*Yes, but I can't remember any of the language, nor anything further than that such language was used.*
Q.	*Did you on that occasion, hear the expression of "Son of a Bitch" used by the Captain?*
A.	*I can't remember that I did. I think had such an expression been used, it would under the circumstances have attracted my attention and I should probably have remembered it.*
Q.	*Have you ever heard Captain Hooker curse his man and call them offensive and opprobrious names?*
A.	*Yes.*
Q.	*Has this occurred rarely and with long intervals or has it been a matter of frequent occurrence?*
A.	*Quite frequently.*
Q.	*Have you ever heard Capt. Hooker apply the epithet of "Black Son of a Bitch" to any of his men?*

A.	*Yes.*
Q.	*Does he, as far as your observation goes, habitually use such expressions when addressing his men?*
A.	*No, they are exceptional.*
Q.	*Were you present at Target Practice last fall on the occasion when Private F. Smith was reprimanded by his Captain for wearing a Government Cap?*
A.	*I was present.*
Q.	*State whether the Captain at that time called Smith a "Son of a Bitch"?*
A.	*I did not hear the captain use any improper language to Private Smith when he reprimanded him for wearing a Government Cap.*
Q.	*Were you present when during September last, Captain Hooker gave his instructions to Corporal Williams, in charge of a Detachment about to proceed to Canada,*[1] *to escort Private Riley back from Paraje?*
A.	*No, but within hearing distance.*
Q.	*Were the instructions at that time given by Capt. Hooker, in your opinion, in any sense improper?*
A.	*I overheard a portion of the instructions given by Captain Hooker to Corporal Williams, in charge of a Detachment about to proceed to Canada to meet Private Riley on his return from Paraje, whither he had been sent with dispatches, and there was nothing improper in what I heard.*

Note

1 Cañada Alamosa, a village near to Ojo Caliente.

Acting Assistant Surgeon C.A. Sewall, U.S. Army, being called and questioned, replied as follows:

Q.	*Were you present at Target Practice last fall on the occasion when Private F. Smith "E" Co. 9th Cav. Was reprimanded by his Captain for wearing a Government Cap?*
A.	*Yes Sir, I was.*
Q.	*State as near as you can the language used by the Captain on that occasion.*
A.	*I don't remember exactly what he said, but I think he scolded him for not wearing his Hat like the rest of his men in his Company. I believe also that he told the Sergeant to put Smith on* ***????*** *until he could find his Hat.*
Q.	*Did you hear Captain Hooker call Private F. Smith a "God damned Son of a "bitch" on that occasion?*
A.	*I did not.*
Q.	*Had he done so could you have failed to have heard it?*
A.	*I could not.*
Q.	*Do you know Private Crawford "E" Co. 9th Cav.?*
A.	*I do.*
Q.	*Have you ever reported him to Capt. Hooker as a malingerer?*
A.	*No – I never have, except incidentally in private conversation with the Capt. When I have so spoken of him.*
Q.	*Is Private Crawford in your opinion a malingerer?*
A.	*Yes Sir.*
Q.	*Has Private McGill of "E" Co. 9th Cav. Ever been under your treatment for any injury or alleged injury to any of his eyes?*

A. *No Sir.*
Q. *If any injury or blemish to any of the eyes of Private McGill exists, please describe it.*
A. *There is a slight indentation? on the inner surface of the lid of the left eye, but in no way affecting its vision.*
Q. *Could this injury have been produced by any external pressure or abrasion?*
A. *It might have, but in order to have produced this deposit it is necessary that there should have existed a predisposition to it – in fact, this indentation? Might have been altogether produced by constitutional tendency, as such a tendency is more likely than any other cause to produce a deposit such as referred to.*
Q. *Is there any evidence of a scar on the exterior surface of the lid of Private McGill's left eye?*
A. *No Sir.*

This practically closes the investigation so far as the allegations, contained in the anonymous letter are concerned. The Statement made by Capt. Hooker should properly have been written by himself, but as he at the time it was taken, suffered so intensely from neuralgia as not to permit him, without great physical discomfort, to engage in labor of that kind and in order not to lose any more time (several days having been lost through sickness of my own) I wrote the statement myself, at the Captain's dictation.

It will be seen that I have not attempted a very minute verification of many of the allegations made against Capt. Hooker. My reasons for this are twofold. In the first place it would doubtless be safer and more satisfactory, should a further investigation be deemed necessary, that the station of the Company be first changed to a larger post, preferably with a Field Officer in Command. The reason for this is obvious. In the second place I find the Negroes so excitable, imaginative and disposed to exaggeration, their minds evidently being intensely wrought upon by real or fancied wrongs, that the only result of carrying out the investigation further, at present would be confusion. Besides it will be found I think that Captain Hooker's own statement corroborates the essential portion of the allegations made.

I am not especially familiar with the methods required to make our colored Soldiers efficient and reliable, but I presume that patience and forbearance are as necessary in the management of them as of White Soldiers. Anger like any other passion increases when constantly indulged and will hardly ever become the proper agent for increasing the efficiency of our Army, whatever material its Soldiery may be composed of. Captain Hooker evidently requires his men to come up to his own standard of efficiency and Soldierly qualifications; this I think can only be expected in exceptional cases of men so recently and suddenly lifted from the deepest possible degradation to the higher level of responsible manhood. Scolding and arbitrary exercise of power only make matters worse. It is evident from the straightforward and manly admissions of Captain Hooker that he believes the course pursued by him towards increasing the efficiency and the discipline of his men to be the only one available. He certainly makes no effort, either to shield himself or to present matters in any but their natural colors. He rather invites responsibility than otherwise. I am convinced that Captain Hooker has in every thing acted for what he believed to be the best interest of the service and with a conscientious sense of duty, whether mistaken or not and I feel it my duty therefore to state that he, in all that relates to the details of service, its systematic division, care of Government Property, the Military Instruction of his men and the Company Commissariat is unremitting and indefatigable in his personal attention and supervision and deserving of great credit.

It is therefore more than unfortunate that Captain Hooker has contracted such strong and seemingly ineradicable prejudices against the colored race as Soldiers. If, as I believe, the ???? ability of Captain Hooker (which, according to all accounts, and perhaps naturally, has largely increased since the loss of the Herd) is in a great measure due to the existing nervous prostration the interests of the service would be observed if "E" Company, 9th Cavalry could, for a time at least, be stationed at a post where the Commanding Officer would be superior in Rank to Captain Hooker. This would relieve the Captain of immeasurable little details, thus making life easier to him and perhaps more satisfactory to his men.

<u>*The loss of the Company Herd*</u>

Extract from Proceedings of a Board of survey, convened at Ojo Caliente, N.M. September 9th 1879.

* * *

Captain A.E. Hooker, 9th Cavalry, the first witness examined by the Board, testified as follows:

* * *

The herd was sent out on the 4th of September as usual, early in the morning, under a guard of five men, a Sergeant commanding, with the usual detailed and stringent instructions as to the care and protection of Animals. The herd was brought in to water about 11 A.M., the Herd Guard at the same time getting their Dinners and the Sergeant reporting as usual for further instructions. The Herd was again taken out about 12 N. and, from subsequent examination of the Ground, was herded some distance from the Main Canon or Valley into some cross Canons about one mile from camp, and was evidently surprised in a sort of trap or cul de sac, where the Indians had been enabled to close in upon and surround it and cut it off from Camp in consequence of an evident failure to post a Vidette and to vigilantly guard the Herd in accordance with instructions. It was not discovered that the Herd had been captured and run off until after 6 P.M. Recall of the Herd, Water and Stable Calls sounded as usual (since August 31st) at 5 P.M., the Company then going out near the water to meet the Herd as it should be driven in at that time.

The Herd not making its appearance immediately caused no immediate alarm, as it sometimes seemed that the Herd Guard would misjudge the time and be somewhat late. About 6 O'Clock however, the first Sergeant took some of the men and went out on a high point in the direction it was supposed the Herd had been grazing and discovered, as he afterwards reported, a cloud of dust some miles distant and in the direction of Red Canon and Luna Spring. It was then getting dark; I at once sent Lieutenant Taylor, mounted on the only remaining Animal, a condemned Cart Mule that had that day been used in the Cart and was therefore in the Corral, and a Non-Commissioned Officer and Six Men, out to explore the ground where the Herd had been grazing, to ascertain if possible, whether the Herd had stampeded or been jumped by Indians and, in the latter case to search for dead bodies.

The next morning I visited the ground in Company with Lieut. Taylor and others (the dead bodies of the Herd guard having been discovered and brought in,) and from personal observation formed the conclusions as to the manner of the Capture, as above set forth in this statement.

My instructions to the Herd guard had evidently been disregarded, first, in taking the Herd into a place where it could be easily surrounded, surprised, and cut off from Camp. Second, in the evident failure to post a mounted Vidette (to be relieved every hour) on the highest point in the vicinity of the Herd, to vigilantly watch all approaches to the ground where the Herd was grazing; and Third, in the evident disregard of my oft repeated instructions, that all of the Herders would remain constantly vigilant, with their Horses in hand when not mounted, in readiness to mount in an instant, in case of danger or uneasiness on the part of the Herd. It had formerly, (some weeks since) been necessary, in order to keep the Horses in serviceable condition, to herd them some distance (four or five Miles) from Camp, from lack of grazing in the immediate vicinity and from the fact that I was prohibited from feeding Hay. But latterly, since rains had started fresh grass in the more immediate vicinity, the Herd guard had been instructed to take the Herd but a short distance from Camp and when leaving the Main canon, or rather valley (in some places from a fourth to half a Mile wide) in search of better grazing to avoid taking the Herd into any place where it could be easily approached, surrounded or surprised by Indians, against whom (more particularly of late) the Men on guard have been daily and constantly cautioned. The Herd guard has been constantly instructed that in case of any approaching or seeming danger at once to close up the Herd and be on the alert to rush or stampede it into Camp; a thing easily accomplished, as has been frequently demonstrated by practice and experience, the horses being disinclined to run in any other direction through play or ordinary fright.

Extract from Proceeding of a Board of Survey convened at Ojo Caliente, N.M. September 9th 1879. Testimony by Lieut. F.B. Taylor, 9th

* * *

To begin at the beginning: On the afternoon of the day on which the Company Herd was captured, Captain Hooker was informed by a Visitor at the Post that Victorio, Nani and some other Apache Chiefs, with about thirty five or forty Indians of their respective bands, had been seen the day before at the Ranches near the head of the Rio Cuchillo Negro, distant about eighteen Miles South from Ojo Caliente. I also learned this news and, though on Sick Report from an illness contracted on a two week's Scout into the Navajoe Country, in which In had recovered some Stock stolen by the Apaches, and from which I had returned only a few days previous, I about 5 O'Clock went to Captain Hooker and said to him that though still under the weather yet if he wanted to send a Scout to the Cuchillo Negro after Victorio, I would go, for I thought that if the Report of his being there was true it was too good a chance to lose to strike the old Chief and punish him.

The Captain gladly accepted my offer and it was arranged that I should start that evening after retreat and together we proceeded to the Corral to pick out the twenty five Men and horses to accompany me. It was then that we discovered that the Herd was not yet in, whereupon we both walked perhaps a hundred yards from the Corral in the direction in which the Company had previously gone to meet the expected Herd. But though we could see the Company waiting from where we stood, still there was no sign of the coming horses. After standing there some minutes the Captain remarked that he hoped nothing had happened to the Herd and that he though nothing had, citing the instance of the Herd once before being equally late in getting in, owing to a misjudging of time and distance from camp by the Non-Commissioned Officer in charge and that the delay on the present occasion would be found to be due probably to the same cause. Just then the First sergeant of the Company came up and reported that he had been over on a certain high ridge, pointing it out, and that he had seen a big cloud of dust like made by moving animals going across in the direction of the Luna [Luera?] *Mountains. At the same time the Captain's brother, Mr W.J. Hooker, who was standing near by with a Glass, espied what appeared to be an Indian Pony coming out of one of the little Canons leading down to the Creek. I remarked that these were two bad signs and, turning to the captain, asked him to let me take the Cart Mule and go out and see what was the matter. The Captain assented and at the same time ordered a half dozen Men to accompany me. The Sun had now set and though we hurried away, it was dark before we reached the herding ground owing to some clouds that quickly arose in the West. However, by examining the ground with the aid of lighted matches, we discovered the track of the Herd as it entered one of the several Canons leading from the water. Ascending this Canon we at last, after much difficulty, owing to the darkness, the wind and a drizzling rain that had meanwhile set in, reached about Nine O'Clock and at about one and a half Mile from Camp, the place where the Herd had been jumped and stampeded, as evidenced by the deeply indented ground. Making a guess as to the direction the Indians would drive the Herd, I at once, without following the Horses' tracks but keeping above them, struck across for a wide, long Canon that I knew led up into the Mountains. Reaching it we then found the trail of the Herd plainly defined, leading to the Northwest. Some moccasin tracks were mingled with those of the Animals as though some Indians were following the running Herd on foot. These tracks were probably made by the two or three Indians who had lingered behind to rob the dead. Returning down the Canon, less than a quarter of a Mile, we came upon the bodies of two of the Herders, the acting Corporal and a Private, cold and stiff in death. After a few moments spent in an unsuccessful search for the bodies of the other three Herders, I left a guard over the dead bodies and returned with two of the Men to camp, reaching there at 10 O'Clock as shown by my watch. The Captain immediately detailed another squad of Men to go out to where the Herd had been jumped to look for the missing members of the guard and the mule that I had been riding was taken from under the Saddle and harnessed to the Cart to bring in the dead bodies: One of the Men that had come in with me going back to guide the party to the locality. This Detachment, together with the first one, returned to Camp about midnight, but had not been able, on account of the broken character of the ground, to find the other bodies. The next morning early, a Detachment of the Company, acting under the Orders of the Company Commander, went out to renew the search for the missing bodies, for we now made no doubt that all the Herd Guard had been Killed, and I followed soon after, though not soon enough however to reach the ground before the three dead Guards had been found and their bodies placed in the Cart. An examination revealed that, like their companions found the night before, the sergeant and remaining two Privates had been shot to death, their arms and accoutrements stripped from their bodies and their pockets rifled and turned.*

Sending the Cart with its ghastly load back to Camp, I proceeded to a careful study of the ground where the Herd had been stampeded, with a view to forming some conclusions as to the manner in which it had been approached and captured by the Indians.

Going back on the trail I found where the Horses had been quietly grazing along. Following up their tracks, they led across one or two little ridges into and across three little short Canons making out from a long Canon running parallel to a high ridge. These little Canons indent the West side of this Ridge (the side opposite or farthest from the Camp) – it was in and on the slopes of these little Canons that the Herd evidently was grazing when surprised by the Indians.

On the eastern slope of the high Ridge just mentioned are two other little short Canons leading up from a long Canon extending back some distance into the Foot-hills. It was up those two little Canons that the Indians had approached the Herd, as shown by their Moccasin and Pony tracks; it was on or near the top of this high Ridge that the Indians had crawled and secreted themselves behind and under some low growing live Oaks, while preparing their Attack upon the Herd, several of the trees bearing in the trampled grass and weeds growing about their roots the marks of concealed Indians. From the crest of this Ridge the Indians could look directly upon the Herd, grazing probably not to exceed forty yards from them down the Slope. Other trees, between this place and the Trail hacked by the Herd in grazing up from Water, also showed signs where Indians had sat or laid concealing, watching the Herd, from time to time falling back from tree to tree before the gradually approaching Horses until they were at last in the place they had designated they should reach before jumping them and Killing the Herders.

The fact that all these Indian Signs I have just remarked were not seen, or if seen were not heeded, by the Herd Guard as they moved with the Herd slowly over the ground containing them, certainly evinces on their part great blindness or heedlessness, the result probably of carelessly and imperfectly performed duty. And had a Sentinel or Herder been posted upon the high Ridge before mentioned, the highest ground in the vicinity, of which no evidence is observable, or had said Ridge even been visited with a view to ascertaining what Kind of ground laid about and behind it, as it would seem should occur to any prudent or vigilant man to do, the Indians hiding thereabouts could not help but be seen and their ???????????? *surprise and attack avoided; or at least a warning would have been gained in sufficient time to enable the Guard to run the Herd out of danger, into the protection of the Post. But no, every thing points to the belief that the Guard was woefully negligent and inattentive, lulled by the long absence of danger into a fancied and fatal sense of security. This circumstance, coupled with the favorable nature of the ground, so aptly described by Captain Hooker in his Statement as a regular Trap, or cul de sac, with a Ridge between them and the Camp to break and turn back the sound of the firing, gave the Indians a fearful advantage which they were quick to take. Jumping the Herd, the Tracks showed that the Indians had forced it out of the little nest of Canons, across a low intervening Ridge and into the long wide Canon before alluded to. It was near the bottom of this low Ridge that the bodies of the two Herders, found the night before, were lying. The body of the Sergeant was found on the extreme northern flank of the running herd as located by the horses tracks. The fourth was killed on the opposite flank, the fifth about midway between the two flanks. The two men first found I think to have been the only ones mounted at the moment the attack was made, several minor circumstances going to show that they were shot from their horses, in the rear of the herd as they were following it. The suddenness of the attack, the probable Complete surprise in fact, I believe to have prevented the remaining three men from mounting their horses and they were, from all appearances, killed on the ground. Killed with 50 Calibre guns as indicated by the empty shell I picked up close by one of the bodies. All the men judging from the positions of the bodies when found, all but one lying with the face in the direction of the fleeing herd, the location of the bodies from where their hats were lying – all betokened that the poor fellows had made a crazed, frantic effort to save the herd, when too late. How futile their efforts the* ***??sad segment??*** *shows I imagine that the herd was jumped between 3 and 4 P.M. for about the latter time it is the custom of the herders to turn it towards Camp, feeding back in anticipation of the ????? This day the herd had not yet been turned, I estimate that there were not above a dozen or fifteen Indians immediately engaged in the attack upon the herd, the balance of the band, if there were more, probably being in waiting some distance off, but ready to join in the stampede as the frightened horses came flying past. But these twelve or fifteen Indians were undoubtedly picked men, well commanded; the unusual size of one of the moccasin tracks noticed giving size to the scarce improbable belief that it was made by foot of big fat Nani himself.*

The Indians did not easily get away with the herd however. Either turned by the herd guard or prompted by force of habit and fear, several of the horses made a dash in the direction of Camp getting some distance away from the main body of the herd, but mounted Indians came sweeping across their front out of a Canon lower down and headed them off and forced them back. Certainly there were Indians enough to accomplish successfully all that they had intended: a squad to kill the herders another to run the herd and still another to ***??cut the deal??*** *and* ***?????*** *up the blunder.*

On my way back to Camp after my examination of the scene of the conflict, as I have narrated, I met Capt. Hooker and party and returned with them to the ground and pointed out the things I had discovered.

* * *

Mr John Sullivan being called and questioned as follows:

Quest. *Please state your name and residence.*

Ans. *John Sullivan, residing at Cañada Alamosa, Socorro County, New Mexico.*

Quest. *Did you visit Ojo Caliente N.M. on or about the time E Co. 9th Cavy herd was captured by the Indians?*

Ans. *Yes sir, I was there that very day.*

Quest. *Give date, month and year?*

Ans. *I do not recollect, it was in August last I think or thereabout.*

Quest. *You say that you were there on the very day that the Indians captured E Co. 9th Cav's herd, this year.*

Ans. *Yes sir,*

Quest. *What time of day did you arrive in Ojo Caliente on that day?*

Ans. *It was about 12 o'clock N. and before 1 o'clock P.M.*

Quest. *I ask, if you know, who was in Command at Ojo Caliente at that time?*

Ans. *Capt. Hooker.*

Quest. *Did you see Capt. Hooker on that day?*

Ans. *Yes sir,*

Quest. *At what time, in the day, did you first see him?*

Ans. *I think it was in the neighborhood of 2 o'clock P.M. couldn't say whether a little before or a little after.*

Quest. *In what place did you see him?*

Ans. *I first saw him in the Commissary store room.*

Quest.	*Please state the nature of your conversation with the Captain at that time.*
Ans.	*I told him that I had come over from Cuchillo Negro to Canada the night before, about midnight, wanting help to go out to the Cuchillo negro to where the sheep an ox herds were grazing on account of the Indians having been there the day before and some of the herders had come in to report it, that there had been thirty five or forty Indians out there and I asked the people from Canada to come up here, so that I could get my rifle and accompany them, my rifle was up here, and to report it in the mean time to Capt. Hooker.*
Quest.	*What reply did Capt. Hooker make to you?*
Ans.	*He felt very much dissatisfied with the people for not coming up here in the first place and notifying him. He said that if the people had come up and reported the fact that he would have started the whole command out.*
Quest.	*How long did you remain with the Captain?*
Ans.	*Well sir, I think an hour at least, talking from the time I met him at the Commissary. After the Captain got through issuing rations we went from the Commissary to his private office where the greatest part of our conversation took place.*
Quest.	*About what time did you leave the Captain?*
Ans.	*I think it was 3 o'clock P.M. May be a little after.*
Quest.	*Did you carry a watch?*
Ans.	*No sir*
Quest.	*How could you ascertain the exact time then?*
Ans.	*Well, before I came up to see the Captain I was in Mr Kelly's house and while there looked at his clock and saw that it was after one but before two o'clock P.M.*
Quest.	*What time of day did you leave Ojo Caliente?*
Ans.	*I left the Post between 5 and 6 o'clock P.M.*
Quest.	*How far is it from here to Cuchillo Negro where the Indians were reported to be?*
Ans.	*Between ten and twelve miles it is supposed to be.*
Quest.	*When did you become aware that the Indians had captured the government herd?*
Ans.	*On the day after the capture.*
Quest.	*Do you happen to know where the Indians went with the herd after they had captured it?*
Ans.	*Only by report I have heard.*
Quest.	*Did you meet Lieutenant Taylor on that day when you said that you met Captain Hooker, and reported to him about the Indians?*
Ans.	*Yes Sir,*
Quest.	*What time of day was it when you met him?*
Ans.	*About 3 or after 3 o'clock P.M.*
Quest.	*How long after 3 o'clock P.M. at the farthest could it have been?*
Ans.	*It must have been close to 3 o'clock, a quarter or half past at the farthest.*
Quest.	*Has Captain Hooker ever ordered you away from Ojo Caliente?*
Ans.	*Yes Sir, with my teams.*
Quest.	*For what offence?*
Ans.	*I know of no offence unless it was to get the teams off from the reservation.*
Quest.	*State if there is any personal feeling of hostility existing on your part towards Captain Hooker.*
Ans.	*None Sir.*

Quest.	*Did you, in Mr Hooker's store at Ojo Caliente, on the day of the capture of the herd, and in the presence of enlisted men of "E" Company, 9th Cavalry, state that you had reported or would report the presence of Indians in this vicinity to Captain Hooker?*
Ans.	*Some enlisted men may have heard me telling Mr Hooker or Mr Kelly about those things.*
Quest.	*Did you at that time tell Mr Hooker, Mr Kelly or any of the enlisted men that the Indians intended to make an attack upon, or try to run off with the Cavalry herd?*
Ans.	*I did not.*

Captain Hooker declining not only to be present while the above testimony was taken, but also his right of cross examination no further questions were asked of Mr Sullivan.

First Lieutenant F.B. Taylor, 9th Cavalry being recalled and questioned replied as follows:

Quest.	*Were you present at Ojo Caliente on the 4th day of September 1879?*
Ans.	*I was.*
Quest.	*State all you know with reference to the time of the alleged visit of an Mr Sullivan and the character of reports concerning Indians alleged to have been made by him to Captain A.E. Hooker, 9th Cav'y, Sept. 4th 1879?*
Ans.	*Between three and four o'clock on the afternoon of September 4th 1879, I saw Mr Sullivan and Captain Hooker standing talking together in front of the latter's quarters. As they separated I called to Mr Sullivan to please come over to my quarters. He did so. I asked him that was he was telling the Captain about the Indians. He replied that he had been telling him about Victorio, Nana and some other Apache Chiefs, with a lot of their Indians, thirty five or forty being seen on the headwaters of the Rio Cuchillo Negro the day before.*
Quest.	*Please state result of these reports with reference to immediate address taken by Captain Hooker?*
Ans.	*I cannot…*
Quest.	*Were any immediate actions or measures taken by him with special reference to the safety of the herd?*
Ans.	*I do not know.*
Quest.	*If any such measures had been taken would you have been likely to know them?*
Ans.	*I think I should.*
Quest.	*Have you visited the ground upon which the Company horses were feeding when being captured by the Indians Sept. 4th 1879?*
Ans.	*I have.*
Quest.	*Was the ground of such a character that if a vidette had been properly posted he could not have failed to discover the approaching Indians?*
Ans.	*Yes.*
Quest.	*Do you think, armed and equipped as the herd guard was on the 4th September, 1879 that, even if it had discovered the Indians shortly before the attack, the guard could have saved the herd or having started the herd toward camp could have saved itself?*
Ans.	*I cannot say.*
Quest.	*Do you consider men armed with pistols only and riding their horses without saddles as able to defend themselves as men armed with Carbines and riding horses fully equipped?*
Ans.	*No.*

Quest. *Do you believe the herd guard at Ojo Caliente, Sept. 4th 1879, to have been derelict in its duty?*

Ans. *I think they must have been.*

Quest. *While at Ojo Caliente and up to September 4th 1879, have you ever received orders from your Commanding Officer to make occasional visits to the grazing Company herd, to ascertain that the herd guard was performing its duty properly?*

Ans. *No.*

Captain Hooker declining not only to be present while the above testimony was taken, but also his right to cross-examination, the witness was dismissed.

Captain A.E. Hooker, 9th Cavalry, being called and questioned replied as follows:

QQuest. *What was the number of men comprising the herd guard at Ojo Caliente, N.M. September 4th 1879, the day your horses were captured by the Indians?*

AAns. *Five men commanded by a Sergeant. The herd guard had previously consisted of eight men which had been reduced to five, owing to a large portion of the Company being on detached service.*

QQuest. *How many men were for duty in your company on the morning of September 4th 1879?*

AAns. *Twenty five privates. A detachment of twenty seven men under Lieutenant Taylor having returned from a scout two or three days previous and expecting to start out another scout within a day or so. I had not increased the guard, it being necessary to give those who had just come in an opportunity to wash, patch up their clothing, clean up their arms &c.*

QQuest. *What was the whole strength of your Company?*

AAns. *Forty seven men, enlisted.*

QQuest. *Could you, without neglecting other equally important duties have detailed a larger herd guard than five men, or did you consider that number of men sufficient?*

AAns. *I could have detailed a larger number but from the circumstances just mentioned, and the fact that the country in the vicinity had been thoroughly scouted during the month of August and all reports agreeing and corroborating that no Indians were on the west side of the Rio Grande at that time, it was thought important that they would return to this side of the Rio Grande, for some days at least and, the guard being instructed to take the herd, but a short distance and not to take it into a locality where it could be cut off from the Camp of the Company, I did consider that number of men amply sufficient, if my instructions were carried out. In some accounts I have found small guards with a moving herd preferable, all the men being necessarily constantly occupied with their duties, as with a larger guard a portion of the men occupy themselves with gambling under a shade tree if the weather is warm, or around a fire if cold and the duty of the vidette in that case simply resolves itself with watching for the approach of an officer; the herd being in the mean time kept close by one or two men without being given proper opportunity to graze, the balance of the men being engaged in the game and the non-commissioned officer in charge probably being the Banker. The reports more particularly referred to above are those of Lieutenant Taylor, on his return from scout last of August, and that of Mr Stackpole at San Jose, which corroborated that of Lieutenant Taylors to the effect that the Indians which had been raiding on this side of the river, had returned to the San Andreas mountains in the vicinity of Fort Stanton with stolen stock. These reports were forwarded to District Headquarters by endorsement under date of September 3rd, 1879 conveying my impression of the probabilities of further depredations on this side of the river, for some time to come.*

QQuest. *Did the Non-Commissioned Officer in Charge of your herd guard September, 4th, 1879 report to you for orders?*

AAns. *He did and received his instructions which were most thorough and explicit, before going on herd.*

QQuest. *Please state as minutely as possible what orders you gave him?*

AAns. *The Sergeant was instructed to take the herd but a short distance up the valley, or main Canon as it is called here, in some places nearly a mile wide and for three or four miles in full view of my Quarters and high points in the immediate vicinity. He was instructed particularly not to permit the herd to go into the side canons to a distance that would render it liable to be cut off from Camp. A mounted vidette to be posted on the highest ground in the vicinity of the herd, overlooking the approach in all directions. This vidette to be relieved every hour, with instructions to keep a vigilant look-out or watch and to notify the Sergeant of the approach of any party or object from any direction, – the Sergeant at once to close up the herd preparatory to stampeding and running it into Camp, an operation which has repeatedly and successfully been performed many times under my instructions and those of my seniors, in command over me. Had these instructions been adhered to it would have been impossible for the guard to have been surprised and the herd captured and run off. The Sergeant was also instructed to bring the herd into water from half past ten to eleven o'clock A.M. when the men were to get their dinner and the Sergeant to report for further orders. The herd was brought in between eleven and twelve o'clock, the Sergeant reported for instructions and was directed to take the herd out again with the same instructions that he had before received.*

QQuest. *Please state, how your herd guard was armed on the 4th day of September 1879?*

AAns. *The herd guard was armed with Colt revolvers Cal. 45. the mounted fighting arm of the Service.*

QQuest. *Give your reasons why the herd guard was armed with pistols only?*

AAns. *The herd was a loose moving herd, the guard not expected to make a stand or fight, except a running hand to hand fight; under any circumstance. The carbines under these circumstances would be a useless incumbrance to the herders*

I have always made this distinction in arming the herd guard, – with a moving, loose herd I have armed the guard with revolvers – with a stationary herd, picketed or sidelined, I have armed the guard with carbines, it being necessary in that case to make a stand, it being impossible to move the herd rapidly and in that case when there was the slightest danger not permitted the herd to go from the protection of the main force – it was however necessary here to give the herd a wide range, there being no grass in the immediate vicinity of the Camp of the Company, and no hay for the horses to eat while standing corralled during the night. My Company here has always been considered an unusually safe herd to give a loose range as from long practice and habit, it was very easily handled and invariably when stampeded would run direct to the stables or picket line. This has occurred frequently in a temporary Camp in the open field.

QQuest. *How were the horses ridden by your herd guard, equipped?*

AAns. *They were equipped with saddle blankets, curcingles and watering bits. The herders being provided with their lariats in order that they might give their horses an opportunity to graze, when their instructions permitted them to be dismounted. The herders in no instance to permit their horses to be beyond the length of a lariat from them and to be in readiness to mount in an instant, ready for any emergency.*

QQuest. *Give your reasons why no saddles were allowed.*

AAns. *They were not deemed necessary, in fact I have found blankets preferable, as with saddles in my experience, more horses have been rendered unserviceable from sore backs, by men on herd guard than all other duties combined. The men are originally taught riding in accordance with the tactics, with the saddle blankets and snaffle bit and in most instances I have found men in my Company to be better riders without, than with, the saddles as liable to injure themselves in a short run, the saddle of course being necessary when the man is to be mounted for any length of time, as for a march. The men as a rule are very cruel to their horses with a curb bit and a snaffle, or watering bit, I have deemed sufficient for herding purposes with the advantage that the horse can graze freely, when an opportunity offers, with a snaffle bit, which cannot be done with a curb. My superiors are in a position to judge whether my horses under my mode of treatment have been relatively in a better or worse Condition than the horses of other Companies.*

QQuest. *What time of day, September 4th, 1879, did one Mr Sullivan visit you?*

AAns. *I left my quarters at 3.30 o'clock P.M. by appointment, to issue rations, went to the Commissary Store room, commenced the issue – had been there probably ten to fifteen minutes when Mr Sullivan, a citizen from Cañada Alamosa, twenty miles below this place came in.*

QQuest. *What reports, with reference to the Indians, if any, did he make to you?*

AAns. *After some general Conversation Mr Sullivan mentioned incidentally saying by the way that he had not come here for that purpose but on other business that he had learned early during the night of the third of September, 1879, from citizens from Cuchillo Negro, thirty eight miles from here by way of Cañada Alamosa, that they were on their way to inform me, that Victorio and thirty five to forty of his band had been seen on the day previous (the evening of the 3rd) near the headwaters of the Cuchillo Negro, which at the nearest point is about eighteen miles from this place and about twenty miles above the town or settlement of Cuchillo Negro; that these Citizens of Cuchillo Negro, who were alarmed about their stock, were persuaded by the Citizens of Cañada Alamosa that it was unnecessary for them to come here and inform me; that they or a party from Cañada Alamosa would return with them at once to Cuchillo Negro and make it all right with the Indians and that they need not apprehend the loss of their stock or words to that effect. Mr Sullivan said further that he favored giving me immediate information and would have come with the party during the night to inform me, but the citizens of Canada prevailed and a party of them left at 2 o'clock A.M. on the morning of the 4th for the Cuchillo Negro, repeating that he did not come for the purpose of giving me the information, it being now too late but, being here on other business, thought that he would give me the information for what it was worth, or words to that effect. I replied that I regretted very much that the citizens of Cuchillo Negro had not been permitted to come through and give me the information at once as in that case I could have been on the headwaters of the Cuchillo Negro, where the Indians were reported to have been, with my Company shortly after daylight that morning, as it was I would be nearly twenty four hours behind the Indians.*

QQuest. *Did you credit these reports?*

AAns. *I did to sufficient extent to make immediate arrangements with the view to starting out with the available force at my command when the moon should rise that night which would be about 9 o'clock.*

QQuest. *Had you, prior to between 3 and 4 o'clock P.M. September 4th, 1879, received any information from any of your subordinates, from any citizens or by letter from any source, that Indians had committed depredations or been seen in the country around your present station?*

AAns. *Aside from depredations in the vicinity of San Jose, forty miles from here, reported in a letter from Mr Stackpole, dated August 31st, which I have previously reported as having accompanied Lieutenant Taylor's report, and depredations committed in the vicinity of Tularosa, some time in August and which had immediate attention at my hands, scouts being sent to that vicinity – none.*

QQuest. *Did Private Woods of your company report to you within a few days before your horses were run off, that he had seen distinct signs of Indians, and that the Indians had attacked a sheep herder and killed some of his stock – all in the near vicinity of your station?*

AAns. *Not to my recollection. Had he made such a report I think I should have remembered it. The mail escort always report to me personally and at once on their return to this place and I invariably question them as to what they have seen or heard en route bearing upon the subject of hostile Indians. The mail escorts are instructed to gather such information and to observe closely both going and coming with a view to the discovery of Indian signs should there be any. I think Private Woods gave me some very garbled rumors bearing upon and growing out of the facts referred to in the report of Lieutenant Taylor and the letter of Mr Stackpole.*

QQuest. *Did Private Willis of your Company request permission on the 4th of last September, to visit Paraje and if so, what was your reply?*

AAns. *He did request permission about that time, some days previous I think, and I told him that I would arrange for him to go down with one of the Mail Parties; subsequently, about the time he expected to go, I told him that his trip to Paraje would have to be deferred for the present, as I was liable to start out with a scout on short notice and day and would require him to accompany me as cook for my mess.*

QQuest. *What were your reasons for considering yourself at that time more particularly liable to go on a scout than at other times?*

AAns. *Well – my reasons will be found in my reply to Mr Stackpole's letter, already referred to, a copy of which will be furnished you [will be appended and marked "A"] and in the fact that I anticipated that the raiding Indians, referred to in Lieut. Taylor's report and in Mr Stackpole's letter as having gone to the vicinity of the San Andreas Mountains, Fort Stanton reservation, with stolen horses, would shortly after the usual rest, start out on another raid plundering the settlements on the Rio Grande and to the westward of here, Tulerosa [Old Fort Tularosa], Alamosa Rito Quinada and the settlements on the headwaters of the San Francisco River all at a distance of from forty to one hundred miles from here and, having endeavored to Impress the Citizens in those various localities with the importance of giving prompt information of the presence or approach of raiding parties of Indians I wished to be readiness with my Company or as large a portion thereof as could be safely spared from this place, to start out at a moments notice in pursuit of the raiders, prepared to follow them to their capture and destruction if possible or at least to drive them out of the settlements and prevent depredations.*

QQuest. *What time of day, September 4th 1879, did you take the first special step to enquire into the safety of your herd of Government horses?*

AAns. *The Sergeant of the horse guard instructions were to graze the herd in towards the Camp in time to be at the water by 5 o'clock P.M., when recall of the herd, water call and stable call were sounded and the first Sergeant marched the Company out to meet the herd in the bottom near the water where they always were caught up easily, watered and brought in fed and groomed. Sometimes it would happen that the Non Commissioned Officer of the horse guard would misjudge the time and be a little late. On this occasion the non appearance of the herd caused no immediate uneasiness. I started from my Quarters over to the*

AAns. (cont.d) *stables, shortly after Stable Call, with a view to their selecting the detachment of men and horses to start out that night on a scout to the headwaters of the Cuchillo Negro for the purpose of finding and following the trail of the Indians reported to me by Mr Sullivan. On passing Lieutenant Taylor's Quarters, on my way to stables, the Lieutenant, who had been on sick report since his return from scout on the last day of August, came out and referring to the report brought in by Mr Sullivan, says "I suppose you want to get off a scout," I replied "Yes, I am on my way now to stables for the purpose of making the detail selecting the men and horses," some of the latter being in very poor condition from a constant service during the last month, the Lieutenant replied "I will go with you." And, referring to my own condition as to health since his return, said, "although far from being well, I think perhaps that I am better able to go out with a scout than you are and if you wish me to go out in command of the scout I will report myself for duty and be in readiness to start out early in the morning." I said, "No, that will not do, the scout must start out when the moon rises tonight and be at the Cuchillo Negro before daylight tomorrow morning. We will go to the stables and select the detail – we can arrange that matter afterwards." As we approached the corral I discovered that the horses were not in, then it first flashed upon me, perhaps the herd had been jumped – to which thought I gave expression – turned on my heel, advancing in the direction from which the herd should approach followed by Lieut Taylor who responded to my expression, that he did not apprehend anything of that kind, saying, that it was not an unusual thing for the herd to be a little late coming in – the non commissioned officer had perhaps misjudged the time again, or something to that effect. As we advanced toward the watering place I saw the Company in the bottom near the water, where the herd was usually caught up, and the first Sergeant on a high point, a little distance across the valley, looking in the direction from whence the herd should come. He directly came back to the Company, marched it back towards where we were standing and reported to me that he saw a large dust several miles off toward and to the right of a point of a mountain in the direction of Luna Springs, which is the first water in that direction and thirty miles from this place. I was satisfied that the herd was gone and beyond recovery, the only animal remaining being a condemned pack mule, which had been used in the cart for police purposes that day. I told the orderly trumpeter to sound the call for retreat, it being then nearly dark, remarking to the Lieutenant that nothing could be done until the moon came up as I could not see tracks in the dark. The Lieutenant volunteered, if I could give him the pack mule, to go over and examine the ground with a view to discovering the bodies of the guard and any indication of what might have transpired. I ordered a detail of a Sergeant and six men to accompany the Lieutenant. He reported on his return, about ten o'clock I think after the moon arose, a discovery of two dead bodies of the guard. Owing to the darkness he was unable to discover the others, for which purposes he returned in the morning with another detail, discovering the bodies of the other three. I deemed the most important step to be taken for the recovery of the herd would be to get immediate information to District Headquarters by telegraph, with a view to getting mounted troops on the trail of the Indians feeling certain that the Indians would make direct for Mexico with the captured herd, and that troops from Bayard, if promptly ordered would have some chance of intercepting them. I at once dispatched a courier on the condemned pack mule referred to, with a telegram to District Headquarters with the report of my loss and the direction the herd had been taken and the probable attempt to escape from the country into Mexico. I deemed it utterly useless to attempt the pursuit dismounted without a single pack mule for transportation of rations or blankets, of a band of Indians mounted on the horses I had lost and through a country utterly destitute of means of subsistence.*

QQuest. *Did you, yourself, or any other Commissioned Officer of your command, while at Ojo Caliente, occasionally visit the Company horses while they were on herd, to see that the herd guard maintained a strict lookout?*

AAns. *I did not go into the herd or the immediate vicinity thereof, but watched the herd closely with my field glass and endeavored, to the best of my ability, to see that the herd duty was well performed. I have found that to be the better way to insure a strict compliance with my instructions than visiting the herd mounted and openly, as in the latter case the vidette was seen to perform his duty in so far as notifying the herd guard of the approach of an officer, that they might, on his arrival at the herd, be engaged in the scrupulous performance of their duty in carrying out the explicit instructions so frequently given them and the importance of which I had so constantly endeavored to impress upon them and more particularly within a few weeks of the time of the capture. Furthermore, I had been since coming to this place with my Company, early in May last, most of the time the only officer present for duty with the Company, overwhelmed with clerical duties and in a condition of health which, had I been a subordinate at a Post or other command would have compelled me to have been a great portion of the time on sick report. I was sick when I received my orders in April last, at Fort Union, to march my Company to this place and the only officer on duty with the Company, my Second Lieutenant being on detached service, my First Lieutenant sick at the Post. Although on sick report myself, I remained on duty with my Company and without assistance made all possible haste to pack up property to be left behind at the Post and to march with my Company, under the orders I had received. I was put on duty by the Surgeon at my own request, to enable me to march with the Company, rather than to have a stranger to the Company detached for that purpose. My First Lieutenant joined me here a convalescent, on the 11th of June last and, much of the time since that, has not been in condition for very active or hard service. He was absent for nearly a month previous to the capture of the Company herd, in command of a scout, from which he returned sick, unable to march with the detachment, being brought in an Army wagon which had been sent out with rations and forage for his detachment. In a letter, or endorsement, of which I did not retain a copy, from want of clerical assistance, written about the last of August, to District Headquarters I think on an endorsement of Lieutenant Taylor's report forwarded on the 3rd of September, I made reference to the great need I had of another officer for duty with my command, my second lieutenant still being absent on detached service and I feeling no confidence whatever in the efficiency of any detached scout or escort that I might send out under command of a non commissioned officer or in any reports or information gained in that manner, except the same would otherwise corroborated. My Company Morning Report shows for duty, during the latter part of August and up to the 4th of September, Privates present for duty ranging from twelve to twenty five, from which it will be seen that it was impossible to keep up a guard in camp, which has been necessary, and at the same time keep up a large herd guard, in addition of the performance of necessary daily and police duties cutting and hauling of wood for the command &c.*

QQuest. *Could you readily command a view of the herd, on its ordinary grazing ground from any point in the immediate vicinity of your quarters?*

AAns. *From the landing of the staircase in the rear of my Quarters, communicating with the upper part of my house an open unobstructed view of the main valley, in some places, nearly a mile wide, can be had, for nearly if not quite four miles by the aid of a good field glass, which I have. From a high point in the immediate vicinity of my Quarters an equally extended view is had of the principal side Canon and other smaller canons opening into the main valley.*

QQuest. *In case armed Indians in force attempted to run off a herd of horses guarded by five men, and had been successful, and these five men thus compelled to fight, would you consider their chances of success, with only pistols to defend themselves with, to be as good as if they had been armed with carbines?*

AAns. *Better, in my opinion – the carbines under those circumstances would be worse than a useless incumbrance. In a running hand to hand fight of that character the pistol would be much the better arm of the two. The carbine, as I understand and have been instructed, being only serviceable as intended for use when troopers are dismounted, in accordance with the tactics, to fight on foot. My Company being well instructed in the use of the pistol and having fired away thousands of rounds of ball cartridges, not to mention blank cartridges, when mounted on a skirmish line, when charging as foragers, or charging in line and by platoons, and under none of these circumstances is the carbine used, except perhaps when firing at long range at a halt on the skirmish line.*

The examination of Captain Hooker here closed, and all the information possible to elicit has now I think been obtained

The <u>facts of the case</u> are as follows:
The herd of "E" Co. 9th Cavalry was, on the morning of the 4th of September 1879, sent out to graze under a guard of five enlisted men. These men were armed with pistols only and their horses were without saddles. The men were ordered to graze the herd in the main valley and not to take the herd so far into any side canons as to make it liable to be cut off (see page [left blank]*) thus leaving the most important portion of the guard's duty, in a measure, dependent upon the discretion and intelligence of the non-commissioned officer in charge. The herd returned a little before noon and was again sent out, and subsequently captured by he Indians but according to all indications, not earlier than four o'clock P.M. The soldiers guarding the herd were all killed. At no time during the summer had a commissioned officer visited the herd.*

Between 3 and 4 o'clock P.M. Captain Hooker received information that Indians were, or had recently been on the Cuchillo Negro. At 5 o'clock P.M. the herd failed to make its appearance. After sundown (certainly not earlier than 6 o'clock P.M.) the first actual step was taken to ascertain what had become of the herd and its herders. The herd was captured about one and a half miles from the Post.

I have visited the ground where the horses were captured and had the places pointed out to me where the dead bodies of the herd guard were found. The ground where the capture was made is so intersected by very deep and narrow depressions, with corresponding intervening ridges, as to form a perfect network and make it utterly impossible for the most vigilant sentry to discover the approach of Indians until the latter were in striking distance. Nobody but an imbecile would ever have brought a herd into such a place, in an Indian Country, and the inference is but natural that if negro soldiers are so careless and worthless as described by Captain Hooker their discretion should not have been depended upon. This much I will say of the dead guard that, having brought the herd to where it was captured, no amount of vigilance, bravery and presence of mind could have saved either them or the herd. The vidette may have been at his post but practically he could see no further than down into the depressions nearest him, the next ridge closed his view and the cuts and depressions entirely out of the vidette's vision communicated with those that were nearest him. It must be remembered that with a moving herd the vidette also is moving. He may have just reached, or been about to reach, the point from which he, with the greatest advantage, could watch over the safety of the herd when the Indians made the attack. The Indians had been concealed in the hills, evidently knowing that it was the custom of the herd guard going from the Post to keep in the main valley, but on their return not always to follow the same safe road. That such was the case is indicated by what took place during the afternoon of Corporal Quarle's reduction, as related by the Captain, (See page [left blank]*) When the herd entered the hills the Indians under absolutely perfect cover swung their flanks around it until the herd was completely enveloped. Escape for either men or horses became simply impossible. Armed with Carbines one* *or more of the men might possibly, from behind a shelter, have kept the Indians off and thus been saved but it is extremely doubtful. The bodies of two of the men were found outside of the ground upon which the horses had been. It is fair to suppose that these bodies were those of the vidette and the other mounted man under whose duty it was to ride around the herd for the purpose of keeping it together. These men had evidently tried to make their escape towards the main valley but were hemmed in and killed.*

White soldiers would under similar circumstances have met with the same fate, and would probably have committed the same error, if left to themselves. Men who have been accustomed to herd for a number of years, without ever meeting with an accident, forget danger, and especially so when a days duty is nearly completed and the herd facing homeward, is gradually moving towards stables and I therefore give it as my opinion that herd guard, in an Indian Country, if the number of animals to be guarded warrants is, is of a sufficient importance to be under the personal supervision of a commissioned officer. It is to be regretted if in this special case neither the number of officers present nor their physical condition permitted such a supervision.

With reference to herding without saddles and carbines I will only say that it is contrary to my personal experience.

Trusting that I have succeeded to give the fullest details possible pertaining to the matter under investigation so as to enable the District Commander without further information to form a correct judgement.

I am Sir Very respectfully
Your obedient servant
(Signed) Charles Steelhammer
Capt. 15th Infy U.S.A.[20]

20 Captain Charles Steelhammer, Ojo Caliente, to AAAG Dist. of New Mexico, Santa Fe, 11 December, 1879, in Letters Received by Headquarters District of New Mexico September 1865-August 1890, RG 393, Microfilm M1088 Roll 38, File 1664-2491, July–Sept. 1879.

Document 9.2

Anonymous Letter from Company E, Ninth Cavalry Denouncing Captain A.E. Hooker, 3[21] September, 1879

Ojo Caliente N.M.
Sept. 3 1879

To the Department Commander of the Mo. Dear Sir, It is with the complaint of your respective Soldiers of Company E, 9th Cavalry. Sir we have call the attention of the Department Commander concerning the great assassinations which occurred near Ojo Caliente NM on or about September 3rd 1879. Sir those soldiers that were slaughtered were Sergeant S. Chapman, Privates J.E. Hoke, S. Graddon, W. Humphrey and Abraham Percival in which Capt Hooker's to blame for the murder of these men mentioned in those few lines, please General search their complaints of which I have made several complaints to the District Commander before this murder was committed, and the men were only armed with Revolvers, 9 or 12 rounds of Pistol Cartridges and the expressions which the Captain made when the men were formed, that he wished that all the negroes were killed, and says that he will try to get as many of the worthless Sons of Bitches killed as he can. Now Dear General if this complaint of these your obedient Soldiers don't take any effect, then General, we don't know who to look for mercy and help, we do believe that you area just officer and will give enlisted men justice. We have sent in several reports to various Headquarters and have not received any satisfaction from either of those mentioned. The Captain has been cautioned several times about the Indians was going to attack our or his herd but he would not pay any attention to the reports which came into him. General we are willing to obey all Military rules and regulations but we are not in discipline enough and our Company Commander is so unofficer like that we cannot obey as good soldiers should obey, and General if you think that these reports are not true why then call on your respective Company "E" which are given up by all of the citizens of New Mexico to be the most disciplined company on the frontier and we shall dear General will seek in yourself and you will find that there are some soldiers in the field which can turn in a true report against his Commanding Officer as well as against soldiers and if we cannot receive satisfaction why then we will report to every Headquarters in the Army.

Sir I truly hope this will tell the Commanding Officers of several Headquarters what the officers in the Indian Territory are a treating soldiers.

Well General we have sent several reports whether your \headquarters have received think as not.

Please reply soon as received and excuse bad writing

From your most truly and obedient Soldiers unrevealed and oblig yours truly Company "E" 9th Cavalry.[22]

21 The date should read 4 September, 1879, but the writer is clearly uncertain as to the exact date of the letter.

22 Anonymous letter from Company E, Ninth Cavalry, in Letters Received, Dept. of Missouri 1868-98, RG 393, Entry A1-1 2601, Box 84.

Document 9.3

Colonel Hatch's Recommendation 13 September, 1880

Headquarters District of New Mexico
Santa Fe, New Mexico, Sept 13", 1880

To the
Assistant Adjutant General
Department of the Missouri
Fort Leavenworth Kans

Sir:
The report of Captain Charles Steelhammer, 15th Infantry, in case of Captain A.E. Hooker was submitted during my absence to Captain Pollock, Acting Assistant Inspector General of the District, who decides Captain Hooker should be brought to trial by Court Martial. Even the occasional and under the greatest provocation of such language as is attributed to Capt. Hooker, in the statement shown by Captain Steelhammer's report and admitted by Captain Hooker, is most censurable, and cannot be too decidedly disapproved, and warrants a trial by Court Martial.

Concerning the loss of his Company horses, my opinion is that Captain Hooker is wholly responsible, which can be decided by a Board of Survey.

The suggestion contained in Captain Steelhammer's report of a station at a post, commanded by a senior, who is a Field Officer, has in effect been answered – Captain Hooker with his Company is assigned to Fort Wingate.

In view of the fact that a large number of the witnesses who would be necessary for the trial, have been discharged, and at this time who are Citizens having gone to distant places, and involving great expense if they could be obtained such trial is not recommended, mainly on the grounds of expense and uncertainty of establishing the Charges before a Court Martial, but steps should be taken to impress upon Captain Hooker in decisive terms the absolute necessity for a discontinuance of such conduct in future.

In extenuation of Captain Hooker's harsh language to enlisted men of his Company, men are always ready to re-enlist with him, and his Company is usually in fine condition, which is the most pertinent answer to the allegation of harsh treatment, and should decide the question in a great manner. In consideration of the above, I recommend no further action.

Very respectfully
Your obedient servant
(Signed) Hatch.[23]

General Pope added the following endorsement

For the reasons as set forth within, the Department Commander will not take further steps to bring Captain Hooker to trial for the offences in question; but that he cannot fail to express his entire disapproval of his conduct, as set forth in the report of Captain Steelhammer: and Captain Hooker is admonished that no consideration of trouble or expense will save him from trial if his conduct is repeated.[24]

23 Hatch to AAG, Dept. of the Missouri, Fort Leavenworth, 13 September, 1880 in Letters Sent by the 9th Military Department, the Department of New Mexico, and the District of New Mexico 1849-1890 M1072 (Record Group 393) Roll 6, Jan 1880-August 1881, Letter No.483, pp.312-313.

24 General Pope's endorsement added to Hatch to AAG, Dept. of the Missouri, 13 September, 1880 in Letters Received by Headquarters District of New Mexico September 1865-August 1890 (Pamphlet Describing M1088 from Record Group 393) Roll 41, July-Dec 1880.

Document 10

Hooker's Account of Events at Ojo Caliente for September 1879

A) To the AAAG, Dist of New Mexico, 5th September 1879

The indians jumped my herd yesterday afternoon while grazing about one mile from camp. Killed all of the herd guard and got off with all of my horses and mules except ten (10) horses and two (2) mules on scout which will not be in for some days am left without a hoof except one condemned pack mule the trail leads in the direction of Suera [Luera?] Springs the Indians will probably divide and make for Mexico. The loss is the result of gross carelessness and neglect on the part of the guard which they have paid with the forfeit of their lives the Indians are supposed to be forty (40) in number including Victorio Nana Sanchez Etc. Also from the Mescalero's Agency my company is absolutely afoot and without means of transportation the indians are probably a hundred miles from here & I am powerless to do any thing except ask for an investigation and a court of inquiry.[25]

B) In his Post Return for September 1879

The command has been employed during the month guarding the public property and supplies at Ojo Caliente N.M and furnishing details for scouts, and escort, and courier, and mail service in addition to herding public animals and performing the usual routine of camp and garrison duties, instructing recruits, Etc.

The herd of Company "E" 9th Cavalry jumped by indians (Victorio's Band) on the 4th, the entire guard surprised and killed, 46 Company horses (for which Capt. A.E. Hooker 9th Cavalry is accountable) 18 mules (for which the Depot Quartermaster at Fort Union N.M. is accountable,) and 4 Officers horses (One the property of Capt. A.E. Hooker, 9th Cavalry, two that of 1st Lt. F.B. Taylor 9th Cavalry and One that of A.A.Surgeon C.A. Sewall U.S.A.) were captured and run off by the indians, and were subsequently mounted and used by them in their continued hostile demonstrations.

On the morning of Sept. 28. the Mail Escort of 5 men of the Company, 1st Sergeant Henry Robinson commanding, was attacked, in the Canon about two (2) miles below Ojo Caliente, by a large party (estimated from 50 to 70,) of hostile (Victorio's band) many of them mounted on cavalry horses, a brisk engagement ensued. The Mail Party (in a 4 mule escort wagon,) rapidly retreating on the camp of the company narrowly escaping capture and death, an attempt to cut off the retreat being frustrated by the most opportune intervention of Sergeant James Williams with a small hunting party of the company, which arrived and opened fire, just in time, at the point in the canon where the hostiles attempted to cut off the retreat of the Mail Party, which together with the hunting party were pursued almost into the camp of the company. The company were at once deployed upon the surrounding hills and remained under arms the remainder of the day, and most of the time to the end of the month, as it was evidently the intention of the hostiles, had they not been discovered in time, to surprise and capture the remaining herd of horses, and mules, and should they have succeeded in drawing the main force of the company out into the mountains to take plunder and destroy the buildings and property, at Ojo Caliente, including the reserve arms, ammunition, and supplies pertaining to the company.

25 Hooker to AAAG, 5 September, 1879 in RG393, Pt3, Entry 439, pp.211-213.

Under cover of night on the 28th a mail party of 15 mounted men, Sergt. Wm. Howard commanding, was sent in to Paraje, (60 miles distance) with the mail and dispatches, running upon a small party of indians in the canon, (above Cañada Alamosa,) but getting through safely. On the return trip, on the night of the 30th, Sergt. Howard's party was attacked by a party of about 20 mounted hostiles near (and about two miles below the town of) Cañada Alamosa, and, after a brisk running fight, succeeded in getting away from the Indians, with the mail, and returned to Paraje, and there awaited assistance from the Company.[26]

26 Returns From U.S. Military Posts 1800-1916 Ojo Caliente, N.M. May 1879-March 1882, Microfilm 617 Roll 877– from Record Groups 393.

Document 11

Morrow's Original Telegram on McEvers' Ranch

Date: Ft Bayard 13
Rec'd: SF 13
To: Loud AAAG

Just Rec'd the following from McEver near Hillsboro. We had a five hours fight here yesterday with all of one hundred Indians we have ten killed and several wounded all our stock is gone have sent every soldier available out with Dawson and Day. L Co has not started yet I hear Beyer and Hugo & Lt Wright are all in the vicinity and should be able shortly to overtake Victorio.
Morrow
Maj. Comd[27]

Compare with the following:

"TELEGRAM."
HEADQUARTERS DISTRICT OF NEW MEXICO,
ACTING ASSISTANT ADJUTANT GENERAL'S OFFICE,

SANTA FE, NEW MEXICO,
September 17th 1879

Major Arnold
Fort Grant, Arizona

Commanding Officer Fort Bayard reports information of a five hours fight with Indians by citizens at McEvers' Ranch near Hillsboro with a loss of ten killed and several wounded. One hundred Indians reported in the fight. Major Morrow has sent out every available soldier in pursuit.
In absence of Col. Hatch
(Signed) Loud
A.A.A. General[28]

27 Morrow to Loud AAAG SF 13 September, 1879, RG 393, Pt 3, Entry 439, p.341.
28 Hatch to Arnold, 17 September, 1879 in RG 393, Part One, Entry 235, p.12.

Document 12.1

Report on Las Animas Canyon Ambush 18 September, 1879

Date: Ft Bayard 23
Rec'd: SF 23
To: Loud SF

Dawson Wright & Day struck Victorio's trail at Head of the Tierra Blanca Canon two days old on the 16th followed it to head of Las Animas River where on the 18th they ran upon the Indians who held a strong position troops were virtually caught in a trap Capt Beyer with his Co and Hugo's came up & took part in fight after fighting all day the troops were compelled to withdraw under cover of darkness with a loss of five men killed & one wounded & 32 horses killed & six wounded. I have sent Blocksoms & Gatewood with their Apache Scouts & Emmet with his Navajos to the scene of the action and follow immediately with all available men of the post my cavy will be principally dismounted Wright with 22 men of C Co is at Hillsboro & will join me. I have ordered Dimmick to meet me at McEvers' Ranch. Purington is here and his Co goes with me. Victorio is said to to [the two 'to's' are in original telegram] *have about 140 men, two Navajo Indians & one citizen were killed in the fight. I will make my base of operations at McEvers' Ranch.*
Morrow
Maj Comd[29]

Compare with the following two reports:

Dawson Wright & Day struck Victorio's trail at Head of the Tierra Blanca Canon two days old on the sixteenth followed it to head of Las Animas River where on the eighteenth they ran upon the Indians who held a strong position. Troops were virtually caught in a trap Capt Hooker with his company and Hugo's came up and took part in fight. After fighting all day, the troops were compelled to withdraw under cover of darkness with a loss of five men killed & one wounded and thirty two horses killed & six wounded. I have sent Blocksoms & Gatewood with their Apache Scouts and Emmet with his Navajos to the scene of the action and follow immediately myself with all the available men of the post. My Cavalry will be principally dismounted. Wright with 22 men of "C" company is at Hillsboro and will join me. I have ordered Dimmick to meet me at McEvers' Ranch. Purington is here and his company goes with me. Victoria is said to have about 140 men. Two Navajo Indians & one citizen were killed in the fight. I will make my base of operations at McEvers' Ranch.
(Signed) Morrow Comd[30]

29 Morrow to Loud AAAG 23 September, 1879, RG 393, Pt 3, Entry 439, pp.344-347; Loud to Hatch, 23 September, 1879, Telegrams Sent Dist. of New Mexico, Vol.2, Jan.–Dec. 1879, RG393, Part 3, Entry 431, p.241; See also McDowell to Commanding General, Mil. Divn. Of the Missouri, 25 September, 1879, 'Victorio Campaign, Feb. 1879-Nov. 1880' in "Special Files" Created by the Military Division of the Missouri. Records of US Army Continental Commands, 1821-1920 Record Group 393 M1495 Microfilm Roll 14.

30 Loud AAA General to AA General Fort Leavenworth 23 September, 1879 in Papers relating to military operations against Chief Victorio's band of Mescalero Apache in southern New Mexico, 1879-81 in Letters Rec'd by the Office of the Adjutant General (Main series). 1871-80, M666. Roll 526; Pope to AAG Mil. Division of the Missouri, 24 September, 1879, 'Victorio Campaign, Feb. 1879-Nov. 1880'

Following telegram received yesterday from Commdg officer Dept Arizona. Major Morrow reports following just received from Col. Hatch ?????? Sept Twenty Third Seventy Nine. Lieuts Dawson Wright and Day struck Victoria trail at head of Serco Blancia Canon two days old on sixteenth followed it to hd of Las animas River where on the eighteenth they ran upon the Indians who held a strong position. Capt Beyer with his company and Hugo came up & took part in fight. After fighting all day the troops were compelled to withdraw under cover of Darkness with a loss of five men & one wounded & thirty two horses killed & six wounded. Morrow has sent Lieut Blocksom & Gatewood Sixth Cavalry with their Apache Scouts & Emmet with Navajoes which arrived at Bayard yesterday to the scene of action & will follow immediately with all available men of Post. Company L Ninth Cavalry & Lt Wright with twenty two men Company C will join tomorrow. Victoria is said to have about one hundred & forty Indians. Two Navajoes & One Citizen were also killed in fight. Morrow will make base operations at McEvers' Ranche.[31]

in "Special Files" Created by the Military Division of the Missouri. Records of US Army Continental Commands, 1821-1920 Record Group 393 M1495 Microfilm Roll 14.

31 McDowell to Adjutant General, Washington D.C. 25 September, 1879 & Pope to Townsend AG Wash. D.C. 18 September, 1879 in Papers relating to military operations against Chief Victorio's band of Mescalero Apache in southern New Mexico, 1879-81 in Letters Rec'd by the Office of the Adjutant General (Main series). 1871-80, M666. Roll 526.

Document 12.2i

Extract from Lewis Kennon's Report on Las Animas Canyon Fight

On September 5, 1879, Companies C and G, Ninth Cavalry, under command of Capt. C.D. Beyer, left Fort Bayard, New Mexico, on a scout against the Apache Indians. Acting Assist. Surg. Lewis Kennon gives the following account of the expedition: "We marched in a southeastern direction until the morning of the 18th, when we came up to Captain Dawson, Ninth Cavalry, with Companies A and B engaged and nearly surrounded by Indians, near the head of the Rio de los Animas. One wounded man, a private, was gallantly brought away by a young officer of the Ninth Cavalry, Lieut. M.W. Day, in the face of a steady fire of 50 rifles. During the retreat in the darkness for some sixteen miles, the wounded were carried astride of pack mules, each one led by a soldier. It was impossible to adopt any other method less painful. It was out of the question to improvise any form of travois, and carrying a man in a blanket at the rate of speed we found necessary was excluded from consideration." The casualties in this engagement consisted of 3 killed and 2 wounded: one of the latter died two days after the injury.[32]

32 Report of Acting Assist. Surgeon Lewis Kennon, in Annual Reports of the War Department 1880: Microcopy M997 Roll 35 1880 Vol. I, p.519.

Document 12.2ii

Lewis Kennon's Letter to the Surgeon General to the Army, 22 September, 1879

Fort Bayard New Mexico
September, 22d 1879

Brigadier General Barnes
Surgeon General USA
General

I have the honour to report my arrival at my post this day on my return from a scout against the Apache indians.

I left this Post on 5th Septr with companies C and G 9th Cav. Captain Beyer commanding scouting in a south easterly direction until the 18th.

On that day being near the head of the Rio de los Animas we saw the indians.

They were in front of and had nearly surrounded Capt Dawson 9th Cav with Companies A and B of that regiment and a few Navajoes.

We remained in front of them all day endeavouring to extricate Capt Dawson's command from its position.

Finally night came on and under cover of darkness he retreated to us and we all together left the field – Travelling about fifteen miles to a safe position.

The loss of the Command was Haines Peter, G Comp 9th Cav: killed and left on field – Crump Jeremiah B Comp 9th Cav. Shot in stomach, brought off field but died next day. Freeland Alfred B Comp 9th Cav shot in thigh now under treatment and two Navajo scouts Sam and Barrajo left dead on field.

The medicines and instruments were captured by the indians the pack mules bearing them having been shot.

I have the honour to be
Very Respectfully
Your Obedient Servant
Lewis Kennon
Acting Assistant Surgeon[33]

33 Kennon to Barnes, 22 September, 1879 in Kennon L.W.C., Personal Papers of Medical Officers and Physicians (Medical Officers Files) RG 94, Entry 561.

Document 12.2iii

Asst. Surgeon R.E. Smith?, Fort Bayard, Letter to Surgeon General of the Army, 25 September, 1879

Fort Bayard New Mexico
September 25 1879

Brigadier General Barnes
Surgeon General of Army
Washington DC
Through General Pope Dept of the Missouri.

General
I have the honor in transmitting this list of killed and wounded to say that the unknown character of these wounds results from the men being abandoned on the field by the troops.

One man a private was gallantly brought away by a young Officer of the 9th Cavalry Lieut Day in the face of a steady fire of fifty rifles. The others were left to their fate.

I have the honor to be
Very respectfully
Your Obt. Servant (No signature but probably R.E. Smith)
Asst Surgeon of Army.[34]

34 RG 98 Fort Bayard Interrement Record NMRA-902(8888). Microfilm held in NMSU archives, Las Cruces, New Mexico.

Document 12.3i

An Account of the Las Animas Fight published in *Thirty Four* 31[35] September, 1879[36]

From Hillsboro.

Hillsboro, New Mexico
Sept., 21st 1879

Dear Thirty Four
Capt. Beyer and Lt. Hugo passed through this place [Hillsboro] on the 13th inst, with about forty men. A number of our citizens joined them. On Sunday morning finding that the trail bore toward the Mimbres it was anticipated that a raid toward that section was contemplated by the Indians. The command accordingly took the shortest trail to the Mimbres. No sign of Indians could be found, the command therefore marched into Fort Bayard to provide additional rations and having replenished took up the line of march across the Mimbres Mountains. On Sunday night Lt Wright with 15 men and 4? Navajo scouts passed through town for McEvers' Ranch after forced march from the Aleman on Jornada del Muerto. Having made the march of 80 miles in 23 hours. He reached McEvers' Ranch on morning of the 15th. Here he awaited the arrival of Capt. Dawson and Lt. Day with 23 men. The remainder of Sunday was spent by the scouts in searching for a trail. This was absolutely necessary on account of the various trails leading from the battle ground of the 11th inst. The troops commanded by Capt. Dawson then took up the trail – then five days old. The trail in many places was bloody, bloody rags, dead cattle only skinned were found in great numbers, while in one place evidence of the burial of a dead Indian was found by which lay a lanced horse. On the morning of the 17th about 9 a.m., at the head of the Las Animas, the Indian scouts reported from signs the immediate presence of the Indians. The trail leading up an almost inaccessible hill. The scouts advancing about 100 yards ahead of the troops. The troops dismounted and followed, carbines in hand and when about 150 yards from the summit, a single shot was fired which killed one of the Navajo scouts, then followed a perfect rain of shot, volley after volley poured down from the hills. Capt. Dawson's, Lieut. Wright's and Lt. Day's horses all fell dead at the first volley. Two soldiers were wounded by the same fire. The officers and men then sought such shelter as was afforded by the rocks. The skirmishers in advance returned the fire of the Indians and endeavoured to advance. The Indians perceiving this delivered a deadly fire upon them from every side. Their position was such that for two full hours they held the soldiers in a position, unable to advance or retire without losing their horses. At length the inspiring blast of the bugle was heard in the distance and then the cheers of the citizens accompanying the troops could be heard. It was Capt. Beyer's command of 69 men including soldiers and citizens. He promptly sent Lt Hugo and Emmet the latter the grandson of Robt. Emmet to aid the citizens and about half of his men to flank the Indians, which was done successfully. They charged and captured the Indians camp which was held only for a short time. The Indians poured in shots from all directions, killing Jack Hagan from Georgetown, one soldier and twelve horses. Finding that they could not hold the camp in the face of a tremendous fire from the unseen enemy, the soldiers and citizens fell back. The citizens who participated in the engagement are all loud in the praise of Lt. Emmet's coolness under fire. Returning to Capt. Beyer, the failure of the effort to hold the camp was reported. Capt. Beyer then endeavoured to attract the attention of the enemy and to draw his fire from Capt. Dawson's command. This with the approach of night enabled Capt. Dawson to retire without further loss,

35 This is a mistake made in the original newspaper. See microfilm and copy held in the Lee C. Myers Papers, NMSU Archives, Las Cruces, New Mexico.
36 Copies also held in the Lee C. Myers Papers, NMSU Archives, Las Cruces, New Mexico.

though, under a heavy fire. Lt Day regardless of his own life carrying a wounded soldier on his back to the main command, a distance of 700 yards. The entire command then retreated to a tenable camp some miles down the Las Animas and reached this place on the 19th acknowledging themselves badly whipped. The following were killed: Jack Hagan[Higgins], Citizen private Haines, Co. G 9th Cavalry and two of the Navajo scouts. Wounded: two privates of Co. B 9th Cavalry and two Navajo scouts. Between 40 and 60 U.S. horses and mules killed – the citizens lost all of their horses. About 20 of Hooker's horses were seen in possession of the Indians. During the fight, one of the Navajo scouts advanced so near to the enemy that he was killed by a pistol shot. Joe Yankie, Bill Buts and Malcolm MacGregor and other citizens who participated in the engagement speak in the highest terms of the courage and daring of both officers and soldiers.

Lt. Wright with 25 men is affording protection to our citizens at this place. The rest of the command have gone to Fort Bayard for fresh horses and supplies. All expressed determination to give Victorio his fill of fighting this time.

Yours
'Haut Gout.'

Document 12.3ii

'Victorio's Victory in the Black Range' published in *Thirty Four* 31 September, 1879[37]

Victorio's Victory in the Black Range.

A miner who participated in the fight interviewed by one of our prominent citizens:

Citizen – Joe, I understand you participated in the fight the other day in the Black Range?

Joe: – 'Yes, sir, I did and we got whipped and run plumb to Hillsboro.' 'Tell us something about the fight.' 'Well, when we came up to the battle ground, we found Lt. Wright with his handful of men surrounded by the Indians, unable to advance or retire. Capt. Beyer then divided his men and ordered half to flank the Indians and keep up a hot fire whether they saw and Indian or not and the other half to charge and storm the Indian camp. The boys took the camp, but the bullets flew so thick they, like the boy who caught the yaller jacket," let it go again and was glad to get out of it. Poor Jack Higgins fell and cried out to the boys to take him out or shoot him through the head, but the boys were running for their lives and the poor fellow was left in the hands of the Indians and nobody knows what become of him. After the boys got out the Indians turned their attention to us (we were the flanking party in a deep rocky canon) and the bullets came whizzing so thick that we were compelled to dismount and seek refuge behind rocks – and sir, we had not more than dismounted before the Indians came right up and took our horses. Then we got orders to retreat and we got out of there.'

'How many men were killed in the fight? 'Jack Higgins[,] one soldier and two of the Navajos one?[38] were killed and four were wounded, two soldiers and two of the Navajoes.[39]' 'Four men killed and four wounded and you ran?' 'Well, about 50 of our horses and mules were missing. They got all of our pack mules with our provisions, ammunition, medicines and the surgeon's implements.' 'Where was Capt. Beyers during the fight?' 'He was on top of the hill giving orders.[']' 'Was he in gunshot of the Indians?' [']Well. A gatling gun might have fetched him.' [']So the Capt. Was pretty safe then?' 'You bet he was, he thought his hair was too good to be lost.' 'You retreated to Hillsboro?' 'Yes, sir, and Capt. Byers went clear into Fort Bayard.'

We understand that Capt. Beyers on his arrival at Fort Bayard was put under arrest by Maj. Morrow for cowardice. The Major with all the men he could raise, started immediately for the Indian camp. The Maj. Said he would take Victorio's camp or else not one of them would return. Maj. Morrow is a brave soldier and we may soon expect some startling news from Victorio's camp

37 This account held in the Lee C. Myers Papers, NMSU Archives, Las Cruces, New Mexico.
38 Not sure what this use of 'one' means.
39 Both spellings of the plural of 'Navajo' are used in this article.

Document 12.4

Lt. Emmett's Account from 'Some Personal Recollections of the Indian Tribes of New Mexico and Eastern Arizona

In September of this year, 1879, while I was in Santa Fe on court martial duty, we received a dispatch that the Apaches had stampeded and driven off to the mountains nearly all of the horses of E. Troop of the regiment. This troop, of which I was 2nd Lieut., although since the beginning of the year I had been detached in charge of scouts, was again stationed at Ojo Caliente. Nothing had been heard of Victorio and his band since their escape to Mexico and the herd had been sent out to graze as usual about a mile from the post under a guard of six armed herders. What exactly happened we never knew, except that the Indians had succeeded in slipping up, stampeding the herd and killing all six herders, probably before the latter had a chance to fire a shot. Indians are wonderfully clever at this sort of thing.

Lone Wolf's band of Kiowas, some years before on the Rio Neuces in Texas, had stampeded the herd of D. Troop of the 9th Cav. In full sight of camp and would have succeeded in carrying them all off had it not been for one very fast, intelligent horse belonging to Lieut. Hughes of the troop. Horses, when stampeding will blindly follow a leader, and this horse led them nearly all back to camp; the Indians not being well enough mounted to head them.

This horse carried his master through the Apache campaign in New Mexico and was killed in the fight with the Utes when D. Troop went to the assistance of the 5th Cav. On the White River, Colorado, at the time of the Meeker massacre.

On hearing the news of the stampeding of E. Troops' herd, I immediately returned to Ft. Bayard in the extreme southern part of the territory, a 48 hours ride by coach in those days. I arrived at Ft. Bayard about 11:00 o'clock at night and by dawn I was on my way with Capt. Beyer of my regiment to join his troop at McEver's Ranch, about 60 miles distant, where I expected to find my scouts. We arrived in the evening and found that the Indians had attacked Hillsborough, a small mining settlement, and after killing some people there and in some neighboring Mexican ranches, had gone into the Black Range toward the head of the Rio Animas. Next morning with C Troop and part of G Troop of the regiment, we took their trail. It was easy to follow as they were nearly all mounted. We soon found that B Troop and my scouts were ahead of us. The following morning, as we were marching up the Rio Animas, through a very rough country, we met a citizen riding for his life to meet us. The man, who was very nearly frightened to death, told us that the Indians had attacked the command ahead of us that morning in some rough cliffs a couple of miles up the stream, and that he was the only man left to tell the tale. We galloped on and soon heard dropping shots, which showed us that our friend's account of the affair was not altogether correct, there being somebody, at least, left to shoot. When we got in sight of the place we found that the Indians had led the troops into a trap between high cliffs. The men had been dismounted and had sheltered themselves from the Indians fire but could not attack, as the cliffs were inaccessible, nor retire without exposing themselves to a very galling fire in crossing the open ground in close range of the Indians.

I noticed that a long spur of mountains ran in the rear of the Indians' position, and Capt. Beyer sent Lt. Hugo and myself with about 35 men to endeavor to get above them and drive them out of the cliffs. This we succeeded in doing after a desperately hard climb, with the loss of two men. The Indians retired to some heights above us, from which, with our small force we could not drive them. Owing to the very rough place in which we were, the Indians could slip up close to us on all sides and our position was fast becoming untenable. The mountain side was very rough and covered with a thick oak scrub. It was almost impossible to see an Indian, as they had covered their bodies with garlands of oak leaves.

Having accomplished the release of the troop held in the cliffs, it was decided to withdraw our men. This was not so easy to do without heavy loss, as there was much open ground to cross in descending the mountains after leaving the brush and rocks from which we were then firing. I was fortunate enough with five men of G Troop to hold the Indians in check till the rest of my party got down the hill, and still more fortunate to get down myself with my five men. Why the Indians let us get away I could never quite explain. They probably did not know at once that we had gone and were afraid to show themselves to get a shot at us as we slipped down the steep hill. This momentary hesitation on their part gave us our chance to cross the dangerous open space.

After our retirement from the mountain, it being then nearly night, no further attempt was made to dislodge the Indians from their stronghold. That night they scattered, and the next we heard of them they were 60 miles away.

For our part in this action, my classmate Lieut. M.B. Day, 9th Cav. and myself were given the "Medal of Honor"; he for carrying off a wounded man under fire from the cliffs where B Troop was first attacked, and to me for covering the retreat of our men from the mountain.

In this affair we lost five men killed and several wounded, probably more than the Indians did.

Document 13

Estimate of Apaches with Victorio 22 September, 1879

Fort Leavenworth Kans Sept 22nd 1879

To: Secretary of War
Washington D.C.

Following telegram just received, relative to outbreak of Indians in New Mexico, is repeated for your information.

Santa Fe, N.M. Sept 21, 1879

General Pope, Ft Leavenworth, Kans.
Comdg Officer Bayard reports numbers of Indians out may be as many as seventy five. Victoria had forty three when he left Mescalero Agency. Is reported to have had about forty when he took horses at Ojo Caliente and began hostilities, and rumours state he was joined afterwards by Indians from Mexico. No information of other Indians being out. Troops in pursuit not yet heard from. Lieut Gatewood with Arizona scouts will be in Bayard today Morrow will hold him until he hears of Victoria. No news from Ojo Caliente. Comdg Officer, Dept Arizona was, Sept 6th, telegraphed Hooker's loss and promised cooperation. Comdg Officer, Camp Grant, Arizona was telegraphed about Hillsboro affair. Will keep you informed.
In absence of Col. Hatch
(Sgd) Loud AAAG
(Sgd) John Pope
Bt. Maj. Gen'l Comdg.[40]

40 Pope to Secretary of War 22 September, 1879 in Papers relating to military operations against Chief Victorio's band of Mescalero Apache in southern New Mexico, 1879-81 in Letters Rec'd by the Office of the Adjutant General (Main series). 1871-80, M666. Roll 526.

Document 14

Bayard Roll Call 24 September/October, 1879

Date: Bayard 24
Rec'd: SF 24
To: AAA Genl SF

Cav officers present seven viz Capts Beyer Dawson & Humphreys 1st Lt Burnham & Humphreys Asst Surg Smith 2nd Lt Emmet. Co A 9th Cavy 21 enlisted men & 6 unserviceable horses Co B 9th Cav 28 enlisted men 7 serviceable & 7 unserviceable horses Co C 9th Cav 32 enlisted men 1 serviceable & 10 unserviceable horses. Co G 9th Cay 38 enlisted men 3 serviceable & 6 unserviceable horses Co H 9th Cav 37 enlisted men & 7 unserviceable horses. Co E 15th Infy 31 enlisted men present. Detachment of 5 men Co E 15th Infy at Knights Ranche. 5 men same Co at Burro Springs. 5 men Co B 9th Cav at Hudson Hot Spring. Det of 10 men 9th Cav at Masons Ranche. Detachment of 4 men 9th Cav at Hay Camp of Contractor near Florida Mts & detachment of 12 men started for McEvers' Ranche. Were sent by order of Maj Morrow to Chases Ranche on Las Animas. Maj Morrow having at his supply camp McEvers' Ranche one ???? Officer Lt Wright & 46 enlisted men.

Beyer
Comdg[41]

41 Beyer to AAAG Santa Fe, 24 Sept/Oct, 1879, RG 393, Pt 3, Entry 439, pp.288-290.

Document 15.1

Morrow's Report on pursuit of Victorio up to 26 September, 1879.

Date: Head of Animas River 26
Rec'd: SF 30
To: Loud AAAG

Indians left Rancheria two days ago leaving three back to watch who left yesterday trail struck Palomas river close to Black Range & there followed the wash of the river easterly. Blocksom & Gatewood are on the trail at present at head of Arroyo Saco five miles from here. I join them this AM trail is made by about 150 animals Indians estimate numbers of hostiles at 75 or 100 including a few women & children. I send dismounted men with Lt Humphreys back to the post. I am confident of catching Victorio. I have made delay to bury the four dead found in Victorios Camp who were killed in the fight with Capt Beyer.
Morrow
Maj. Comd[42]

42 Morrow to Loud AAAG 26 September, 1879, RG 393, Pt 3, Entry 439, pp.361-362; See also Hatch to AAG Fort Leavenworth, 30 September, 1879, Telegrams Sent Dist. of New Mexico, Vol.2, Jan.–Dec. 1879, RG393, Part 3, Entry 431, p.259.

Document 15.2

Morrow's Report on his Campaign against Victorio submitted 5 November, 1879

Fort Bayard, New Mexico
November 5th 1879

To the
Actg. Asst. Adjutant General
District of New Mexico
Santa Fe, N.M.

Sir
I have the honor to report operations against the hostile Indians under Chief Victoria by Troops from this and neighboring Posts under my Command. On August 31st 1879 I received a letter from Agent Russell of the Mescalero Indians, enclosing one from ex-Agent Godfrey informing the Commanding Officer of this Post that Victoria's Band of "Warm Springs Apaches" had left that Reservation and were going west and were now supposed to be in the Socorro Mountains, immediately upon receipt of this information, Sept 5th I sent Lieut Wright 9th Cavalry, with Indian scouts and 15 enlisted men, Comp. "B", 9th Cav., to the Socorro? Mts., ordered Captain Beyer with his Company "C", 9th Cav., to the Caballo Mts., and Lieut Hugo with "G" Co, 9th Cav., out the U.S. Road towards Ojo Caliente; On the 11th inst, I heard of the loss of Captain Hooker's Horses and at once dispatched couriers after Capt. Beyer and directed him to take up the trail at once in the vicinity of Luera Springs and push on vigorously, on the 13th I sent Captain Dawson with Lieut Day, with 17 men of "A" and five men of "B" Comp. 9th Cav., and three Navajo Scouts to McEvers' Ranche to take the trail from that point, communicate with Capt. Beyer and report to him, I also communicated with Lieut. Wright at the Aleman and directed him to go at once to McEvers' Ranche and report to Captain Dawson, he reported on the 15th inst. And Captain Dawson took up the trail on the 16th for information respecting his further movements, attention is respectfully invited to his report enclosed herewith, marked "A" and to the Report of Captain Beyer, marked "C", as will be seen by the latter report Capt. Beyer returned to this point on the 22nd Sept., having been unable to dislodge the enemy, (and I will here state that Captain Beyer did the only thing that could have been done under the circumstances. I have since been over the field and am certain that Captain Dawson's Command would have been annihilated but for Captain Beyer's timely arrival.)

At daylight the following morning I moved with all the available strength of the Command, including two Companies of Indian Scouts from Arizona under Lieuts. Blocksom and Gatewood, 6th Cav., numbering 191 Enlisted Men and 6 Officers, (73 of these Men and 36 Indian Scouts were dismounted) and proceeded to the scene of the late hostilities. The 1st night I encamped on the Mimbres near Thompson's Ranche and from there detached Lieut. Blocksom with his and Lieut. Gatewood's Indians and detachments to take the trail via Willow Springs, whilst I with the rest of the Command was to go over the Gaballan [Gavilan?] *trail to McEvers, thence over Dawson's trail so that the two commands would strike the hostile camp at the same hour on either side, I reached the Camp on the 26th about noon and after dismounting the Cavalry & securing horses &c. moved upon the camp so that I would strike it simultaneously on both flanks. The movement was executed satisfactorily, but the enemy was no longer there, having been gone about three days. That evening I received a courier from Lieut. Blocksom with the information that he was on the trail about four miles north of me. It being night, I went into Camp. The next morning I ordered the dismounted Men and those without horses (83) in charge of Lieut Humphrey & took the trail up to the Indian Camp, on which Captain Dawson had been attacked. He described the nature of the country, and I will merely state, that it took me one hour and twenty minutes to ascend to the Indian Camp and under fire it would have been an absolute impossibility for any number of men to have taken the position by storm, as it was as much as my Command could do to take it without having anybody on top to shoot at us: At 3:30 P.M. I camped on the Arroyo Seco on Blocksom's and the hostile trail. The next day about 12 miles from Arroyo Seco N.E. found Lieut. Blocksom's Horses and Pack Mules and learned that he with his Command had moved out on foot about 1 O'Clock in the night to surround an Indian Camp and attack at daylight. They accomplished the feat, but as in the former case the Indians had decamped, leaving however about 20 or 30 Horses behind them. I put the Command in camp here (see Lieut. Blocksom's Report, marked "D".)*

Monday 29th broke Camp at 1:30 P.M. This late start was rendered necessary by having the Scouts out looking up the hostile Camp. I followed trail in the direction of the Cuchillo Negro. After marching over very rough Country a distance of 8 miles, found our Scouts awaiting us with the information that they had found the hostiles and unfortunately for us had been seen by them. Although it was 5 P.M. I ordered an immediate attack, knowing that Victoria would not wait until morning. The Indian Scouts under Blocksom and Gatewood rushed immediately to the assault and got possession of the hostile Camp. The Troops followed under fire from the surrounding hills. The firing was kept up until after ten O'Clock, when I ordered the Command to unsaddle and go into Camp. No one was hurt on our side. In this affair three hostiles were killed and left in their Camp fifteen Horses saddled and packed and a lot of loose stock captured. The next morning at daybreak whilst we were eating our breakfast the vidette on post on a bluff overlooking Camp, was killed and the Indians opened a hot fire into the Camp from that and neighboring Cliffs. The 6th Cavalry Detachment was not attacked, but upon hearing the firing came quickly to our assistance and dislodged the enemy from the bluffs on the left. I charged the hill directly over Camp where the vidette had been killed and drove the enemy off, then joined by Blocksom's Indians followed the retreating hostiles and kept up a running fight until after two O'Clock P.M., the hostiles as soon as driven from one position seeking another in rear. At 3 P.M. I returned to my Camp, ordered the Command to saddle up and marched to the head of the Cuchillo Negro (first water)

The next day, October 1st I took up the trail and after marching three miles, the Indian Scouts captured a squaw and child. She said that she had run away as did all of the squaws during the fight of the night before, and was now trying to find her way back to Victorio. She also stated that he was going to the Mogollon Mts. I went into Camp here and sent the Indian Scouts out to find Victorio's Camp, which I was sure would not be far. He was evidently carrying a number of wounded with him, amongst others his son "Washington". Scouts returned at sundown and reported hostile Camp about four miles in an air line from the Camp, from which we had routed them. At Moonrise started Lieut Blocksom and his Command in front with orders to place himself on the west side of the Camp, and I moved out at 12:15 M. so that we would both strike it at daylight.

We reached our respective positions simultaneously just at break of day. The Indian Camp fires were burning and the scrub Cedar trees in his Camp were festooned with fresh beef. We could also see that the hill was strongly fortified at every possible point. Our scouts on the west side advanced with Cat like stealth and were shortly in possession of the works. The slippery enemy had again eluded us. Had Victorio held his position, nothing but Artillery could have dislodged him, except at a fearful sacrifice of life. He certainly would have Killed half the Command, before we could have taken his position. I returned to my horses and sent the Scouts to follow a trail (October 3rd) remained in Camp balance of the day. Scouts returned reporting trail leading to the Mogollon Mts., via Malpais Creek, this confirmed story of the Squaw. Knew that the trail would have to cross North Star Road either at Diamond Creek or Malpais Creek, though it best to go by Ojo Caliente, distant 15 miles and cut the trail, would save time and get my Horses shod, draw Rations and Ammunition.

October 4th Marched to Ojo Caliente and sent to Bayard for more men to come and relieve those men with me who were worn out and dismounted.

October 5th Left Ojo Caliente and marched to Shaw's Ranche on U.S. road.[43]

October 6th Left Shaw's Ranche at 7 A.M. and marched to Sherman's Cienega on U.S. Road, where I was joined same day by Captain Purington, 9th Cav. With a Command composed of Captain Campbell.

---

43 This looks like U.S. Road but handwriting might possibly mean N.S. road i.e. North Star Road?

Lieut. Glass, & Co. "A", 6th Cav. (25 Men) Lieut. Maney, 15th Infty and 25 San Carlos Indian Scouts, Capt. Beyer, 9th Cav., in all 113.

October 7th Having learned from Purington that there was no trail crossing U.S. road, immediately sent all of the Scouts back to last Camp over the Mountains to take up the trail and send in word where to strike it.

October 8th remained in Camp awaiting Report of Scouts.

October 9th Scouts came back at noon and reported that the trail led to the San Mateo Mts., started at 1 P.M., sent Beyer Dimmick, Doctor Smith, Lieuts. Emmet and Wright back to Post with all of the dismounted Men and worn out horses. Lieut. Blocksom's Command was also ordered back, the term of Service of his Indians having expired. The force thus sent back numbered 110 enlisted men & Indians.

October 10th Marched to Ojo Caliente where my Scouts reported that the trail was running South from Cañada Alamosa.

October 11th Marched through the Canada to the town of that name and camped.

October 12th Followed trail to Chase's Ranche on the Cuchillo Negro.

*October 13th Broke Camp at * A.M. (raining very hard) followed trail South to the Palomas. Found Indian Camp four days old, continued on trail about four miles South and found another Camp on a dry Creek (water in holes)*

October 14th Started Indians out at day break and followed at 11 A.M., with the Command. Marched South East until 5:30 P.M., over fearfully rough trail through drenching rain, lost five Horses and one Mule.

October 15th Followed the trail South through "Placer Diggings". Mr Chase here overtook us and reported Squaw trail to our left about two miles, but I was on main trail and would not leave it. Knowing that they would all come together eventually. He also told me of the burning of McEvers' Ranche, and went into Camp. Sometime after midnight a Citizen rode into Camp and reported Indians at Lloyd's Ranche. At day break sent Indians with Gatewood and Lieut. Glass with detachment 6th Cav. To ascertain truth of Report. Also sent to Bayard for 30 days more Rations.

October 17th Remained in Camp, shoeing animals and awaiting Report of Scouts. Courier came from Cummings reporting that the hostiles had sacked Santa Barbera and Killed a great many people; at 6:30 runners came in from Gatewood confirming somewhat of the above and reporting trail going towards Florida Mountains.

October 18th Left Camp at day break and marched direct to Cummings, where Lieut Gatewood and his Command were awaiting for me. We were all out of Rations, sent a party to hurry up the Supply Train. They found the Train on Mule Springs Road and brought it into Camp at midnight. Couriers arrived from Captain Carroll with letter from that Officer, reporting to me for duty, he being at Ojo Caliente.

As I was quite sure that Victorio would try to enter the Mogollon Mts. By his old trail by the Hatchet Mountains, Mule Springs and the San Francisco River, I sent order to Captain Carroll to move at once down the North Star Road to Diamond Creek, where he would be joined by Lieut Maney and his Indian Scouts. He would there take Victorio's old trail through the Mogollon Mountains towards the San Francisco River, go to Mule Springs, thence ????? on the old trail to the Burro Mountains, when, if Victorio had gone that way, his Column would have struck him about the same time I would by following Victorio's trail.

October 19th Remained in Camp dividing Rations, shoeing Horses, culling out the unserviceable, owing to limited number and poor condition of Pack Mules – could only carry fifteen days Rations, I therefore ordered Lieut. Wright to take the balance to McEver's Ranche and there establish a Supply Camp. Started Lieut. Gatewood and his Indians out on the trail to the Florida Mountains.

October 20th Moved the Command on trail to the Florida Mountains and camped at Beyers Spring.

October 21st Marched South to the Tres Hermanas and overtook my Scouts in Camp.

October 22nd Lieut. Gatewood and his Indians with Lieut Schaeffer 9th cav. and Detachment started at daylight. I followed with Command at 9 A.M., marched S.E. to Palomas Lake about four miles South of the Mexican Border, went into Camp and waited the Report of Lieut Gatewood.

October 23 Dispatched Couriers after Lieut Gatewood to tell him of a smoke I could see in Potrillo Mts. And direct him to investigate it.

October 24th Corporal returned at sundown Gatewood's Scouts out hunting cause of smoke.

October 25th Lieut. Gatewood returned, his Scouts could find no trail or signs of smoke, but I was confident that the smoke indicated Indians and marched the Command to the place, about twenty five miles, and found trail and camp about four days old, also evidence of several wounded. The Indians had used up all of the Water which had been in the tanks and we were forced to make a dry Camp. At daylight of the 26th took up the trail and after marching three miles found another deserted Camp, Tanks also dry. Trail ran S.E. into Old Mexico, followed it steadily until sundown found two small holes of rain water in the prairie, where some few men in advance got a drink.

October 27th Took up the trail again at daylight, followed it steadily until sundown, when our Scouts who were in advance sent word back that there was dust ahead, just entering the Mountains, I halted the Column and rode up and satisfied myself that it was made by mounted Indians. I sent the scouts ahead to reconnoitre the ground and as soon as it was dark enough to hide my dust, followed. I was anxious to get to the Corralitos River, which I knew to be somewhere in the direction in which I was marching and probably not more than five or six miles distant. (I had no guide who Knew the Country). My horses and mules were dropping down every mile, for want of water. Upon approaching the Mountains where I had seen the dust my Scouts came running back with the Report that the Indians were fortified on the hills in front, on either side of the trail, ready to open on me so soon as the Command should have well into the Canon. I immediately turned the head of the column to the left, moved up under cover of Mountains, dismounted and prepared to fight on foot. I did not wish to attack until daylight and sent the Scouts up to locate the Camp and the different positions, but the Mules and Horses cried so loudly and particularly for water that our presence was quickly discovered and the moment our Indians reached the crest of the first hill they were fired upon. I immediately advanced with the Command leaving a sufficient guard for the Horses. We had no trouble in dislodging the enemy from the two hills which they then occupied, as we took them in rear and their Breastworks were made to face the trail which led through the Canon. They leaped over the works, across the Canon trail, and into the works on the opposite hills. We kept up a lively fire and followed at a run until we commenced to ascend the hills upon which they were fortified and in strong force, where we had to take it slowly owing to the difficulty of climbing. When we had reached within about thirty yards of the top and all exposed in the bright light of a full moon, they opened upon us with a rattling volley with slight effect, however as they fired too high, three of the Scouts were hit, one killed and two wounded. We tried persistently to advance, but could not do it. I then tried to flank hill and sent Lieut. Gatewood around to the right to attack and the moment he opened fire I was to advance. He succeeded most gallantly in getting up within ten feet of the Breastworks and held his ground there until he got out of ammunition, the enemy in the meantime rolling rocks down upon him during his siege. I tried again and again to take the works in my front, but could not succeed, opposed as much by natural obstacles as by the enemy, as I was afraid of waisting[44] all of my ammunition in futile efforts, I determined to withdraw to the hills from which we had just driven the enemy and wait until after daylight. I accordingly at 10 O'Clock A.M.,[45] directed the retirement. Upon returning to my Horses I found them in such a condition, that unless they had water very soon, I would have to take my whole Command back on foot, they having been three days and nights without any. The men also suffering and I determined to take the Command to the River, which I knew to be near and[46] come back on foot at daylight to settle the business. I accordingly collected the Command and moved out unmolested toward the River, which I reached at 5 A.M., it being twelve miles instead of three or four as I had supposed. I unsaddled and put the Command into camp, where in a few minutes all but the guard, were asleep completely worn out.

I had intended to move back at night and strike again at daybreak, but upon an inspection of the Command found that I could not if without serious loss and no corresponding gain, as my stock was broken

44 As spelled in original document.
45 I suspect that the Major may mean P.M.
46 As phrased in original document.

down and there was not enough ammunition left to last three hours and I knew it would take a whole days hard fighting to dislodge him from his present position and then we would have to repeat the operation indefinitely suffering loss all the time, whilst we were inflicting none. I had accomplished my object so far as the means at my disposal would permit, had punished Victorio severely and had driven him from the Country which he declared he would never leave, I therefore remained in Camp that day to rest and on the 29th moved over to the Corralitos River and encamped.

October 30th Marched to Palomas Lake and camped.

October 31st Sent Captain Campbell, 6th Cav. And Lieut Gatewood with their Commands to Cummings and went with the rest of the Command to Fort Bayard via Hot Springs, arriving on the 2nd instant. The rest of the Command arrived on the day following. My Command during the last affair consisted of 81 enlisted Men and 18 Indian Scouts. About one half the men were left with the Horses and in possession of the hills from which we had driven the enemy and which it was necessary to hold in order to protect the Horses. Only about forty men were or could have been engaged and we were outnumbered three to one by the enemy. The Officers and the Men all behaved gallantly throughout the entire campaign. I would have to mention the names of some enlisted men of the 9th cavalry, who behaved exceptionally well during the affair of the 29th of September, other men doubtless behaved as well, but these happened to come under my immediate observation.

Sergt. Thomas F. Fredericks	*Co "H", 9th Cav.*
Sergt. David Badie	*Co "B", 9th Cav.*
Corporal Charles A. Parker	*Co "G", 9th Cav.*
Sergt. Nathaniel Howard	*Co "L", 9th Cav.*
Trumpeter Louis T. Green	*Co "H", 9th Cav.*
Pvt. Issac Holbrook	*Co "H", 9th Cav.*
Pvt. Wm. Jones	*Co "L", 9th Cav.*

To Captain Campbell and his Company "A", 6th Cav. I am indebted for gallant and efficient service and to Lieuts. Blocksom and Gatewood, 6th Cav. with their invaluable Indian Scouts is due the entire credit of Victorio's expulsion from the Country, as I Know that without the assistance of Indians the Command would never have been able to have followed Victorio's trail.

Captain Campbell's Report and field notes of the Expedition is enclosed, Marked "E"

Very respectfully
Your obedient Servant
(Signed) A.P. Morrow
Maj. 9th Cav.
Comdg. Post.[47]

47 Morrow to AAAG Dist. Of New Mexico, 5 November, 1879 in Papers relating to military operations against Chief Victorio's band of Mescalero Apache in southern New Mexico, 1879-81 in Letters Rec'd by the Office of the Adjutant General (Main series). 1871-80, M666. Roll 526; RG393, Letters Received by Headquarters District of New Mexico September 1865-August 1890, M 1088, Roll 37 (Oct-Dec 1879); See also Pope to AAG HQ Divn. Of the Missouri, 4 November, 1879, 'Victorio Campaign, Feb. 1879-Nov. 1880' in "Special Files" Created by the Military Division of the Missouri. Records of US Army Continental Commands, 1821-1920 Record Group 393 M1495 Roll 14 & Humphreys to AAAG, Dist. Of New Mexico, 5 January, 1880, 'Victorio Campaign, Feb. 1879-Nov. 1880' in "Special Files" Created by the Military Division of the Missouri. Records of US Army Continental Commands, 1821-1920 Record Group 393 M1495 Roll 14.

Document 15.3

Lt Blocksom's Report on Field Service between 24 September & Early October, 1879

Left Bayard on 24th Sept with about 55 men, 6th Cav, Co's "A" and "C" Indian Scouts, Lt. Gatewood Commanding Co. "A": Struck Victorio's trail on the 27th about 75 miles north east of Bayard in Black range; Sent ?Conner? back by order to Maj. Morrow who had left Bayard the same day I did; he was about 15 miles behind: joined me next day with a force of about 200 men, 9th Cav. Indian Scouts in advance discovered Victorio's Camp on the Evening of the 29th. I, with the detachment of the 6th Ca. being ahead of the rest of the column, was ordered by Maj. Morrow to dismount my men and follow the scouts, who were then about a mile ahead; While dismounting, the scouts Commenced firing and I started in the direction of the firing as rapidly as possible, reaching the scouts in about 20 minutes; they were then about 2 miles from where we had dismounted, had driven the hostiles off but could not tell where they had gone, as it was now quite dark; tried for about half an hour to find their trail but could not do so. Was then joined by Maj. Morrow, with the greater portion of his force who concluded to go back where we had first stopped and camp. He camped about half a mile from me. Ordered me to send scouts out at daylight to hunt up trail which I did. About 7 O'clock the next morning heard heavy firing down at his camp and immediately sent Lt Gatewood with 30 men there and followed as soon I had established a proper guard. The hostiles had killed a picket on a high peak over his camp (in a Canon) and were firing into it. Lieut Gatewood with his detachment was half way up a mountain on the other side of the camp soon reaching the top. I followed the detachment, which was then delivering such a continuous firing that the hostiles could do no more damage on the camp below. Maj. Morrow in the meantime had charged up the other peak with 30 men about 7 or 8 only of whom followed him to the top. He had nearly reached the top when the Indian Scouts with guides Dunn and Borman who were about 3 miles off when the fight began, came along a ridge leading to the peak, poured a heavy volley into the hostiles, drove them off and followed them about three miles, where they took up an almost impregnable position, in a huge rocky natural fortress surrounded on nearly every side by deep canons. Maj. Morrow concluded not to follow them any further until we could reach water, we then having had none for over 24 hours. We packed up and left camp about [Last seven words scored out] *It was impossible to tell how many of the hostiles were killed, as the country was so rough that they could easily hide or carry off their dead before we could reach them. The scouts discovered 4 dead bodies; two bucks, one squaw and one child – the hostiles probably numbered between 40 and 50 – We left Camp about noon, reaching water in about five or six hours – We discovered their camp again some two or three days after Lt Gatewood and myself made a night march upon it with the Scouts, followed by Maj Morrow but the hostiles had fled during the night, leaving their fires burning, meat cooking ???? and we had to go back to camp. I saw no more of the hostiles, as I was ordered in a few days after to return by Maj Morrow, the time of my Indian Scouts being overdue, After the fight, Scouts captured one squaw and child – Scouts recaptured 15 or 20 of Capt. Hookers horses, and captured about 50 head of hostiles horses.*[48]

48 RG 393, Part 1, Entry 240.

Document 15.4

Lt Gatewood's Report on field Service between 8 September & 4 November 1880

(Written 20th December 1879)

Fort Apache A.T.
Dec. 20, 1879.

To the
A.A.A.G. in the Field
Fort Lowell
(Through Postmaster) A.T.

Sir

I have the honor to submit the following report of the field service of Co "A" Indian Scouts since Sept. 8. 79: At that date, the command, consisting of eighteen scouts (two sick, I left behind) and a Cavalry detachment of nineteen men, left this post in obedience to telegraphic orders from the Comd'g Officer in the Field, to watch the New Mexico line south eastward. The Warm Spring renegades were expected to try to come on the San Carlos Reservation. A thorough scout was made of that part of the country as far south as the Gila River, without discovering any signs of hostiles. While encamped on that river, I received an order to report for duty to Maj. A.P. Morrow, 9th Cav, at Fort Bayard N.M. & so reported on the 20th of Sept. Lt. A.P. Blocksom having arrived the next day with his scouts, mine were joined with his, & both ordered across the Mimbres Mountains, to the scene of a fight between Victorio's band & some 9th Cav. Troops under Capt. Beyer, of that Reg't. I served under the immediate command of Lt. Blocksom from that time until about Oct. 8. when he returned to this Department to discharge his scouts. The scouts having ascertained the direction of the trail of Victorio's band after the fight in the Black Range, on the 10th [October] *the whole command under Maj. Morrow, left Ojo Caliente, N.M., in pursuit, and on the 15th arrived at McEver's Ranch which is about 12 miles south of Hillsboro. During the night news came, to the effect that Indians were committing depredations along the Rio Grande, at a town called Santa Barbara & at Lloyd's Ranch. The latter place was said to be twelve miles from McEver's. Early next morning I was sent with my command, Lt. Maney's scouts from Fort Bayard & a detachment from Co. "A" 6th Cav under Lt. J.N. Glass, to the scene of these ?atrocities?, rationed for two days. The march instead of twelve, proved to be thirty, miles and the killing of fourteen men had taken place five days before. I followed the trail southward towards the Goodsight Mountains, to within twenty miles of Old Fort Cummings, & having reported the fact to Maj. Morrow, went to that place to await the arrival of the rest of the troops & to get supplies. I arrived there on the 17th.*

The Good Sight Mountains, about fifteen miles east of Old Fort Cummings, extend almost north and south, and from the point where I left the trail of the hostiles, there is no water southward for about seventy-five miles, except what may accumulate in holes from rains, & these tanks do not last long

The whole command having arrived at Cummings, Lt Glass & myself, with his ????? detachment & scouts, left about sun-set for the Floridas. The country between those mountains & Cummings being flat & the distance about twenty-five miles, the march was made at night, so that the troops might not be seen by any of the hostiles on the lookout. After entering the mountains & taking a few hours sleep, the scouts were deployed through them, & we camped the next day on the south side. No sign of Indians was found. Another day's march brought us into the Tres Hermanas, where the main column arrived on the 20th, having marched from Cummings in two days, The general direction so far was nearly south, & about parallel to that of Victorio. The march from Tres Hermanas on the 21st was south westerly, to Palomas Salt Lake about five miles south of the Chihuahua line. From this place, I was again sent ahead, fifteen miles further on, and lay over a day on the Coralitos River to scout eastward. Still no sign of Indians & I returned to

Polomas Lake, where the main body of troops were yet encamped. On the 25th a move was made to the east into the ?Potrillo? Mountains – an extension of the Goodsight, – and Victorio's trail was found the next day & followed till about 9 P.M. Very little water had been found during these two days. About 7.30 P.M. the next day (27th) after a long march over a sandy country, the Guzman Mountains were reached, & the position of the hostiles discovered. An attack was immediately made, driving them from positions on two ridges. An advance on another was made, a bluff at the top was found which could not be seen at a distance in the darkness. A volley from the top of this last ridge Killed one of my scouts and wounded another. The firing became rapid for about an hour, & then desultory until about 2 A.M., the 28th, the command was withdrawn for the purpose of obtaining water. After climbing thus for several hours through the mountains, many men were exhausted & suffered from thirst. A spring was reached, just before day the 28th where the troops rested a day, & then returned to Fort Bayard, arriving there about the 4th of November. I scouted the country from Fort Bayard here & I found no signs or trails of Indians

I desire particularly to call attention of the Commanding Officer in the Field to the fact, that never but once has a medical officer accompanied my command. This has its effect on men, I believe, having overheard by chance, such remarks as "no doctor as usual." One scout died last May of Pneumonia, from want of proper treatment & another was saved by timely arrival at Ojo Caliente, N.M. where he received medical attention.

Having served under the immediate command of Lt. Blocksom or Maj. Morrow, all the time, except what is mentioned above of detached scouts, I respectfully beg leave to refer to their reports for a more detailed account.

I am, sir,
Very respectfully
Your Obed't serv't
Chas B. Gatewood
2nd Lt 6th Cav
Comdg Co "A" Ind. Scouts[49]

49 RG 393, Part 1, Entry 240.

Document 16

Morrow's Report on Cuchillo Negro Fight 29/30 September, 1879

Date: Ojo Caliente, Oct 1st 1879
Rec'd: Santa Fe Oct 3rd 1879
To: AAAG Santa Fe

Telegram by courier to Paraje and by mail to Socorro.

The following received this morning at 6 AM from Major Morrow.

Chaves Ranche
Rio Cuchillo Negro
September 30 1879

To Captain Hooker
I struck Victorio yesterday at 3.30 PM and fought him until about 10, drove him off, inflicting severe punishment. Found three of his dead on the field this AM. This morning, whilst we were at breakfast, he attacked my camp and we fought him hard until 3.30. He had all the surrounding points fortified. We however dislodged him. There is evidence in his camp of many having been killed and wounded. I was obliged to come to this point for water and to save my animals, which were in a canon, exposed to Victorio's fire from the Mountains.

Our Indian scouts captured a great many horses and mules in all about 60, among them 12 or more of your horses and the mules they captured from Beyer. Victorio is still near the head of the Cuchillo Negro and I will attack him again in the morning. I need more men and particularly more ammunition. I wish you would send as many cartridges as you can spare, by the courier party when they return to-morrow; if you can send 15 or 20 men they will be of service. Victorio is in an almost inaccessible country and it may take several days hard fighting to drive him out.

Lost two men and some horses killed today. I will send here with a dispatch to Col. Purington asking for the Indian Scouts and all the men he can muster to be sent to me at once, also for rations as some of the Companies are nearly out. Dimmick's Company has only two days, can you send us any. Mr Pates a citizen, goes in with couriers. If you can provide him with rations, please do so. Please notify District Head Quarters and tell Loud that Victorio is evidently determined to fight it out on this line and so am I. But I want more men. My command is nearly used up. We will be out of rations on the 2nd, 5th and 7th respectively. Can you help me out until I can get some from Bayard.

Morrow
Maj. Comdg

I will supply Major Morrow's command with one thousand complete rations and two thousand cartridges. I cannot spare any troops at present as the Indians are constantly vibrating between Major Morrows command and mine, ready to jump this place when I leave it.

The last mail escort of five mounted men, which left here on the 28th of September I fear has been captured and I sent Lieut Taylor with twenty dismounted men under cover of night to escort these dispatches and look after the missing detachment. Send me five thousand carbine cartridges cal. Forty five. I send ration returns by mail.

Hooker

Capt. Com'd'g[50]

50 Hooker to AAAG SF 1 October, 1879, RG 393, Pt 3, Entry 439, pp.326-333; Loud to Willcox, 4 October, 1879, Telegrams Sent Dist. of New Mexico, Vol.2, Jan.–Dec. 1879, RG393, Part 3, Entry 431, pp.280-281; See also Arnold to AAG Dept. Arizona, 4 October, 1879, Troops in Southeastern Arizona, Dept. of Arizona, RG393, Part 1, Entry 232, Vol.4, 3 July, 1879–13 Dec., 1879, Letter No.179, pp.114-115; Hatch to Willcox, 7 October, 1879 in Papers relating to military operations against Chief Victorio's band of Mescalero Apache in southern New Mexico, 1879-81 in Letters Rec'd by the Office of the Adjutant General (Main series). 1871-80, M666. Roll 526.

Document 17

Morrow's Request for Mountain Howitzers

Date: Ojo Caliente Oct 5th 1879
Rec'd: Santa Fe Oct 6th 1879
To: Loud AAAG SF

Victorio has left the Miembres and Black Range and taken to the Mogollon Mountains. I am on his trail and will push him hard. I think he will go thro' the Burro Mountains to Mexico, I which event I will follow him. Captain Hooker has reshod my command and furnished it with rations and 2000 rounds carbine ammunition. Yesterday captured a squaw and child. Have all the men I want, but would like to have two or three jackass howitzers. Victorio always selects high points in the mountains for his camps and they are practically inaccessible to the troops and as they are strongly fortified, they can be taken only by storm and consequently great mortality upon the part of the troops and none at all upon the part of the Indians. There are some guns at Fort Union Arsenal adapted to mountain service, that would be of great assistance to me. I hear that the Governor of New Mexico has requested federal assistance he is acting without knowledge of the situation. Volunteers would be of no service. I have troops enough to whip Victorio but as I telegraphed at ?????, it will take two months to do it.
Morrow
Maj. Com'd'g

Forwarded by courier to Socorro at ? pm
Major Morrow left here at 1 PM his main force having left earlier. It is not improbable that the Indians will scatter in his front and consolidate again in this vicinity. Courier will remain at Socorro 24 hours. Lieut Taylor reports by mail, reports Indians in vicinity of Canada and San Jose watching for mail escorts.
Hooker
Capt Com'd'g.[51]

51 Hooker to Loud AAG 5 October, 1879, RG 393, Pt 3, Entry 439, pp.320-324; See also Loud to Hatch, 6 October, 1879, Telegrams Sent Dist. of New Mexico, Vol.2, Jan.–Dec. 1879, RG393, Part 3, Entry 431, pp.288-289.

Document 18.1

McEver's Report on the burning of his Ranch in October 1879

I give the facts in regard to the attack made in this place last Friday, 10th October. Myself and Jacob Arnett started to my cornfield after a load of fodder. We had just gotten up on one side of the field where we had upset a load the day before, and was loading it on the wagon when Mr Luiklas and Mr Campbell came by on their way to Hillsborough. They had just passed us and gotten out of sight over the hill, when I heard about five or six shots fired at them. I jumped from the wagon and while in the air, before I struck the ground, there was a volley about seventy five shots came from the corn shocks to our right and not over thirty steps distant. We had barely about twenty feet to run to get into some sun flowers that stood very thick and tall, and the red devils must have fired fifty shots at us before we could get that distance. The Indians then made a rush for us firing very rapidly over us and around us. They came up to within thirty or forty feet of us, stationed their guards all around us, and kept us there while the main body made for the Ranch, captured the herds, burned and robbed the house, killed the horses in the wagon, captured one horse and one mule, 1400 rounds of Government ammunition and 100 rounds of private ammunition. They kept us corraled from nine o'clock in the morning until nine at night and you can imagine that it was a very long day. We have lost everything that could by burned or destroyed.

Very Respectfully Yours,
H.D. McEvers[52]

52 Letter to the *Grant County Herald* published 18 October, 1879.

Document 18.2

Sarah Gibson's Account of the Attack upon McEvers' Ranch October 1879

Mr McEverett [McEvers] and a hired hand was out in the field with a wagon and horses hauling corn fodder, which was piled in shocks. They felt uneasy still, for they carried their guns with them and set them down by the wagon. Everything looked nice and peaceful, but they were suddenly surprised by about fifteen shots by some more men nearby and several red men jumped from beneath the shocks of fodder from all over the field. The men jumped from the wagon just as the bullets passed over their heads.

When they (the Indians) started shooting at them, they run for shelter in the tall sunflowers, which grew all around them. The women from the house started outside and could see someone from the Gibson ranch and waved. The man, who was wounded before, [10/11 September, 1879] was going to Gibson's and heard the shooting. Also, the children, Bill [Gibson] was not at home, having gone with the team several hours before to Irvins [Irwin's] to go out on the prairie to haul hay. Mrs Gibson sent the man when he got there at top most speed to stop them if possible. The women from Gibson's waived [waved?] for him to come on down there, they thought it better for them to run from danger than face it, so they waived them (McEverett's) to come on down there, which they did. The girl, about 17 years old, tried to ride her pony away which she thought a great deal of, but it was the pony the Indians wanted and they began shooting at her until she had to leave her pony and fly, which she did, never looking back or stopping for water, but just kept ahead until she reached Irvins. Soma [some] of the boys from Gibsons come running in crying "here they come Ma". This excited them all so they began getting the little ones together for a run to the lower ranch where all the men were. John run to the top of the hill and shouted, "here they are". The mother took one of the twins and a box of cartridges. Mollie, the oldest daughter, took the other twin and Polly, the other girl, took a small youngster named Lane. They started on a run when John said, "here they are". Imagine the excitement. The mother started to exchange loads with Polly as Lane was too heavy for her small arms, to run, and on doing so she dropped the box of cartridges in the dirt and had to stop to pick them up. She thought of the quickest way of doing it, as one will in a tight place, by scooping them up dirt and all in Lane's hat. By this time, Mrs. McEverett caught up with them and picked Annie, another one that couldn't run, up across her shoulder and away they went. By the time they was well around the point of the hill, here come Bill and the men with the hay wagon. They were glad of this for the Indians were getting pretty close. While they were all piling in the wagon, one of the men started after a horse, which was tied in the pasture, but the Indians began shooting at him over the heads of the others in the wagon. They wanted the horse. (The man, Coffee, got to Irvins just as the men were getting on the wagon to leave for the hay). They all found shelter in Irvins house which was made of small pickets.

Here they stayed until the next day before anyone ventured out. While there, everything seemed quiet and they didn't think there were any Indians anywhere. So they were all brave enough to get out and look around. Bill was one of them who was always there when any fighting or excitement was going on. They could not see or hear any Indians, so Bill and Mr. Irvins were standing by the wagon with a post between them facing each other and talking it over, when Whiz, Buzz, a bullet hit the post which was sticking up just between them and another one hit the ground between young Irvins' legs. This caused a scatterment for shelter again where they remained until someone come from town. How did they get word? Listen! You remember Mr. McEverett and his hired man run into the sunflowers to hide at the beginning? Neither knew where the other one was all this time. The hired man found his way out during the night and away to town, where he gave the alarm. Mr McEverett ventured out from hiding about nine o'clock at night and went to his home, or where his house was that day, for the Indians had blown the house up with powder that was in the house, first removing the bedding, trunks and clothing. The beds they put in one pile and burned. The clothes they took from the trunks and others and hung them across some poles, which were in the yard used as tying places, and set fire to them.

In one of the trunks was a packet where the girl had put a ten-dollar bill. This they [the Apaches] had not found. From here, Mr McEverett made his way to the Gibson place, but it was deserted. So he went cautiously to the Irvins place, hiding and listening several hours to be sure the occupants were white before he made his appearance and presence known at the house. No doubt he expected to find some or maybe most all of them murdered but no, not one even hurt, except from fright. When he found they were white he hollered and you may be sure there were some proud people there. They all thought sure he was killed. But it was sad to see their home all tore up. But they built again and stayed there.

The Gibsons left right after that raid and went back to Hillsboro and after they left, the same Indians came back and made another raid. They were sure thankful they were not there then.[53]

53 Gibson, S. *'From the Archives: Sarah Gibson's Story' Hillsboro Historical Society, February 2016, Vol. 9, No.1,* p.5-6.

Document 19.1

Initial Report of Attacks on Colorado

Date: Bayard 13
Rec'd: SF 13
To: AAAG SF

Just recd the following Colorado 13 C.O. Bayard The Indians are here in force have killed some more men Signed????? ???? [Name illegible]
Beyer
Comd[54]

54 Beyer to AAAG SF 13 October, 1879, RG 393, Pt 3, Entry 439, p.314.

Document 19.2

Rynerson Expedition Sets Out 14th October 1879

Date: Mesilla Oct 14th
Rec'd: SF
To: Lt Allen

Over ninety men armed and mounted left Mesilla at 12 today for Masons Ranche
Mesilla Op

For Capt Loud
District Hd Qrs[55]

See also:

Date: Unknown
To: Capt Loud

Op. Mesilla reports company of over one hundred men armed and mounted, started at 1 o'clock.
Frost[56]

55 Mesilla Operator to Lt Allen 14 October, 1879, RG 393, Pt 3, Entry 439, p.307.
56 Frost to Loud, RG 393, Pt 3, Entry 439, p.310.

Document 19.3

Report on Casualties from Van Patten's Expedition

Date: ??Mesilla?? 14
Rec'd: SF 14
To: Lt Allen

Messenger from Masons Ranche arrived last night with report of Dr Lyons of Mounted Company from Mesilla, stating that Wm T Jones of Mesilla and four Mexicans from Cruces were killed in Indian fight.
Mes Op

??? from Original of Frost Mesilla Op.[57]

57 Mesilla Operator to Lt Allen 14 October, 1879, RG 393, Pt 3, Entry 439, p.313.

Document 19.4

Van Patten & Wagon Train Report

Date: Bayard 16
Rec'd: SF 16
To: AAAG SF

In answer to enquiry regarding the fight between Co of Citizens and Indians near Colorado The following dispatch just received Mesilla 15 C.O. Bayard The fight took place as reported but only five killed wagon train attacked about same time 12 bodies found no important information since second company left the Indians are supposed to be in vicinity of Colorado.
Signed Operator
Beyer
Comdg.[58]

58 Beyer to AAAG SF, 16 October, 1879, RG 393, Pt 3, Entry 439, pp.303-304.

Document 19.5

Col Rynerson's Report of 16 October, 1879

Date: Mesilla Oct 17th
Rec'd: SF
To: Lt Allen

Colonel Rynerson writes as follows from Colorado 16th. Arrived here last night buried ten Mexicans on side of road massacred by Indians 8 miles beyond Masons Ranche; teams stolen and butchered. Outfit from El Paso, Mexico. Also buried 4 men ????? Lyons and Van Pattens party. Have sent body of W.T. Jones to Mesilla, others too much decomposed. Been to Loyd's Ranche, totally destroyed by Indians, cattle all stolen. Indians all left for Florida Mountains. No casualties in our party. People south should guard against Indians. We have no rations for long campaign. Lyons and van Pattens party fought whole band of Indians, miracle any of them escaped. Indians horribly mutilated body of Clito Sanches, who made a desperate resistance. Morrow arrived at Loyd's Ranche.
(Sig) H.S. Rynerson.

Volunteer just arrived. Have buried sixteen men on trip. Seven others could not find.
Mesilla Op[59]

59 Mesilla Operator to Lt Allen 17 October, 1879, RG 393, Pt 3, Entry 439, pp. 300-302; Loud to AAG Fort Leavenworth, 17 October, 1879, Telegrams Sent Dist. of New Mexico, Vol.2, Jan.–Dec. 1879, RG393, Part 3, Entry 431, pp.330-331.

Document 19.6

Mason's Appeal for Aid to Col. Hatch 18 October, 1879

Masons Ranch NM Oct 18

Col Hatch

Sir i received your Note regarding indians in reply i must say that i Don't Know an indian that come from mexico from any other But one week ago there was 10 ten men Killed 6 six miles from here on the road Some of them were Burned to Death, their train robed[60] *and Cattle Killed. 5 Five miles from there towards my other Ranch there was 5 men Killed.*

At my Stock Ranch my Partner was Killed The Ranch Burned the cattle Killed Horses drove off and everything Destroyed.

There was a large emigrant train passed by Here about a week ago, they heard they indians were close to them so they turned and Come Back to the ranch just in time to save their lives But had to leave their loaded wagons which was Plundered in less than two Hours afterwards there was 12,000 pounds of Goods for Silver City taken there was two familys from Texas left without anything Even the Childrens Clothing.

As to this ranch i am in a Bad fix i can get Nobody to cut Hay or Haul wood every Body is afraid to leave home

I cant even Get freight Here from Mesilla i have 10 Soldiers here Belonging to the 9th Cavalry without Horses they are No good whatever i cant get them to stand a guard

i am entirely at the mercy of the indians

i wish you Could Send me a little Protection i havent even a courier I could send for Help in case the Ranch was atacked

Thanking you and the Government
For past favors
I remain yours
Respectfully
R S Mason
PS Please excuse writing with Pencil.[61]

60 I have reproduced this letter as it appears in the microfilm including style and spelling errors.
61 Mason to Hatch, 18 October, 1879 in Letters Received by Headquarters District of New Mexico September 1865-August 1890 (Pamphlet Describing M1088 from Record Group 393) Roll 39, Oct-Dec 1879.

Document 19.7

Home Again'. Rynerson's Expedition as reported in *Thirty Four*

22 October, 1879

HOME AGAIN

Col. W.L. Rynerson and men who left this place and Mesilla last Tuesday, 14th, for the battle ground to bury the bodies of the unfortunate men of Van Patten's party, arrived here last Friday.

In order to give a correct statement of their march, we visited numerous persons of the party, both Americans and Mexicans and we have the following: After leaving Mesilla last Tuesday, the command not yet organized, proceeded to the top of the mesa above Picacho where an election was held with the following result: W.L. Rynerson, Capt. Jno S. Crouch, 1st Lt. Don Guadalupe Ascarte 2d Lt. The company then being organized, proceeded to Mason's Ranch where they arrived during the night and where they found Van Patten and the survivors of his party. The account of their fight with the Indians was listened to with interest by all the command who had arrived and who expected that more of them would on the following day share the same fate of the five men who had been left dead on the battle field. During the night some person on the ranche discouraged some of Col. Rynerson's men by telling them that if they attempted to bury those bodies they would all surely be killed; and urged and advised them not to go. Consequently, on the following morning, after the Capt. had given orders to get ready to march, he found that the spirit of some of his men had been tampered with, whereupon he made a short speech and told them that those bodies were laying on the plain and being eaten by coyotes and that it was their duty to bury them if possible; that probably they should have to fight and in case they should, he would not require them to do so unless they had something near an even show and in case there was an even show that he was going to whip the Indians; and those who did not wish to go could fall out of line. Twelve men fell out. The Capt. gave orders to forward march when the men gave three hearty cheers for their Capt. and the 12 fell in the ranks and marched on. Dr W.B. Lyon, J.B. Hinds, and Filomon Barela, (of the Van Patten party) fell in with the command to see it out. Van Patten and the balance of his men returned to Las Cruces.

The Capt. then ordered Doctor Montero with 10 men to keep 200 yards ahead of the command: David Wood with ten men on one flank and a gentleman from Dona Ana on the other, keeping 200 yds. on each side of the command. Four miles the other side of Magdalena canon, the command came upon a train of wagons and carretas, apparently from Mexico. The most of the cattle shot dead in the yokes, others breathing. 10 dead bodies lay under the wagons and among the dead cattle. The Capt. after placing his men on guard to prevent any surprise from the Indians, detailed a party to bury the dead. One man was found dead in his carreta leaning up against a box and his cattle grazing around. Some women and children's clothing were found strewed about, evidently the women and children were taken and are in the hands of the Indians. The guns which were muzzle loading were broken over the wagon wheels and left. A lot of flour that had been shipped to Mr Hughes, Silver City, was scattered over the ground and the sacks taken by the Indians. After having buried these bodies, the command proceeded to the place where Van Patten's comrades had been killed. The first body found was that of W.T. Jones which was found about one mile from where the party had been attacked. The other bodies were found from one to three miles apart. Jones' body was in a state of decomposition and it was suggested that it be buried there. But Doctor Lyon said that he could prepare the bodies so that they could be taken in, whereupon Jones' body was put into the wagon and the wagon drove to the next body which was so mutilated and decomposed that the driver said he would not take it unless some one else would drive the team. A dissatisfaction arose when Col. Rynerson said that all the bodies must be taken or buried as they found them. An attempt was made to get the other bodies to the wagons but it was pronounced impossible, when Col. Rynerson ordered that Jones' body which had been rolled up in a wagon sheet and in the wagon, to take it out and bury it, but Don Pablo Melendres and other Mexicans insisted that as the body was in the wagon to let it remain. The Col. then asked if all were satisfied, if not the body would be taken out and buried. All being satisfied, the bodies were buried, which took the balance of the day as they were so scattered and hard to find. The battle ground showed evidence of a hard fight and all agree that the escape of the small party was owing to their bravery and good management. The command then pushed on and arrived at Colorado about 1 o'clock[62] the next morning where they rested until after break-fast. The command then reinforced by the Colorado people, which swelled their number to 100, marched for Lloyds ranche where they reached in a few hours, but the Indians had all gone. Five more bodies were buried there. Not a living thing could be found on the ranche. All the chickens had been killed and left to rot, about 100 head of cattle had been shot down and but a small piece of flesh taken from some of them, and about 100 head of Lynch Bro's. fine imported bucks had been killed. The Indians are headed by Victorio and have gone to the Florida Mountains. Maj. Morrow's command is after them but they are about four days behind the Indians.

62 As spelled in original document.

Document 20

Sheridan's Resume of Events in New Mexico from Victorio's Breakout to the 22 October, 1879.

(Excerpt from summary of operations against hostile Indians in Division of Missouri since 25 October, 1878)

In New Mexico a band of Apaches under the Chief Victoria, broke away from their reservation, to which they had gone reluctantly, and the result has been bloodshed expense and anxiety. They have killed five soldiers, two scouts, and fifteen or sixteen citizens, including one if not more families of women and children, but to some extent have already been punished by the troops, who are still in pursuit. The most recent information from New Mexico, though not yet officially confirmed, goes to show that great destruction to life and damage to property has been committed in the Mesilla Valley by these same Indians, although they are constantly and energetically pursued by our troops. Their tactics being to attack and plunder some given point, then to scatter like quails and meet again at some other distant point previously understood, for plunder and again scatter, therefore it is exceedingly difficult for our troops to over-take and punish them. At present, however, the prospect looks fair that they will soon be overtaken and killed or captured.[63]

63 Sheridan to Townsend, AG Army 22 October, 1879, RG 393, Part 1, Entry 2538, p.213.

Document 21.1

Lt Finley's Account of the Expedition into Mexico and Fight with Victorio at Guzman Mountains – 4 November, 1879

Fort Bayard
Nov. 4th 1879

...I had a pleasant but very monotonous trip from Santa Fe to Bayard, part of the time we were rather afraid of an attack by Indians as our train held arms and ammunition for the citizen volunteers down here. We made a camp one night on a stream called the Matcho – it was in the Indian country just after leaving Hillsboro, where I mailed my last letter to you. It was raining hard and we had to stay up all night watching for the "poor los", they were around but didn't attack as we had about 30 men in all and they were probably but a small band watching us. We brought our arms through safely and came here the 16th of October. My company was in the field and I thought it would be some time before I would get a chance to join it but a courier came in from Maj. Morrow ordering rations etc to be sent out the next day, so I applied to be sent out to my company along with the supply train. I had some trouble in getting a mount but finally obtained a small but strong mule from the Quarter-master also a pair of soldiers pants, a couple of pr's of socks etc and a pair of boots – then from another officer I got an old ragged blouse and a white felt slouch hat from the store – also a pair of blankets from the Q.M. We started out at 4 P.M. on the 17th – marched till 11P.M. – started again at 8 A.M. – marched till 3 A.M. the next day when we reached Morrow's camp. I reported for duty and found 5 Second Lieuts. whom I had known at the Point and they gave me a warm reception – one of them was sent off on a separate scout but the rest of us hung together. One day later we broke camp and moved southward to intercept Victoria and his band. We went some 20 or 25 miles into <u>Old Mexico</u> and finally cut his trail apparently about 3 days old. Water was very scarce and we made very long marches through rough country so our stock suffered considerably – every day some horses and mules were abandoned and shot. We found several that had been killed by Victorio.

On the night of the 24th we camped at a mud hole which contained enough water for the command (about 150 men altogether and 200 head of stock) – on the 25th we found no water – on the 26th we struck a hole with enough water for about half the horses but so poor in quality that the men could not drink it. About 4 P.M. on the 27th one of our Indian scouts (who always go ahead) came back from the top of a hill and made motions that he wanted the field glasses and reported a cloud of dust in the distance. The command was halted and the officers went up on the hill. With the glasses we could see about ten miles away across the prairie some men and ponies just filing around the base of a hill, into a canon, they were immediately pronounced to be Indians. We waited until nearly dusk so that they could not observe us and then started after them, as we travelled across the prairie the moon rose, almost full, it was one of the most beautiful nights I ever saw. We reached the hill about 8½ P.M. The plan was to camp quietly until daybreak and then attack the Indians who we supposed were camped a mile or so in the mountains and were ignorant of our approach. Just as we reached the hill our Indians came running back saying the Chirikowas (hostiles) were camped about 1500 yards away. Then we moved off under cover of the hill and prepared for a night attack. It turned out that the Chirikowas had laid a beautiful little plan to ambush the whole command but Morrow was too sharp for them. They had the hills on both sides of the trail fortified by breastworks of rock. Morrow instead of going up the trail and took the Indians there in the rear and drove them to their principal fort on the other side – this was an isolated hill strongly fortified and under the circumstances almost impregnable. Right before this hill was another smaller ridge about half as high. We chased them as far as this and as our line charged up the ridge the Indians fired one volley and then fled to their fort. They killed one of our Indians and wounded two others. For three hours longer we lay behind the rocks on that ridge, both sides doing considerable shooting but inflicting no damage. We would watch until we saw the flash of a gun from their hill and then fire at that spot. One party of 8 men were sent around on their flank and probably killed two or three. When I say "we" in all this I don't mean that I was in it all. When we first heard our Indians firing ahead I like a greenhorn started up the hill on a dead run – now these hills are covered with huge rocks called mal-pais (literally "bad country") with sharp jagged edges and so thickly laid on the hill that there is not a blade of grass or a bare spot on them – you can imagine it is pretty hard climbing – of course we were dismounted. When I got half way up I had to stop and rest and when I finally reached the top I was completely exhausted. I couldn't have moved a step further for a fortune. Just then I was ordered with another officer and a detachment of five or six men to hold the top of the hill and watch over the camp. Well, after I had recovered my wind to some extent our troops had occupied the ridge I spoke of – we could see the firing and now and then we would get a shot up in our direction. I felt rather ashamed at not being able to keep up with my company so I told Lt. Day who was with me that I was going over there. A Mexican guide had been sent for Maj. Morrow to come to the ridge and I told him that I would go along, so we climbed down the hill and went across the bottom to the ridge. As we went across we would watch for a flash from the Indian fort and then drop down behind a rock or a sand hill, the Indians could see us in the moon-light and made it pretty lively for one little stretch of a hundred yards or so, but it was a bad light for aiming and we came through all right. To cut a long story short we had to withdraw and go 15 miles for water. Men and beasts were suffering greatly from thirst and were exhausted having marched over 40 miles and fought and climbed for 4 hours.

We reached water at 5 A.M. staid one day to recruit(?) [regroup?] *and then pulled out for home. In the engagement we lost one white soldier and one Indian killed. What the Indian loss was we don't know. During the fight we could hear the squaws inside the fort "making medicine" – singing and howling at a great rate – and Victorio was shouting continually, he said he could whip the whole 9th Cav. and had more rations than we had so we could not starve him out…*

Your loving Son
Walter.[64]

64 Letter dated Fort Bayard, 4 November, 1879 in The Walter Lowry Finley Collection.

Document 21.2

Lt Gatewood's Account of the Expedition into Mexico and Fight with Victorio in the Sierra De Guzman

We marched in the broiling heat all day in a south-easterly[65] direction, and about dark found a small tank of water in the rocks near the foot of the Goodsight[66] Mountains, which furnished perhaps half a pint to each man and animal. There we camped for the night. Early the next morning, as soon as the trail could be seen, we were on our way. All next day the command plodded along through the sand and heat, across the desert north of the Guzman Mountains. The trail wound among sand hills and lava beds, tending generally southward. Horses and mules began to grow leg weary and suffer from thirst and the heat, and for every horse that was shot by the rear guard a soldier was placed on foot. Thus man and beast trudged along, frequent halts being made to allow a little rest for the weary. About 9 o'clock we found a pool of mud in an alkali flat, and camped there for the night. It had been a pool of impure water, but the hostiles that day had driven their horses through it and it had been so thoroughly stirred up that it was about the consistency of thin mortar. Men and animals tried to drink it, but not with much success. In the two days' march fully seventy miles had been covered, and not a drop of water in the whole command. An unknown country still lay ahead, and the outlook was not encouraging but the hope of overtaking the enemy and giving him a well deserved punishment spurred the men into extra efforts. Besides, it was more than probable that by proceeding on our way, water would be reached sooner than by retracing our steps, or by making a day's march to the west into the Hatchet Mountains, where it was known water could be had. So bright and early the next morning march was resumed. The number of animals killed by the rear guard increased, the sun seemed to beat down hotter and hotter as the march continued. Men began to offer a month's pay, or all that they had, for just one swallow of water. There was no singing, no joking, no conversation, no smoking in the column, and the banjo of a colored soldier that used to enliven the men was silent. The Indian scouts, who always marched on foot, were more used to hardships, but even they began to show the effects of marching under such conditions. Several times we passed places where the wily savages had laid in ambush, but abandoned them evidently on account of the extreme caution with which such places were approached. In the afternoon we found a tank of clear and cool water, but alas! A coyote had been killed and disembowelled in it, and it had been otherwise disgustingly poisoned. It was difficult to keep many of the men from drinking it. Several had been made very sick by swallowing it. Some of the dismounted men were in serious condition, and had to be packed along on the best of the remaining horses and mules. Thus the command dragged its weary length along until after dark we entered the projecting ridges of the Guzman mountains, twenty miles perhaps from Janos Chihuahua, Mexico. Here the very plain trail ran between two parallel ridges covered with bushes and rocks, and a line of warriors in each ridge, hidden in the bushes and behind the rocks, waited for us to march along in the open come within easy range. But our scouts were not to be deceived by the evidences on the trail that the enemy had passes through hurriedly, and was trying to get away… The full moon had just arisen, and in that clear atmosphere one could see a man at considerable distance. How they must have chuckled to themselves as they watched us coming, and gloating over the victory so easily to be

65 See also Morrow to AAAG Dist. Of New Mexico, 5 November, 1879 in Papers relating to military operations against Chief Victorio's band of Mescalero Apache in southern New Mexico, 1879-81 in Letters Rec'd by the Office of the Adjutant General (Main series). 1871-80, M666. Roll 526.

66 I suspect that Gatewood means the Potrillo Mountains here and, as noted earlier, Gatewood had stated that the Potrillo Mountains were effectively a continuation of the Goodsight Mountains.

obtained. Some of our scouts succeeded in getting to the rear of one of the lines without attracting attention and a volley from them, followed by the advance of a line of dismounted soldiers, caused a precipitate evacuation of their strong position. They rallied on a higher ridge, a few hundred yards further on which they held until the flashes from the two opposing lines almost overlapped. But the Apaches can't stand close quarters; they broke and ran, as they always will. Our men steadily advanced, though it was evident by this time that the enemy outnumbered us considerably, and we were into a rougher and more broken mountain region, with which, of course, they were perfectly familiar, and of which we were totally ignorant. Water was probably there if it could be found. Again they took up a position still higher, and again the men responded to the "Forward march" of the commander, and splendidly climbed the mountain side. The Indians seemed to have plenty of ammunition which they rapidly expended in improved Winchester rifles, for when our line arrived within point blank range the whole top of the mountain was a fringe of fire flashes. Stationed with a few men on a peak to the left and rear of our skirmishers and somewhat above the hostiles, I had a good chance to witness this part of the fight. Nearer and nearer to the top of the ridge approached the flashes from our Springfield carbines and the reports from their Winchesters above were so frequent as to be almost a continuous roar. It seemed to me that fully half the men must be disabled, yet their return fire was brisk enough, as they slowly advanced. Suddenly the firing ceased; the rumbling and crashing of large stones down the side of the mountain could be heard; the line had run up against a palisade of solid rock, twenty feet high or more, which they could not climb, and which had not been noticed because the moon was rising behind the enemy's position and the palisade was hid in shadow. From this place the hostiles were rolling heavy stones down among our men, but luckily, none were hurt though several had been killed and several more wounded during the heaviest fusillade.[67]

67 Gatewood, 1894, pp.103-104.

Document 22.1

US Consulate in Chihuahua Report on the Candelaria Mountains Affair as reported by Mexican Sources 14 November, 1879

Department of State:
Washington December 4 1879

The Honorable
George W. McCrary
Secretary of War

Sir:
I have the honor to transmit herewith a copy of a dispatch No.34, dated November 14th, from the Consul at Chihuahua, in relation to Indian depredations in Northern Mexico. It would seem that the Indians complained of said from our side of the border.
I have the honor to be Sir
Your obedient servant
(Signed)
Mr W M. Evarts

Inclosure – Copy of dispatch No.34, dated November 14, 1879

Inclosure

No 34

U.S. Consulate,
Chihuahua, Nov. 14. 1879.

Hon. W. Hunter
2d Asst. Secretary of State,
Washington D.C.

Sir:
I enclose you a copy of a translation of a document sent to this capital from the Rural Judge at Carmen.

This document speaks for itself and needs no comment from me. It tells its own horrible story of butchery by the devilish fiends who are fed and clothed by the U.S. Government and who leave their reservations whenever they see fit to do so and leave their trail of desolation, murder and fiendish lust wherever they may chance to pass.

The Indians who were engaged in this horrible slaughter are said to be from the Tulerosa Reservation, and are by no means a very large band, but they successfully ambushed the first party mentioned, at a water hole and at the first fire killed nearly the entire party. The assisting party were also ambushed with horrible results.

I knew some of these men who were killed and they are indeed a loss to the State and the community which they governed.

The first question naturally is: How can this state of affairs be prevented? I think I can answer it: By a hearty cooperation in a war of extermination begun at the same time on both sides of the Rio Grande and with the mutual understanding that a party out after hostile Indians shall pass the boundary line as often as it is necessary for them to do so. This arrangement can be easily effected, and so far as the States of Chihuahua and Sonora are concerned, it can be entered into with perfect safety. If you will examine the reports of the officers of the U.S. Army who have had occasion to be near the line, I am sure that they will say that the ranche-men and large haciendas would gladly welcome the troops of the States of Government into Mexico with all the assistance they themselves were able to give as guides or in other ways

I think the General Government of Mexico could be easily induced to put three hundred men in Chihuahua for this purpose, and the State Govt., I am sure, were it able to do so, would drive the Indians from Casas Grandes and from the State.

In conversation with the prefector of Casas Grandes on this question, he said: "what am I to do? My only safety is in peace with them as I am not strong enough to defend myself should I incur their enmity."

While in this city he received letters from his place telling him that many new Indians had arrived at his place. He was of the opinion that while some of Victoria's Indians may have visited Casas Grandes, he does not think that Victoria was himself there. Chief Juh claims to have been in the fight when they captured – so he says – a whole wagon load of ammunition from the soldiers. He lost two of his principal chiefs in this or some of his other fights.

I have presented to you my plan of getting rid of these Indians. If you drive them out of New Mexico or Arizona they will take refuge in the mountains of Chihuahua, and from these fastnesses they will from time to time raid forth and depredate across the line and will probably be good Mexican Indians so long as it is policy for them to do so; but if they are attacked from both sides at once, and learn to their sorrow that there is no more line to shield them, they may be content to go back and surrender their arms and ponies and stay on their reservations.

One may study the Indian character and moralize over his lamentable condition, but his ideas are not firmly fixed on the Indian question until he has been chased by them and then his mind is settled on the question forever. Any one who has been upon the frontier knows the present Indian system to be the grandest kind of a fraud and I have never yet talked with a frontiersman who endorsed the system and I have made it a duty to ask the opinion of those whom I considered competent to judge of the situation.

I am Sir
Your most obedient servant
(Signed)
Louis H. Scott.

Enclosure – one copy in translation of document from the Rural Judge at Carmen.

Translation from a copy of the original
From the Rural Judge of the town of El Carmen, State of Chihuahua, Mexico

Just at this moment 10:30 P.M. I have sent an armed force to the town of Carrisal on petition of the Mayor of said town for the use described in the following communication, which I have just now received, it having been five days on the road.

Town of Carrisal
State of Chihuahua, Mex.

Sir Lie Jacques
El Carmen

There have just now arrived here twenty men of the ones I had sent to the succour of others which I had previously sent and these have informed me that they have returned horseless, and the Indians have killed 15 of their number while they were bringing 18 of the first force killed also by the Indians. In consequence of this I have thought proper to advise you not to make another movement of the same nature until a sufficient force is mustered. The dead bodies remained on the field unburied on account of the Indians have taken an advantageous position on the Tinaja De La Candelaria, overlooking the main road between El Paso and La Salada. Therefore I believe that only by mustering a competent force of about 200 men can the dislodgement of the Indians from their present position be attempted, or the burial of the dead which I repeat are more than thirty. You will therefore please send a force for a regular campaign as soon as possible, to be rendezvoused in this town; trying all your power to do the same in adjoining farms and please send this communication to the Capital of the State

I enclose a list of the dead as far as it is known.

Carrisal Nov. 9, 1879

(signed) E. Martinez

List of the men of the first force:

Killed	*Josi Rodriguez*
Killed	*Maurico Salis*
Killed	*Flamencia Villuneuva*
Killed	*Yues Ortega*
Killed	*Hernujildo Ruis*
Killed	*Enlatio Villaneuva*
Killed	*Josi Ma Hernandez*
Killed	*Serafino Tuilillo*
Killed	*Josi Ma Salis*
Killed	*Santas Contreras*
Wounded	*Herculano Hernandez*

Of the force sent to the rescue of the above, the following are killed.

Commander Josi Ma Rodriguez
Jesus Dominguez
Tubuscio Contreras
Francito Servantes
Desirerio Sanchez
Juan Alanan
Jesus Vaca
Guadalupe Ruiz
Julio Hernandez
Luis Nunez
???? Huano

and two strangers whose names are unknown.

Influenced by the foregoing communication, I suspended the march of the force I had got up until I could muster from the farm thirty men in all that they in company with the force from the farm of San Lorenzo, should go immediately to Carrisal to severely chastise the Indians that have caused us to mourn over the loss of influential men like Sr. Rodriguez and Sr. Dominguez, who have rendered the State important and valuable service.

As soon as the force from San Lorenzo presents itself here, my force of 30 men will be ready to accompany them to Carrisal, to punish the Indians. At the same time it is absolutely necessary that, without any loss of time, you should send this communication to the Capital of the State that the authorities there may entertain this important subject, and leave aside for a moment our political contention.

Liberty in the Constitution.

Town of El Carmen, Nov. 9. 11. P.M. 1879.

(Signed A. Jaquez

Note: I have just now also written for an assistant force from the towns of Galeana and Valle de San Buenaventura, in order to organize the campaign asked for by the Mayor of Carrisal
(Signed) Jaquez

At (2 A.M.) of this day I received the above communications which continue in their route for the information of the respective parties below.
Liberty in the Constitution
San Lorenzo Nov ber 10th 1879
Signed F. Rubaliano

To the Authorities in the farms of "San Lorenzo", "Plan de Alamos", "Ojo de la Laguna", "Encinillas", Sauz, town of Sacramento and the City of Chihuahua.[68]

(Note this information reached HQ of the US Army on 10 December, 1879, passed to HQ Division of the Missouri then on to the Department of the Missouri on the same day, finally reaching HQ Dist of New Mexico on the 24 December, 1879.)

68 Scott to Hunter, 2nd Assistant Sec of State, Washington D.C., 14 November, 1879 in Consular Despatches Chihuahua Mexico 1830-1906 M289 Roll 1 30 November, 1830-13 May, 1901; RG393, Letters Received by Headquarters District of New Mexico September 1865-August 1890, M 1088, Microfilm Roll 37 (Oct-Dec 1879); See also Papers relating to the Frelinghuysen-Romero Agreement of July 29, 1882, providing for reciprocal crossings of the international boundary by troops of the United States and Mexico in pursuit of hostile Indians, Feb. 1862-June 1867; Letters Rec'd by the Office of the Adjutant General (Main Series), 1881-1889. Microfilm 689 Roll 81.

Document 22.2

James Kaywaykla's account of the Ambush In the Candelaria Mountains

There was much vegetation up on the mesa and especially along the rim. It afforded fine concealment for those watching the canyon. At our backs was an arroyo for concealing the horses, which were kept saddled. Beyond the mesa was a long gradual slope to the south offering easy retreat. As usual, sentinels were posted in all directions. Grandmother took her place on the edge overlooking Nana's men. At points commanding the mouth of the canyon, men were stationed to signal if the enemy approached from the west.

The sentinels were provided with bits of mirrors to flash warnings. When General Miles wrote of his campaign against the Apaches he assumed that we knew nothing of the heliograph.[69] He was mistaken. My people did not know the Morse code, but they had learned that mirror flashes warned soldiers and ranchers of our movements; and they, too, made use of the device. I've often wondered why so much has been written about smoke signals. As far as I know they were not much used.

On the northern slope of the canyon, overlooking the little stream, Victorio stationed a few picked men. Nana led another few up the south slope and placed them behind boulders. Victorio stayed on the mesa with us until warning flashes from the points of entrance indicated the approach of the enemy. He lay on the rimrock, peering through field glasses, the first I had seen.

"Mexicans, but not cavalry," he said. And he took his men and joined Nana. Siki Mother and Blanco's wife checked the horses, tied their equipment to the saddles, and hobbled their mounts. Mother was the first to spy the riders, tiny specks moving towards the canyon. Slowly they increased in size and rode single file up the little stream. They dismounted, drank, watered their horses, and then rode straight into our ambush. Kaytennae let every man pass the boulder behind which he lay before opening fire. Those on the left killed every horse before starting on the men. Two of the twelve fell, as the Mexicans retreated up the south slope where Nana's forces were hidden. It was over very quickly. The warriors walked among the bodies collecting rifles and ammunition belts. A body moved and was impaled on a spear. The warriors took shirts and saddles, and toiled up the slope to the mesa.

The men were not tortured; the bodies were not mutilated. I know for I lay on my belly and watched this thing happen. I have seen hundreds killed, none tortured. Mutilation that has occurred was done after death, and that for the purpose of avenging mutilation perpetrated on the body of Mangas Coloradas. Nor did Victorio's band scalp. I never saw a scalp taken, and I was with his band until he died…The chief came, but did not give the order to mount. We remained in camp. There was not even a victory dance though many of the young men wanted one. We remained as we had been with guards posted…A second band of ricos came in search of those who had died. The vultures and wolves had left little of the first party. They left little of the second. And this was done without any Apaches being wounded.

Then Victorio gave orders to ride.[70]

69 See Miles, 1932, pp.195-196; 2001, p.539 for his version of events. See also Neifert, 2001, pp.560-561.

70 Ball, 1970, pp.13-14 & p.15.

Document 22.3

Baylor and Gillett's Reconstruction of the Candelaria Mountains Massacre

Baylor's Account

The First Ambush:

After Major Morrow's defeat the Indians probably 200 in number, came down about 55 miles due west of here, and camped in the Candelaria Mountains, a group of peaks surrounded by open plains. They had splendid water, grass and plenty game, and probably intended to winter, but a party of 15 Mexicans – the best citizens of Carisal – finding a trail, followed it and were led into an ambuscade and all killed.

The scene of the conflict was perfectly horrible. I saw in one little narrow parapet, which the beleaguered Mexicans had hastily thrown up, seven men piled up in a space 6x7 feet. The Indians had shown great cunning, as they have though all this campaign. The trail passed a low place between and commanded by, three rocky peaks. The Mexicans were fired upon from one side just as they reached the crest of the mountains; they had evidently dismounted and ran into the rocks on the opposite side, when the Indians began killing the horses that they had tied, and opened fire on them from nearly overhead and a peak out to one side. They were all killed. A letter written by them asking for help was found outside their breastwork, and near the body of two men who had evidently attempted to escape but were riddled with balls.

Thirty five more men – nearly the entire fighting force of Carisal – went out to look for their kindred, and the Indians so managed to drive them into the same slaughter pen, and eleven of them were killed, near the same spot, three ran some distance and their bodies were not found. We buried 26, and 3 were still missing.[71]

The Second Ambush:

It was evident that the last party had found the bodies of their kinsmen and collected and put them in a big crevice in the rocks and had begun to cover them with loose stones, the Indians watching them all the time, just as a cat plays with a mouse before killing it. They opened fire on them when all probably had set their guns against the rocks and were busy in the last sad rites of burying their loved ones, little dreaming it was soon to be their own grave.[72]

Gillett's Account

The First Ambush:

From his position on the tall peaks Victorio had seen the little body of Mexicans long before they struck his trail and, knowing that they would never come upon the Candelarias after seeing the size of his trail, he sent forty or fifty of his warriors to form an ambuscade where the trail crosses the crest between two peaks. He must have been with the braves himself, for the thing was skilfully

71 Lt Baylor to Gen. J.B. Jones, Adjutant General, Austin, Texas, 3 December, 1879 'Victorio Campaign, Feb. 1879-Nov. 1880' in "Special Files" Created by the Military Division of the Missouri. Records of U.S. Army Continental Commands, 1821-1920 Record Group 393 M1495 Microfilm Roll 14; As above in Papers relating to military operations against Chief Victorio's band of Mescalero Apache in southern New Mexico, 1879-81 in Letters Rec'd by the Office of the Adjutant General (Main series). 1871-80, M666. Roll 526; See also Thrapp, 1974, p254, see also Baylor, 1996, pp.287-288. Wellman states that the site was reached approximately two weeks after the ambush (Wellman, 1957, p.163).

72 Baylor, 1996, pp.287-288.

planned and executed. On the north side of the trail there were only a few boulders, but south side the hills were very broken, rising in rough tiers of stones. The Apaches hid in these rocks and awaited their victims. On November the 7th, the Mexicans entered the narrow defile and as soon as they were between the two parties of Indians concealed on each side of the pass the Apaches on the north side of the trail fired a volley at them. The Mexicans thereupon made for the rocks on the south side, when the redskins in the cliffs above opened fire on them. Caught in this death trap, the entire force was massacred…When I walked over the ground some time afterward I saw where one Mexican had got into a crevice from which he could shoot anyone coming at him from east or west. He was hidden also from the Indians in the cliffs above him, but his legs were exposed to the warriors on the north side and they had literally shot them off up to his knees. I also found seven dead Mexicans in a small gully, and on a little peak above them I discovered the lair of one old Indian who had fired twenty seven shots at the tiny group until he had killed them all, for I found that number of .45-70 cartridge shells in one pile. Practically all the horses of the Mexicans were killed.[73]

The Second Ambush:

As it was supposed that only a small band of Apaches bent on horse stealing was in the Candelarias, another small band of fourteen men volunteered to go and see what had become of their friends and kindred. Don Jose Mario Rodriguez was appointed commander, and the little party took the trail of their comrades with sad foreboding. Old Victorio, from his watch towers in the Candelarias, saw this rescue party and prepared for its destruction. The signs indicated that the second party had walked into the same death trap as the first, but its members had scattered more in fighting and many of them were killed on the southern slope of the hills. Two had attempted to escape on horseback, but were followed and killed. I found one of these unfortunates in an open plain some six hundred yards from the hills. He had been surrounded, and seeing escape was impossible, had dismounted, tied his horse to a Spanish dagger plant, and put up a good fight. I found thirty or forty cartridge shells near where he had fallen. His pony had been killed and the dagger plant shot to pieces. The Apaches had cut off his right hand and had carried away his gun, six shooter, saddle, and bridle.[74]

73 Gillett, 1976, pp.162-163.
74 Gillett, 1976, p.163-164.

Document 23

US Consulate in Chihuahua Report on Apache Raids in Chihuahua 28 November, 1879

Department of State
Washington December 16 1879

The Honorable
Alexander Ramsey
Secretary of War

Sir
Referring to previous communications upon this subject I now have the honor to transmit herewith for your information, a copy of dispatch No. 36 of the 28th inst. From the Consul at Chihuahua, in relation to the presence of hostile bands of Indians in that state.
I have the honor to be, Sir,
Your obedient servant
(Signed) Wm. M. Evarts

No. 36

U.S. Consulate
Chihuahua Nov. 28 1879

Hon. W. Hunter
2nd Asst. Sec. of State
Washington D.C.

Sir
I beg to acknowledge the receipt of your dispatches dated Oct. 29th (No.26) and Nov. 10 (No.27) and they have my careful attention.

In regard to the enclosure from the War Department with letters from the Commanding Officer in New Mexico, I have this to say: I have read all the correspondence carefully and I have long since made corrections of my dispatch of July 20th. At the time of writing that dispatch, I did not know of the presence of Juh and his band, had never heard of any depredations they had committed, and consequently could make no report upon them.

This band of Indians were on Reservations about three years ago, if I am correctly informed, and first went into Sonora, where they remained until this spring, when it appears they made a raid into Arizona, and stole some mules, stock etc., and then came into Mexico, settling at Casas Grandes. I am reliably informed that Juh sticks pretty closely to the mountains, and does not like to talk or be interviewed, but he has at times told of his exploits. I had a call this morning from Thos. Parker, whose brother is an officer in the Arizona Indian Scouts. Mr Parker has jus passed through Casas Grandes (on 27th inst.) and reports only two Indians there, Juh and the others have gone, most probably to join Victoria, who I now learn for a certainty, is in the State at the head of forty-five warriors, all well armed. Juh's Indians are not well armed, but Victoria has plenty of ammunition and needle=guns in abundance.

Morrow ran Victoria sixty miles this side of the line, and fought him at La Laguna Busman [Guzman?] *about the first of this month*

About this time, or before, he was joined by Juh, who in reality belongs to the same tribe of Indians as Victoria, but these two worthy cut-throats have not been able to agree for years, and personally are not friends.

After their fight with Morrow, they crossed to the Candelaria Mountains, where they got in their terribly bloody work on the Carrizal party – where they killed over thirty Mexicans and some splendid citizens.

On the 23rd inst. They attacked Galliana, taking sixty to seventy horses and killing two men and badly wounding one other, who however will live. The next day they attacked San Lorenzo, killing three men and taking 200 horses, which had just been gathered for the purpose of driving them near this City for protection.

At Salada, before they attacked Galliana, they captured a whole train, which they destroyed, killing all the train men, whose exact number I am unable to learn, but which was probably not less than twelve. From San Lorenzo they went to Santa Clara, where my last advices leave them.

When Juh came to Casas Grandes, he sued for peace, and as the State Govt had not force to send against him, he was left unmolested, as none of the ranchmen were willing to take the responsibility of driving him away, being willing to be at peace if the Indians did not molest them. I have heard that the Indians were offering stolen mules for sale, and it is quite likely that they succeeded in disposing of them, and all the rest of their stolen plunder.

Victoria never asked for peace, but went right to work killing every one he could find. The entire country north of the city is demoralized and they claim Victoria has a large band with him. Mr Parker crossed their tracks and at one time saw their horses and does not think they number more than a hundred men. I am confident there are not over one hundred and fifty at an outside figure.

That the Indians of Juh have been harbored at all, I am sure is for the reason that there were no means to punish them. Gen. Trevino with 500 soldiers arrived here this week, and he said he will as soon as he has settled the political matters which have disturbed us for the past month, send a force against these Indians. If a movement is made by Morrow at the same time, they will bag the whole lot, but this thing of one side chasing them across the line, and then in a month have the other side chase them back again, is in my opinion, a poor way to fight them, and should be abandoned. I would earnestly request that some steps be taken for concerted action against these hostile Indians and if you think proper I would endeavor to establish an understanding here with the State Govt, that any force in pursuit of Indians can follow them into this state, and fight them wherever found. I am sure in the face of what has occurred, that not only permission will be granted, but that our forces will have the hearty co-operation of the inhabitants of Chihuahua, who have for the past hundred years waged a volunteer warfare against the Apaches.

In regard to the cattle stolen from Corralitas, I have nothing to retract, and the less the interested parties regard it (I mean the purchasers) the better it will be for them. I do not think they will court any enquiry on the subject.

I am, Sir,
Your most obdt. Servant
(Signed) Louis H. Scott.
U. S. C.[75]

75 Scott to Hunter, 2nd Assistant Secretary of State, Washington D.C. 28 November, 1879 in Consular Despatches Chihuahua Mexico 1830-1906 M289 Roll 1, 30 November, 1830-13 May, 1901; Evarts, Dept. of State to Alexander Ramsey, Secretary of War, 16 December, 1879, 'Victorio Campaign, Feb. 1879-Nov. 1880' in "Special Files" Created by the Military Division of the Missouri. Records of US Army Continental Commands, 1821-1920 Record Group 393 M1495 Microfilm Roll 14 see same letter in Papers relating to the Frelinghuysen-Romero Agreement of July 29, 1882, providing for reciprocal crossings of the international boundary by troops of the United States and Mexico in pursuit of hostile Indians, Feb. 1862-June 1867; Letters Rec'd by the Office of the Adjutant General (Main Series), 1881-1889. Microfilm 689 Roll 81.

Document 24

Background to, and Diplomatic Implications of, the Acceptance by the Chiricahuas, led by Juh, of San Carlos as their Reservation

Headqrs Dept of Arizona
April 3. 1880

Fremont John C. To his Excellency
Governor of Arizona Territory

Sir:

I have the honor to acknowledge the receipt of your communication of the 16th ultimo, enclosing a communication from the Governor of Chihuahua, with enclosures demanding the delivery to his Government of the Indians recently transferred to the San Carlos Reservation, and to communicate for your information the following:

In consequence of depredations committed by the Chiricahua Indians in southern and south-eastern Arizona, in April 1876, the Interior Department ordered the removal of that tribe from their Reservation near Fort Bowie A.T., to the San Carlos Indian Reservation, and the Commanding Officer of his Department was directed to assist in their removal, which was effected in May 1876.

Tahza, son of Cochise and Chief of the northern Chiricahuas, consented to the removal, Eskinya, Juh, Jeronimo and Nolgee, Chiefs of the southern Chiricahuas opposed it.

Just prior to the movement being affected, the respective followers of Tahza and Eskinya, met and fought among themselves, near Fort Bowie, A.T., June 7th 1876; in this fight Eskinya was killed; Juh, Jeronimo and Nolgee with their followers making their escape towards Chihuahua in Mexico. It was subsequently ascertained that a large portion at least of this party visited the Agency of the Southern Apaches at Ojo Caliente, New Mexico.

A decision of the Secretary of the Interior to the effect that the Chiricahua Indians who had taken refuge on the Southern Apache Agency, New Mexico, were to be allowed to remain there, was received by the Department Commander on the 22nd August 1876.

November 15. 1876, M.A. Sweeny, Acting Indian Agent San Carlos, reported he had received information from Indians, that nearly all the Chiricahuas who failed to move to San Carlos, were at that time at the Southern Apache Agency.

Lieut. Rucker had an engagement January 9. 1877, with a party of renegades in Ludendorf Mountains New Mexico, in which engagement a nephew of Jeronimo, was captured; and it is probable that these renegades were a part of Jeronimo's followers.

Lieut. Henely reported March 17. 1877, that he saw Jeronimo at the Agency in New Mexico; that he had just returned from a raid with one hundred (100) horses; that he was indignant because he could not draw rations for the time he was absent.

Indian Agent Clum, was directed by the Interior Department, March 20 1877 to remove to the San Carlos Reservation, such of the Chiricahuas as were then at the Agency in New Mexico, in which movement the military was to assist. These Indians (their number is unknown to me) were turned over to Agent Clum, May 4. 1877.

December 12. 1877, Agent Hart reported depredations committed by Juh and Nolgee at Ash Springs, Stein Peak Mt: Juh and Nolgee were traveling south.

August 9. 1878, Lieut. L. A. Abbott, 6th cavalry reported the departure of Jeronimo from the San Carlos Reservation.

July 18. 1879, Lieut. C.B. Gatewood, 6th Cavalry, reported that Jeronimo had left Juh in Mexico and that the former would probably turn up in Arizona.

August 9. 1879, the Commanding Officer Camp Thomas A.T. reported that Juh, with eighty (80) followers, was at Casas Grandes, Mexico, and that it was his belief that the Mexican authorities were willing to surrender them to our Government.

On November 28. 1879, the United States Consul at Chihuahua, Mexico, in writing to the Secretary of State, Washington D.C. says: "This band of Indians were on Reservation about three years ago, if I am correctly informed, and first went into Sonora, where they remained until the Spring, when it appears, they made a raid into Arizona and stole some stock, mules etc. and then came into Mexico, settling in the mountains near Casas Grandes. XXXXX. *When Juh came to Casas Grandes he sued for peace and as the State Government had not force to send against him, he was left unmolested; as none of the ranchmen were willing to take the responsibility of driving him away, being willing to be at peace if the Indians did not molest them."*

In the Summer of 1879, the Agent at San Carlos reported to me that steps should be taken to secure the return of the renegade Chiricahuas to their Reservation, but that he was powerless without the assistance of the military.

Upon sounding the leading Chiricahuas left at San Carlos, they made known to me through my Chief Scout, Archie McIntosh, the desire to have the renegades of their tribe brought to that Reservation: whereupon I entered into negotiations, through the Indians at San Carlos, for the return of their brethren.

Certain men of the tribe communicated with the renegades in Mexico, and the latter agreed to return to the Reservation, provided they were assured of protection: they were informed that if they would return to the Reservation and conduct themselves well, they would be protected.

On or about December 18. 1879, these renegades (one hundred and two (102) in number) arrived in the vicinity of Camp Rucker, where they were received by Lieut. Haskell, my Aide-de-Camp and Archie McIntosh, Chief Scout, by whom they were conducted to San Carlos.

Since the surrender of the Indians it is understood that they have conducted themselves in a satisfactory manner. It is known that Juh, Jeronimo and their followers are not Mexican Indians and therefore do not come within the provisions of the letter of the Secretary of State, dated October 10, 1879, (copy herewith,) and that their delivery by this Government to the Mexican authorities, would be a breach of faith and is therefore disapproved on the following grounds, viz: First the Indians are American Indians. Second, they returned on the faith of my promise that they would be received and protected and their surrender would therefore be a gross breach of faith, which would be both wrong and work disastrously to ourselves as well as to our neighbors, the Mexicans. Third; that having allowed these Indians to reside unmolested on Mexican soil at Casas Grandes, from whence they made raids on us, the Mexican authorities cannot find fault with us for receiving the same Indians and putting a stop to their raids on the Mexican people; of which raids there have been no complaints since the date of their surrender to me at Camp Rucker. Fourth, we have effected the separation of Juh and Jeronimo from Victoria; and by the use of the very Indians in question, we are assisting Gen'l Hatch to operate against Victoria in New Mexico; therefore military policy will not allow their being given up, even if there were doubts as to the justice of the case; and this military policy is as much for the benefit of our Mexican neighbors as for ourselves against a common enemy.[76]

76 See also Martin to AG, Military Division of the Pacific, Presidio San Francisco, 11 September, 1880, where he notes that no more was heard of this application to return Juh and his followers to the Republic of Mexico (RG393, Part 1, Entry 169, Vol. 10, p.419).

Very Respectfully
Your obedient servant
O.B. Willcox
Colonel 12th Infantry
Bvt Maj Gen'l (assigned)
Comdg Department.[77]

77 Willcox to Fremont, Governor of Arizona Territory, 3 April, 1880, RG393, Part 1, Entry 169, Vol. 10, pp.137-140; See also Report of General O.B.Willcox, 11 September, 1880, in Annual Reports of the War Department 1880 : Microcopy M997 Roll 35 1880 Vol. I, p.207.

Bibliography

Primary Sources

National Archives Washington D.C. Microfilm Sources

Roll(s)	File	Description
Letters Rec'd by the Office of the Adjutant General (Main series). 1871-80. RG94, M666, 593 rolls)		
24	2465 AGO 1871	*Correspondence relating to the selection by Vincent Colyer of the Board of Indian Commissioners of sites for Apache Indian reservations at Tularosa Valley, and White Mountain, New Mexico Territory, and at Camp Grant and Camp Verde, Arizona Territory, 1871-72. Included is the order by General George Crook that the Apaches move onto the reservations by Feb 15, 1872, or be considered hostile.*
123	3383 AGO 1873	*Correspondence relating to the agreement with Cochise, chief of the Chiricahua Apache, negotiated by Gen. Oliver O. Howard and to Gen. George Crook's criticism of the agreement and his request to be allowed to subdue Cochise with force 1873-74*
265	2576 AGO 1876	*Correspondence relating to the removal of the Chiricahua Apache Indians to the San Carlos Indian Agency, Arizona Territory, 1876-77.*
326	1927 AGO 1877	*Correspondence relating to the arrest and removal of Geronimo's band of renegade Chiricahua Apache Indians from Ojo Caliente, New Mexico Territory, to the San Carlos Indian Agency, Arizona Territory, 1877*
366	5705 AGO 1877	*Correspondence relating to military operations against the Warm Springs Indians who fled from the San Carlos Indian Agency, Arizona Territory, 1877-79*
526-528	6058 AGO 1879	*Papers relating to military operations against Chief Victorio's band of Mescalero Apache in southern New Mexico, 1879-81, and one letter dated Mar. 13, 1886.*
Letters Rec'd by the Office of the Adjutant General (Main Series), 1881-1889. M689. 740 rolls. DP		
44	4746 AGO 1881	*Correspondence and reports mainly concerning efforts to capture hostile Apache Indians who were terrorising the border region of the District of New Mexico, July-Dec. 1881.*

Roll(s)	File	Description

Returns From Regular Army Infantry Regiments June 1821-December 1916-1916 (Pamphlet Describing M665 from Record Groups 94 & 391)

Roll (s)	File	Description
166	N/A	*15th Infantry Jan. 1873-Dec. 1880*
167	N/A	*15th Infantry Jan. 1881-Dec. 1889*

Letters Rec'd by the Office of the Adjutant General (Main Series), 1881-1889. M689. 740 rolls. DP

77	364 AGO 1882	*Papers and a report of Mar. 4, 1882, from the Secretary of War relating to a statement of expenditures for Indian wars and for the observation and control of Indians from July 1, 1871-June 20, 1882*
81	663 AGO 1882	*Papers relating to the Frelinghuysen-Romero Agreement of July 29, 1882, providing for reciprocal crossings of the international boundary by troops of the United States and Mexico in pursuit of hostile Indians, Feb. 1882-June 1887*

Returns From Regular Army Cavalry Regiments 1833-1916 (Pamphlet Describing M744 from Record Groups 94 & 391)

43	N/A	*4th Cavalry 1887-1883*
63	N/A	*6th Cavalry 1875-1880*
64	N/A	*6th Cavalry 1881-1887*
88	N/A	*9th Cavalry 1873-1880*
89	N/A	*9th Cavalry 1881-1887*
96	N/A	*10th Cavalry 1873-1880*

Returns From U.S. Military Posts 1800-1916 (Pamphlet Accompanying M617 – from Record Groups 393)

87	N/A	*Bayard, Fort, N. Mex Aug. 1866-Dec. 1879*
88	N/A	*Bayard, Fort, N. Mex Jan. 1880-Dec. 1894*
117	N/A	*Bliss, Fort, Tex. Jan. 1872-Dec. 1885*
242	N/A	*Concho, Fort, Texas Jan 1879-June 1889*
262	N/A	*Craig, Fort, N. Mex Jan. 1871-June 1885*
298	N/A	*Davis, Fort, Texas Jan 1879-June 1891*
877	N/A	*Ojo Caliente, N. Mex May 1879-Mar. 1882*
1217	N/A	*Stanton, Fort, N. Mex Jan. 1868-Dec. 1877*
1218	N/A	*Stanton, Fort, N. Mex Jan. 1878-Dec. 1887*
1449	N/A	*Wingate, Fort, N. Mex Jan. 1872-Dec. 1882*

Microcopy M997: Annual Reports of the War Department

26	N/A	*1876 Vol. I-II*
27	N/A	*1876 Vol. II-IV*
28	N/A	*1877 Vol. I-II*
29	N/A	*1877 Vol. III-IV*
30	N/A	*1878 Vol. I-II*
31	N/A	*1878 Vol. II*

Roll(s)	File	Description
32	N/A	*1878 Vol. III-IV*
33	N/A	*1879 Vol. I-II*
34	N/A	*1879 Vol. II-IV*
35	N/A	*1880 Vol. I-II*
36	N/A	*1880 Vol. II*
37	N/A	*1880 Vol. III-IV*
38	N/A	*1881 Vol. I-II*
39	N/A	*1881 Vol. II*
40	N/A	*1881 Vol. III-IV*

"Special Files" Created by the Military Division of the Missouri.
Records of US Army Continental Commands, 1821-1920 M1495 (Record Group 393)

14		*Disturbances at El Paso, TX, Sept. 1877-May 1878* *Victorio Campaign, Feb. 1879-Nov. 1880*

Letters Sent by the 9th Military Department, the Department of New Mexico, and the District of New Mexico 1849-1890 M1072 (Record Group 393)

6		*Name and Subject Index to Volume 18 1878* *Volume 18* *Name and Subject Index to Volume 19 Jan–Oct 1879* *Volume 19 1879* *Name and Subject Index to Volume 20* *Volume 20 1880* *Name and Subject Index to Volumes 20 and 21 1881* *Volume 20 Jan 1880–Aug 1881*
7		*Name and Subject Index to Volumes 20 and 21 1881* *Name and Subject Index to Volume 21 1882* *Name and Subject Index to Volumes 21 and 22 1883* *Volume 21 Aug. 1881–Aug.1883* *Name and Subject Index to Volumes 21 and 22 1883* *Volume 22 Sept. 1883–July 1887* *Volume 23 July 1887–Sept. 1890*

Headquarters Records of Fort Cummings, New Mexico, 1863-1873 & 1880-1884 M1081
Rolls 1, 2, 3, 5 & 8

Letters Received by Headquarters District of New Mexico September 1865-August 1890 (Pamphlet Describing M1088 from Record Group 393)

37	658-1658	*Apr.–June 1879*
38	1664-2491	*July–Sept. 1879*
39	2506-3485	*Oct.–Dec. 1879*
40	806-1790	*Jan.–June 1880*
41	2103-4519	*July–Dec. 1880*
42	5-1544	*Jan.–Apr. 1881*
43	1568-4364	*May–Oct. 1881*
44	4368-5690	*Nov.–Dec.1881*

Roll(s) File Description

HQ Records of the District of the Pecos 1878-1881 Microcopy M1381
Rolls 1-5

Consular Despatches Chihuahua Mexico 1830-1906 M289
Rolls 1-2 Nov 30th 1830-May 13th 1901

Consular Despatches Cuidad Juarez (Paso del Norte) M184
Roll 2 Jan 16th 1871–Dec 31st 1884

National Archives Washington D.C. Non-Microfilm Sources

Record Group 94, Bi-Monthly Muster Rolls:	Co A 4th Cavalry Regiment 1880
	6th Cavalry Regiment 1880
	9th Cavalry Regiment 1879-1881
	10th Cavalry Regiment 1880
	15th Infantry Regiment 1879-1881

Record Group 94, Entry 257, Medical History, Fort Bayard, New Mexico Vol. 896.

Record Group 94, Entry 297, Personal Record Files.

Martin B. Hughes	Box 483 AA1-10
John F. Guilfoyle	Box 481 AB1-18
Adam Kramer	Box 33 AC1-5
James H. French	Box 448 AD1-AD5
Matthias W. Day	Box 1 AE1-AE11
Henry Carroll	Box 476 AF1-AF12
John Conline	Box 279 AG1-AG16
Thomas Cruse	Box 1428 AI1-3
Eugene D. Dimmick	Box 1496 AJ1-17
Michael Cooney	Box 1067 AK1-AK5
George R. Burnett	Box 941 AL1-AL12
Patrick Cusack	Box 49 AN1-AN6
Samuel Woodward	Box 426 AO1-AO4
Augustus P. Blocksom	Box 463 AP1-AP11
Nicholas Nolan	Box 857 AQ1
Stephen C. Mills	Box 829 AR1-AR10
Leighton Finley	Box 600 AS1-AS2
Frank B. Taylor	Box 501 AT1-AT3
Henry H. Wright	Box 334 AU1-AU29
George W. Smith	Box 309 AV1-AV3
Louis H. Rucker	Box 180 AW1-AW4
Albert P. Morrow	Boxes 71 & 72 AX1-AX10
Tom Jeffords	Box 654 AY1
William H. Hugo	Box 526 AZ1-AZ6

Record Group 94, Entry 561 Personal Papers of Medical Officers and Physicians ("Medical Officers Files": Kennon, L.W.C. 1853-79, Box 1112
Record Group 391, Entry 734, Regimental Histories 4th Cavalry 1855-1926.
Record Group 391, Entry 744, Miscellaneous Records 1880-1914 Orders/Letters 4th Cavalry.
Record Group 391, Entry 841, Reports and Tabular Statements of Scouting Expeditions 1867-1891.
Record Group 391, Entry 909/911/919, Regimental Orders Issued 1876-1879.
Record Group 391, Entry 920, Letters, Telegrams and Endorsements Sent: and General and Special Orders and Circulars Issued by a Battalion July – September 1880.
Record Group 391, Entry 921, Letters & Telegrams sent by the Battalion on the Southern Pacific Railway at Separ NM Sept-Nov 1881.
Record Group 391, Entry 922, Letters & Telegrams Received by the Battalion on the Southern Pacific Railroad at Separ NM Sept-Nov 1881.
Record Group 391, Entry 923, Orders Issued by the Battalion on the Southern Pacific Railroad at Sepr NM Sept-Nov 1881.
Record Group 391, Entry 925, Endorsements Sent 1873-85, 10th U.S. Cavalry.
Record Group 391, Entry 933, Regimental History 1866-98, 10th U.S. Cavalry.
Record Group 393, Letters Received Dept. of the Missouri 1868-98 Entry A1-1 2601 Boxes 83-98
Record Group 393, Part 1, Entry 169, Letters Sent Vol. 9. Dept of Arizona 1879
Letters Sent Vol. 10. Dept of Arizona 1880
Letters Sent Vol. 11. Dept of Arizona 1881.
Record Group 393. Part 1, Entry 181, Letters Received, Dept of Arizona 1881.[1]
Record Group 393. Part 1, Entry 183, Dept of Arizona & District of New Mexico: General Orders, Circulars and Court Martial Orders 1870-1881.[2]
Record Group 393. Part 1, Entry 184, Dept of Arizona: Special Orders 1879-1881.
Record Group 393. Part 1, Entry 185, Dept of Arizona: General and Special Orders and other Orders Issued and Received.[3]
Record Group 393. Part 1, Entry 187, Dept of Arizona, Manuscript Reports 1880-85.
Record Group 393. Part 1, Entry 204, Dept of Arizona, Miscellaneous Records 1879-1880.
Record Group 393, Part 1, Entry 232, Dept of Arizona: Field Records – Troops in Southeastern Arizona 1878-1881.
Vol. 2. – September 1st 1878 – May 27th 1879.
Vol. 3. – May 27th 1879 – July 3rd 1879.
Vol. 4. – July 3rd 1879 – December 13th 1879.
Vol. 5. – December 13th 1879 – May 7th 1880.
Vol. 6. – May 7th 1880 – May 18th 1880.
Vol. 7. – May 16th 1880 – September 6th 1880.
Vol. 8. – September 6th 1880 – December 12th 1880.
Record Group 393. Part 1, Entry 235, Dept of Arizona: Letters and Telegrams Rec'd 1878-1880.[4]
Record Group 393. Part 1, Entry 236, Dept of Arizona: Troops in South East Arizona Telegrams 1880.

1 I have photocopied all the material cited. I have numbered each photocopy in the order that I discovered them. In the text of this book they are cited as follows: (Sender to Recipient with date, RG393, Pt.1, Entry 181, page number (This number refers to the number that I have assigned to the telegram copy in my own files.)).
2 See Footnote 1.
3 See Footnote 1.
4 See Footnote 1.

Record Group 393. Part 1, Entry 238, Dept of Arizona: General Orders and Field Orders July 1879 – January 1881.
Record Group 393. Part 1, Entry 239, Dept of Arizona: Special Orders Vols. I & II October 1879–January 1881.
Record Group 393. Part 1, Entry 240, Dept of Arizona: Miscellaneous Records 1878-1880.
Record Group 393. Part 1, Entry 244, Dept of Arizona: District of Apache – Telegrams Received 1881.
Record Group 393. Part 1, Entry 2538, Division of the Missouri: Letters Sent Vol. 6 1879-1881.
Record Group 393. Part 1, Entry 2539, Military Division of the Missouri: Press Copies of Letters and Endorsements Sent, Vols. 11-14 1879-1881.
Record Group 393. Part 1, Entry 2546, Military Division of the Missouri: Letters Received 1879-1881.[5]
Record Group 393. Part 1, Entry 2551, Military Division of the Missouri: Annual Reports of Departments 1879-1881.
Record Group 393, Part 3, Entry 431, District of New Mexico:
Telegrams Sent Vol. 2 – Jan. to Dec. 1879.
Vol. 3 – Jan. to Nov. 1880.
Vol. 4 – Nov. 1880 to Jan. 1881.
Vol. 5 – Feb. to Dec. 1881.
Record Group 393, Part 3, Entry 439, District of New Mexico: Telegrams Received 1870-1885 (Unarranged)[6]
Record Group 393, Part 3, Entry 440, District of New Mexico, Mail Copies of Telegrams Received 1880-1885 (Unarranged).[7]
Record Group 393, Part 3, Entry 446, District of New Mexico, Printed Special Orders 1869-1888.
Record Group 393, Part 3, Entry 450, District of New Mexico Printed Special Orders 1869-1888.[8]
Record Group 393, Part 3, Entry 451, District of New Mexico, Circular Letters Issued 1876-84.
Record Group 393, Part 3, Entry 453, District of New Mexico, Special Orders Rec'd from Sub-Commands.
Record Group 393, Part 3, Entry 472, District of New Mexico, Miscellaneous Records 1868-1889.
Record Group 393, Part 3, Entry 474, District of New Mexico, Press Copies of Letters and Telegrams Sent by Commander Hatch in the Field 1877 Ojo Caliente.
Record Group 393, Part 3, Entry 475 District of New Mexico General and Special Field Orders, Letters and Telegrams Volume 4-7.
Record Group 393, Part 3, Entry 477, District of New Mexico, Letters and Endorsements Sent 1877-1887.
Record Group 393, Part 3, Entry 479, District of New Mexico, Letters Received at AAG 1872-1880.
Report of the Commissioner of Indian Affairs, Dept. of the Interior, Office of Indian Affairs. Washington November 1 1880.
John H. Ware V. the U.S. & Apache Indians, Depredation Claim No. 4584, 16E3/3/6/5 Box 375.

5 See Footnote 1.
6 Note: There are several problems with this material. Some of the telegrams are not clearly dated. They are not stored in order and some are illegible. I photocopied all the telegrams cited. I have numbered each telegram photocopy in the order that I discovered them. See also Footnote 1.
7 See Footnote 1.
8 Note that these also contain Special Field Orders issued by Headquarters in the Field.

Government Documents

Chronological List of Actions, &c., with Indians, from January 1, 1866 to January 1891. *Adjutant General's Office.*

Record of Engagements with Hostile Indians within the Military Division of the Missouri from 1868 to 1882. Compiled from Official Records. Headquarters – Military Division of the Missouri, Chicago Illinois, August 1st 1882: *Lieutenant General P.H. Sheridan Commanding*

New Mexico State University Archives

RG 98 Fort Bayard Interrement Record NMRA-902(8888).

Microfilm held in NMSU archives, Las Cruces, New Mexico

Lee Myers Papers: Boxes 6 & 7/25

The Newberry Library, Chicago

Records of the New Mexico Superintendency of Indian Affairs 1846-80, Microfilm Roll 24 1875-80

Documents courtesy of William A. Dobak

Parker to CO Fort Wingate, 10 August, 1881, Department of Missouri, Letters Received, 6552 DMo 1881

Parker to A.A.A.General, District of New Mexico, Santa Fe N.M., 13 August, 1881, Department of Missouri, Letters Received, 6552 DMo 1881

Carroll to Acting Assistant General, District of New Mexico, Santa Fe, N.M. 17 October, 1881, Department of Missouri, Letters Received, 7266 DMo. 1881

Gardner to The Adjutant Batt. Ninthh Cavalry In the Field, Separ S.P.R.R., N.M. 28 October, 1881, Department of Missouri, Letters Received, 7320 DMo. 1881

Gardner to The Adjutant Batt. Ninth Cavalry, Separ S.P.R.R., N.M. 31 October, 1881, Department of Missouri, Letters Received, 7320 DMo. 1881

Carroll to A.A.A. General, Dist. Of New Mexico, Santa Fe N.M. 31 October, 1881, Department of Missouri, Letters Received, 7330 DMo. 1881

Van C. Smith to Capt. Carroll Separ N.M. 23 October, 1881, Department of Missouri, Letters Received, 7330 DMo. 1881

Following to do with a discussion concerning the relocation of Mescalero and San Carlos Reservations to Indian Territory Late 1881-1882

Bradley, CO Fort Wingate, to HQ District of New Mexico, 1 February, 1882, Department of Missouri, Letters Received, 710 DMo. 1882

Mackenzie, to AAG Dept. Of Missouri, 5 February, 1882, Department of Missouri, Letters Received, 710 DMo. 1882

Kirkwood, Secretary of the Interior to The Secretary of War 11 January, 1882, Department of Missouri, Letters Received, 710 DMo. 1882

Randall, Capt. Twenty-Third Infantry CO Fort Reno, Indian Territory to Assistant Adjutant General, Department of the Missouri, 28 January, 1882, Department of Missouri, Letters Received, 710 DMo. 1882

Guy V. Henry, Major Ninth Cavalry, Fort Sill to Assistant Adjutant General, Department of the Missouri, 27 January, 1882, Department of Missouri, Letters Received, 710 DMo. 1882

Documents courtesy of Berndt Kuhn

'Terrassas Talks' *Daily New Mexican* 30 October, 1880

'Greeting the Victors' Victory Parade in Chihuahua City as reported in the *Daily New Mexican* 2 December, 1880

Price to Act. Asst. Adjt. General, District of New Mexico, 25 July, 1873 in Letters Received, District of New Mexico, RG393.

Documents courtesy of Daniel D. Aranda

David L. Hughes' 'An Early Chapter in the life of Apache Bill'

Parks, H.L. "Gavilan Canyon Fight – August 19, 1881" Letter dated 28 April, 1956

Fountain to Bureau of Pensions, Dept. of the Interior, 12 September, 1912

MacPherson Letters 1 January, 1879 to 3 September, 1880, University of Virginia at Charlottesville

Lt. M.B. Hughes to CO Ojo Caliente, 10 November, 1877

Statement of Apache Indian Chiefs, Fort Wingate, 24 October, 1877 in Letters Received, District of New Mexico 1877

Joaquin Terrazas to Genl. G.P. Buell 12 November 1880

Anon. 1, "Gavilan Canyon Fight – August 19, 1881". *This document mainly quotes the Annual Report of the Secretary of War 1881, but includes some comments concerning US Army failures in Korea suggesting that this was written in the 1950s.*

Anon. 2, "Fort Selden History: Month 1"

Misc. 1, "The Jim Santiago, Vidal Trujillo Gonzales Family" by Vidal T. Gonzales

Misc. 2, "Appendix A: Council of Mimbres Apaches held at Fort Tulerosa [Old Fort Tularosa] September 11 [12] 1872" RG 75 in National Archives also in Arizona Historical Society Microfilm MC 4

Source: Ed Sweeney via Dan Aranda

Misc. 3, "Spots of Interest in the Area". *This is a page-long article in three columns concerning the events surrounding the death and commemoration of Jim Cooney.*

Misc. 4 "The Indian War in the Lava Beds". *Cuttings relating to the ambush of Eugene Van Patten's posse and other attacks perpetrated by Victorio's Apaches in October 1879.*

Misc. 5 Declaration of Fransisco Montoya and supporting statement of Jose Abatos concerning and attack on Montoya's freight train in early May 1880.

Document sent by Karl Laumbach & Daniel D. Aranda

'The Pursuit of Victorio' By Captain Jack Crawford: Socorro County Historical Society, Publications in History, Volume 1, February 1965

Papers Held in the Gatewood Collection

Report of Captain C.B. McLellan, 6th U.S. Cavalry, May 16, 1880, On Operations in the District of New Mexico.

Report of Colonel E.A. Carr, 6th U.S. Cavalry, August 29, 1880, on Field Operations in South-Eastern Arizona.

Keith Humphries Collection, Geronimo Springs Museum, Truth or Consequences, New Mexico.

William M. Bates Interview Notes c. 1940

Fort Davis Museum Archive

Robert Grierson's Diary, 10th July to 1st September 1880.

Special Collections, University of Arizona Library, Tucson

Leighton Finley Diary, 25th July to 15th November 1880.

Useful Biographical Sources

Browning, J.A. (1992), *The Western Reader's Guide: A Selected Bibliography of Nonfiction Magazines 1953-91* (Barbed Wire Press: Stillwater Oklahoma)

Browning, J.A. & McCravey, J.B. (2000), *A Complete Guide to Hunter's Frontier Times* (Eakin Press: Austin Texas)

Contemporary Newspapers

Grant County Herald & New Southwest 1879-1881

Thirty-Four 1879-1880

Microfilms Courtesy of Ed Sweeney.

Crimmins, Colonel M. L. "The Mescalero Apaches" *El Paso Times* Sunday, May 31, 1931 & Sunday, June 7, 1931

Las Vegas Daily Gazette, 30 December, 1882.

'Nutt in a Nutshell' by 'Rambler', http://chroniclingamerica.loc.gov/lccn/sn90051703/1882-12-30/ed-1/seq-4/#date1=01%2F01%2F1882&sort=date&date2=12%2F31%2F1882&searchType=advanced&language=&sequence=0&index=19&words=Kingston&proxdistance=5&state=New+Mexico&rows=20&ortext=&proxtext=&phrasetext=&andtext=kingston&dateFilterType=range&page=3

The New York Times

'Punishing Victorio's Band', 30 July, 1880.
http://query.nytimes.com/mem/archive-free/pdf?res=9E05E1D81630EE3ABC4850DFB166838B699FDE

'Victorio's Murdering Band', 28 August, 1880
http://query.nytimes.com/mem/archive-free/pdf?res=9A0DEFDB153BE033A2575BC2A96E9C94619FD7CF

'Outrages by Victorio's Indians', 10 September, 1880
http://query.nytimes.com/mem/archive-free/pdf?res=9805E0D8143FEE3ABC4852DFBF66838B699FDE

'The Death of Victorio', 28 October, 1880
http://query.nytimes.com/mem/archive-free/pdf?res=9B07E5DE173FE533A2575BC2A9669D94619FD7CF

'The End of Victorio', 29 October, 1880
http://query.nytimes.com/mem/archive-free/pdf?res=9E02E7DA153BE033A2575AC2A9669D94619FD7CF

'The Murdering Apaches', 31st January 1881
http://query.nytimes.com/mem/archive-free/pdf?res=9806E4DA1F3AE533A25752C3A9679C94609FD7CF
'American Surveyors Murdered: Thirteen Men of the Mexico Central Force Found Dead' 7th July 1881
http://query.nytimes.com/mem/archive-free/pdf?res=9A02EFDC103CEE3ABC4F53DFB166838A699FDE

From the Walter Lowry Finley Collection (AC 083-p), Angélico Chávez History Library, Museum of New Mexico, Palace of the Governors, Santa Fe, New Mexico, U.S.A.

Weekly New Mexican, 27 September, 1879, p.2, c.2.
'The Fight on the Animas', *Weekly New Mexican*, 11 October, 1879, p.1, c.3.
'The Indian War in the Southwest', *Weekly New Mexican*, 11 October, 1879, p.2, c.1.
'Victorio the Indian Chief' *Weekly New Mexican*, 18 October, 1879. p.1, c.4.
'Indian News' *The New Mexican*, 18 October, 1879, p.2, c.5.
'The latest Indian News. Major Morrow follows Victoria into Mexico, and has a fight with him. The Savages are Dispersed with Heavy Loss.' *Weekly New Mexican*, 8 November, 1879, p.2, c.3.

Secondary Sources

Books

Adam, G.G.	2001	"Resolution Adopted at Meeting of Residents of Cochise County, Arizona, Regarding Outbreak of Indians From San Carlos Reservation" in Cozzens, *Eyewitnesses to the Indian Wars 1865-1890 Volume 1: The Struggle for Apacheria* (Stackpole Books: Mechanicsville) 414-424 First Published 1885
Aleshire, P.	1998	*Reaping the Whirlwind: The Apache Wars* (Facts on File: New York)
Alba, V.	1973	*A Concise History of Mexico* (Cassell: London)
Alonso, A.M.	1997	*Thread of Blood: Colonialism, Revolution, and Gender on Mexico's Northern Frontier* (The University of Arizona Press: Tuscon)
Altshuler, C.W.	1991	*Cavalry Yellow & Infantry Blue: Army Officers in Arizona between 1851 and 1886* (Arizona Historical Society: Tuscon)
Anderson, F.	2000	*Crucible of War: The Seven Years' War and the Fate of Empire in British North America. 1754-1766* (Faber & Faber: London)
Astor, G.	1998	*The Right to Fight: A History of African-Americans in the Military* (Presidio: Novato CA)
Ball, E.	1970	*In the Days of Victorio: Recollections of a Warm Springs Apache* (The University of Arizona Press: Tucson)
Ball, E., Henn, N. & Sánchez, L.A.	1980	*Indeh: An Apache Odyssey* (University of Oklahoma Press: Norman)
Bancroft, H.H.	1889	*The Works of Hubert Howe Bancroft, Vol. XVI: History of the North Mexican States & Texas Vol. II 1801-1889* (The History Company: San Francisco)
Basso, K.	1996	*Wisdom Sits in Places: Landscape and Language Among the Western Apache* (University of New Mexico Press: Albuquerque)

Barnes, W.C.	1982	*Apaches & Longhorns: The Reminicinces of Will C. Barnes* (The University of Arizona Press: Tuscon) Copy of Edition Published in 1941
Barnes, W.C.	2001 (i)	"The Apaches' Last Stand in Arizona: The Battle of Big Dry Wash" in Cozzens, *Eyewitnesses to the Indian Wars 1865-1890 Volume 1: The Struggle for Apacheria* (Stackpole Books: Mechanicsville) 267-285 First Published 1931
Barnes, W.C.	2001 (ii)	"In the Apache Country" in Cozzens, *Eyewitnesses to the Indian Wars 1865-1890 Volume 1: The Struggle for Apacheria* (Stackpole Books: Mechanicsville) 615-624 First Published 1887
Barney, J.M.	1996	*Tales of Apache Warfare: True stories of Massacres, Fights and Raids in Arizona and New Mexico* (Trail to Yesterday Books: Tuscon) First published in 1933
Baylor, G.W. (Thompson, J.D. ed)	1996	*Into the Far Wild Country: True Tales of the Old Southwest* (Texas Western Press, The University of Texas at El Paso: El Paso)
Beck, W.A. & Haase, Y.D.	1969	*Historical Atlas of New Mexico* (University of Oklahoma Press: Norman)
Beck, W.A. & Haase, Y.D.	1989	*Historical Atlas of the American West* (University of Oklahoma Press: Norman) *Historical Atlas of the American West* (University of Oklahoma Press: Norman)
Benson, H.C.	2001	"The Geronimo Campaign" in Cozzens, *Eyewitnesses to the Indian Wars 1865-1890 Volume 1: The Struggle for Apacheria* (Stackpole Books: Mechanicsville) 552-556 First Published 1909
Betzinez, J.	1987	*I Fought with Geronimo* (University of Nebraska Press: London) First published by Stackpole 1959
Beyer, W.F. & Keydel	1971 (i)	"The Battle of Cuchillo Negra Mountains" cited in J.M. Carroll (ed), *The Black Military Experience in the American West* (Liveright: New York)
Beyer, W.F. & Keydel	1971 (ii)	"The Battle of Carrizo Canyon Mountains" cited in J.M. Carroll (ed), *The Black Military Experience in the American West* (Liveright: New York)
Beyer, W.F. & Keydel	1971 (iii)	"The Battle of Gavilan Canyon" cited in J.M. Carroll (ed), *The Black Military Experience in the American West* (Liveright: New York)
Beyer, W.F. & Keydel	1971 (iv)	"The Battle of Membres Mountains" cited in J.M. Carroll (ed), *The Black Military Experience in the American West* (Liveright: New York)
Beyer, W.F. & Keydel	1971 (v)	"The Battle of Las Animas Canyon" cited in J.M. Carroll (ed), *The Black Military Experience in the American West* (Liveright: New York)
Beyer, W.F. & Keydel	1971 (vi)	"Tularosa" cited in J.M. Carroll (ed), *The Black Military Experience in the American West* (Liveright: New York)
Bigelow, J.	1986	*On the Bloody Trail of Geronimo* (Westernlore Press: Tuscon) First Published 1886-1887
Billington, M.L.	1991	*New Mexico's Buffalo Soldiers 1866-1900* (University Press of Colorado: Niwot)

Birtle, A.J.	2001	*U.S. Army Counterinsurgency and Contingency Operations Doctrine 1860-1941* (Center of Military History, United States Army: Washington D.C.)
Blevins, W.	1993	*The Wordsworth Dictionary of the American West* (Wordsworth Editions: Ware)
Blyth, L.R.	2012	*Chiricahua and Janos: Communities of Violence in the Southwestern Borderlands* (University of Nebraska Press: Lincoln)
Bourke, J.G.	1980	*On the Border with Crook* (Time Life: New York) First published by Charles Scribners Sons 1891
Bourke, J.G.	1987	*An Apache Campaign in the Sierra Madre: An Account of the Expedition in Pursuit of the Hostile Chiricahua Apaches in the Spring of 1883* (University of Nebraska Press: London): First published by Charles Scribner's Sons 1886
Bourke, J.G.	2001 (i)	"Crook's Campaign in '72" in Cozzens, *Eyewitnesses to the Indian Wars 1865-1890 Volume 1: The Struggle for Apacheria* (Stackpole Books: Mechanicsville) 141-143 First Published 1883
Bourke, J.G.	2001 (ii)	"With Crook in the Sierra Madre" in Cozzens, *Eyewitnesses to the Indian Wars 1865-1890 Volume 1: The Struggle for Apacheria* (Stackpole Books: Mechanicsville) 346-385
Bowles, N.	1998	*Government and Politics of the United States 2nd Edition* (MacMillan Press: Basingstoke)
Boyer, R.M. & Gayton, N.D.	1992	*Apache Mothers and Daughters* (University of Oklahoma Press: Norman)
Brown, D.	1970	*Bury My Heart at Wounded Knee* (Vintage: London)
Bryan, H	1998	*True Tales of the American Southwest: Pioneer Recollections of Frontier Adventures* (Clear Light Publishers: Santa Fe)
Buchanan, K.M.	1986	*Apache Women Warriors* (South-western Studies No 81; University of Texas at El Paso: El Paso Texas)
Burton, A.T.	1999	*Black, Buckskin and Blue: African-American Scouts and Soldiers on the Western Frontier* (Eakin Press: Austin Texas)
Callinicos, A	1999	*Social Theory: A Historical Introduction* (Polity: Cambridge)
Carmony, N.B.	1996	*The Civil War in Apacheland: Sergeant George Hand's Diary- California, Arizona, West Texas, New Mexico 1861-1864* (High Lonesome Books: Silver City)
Carr C.C.C.	2001	"The Days of the Empire-Arizona 1866-1869" in Cozzens, *Eyewitnesses to the Indian Wars 1865-1890 Volume 1: The Struggle for Apacheria* (Stackpole Books: Mechanicsville) 18-35 First published 1889
Carroll, J.M.	1971	*The Black Military Experience in the American West* (Liveright: New York)
Cashin, H.V.	1993	*Under Fire with the Tenth U.S. Cavalry* (University Press of Colorado: Niwot) First Published by F. Tennyson Neelyin 1899
Chisman, C.	2001	"The Apache Campaign of 1885-1886" in Cozzens, *Eyewitnesses to the Indian Wars 1865-1890 Volume 1: The Struggle for Apacheria* (Stackpole Books: Mechanicsville) 540-545 First Published 1927
Chun, C.K.S.	2004	*US Army in the Plains Indian Wars 1865-91 (Battle Orders Number 5)* (Osprey Publishing: Oxford)

Clarke, P.H.	2001	"A Hot Trail" in Cozzens, *Eyewitnesses to the Indian Wars 1865-1890 Volume 1: The Struggle for Apacheria* (Stackpole Books: Mechanicsville) 630-641 First Published 1894
Clausewitz, C.	1968	*On War* (Penguin: London)
Clendenen, C.C.	1969	*Blood on the Border: The United States Army and the Mexican Irregulars* (Collier-Macmillan: London)
Clifford, F. & Nolan, F. (editor)	2011	*Deep Trails in the Old West: A Frontier Memory* (University of Oklahoma Press: Norman)
Cocker, M.	1999	*Rivers of Blood, Rivers of Gold: Europe's Conflict with Tribal Peoples* (Pimlico: London)
Coffer, W.E.	1982	*The Story of the Indians of Arizona and New Mexico* (Van Nostrand Reinhold Company: New York)
Coffman, E.M.	1986	*The Old Army: A Portrait of the American Army in Peacetime 1784-1898* (Oxford University Press: Oxford)
Cole, D.C.	1988	*The Chiricahua Apache 1846-1876: From War to Reservation* (University of New Mexico Press:Albuquerque)
Collins, C.	1994	*The Great Escape: The Apache Outbreak of 1881* (Westernlore Press: Tuscon Arizona)
Collins, C.	1999	*Apache Nightmare: The Battle at Cibecue Creek* (University of Oklahoma Press: Norman)
Cozzens, P.	2000	*General John Pope: A Life For The Nation* (University of Illinois Press: Urbana)
Cozzens, P.	2001	*Eyewitnesses to the Indian Wars 1865-1890 Volume 1: The Struggle for Apacheria* (Stackpole Books: Mechanicsville)
Cozzens, P.	2005	*Eyewitnesses to the Indian Wars 1865-1890 Volume V: The Army and the Indian* (Stackpole Books: Mechanicsville)
Cremony, J.C.	1983	*Life Among the Apaches* (University of Nebraska Press: London) First published by A. Roman and Company 1868
Crick, B	2005	*In Defence of Politics 5th Edition* (Continuum; London)
Crook, G.	2001 (i)	"Apache Affairs: An Interview with General Crook" in Cozzens, *Eyewitnesses to the Indian Wars 1865-1890 Volume 1: The Struggle for Apacheria* (Stackpole Books: Mechanicsville) 396-404 First Published 1883
Crook, G.	2001 (ii)	"Resume of Operations against Apache Indians, 1882 to 1886" in Cozzens, *Eyewitnesses to the Indian Wars 1865-1890 Volume 1: The Struggle for Apacheria* (Stackpole Books: Mechanicsville) 569-589 First Issued in 1886
Crook, G.	2001 (iii)	"The Apache Problem" in Cozzens, *Eyewitnesses to the Indian Wars 1865-1890 Volume 1: The Struggle for Apacheria* (Stackpole Books: Mechanicsville) 593-603 First Published 1886
Cruse, T.	1987	*Apache Days and After* (University of Nebraska Press: London) First published by The Caxton Printers Ltd 1941
Cruse, T.	2001	"From Hembrillo Canyon to Chevelon's Fork" in Cozzens, *Eyewitnesses to the Indian Wars 1865-1890 Volume 1: The Struggle for Apacheria* (Stackpole Books: Mechanicsville) 262-266 Letter written May 25th 1883

Dale, E.E.	1949	*The Indians of the Southwest: A Century of Development under the United States* (University of Oklahoma Press: Norman)
Daly, H.W.	2001	"The Geronimo Campaign" in Cozzens, *Eyewitnesses to the Indian Wars 1865-1890 Volume 1: The Struggle for Apacheria* (Stackpole Books: Mechanicsville) 447-487 First Published 1933
Davis, B.	1976	*The Truth About Geronimo* (University of Nebraska Press: London) First published by Yale University Press 1929
Davis, B.	2001	"The Difficulties of Indian Warfare" in Cozzens, *Eyewitnesses to the Indian Wars 1865-1890 Volume 1: The Struggle for Apacheria* (Stackpole Books: Mechanicsville) 488-494 First Published 1885
Debo, A.	1993	*Geronimo: The Man, His Time, His Place* (Pimlico: London)
Deverell, W.	1996	'Fighting Words: The Significance of the American West in the History of the United States', in C.A. Milner, *A New Significance: Re-Envisioning the History of the American West* (Oxford University Press: Oxford), pp.29-55
Discussion Forum II,	1968	'Discussions Part II', in R.B. Lee & I. DeVore, *Man the Hunter* (Chicago Aldine Publishing: Chicago)
Dixon, D.	1994	*Hero of Beecher Island: The Life and Military Career of George A. Forsyth* (University of Nebraska Press: London)
Dobak, W.A. & Phillips, T.D.	2001	*The Black Regulars 1866-1898* (The University of Oklahoma Press: Norman)
Downey, F. & Jacobson, J.N.	1973	*The Red-Bluecoats: The Indian Scouts* (Old Army Press: Fort Collins)
Driver, H.E.	1961	*Indians of North America* (The University of Chicago Press: London)
Dunlay, T.W.	1982	*Wolves for the Blue Soldiers* (University of Nebraska Press: London)
Dunn, J.P.	1958	*Massacres of the Mountains: A History of the Indian Wars of the Far West 1815-1875* (Archer House: New York)
Eaton, G.O.	2001	"A String for the Bow" in Cozzens, *Eyewitnesses to the Indian Wars 1865-1890 Volume 1: The Struggle for Apacheria* (Stackpole Books: Mechanicsville) 177-181 First published in 1938
Edge, R.J.	1971	"Braves of all Colors: The Story of Isaiah Dorman Killed at the Little Big Horn" cited in J.M. Carroll (ed), *The Black Military Experience in the American West* (Liveright: New York)
Elliott, C.P.	2001	"The Geronimo Campaign of 1885-1886" in Cozzens, *Eyewitnesses to the Indian Wars 1865-1890 Volume 1: The Struggle for Apacheria* (Stackpole Books: Mechanicsville) 427-446 First Published 1910
Evans, R.K.	2001	"The Indian Question in Arizona" in Cozzens, *Eyewitnesses to the Indian Wars 1865-1890 Volume 1: The Struggle for Apacheria* (Stackpole Books: Mechanicsville) 604-614 First Published 1886
Farrow, E.S.	2000	*Mountain Scouting: A handbook for Officers and Soldiers on the Frontiers: Foreword by Jerome A. Greene* (University of Oklahoma Press: Norman) First published by E.S. Farrow New York 1881
Faulk, O.B.	1969	*The Geronimo Campaign* (Oxford University Press: Oxford)
Faulk, O.B.	1974	*Crimson Desert: Indian Wars of the American Southwest* (Oxford University Press: New York)

Finerty, J.F. 2001 "On Campaign after Cibecue Creek" in Cozzens, *Eyewitnesses to the Indian Wars 1865-1890 Volume 1: The Struggle for Apacheria* (Stackpole Books: Mechanicsville) 236-261 First Published 1881

Fish, C. R. 1923 *American Diplomacy* (Henry Holt & Co.: New York)

Flanagan, M. 1999 *The Complete Idiot's Guide to the Old West* (Alpha Books: New York)

Flayderman, N. 1977 *Flayderman's Guide to Antique American Firearms...and their Values* (Follett Publishing Company: Chicago)

Forbes, J.D. 1994 *Apache, Navaho, and Spaniard 2nd Edition* (University of Oklahoma Press: Norman)

Foster, J.W. 1900 *A Century of American Diplomacy: Being a Brief Review of the Foreign Relations of the United States 1776-1876* (Houghton & Mifflin: Cambridge)

Fowler, A. 1996 *The Black Infantry in the West 1869-1891* (Greenwood Press: New York)

Fox *et al*, 1993 *Archaeology, History and Custer's Last Battle: The Little Big Horn Re-examined* (University of Oklahoma Press: London)

Frazer, R.W. 1965 *Forts of the West: Military Forts and Presidios and Posts commonly called Forts West of the Mississippi River to 1898* (University of Oklahoma Press: Norman)

Fuller, W.D. 2005 "Hunting with Apaches" in Cozzens, *Eyewitnesses to the Indian Wars 1865-1890 Volume V: The Army and the Indian* (Stackpole Books: Mechanicsville) 465-468 First published in 1872

Genung, C.B. 2001 "Indians and Indigo" in Cozzens, *Eyewitnesses to the Indian Wars 1865-1890 Volume 1: The Struggle for Apacheria* (Stackpole Books: Mechanicsville) 71-84 First published in 1911

Gibson, M. 1974 *The American Indian: From Colonial Times to the Present.* (Wayland Publishers: London)

Gillett, J.B. 1976 *Six Years with the Texas Rangers 1875 to 1881* (University of Nebraska Press: London) First published by Yale University Press 1925; Gillett copyright taken out in 1921

Glass, E. 1971 "Early Field Service" cited in J.M. Carroll (ed), *The Black Military Experience in the American West* (Liveright: New York)

Goodwin, G. 1998 *Western Apache Raiding and Warfare* (The University of Arizona Press: Tuscon)

Grant, A. 1994 *The American Political Process 5th Ed.* (Dartmouth: Aldershot)

Griggs, G. 1974 *History of the Old West* (Bronson Printing Co,: Las Cruces N.M.)

Griffen, W.B. 1988 *Apaches at War and Peace: The Janos Presidio, 1750-1858* (University of Oklahoma Press: Norman)

Haley, J.E. 1952 *Fort Concho and the Texas Frontier* (San Angelo Standard-Times: San Angelo, Texas)

Haley, J.L. 1981 *Apaches: A History and Culture Portrait* (University of Oklahoma Press: Norman)

Hatfield, S.B. 1999 *Chasing Shadows: Apache and Yaquis Along the United States-Mexico Border, 1876-1911* (University of New Mexico Press: Albuquerque)

Hay, C. 1995 'Structure and Agency' in D. Marsh & G. Stoker, *Theory and Methods in Political Science* (MacMillan: Basingstoke)

Heitman, F.B.	1903	*Historical Register and Dictionary of the United States Army 1789-1903* (Government Printing Office: Washington D.C.)
Hill, E.E.	1979	"John Q. Smith 1875-1877" in Kvasnicka, & Viola (Eds) *The Commissioners of Indian Affairs, 1824-1977* (University of Nebraska Press: London)
Hook, J.	1987	*The Apaches* (Osprey Publishing: London)
Hughes, F.G.	2001	"The Military and Cochise" in Cozzens, *Eyewitnesses to the Indian Wars 1865-1890 Volume 1: The Struggle for Apacheria* (Stackpole Books: Mechanicsville) 132-137 First Published in 1886
Humphries, K.	1988	*Apache Land From Those Who Lived It* (The Printing Corner: El Paso Texas)
Hyde, A.F. & Deverell, W.	1996	'Reintroducing a Re-envisioned West', in C.A. Milner, *A New Significance: Re-Envisioning the History of the American West* (Oxford University Press: Oxford), pp.300-305
Jennings, F.	1988	*Empire of Fortune: Crowns, Colonies, and Tribes in the Seven Years War in America* (WW Norton & Company: London)
Jett, W.B.	2001	"Engagement in Guadalupe Canyon" in Cozzens, *Eyewitnesses to the Indian Wars 1865-1890 Volume 1: The Struggle for Apacheria* (Stackpole Books: Mechanicsville) 495-496 First Published in 1937
Johnson, M.	1992	*The Native Tribes of North America: A Concise Encyclopedia* (Windrow & Greene: London)
Katcher, P.	1985	*US Cavalry on the Plains 1850-90* (Osprey Publishing: London)
Katz, W.L.	1996	*The Black West: A documentary and Pictorial History of the African American Role in the Westwards Expansion of the United States* (Simon & Schuster: London)
Kavanagh, T.W.	1996	*The Comanches: A History 1706-1875* (University of Nebraska Press: London)
Keenan, J.	1997	*Encyclopedia of American Indian Wars 1492-1890* (ABC-CLIO: Oxford)
Kemble, E.C.	2001	"Victorio and His Young Men" in Cozzens, *Eyewitnesses to the Indian Wars 1865-1890 Volume 1: The Struggle for Apacheria* (Stackpole Books: Mechanicsville) 203-210 First Published 1880
Kenner, C.L.	1999	*Buffalo Soldiers and Officers of the Ninth Cavalry 1867-1898* (The University of Oklahoma Press: Norman)
Knight, O.	1960	*Following the Indian Wars: The Story of the Newspaper Correspondents Among the Indian Campaigns* (University of Oklahoma Press: Norman)
Knight, O.	1978	*Life and Manners in the Frontier Army* (University of Oklahoma Press: Norman)
Kraft, L.	2000	*Gatewood & Geronimo* (University of New Mexico Press: Albuquerque)
Latane, J.H. & Wainhouse, D.W.	1940	*A History of American Foreign Policy 2nd Edition* (Odyssey Press: New York)
Laughlin, W.S.	1968	'Hunting: An Integrating Biobehavior System and Its Evolutionary Importance', in R.B. Lee & I. DeVore, *Man the Hunter* (Chicago Aldine Publishing: Chicago)

Laumbach, K.W.	2001	*Hembrillo, An Apache Battlefield of the Victorio War: The Archaeology and History of the Hembrillo Battlefield* (Prepared for the White Sands Missile Range, New Mexico by Human Systems Research Inc)
Laumbach, K.W., Scott, D.D. & Wakeman, J.	2005	*Conline's Skirmish: An Episode of the Victorio War. Archaeological and Historical Documentation of an 1880s Skirmish Site on White Sands Missile Range.* (Prepared for The Directorate of Public Works, White Sands Missile Range, New Mexico by Human Systems Research Inc.)
Leckie, W.H.	1967	*The Buffalo Soldiers: A Narrative of the Negro Cavalry in the West* (University of Oklahoma Press: Norman)
Leckie, S.A. (Editor)	1989	*The Colonel's Lady on the Western Frontier: The correspondence of Alice Kirk Grierson.* (University of Nebraska Press: London)
Leckie, W.H. & Leckie, S.A.	1984	*Unlikely Warriors: General Benjamin Grierson and His Family* (University of Oklahoma Press: Norman)
Leckie, W.H. & Leckie, S.A.	2003	*The Buffalo Soldiers: A Narrative of the Black Cavalry in the West – Revised Edition* (University of Oklahoma Press: Norman)
Lee, R.B.	1968	'What Hunters Do for a Living or, How to Make Out on Scarce Resources', in R.B. Lee & I. DeVore, *Man the Hunter* (Chicago Aldine Publishing)
Lee, R.B. & DeVore, I.	1968	Problems in the Study of Hunters and Gatherers', in R.B. Lee & I. DeVore, *Man the Hunter* (Aldine Publishing: Chicago)
Leftwich, A	1983	*Redefining Politics; People Resources and Power* (Methuen: London)
Leftwich, A	1984	*What is Politics? The Activity and its Study* (Blackwell: Oxford)
Leftwich, A	2004	*What is Politics? The Activity and its Study* (Polity: Cambridge)
Lekson, S.H.	1987	*Nana's Raid: Apache Warfare in Southern New Mexico 1881* (South-western Studies No 81; University of Texas at El Paso: El Paso Texas)
Lewis, J.E.	1996	*The West* (Siena: Bristol)
Lloyd, F.	2001	"A Profile of the San Carlos Agency" in Cozzens, *Eyewitnesses to the Indian Wars 1865-1890 Volume 1: The Struggle for Apacheria* (Stackpole Books: Mechanicsville) 324-331 Letter written Feb 10th 1883
Lockwood, F.C.	1987	*The Apache Indians* (University of Nebraska Press: London) First published by MacMillan New York 1938
Longstreet, S.	1970	*War Cries on Horseback: The History of the Indian Wars* (Sphere: London)
Loring, L.Y.	2001	"Report on [the] Coyotero Apaches" in Cozzens, *Eyewitnesses to the Indian Wars 1865-1890 Volume 1: The Struggle for Apacheria* (Stackpole Books: Mechanicsville) 182-202 First Published 1875
Ludwig, L.L. & Stute, J.L.	1993	*The Battle at K-H Butte: Apache Outbreak – 1881: Arizona Territory* (Westernlore Press: Tuscon Arizona)
Mails, T.E.	1974	*The People Called Apache* (BDD Illustrated Books: New York)

Maus, M.P.	2001	"Chasing Geronimo through the Sierra Madre" in Carmony, N.B. & Brown, D.E. (Eds) *Tough Times in Rough Places: Personal Narratives of Adventure, Death and Survival on the Western Frontier* (The University of Utah Press: Salt Lake City) 237-252 First Published 1896
McAnulla, S.	2002	'Structure and Agency' in D. Marsh & G. Stoker, *Theory and Methods in Political Science* 2nd Edition (Palgrave MacMillan: Basingstoke)
McChristian, D.C.	1995	*The US Army in the West, 1870-1880: Uniforms, Weapons, and Equipment* (University of Oklahoma Press: Norman)
McCracken, H.(Editor)	1960	*Frederic Remington's Own West: Written and Illustrated by Frederic Remington* (The Dial Press: New York)
McKenna, J.A.	1963	*Black Range Tales Chronicling Sixty Years of Life and Adventure in the Southwest* (Rio Grande Press: Chicago)
Merritt, W.	2001	"Incidents of Indian Campaigning in Arizona" in Cozzens, *Eyewitnesses to the Indian Wars 1865-1890 Volume 1: The Struggle for Apacheria* (Stackpole Books: Mechanicsville) 155-161 First published 1890
Miles, N.A.	2001	"On the Trail of Geronimo" in Cozzens, *Eyewitnesses to the Indian Wars 1865-1890 Volume 1: The Struggle for Apacheria* (Stackpole Books: Mechanicsville) 536-539 First Published in 1911
Miller, L. (Editor)	1995	*From the Heart: Voices of the American Indian* (Pimlico: London)
Moore, W.H.	1994	*Chiefs, Agents & Soldiers: Conflict on the Navajo Frontier 1868-1882* (University of New Mexico Press: Albuquerque)
Morrison, K.	2006	*Marx, Durkheim and Weber 2nd Edition* (SAGE:London))
Neifert, W.W.	2001	"Trailing Geronimo by Heliograph" in Cozzens, *Eyewitnesses to the Indian Wars 1865-1890 Volume 1: The Struggle for Apacheria* (Stackpole Books: Mechanicsville) 557-561 First Published 1935
Nickerson, A.H.	2001	"An Apache Raid, and a Long Distance Ride" in Cozzens, *Eyewitnesses to the Indian Wars 1865-1890 Volume 1: The Struggle for Apacheria* (Stackpole Books: Mechanicsville) 107-112 First Published in 1897
Nisbet, R.A.	1966	*The Sociological Tradition* (Heinemann: London)
O'Neal, W.	1991	*Fighting Men of the Indian Wars: A Biographical Encyclopedia of the Mountain Men, Soldiers, Cowboys and Pioneers Who Took Up Arms During America's Westward Expansion.* (Barbed Wire Press: Stillwater Oklahoma)
Ogle, R.H.	1970	*Federal Control of the Western Apaches 1848-1886* (University of New Mexico Press: Albuquerque)
Opler, M.E.	1969	*Apache Odyssey: A Journey between Two Worlds* (Holt, Rinehart and Wilson: London)
Opler, M.E.	1994	*Myths and Legends of the Chiricahua Apache Indians* (University of Nebraska Press: Lincoln) First published by the American Folk-Lore Society 1942

Opler, M.E.	1996	*An Apache Life-Way: The Economic, Social, & Religious Institutions of the Chiricahua Indians* (University of Nebraska Press: Lincoln) First published by the University of Chicago Press 1941
Panzeri, P.	1995	*The Little Big Horn 1876: Custer's Last Stand* (Campaign series No. 39; Osprey: London)
Parker, J.	1929	*The Old Army Memories 1872-1918* (Dorrance & Co: Philadelphia)
Parkman, F.	1908	*The Conspiracy of Pontiac and the Indian War after the Conquest of Canada Vol. II* (JM Dent & Sons: London)
Pegler, M.	1993	*US Cavalryman 1965-1890* (Warrior Series 4; Osprey: London)
Pettit, J.S.	2001	"Apache Campaign Notes-1886" in Cozzens, *Eyewitnesses to the Indian Wars 1865-1890 Volume 1: The Struggle for Apacheria* (Stackpole Books: Mechanicsville) 532-535 First Published 1886
Pletcher, D.M.	1978	"Manifest Destiny" in De Conde (Ed), *Encyclopedia of American Foreign Policy: Studies of the Principal Movements and Ideas Volume II*, (Charles Scribners Sons: New York) 526-534
Rakocy, W. & Jones, R.S. (Editors)	1977	*Mogollon Diary 1877-1977* (Rio Bravo Press)
Rakocy, W.	1983	*Ghosts of Kingston Hillsboro N. Mex. A Pictorial Documentary of the Great Black Range Country ca. 1880's* (Bravo Press: El Paso)
Randall, A.F.	2001	"In the Heart of the Sierra Madre" in Cozzens, *Eyewitnesses to the Indian Wars 1865-1890 Volume 1: The Struggle for Apacheria* (Stackpole Books: Mechanicsville) 394-395 First Published 1883
Rathbun, D.C. & Alexander, D.V.	2003	*New Mexico Frontier Military Place Names* (Yucca Tree Press: Las Cruces)
Reedstrom, E.L.	1990	*Apache Wars: An Illustrated Battle History* (Sterling Publishing Co.: New York)
Rickey, D.	1963	*Forty Miles a Day on Beans and Hay: The Enlisted Soldier Fighting the Indian Wars* (University of Oklahoma Press: Norman)
Rice, M.M.	2001	"Across Apache Land" in Cozzens, *Eyewitnesses to the Indian Wars 1865-1890 Volume 1: The Struggle for Apacheria* (Stackpole Books: Mechanicsville) 502-508 First Published 1895
Ridley, J.	1993	*Maximilian and Juarez* (Constable: London)
Rister, C.C.	1928	*The Southwestern Frontier* (Arthur Clark Company: Cleveland)
Roberts, D.	1998	*Once They Moved Like The Wind: Cochise, Geronimo and the Apache Wars* (Pimlico: London)
Robinson III, C.M.	2001	*General Crook and the Western Frontier* (The University of Oklahoma Press: Norman)
Robinson, S.	2000	*Apache Voices: Their Stories of Survival as Told to Eve Ball* (University of New Mexico Press: Albuquerque)
Rostow, E.V.	1993	*A Breakfast for Bonaparte: US National Security Interests from the Heights of Abraham to the Nuclear Age* (National Defense University Press: Washington D.C.)
Ruhlen, G.	1971	"Quitman: The Worst Post at Which I Served" cited in J.M. Carroll (ed), *The Black Military Experience in the American West* (Liveright: New York)

Russell, S.	1986	"The Social Construction of Artefacts: A Response to Pinch and Bijker" *Social Studies of Science* Vol. 16, SAGE, London, 331-46
Sanchez, R.	200	*Cochise Remembers: A Story of Discovery and Reconciliation in New Mexico Genealogy and Family History* (R&R: San Diego)
Safford, A.P.K.	2002	"Something About Cochise" in Cozzens, *Eyewitnesses to the Indian Wars 1865-1890 Volume 1: The Struggle for Apacheria* (Stackpole Books: Mechanicsville) 124-131 First published 1872
Scott *et al*	1989	*Archaeological Perspectives on the Battle of the Little Bighorn* (University of Oklahoma Press: London)
Scott *et al*	1998	*They Died With Custer: Soldiers Bones from the Battle of the Little Bighorn* (University of Oklahoma Press: Norman)
Schubert, F.N.	1995	*On the Trail of the Buffalo Soldier: Biographies of African Americans in the U.S. Army 1866-1917* (Scholarly Resources: Wilmington, Delaware)
Schubert, F.N.	1997	*Black Valor: Buffalo Soldiers and the Medal of Honor, 1870-1898* (Scholarly Resources: Wilmington, Delaware)
Schubert, F.N.	2003	*Voices of the Buffalo Soldier: Records, Reports, and Recollections of Military Life and Service in the West* (University of New Mexico Press: Albuquerque)
Shaffer, D.R.	1999	*Developmental Psychology: Childhood & Adolescence 5th Edition* (Brooks Cole Publishing Co: London)
Shipp, W.E.	2001	"Captain Crawford's Last Expedition" in Cozzens, *Eyewitnesses to the Indian Wars 1865-1890 Volume 1: The Struggle for Apacheria* (Stackpole Books: Mechanicsville) 516-531 First Published in 1892
Sieber, A.	2001	"Military and Indians" in Cozzens, *Eyewitnesses to the Indian Wars 1865-1890 Volume 1: The Struggle for Apacheria* (Stackpole Books: Mechanicsville) 290-294 First Published 1882
Skogen, L.C.	1996	*Indian Depredation Claims 1796-1920* (University of Oklahoma Press: London)
Smith, S.L.	1990	*The View from Officer's Row: Army Perceptions of Western Indians* (University of Arizona Press: Tuscon)
Smith, T.T. (Editor)	1994	*A Dose of Frontier Soldiering: The Memoirs of Corporal E.A. Bode, Frontier Regular Infantry, 1877-1882* (University of Nebraska Press: Lincoln)
Sonnichsen, C.L.	1973	*The Mescalero Apaches 2nd Edition* (University of Oklahoma Press: London)
Spicer, E.R.	1962	*Cycles of Conquest: The Impact of Spain, Mexico, and the United States on the Indians of the Southwest, 1533-1960* (The University of Arizona Press: Tuscon)
Spude, R.L.	1992	"Native Americans and Gold Rushes. Two Views: 1860s Arizona and the Apache, 1900s Alaska and the Eskimo" in K. Tenfelde, in *Towards a Social History of Mining in the 19th and 20th Centuries: Papers Presented to the International Mining History Congress Bochum, Federal Republic of Germany, September, 3rd-7th 1989 (Verlag C.H. Beck: Munchen)*

Steffen, R. 1978 *The Horse Soldier 1776-1943 Volume II: The Frontier, the Mexican War, the Civil War, the Indian Wars 1851-1880* (University of Oklahoma Press; London)

Stockel, H.H. 1991 *Women of the Apache Nation: Voices of Truth* (University of Nevada Press: Reno & Las Vegas)

Stockel, H.H. 2004 *On the Bloody Road to Jesus: Christianity and the Chiricahua Apaches* (University of New Mexico Press: Albuquerque)

Stout, J.A. 1974 *Apache Lightning: The Last Great Battles of the Ojo Calientes* (University of Oxford Press: New York)

Sweeney, E.R. 1991 *Cochise: Chiricahua Apache Chief* (University of Oklahoma Press: Norman)

Sweeney, E.R. 1992 *Merejildo Grijalva: Apache Captive, Army Scout* (The University of Texas at El Paso: Southwestern Studies Series No 96, El Paso

Sweeney, E.R. (Editor) 1997 *Making Peace with Cochise: The 1872 Journal of Captain Joseph Alton Sladen* (University of Oklahoma Press: Norman)

Sweeney, E.R. 1998 *Mangas Coloradas: Chief of the Chiricahua Apaches* (University of Oklahoma Press: Norman)

Tate, M.L. 1999 *The Frontier Army in the Settlement of the West* (Oklahoma University Press: Norman)

Thompson, E.N. 1971 "The Negro Soldier and His Officers" cited in J.M. Carroll (ed), *The Black Military Experience in the American West* (Liveright: New York)

Thompson, C. 1985 *History of Marfa and Presidio County, Texas 1535-1946. Volume One, 1535-1900* (Nortex Press: Austin)

Thrapp. D.L. 1964 *Al Sieber Chief of Scouts* (University of Oklahoma Press: London)

Thrapp, D.L. 1967 *The Conquest of Apacheria* (University of Oklahoma Press: London)

Thrapp, D.L. 1972 *General Crook and the Sierra Madre Adventure* (University of Oklahoma Press: London)

Thrapp, D.L. 1973 *Juh: An Incredible Indian* (South-western Studies No 39 University of Texas at El Paso: El Paso Texas)

Thrapp, D.L. 1974 *Victorio and the Mimbres Apaches* (University of Oklahoma Press: London)

Thrapp, D.L (Editor). 1979 *Dateline Fort Bowie: Charles Fletcher Lummis Reports on an Apache War* (University of Oklahoma Press: Norman)

Thrapp, D.L. 1988 *Encyclopedia of Frontier Biography Vol I-III* (University of Nebraska Press in association with The Arthur H. Clark Company: London & Spokane)

Turney-High, H.H. 1991 *Primitive War: Its Practice and Concepts* (The University of South Carolina Press: Columbia)

Twitchell, R.E. 1963 *The Leading Facts of New Mexican History* (Horn & Wallace: Albuquerque)

Upham, F.K. 2001 "Incidents of Regular Army Life in Time of Peace" in Cozzens, *Eyewitnesses to the Indian Wars 1865-1890 Volume 1: The Struggle for Apacheria* (Stackpole Books: Mechanicsville) 85-93 First Published 1885

Utley, R.M. 1963 *The Last Days of the Sioux Nation* (Yale University Press: New Haven)

Utley, R.M.	1967	*Frontiersmen in Blue: The United States Army and the Indian, 1848-1865* (University of Nebraska Press: London)
Utley, R.M.	1973	*Frontier Regulars: The United States Army and the Indian, 1866-1891* (University of Nebraska Press: London)
Utley, R.M.	1977	*A Clash of Cultures: Fort Bowie and the Chiricahua Apaches* (National Park Service: Washington D.C.)
Utley, R.M.	1984 (i)	*The Indian Frontier of the American West 1846-1890* (University of New Mexico Press: Albuquerque)
Van Alstyne, R.W.	1978	"The Monroe Doctrine" in De Conde (Ed), *Encyclopedia of American Foreign Policy: Studies of the Principal Movements and Ideas Volume II*, (Charles Scribners Sons: New York) 584-596
Van Orden, J.	1991	*Geronimo's Surrender: The 1886 C.S. Fly Photographs* (Arizona Historical Society: Tuscon)
Wakeman, J. & Laumbach, K.	1999	'Victorio's Escape: GPS and Archaeology Recount the Tale of an Apache Battle' in K.L. Feder, *Lessons from the Past: An Introductory Reader in Archaeology* (Mayfield Publishing Company: London)
Watson, J.W.	2001	"Scouting in Arizona, 1890" in Cozzens, *Eyewitnesses to the Indian Wars 1865-1890 Volume 1: The Struggle for Apacheria* (Stackpole Books: Mechanicsville) 642-648 First Published 1897
Watson, J.W.	1976	*Chronological List of Engagements between the Regular Army of the United States and various tribes of Hostile Indians which occurred during the years1790-1898 inclusive* (AMS Press: New York)
Watt R.N.	2012	*Apache Tactics 1830-1886* (Osprey Publishing: Oxford)
Watt R.N.	2014	*Apache Warrior 1860-1886* (Osprey Publishing: Oxford)
Wellman, P. I.	(No date)	*Death in the Desert* (W. Foulsham & Co for the Fireside Press: London)
Wellman, P. I.	1957	*Death in the Desert* (Transworld Publishers:London)
Wharfield, Col. H.B.	1971	"The Tenth Cavalry in the Early Days" cited in J.M. Carroll (ed), *The Black Military Experience in the American West* (Liveright: New York)
Wheeler, K.	1978	*The Old West: The Scouts* (Time-Life Books: Alexandria Virginia)
White, J.M.	1979	*Everyday Life of the North American Indian* (Book Club Associates: London)
White, R.	1991	*"It's Your Misfortune and None of My Own": A New History of the American West* (University of Oklahoma Press: London)
Woodburn, J.	1968	'An Introduction to Hadza Ecology', in R.B. Lee & I. DeVore, *Man the Hunter* (Chicago Aldine Publishing: Chicago)
Wooster, R.	1988	*The Military and United States Indian Policy 1865-1903* (Yale University Press: London)
Worcester, D.E.	1979	*The Apaches: Eagles of the Southwest* (University of Oklahoma Press: Norman)
Wormser R.	1966	*The Yellowlegs: The Story of the United States Cavalry* (Doubleday: New York)
Wright, H.R.	2001	"In the Days of Geronimo" in Cozzens, *Eyewitnesses to the Indian Wars 1865-1890 Volume 1: The Struggle for Apacheria* (Stackpole Books: Mechanicsville) 497-501 First Published 1905

Journals

The *Army and Navy Journal* – Vols. 16-18 (August 1879 – July 1882)

Aceves, J.	"Who was Victorio? By Don Jesus Tarin as told to Jose Aceves" *Frontier Times* (September 1963), 24-25 & 71
Aranda, D.D.	"An Episode From Victorio's War," *Real West* (February 1984), 14-19
Aranda, D.D.	"Apache Depredations in Dona Ana County: An Incident in Victorio's War," *Southern New Mexico Historical Journal* Vol. 3, 1995, Issue 1, 2-8
Ayres, J.	"A Soldier's Experience in New Mexico," *New Mexico Historical Review*, Vol. XXIV, No. 4 (October, 1949), 259-66
Ball, L.D.	"Militia Posses: The Territorial Militia in Civil Law Enforcement in New Mexico Territory, 1877-1883," *New Mexico Historical Review*, Vol 55, No. 1 (January, 1980), 47-69
Ball, Eve.	"The Fight for Ojo Caliente," *Frontier Times*, Vol. XXXVI, No. 2 (Spring, 1962), 22-23, 40
Balmer, J.W.	"It was only 75 Years Ago" *The English Westerners Brand Book* Vol. 3, No. 1 (November 1956) 1-7
Baylor, G.W.	"The Old Frontier; Events of Long Ago" *Frontier Times* Vol. 2, No.11, (August 1925), 12-13
Bernstein, J.H.	"Secrets of Los Ladrones: Mysteries Shroud remote Rio Grande Valley Range," *New Mexico Magazine* Vol. 72, No 7 (July 1994), 72-79
Billington, M.	"Black History and New Mexico Place Names," *Password* Vol. XXIX, No. 3 (Fall, 1984), 107-113
Bond, H.M.	"The Negro in the Armed Forces of the United States Prior to World War I," *Journal of Negro Education,* Vol. 12, Issue 3, (Summer 1943), 268-287
Boucher, L.H.	"Fort Cummings, Desert Sentinel,"*Real West*, Vol. XIII, No. 81 (April, 1970), 6, 44-47
Brumwell. S.	"A Service Truly Critical: The British Army and Warfare with the North American Indians, 1755-1764" *War in History*, Vol. 5, No 2 (1998) 146-75
Clum, J.P.	"Geronimo," *New Mexico Historical Review,* Vol. III, Nos. 1,2,3 (January, April, July 1928), 1-40, 121-44, 217-64.
Clum, J.P.	"The Apaches," *New Mexico Historical Review,* Vol. IV, No. 2 (April, 1929i), 109-127
Clum, J.P.	"The San Carlos Police," *New Mexico Historical Review*, Vol. IV, No. 3 (July, 1929ii), 203-219
Clum, J.P.	"Apache Misrule," *New Mexico Historical Review,* Vol. V, Nos. 2 & 3 (April, July 1930i), 138-153, 221-239
Clum, J.P.	"Victorio," *Arizona Historical Review*, Vol II, No. 4 (January, 1930ii), 74-90
Crimmins, Col. M.L.	"Colonel Buell's Expedition into Mexico in 1880," *New Mexico Historical Review*, Vol. X, No. 2 (April 1935), 133-142
Crimmins, Col. M.L.	"The Mescalero Apaches" *Frontier Times* Vol. 8, No.12, (September 1931), p.551

Cutter, D.C. "The Legacy of the Treaty of Guadalupe Hidalgo," *New Mexico Historical Review*, Vol. 53, No. 4 (October, 1978), 305-315

Dinges, B.J. "The Victorio Campaign of 1880: Cooperation and Conflict on the United States – Mexico Border," *New Mexico Historical Review*, Vol. 62 No. 1, (Jan 1987), 81-94

Dinges, B.J. "Leighton Finley: A Forgotten Soldier of the Apache Wars" *The Journal of Arizona History*, Vol. 29, No.2, (Summer 1988), 163-184

Elliott, C.P. "An Indian Reservation Under General George Crook," *Military Affairs*, Vol. 12, Issue 2 (Summer 1948), 91-102

Ellis, R.N. (Ed) "The Apache Chronicle," *New Mexico Historical Review*, Vol. XLVII, No. 3 (July, 1972), 275-282

Gatewood, C.B. "Campaigning Against Victorio in 1879," *The Great Divide*, (April, 1894), 102-104

Gibson, S. 'From the Archives: Sarah Gibson's Story' *Hillsboro Historical Society*, February 2016, Vol. 9, Number 1, 4-7
Richard E. Mitchem of Cedar City, Utah sent the story below to Sonja. We've seen several accounts of the 1879 Apache attack on McEver's Ranch, but this is the only first-hand description we've seen, told by one of the women who was living at the cienega, when the attack occurred. Mr. Mitchem received this manuscript from Judith Crawford of Deming, NM.

Gillett, J.B. "Injun Fighting With The Texas Rangers" *Frontier Times* Vol. 3, No. 9, (June 1926)

Greever, W.S. "Railway Development in the Southwest," *New Mexico Historical Review*, Vol. XXXII, No. 2 (April, 1957), 151-203

Hall, M.H. "Colonel James Reily's Diplomatic Missions to Chihuahua and Sonora," *New Mexico Historical Review*, Vol. XXXI, No. 3 (July, 1956), 232-242

Harnin, W. "Apache Siege at Alma" *True West* (June 1956) 8-10 & 30

Hart, R.L. "Colonel Hatch and the Territorial Press during the Victorio War" *Southern New Mexico Historical Review* Vol. VI, No. 1, (January 1997) 44-49

Hastings, J.K. "A Boy's-Eye View of the Old Southwest," *New Mexico Historical Review*, Vol. XXVI, No. 4 (October 1951), 287-301.

Hunter, J.M. "The Fierce Apache Indians" *Frontier Times* Vol. 21, No. 7, (April 1944), p.299

Janda, Lance. "Shutting the Gates of Mercy: The American Origins of Total War, 1860-1880" *The Journal of Military History*, Vol. 59, Issue 1 (Jan 1995), 7-26

Johnson, B.C. "The Death of Victorio: Beck's Account" *The English Westerners Brand Book* Vol. 3, No. 9, (July 1957) 9-11

Jones, Calico. "Nana: The Vengeful Ghost of the Apaches" *Western Digest* (November 1969), 52-61 & 74-81

Jones, Calico. "Victorio's Vengeance Raid," *Real West*, Vol. XIII, No. 81 (April, 1970), 31-35,55,77

Jones, O.L. "Lew Wallace: Hoosier Governor of Territorial New Mexico, 1878-81" *New Mexico Historical Review*, Vol. 60, (April, 1985), 129-158

Kayser, D. "The Southern Apache Agency" *El Palacio* Vol. 79, No. 2, (1973i), 16-23

Kayser, D.	"Fort Tulerosa [Old Fort Tularosa]: 1872-1874" *El Palacio* Vol. 79, No. 2, (1973ii), 24-27
Kaywaykla, J., as told to Eve Ball.	"I survived the Massacre of Tres Castillos," *True West*, Vol VIII, No. 6 (July-August, 1961), 22-23, 38.
Kaywaykla, J., as told to Eve Ball.	"Nana's People," *True West*, Vol X No. 6 (July-August, 1963), 20-21, 66-67.
Leonard, T.C.	"Red, White and the Army Blue: Empathy and Anger in the American West," *American Quarterly*, Vol. 26, Issue 2 (May 1974), 176-190
Matthews, J.	"Squarely Fought: Fort Concho and the Campaign against Victorio, 1880," *West Texas Historical Association Year Book*, Vol. 69, (1993), 34-44
McChristian, D.D.	"Grierson's Fight at Tinaja de las Palmas: An Episode in the Victoria (sic) Campaign," *Red River Valley Historical Review*, Vol. 7, (Winter 1982), pp.45-63
Meyer, D.L.	"Early Mexican-American Responses to Negative Stereotyping," *New Mexico Historical Review*, Vol. LIII, No. 1 (January, 1978), 75-91
Miles, Bob.	"Nine Against a Hundred" *Old West* (Fall 1971), p.20
Miles, N.A,	"How U.S. Troops Caught Geronimo" *Frontier Times* Vol. 9 (February 1932), 193-196
Miller, H.	"Nana's Raid of 1881," *Password,* Vol. XIX, No 2 (Summer 1974), 51-70
Miller, D.A.	"The Role of the Army Inspector in the Southwest: Nelson H. Davis in New Mexico and Arizona, 1863-1873" *New Mexico Historical Review* Vol. 59, No. 2 (April 1984), 137-164
Myers, L.	"Fort Webster on the Mimbres River," *New Mexico Historical Review*, Vol. XLI, No. 1 (January, 1966i), 47-57.
Myers, L.	"The Enigma of Mangas Coloradas' Death," *New Mexico Historical Review*, Vol. XLI, No. 4 (October, 1966ii), 287-304
Myers, L.	"Military Establishments in Southwestern New Mexico: Stepping Stones to Settlement," *New Mexico Historical Review*, Vol. XLIII, No. 1 (January, 1968), 5-48.
Nolan, F.	"Van C. Smith:'A Very Companionable Gentleman'" *New Mexico Historical Review* Vol. 72, No. 2 (April 1997), 153-170
Nolan, F.	"The Men of Fort Stanton," *Quarterly of the National Association for Outlaw and Lawman History*, Vol. 18 (Oct 1994), 37-45
Nolan, P.T.	"Captain Jack Crawford: Veteran and Western Hero," *Real West*, Vol. XIII, No. 81 (April, 1970), 19-22 & 63
Norton, H.S.	"Kaytennae and the End of the Apache Wars" *True West* (June 1988), p.14
O'Neal, B.	"Captain Henry Carroll: Southwestern Indian Fighter" *Real West* (June 1982), p.55
Ogle, Ralph H.	"The Apache and the Government – 1870's," *New Mexico Historical Review*, Vol. XXXIII, No. 2 (April, 1958), 81-102
Opler, M.E.	"A Chiricahua Apache's Account of the Geronimo Campaign of 1886," *New Mexico Historical Review*, Vol. XIII, No. 4 (October, 1938), 360-386.
Opler, M.E. & Hoijer, H.	"The Raid and War-Path Language of the Chiricahua Apache," *American Anthropologist* Vol. XLII, (Oct-Dec 1940), 617-34

Opler, M.E. & C.H. Opler. "Mescalero Apache History in the Southwest," *New Mexico Historical Review*, Vol. XXV, (January, 1950), 1-36

Porter, K.W. "Contacts in Warfare" *Journal of Negro History* Vol. 17, Issue 3, (July 1932), 298-306

Porter, K.W. "Notes Supplementary to 'Relations between Negroes and Indians" *Journal of Negro History* Vol. 18, Issue 3, (July 1933), 282-321

Porter, K.W. "Negroes and Indians on the Texas Frontier, 1831-1876," *Journal of Negro History* Vol. 41, Issue 3 (Jul., 1956i), 185-214

Porter, K.W. "Negroes and Indians on the Texas Frontier, 1831-1876," *Journal of Negro History* Vol. 41, Issue 4 (Oct., 1956ii), 285-310

Powers, N.B. "A Ride From Geronimo, The Apache," *New Mexico Historical Review*, Vol. XXXVI, No. 2 (April, 1961), 89-96

Rasch, P.J. "The Death of Victorio" *The English Westerners Brand Book* Vol. 11, No. 3, (April 1960), 9-10

Reddick, L.D. "The Negro Policy of the United States Army, 1775-1945" *Journal of Negro History* Vol. 34, Issue 1, (Jan 1949), 9-29

Reeve, F.D. "The Federal Indian Policy in New Mexico, 1858-1880," *New Mexico Historical Review*, Vol. XII No 3 (July 1937), 218-269 & Vol. XIII Nos.1,2,3 (January April and July 1938) 14-62, 146-191, 261-313

Remington, F. "A Scout with the Buffalo Soldiers" *The Century Illustrated Monthly Magazine* New Series Vol. XV, (November 1888-April 1889), 899-912

Rolley, LaNelda "Buffalo Soldiers Ride Again: Belated Recognition extended to Black Regiments" *New Mexico Magazine* Vol. 72, No. 7, (July 1994), 26-31

Rosson, M. "The Pursuit of Victorio", *Real West* March 1980, p.26 repeated in *Real West* Special Issue 1981 p.14

Russell S. "The Social Construction of Artefacts; A Response to Pinch and Bijker" *Social Studies of Science*, (1986), 16, pp.331-346. (London: SAGE)

Sayles, S. "The Romero-Frelinghuysen Convention: A Milestone in Border Relations," *New Mexico Historical Review*, Vol. LI, No. 4 (October, 1976), 295-311

Schwatka, F. "Among the Apaches" *The Century Illustrated Monthly Magazine* New Series Vol. XII, (May 1887-October 1887), 41-52

Sharp, K. "Last Words on Victorio" *The English Westerners Brand Book* Vol. 3, No. 10, (August 1957), 11-12

Smith, R.A. "Apache Plunder Trails Southwards, 1831-1840," *New Mexico Historical Review*, Vol. XXXVII, No. 1 (January 1962), 20-42

Smith, R.A. "The Scalp Hunt in Chihuahua-1849," *New Mexico Historical Review*, Vol XL, No. 2 (April, 1965), 116-40

Sowell, A.J. "A Tragedy Of The Texas Frontier" *Frontier Times* Vol. 22, No. 10, (July 1945), 290-292

Steelhammer, C. "With the Apache Indians during the Revolt of 1879," *Military Affairs*, Vol. 18, No.2 (Summer 1954), 86-88

Tate, M.L. "John P. Clum and the Origins of an Apache Constabulary, 1874-1877" *American Indian Quarterly* Vol. 3, No.2 (Summer 1977), 99-120

Temple, F.M. "Federal Military Defense of the Trans-Pecos Region 1850-1880," *West Texas Historical Association Year Book*, Vol. 30, (1954), 40-60

Temple, F.M.	"Colonel Grierson in the Southwest," *Panhandle Plains Historical Review*, Vol. 30, (1957), 27-54
Temple, F.M.	"Colonel B. H. Grierson's Victorio Campaign," *West Texas Historical Association Year Book*, Vol. 35, (1959), 99-111
Temple, F.M.	"Colonel B.H. Grierson's Administration of the District of the Pecos" *West Texas Historical Association Year Book* Vol. 37, (October 1962), 85-96
Utley, R.M. (1984ii)	"The Buffalo Soldiers and Victorio" *New Mexico Magazine* 62: 3 (March 1984) ????????????????????
Wasson, J.	"The Southwest in 1880," *New Mexico Historical Review*, Vol. V, No. 3 (July, 1930), 263-287
Watt, R.N.	"Raiders of a Lost Art? Apache War and Society" *Small Wars & Insurgencies* Vol. 13, No. 3, (Autumn 2002), 1-28
Watt, R.N.	"'Horses Worn to Mere Shadows': The Effects of Campaigning against Apaches upon the Ninth U.S. Cavalry Regiment in New Mexico Territory 1879-1881" *New Mexico Historical Review*, (Spring 2011), 197-222
Watt, R.N.	"Apaches Without and Enemies Within: The U.S. Army in New Mexico 1879-1881" *War in History*, Vol. 18, Issue 2, (April 2011), 148-183
Watt, R.N.	"Victorio's Military & Political Leadership of the Warm Springs Apaches" *War in History* Vol. 18, Issue 4, (November 2011), 457-494
Watt, R.N.	"A Reevaluation of Colonel Benjamin H. Grierson's Trans-Pecos Campaign Against Victorio, July-August 1880." *Southwestern Historical Quarterly*, Vol. CXVIII, No.3, (January 2015), 240-261
Watt, R.N.	"'An Exodus to Nowhere'?: Victorio's Tres Castillos Campaign, September-October 1880" *The Journal of Military History*, Volume 80, No.4, (October 2016), 1037-1072
White, R.	"Race Relations in the American West," *American Quarterly*, Vol. 38, Issue 3 (1986), 396-416
Wilks, J.	"A Negro Trooper Of The Ninth Cavalry" *Frontier Times* Vol. 4, No.7, (April 1927), p.11
Wilson, J.P.	"How the Settlers Farmed: Hispanic Villages and Irrigation Systems in Early Sierra County, 1850-1900" *New Mexico Historical Review* Vol. 63, No. 4, (Oct 1988), 333-356
Woodward, A.	"Side Lights on Fifty Years of Apache Warfare" *Arizoniana* Vol. 11, (Fall 1961), 3-14
Worcester, D.E.	"The Beginnings of the Apache Menace of the Southwest," *New Mexico Historical Review*, Vol. XVI, No. 1 (January, 1941), 1-14
Worcester, D.E.	"The Apaches in the History of the Southwest," *New Mexico Historical Review*, Vol. L, No. 1 (January, 1975), 25-44
Yarbrough, L.	"Victorio, The Desert Fox" *Real West* (June 1969), 10-12, 65-66 & 69

Modern Newspaper Articles

Abarr (i), James. "Mining Memories," *Albuquerque Journal* October 18, 1998

Abarr (ii), James. "Desolate Outpost," *Albuquerque Journal* August 30, 1998

Associated Press, "1879 Battle Commemorated," *The Arizona Republic*, June 16, 1999

Digest, "Victorio's Name Cleared," *Albuquerque Journal*, July 4, 1995

El Paso Times 1st March 1942, "Apaches In Ambush Between Hillsboro, Lake Valley Killed 18 Frontiersmen, Buried In Single Grave On Spot Where They Fell"

Evening Review, The, Saturday 17th June 1882

Frentzel, Martin. "Trailing the Buffalo Soldiers," *Albuquerque Journal*, Dec 12, 1996

Jackson, David G. "Group Hikes Into History," *Albuquerque Journal*, November 16, 2000

The Los Angeles Times, "Leading the Charge: Danny Glover brings 'Buffalo Soldiers,' a Chronicle of the Famed Black Cavalry Corps to TNT," cited in the *Fort Worth Star-Telegram*, December 5, 1997

Lumpkin, John J. "Scientists Rewrite Cavalry, Apache Battle History," *Albuquerque Journal*, April 23, 1999

Neel, Ellis "Rewriting History: Buffalo Soldier Grit Backed by Evidence" Alamogordo Daily News cited in *The Denver Post* May 2, 1999.

Perez, L. "Memoir Recounts Death of Apache Chief Victorio" *Silver City Daily Press* Tuesday, June 30, 1998

Reed, Ollie Jr. "Colonel Lauded for Grave Work: Relocation Effort Leads to Prestigious Award," *The Albuquerque Tribune* cited in *The Denver Post*, June 20, 1999

Rene Romo Journal Southern Bureau, "Cavalrymen Honored Century After Battle," cited in *Albuquerque Journal*, September 14, 1996

Roberts, Chris. "Honoring Warriors," *Albuquerque Journal*, June 22, 1997.

Rocky Mountain News, "Apache Chief to be Honored: 19th Century Leader Victorio to be Inducted into Indian Hall of Fame in Oklahoma Ceremony" *Rocky Mountain News* August 18, 1991.

Saunders, Dusty. "A Wild Ride with 'Buffalo Soldiers' TNT Film Features Blacks' Encounters with Apaches and with White Military," *Rocky Mountain News*, December 7, 1997

Simmons, M. "New Mexico Scrapbook: Miners Flocked to Florida Mountains" *El Paso Times* 22nd January 1995

Sun-News. "Scientists Rewrite Cavalry, Apache Battle History" *Sun-News* Saturday, April 24, 1999

Whitney Herb. "He was a Guerrillla Fighter without Peer whose Nickname became a Battle Cry... Geronimo!," *The Arizona Republic* August 31, 1986

Internet Sites

Alma – New Mexico Ghost Town (*downloaded 24/03/2001*)
http://www.ghosttowns.com/states/nm/alma.html

Ambush in Massacre Canyon: by G. Ballinger (*downloaded 17/03/99)*
http://www.zianet.com/wblase/courier/ambush.htm

American Life Histories: Manuscripts from the Federal Writers' Project. 1936-1940 (*downloaded 03/03/2001* – See following entries)

Abran Miller
http://lcweb2.loc.gov/cgi-bin/query/D?wpa:41:./temp/~ammem_3Uyf::

Early Days Around Silver City
http://lcweb2.loc.gov/cgi-bin/query/D?wpa:15:./temp/~ammem_3Uyf::

Early Days In Silver City and Grant Co.
http://lcweb2.loc.gov/cgi-bin/query/D?wpa:1:./temp/~ammem_rPD9::

Incidents of the Early '80s
http://lcweb2.loc.gov/cgi-bin/query/D?wpa:4:./temp/~ammem_6794::

J.C. Brock
http://lcweb2.loc.gov/cgi-bin/query/D?wpa:14:./temp/~ammem_3Uyf::

J.F. Henderson
http://lcweb2.loc.gov/cgi-bin/query/D?wpa:39:./temp/~ammem_3Uyf::
J.H. (Jake) Byler
http://lcweb2.loc.gov/cgi-bin/query/D?wpa:44:./temp/~ammem_3Uyf::
Jose Apodaca
http://lcweb2.loc.gov/cgi-bin/query/D?wpa:17:./temp/~ammem_3Uyf::
Killing of Charlie Bachelor
http://lcweb2.loc.gov/cgi-bin/query/D?wpa:9:./temp/~ammem_3Uyf::
Louie Taren
http://lcweb2.loc.gov/cgi-bin/query/D?wpa:21:./temp/~ammem_3Uyf::
Mexican Boy Captured by Apache Indians
http://lcweb2.loc.gov/cgi-bin/query/D?wpa:3:./temp/~ammem_6794::
Mogollons of the Early Days
http://lcweb2.loc.gov/cgi-bin/query/D?wpa:1:./temp/~ammem_38gG::
Mr Eugene McCrohan
http://lcweb2.loc.gov/cgi-bin/query/D?wpa:1:./temp/~ammem_E2JH::
Mrs O.S. Warren
http://lcweb2.loc.gov/cgi-bin/query/D?wpa:18:./temp/~ammem_3Uyf::
Old Timers Dictionary
http://lcweb2.loc.gov/cgi-bin/query/D?wpa:23:./temp/~ammem_3Uyf::
The Alma Massacre
http://lcweb2.loc.gov/cgi-bin/query/D?wpa:2:./temp/~ammem_BRbY::
The Alms Massacre
http://lcweb2.loc.gov/cgi-bin/query/D?wpa:5:./temp/~ammem_6794::
Aragon – Fort Tularosa – New Mexico Ghost Town (*downloaded 12/12/2000*)
http://www.ghosttowns.com/states/nm/aragon-forttularosa.html
Benjamin H. Grierson by Chuck Barth, Tuscon Arizona (*downloaded 15/05/2001*)
http://www.cia-g.com/~rockets/NMGrierson.htm
The Buffalo Soldiers (1) (*downloaded 15/01/2000)*
http://www.zianet.com/wblase/courier/buffalo.htm
Buffalo Soldiers (2): Synopsis of TNT's Buffalo Soldiers: (*downloaded 13/09/99)*
http://turnerlearning.com/tntlearning/buffalo /entire.html
Buffalo Soldiers & Indian Wars (*downloaded 20/03/2001-05-17*)
http://www.buffalosoldier.net/index.htm
The Bulletin – Serving Las Cruces and the Mesilla Valley for Thirty Years. (*downloaded 15/01/2000)*
http://www.zianet.com/bulletin/1999/04_29_99/plaque.html

Articles

Plaque Commemorates 1880 Battle in San Andres – M. Jaxson
Space Age Science Yields New View of Hembrillo Battle – J. Eckles
Cabinet Members Under Hayes (*downloaded 24/10/05*)
http://www.infoplease.com/ipa/A0101224.html
Cabinet Members Under Garfield (*downloaded 24/10/05*)
http://www.infoplease.com/ipa/A0101226.html
Cabinet Members Under Arthur (*downloaded 24/10/05*)
http://www.infoplease.com/ipa/A0101228.html

Chief Victorio (*downloaded 10/03/2001*)
http://www.kingsnake.com/hudspeth/victorio.htm
Chiz – New Mexico Ghost Town (*downloaded 12/12/2000*)
http://www.ghosttowns.com/states/nm/chiz.html
Chloride, Sierra County NM (*downloaded 03/03/2001*)
http://village.globaldrum.com/sierra_newmexico/chloride.htm
Clairmont – New Mexico Ghost Town (*downloaded 24/03/2001*)
http://www.ghosttowns.com/states/nm/clairmont.html
Claridge, D. – Geronimo and Victorio – A Comparative Study (*downloaded 12/12 2000*)
http://www.zianet.com/snm/geronvic.htm
Cooney – New Mexico Ghost Town (*downloaded 12/12/2000*)
http://www.ghosttowns.com/states/nm/cooney.html
Cuchillo – New Mexico Ghost Town (*downloaded 12/12/2000*)
http://www.ghosttowns.com/states/nm/cuchillo.html
Electric Scotland.Com: Deaths which Occurred October 14th *(consulted 15/01/2000)*
http://www.electricscotland.com/history/today/1014.htm
Fort Davis Museum – Planning Outline for Rattlesnake Springs Exhibit *(downloaded 15/05/2001)*
http://turnerlearning.com/tntlearning/buffalo/davis.html
Fort Selden: New Mexico Territory-8 May 1865-April 1889 (*downloaded 15/01/2000)*
http://www.zianet.com/wblase/courier/fts.htm
General Sherman's Opinion – New Mexico History Index (*downloaded 13/12/2000*)
http://www.cia-g.com/~rockets/shermanopinion.htm
Glenwood New Mexico (Ref to approx location of the Cooney Fight of April 29th 1880) (*downloaded 06/08/99)*
http://www.zianet.com/snm/glenwood.htm

The Handbook of Texas Online

Baylor, George Wythe (1832-1916): by T.W. Cutrer (*downloaded 13/09/99)*
http://www.tsha.utexas.edu/handbook/online/articles/view/BB/fbaar.html
Buffalo Soldiers: by M. Odintz (*downloaded 13/09/99*)
http://www.tsha.utexas.edu/handbook/online/articles/view/BB/qlbl.html
Byrne, James J: by T.W.Cutrer (*downloaded 11/07/2000*)
http://www.tsha.utexas.edu/handbook/online/articles/view/BB/fby5.html
Eagle Spring no named author (*downloaded 10/09/99)*
http://www.tsha.utexas.edu/handbook/online/articles/view/EE/rpel.html
Flipper, Henry Ossian (1856-1940): by B.J. Dinges (*downloaded 13/09/99)*
http://www.tsha.utexas.edu/handbook/online/articles/view/FF/ffl13.html
Gillett, James Buchanan (1856-1937): by M.F. Peirce (*downloaded 13/09/99)*
http://www.tsha.utexas.edu/handbook/online/articles/view/GG/fgi25.html
Grierson, Benjamin Henry (1826-1911): by B.J. Dinges (*downloaded 10/09/99)*
http://www.tsha.utexas.edu/handbook/online/articles/view/GG/fgr59.html
Rattlesnake Springs, Battle of.: by B.J. Dinges (*downloaded 10/09/99)*
http://www.tsha.utexas.edu/handbook/online/articles/view/RR/qfrpg.html
Tinaja De Las Palmas, Battle of: by D.C. McChristian (*downloaded 13/09/99)*
http://www.tsha.utexas.edu/handbook/online/articles/view/TT/qftl.html
Van Horn, Texas. by M.D. Kohout (*downloaded 11/06/2001*)
http://www.tsha.utexas.edu/handbook/online/articles/view/VV/hgv1.html

Hembrillo Battlefield (Public Affairs Office: White Sands Missile Range) (*downloaded 14/09/99)*
http://www.wsmr.army.mil/paopage/Pages/facts.htm

Hillsboro – New Mexico Ghost Town (*downloaded 12/12/2000*)
http://www.ghosttowns.com/states/nm/hillsboro.html

Hurst (1), J.W. – Kas-Tziden's Fury (Nana's Raid) (*Downloaded 12/12/2000-12-15*)
http://www.zianet.com/snm/nana.htm

Hurst (2), J.W. – Victorio and the Reservation System – A Prescription for Disaster
http://www.zianet.com/snm/victorio.htm

'Indian War Period Medals of Honour' (*downloaded 17/03/99)*
http://www.army.mil/cmh-pg/mohind.htm

Konstantin, P. – May 23rd to 31st in North American History (*downloaded 01/06/2001*)
http://members.tripod.com/~PHILICON/May4.html

Lake Valley – New Mexico Ghost Town
http://village.globaldrum.com/sierra_newmexico/lakevall.htm

Lake Valley – Sierra County NM (*downloaded 12/12/2000*)
http://www.ghosttowns.com/states/nm/lakevalley.html

Las Animas Canyon 1879-1997 by A. Apostolides (*downloaded 18/05/9)*
http://www.zianet.com/institute/LasAnim.htm

Library of Congress 'Chronicling America' website (http://chroniclingamerica.loc.gov/) First accessed July 2014. This is a very useful site for searching old US Newspapers for articles on the Victorio Campaign. The simplest way to progress is to enter names or incidents into the search engine and take it from there….

Map of New Mexico 1895 (*downloaded 06/08/99*)
http://fermi.jhvapl.edu/states/1895/nm_1895.jpg

Monticello or Placita – New Mexico Ghost Town. (*downloaded 12/12/2000*)
http://www.ghosttowns.com/states/nm/monticello.html

Ninth Cavalry Cemetery Dedication…site of the Battle of Las Animas in New Mexico: by K. Dusenberry, (*downloaded 14/09/99*)
http://www.coax.net/people/lwf/cem_ded.htm

The Ninth Regiment of Cavalry – Lt G. Hutcheson (Reprinted from Journal of the Military Service Institution, Vol. XVI, No 75, May 1895) *This article is also available from the US Army Center of Military History webpage* (*downloaded 14/09/99)*
http://www.coax.net/people/lwf/9thcav.htm

Perspectives: Between 1865 and 1890, 18 'buffalo soldiers' won the Medal of Honor in the American West. (*downloaded 15/05/2001*)
http://www.thehistorynet/MilitaryHistory/articles/1997/02973_text.htm

Outside View of New Mexico – New Mexico History Index (*downloaded 13/12/2000*)
http://www.cia-g.com/~rockets/dNMhist.view.htm

Royal City News – Victorio by C. Bennett. (*downloaded 14/08/2000*)
http://www.royalcity news.com/actio...p.section1.las&issue_name=curren[9]

Scientist Rewrite Cavalry/Apache Fight History (*downloaded 14/12/2000*)
http://www.webarchives.net/scientists_rewrite_cavalry.htm

Schubert, Frank N. "Remembering the Buffalo Soldier: Memorials to Black Soldiers of the Indian War Era" *(downloaded 12/11/2002)*
http://www.captainbuffalo.com/memorials.html

9 This webpage is one of the better summaries of the Victorio stories, though by no means complete or accurate. However, I had problems printing off the page and as such do not have a full web address available. I do have a copy of the article available for viewing.

USACMH – The US Army Center of Military History webpage.
Capt W.H. Carter – The Sixth Regiment of Cavalry
Lt J. Bigelow – The Tenth Regiment of Cavalry
Appendix 4 – Dates of Important Campaigns.
The U.S. Cavalry Versus The Indians 1832 through 1898 (*downloaded 15/05/2001*)
http://members.aol.com/aacsgtmike/indians.html
The United States Army Military History Institute webpage
http://carlisle-www.army.mil/usamhi/DL/
Victorio Canyon – Diablo Mountains (*downloaded 10/03/2001*)
http://www.kingsnake.com/hudspeth/victorio_canyon.htm
Wakeman, J.(New Mexico State University) Laumbach, K. (Human Systems Research Inc.) (*downloaded 14/04/99)*
http://www.gpsworld.com/feature/1097victorio/bottom.htm
West Point Pioneer: Henry Ossian Flipper: by L.R. Jordan (*downloaded 09/03/99)*
http://www.aog.usma.edu/Pubs/Register/Flipper.htm
White Sands & Lake Lucero (*downloaded 26/02/2001*)
http://www.geocities.com/Athens/Parthenon/5883/whitesan.htm
24th U.S. Infantry at Fort Davis Texas (*downloaded 14/09/1999*)
http://www.coax.net/people/lwf/24th_fd.htm

Masters Thesis

Major Eric Leon Bradley, *Factors Influencing the Impacts on Security of Manning Military Posts on the United States-Mexico Border from 1865-1916*, A thesis presented to the Faculty of the U.S. Army Command and General Staff College in partial fulfilment of the requirements for the degree Master of Military Art and Science Military History, (Fort Leavenworth: Kansas, 2007) http://stinet.dtic.mil/cgi-bin/GetTRDoc?AD=ADA471719&Location=U2&doc=GetTRDoc.pdf (*Downloaded 12th June 2008*)

Maps

US Geological Survey Topographical 1:250,000 scale Maps
NI 12-6 – St Johns
NI 12-9 – Clifton
NI 12-12 – Silver City
NH 12-3 – Douglas
NI 13-4 – Socorro
NI 13-7 – Tularosa
NI 13-10 – Las Cruces
NH 13-1 – El Paso
NI 13-5 – Ft Sumner
NI 13-8 – Roswell
NI 13-11 – Carlsbad
NH 13-2 – Van Horn
NH 13-5 – Marfa
NH 13-8 – Presidio

Maps from the Instituto Nacional De Estadistica Geografia e Infromatica, (INEGI) Estados Unidos Mexicanos

H12-2 – Nogales
H12-5 – Cananea
H12-8 – Hermosillo
H12-3 – Agua Prieta
H12-6 – Nacozari
H12-9 – Madera
H13-1 – Cuidad Juarez
H13-4 – Nuevo Casas Grandes
H13-7 – Buenaventura
H 13-10 – Chihuahua
H13-5 – San Antonio Del Bravo
H13-8 – Ojinaga
H13-11 – Cuidad Delicias

David Rumsey Map Collection:

Historic Maps 77. Part of Central New Mexico. by Wheeler, G.M. from 1882 http://www.davidrumsey.com/detail?id=1-1-384-0091&name=77.+Part+of+Central+New+Mexico

AAA Arizona & New Mexico Road Map 1999

Index

INDEX OF PEOPLE

INDEX OF PLACES

INDEX OF MILITARY FORMATIONS & UNITS

INDEX OF MISCELLANEOUS & GENERAL TERMS